Thailand

Political History
and
Buddhist Cultural Influences

To

The People of Thailand

Thailand

Political History
and
Buddhist Cultural Influences

by

Kanai Lal Hazra

Vol I: Political History

Decent Books
New Delhi

Published and Printed by:
Decent Books
D-36/A-1, Mohan Garden
Najafgarh Road
New Delhi - 110 059

Distributed by:
D.K. Printworld (P) Ltd.
Regd. office : *'Sri Kunj'*, F-52, Bali Nagar
New Delhi - 110 015
Phones : (011) 545-3975, 546-6019; *Fax* : (011) 546-5926
E-mail: dkprint@4mis.com

ISBN 81-86921-12-5 (Set)
ISBN 81-86921-13-3 (Vol. I)
ISBN 81-86921-14-1 (Vol. II)

First Published in India in 2000

Preface

THIS book entitled 'Thailand' throws flood of light on Thailand's political, religious, art and literary history from the earliest times to the present day, i.e., 1998. The first chapter in its discussion presents an authoritative and up to date account of Thailand's political history and mentions its economic world and also other valuable matters in this connection. The second chapter deals with the introduction, rise and development of its Buddhism. The third chapter is a study on its Buddhist art. The fourth chapter describes its Buddhist literature. The fifth chapter is a conclusion.

I express my deep gratitude to my friends Prof. Dr. G.D.K. Nanayakkara and Dr. Daya Amarasekera of the University of Peradeniya, Sri Lanka and Dr. Mrs. Manikuntala Halder (De) and Prof. Dr. M.K. Ganguly of the University of Calcutta for taking personal interest in my work. My thanks are also due to my brother Mr. Subodh Kumar Hazra, my niece Mrs. Pratima Haldar, her husband Mr. Pranab Kumar Haldar and my another niece Mrs. Malaya Paul and her son Mr. Biswarup Paul for their keen interest in the publication of this book. My thanks are also due to the librarian and the deputy librarian Mr. Chitta Patra of the Indian Museum Library, Calcutta for helping me to use books in this library.

I must be thankful to my publisher for the publication of this book.

Kanai Lal Hazra

Contents

Volume I

Political History

	Preface	v
	Abbreviations	ix
1.	Thailand's Political History	1

Volume II

Buddhism and its Influence on Thai Culture

	Abbreviations	vii
2.	An Account of Thailand's Buddhism : Its Introduction, Rise and Development	339
3.	Thailand's Buddhist Art	407
4.	A Survey of Thaland's Buddhist Literature	485
5.	Conclusion	531
	Bibliography	551
	Index	559

Abbreviations

AA	:	*The Asian Age*, Calcutta.
AAT	:	*Art and Archaeology in Thailand*, Published by the Fine Arts Department. In Commemoration of the 100th Anniversary of the National Museum, Thailand.
AB	:	*Ananda Bazar Patrika*, Calcutta.
ABGPN	:	*A.B. Griswold and Prasart na Nagara*, A Pali Inscription from Vat Sri Ratnamahadhatu, Subarnapuri.
ACHBAS	:	*A Concise History of Buddhist Art in Siam*, Reginald Le May.
AHS	:	*A History of Siam*, W.A.R. Wood.
AHSEA	:	*A History of South-East Asia*, D.G.E. Hall.
ANAEI	:	*A New Account of the East Indies*, Alexander Hamilton.
ASEAW	:	*Ancient South-East Asian Warfare*, H.G.Q. Wales.
Baa	:	*Buddhist art and architecture*, Robert E. Fisher.
BACSEA	:	*The Buddhist Annals and Chronicles of South-East Asia*, K.L. Hazra.

Bapat	:	*2500 years of Buddhism*, P.W. Bapat.
BEA	:	*Buddhism in East Asia*, Sukumar Dutt.
BEFED	:	*Bulletin l'Ecele Francaise d'Extreme Orient*, Hanoi.
BEFEO	:	*Bulletin do l'Ecole Francaise d'Extreme Orient*, Hanoi.
BM	:	*British Malaya*, A Lennex Mills.
CDSEA	:	*Collective Defence in South-East Asia*, Chatham House Report, London.
Chdv	:	*The Chamadevivamsa, G. Coedes, Documents sur l'histoire politique at religiouse du Laos Occidental, Bulletin de l'Ecole Francaise d'Extreme Orient, XXV*, Hanoi.
Damrong	:	*Prince Damrong,'The story of the records of Siamese history'*, The Siam Society, Fiftieth Anniversary Commemorative publication, *The Siam Society Journal*, vol. I.
DRTS	:	*Description du Royaume Thai au Siam*, Jean Baptiste Pallegeix.
DSEA	:	*The Diplomacy of South-East Asia*, Russel H. Fifield.
DVP	:	*Dīpavaṁsa*, ed. H. Oldenberg.
ECT	:	*Economic Change in Thailand since 1850*, James C. Ingram.
ET	:	*The Economic Times*, Calcutta.
FYS	:	*Five Years in Siam*, H.W. Smyth.
GRAHAM	:	*Siam*, W. A. Graham.

HB	:	*Hinduism and Buddhism*, Sir Charles Eliot.
HPWT	:	*History of Protestant work in Thailand*, Kenneth E. Wells.
HTBSEA	:	*History of Theravāda Buddhism in South-East Asia*, K.L. Hazra.
ICS	:	*The Indian Colony of Siam*, P.N. Bose.
IICSEA	:	*Influence of Indian culture in South-East Asia*, R.C. Mazumdar.
ISEA	:	*India and South-East Asia*, R.C. Majumdar.
IWGS	:	*The Impact of the West on the Government of Siam*, Walter F. Vella.
JECSCC	:	*Journal of an Embassy to the Courts of Siam and Cochin China*, John Crawford.
JKM	:	*Jinakālamalī*, G. Coedes, BEFEO,Vol. XXV, Hanoi, 1925.
KM	:	*King Mongkut*, Frankfurter, O, Journal of Siam Society.
LBS	:	*Le bouddhisme a Siam*, Lean Feer. Memoire de la Societe Academique Indo-Chineise de France I.
LEHII	:	*Les Estate Hindouises d'Indochina at d'Indonesia*, G. Coedes.
LV	:	*Locust Valley*, Augustin.
LVRRM	:	*La Vie religiouse du Roi Mongkut*, R. Lingat.
Mahabodhi	:	*Buddhism in Thailand*, Ven. P. Amara

		Thera, *The Mahabodhi*, Nov-Dec, 2521-1997, Vol. 85, Nos. 11-12.
Mhv	:	*Mahāvaṁsa*, W. Geiger.
MKS	:	*Mongkut, King of Siam*, Abbot Low Moffat.
MTI	:	*Mangalartha Temple Inscription.*
PLC	:	*The Pali Literature of Ceylon*, G.P. Malalasekera.
Sas	:	*Sāsanavaṁsa*, M. Bode.
SASP	:	*Some Aspects of Siamese Politics*, John Coast.
SC	:	*Siam and Combodia*, Rachel Wheatcroft.
SCR	:	*Some Siam, the crossriads*, Josiah Crosby.
SEA	:	*South-East Asia*, John F. Cady.
SGEC	:	*The Sheaf of Garlands of the Epoch of the Conqueror*, N.A. Jayawickrema, Being a translation of the Jina Jina-kalamalipakaranam of Ratanapanna Thera of Thailand, PTS, Translation Series.
SGEC	:	*'The Sheaf of Garlands of the Epochs of the Conqueror'*, Pali Text Society, Translation Series, no. 36, N.A. Jayawickrema.
SSJ	:	*The Siam Society Journal*, Vol. II.
STC	:	*Siam in the Twentieth Century*, John Garden Drummond Campbell.

SUR	:	*Siam under Rama III*, Walter F. Vella.
TAII	:	*Thai Art with Indian Influences*, Premsak Jermswatdi.
TAIL	:	*Thai Art with Indian Influences*, Premsak Jermswatdi.
TAKE	:	*The Ancient Khmer Empire*, L.P. Bridggs.
TAT	:	*The Arts of Thailand*, S.V. Beek and L.D. Jettoni.
TCICSCL	:	*Travels in the central parts of Indo-China, Siam, Combodia and Laos during 1859-60*, Henry Mouhet.
TDMKJS	:	*A True Description of the Mighty Kingdom of Japan and Siam*, Joest Schouten.
TESG	:	*Thailand, Economic Survey Group, Report on Economic Development Plans*, Bangkok.
THRAF	:	*Thailand, Human Relations Area Files*, Thomas Fitzsimmons.
TG	:	*The Telegraph*, Calcutta.
Thailand	:	*Thailand*, Swami Sadananda.
TKHAAT	:	*The Kingdom of Haripunjaya, Art and Architecture-Thailand*, Srisakara Vallibhotana.
TLP	:	*Thailand: Land and Peoples*, Prachoem Chomchai.
TMGI	:	*The Making of Greater India*, H.G.Q. Walas.

TMSEA	:	*The Making of South-East Asia*, G. Coedes, tr. by H.M. Wright.
TPSCHRAF	:	*Thailand: Its People, Its Society, Its Culture, Human Relations Areas Files*, Wondell Blanchard.
TSM	:	*The Statesman*, Calcutta.
TSR	:	*The Siam Repository*, Sannel J. Smith.
TSRWR	:	*The Siam Rath Weekly Review*, August 29, Bangkok.
URPAA	:	*Une Recension Palie Des Annales d'Ayuthia*, G. Coedes, *Bulletin de l'Ecole Francaise d'Extreme Orient*, XIV, Hanoi,
Wyatt	:	David K. Wyatt, Chronicle Tradition in Thai Historiography, South-East Asian History and historiography, ed. C.D. Cowan and O.W. Walter.

1

Thailand's Political History

THAILAND with an area of 380,400 square miles and a population of about 25,520,000 is situated between 6-21° N latitude and 97-196° E longitude. The population indicates an increase of 2.8 per cent over the previous decade. The increase has taken place owing to the availability of better medical services which have resulted in a fall in death rate.

The original name of Thailand was Siam. Several Chinese annals, Sanskrit literature and chronicles of Sri Lanka refer to it. This shows that the name was very ancient one. The change in the official name for the country was from Siam to Thailand in June 1939 and it has become known by it. From the Thai people it has adopted its name. They migrated to this country from the hilly northern side and in course of time they became the rulers of the entire country. Thailand means 'land of the free people' and this title is justified because Thailand is the only South-East Asian country that never became a colony of an European power. On a map it looks like a blooming flower on a stem and this stem is the Thai portion. It "like the shadowy outline of the shrunken face and trunk of an elephant" is surrounded by the Gulf of Siam on one side and Kampuchea (Camboja, Cambodia). Laos, Myanmar (Burma) and Malay on its other side. The Salween river divides Thailand from Myanmar and the Mekong river exists as a dividing line between eastern Thailand and Laos. The country is divided into four main geographic regions.

The north, where several important rivers originate, is crisscrossed by teak-covered mountains and fertile valleys. The country's highest point, Inthamon Peak (8,452 feet; 2,576 meters), is located in this area. The most heavily populated region is the alluvial central plain, where the country's commerce, industry and farming activities are mainly concentrated. A vast complex of canals and irrigation projects, fed by the Chao Phraya River system, waters the land. North-eastern Thailand, the third region, consists of a sandy, dry plateau that generally cannot retain sufficient water for irrigation. The heavily forested south, a 470-mile (750 km) portion of the Malay Peninsula, contains much of Thailand's mineral wealth.

Thailand is the country where its people belong to the Thai ethnic group. This includes the northern Thais (or Lao) who have connection with the people of neighbouring Laos. There are many people who have Chinese background and there are also Malays in the country. Hill tribesmen are living in the western and northern regions.

According to historians, the Thais took their origin in north-western Szechwan in China several thousand years ago. They were compelled to migrate south because of conflict with the Chinese. They founded a kingdom called Nanchao in south China in the seventh century AD. Charles Eliot states that[1] the Thai (in the form Tai) was the racial name of several tribes of the southern provinces of China. From there they began to move and took shelter from Laos to Assam and the middle section arrived in the Menam Valley. They came to a century which was the Mon region in central Thailand and this century was quite different from their own. The Siamese people said that they have adopted the name Thai (free) when they were able to throw away the

1. *HB*, MI, p. 79.

influence of the Cambodians. The name Siam, Syam or Syama has been identified with the Sanskrit Syama, dark or brown. Possibly, the names Shan and A-hem are variants of the same word and it seems that Syama is not its origin and it is very probable that it is an artificial distortion. The name Lao was the another branch of the same race and these people settled in a country which became known as Laos and they came to this place before the Thais migrated to Thailand. The Thais or the Tais gradually established small principalities and their important region was Lamphun on the western side of the Mekong. Then they moved into the kingdoms of Svankalok, Sukhothai (Sukhodaya) and Lavo (Lopburi), the vassal states of Combodia. Another branch of the Thias in the beginning of the twelfth century AD went towards the southern sides. The Combodian empire tried its best to control these people for sometime but in the second half of the thirteenth century AD they declared their independance and they established an independent state and its capital was Sukhodaya or Sukhothai. In AD 1287 when the Thais conquered Thailand, three Thai leaders came to an agreement for division of the conquered regions. Mangroi and Rama or Ram Khamheng were two important leaders of this pact. The former received the whole of northern Thailand and central and southern Thailand came under the control of the Thai leader, Rama Khamheng.[2]

The original people of Thailand were the mens. In ancient times they took shelter in the valley of the Menam river and along the lower portion of its tributaries. They were the inhabitants of central Thailand which comprised the 'trunk of the elephant' and it extended along the two-thirds of the Malay Peninsula. Lavo or Lopburi was mentioned as an important place of Mon life and culture. From the archaeological finds discovered at the Menam valley, it is clear that this region flourished from the sixth or seventh centudry AD onwards. The Dvāravatī kingdom

2. *BEA*, p. 73.

in the lower Menam valley in lower central Thailand was another Mon kingdom in the seventh century AD. The Chinese travellers Hiuen Tsang and I-tsing and also the texts of several writers mention it as T'o-lo-po-ti which was located between the Pyu kingdom of Sirikhotta (Prome) in lower Myanmar and Icānapura of the Khmer kingdom. George Coedès and other scholars refer to it as Dvāravatī. The archaeological remains show that this kingdom was established in the sixth or seventh century AD. The Mon people used to live in this kingdom. Their capital was at first at Nagarama Patha or Nagara Prathama or Nakorn Patom or mere usually Phra Pathom which was about thirty miles west of modern Bangkok and later at Lavo or Lopburi. The Dvāravatī kingdom was able to extend its political influence up to Haripuñjaya (Lamphun, Lampun or Lampoon) in northern Thailand. During the twelfth century AD the lower Menam valley which the Khmers captured from the Mons, both Lavo and Sukhodaya accepted the paramountcy of Combodia. From paleographical evidences found at Angkor Wat, troops of Suryavarman II whose title was Paramavishnu were recruited from Lavo and Syam Kut (the Sukhodaya principality). Lopburi declined when Śrī Indrāditya, the Thai chieftain, everthrew the Khmers from the Sukhodaya region. A new epoch in architecture distinct from that of the Khmer's as ushered in Lopburi P'ra Itarai in the eighteenth century AD wanted to reconstruct the town as his summer residence during peaceful days and he tried to fortify it as an emergency capital in case Ayuthia was invaded. When he decided to rebuild it, he was helped by Constance Phaulkon, a Greek adventurer. He reconstructed the old town with a new citadel, a royal palace, an outer wall and a water system. The town of Lopburi flourished under Ayuthia and it continued to develop so long Ayuthia remained the capital. But it declined when the centre of the central Thai authority was moved to Bangkok.

The Haripuñjaya kingdom occupied an important place in the political history of Thailand. The *Jinakālamālī*, a text of the first half of the sixteenth century AD, indicates that there was some political alliance between the kingdom of Haripuñjaya, Rāmaññanagara (this state was situated between Lopburi and Ayuthia or Ayudhya) and Lopburi. It states that in the second half of the seventh century AD the sage named Vāsudeva founded the city of Haripuñjaya. Then the princess Cammadevī, the daughter of the king of the city of Lopburi and the wife of the provincial ruler of Rāmaññanagara, began to rule at Haripuñjaya in about AD 663. It is said that the king of the city of Lopburi sent his daughter to become the ruler there on the advice of a Buddhist monk and a layman of Haripuñjaya. After leaving her husband she came to Haripuñjaya with soldiers and 500 great elders who were well-versed in the three Piṭakas in the second half of the seventh century AD Lopburi was her home. The lower Menam valley was dominated by a Mon-speaking race. The story of the *Jinakālamālī* gives us indication about the introduction of the Mon culture to Haripuñjaya in the second half of the seventh century AD. In the tenth century AD the friendly relations that existed between Lopburi and Haripuñjaya in the early period seem to have been strained. The *Jinakālamālī* mentions that towards the end of the tenth century AD the king of Haripuñjaya invaded the city of Lopburi. In about middles of the eleventh century AD in the reign of Kambala of Haripuñjaya an epidemic of plague raged for six years and the people of Haripuñjaya in order to escape from it first fled to the city of Sudhammangara (Thaton) in lower Myanmar and then went to Haṁsāvatī (Pegu) in lower Myanmar. But they then returned to Haripuñjaya when the epidemic of plague had subsided. It is very possible that some Mon people from Lower Myanmar came to Haripuñjaya with the Mon people of Haripuñjaya and they settled there. That Myanmarese influence was felt in the Haripuñjaya kingdom and it is confirmed by the fact that several scholars have discovered Myanmarese characters of the eleventh century AD in several Mon inscriptions at Haripuñjaya dated in the eleventh century AD. All these facts give an idea about Mon influence in

Haripuñjaya in the upper Menam valley. Meng Rai or Mangrai, the Thai chief of Chieng Rai, after a long series of campaigns finally in AD 1290-2 conquered the Haripuñjaya kingdom and founded the kingdom of Chiengmai or Xieng Mai or May or Nabbisipura which became the most important region in northern Thailand from that time onwards.

Mr. Srisakra Vallibhetama gives an account of the kingdom of Haripuñjaya. He described,[3]

> The existence of the kingdom of Haripuñjaya as the early urban development of northern Thailand is supported by three major kinds of evidence that validate each other — written documents, sites of ancient towns and archaeological monuments and objects. From reliable chronicles namely Jinakalamalipakorn, Chamadeviwengsa and Tamnan Munsasana, the origin of Haripuñjaya begins with myth which contains some elements of truth that can be elicited through anthropological study and analysis.
>
> Interpreting in terms of ethnological viewpoint, the lower Chiengmai valley — the area around the slope of Doi Suthep which is drained by the rivers Mae Khan and Mae Ping was occupied by an ethnic group called the Meng who divided among them into four totemic groups namely the deer, the elephant, the rhinoceros and the cow. These people seemed to have been living in tribes practising dry rice cultivation as their main economic concern. Later on the area was penetrated by newcomers from central Thailand who were better off with the Indian civilisation. They had as their leader the hermit Vasuthep who soon married the native girl of the deer tribe. Cultural intercourse between the two groups resulted in a shift from dry rice to wet rice ceremony,

3. *AAT*, pp. 279 ff.

the expansion of the farming area into the flooded land and foundation of the city of Migkhasangara Nakhon. Urban life began and social class developed. However, this city did not last long for it was destroyed by flood and finally abandoned in favour of the new one — the city of Haripuñjaya.

Vasuthep, the founder of the city, saw no qualified person among the native to put into the throne and then turned to invite Chamdevi, the daughter of the king of Lavo, who was probably related to him through either the affinal or consanguinial tie. The coming of Chamdevi to Haripuñjaya is of a great socio-cultural change in the northern society. Hīnayāna Buddhism was officially introduced into the kingdom; the Wat and the Monk organisation were established. More people from the central moved in; many of them were specialists of various kinds who were capable to transform the kingdom into an Indianised state as these found in the central. Haripuñjaya became an urban centre where people of different ethnic origins were arranged to live together under one sovereign. The royal family played a crucial role in integrating the people under one culture. This was achieved by means of teaching Buddhism and establishing monasteries in one way and encouraging intermarriage among the people of different groups in the other. For the latter, Chamdevi set an example for her people by marrying her son to the daughter of Nai Khan Kwaya who was the Meng and the daughter of Khun Vilangka, the Lua cheiftain who surrendered to her after a long conflict.

The reign of Chamdevi marked the period of building up and expansion of the kingdom; one of her son, Inthavorn went across the Khun Tan Range to the Lampang valley to found Khelang Nakhon as the second city of

Haripuñjaya. After her, the kingdom was firmly established, although sometimes it was taken and ruled by monarchs from other regions. Throughout its history, Haripuñjaya seemed to have been related socially and culturally with the kingdom of Lavo in central Thailand and the Mon kingdom in the Salwin River basin. At the end relationship with Lavo became strained through conflict and wafare, while that with the Mon was friendly and helpful. When cholera broke out in Haripuñjaya, large number of its population evacuated into the Mon country and took refuge there for several years. This incident brought the Haripuñjaya people closer to the Mon and it reflected through the use of the Mon script and language in the inscription stones. Such resemblance caused several scholars to attribute the ethnic origin of the Haripuñjaya people to the Mon.

Apart from relationship with other countries, the story of Haripuñjaya is concerned with patronising and promoting the Buddhist religion. Two pious kings worthy to be mentioned are Adityaraj who built the *wat* and the *stupa* housing the Relics of the Buddha (Wat Phara Dhat Lamphun) and Sabbadhisiddhi, who constructed several wats, devoted large number of land to the monks and abdicated for entering the monkhood for a period of time during his reign. After Sabbadhisiddhi, the kingdom seemed to decline and at the end was conquered by king Mengrai from the Chiengrai valley who annexed it to the kingdom of Lan Na which was founded in AD 1296.

Prior to 1965 archaeological data concerning the kingdom of Haripuñjaya was limited to ancient monuments and objects found in Lamphun, its old capital. This seemed to imply that the whole kingdom existed only within one single city. Recent field research conducted by the author and his colleagues has revealed more data to support and validate what had been recorded in the written documents. From new data, the Haripuñjaya proper consists of five ancient towns distributed in the lower Chiengrai valley and a part of the Lampang valley.

In Chiengrai valley, the Haripuñjaya towns are geographically distributed between latitudes 18"30' North to 18"38' North and longitudes 98"50' East to 99"65' East grouping in the plain that extends from the slope of Doi Suthep and that is drained by the Mae Ping River and its tributaries, the Mae Khan and Mae Kwuang. There are altogether four towns namely Lamphun, Vieng Mane, Vieng the Karn and Vieng Thoh. They are of an irregular plan surrounded by earthen-wall meat; each is located in the area near to an old water course which was once a river. The distance among these towns is about 7-8 km from one another, indicating that a journey from one city to another can be completed whithin one day. Residential area is not confined within the city wall but extended around the city and also along the banks of the waterway. Such an evidence can be traced through remains of the ancient wats which marked the community centres.

In Lamphang valley where the city of Khelang Nakhon was located, as it is mentioned in the chronicle, the exact location of this city has not yet been point out but it is likely to be included in the same area with the old city of Lampang on the morthern bank of the Wang River which is now in the muncipality of Lampang. This is because there are some traces of wall and meat that appear in the aerial photograph suggesting that two towns overlapping each other. Further, some archaeological evidences namely the remains of *stūpa*s. Stuco image of the Buddha and decrorative designs of the Haripuñjaya style have been found in an old wat close to the city.

Next to the sites of the ancient cities and towns, the archaeological monuments and objects seem to be significant in verifying the existence of the kingdom of Haripuñjaya. There presence *in situ* does not only tell the date and chronology of each locality and town but also indicates its history, belief system, level of technology and the cultural contact with other regions. Most of these evidences are religious monuments and objects belonging to the Hīnayāna tradition which in their turns, can be classified into *stūpa*s, image of the Buddha, decorative designs and motifs, printed Buddha, inscription stones, mortuary bowls and pots and boundary stones, marking the sacred sites.

The Haripuñjaya *stupa*s, so far remained, have a distinctive style that can be divided into at least four types, pyramidal-storied structure, an octagonal-shaped *stupa*, the Sri-Vijaya-like *chetiya* and an octagonal storied *stupa*. Among them the first type seems to be very popular and it became a model for many *stupa*s of the later period. The images of the Buddha are viewed into the early and the later types. The early type has a rather round and smooth face reflecting some facial characteristics influenced by the Dvaravati school from the central while the later type has a long face and baldging eyes expressing the indigenous character of its locality. Stucco decorations of the *stupa*s and the printed Buddha help to indicates art influence from the Sri-Vijaya, Pala and Lopburi schools that spread from the central to the north, while the inscription stones are of the Mon scripts and language indicates social and cultural relation between Haripunjaya and the Mon of the Salwin River Valley. Mortuary bowls and pots incised with symbolic designs tell of a funeral cult and the magico-religious belief of the indigeneous people. Such a practice seems to have a counterpart only in Southern Thailand which is in the sphere of the Sri-Vijaya cultural influence. The upright stones which are found marking the sacred monuments are similar to those found in the north-east. They are perhaps an element of the megalithic culture shared among the indigenous people of South-East Asia.

Observing from most of the ancient sites, the Haripunjaya cultural materials are associated with those of the Lan Na, so it corresponds to the written documents that the kingdom had collapsed and became a part of the new kingdom. Although Haripunjaya has already ceased to exist, its culture still persists; the city of Lamphun, its capital has been restored and preserved as the religious centre of the north for several centuries. Even to-day some of its magical elements such as printed Buddha and votive tablets are sought incessantly by large number of people who believe in their magical qualities.

The Thais are said to have originally belonged to Yunnan of China and they began to settle in the Menam valley from the eleventh century AD onwards. They settled in northern Thailand and also in north-central Thailand. One branch reached Khamphaeng Phet on the Mae Phing river in central Thailand and Lopburi in southern Thailand. Kublai Khan, the Mongol leader, conquered the kingdom of Nanchao in China in about AD 1253 and owing to this invasion many Thais from Nanchao arrived in northern, central and southern Thailand and in this way they settled themselves in Thailand.

The Sukhot'ai or Sukhothai or Sukhodaya Dynasty

We do not know much about the origin of the Thai kingdom of Sukhodaya in Thailand. An inscription discovered at Sukhodaya throws a considerable light on it. It says that a Kamboja General went to fight against two Thai chiefs who were Pho Khun Bāng Klāng Thao and Pho Khun Phā Muang, chief of Muang Rāt. The former occupied Sajjanālaya and the latter with his army came there for his help. The Kamboja or Kambuja army captured Sukhodaya but was unable to proceed further because the army was defeated by the Thai chief Pho Khun Phā Muang who then arrived in Sukhodaya and gave the charge of its government to Pho Khun Bāng Klāng Thao. But the latter did not like to enter the city. Then his army was removed by the former and when Bāng Klāng Thao arrived in Sukhodaya, he formally consecrated him to the throne of Sukhodaya and he took the name of Śrī Indrapatindrāditya with the title Kamraten Añ Phā Muang which was conferred on him by the ruler of Kambuja. The passage of the inscription describes that Pho Khun Phā Muang was a vassal chief and the marriage took place between him and the daughter of the king of Kambuja. The former was the suzerain ruler and conferred on his ally, the position and titles which the suzerain king of Kambuja had offered to him. This incident shows that north Thailand was virtually liberated from the influence and control of Kambuja. It is interesting to note here that although north Thailand became free from the influence of Kambuja, yet the new ruler and his successors used the old Kambuja titles. Thus Pho Khun Phā Muang liberated Thailand from Kambuja suzerainty. According to the inscription found at Sukhodaya, Phā Muang had married the daughter of the king of Kambuja and received the sacred sword, the honorific title named Śrī Indrapatindrāditya and a formal investiture from him. All these facts identify him with king Śrīndravarman of Kambuja who had married the Kambuja ruler Jayavaraman VIII's daughter. Cheu Ta-kuan went to the court of Srīndravarman with the Chinese embassy in AD 1296 and he referred to this king:

> The new king is the son-in-law of the old. He had adopted a military career. His father-in-law loved his daughter who stole the golden sword (of the king) and took it and gave it to her husband. The son, thus deprived of succession, plotted to raise an army. The new king came

> to know of it, cut off the fingers of his feet and shut him up in a dark chamber.

A Kambuja inscription which partly corroborates the account of Cheu Ta-Kuan, mentions that Jayavarman VIII in favour of his son-in-law abdicated the throne. According to the custom in Kambuja, the prince who was consecrated as heir-apparent with the title Sri Indrapati or Indrāditya became known as Śrīndravarman on accession to the throne. R.C. Mazumdar says that

> we have a remarkable coincidence, both in name and the three special circumstances (marriage of the king's daughter and the possession of the sword, indicating investiture as heir-apparent) between the Kambuja king Śrīndravarman and the cheif Phā Muang. Besides, the fact that this chief, although son-in-law of the Kambuja king, was opposed by an 'audacious Kambuja general' would be explained by the rivalry between Śrīndravarman of Kambuja and his brother-in-law referred to by Cheu-Ta-Kuan. Such coincidences cannot be dismissed as casual and we are justified in presuming the indentity of the two. In that case we must held that prince Śrīndra-varman was invested as regent or viceroy over Siam during the reign of his father-in-law, and the struggle for succession with his brother-in-law, which took place during the reign of the old king, he had the assistance of the Thai chief whose services he rewarded by his appointment as vassal chief of Sukhodaya, nominally under his suzerainty. It was probably not long before the chief of Sukhodaya became too powerful and challanged the authority of Kambuja, and the 'recent wars with the Siamese which devastated Angkor region' as reported by Cheu Ta-Kuan might refer to the civil war or to the latter stage of this war for liberation. In any case we are justified in presuming that the rise of

> Sukhodaya as an independent kingdom was probably due to the civil war between Śrīndravarman, the son-in-law of the king Kambuja, and his brother-in-law.

If we accept the above-mentioned facts then we can refer to the accession of Indrāditya to the reign of Jayavarman VIII who occupied the throne in AD 1243 or somewhat later. But the current view is that Indrāditya established the kingdom of Sukhodaya in AD 1218. The Nagara Jum inscription says,

> The year in which Phrayā Mahā Dharmarāja constructed (or commenced) the Phra Dhātu, the age of Mon was lowered below 100 years. That was 139 years ago, and the year of the reduction is really the year of Hare.

Mr. P. Patithuguenin who translated the above inscription states,

> If this phrase has any sense it appears to convey that 139 years before 1279, i.e., in Śaka 1140 (AD 1218), which was really a year of Hare, under a king named Phrayā Mahā Dharmarāja an important social revolution took place, which could well be, as already remarked by Lajonquiere, the date of accession of the first king of Sukhodaya. It is not then Śrī Sūrya Phra Mahā Dharmarājādhirāja who reigned from Śaka 1276 to 1298, but one of his predecessors more than a century ago, who is the Phrah or Bā Thammarat of the tradition and who could not be any other than Indrāditya.

It is very different to accept the date of accession of Indrāditya in AD 1218 on the basis of the above theory. According to the inscription of Rama Khamheng, the king, who was the third son of Indrāditya and the third king of dynasty, ascended the throne of Sukhodaya between AD 1283 and 1292. This gives the date of the accession of Indrāditya sometime about the middle of the thirteenth century AD. The *Jinakālamālī*, the Pāli chronicle, mentions the accession of Phra Ruang, the founder of the

Sukhodaya dynasty in AD 1265. Prince Damrong identifies Phra Ruang with Indrāditya and George Coedès agrees with him. According to scholars, Indrāditya ascended the throne of Sukhodaya in AD 1256. R.C. Mazumdar refers to AD 1256 as the date when Indrāditya first became a ruling chief and he says further that this was not the date of his conquest of Sukhodaya. The first part of Rama Khamheng's inscription gives us an idea that Sukhodaya was not a very important kingdom during the time of his father and elder brother who ruled before him, and its greatness and importance really began from his reign. R.C. Mazumdar states that we cannot rule but altogether the possibility that Indrapatindrāditya who by the son-in-law of the Kambuja king was formally consecrated at Sukhodaya after the defeat of the Kambuja general was no other than Rama Khamheng himself, and he took the name of Indrapatindrāditya from the name of his benefactor (Indrabhūpati) and his own grandfather Indrāditya. Rama Khamheng in his inscription says that he conquered a very wide area and captured several regions of Kambuja. Cheu Ta-Kuan wrote an account on Kamboja in AD 1296 or AD 1297 and mentions the devastation of the country in the recent wars with Thailand. The Sukhodaya inscription describes a fight which took place between a Kambuja general and the son-in-law of the Kambuja king allied with a Thai chief of Thailand. All these facts discuss the different episodes in the struggle between the son and son-in-law of Jayavarman VIII, the Kambuja king. This civil war probably took place sometime before the end of the reign of this king in AD 1295 or 1296. Because from the Mangalārtha Temple inscription we learn that Jayavarman VIII abdicated in favour of his son-in-law. R.C. Mazumdar states,

> But although this may be justly regarded as a weak argument against the obvious inference from Cheu Ta-Kuan's statement, quoted above, it is to be noted that we cannot reject the idea of a civil war taking place long before the end of Jayavarman's reign without upsetting some

> of the generally accepted views of historical event. For, apart from all speculative theories on the indentification of Phā Muang, the broad fact remains that he, a son-in-law of the ruling king of Kambuja, fought with a Kambuja General near Sukhodaya. Although this cannot be precisely dated it could hardly have taken place in AD 1295 or 1296. When King Rama Khamheng must have, according to the generally accepted view based on Sukhodaya Inscription, thoroughly established his power over Sukhodaya and an extensive region round it, and we can hardly think of a Kambuja prince defeating a Kambuja General and consecrating an allied chief as ruler over Sukhodaya. On the other hand it difficult to explain away the incident by referring it to the reign of any other king of Kambuja.... There are no remarkable grounds to place the foundation of Sukhodaya by Indrāditya before AD 1243. When Jayavarman VIII ascended the throne, and the fight between the Kambuja general and the son-in-law of the Kambuja king, referred to in the Sukhodaya inscriptions can only refer to a civil war in his reign.

The war of succession to the throne took place between Śrīndravarman and his brother-in-law and probably this happened long before AD 1275. The Bantei Srei inscription of Śrīndravarman describes that the earth is congratulated on its deliverance, by a young king, from the thorns and brambles which had grown up during the reign of an old king. This indicates that Śrīndravarman was a young man when he took the throne in AD 1295 or 1296. The reference to the thorns and brambles during the reign of the old King Jayavarman VIII shows the true picture of his regin. He in his old age announced Śrīndravarman, his son-in-law, as his successor and appointed him as governor of Western provinces including Thailand. Then his son to defend his right stood against his father's decision and for this reason a civil war took place between him and his brother-in-law and they fought against each other in Thailand. Kublai Khan conquered the Thai kingdom of Nan Chao and the Thais moved towards the south, and Śrīndravarman got their support and he offered large rewards and concessions. He was very pleased with a Thai chief (either Indrāditya or Rama Khamheng) and he consecrated him as king of Sukhodaya and he gave him independence and suzerainty over Thailand. He took their help to defeat his brother-in-law and to imprison him and he waited for sometime when the old king abdicated in his favour. He then ascended the throne. The civil war brought political troubles at home and abroad but produced a very significant event no doubt. The Sukhodaya kingdom of Thailand was founded at this time.

In about the middle of the thirteenth century AD two small states Muang Bang Yang (Mo'an Pan Yan) and Muang Rat (Mo'an Rat) were governed by two Thai chiefs and they were Bang Klang Thao or Pan Klan Dav and Pha Muang or Pha Mo'an under Khmer sovereignty. These two states revolted against the Khmer governor at Sukhodaya and at Sri Sachanalai or Si Satchanalai or Sawankhalok or Sajjanālaya and established the first independent Thai kingdom of Sukhodaya in north-central Thailand. They became rulers of Thailand and thus they were able to put an end to the political supremacy of Cambodia over them. The chief of Muang Bang Yang became the first ruler of the dynasty and he took the title of Indrapatindrāditya or Śrī Indrāditya or Śri Int'arat'itya. Thus was founded the Thai state of Sukhodaya,[4] and this was an important event in the political history of Thailand.

Ram or Rama Khamheng, Rama the Brave (AD 1275-1317 or 1283-1317) was the next ruler of Sukhodaya. He occupied the throne after his father Śrī Indrāditya. He may justly be called the first Thai king of Thailand. Śrī Indrāditya had three sons. The first or the eldest died young and the second ruled for a few years only. He was Ban Muang. Rama Khamheng was the

4. *AHSEA*, p. 936.

youngest. In AD 1275 he reigned his father's kingdom. He ruled over the central and southern regions of Thailand and his capital was at Sukhodaya which was situated in southern Thailand. Between AD 1283 and AD 1287 he occupied the places of the Mons of the Menam valley and established the Thai rule for Khmer over the region which included much of the upper Mekong area as well. In AD 1287 Mangrai, Rama Khamheng and Ngam Muang, the chief of P'ayao not only established friendship but also came to an argument. This year witnessed the decline of the Khmer power as well as the disappearance of a strong Myanmar and this gave an opportunity to the Thais to expand their territories. Rama Khamheng occupied an important place in the political history of Thailand as a renowned statesman. During his rule Sukhodaya has been mentioned as the 'cradle of Siamese civilisation'. He established friendly relations with the imperial court of China. He visited China in AD 1294 and in AD 1300 and he married a Chinese princess there in AD 1300 and many ceramic workers from China came to Thailand with him. They were regarded as the pioneers of the ceramic art of Thailand. The pioneers of ceramic industry in Thailand were the Chinese potters from Chihili who came in a batch of three to five hundred at the invitation of king Rama Khamheng of Sukhodaya. Swami Sadananda says,

> Without assailing the truth of the presence of Chinese artisans at Sukhothai during Ram Kamhaeng's reign, suffice it is state that some eight hundred years before Siam may be said to have begun the manufacture of glazed porcellanous utensils. And to the first Thai colonists of the area where the Mekong rises goes the credit of this innovation.

During the rule of Rama Khamheng Sukhodaya became prosperous and it was ruled justice and magnanimity. From his subjects — the Mons and the Khmers, he adopted the script which he introduced for reducing the Thai language to writing in AD 1283. There was no alphabet for his people and he discovered one. For their use he wanted to adopt an official language and he used the new characters for the first time in his famous inscription of AD 1292 at Sukhodaya and this inscription was regarded as the oldest extant specimen of the Thai language. His script or alphabet became well-known in Thailand as 'Sukhodaya script', and it was used throughtout Thailand. Charles Eliot says that this alphabet was taken from Cambojan but some of the letters particularly in their later shapes indicate that the Mon or Talaing script made a great influence upon it. It seems that the modern Cambojan alphabet is 'little more than an elaborate form of Siamese' and for ecclesiastical purposes in Thailand the Thais used it very much. Charles Eliot describes furthur that

> this script subsequently developed into the modern Siamese writing which, though it presents many difficulties, is an ingenious attempt to express a language with tones in an alphabet. The vocabulary of Siamese is not homogeneous: it comprises (a) a foundation of Thai, (b) a considerable admixture of Khmer words, (c) an element borrowed from Malay and other languages, and (d) numerous ecclesiastical and learned terms taken from Pāli and Sanskrit. There are five tones which must be distinguished, if either written or spoken speech is to be intelligible. This is done partly by accents and partly by dividing the fourty-four consonants (many of which are superfluous for other purposes) into three groups, the high, middle and deep.

Swami Sadananda mentions about the evolution of Siamese alphabet and literature. He states,

> Though the Thai characters might have originated long while back, they must have been profoundly impressed by these of the Khmers. The language of the Thai covers

an extensive terrain which only modern means of quick transport and communication has shortened the time taken in covering it. As this was not possible before the end of the ninteenth century the manner of writing and the way of pronouncing the same word has been varied. Some of them retained Hindu alphabet while others have altered it. Some are inclined to write in horizontal line and others prefer vertical columns. Some have preserved the origal forms and others have transformed them. Some write from right to left whereas others do the reverse way. But not untill king Ram Kamhaeng ascended the throne at Sukhodhya, the final forms of the Siamese letters were decided upon. Ram Kamhaeng's own inscription states, 'Hereofore these strokes of Thai writing were not. In 1205 of the era, year of the Goat, Prince Khun, Ram Kamhaeng sought and desired in his heart and put into use these strokes of Thai writing. And so these strokes of Thai writing because that Prince employed the same.' It clearly paints to the fact that Ram Kamhaeng did not invent Thai alphabet nor the script but simply elaborated. The initiative he took in AD 1283-84 was at first slow in its application, but it tolled the death-knell to the archaic Mon scripts which had been hitherto exclusively used in all writings of Siam. For the reformation of the alphabet and its spread in the country King Ram Kamhaeng had to take help of the teachers of Pāli from Ceylon. He could count among the learned men of his line the head of the religious body who knew by heart the three Piṭakas and it was notably under his direction that the Thai evolved the script of the nation. It was one thing for an enthusiast like king Ram Kamhaeng to evolve a new script and have a tablet engraved in the same characters for commemorating the occasion, it was quite another matter to ensure its application nationwide. The Khmers and their late subjects like Mons were naturally loth to forego all of a sudden the manner of writing they were as long familiar with in preference to new one their conqueror wished to impose upon them. Besides, the Aryanised races could only think even of their mundane affairs in the light of their religion. The literacy efforts of the age were confined to the belief they cherished. Hence composing or transliterating chiefly centred round religious themes and dogmas which only monks were educated enough to undertake. The preponderance or the diminution of works on any special tenets varied directly with their growth or their decline in popularity. Moreover, monasteries were not only depositions of manuscripts but monks were also largely responsible for the speed of sacred and secular education. King Tissaraja might be hailed as having given an impetus in the right direction to the literary movement of the day when he established the direct spiritual bondage between his principality and Ceylon. In AD 1361 the Ceylonese Theras visited the Sukhothai monasteries but a steady in-flew of Pāli texts and annotations only ensued when the Siamese started voyaging to and studying at the fountain-head of Theravadism. This promoted the transliterations of Pāli works into the script of the country and the Kamhaeng alphabet had at last a fair chance of being accepted by the majority.

Sukhodaya's geographical situation no doubt helped it very much to play a great role as the cradle of Siamese civilisation. George Coedès remarks,

> From Cambodia the Siamese assimilated its political organisation, material civilisation, writing and a considerable number of words. Many Siamese artists learned from Khmer artists and transformed Khmer art according to their own genius, and above all under the

> influence of their contact with their Western neighbours, the Mons and Burmese. From these latter the Siamese received their juristic traditions, of Indian origin, and above all Sinhalese Buddhism and its artistic traditions.

Rama Khamheng's inscription gives us an account of his conquests. It describes,[5]

> Rama Khamheng is sovereign lord of all the T'ais. . . . He has conqured the multitude of his enemies, possessing spacious cities and numbers of elephants. Eastwards he has conquered the land up to Saraluang (P'ichit), Song K'we (P'isnulok), Lum (Lomsak), Bachay, Sakha up to the banks of the Mekong and as far as Vieng Chan, Vieng Kham which mark the frontier. Southwards he was subdued the country up to Khient'i (on the Meping between Kamp'engp'et and Nakhon Savan), P'rok (Pakna P'O), Sup'annaphum, Ratburi, P'etchaburi, Si Thammarat (Ligor), up to the sea, which marks the frontier. Westwards he has conquered the country up to Mueng Chot (Me Sat), Hangsavati (Pegu) and up to the sea which marks the frontier. Northwards he has conquered the country up to Mueng P'le (P're), Mueng Man, Mueng P'lua (on the river of Nan), and on the other side of the Mekong up to Mueng Chava (Luang Prabang) which marks the frontier.

It is very difficult to check up this list given in it in every detail. From it we learn that the Sukhodaya kingdom was able to extend its territory on the coast to the banks of the Mekhong and also to Chava (or Luang Prabang); on the south up to the sea, as far as Śrī Dharmarāja or Ligor; and on the west up to Haṁsāvatī or Pegu. Rama Khamheng became well-known in Thailand's history as a king of wisdom and learning and a skilled diplomatist. He showed his great respect towards justizce and he promoted peace

5. *AHSEA*, pp. 172-174; *LEHII*, p. 342.

He created through his genius a name not only for himself but the state he reigned. It was he who transformed the small principality of Sukhodaya a first rate power not only by conquest alone but also by his fine administrative qualities. "In every way he deserves to be acclaimed the first national king and here Siam (Thailand) ever saw". He built a formidable fortress with triple walls, four fortified gates, palaces and lakes at Sukhodaya. He took several aspects of the military organisation of the Mongols and also their threefold division of society and he introduced them into his country. In the epilogue to his inscription he says,

> Rama Khamheng sought to be ruler and lord over all the Thai, to be preceptor and instructor to all the Thai, to know true virtue and righteousness. Among Mon that live in the realm of the Thai, for knowledge and insight, for bravery and daring, for energy and force, there cannot be found a man equal to him. . . .

His reign came to an end before AD 1218. According to a tradition, his disappearance took place in the rapids of the river Sawankhalok.

Rama Khamheng was succeeded by his son Lo T'ai or Lo Thai or Loe Thai (AD 1317-47). Some writings refer to him as Sua T'ai or the 'tiger of the T'ais'.[6] He was a weak ruler and he did not take any interest in the political matters of his kingdom and under him the power of Sukhodaya declined. Most probably, he died in AD 1347. The next ruler was his son Lut'ai or Lu Thai,[7] who was a viceroy at Si Satchanalai or Sawankhalok. In AD 1347 he went to Sukhodaya where troubles broke out at the death of his father. He seized the city and occupied the throne and took the title of Śrī Sūryavaṁsa Rāma Mahādharma-rājādhirāja. He also became known as T'ammaraja Lut'ai or

---

6. *AHSEA*, p. 175.
7. *Ibid.*, pp. 175 and 936.

Dharmarāja. Like his father he was a religious person and he had no feelings for military conquests. An inscription gives an account of him. It describes,

> The king observed the ten royal precepts. He showed mercy towards all his subjects. When he saw another man's rice he did not covet it, and when he saw another's wealth he did not behave unworthily. . . . If he arrested people guilty of cheating or insolence, those who put poison in his food so as to cause him illness or death, he never killed or beat them, but forgave those who behaved evilly towards him. The reason why he repressed his heart and restrained his temper, and did not give way to anger when he might have done, was that he desired to become a Buddha and to take every creature beyond the ocean of the affliction of transmigration.

In order to join the Buddhist monastery, he gave up his job and resigned his crown. The next ruler was his son T'ammarāja II. He occupied the throne in AD 1730. His son T'ammarāja III ascended the throne in AD 1406 after him. The next ruler was his brother T'ammarāja IV. He captured the throne in AD 1419. It may be noted here that T'ammarāja IV and other rulers who came after him were mentioned as merely hereditary governers under Ayut'ia or Ayuthia.

The Ayudhya or the Ayuthia dynasty

From a tradition we learn that a powerful and an ambitious Thai prince of the Chiengsen house and Mangrai, the founder of Chiengmai also belonged to it brought Lavo under his control and received the acknowledgement of his suzerainty from the Sukhodaya ruler Lu T'ai or Lu Thai by using force. He then founded the Ayudhya or the Ayuthia dynasty in AD 1350 and established his capital Dvāravatī Śrī Ayudhya on an island in the Menam in southern Thailand. Thus the middle of the fourteenth century AD witnessed its rise and growth. Ayuthia or

Ayut'ia or Ayodhia remained as the capital of the Thai people up to AD 1767 when a Myanmarese invasion took place. There were about thirtythree Thai kings of Ayuthia. The first ruler of this kingdom was Ramadhipati or Rama T'ibodi. It became a powerful kingdom and it brought under its control both the middle and the lower Menam valleys and an important portion of the Malay Peninsula, including Tenasserim and Tavoy and also restricted Sukhodaya in every way by using force[8] and it remained as its vasal state. It also wanted to subdue Cambodia and its capital Angkor. According to O.W. Walters[9] during Ramadhipati's rule the Thais were able to capture Angkor and it took place in AD 1369. But the ruler died in this year. Lawrence Palmer Briggs thinks that the conquest of Angkor did not occur untill AD 1431. Ramadhipati introduced the Thai Law Code. It gave the basic principles of Thai law for centuries up to the reign of Chulalongkorn and modern legislators in their legislations followed them very much. The king died in AD 1369. His son prince Ramesuen, the Governor of Lopburi, succeeded him. He was unable to acquire good name as a ruler and he became very unpopular. In AD 1370 he abdicated and his uncle occupied the throne as Boromoraja I or Paramaraja I (AD 1370-88). Under his rule Ayuthia was able to extend its territory further in northern Thailand and it re-restablished its authority over the upper Menam valley. In AD 1371 he invaded the northern kingdom and captured several towns. Due to his aggressive attitude towards northwards, Chiengmai became furious and for this reason trouble started and Chiengmai's relation with Ayuthia became very bad and a struggle began which continued for several countries. Boromoraja I's son was T'eng Lan. He was a boy of fifteen when he ascended the throne of Ayuthia after his father's death. But he was murdered by Ramesuen, the ex-king and the latter captured the throne and ruled until

8. *AHSEA*, p. 176; *SEA*, p. 146.
9. *Ibid.*, p. 177.

AD 1395. He invaded the Khmer lands and in AD 1389 due to his invasion Angkor fell. The next ruler was Ram Raja, who was a son of Ramesuen. But in AD 1408 he was dethroned by a palace revolt and Boromoraja I's nephew occupied the throne and he became known as Int'araja (AD 1408-24). He had three sons. When he died a struggle between the two elder ones broke out for the throne. But they were killed when an attempt was made to settle it by personal combat on elephants. Then the youngest brother ascended throne of Ayuthia and he became known as Boromoraja II (AD 1424-48). He was mentioned as a conqueror of Angkor. He wanted to install a Thai puppet king upon the throne of Cambodia but he was not successful. He then wanted to see Cambodia a vassal state, but his mission was not fulfilled. From the Combodian chronicle we learn that the Thais were unable to capture any territory when a struggle broke out between them in AD 1431-2. In AD 1438 Ramesuen, the eldest son of Boromoraja II, became the governor of P'itsanulok and Boromoraja II gave his approval. Then in AD 1442 when a succession struggle began in Chiengmai and the king of Ayuthia took part in it. But he was defeated by the Chiengmai army. During this campaign the king became ill and he died in AD 1448 when he took the leading part to invade the Chiengmai territory.

The next ruler was Ramesuen (AD 1448-88).[10] He became known as Boromo Trailokanat or Trailok. He was an able ruler and good statesman. He tried to centralise system of administration. He re-organised the central administration on a departmental basis and he raised the rank of its principal officers. He made a great distinction between the five great civil departments and the military administration. These were the civil departments — the Ministry of the Interior and the chief minister was its head; the Ministry of Local Government for the city and province of Ayuthia; the Ministry of Finance for foreign trade; the Ministry of Agriculture for cultivation and land tenure

10. *AHSEA*, p. 179, *SEA*, p. 147.

and the Ministry of the Royal Househeld for Palace Affairs and Justice. A division also took place in the military administration and it was divided into several departments. Their heads occupied the position of ministers. In AD 1450 Trailok declared a Code of Palace Law. It mentioned the obligations of tributaries to the Thai Court and referred to the positions of Court personnel and princely descendents.

> The code borrowed from Cambodia the principle that princely status was subject to progressive reduction in rank, one grade per generation through five levels, until it degenerated to mere freedom status to the end.

It codified and also clarified existing custom. It described the tributary states and the form of their tribute, stated the relative rank of all classes at Court from queens and royal princes downwards, gave an account of ceremonies, discussed functions of officials and mentioned punishments. King Trailok saw many diffuculties in law of succession. For this reason he introduced a second or vice-king called the Uparat as the heir apparent. He laid down rules relating to the status of the different classes of people and also mentioned amounts of land to each person. Under the social system of Thailand every Thai man used to possess an amount of land and this they used to get according to his status. This system no doubt gave a framework to society. Trailok regulated the Sakdi Na grades. Each official used to receive the amount of land introduced by the Sakdi Na and he used to live on the revenue got therefrom. This was the financial condition of each official begare salaries were introduced in the second half of the nineteenth century AD. According to a Man's Sakdi Na grade, the Court used to impose the amount of the fine and for his murder the compensation was also paid according to it. Trailok's reign witnessed war with Chiengmai. But he could not do anything in a definite way. In the meantime smallpox broke out in his kingdom. He expected threat from Chiengmai and it was for this reason he transferred his headquarters from Ayuthia to P'itsanulok in AD 1463 and it became his capital. In AD 1461 the Chiengmai army captured Sukhodaya and occupied P'itsanulok. But an invasion from Yunnan had compelled the army people to retire to protect their own teritories and the Thais in AD 1462 were able to recapture Sukhodaya. But Chiengmai kept Sawankhalek in its possession. After sometimes the former again attacked Sukhodaya. The Thais chased the enemies as far as Doi Ba and they were checked and they returned to their capital. After this war there was peace for several years. In the meantime Trailok became a monk and lived in a monastery for sometime. In order to weaken Chiengmai a Myanmarese monk was sent by him to Chiengmai to saw dissension at the Court of Chiengmai. In order to obtain the same object he also sent a mission in the next year and the leader was a brāhmaṇa. But the Chiengmai Court was able to discover the plot and the brāhmaṇa and the Myanmarese monk with stones tied to their necks were thrown into the river. There was no peace at all and the war began in AD 1494 and it continued for the next quarter of a century.

Trailok died in AD 1488. But before his death he made prince Jott'a as Maha Uparat, i.e., second king or vice-king.[11] But he was not his eldest son. After Trailok's death Boromoraj III (AD 1488-91), his eldest son, ascended the throne and Ayuthia again became his capital and Jai Jott'a as Maha Uparat became the governor of P'itsanulok. After the death of Boromoraj III, Jai Jott'a, his brother, as Rama T'ibodi (AD 1491-1529) succeeded him. Duarte Fernandez, the first envoy of the Portuguese conqueror of Malacca, visited his Court. Rama T'ibodi allowed the Portuguese to trade at Ayuthia, Nakhon Sritammarat, Patani, Tenasserim and Mergui. Ayuthia's fresh trouble again started with Chiengmai. One of the Thai Royal princess, who took the yellow robe brought a white crystal image of the Buddha to Ayuthia from Chiengmai. For this reason the king of

11. *AHSEA*, p. 183.

Chiengmai made an attack on the Thai region and Rama T'ibodi established the image. In AD 1508 the former invaded Sukhodaya and the Thais also in return attacked Chiengmai. In AD 1513 the Chiengmai army not only disturbed Sukhodaya by invasion but also brought many prisoners of war and booty to Chiengmai from Sukhodaya. After two years they captured Sukhodaya and Kamp'engpet but the Thai king led a large Thai army and he fought bravely and he defeated them on the banks of the Ma Wang river near Nakhon Lamp'ang. Rama T'ibodi re-organised the whole military system upon the basis of compulsory service. He divided the kingdom into military divisions and sub-divisions and asked all man of eithteen and over to enrol their name for call-up, if and when needed. The next ruler was Boromoraja IV (AD 1529-34) who established peace with Chiengmai. For this reason he made an agreement with Chiengmai. He was the son of Rama T'ibodi. Ratsada, his son, ascended the throne in AD 1534 after him. Then came P'rajai who was Boromoraja IV's half brother. He occupied the throne in AD 1534. He invaded Chiengmai and princess Maha Tewi resisted this attack of the Ayuthian ruler. When P'rajai returned home from his campaign against Chiengmai, then T'ao Sri Suda Chan, one of his four senior non-royal consorts, poisoned him and she was pregnant by her lover. Her own son Koe Fa, who was a boy of thirteen, occupied the throne of his father as king in AD 1546. Then T'ao Sri Suda Chan placed her lover Khun Worawongsa on the throne in AD 1548. But after two months, at a royal banquet they were murdered. It is said that they were killed in the royal barge while they were on their way to an elephant hunt. The next ruler was Prince T'ien, who was a younger brother of P'rajai. He with the title of Maha Chakrap'at ascended the throne of Ayuthia in AD 1549 under the instruction of the leaders who played their great roles to kill T'ao Sri Suda Chan and her lover. This event took place in AD 1549. W.A.R. Wood in his *History of Siam* (p. 112) mentions this event in AD 1549. But D.G.E. Hall refers to this event a year earlier. Because the Myanmarese chronicles describe that Tabinshwehti (AD 1531-50) invaded Thailand towards the end of the year of Maha Chakrap'at's accession to the throne. Bayinnaung, who was a king of Myanmar, wanted to receive submission of all the Thai states to his authority and he demanded a couple of white elephants from Maha Chakrap'at and the latter flatly refused it. After the close of the wet monsoon of AD 1563 the Myanmarese forces proceeded towards Ayuthia. They after crossing the Sittang valley, Chiengmai, Kamp'engp'et and Sukhodaya arrived in Ayuthia and they were able to capture it in February AD 1564 and they did not get any resistance from the Ayuthian forces. They brought king Maha Chakrap'at and all the family members of the royal house to Myanmar as hostages. They then made Maha Chakrap'at's son Mahin as vassal ruler and a Myanmarese garrison was posted at Ayuthia to control him. Mahin was a boy of sixteen and he became a ruler of Ayuthia in AD 1569. Under the supervision of the Pre-Myanmarese ruler of P'itsanulok prince Mahin used to function as a ruler of Ayuthia. But he tried always to throw away the influence of Bayinnaung. He made an alliance with Sett'at'irat of Vieng Chang and they in AD 1566 invaded P'itsaunlok but due to the arrival of the Myanmarese army they then abandoned this idea. In the meantime Maha Chakrap'at became a monk in Myanmar and King Bayinnaung allowed this captive ruler to return to his country on a pilgrimage. But after his arrival in Ayuthia he threw off the yellow robe and he and the prince jointly attacked P'itsanulok. On seeing it Bayinnaung invaded Ayuthia for the second time in AD 1568. Ayuthia resisted it very bravely and Sett'at'irat also helped it by sending a force but the Myanmarese forces drove it off. During this invasion Maha Chakrap'at had died and prince Mahin also died as a prisoner while he was going to Pegu in Myanmar. Then Bayinnaung placed Maha T'ammaraja, the Pre-Myanmarese ruler of P'itsanulok, as the vassal ruler of Ayuthia in AD 1569. The former then moved to Vien Chang to punish its ruler. Many people from Ayuthia at this time went to lower Myanmar to settle there. For about next fifteen years Ayuthia was under the control of Myanmar. At this time Thailand adopted the Myanmarese Era which began in AD 638. In order to distinguish it from the Maha Sakarat which began in AD 78, it became known as the Chula Sakarat. When Chulalengkorn came to power in Thailand, he then adopted the European calender in AD 1887 and then there was no official use of it.

The next ruler of Thailand was Pra Naret, the 'Black prince'. He was the elder son of T'ammaraja, who was a vassal ruler of Ayuthia.[12] He as a hostage was in Myanmar for about six years and he knows Myanmar's military methods.[13] In AD 1571 he was a boy of sixteen and Bayinnaung, the Myanmarese ruler, allowed him to return to Ayuthia. He was a brave person and he became the leader of Thailand's nationalist independence struggle. He proved himself as a prominent leader for his "effective and courageous military leadership against the invading Cambodians". Nanda Bayin of Myanmar wanted to kill him but the Mon chiefs disclosed this matter to him. He then went to Pegu in Myanmar and tried to attack it. He brought a large number of Thai prisoners, who were captured by Bayinnaung from Myanmar to Thailand. Nanda Bayin attacked Ayuthia in December AD 1584 through the Three Pagodas Pass, midway between Moulmein and Tavoy and the Chiengmai army joined him, but each force was defeated separately by Pra Naret. In November AD 1586 three Myanmarese armies proceeded to attack Ayuthia and it was captured by them from January to June AD 1587. But this invasion did not bring a good result. Then Pra Naret turned his attention towards the Combodians instead of Myanmar and he nearly made his effort fruitful to capture their capital but owing to short supplies he abandoned his plan and returned home. In AD 1590 Pra Naret ascended the throne of Ayuthia after the death of his father T'ammaraja and he took

---

12. *AHSEA*, p. 271; *SEA*, p. 192.
13. *ASEAW*, pp. 118-20.

the title of Naresuen. In AD 1592 he defeated the Myanmarese armies and there were led by the heir apparent to the Pegu throne and he was killed at Nong Sa Rai before he was able to reach Ayuthia. The former conquered Tavoy and the Tenasserim coast in AD 1593 and also Moulmein and Martaban. After the defeat of the Myanmarese in February AD 1593 he turned his attention to attack the capital of the Cambodians. He conquered the Cambodian capital Lovek in AD 1594 and established many captives who were brought from Cambodia to several parts of northern Thailand. The king of Lovek fled to Luang Prabang. In the next year the Myanmarese viceroy requested Naresuen's aid to help him against Luang Prabang's invassion and he regained Thailand's control over Chiengmai and it came under the rule of the Ayuthian ruler. In AD 1595 the Thais attacked Pegu but their mission was not fulfilled. Naresuen wanted to capture Nanda Bayin and for this purpose he proceeded towards northwards to invade Toungee but he was defeated and he returned home. After sometime Nanda Bayin was murdered. Thailand took the control of lower Myanmar from Martabon southwards under Naresuen. The latter was a great ruler of Thailand. He occupied 'one of the most honoured places' in his country's history. It was due to his able leadership, Thailand gained its independence. He liberated Thailand from the rule of the Myanmarese. When he failed to capture Toungee in AD 1600, he then showed his keen interest in the Shan States and they became independent countries after the defeat of Nanda Bayin in AD 1599. The former died in AD 1605.

Ekat'etsarat ascended the throne of Ayuthia in AD 1605 after the death of his brother Naresuen. He was the 'white king'.[14] His representatives received Dutch and English ship captains at Aceh in Sumatra and they invited both companies to trade with Thailand. He was a ruler who did not take any interest in war and his aim was to do something for financial reform and trade.

14. *ASEAW*, p. 357.

The Dutch not only interested to connect trade with his country but they established one factory at Patani in AD 1602 and another at Ayuthia. The Japanese and the Chinese also had trade connections with Thailand. The Japanese were regarded as the first foreign traders who established their trade connection with Thailand. The Dutch faced a very strong opposition of the Portuguese and the Japanese in their trade at Patani and Ayuthia but the rulers of these places gave them a warm welcome and they gave them facilities to trade at these places. Maurice of Nassau received in AD 1609 at the Hague a Thai mission from Ayuthia. This was for the first time the Thais went to Europe. King Ekat'etsarat took monopoly control over all items of foreign commerce and both export and import policies were under the strict control of the king. He introduced a new tax on ships and markets. The Thais wanted to encourage the revival of the isthamian portage trade which was suspended for a very long time.

Int'araja II, who was the son of Ekat'etsarat, occupied the throne of Ayuthia in AD 1610 after his father.[15] He was known as Songt'am, 'the Just'. He resigned up to AD 1628. He not only overcame political difficulties but also controlled very firmly. His reign witnessed a Japanese rising and their patron was a minister who was executed because it was due to him the death of the Maha Uparat took place in the previous reign. They not only sacked Ayuthia but also established their hold at P'etchaburi. The king of Luang Prabang also attacked Thailand. Songt'am played his vital role to drive away the armies from Laos and he defeated the Japanese and he acted very firmly. P'etchaburi became powerless. The Japanese came to an agreement with the king of Ayuthia and they remained as the royal body-guards. Peace was established in AD 1612. In spite of the opposition from the Dutch Songt'am allowed a factory of the East India Company at Ayuthia and he also received a complimentary letter from

15. *AHSEA*, pp. 257-62.

King James I of England. He had a trouble with the Myanmarese and then he had the peace agreement with them in AD 1618. Tavoy was kept under his control and he accepted the control of the Myanmarese of Chiengmai in the north-west. In AD 1622 the Thais tried to establish their control over Lovek but they failed to do it. King Songt'am did his best to get support of the Dutch and the English against Cambodia but they never allowed themselves to support him in his activities against the Cambodians. Cambodia was able to retain its independence. Although he was in trouble with Cambodia, Luang Prabang and Japan, yet he was a peaceful and religious person and he was a monk for sometime. He disliked war very much. The East India Company closed its factories at both Patani and Ayuthia in AD 1622 and it was unable to establish regular trade with Thailand for thirty-seven years. The Dutch factory at Patani was also closed. This company could not do well in its trade there.

The next ruler of Ayuthia was Jott'a (AD 1628), who was a son of Songt'am.[16] P'ya Sri Worawong, a cousin of Songt'am was the real ruler and Jott'a was a puppet in his hands and he used to rule under his direction. At'ityawong, a brother of Jott'a ascended the throne in AD 1630 after him. A powerful minister captured the throne of Ayuthia in AD 1630 and he took the title of Prasat T'ong, the king of the Golden Palace. He poisoned Songt'am and his two sons were eliminated by him. He was a very bad person. The Ayuthian people used to call him 'the bottled spider'. When the Japanese leader Yamada stood against him at the time of his usurpation, he poisoned him and he tried to kill the Japanese people in Ayuthia in AD 1632. But he was unsuccessful and many Japanese left Thailand by sea. He then expelled the survivors from his kingdom. The Dutch people became his close friends and they gave him assurance that they would support him against his enemies. In AD 1632 he received a letter from prince Frederick Henry of the Netherlands who sent

16. *AHSEA*, p. 360.

his congratulations for his accession to the throne of Ayuthia. In AD 1634 he allowed the Dutch to construct a " 'stone lodge, with fit packhouses, pleasant apartments and a commodious landing place' on the river-bank at Ayuthia". But his relation with the Dutch became very bad in AD 1636 when the Dutch did not help him. The queen of Patani mentioned him as a 'rascal, murderer and traitor'. He attacked Patani in AD 1632 and in AD 1634, but he failed very miserably. The Dutch did not help him in his first attempt in AD 1632, but in AD 1634 the Dutch sent their help but it was too late. In AD 1636 Prasat T'ong wanted to attack Patani but with the help of the Dutch there was an agreement between the two countries. The former's relation with Patani became very bad in AD 1639, 1648 and 1654. But he established a friendly term with the Dutch for sometimes. In AD 1649 the Dutch wanted to attack Ayuthia when he was unable to satisfy their certain demands. Its result was very bad. The Dutch factory was captured and its inmates were killed. Five years later another trouble arose. The Dutch refused to help Prasat T'ong against Singora, who rebelled. On this occasion the Dutch ship demonstrated in the Gulf of Siam. The Ayuthian ruler then changed his attitude and the peace was established. Although he became well-known for his some creditable reforms, yet it "exhibited periodic orgies of vindictiveness which counted victims by the thousands".

Prasat T'ong died in AD 1656 and two kings ascended the throne after him. But they were murdered. They ruled for a very short period. They were Chao Fa Jai (AD 1656) and Sri Sut'ammaraja (AD 1656).[17] The former was a son of Prasat T'ong and the latter was his brother. Then his younger son took the throne. He was Narai and he ruled for thirty-one years (AD 1657-88). He was energetic, very lively and well-mannered. He showed his friendly attitude towards all his subjects and he did not like war. His reign witnessed Ayuthia's struggle with Myanmar for Chiengmai. He wanted to make his country free from the

17. *AHSEA*, p. 937.

economic control of the Dutch. Because the Dutch people controlled his country's economy very tightly. Narai, in order to take the help of Louis XIV of France, established his contact with him. In AD 1660 he went northwards with a large force but he had to retire. In AD 1661 a large Myanmarese force invaded Thailand by the Ataran river and the Three Pagodas Pass towards Kanburi but they were driven away by the Thias. In AD 1662 the Thais not only raided Myanmar but also occupied Chiengmai. At that time king Pyo of Ava of Myanmar became helpless and he could not do anything for it. In AD 1664 the Chiengmai people revolted against the Thais who were compelled to leave that place owing to them. A Myanmarese prince then became a vassal ruler or Ava at Chiengmai and the Myanmarese controlled it up to AD 1727. Narai invited refugees of the English company in AD 1659 to establish their factory at Ayuthia again and in AD 1661 the English factory was re-opened there. He allowed Bishop Lambert de La Motte of the French Société, Pallu, Bishop of Heliopolis and four priests to construct a church and a seminary at Ayuthia. The Dutch people became very angry when they saw that the English and the French were favoured by him and they wanted special commercial privileges from him. When he rejected it, the Dutch people in AD 1664 blockaded the entrance of the Menam river and he then was forced to sign in August AD 1664 a new treaty. He granted the Dutch the monopoly of the trade in hides and he also prohibited the use of the Chinese and the Japanese sailors on Thai vassals. He was worried for their victory and he tried to do something against them. In this matter he wanted the support of the East India Company and for this reason the English factory at Bantam requested London to help him. But the Ayuthia factory was under the control of Fort St. George on the Coromandal Coast and it did not like to help him in this matter. At that time the company in Ayuthia was very much mismanaged and the factory became sick and was completely ruined and the English trade in Thailand became so bad that it came under the control of interlopers in his time. In

AD 1673 Monsingnor Pallu went to Europe and then returned to Thailand and he brought a personal letter for the king from Louis XIV of France. Then the two bishops Pallu and Lambert requested the king to establish his contact with the Court of Versailles and to send a diplomatic mission there. The Court of Versailles on seening the activities of its missionaries thought that the conversion of Thailand to Christianity was imminent. The English factory was re-opened in AD 1674. The Bantam Council appointed George Burnaby in AD 1678 to investigate the matter relating to the mismanagement of the English factory. After his arrival in Ayuthia George White joined the East India Company at the request of Burnaby, who was then in Ayuthia. They then engaged Phaulkon, whose real name was Constantin Hierachy or Constantine Phaulkon, to do private trading ventures. He was a Greek seaman, adventurer and a linguist. Then in AD 1680 P'ya Kosa T'ibodi, the Thai Minister of the Treasury, appointed Phaulkon as an interpreter and he joined the Thai royal service. The Thai minister was very much impressed by his ability and soon he became Ayuthia's Superintendent of Foreign Trade and director of foreign policy. He showed his efficiency in his office and soon he became an important person in Ayuthia's foreign office. He was regarded as the dominant personality in the Ayuthian government. In AD 1680 Narai sent an embassy to the Court of Varsailles but it was unable to reach there. He received the news of this disaster in September AD 1683. He then sent two minor officials to France and he requested Louis XIV to send a French ambassador to Ayuthia to sign a treaty. These two officials left Ayuthia in January AD 1684 for France via England. According to Narai's request, Louis XIV sent the Chevalier de Chaumont as his accredited ambassador to the Court of Ayuthia together with many priests and Jesuits. He despatched them with an idea that Narai would be converted to Christianity by them. The embassy from France reached Ayuthia in October AD 1685 and the Ayuthian king received the French ambassador with pomp and grandeur. But the Chevalier de Chaumont was a religious fanatic and he was not interested in the negotiation of commercial concessions and Narai and Phaulkon wanted a political alliance with the French government against the Dutch. Phaulkon, who acted as an interpreter to all royal audience, moved in a very diplomatic way and managed the Chavalier de Chaumont in such a clever manner that the latter publicly announced a French alliance with the Ayuthian king. In return he made a draft agreement relating to "trading concessions, privileges for missionaries and the promise of the cession of Singora, near to Patani on the coast of the Malay Peninsula, as a French garrison town" and its object was to resist the Dutch from any military action against Thailand. France gained substantial commercial concessions, there was no bar in its trade, there was a monopoly in the export of pepper and there was also a partial monopoly in the export of tin. The Chevalier de Chaumont went to France in December AD 1685 and he took with him Kosa Pan, a high official of the Court of Ayuthia, as ambassador to Versailles to make arrangements for sending of the French troops to Singora. They with the Jesuit Pora Tachard came to France in AD 1886. According to Louis XIV's advisors, although Singora occupied an important position, yet it was not near the capital, Ayuthia. Its position was far away from it. "It was too remote to be use to France". Kosa Pan did not know anything about their plan. He was quite ignorant of it. The French people made arrangements in such a way that it was not possible for him to know about their movements. A squadron of six warships moved towards Thailand from Brest with 636 soldiers under the leadership of Marshal Desfarges of March 1, AD 1687. Kosa Pan, two French plenipotentiaries, Claude Coberet de Boullay, a director of the Compagnie des Indes and Simon de la Loubero, Pora Tachard and several Jesuits want with them. Pora Tachard was given charge to request Phaulkon to accept Bangkok as substitution for Singora. He was also given power to do something for the arrangement of posting a French governor and garrison to Mergui for French trade with the Coromandel Coast in particular and India in general. If Phaulkon accepted his proposal, then he would become a count of France and a Knight of the Order of St. Michael. If he opposed it, then Marshal Desfarges was told to capture Bangkok by using force. He then came to an agreement with them. He wholeheartedly supported the French plan. James II occupied the throne of England in AD 1685 and in AD 1686 a council was held at the Windsor Castle under his leadership and in it he took a decision to forbid British subjects from serving in the ships of foreign rulers in the East. In June AD 1687 the two English warships, the Curtana and the James reached Margui with king James II's letter relating to his decision at the Windsor Castle. At that time Samuel George White feared an English attack and he planned to return home by his ship the Resolution. He and all the English people in the town then decided to leave the Thai service. Anthony Weltdon or Waldton, the commander of the expedition, accepted Samuel George White's submission at its face value. But after several days, due to fire from the Thai batteries in the ships, the James sank and the Thai troops attacked the English people and they were killed by them. Samuel George White and Anthony Weltdon anyhow escaped from this attack and they with their ships, the Resolution and the Curtana took shelter in one of the islands of the Archipelago. From there Samuel George White returned to England with the permission of Anthony Weltdon and the latter then came to Madras from there. The French squadron under the command of Marshal Desfarges started for Thailand from Brest. When the East India Company of England know it, it thought that the position of its shipping in the Bay of Bengal would be in trouble if the French would capture Margui on the eastern side in addition to Pondicherry on the Coromandel Coast. King Narai then secretly advised Governor Elihu Yale of Madras to capture Mergui before its occupation by the French. Elihu Yale received it in August AD 1687 and he sent a frigate to disturb Anthony Weltden's plan of blockading the port with his two ships. But he could not do anything and he was compelled to surrendor to Dubruant, who already took its control. At this time Thailand's relations with the East India Company became very bad. When king Narai established his close contact with the Court of Versailles, Phaulkon then took a more uncompromising attitude towards the Dutch trade. In AD 1686 the Dutch company had to close its factory because of its bad relations with Thailand. When Marshal Desfarges made an expedition in AD 1687 then the Thai people thought that the Dutch would declare war against Thailand, but it did not occur. The Dutch wanted to wait and to watch the feelings of the Thai people because their forces came very close to Ayuthia. But the force were very small. In the meantime, Phaulkon in order to support the demands of the Jesuits quarrelled with Bishop Laneau, who was the head of the Missions Etrangeres at Ayuthia and the French camp did not take it lightly. King Narai became very ill at Lopburi in March AD 1688 and was too weak to do his royal activities. On seeing this situation P'ra P'etraja, the general in charge of the royal elephants, tried to establish his position boldly with a view to obtain control over the palace. Phaulkon then called General Marshal Desfarges to help him. Several thousand armed Thai people demonstrated and P'ra P'etraja took the office as regent. He then arrested Phaulkon in the middle of May AD 1688. The French people were quite helpless to save him and his and came to an end probably in the last week of June or in the first week of July AD 1688. He died in prison and the French garrisons were expelled. King Narai died probably in the month of July or August AD 1688.

P'ra P'etraja became king of Ayuthia (AD 1688-1703) after the death of Narai.[18] In September AD 1688 there was a settlement between him and the French and the French troops took their departure at the end of November AD 1688. The two sons of Marshal Desfarges and the Catholic bishop remained there as hostages. At Mergui Dubruant had to face with hostile forces

---

18. *AHSEA*, pp. 372 and 937.

and he suffered very much. His many soldiers died and he then went to Pondicherry with some of his garrison. Marshal Desfarges towards the later part of AD 1689 in order to establish French influence in Thailand captured the island of Puket, "better known as Junk Ceylon, the European corruption of its Malay name Ujung Solang". It was for this reason the Thais became very angry with the French people and many French people and the bishop who used to live at Ayuthia were killed. On seeing it, Pere Tachard to stop further trouble came to Ayuthia and he delared that his mission was to establish peace on behalf of Louis XIV and then Marshal Desfarges went to Pondicherry and from there he left for home. Pora Tachard was unable to get anything from his negotiations and he went to Pondicherry towards the end of AD 1690. But there was no more of the persecution of the Christians, the French became free and the missionaries were allowed to do their works peacefully. At that time France started war with the Grand Alliance in Europe and Louis XIV for the time being stopped his plan for the conversion of Thailand. After sometime Pera Tachard went to Thailand again to talk with the Thai authorities, but there was no result from it. The East India Company's relation with Thailand was not good. Because the agent of the company claimed a debt of 65,000 pounds and Anthony Weltdon told the Thai government at Margui to pay them. The relation was so bad that there was no hope of re-opening the English factory at Ayuthia. In the beginning of the eitghteenth century AD the English people tried to re-open a naval repair station at Thailand, but due to the opposition of the Thais, they were unable to do it. Then they moved the port of Syriam in Myanmar and the French people also followed them. P'ra P'etraja was the usurper. He played his great role to save his country from the domination of the French. He overthrow Phaulkon, stopped the French threat, took the control of the government and fought against many people who revolted during his rule. He ruled for fifteen years but his reign was not peaceful. "He earned a reputation for intemperance, cruelty and moral depravity matched by few other rulers in Siam's history." There is a controversy relating to the date of his death. The P'ongsawadan, a Thai chronicle, mentions that he died in AD 1697. There were internal disorders in his kingdom. In AD 1690 an imposter, who declared himself as a brother of king Narai, tried to capture Ayuthia. Nakhon Nayek, Lopburi and Saraburi, the three districts supported him very much but while he was attacking Ayuthia on the back of the elephant, he was wounded and captured and his elephant was shot down. The rebellious districts became so much upset to see his defeat that many people from these places took shelter in Myanmar. In the next year the two provincial governors rebelled. One was at Korat in the north and the other was at Nakhon Srit'ammarat in the Malay Peninsula. P'ra P'etraja got the control of Korat with the help of fyling kites after much difficulty. Flaming torches were attached to them and they began to set fire to the roofs of the houses with their help. The rebel governor then left the city and went to Nakhon Srit'ammarat to join its rebels. P'ra P'etraja attacked the Nakhon Srit'ammarat rebels in AD 1692 and the Korat governor was killed in this fighting. The governor of Nakhon Srit'ammarat after killing his wife and family left the city in a boat with fifty followers. He was an old friend of the admiral who commanded the royal fleet. The latter was killed and his head was placed at the city gate. Because he helped the former. Korat faced another trouble in AD 1699 by a magician and his twenty-eight followers. The governor and his people became helpless and they were afraid to see his magic powers. But the leaders and his twenty-eitht followers surrendered when they were threatened by the royal forces.

The next ruler was Uparat, who was a son of P'ra P'etraja. He ascended the throne of Thailand for a very short period (AD 1703-09).[19] He became known in Thailand's history as P'rachae Sua, 'King Tiger'. He was a cruel ruler. T'ai Sra was P'rachae

19. *AHSEA*, p. 455.

Sua'a eldest son. He ascended the throne of Ayuthia in AD 1709 and he ruled up to AD 1733. He fought against the growing influence of the Nguyen rulers in Hue in Vietnam. In AD 1715 and AD 1717 two large Thai expeditionary forces invaded Cambodia in two ways — one attacked against the coastal districts and the other moved against Udong, Keo Fa's capital. The southern force failed to do anything and it was completely destroyed by storm. The northern force attacked the capital and it defeated the Cambodians several times when they met. Keo Fa showed his allegiance to Thailand and he sought Thailand's help against Hue in Vietnam. But T'ai Sra did not express his desire to help him and in course of time the Nguyen rulers became masters of further Cambodian provinces. John F. Cady states that

> the position of the European foreigner in 1720 was described as unenviable. The Dutch factory still dealt in skins, tin and spanwood indended mainly for the Japanese market, but commercial intercourse under the royal monopoly was becoming increasingly difficult. The suspicion of European traders in particular outweighed the court's interest in either bribes or imported luxuries. A highly irresponsible Persian was apparently acting as Shahbandar. It would be the mid-nineteenth century before Siam's rulers would again welcome the foreigner. The Octogenarian French bishop of the Missions Etrangeres in 1720 operated a church and a seminary at Ayuthia. But Christian converts were very few and often insincere. The completely renegade Portuguese Christian community was served by priests whose conduct was allegedly scandalous.

T'ai Sra died in AD 1733. After his death there was a struggle for the throne between his younger brother, the Uparat and his second son, prince Ap'ai.[20] The Uparat was able to win this battle

20. *AHSEA*, pp. 455-6.

of succession. He became known in Thailand's History as Maha T'ammaraja II or as King Boromokot (AD 1733-58). He was a very dangerous person against his opponents and he showed his revengeful attitude towards them. But afterwards he reigned very peacefully and his period is referred to in Thailand's history as a golden age. He was a peace-loving ruler. He did not like to give a daughter in marriage to the Mon King, Siam Htaw 'Saming T'eh' in Thai. He did not appreciate the idea of his daughter's marriage with the Mon king. Due to the Mon rising in AD 1740 the Myanmarese governors of Martaban and Tavoy in Myanmar went to Ayuthia. At that time the relations between Ava in Myanmar and Ayuthia became very good and a Myanmarese embassy was established in Ayuthia in AD 1744. A Thai mission went to Ava in AD 1746. Saming T'eh was dethroned in AD 1747 and he took shelter in the city of Chiengmai in northern Thailand. But he tried to recapture his throne but he was not successful. He did not get any help from Boromokot. The latter put him on a Chinese junk which proceeded towards China. He got down near the coast of Annam and returned to Chiengmai. Boromokot died in AD 1758.

The next ruler of Ayuthia was Ut'ump'en, the second son of Boromokot. He ascended the throne in AD 1758.[21] But it was not possible for him to rule the country. It was very difficult for him to remain as a king. Then he joined a monastery as a Buddhist monk and he asked his brother to occupy the throne. The new ruler was Boromoraja V or Ekat'at (AD 1758-67). He was the last ruler of the Ayuthian dynasty. In AD 1758 king Alaungpaya of Myanmar attacked Thailand and captured Ayuthia. He became very angry with the Thai authorities because the latter refused to surrender Mon rebels who took shelter in Thailand. Alaungpaya wanted to repopulate lower Myanmar with Mon and Thai captives and for this reason he invaded Ayuthia. He attacked Thailand via the Tenasserim area and he reached in April AD

21. *AHSEA*, p. 456.

1760. He was injured and he died while he was returning to Myanmar before the beginning of the wet monsoon of AD 1760: Hsinbyushin, his younger son came to the throne of Ava in Myanmar in AD 1763. He then started to invaded Ayuthia again. The Myanmarese invasion of Thailand began in AD 1766. A Myanmarese force then arrived to seize Mergui and Tenasserim and soon it captured all the Thai states in the Malay Peninsula. But its progress was checked at P'etchaburi by P'ya Taksin, who was a Chinese general in Thai services. He was regarded as the saviour of Thailand. In AD 1765 three Myanmarese armies — one from Chiengmai, a second by the three pagodas route and the third from the south attacked Thailand. King Hsinbyushin arrived in Ayuthia by the route of Chiengmai and Vientiane. He and other Myanmarese forces attacked Ayuthia. In February AD 1766 they seized Ayuthia. The Thais, who did not like to surrender, protected their capital up to April AD 1767 it came under the control of the Myanmarese in the last week of April AD 1767. When there was no hope then P'ya Taksin left the place for Rayong on the Gulf of Siam. The Myanmarese not only captured Ayuthia but they also completely destroyed the city. They looted it thoroughly. When it fell at their hands, king Boromoraja took his disappearence and the Thai people never heard of him again.

The Bangkok dynasty

Phaya Tak Sin or P'ya Taksin was half-Chinese. But he took the leading part against Myanmarese domination in Thailand. After Ayuthia's fall, he extended his control over several neighbouring districts. In June AD 1767 he attacked and occupied Chantabun.[22] This success made him very popular and soon he got his many followers. In October AD 1767 he moved up to Menam and captured T'anaburi (Bangkok) and expelled the Myanmarese viceroy and was able to occupy Ayuthia again in AD 1778. He

22. *AHSEA*, p. 458.

invaded the camp of the main Myanmarese occupation force at Three Bo Trees which was very close to Ayuthia and he completely defeated it and he got his victory and occupation. He eliminated the legal heir to the throne and then he ascended the throne. At first he wanted to establish Ayuthia as his capital, but for his personal safety and on the advice of soothsayers, he then selected Bangkok as the place for his new capital. Officially Bangkok became known as the capital of Angels, the seat of the government. P'ya Taksin celebrated his coronation at T'annaburi (Bangkok). At that time the Governor of Nakhon Srit'ammarat, who controlled the peninsular provinces, declared his independence and took the title of king Musica. A son of king Boromokot who ruled over Korat and the eastern provinces declared himself as a king. The governor of P'itsanulok also announced himself as king Ruang. A Buddhist monk named Ruan in the extreme north of his provinces made himself a ruler of a theocratic state which became known as the kingdom of Fang. The Myanmarese solidly controlled Ratburi on the Mekhlong river and they kept a strong force and a fleet of boats. When the Chinese started their retreat from Ava in Myanmar in AD 1768, then King Hsinbyushin of Myanmar requested the Myanmarese governor of Tavoy to establish his connection with the Ratburi force to attack Bangkok jointly. But P'ya Taksin not only occupied Ratburi but also stopped the advancement of the governor of Tavoy's force. He defeated the Myanmarese fleet. He invaded P'itsanulek in May AD 1768. At that time king Ruang declared himself as Thailand's king. But immediately afterwards his death took place and his region was occupied by the monk king of Fang. After monsoon P'ya Taksin made an attack upon the Korat region and he was very successful and he defeated its ruler. Cambodia's king Rama T'ibodi, who was known as Ang Non, fled to Bangkok when he was driven out by Ang Tong, his brother, P'ya Taksin, in order to re-establish the exiled king on the throne, sent his Korat force to capture Siemreap and Battambang. At that time he was also busy to punish king Musica of Nakhon

Srit'ammarat. But his armies were defeated and they left Cambodia. He captured P'itsanulok and the kingdom of Fang. Then he occupied Ha-tien and he marched towards Phnom Penh and he dethroned Ang Tong and restored Ang Non. The latter with his help ascended the throne of Cambodia. But in AD 1722 Ang Tong with the help of the Vietnamese force defeated the Thai armies and re-captured his capital. But in AD 1773 the Thai nominee again was able to establish himself as king. Thailand under the rule of P'ya Taksin became the commanding power in Cambodia. In AD 1772 and 1773 Hsinbyushin attacked Thailand but he was unsucessful. In January AD 1775 P'ya Taksin captured Chiengmai in northern Thailand. In February AD 1775 a Myanmarese force took the control of Ratburi. But P'ya Taksin occupied it in April AD 1775. After sometime the Myanmarese armies again tried to re-capture Chiengmai from Chiengsen. But they were unable to recover it. In January AD 1776 Maha Thihathura of Myanmar occupied Sukhodaya. He then seized P'itsanulok. After Hsinbyushin's death, Singu his son became ruler of Ava. He attacked Thailand to recapture Chiengmai. But in September AD 1776 the Thais drove out the attackers. Chiengmai's governor and most of its inhabitants did not like to stay in that city and they took their shelter at Lampang. P'ya Taksin was able to reunite Thailand after driving the Myanmarese out of his country. In AD 1778 the king of Luang Prabang accepted Thai suzerainty. In AD 1781 General Chakri or Chao Phayo Chakkri with a Thai force proceeded towards Cambodia to establish Thai suzerainty and to place Prince in P'itok on the throne. But he returned immeadiately because the Thai people revolted in Ayuthia. The rebel Ayuthians declared that they wanted to kill P'ya Taksin, the insane king, and to see General Chakri on the throne as their ruler. P'ya Sank'aburi, a palace official, became the leader of the rebels and he came to Bangkok, and by his order P'ya Taksin left the palace and became a monk to live in a monastery. He was ousted from his power in AD 1781 by him. In the absance of Chakri he wanted to establish himself as king Chakri got this news from P'ya Suriya, the governor of Korat. The former reached there and the people of Ayuthia requested him to accept the crown. General Chakrai in AD 1782 became the king of Bangkok and he took the title of Rama T'ibodi. At that time P'ya Taksin was about forty-eight years of old. But he was not the right person to rule the country. Because there were mental disorders in him.

A new dynasty of kings took its name from Generalissime Chaopaya Chakri and this dynasty practically saved the kingdom from the Myanmarese. In it till AD 1910 there were six kings each with the surname Rama. King Rama I (AD 1782-1809) was regarded as the founder of Thailand's Chakri dynasty. His capital was at Bangkok and for this reason it became known as the Bangkok dynasty. He was P'ra P'utt'a Yot Fa Chulalok and he was half Chinese. His reign witnessed a great struggle with Myanmar. He tried to consolidate his kingdom and to reorganise its administration. For a brief period he held the Tenasserim provinces of Mergui and Tavoy and then in AD 1792 he gave them to Myanmar. He was mentioned as the founder of modern Bangkok. P'ya Taksin built his capital at Dhonburi on the opposite side of the river Menam. Rama I constructed his palace on the opposite side of the river at Bangkok and for its fortification two walls were erected by him. He re-organised the central government and aslo he organised the administration of the provinces in a proper way. Under his rule Thailand at the beginning of the nineteenth century AD became very powerful. In order to face the renewed attacks of Myanmar's king Badawpaya, and to fight against him with vigour and energy, he showed his keen interest in the defence of his country and for this reason he thoroughly organised it and gave a new look in it. Thus he made during the early period of his reign. The Myanmarese armies attacked his kingdom very often and for this reason he did not find time to assert his claims to Cambodia. During his reign the Tayson rebels and Nguyen Anh were quarrelling among themselves and taking this opportunity, he restored Cambodia's king Anh Eng to the throne of Udong, the capital of Cambodia in AD 1795. He sent him with the Thai forces under the command of Bon, who was the pre-Thai governor of the frontier provinces of Battambang and Siemreap (Angkor). This pro-Nguyen boy-king took shelter in Bangkok from the Tay-son. At this time Cambodia fully came under the control of Thailand. Rama I in AD 1795 captured several Cambodian provinces to the north of Battambang and they were Mongkolbaurey, Sisophon and Korat. He also annexed Battambang and Siamreap (Angkor). Gia Long founded the empire of Vietnam in AD 1802 and allowed Cambodia to recognise the suzerainty of Thailand and Vietnam. Rāma I made no objection for it. He revised the Thai Law Code and he had a great name for his poetical composition. He was the author of the *Ramakien*, a classical work in Thai literature. It was composed in verse in the form of recitatives for singing to the accompaniment of dance. It can be mentioned as the first systematic Thai version of the story of Rāma, hero of the *Rāmāyaṇa*. Rama I played a great role to control prevalent superstitions among the Thai people. He suppressed the worship of the Guardian Deity of the Realm and he gave order that it should be placed strictly subordinate to Buddhist faith. The king mentions in one of his decrees:

> Men's mind must not go astray to other refuges . . . such as spirits and genii. A liberal man, even if he wished to honour such (non-Buddhist) agencies as the tutelary spirits, would do so by regarding them as benevolent ones which might ward off misfortunes, but they should never value them over and above the virtues of the Three Gems. A less informed man when faced with misfortune as a result of his own past misdeed, might come to think that the Three Gems were no longer able to give help and thus forsake them for superstition. He is thus rendered a headless trunk destined for partition. It is

> therefore commanded by his majesty that henceforward, should there be alters of spirits of whatever species, even these of such a spirit as is known to be the Guardian of the Realm, it will be the duty of the officers of the administration to repair and honour them (as of yore by the people), but not to be held high to such a degree as to over stop the honour rendered to the Three Gems. And no sacrifice by killing of living animals is permitted.

Rama II was Rama I's son. He ruled for sixteen years (AD 1809-24).[23] Thailand's history never mentions him as an aggressive ruler. He did not show his great interest in the administration of his government's affairs. He was fond of literature, religious monuments and palace extension. In AD 1814 the Bangkok government sent an army to Korat and it captured several regions between the frontier of the province of Prohn-Top and the Dangrok mountains and also the province of Mlou-pray and Tonle-Ropou and also Stung Trong. By this attack Thailand possessed territories in the north of Cambodia. In AD 1821 Rama II's army attacked the state of the Sultan of Kedah and he took shelter in Penang. From this time Thailand began its political pressure upon the Malay states. Rama II in AD 1818 received a Portuguese envoy, Carlos Manuel Silveira and there was a commercial agreement between them and the latter used to look after Portuguese trade in Thailand. He was like a Portuguese council. He received the Thai title of 'luang' and possibly, he acted and worked under the Thai authority. At this time an English trader named John Hunter was allowed to live there. The East India Company tried to remove the restrictions upon the trade of the British subjects in Thailand. For this purpose the Government of India sent letters and presents to Bangkok in AD 1818 and 1819 but nothing was happened. In order to collect information and to talk with the Thai ministers to remove these conditions a Singapore merchant named Morgan

23. *AHSEA*, p. 465; *SEA*, p. 325.

in a private capacity came to Bangkok in AD 1821 with the approval of Governor Philips of Penang. The Government of India attempted to take this matter officially and John Crawfurd in AD 1821 also moved to do something in this matter. The Thai Government never accepted their proposal and did not like to make an agreement with them. But foreign individual traders were allowed to settle in Bangkok by this government.

The death of Rama II took place in July AD 1824. At this time the first Anglo-Myanmarese war started. Prince Maha Mongkut was the eldest son of Rama II by a royal mother. Every body expected to see him as king of Thailand. When his father died, he was a Buddhist monk. But a court clique allowed the dead king's eldest son who was not by a royal mother on the throne of Bangkok. He became known as Rama III (AD 1824-51).[24] He was P'ra Nang Klao. His reign has been mentioned as a 'somewhat unprogressive' one. He adopted the old-fashioned traditionalist attitude. Britain was engaged in war with Myanmar and Thailand did not show any interest in it and did not like to take part in it to support Britain. In AD 1824-25 Britain adopted policies to deal with Thailand's affairs. Governor Fullerton of Penang knew that Bangkok told the Raja of Liger to impose Thailand's authority in the straits area of Malay. He knew Thailand's attitude very well and for this purpose he proposed to take a bold policy towards Thailand. Although Thailand opposed, yet he wanted to restore the Kedah Sultan and to support and to give help to other Malay states, especially Perak and Selanger which faced trouble by the imposition of Thailand's control. Perak with the help of Solanger declared its independence from Thailand in AD 1822. The East India Company proposed to send Captain Henry Burney, the second ambassador to Bangkok. But he in AD 1826 concluded a treaty. At first there was an expectation to offer the conquered Myanmarese province of Tenasserim to Thailand but the latter's attitude on all matters was not very friendly and for this reason

24. *AHSEA*, p. 467; *ibid.*, p. 334.

the matter was not considered. When Captain Henry Burney went to Thailand there was an idea to resurrect the old Mon kingdom of Pegu in lower Myanmar. At that time thousands of refugee Mons used to live in Thailand. But Captain Henry Burney neither found any one of the royal family nor any suitable candidate outside it in Thailand for the throne. He was told to search for any one of the old Mon royal family from the Mons who used to live in Thailand as refugees fora possible candidate for the throne. In June AD 1825 there was an agreement. The 'independence' of the Malay states were mentioned in such a way as to allow all the Sultans to send the traditional tokens of vassalage status to Bangkok. The Sultan of Perak was allowed to send the symbols of tribute to Bangkok if he wanted to do so. Thailand promised that it did not like to obstruct the rights previously enjoyed by the British to trade with Trengganu and Kalantan and Britain also promised that it did not want to disturb the states in question on any pretext whatsoever. Captain Henry Burney offered 4,000 dollars a year for the withdrawal of the Thai troops from Kedah and the re-establishment of the Sultan, but Bangkok refused this offer. It wanted that Britain would agree to remove the Sultan from Penang to Malacca and would help to obstruct the exiled ruler if he wanted to return to Kadah by force. Governor Fullerton did not accept this proposal but these terms were accepted by Bengal. The British people were allowed to trade only in accordance with local custom. They were permitted to rent land and to build factories if they obtained permission from the authorities and resident Britons were subject to the Thai Courts. Rice for the exportation and opium for the importation were forbidden. A consolidated custom's levy based on the depth of a ship's beam was introduced in place of the previous eight per cent of valorem duty. Distressed seaman would get aid. Regarding the area of commercial concessions Thailand granted very little. This treaty was signed at Trang in AD 1827. Captain Henry Burney did not want to establish a consulate. He "predicted that any enforced presence of a British consul in Bangkok would broad war within six months". An envoy from the United States of America reached Bangkok in AD 1833. He made a treaty relating to the treatment of American citizens who visited Thailand. At that time Captain Henry Burney and Roberts, the American envoy, requested the king of Bangkok to give permission to establish consuls but the king never allowed to do it. In AD 1828 during Rama III's reign not only the Laos kingdom of Vientiane was extinguished but its capital was totally destroyed. This helped him to do something for the re-establishment of the control of Thailand over Cambodia. In AD 1831 P'ya Bodin, the conqueror of Vientiane, defeated the Cambodian army at Kampengchhnang and King Chan took shelter in Vinhlong and the Thai army captured Phnom Penh, Oudong and Chandoc. But the eastern provinces stood against the Thais. P'ya Bodin want to capture Vinh-long but his whole flotilla of war boats was lost by him. The Thai pell-mell was driven away by about 15,000 Vietnamese troops of the Emperor Minh-Mong and they restored Ang Chan on his throne. In December AD 1834 Ang Chan died and Ang May, a young princess, became queen under the direction of Ong Kham-Mang, the Vietnamese Resident. Minh-Mang then re-organised the administration of Cambodia, and the kingdom was divided into thirty-three provinces and they received new names. After seven years the Cambodians revolted against the rule of the Vietnamese and they requested Thailand for help and asked Prince Ang-Duong, who used to live at that time under the protection of Thailand, to occupy the throne. Then P'ya Bodin, the General, went for the second time in AD 1841 to re-establish the influence of Thailand there. He and king Ang-Duong were unable to drive out the Vietnamese army and in AD 1845 there was an agreement. Then under its agreement both Thailand and Vietnam jointly protected Cambodia. Two years later the coromation of Ang-Duong took place. Afterwards he sent his eldest son Ang Votey, who became known as king Narodom (AD 1860-1904), to Bangkok for his education. Rama III played a great role upon him because he allowed Ang-Duong's sons to work in the Bangkok government for the purpose of training. He also supported Cambodia for the development of Buddhism and he stood against the threats of Confucianist Vietnam. Both Britain and the United States before Rama III's death tried to gain more reasonable terms for their merchants. The British people felt frustrated to see the results of Burney treaty. They told about royal monopolies, especially in sugar and the prohibition of the teak trade. Sir James Brooke of Sarawak was mentioned as the British plenipotentiary and he reached Bangkok in August AD 1850. King Rama III wanted to establish good relations with Britain. But owing to his illness, he was unable to meet and to talk with him and to make a satisfactory treaty. The American Ballestier came to Bangkok after Sir James Brooke. He came there to discuss the grievances of the American citizens from the Bangkok and tried to gain a new and more favourable treaty in Bangkok government. But his mission was not fulfilled. King Rama III did not meet him and he was unable to present the president's letter. The Bangkok ministers never discussed trade matters with him. King Rama III in April AD 1851 died. His rule was effective and vigorous because it re-established royal and national prestige and it also helped to strengthen vassal control. By his good administrative system, dynamic role and good diplomacy he not only enhanced the power and the fame of his country but his government also became very strong at the time of his death. Although he could not expand his power and influence in Tanasserim, Cambodia and Malay, yet he gained very much in the last years of his reign by his rule. The foundation of the kingdom became very solid in AD 1851 than what it was in AD 1824 at the time of his accession to the throne. During his reign Thailand's ports were busy with commercial activities. British ships did not come very often to Bangkok because larger European vassals had to pay heavy duties but the smaller Chinese junks did not pay any duty. Two or three cloth-laden ships per year visited Bangkok from Coromandel Coast of India. The opium market in Bangkok flourished very much because the Chinese ships from Canton and from Singapore played their great role in it. The influx of silver due to Bangkok's favourable trade balance helped very much to move the country in the direction of a money economy. Slowly Rama III's government raised its income which amounted to double in AD 1850 than what it earned in AD 1824.[25] At the invitation of Thailand an American treaty of commerce was negotiated in AD 1833. Thailand wanted it for two reasons . . . it needed the regular importation of arms and tried to solve the problem against the threat of a British monopoly. The American negotiation did not deal with boundary problems and other political matters. It helped to moderate port duties and allowed to establish a consulate. But until AD 1856 no American consul came to Bangkok. It also gave permission for the entry of American Protestant missionaries in Thailand, although we learn from the historical records that many protestant missionaries from America arrived in Bangkok in AD 1831. Six Roman Catholic churches existed in Thailand in AD 1828. In the same year Carl Gutzlaff, a protestant missionary-linguist from Netherland, came to Thailand. He was there for three years. During his stay he translated the New Testament into imperfect Thai language, made a Thai-English dictionary, and did further Bible translations into Combodian and Lao. He in AD 1831 went to China from Thailand. The arrival of the first American Board Protestant missionaries took place there in AD 1831 and missionaries of the Presbyterians arrived there in AD 1840. The Catholics and the Protestants adopted various activities for the growth and development of missionary programmes. The Catholics followed the familiar pattern of the church and chapel ministry of the sacraments, seminary and school training for youth and the organisation of an indigenous monastic order. The American Protestants engaged themselves in translation, publication, medical missions and secular education. King Rama III at first

25. *SEA*, p. 338; *SUR*, pp. 19-20, 177-8.

did not object the activities and the programmes of the missionaries in his kingdom but afterwards he did not like the works of the Catholics. He was so much angry with them that in AD 1848 he not only ordered to destroy all Christian centres of worship, but also eight Catholic priests were expelled by him. The American Baptist Mission Press was destroyed by fire in AD 1850 and many books relating to the Christian religion were completely destroyed and employees who worked for the missionaries were imprisoned in AD 1850. Rama III in order to make profit in the foreign trade increased the price of exported sugar by 40 per cent. He with an idea to earn more profit from exports of several items such as sampan woods (for dyes), dried meat and fish, pepper and edible birds' nests employed Chinese tax farmers. He also built and operated European model ships for the purpose of his own use and also the nobles and they were duty-free. It was due to his discriminatory policy only five British vessels visited Bangkok in AD 1849. In AD 1850 Sir James Brook arrived in Bangkok from England and he requested the king for a resident consulate, extra territorial privileges for foreigners, freedom to trade, purchase land and worship and also wanted to find a policy to moderate tax systems. But the king was not happy with his arguments and did not sign any new treaty. Because he wanted to maintain his traditional tax-farming method of earning revenue and did not like to see the foreigners to engage themselves in his business world.

Kingship and Government in the nineteenth century AD in Thailand

The ruler of Thailand was regarded as a reincarnated deity, a *cakravartin*, or universal emperor and he was referred to as a destined Buddha or Bodhisattva. The sacred palace site was occupied by him. Brāhmaṇa priests, who made no influence on governmental administration, played their roles at Court to perform ceremonial and magical functions. The king was a sacred person and his authority was absolute. All the land and also the bodies of his subjects who were his moveable properties were owned by him. He was totally responsible for the welfare of his subjects. He became known as the incarnation of the authority of the state and it was for this reason he according to his satisfaction introduced and promulgated law, appointed high officials and had the power to raise or to dishonour social rank. In order to increase royal revenues he developed canal, land and trade and in this way he promoted public welfare. The Senabodi which had the heads of the six chief departments of his government was consultative council. There were three very important departments which used to deal with the affairs of the north (Myanmar frontier defence), south (the Malay frontier), and commerce and foreign relations. The three top officials, who dealt with military and revenue matters and the posts appointed on the basis of a hereditary used to enjoy a considerable measure of autonomy. Local chiefs acted as governers in the four Lactian provinces in the north and in Liger and in Singora in the peninsula. Other Malay vessel sultans used to pay tribute to the king. Several officials who acted at the royal pleasure were the heads of several departments of the capital, the palace and the lands. Judicial, administrative and revenue functions were not considered into specialised services. Court princes, especially the vice-king or Uprat were often mentioned as nominal chiefs of the six major departments 'with appropriate access to income sources'. Princes were not appointed for the post of provincial governors. The performances of all high officials and governors, especially those located near the capital were checked by censors. By means of monopolies, custom dues and tax farmers the government brought all foreign trades under its control and it gave guarantee from external danger and it remained busy for order and security. It was not responsible for local police protection against bandit outlaws. Local mediators took steps to settle all civil suits. In criminal cases when a member of the group committed offences then relatives and neighbours were compelled to give answer for offences and to help to arrest the criminal. Central government's officials were gready and corrupt and the people used to avoid them as far as possible. Thailand's social status mainly depended on royal preferment. The sons of high officials were appointed as pages at the palace and selected daughters of governors and vassal princes as political hostages used to join the royal harem. The capital was regarded as the focal point of political power, cultural standards, social preferment and wealth. Walter F. Vella remarks,

> Popular respect for authority reflected habits of deference which was related quite as much to the Chinese pattern of family relationships as to the Indian tradition of divine kingship.

Governors used to send a portion of the provincial revenues to the capital and also demanded from the people corvèe labour on public demands which amounted three or four months of duty per year and also military service. Wealthy resident patrons in the name of the king used to collect and transmit the required dues and obligations. The patron used to protect his clients from rapacity and injustice and the clients used to take money from the former when they were in need of money. There were registrations of service dues. The status of every male was tattooed on his wrist. If a client was not happy with his patron, then he had the right to change him. When he was burdened by debt, he then sold himself and his family into slavery and the patron then did not got his services. It was the duty of the patron to save, protect and guide his clients from desperates insolvancy, The land was owned by a family.

Social characteristics in Thailand in the nineteenth century AD

In the early nineteenth century AD Thailand's one-third of population was slave. The master used to pay the requisite royal dues and in return he used to got the slave's services. There were pagoda slaves and debtor slaves and the status of these categories of slaves 'could approximate that of the freeman'. Prisoners of war were regarded as chattels or movable properties of the king who used to give him slave troops. The Myanmarese, Laoctians, Cambodians or Malayasians used to reside in compact national units. Like the ordinary Thai freemen, the prisoner slaves used to live in the same way except for the performance of their royal obligations of military service. The Chinese people were busy in foreign trade, opium smuggling, etc. Commercially, Bangkok was mentioned as a Chinese city. The Chinese people were hard-working people. They were engaged in the construction of public works and they had a very good name for their love for jobs. In place of personal services they used to pay a poll tax. They remained in the posts of tax farmers. Although their societies were very active for self-protection, yet they sometimes were busy in organised crime such as smuggling and thievery. The relation between the Chinese people and the Thais became very bad after AD 1837 and there was a chance of the development of open rebellion in AD 1848. John Crawfurd describes that the Thais were peace-loving people, obedient, orderly, cautious, affectionate, etc., and their standards of domestic life were high. Their system of divorce was very easy and polygamy was very common for the rich people only. John Crawfurd refers to Thai officialdom "as rapacious, defective in candor and sincerity, and inordinately vain in its assumption of national superiority". He mentions officials as objectly servile towards superiors but disdainful toward inferiors. The Thais were easy going, fun-loving and a self-centred people and they never worried about tomorrow. They showed their indifferent attitude towards problems and they never involved themselves directly. They were tactful and unobtrusive. They were not efficient and progressive but they accommodated themselves to changing circumstances.

Prince Mongkut in April AD 1851 ascended the throne of Bangkok while Rama III was still on his deathbed. He was the eldest son of King Rama II and his queen Sri Suriyendra and he was born on Thursday, October 18, AD 1804.[26] His father gave his name Chau Fa Mongkut Sammatt Wongs which means His Royal Highness the Crown Prince or the High Prince of the crown. Like other princes of a royal family he received his early education which included Thai history of the heroic deeds of former kings and the ancient art of war, geography, and also literature and poetry in Thai and Pāli. He also studied the rudimentary precepts of Buddhism together with various maxims from the code of morality of kings. He received a thorough knowledge of royal ceremonise and customs. But his knowledge of the great contemporary world outside the palace was very little. His world moved round the world of the Grand Palace. His father, King Rama II, who was well-known for the poetical writings in the Thai language, personally supervised his education. It was due to his influence Mongkut in later life became famous in Thailand's literary world for his writings which were very beautiful and effective.[27] It was the custom in Thailand that boys who belonged to the royal family twice used to join the Buddhist *saṁgha*, first as a boy and afterwards as a young man. Therefore, Mongkut when he was only fourteen years old entered the Buddhist *saṁgha* as a novice and remained there for seven months. Afterwards, at the age of twenty, he joined the Buddhist *saṁgha* when he was a father. In the meantime King Rama II died and he had not announced the name of his successer before his death. Although Mongkut was the rightful heir to the throne, his elder half-brother Pra Nang Klao, who was born in AD 1787 of a mother not of royal blood, occupied the throne in AD 1824 and became known in Thailand's history as King Rama III. He was a quite experienced man in Thailand's political world. He occupied an important position in the reign of his grandfather and he was a minister of foreign affairs during his father's reign. At that time Mongkut was only twenty years old and was not a

---

26. *MKS*, p. 1.
27. *LVRRM*, p. 132.

well-known figure in Thailand's political world. He had no experience in the affairs of state. When he saw his brother Pra Nang Klao on the throne he then announced his desire to remain as a monk in the Buddhist *saṁgha*. He was known in the monastery as Makuto Bhikkhu, Mongkut, the Beggar. At first he joined the Wat Samorai or the monastery Samorai where Rama I and Rama II used to live as monks and had studied the sacred scriptures and took their religious training and advice from the Buddhist monks. He then joined another monastery where he devoted his time and energy to study the original sacred Pāli texts and he did very well in the examinations. At that time the Buddhist *saṁgha* of Thailand had sunk to a very low level of degeneracy. They set aside the study of the Dhamma and the Vinaya and they restored to the study of astrology, medicine and devil worship. Mongkut felt frustrated on seeing the religious condition of the country and he wanted to leave the Buddhist *saṁgha*. But under the guidance of a Buddhist monk from Pegu in Myanmar he joined the Wat Samorai where he propagated Buddhism and this brought about a great reform in the Buddhist *saṁgha* and a renaissance of religion in Thailand. As a monk he led a very simple and pious life. He used to beg his food daily. In summer and winter seasons he used to go to sacred places, used to meet many people and used to discuss with them many religious problems. Within a very short time he knew the Laotian, Cambodians, Vietnamese, Peguan, Myanmarese, Malay and Hindustani languages.[28] He took keen interest in history. During his stay at the Wat Samorai he was greatly influenced by the French prelate Bishop Pallegoix who used to live close to his place. From him he learnt Latin, mathematics and astronomy and the latter taught him not only Pāli but also the Thai language. Another missionary priest named the Reverend Jesse Caswell taught him English. He took keen interest in the scientific knowledge of the west and he learnt much from the American

28. *LBS*, p. 155.

missionaries about the major Western countries.[29] According to the advice of Rama III he in January AD 1837 became Abbot of the Wat Pawaranivesa. As a monk he founded a new sect the Dhammayutika or the Dhammayutta in AD 1837. He established his contact with Sri Lanka.

King Rama III died in AD 1851. He was succeeded by Mongkut who took the title of Phra Chom Klao or His Majesty Phra Baht Somdoch Phra Paramendr Maha Mongkut Phra Bhom Klao Chao Yu Hua.[30] He also became known as Rama IV. During his rule Thailand "may be said to have passed from the middle ages to modern times".[31] He was a very remarkable person. He was one Thai king whose fame travelled beyond the frontiers of his kingdom not only as an able king and statesman but also as one of those few heroes who by their piety and reforming zeal carved out a place for themselves in the political and religious history of Thailand. He was an active, enlightened and progressive monarch. He worked hard for the moral, intellectual and social uplift of the Thai people. He as a monk lived in the monastery for twenty-six years. His pilgrimages, preaching and his simple monastic life of twenty-six years had a great effect in his mind and made him not only an accomplished person but also helped him to rule the country efficiently as an enlightened ruler.

> The equality and simplicity of monastic life disposed him to come into direct touch with his subjects and to adopt straightforward measure which might not have occurred to one who had always been surrounded by a wall of ministers.

Under his personal care and observation, his subjects were always dutiful to their parents, offered gifts to the poor and deserving and practised non-injury and tried to lead a pious life. He always

29. *DRTS*, II, p. 126; *AHSEA*, p. 666.
30. *TSRWR*, August 29, 1957, p. 12.
31. *HB*, III, p. 87.

wanted to see that his subjects should be law-abiding, virtuous and charitable to all. He always encouraged his people to do works of social value. He was a king of advanced ideas. His reign was peaceful and prosperous. He established the position of Thailand with a strong foundation. He was forty-seven years old at the time of his accession to the throne. He was mentioned as a self-reliant man, outspoken and fearless and he used to perform his work under conviction rather than from expediency. He was a tireless worker and in his personal wants he was very frugal. He had no faith in war. He modernised his country and opened his country's doors for the Western world. For the growth of his country's economy, for the development of his educational system and to work with his government, he invited foreign experts to come to his country. He even wrote articles for the *Siam Times*, a Westerner's local newspaper. He always showed his conservative attitude relating to privileges of the nobility. He even controlled his all advisors very strictly. Many foreign missionaries were his personal friends. So his reign marked a great change in the position and in the status of the foreign missionaries. He protected all Christian subjects who were Catholics and Protestants in his kingdom. Bishop Pallegeix went to Europe in AD 1852 from Thailand and he took with him the king's letters of regard which were addressed to both Louis Napoleon of France and to the Pope. He arranged three wives of American missionaries as tutors for his chief queens to study English. In AD 1852 in Bangkok he started a Christian day school for children. With his permission a Protestant missionary office began to work at Chiengmai in AD 1863. In the early months of AD 1855 he signed the Treaty of friendship and commerce with Britain. Sir John Bowring who served as British consul at Canton from AD 1849-52 played a great role to conduct the negotiations. This treaty refered to important concessions to British merchants and the terms of the treaty declared extra territorial rights for the British subjects. It mentioned the duty payable on goods imported by the British traders, and the duty was three per cent *ad valorem*. It said that a single uniform duty on items for export and a maximum three per cent duty on imports were discussed and were written in it. It also allowed the import of opium duty-free but subject to certain necessary restrictions, and also told that according to an agreed schedule exports were subjected to duties. From this agreement it is known that the British subjects got right to buy or rent land near Bangkok, to build residences, to travel a day's journey inland from Bangkok and no additional charges were imposed on them. Sir John Bowring declared that these provisions 'involved a total revolution in all the financial machinery of the Government'. They brought about a great change in the whole system of taxation. This treaty referred to a residence of a British counsul at Bangkok who had the right to deal with civil and criminal jurisdiction over all British subjects in Thailand. "They were thus made independent of the Siamese courts and answerable to the consul alone."[32] King Mongkut first hesitated to accept this proposal. Because he feared that he would not be in a position to bring the consul under his control. But Sir John Bowring assured him that only competent persons would get this appointment. Thailand's treaty with the British government attracted the attention of other persons and they showed their keen interest to sign similar treaties with King Mongkut's government. Thus, he signed treaties with France and the United States in AD 1856, with Denmark and Hanse cities in AD 1858, with Portugal in AD 1859, with Holland in AD 1860, with Prussia in AD 1862 and with Belgium, Italy, Norway and Sweden in AD 1868. An official Thai embassy was established in Paris in AD 1861. The British trade took great advantages from the Thai government's policy which made a great change in its attitude. Singapore and Hong Kong did good business from Thailand's ports. The British Bombay-Burmah Corporation engaged itself in the teak industry in the forests of northern Thailand. Several

32. *AHSEA*, p. 669.

British firms had their foreign business in Bangkok and Britain invested largest capital in business in that country. King Mongkut also employed foreigners to reorganise the government services. His relations with France at first was very good. Napoleon III's envoy received a hearty welcome at Bangkok in AD 1856. King Mongkut gave permission to French missionaries to construct schools, seminaries and churches in his kingdom. Due to keen competition with the Brithish traders, French business people were unable to do well in their trades in Thailand. When France started to expand in Cochin China, then the trouble began with Thailand's interest in Cambodia. The treaty of AD 1867 allowed Thailand to surrender its claims over Cambodia in return for France's declaration of its rights over Battambang and Siemreap, the old Cambodian provinces and the French explored the middle and the upper Mekong only. All these facts helped king Mongkut to think about Napoleon III's imperial ambitions and for this reason he wanted to establish his contact with Britain very closely. He showed his great interest in science. A total eclipse of the sun was occurred on August 18, AD 1868 and the Thai people were able to see it. Sam Roi Yot on the Gulf of Siam which was about 140 miles south of Bangkok and which was on the western coast of Thailand was selected as the spot by a French scientific expedition to study it and king Mongkut did everything for its success. He constructed houses for his guests and himself and eracted platforms and cleared jungles to observe it. Sir Harry Ord, the Governor of the Straits Settlements and his wife and also all the Europeans in Bangkok and the Thai people took part in this scientific expedition and they saw the eclipse very well. King Mongkut got malaria from this place and he died in September AD 1868 due to fever. Practically, he died "philosophically, without fear or complaint, appropriately in pursuit of his consuming desire to learn". A scholar refers to him

> as a man who respected learning. . . and know the advantage of being able to think, to study, to devise. He

> was not himself content with the old ways of Siam. . . . It was good as far as it went.

In the nineteenth century when all other states of South-East Asia came under the control of the European powers, Thailand under his rule was able to preserve its indipendence. He abolished slavery, gambling and using of liquor and wine and developed the construction of waterways and roads. He spoke against smoking of opium. He patronised shipbuilding and he played a great role for the progress of the teaching of the foreign languages. He constructed a mint in the palace and he introduced flat coins in place of the rounded lumps of gold or silver in Bangkok. He encouraged Westerners to accept job as administrators in his kingdom. He improved the status of women and children. He was determined to modernise his kingdom. For this reason he took the services of the wives of American missionaries to teach Thailand's women. In order to teach his children he brought Mrs. Anna Loonowens, a widow English lady, from Singapore. Several English men were invited by him to work as harbour-masters and commanders of a mercenary police force from Singapore worked in his government. He also appointed a Frenchman to command and to drill the royal army. Another Frenchman acted as the royal bandmaster. An American acted as the head of the newly established Thai custom office. Another foreigner became the director of the mint. Rev. S.G. Macfarland, an American missionary, compiled English to Thai dictionary. King Mongkut connected Bangkok with the new Moulmein to Singapore telegraph line. He also introduced steamers and their services on the river and he also gave permission to use bricks for the construction of houses in Bangkok. He appointed about eighty Europeans in his administration. He wanted to make end the Chinese domination of Thailand's foreign trade and he brought Chinese economic leadership into a different relationship to the government. In AD 1850 in Thailand the Chinese population was about 300,000. In AD 1852 the Chinese opium farmers took the charge of the opium control system. When the European treaties began to carry out successfully, then the economic base of Chinese leadership in Thailand moved in a large measure from foreign commerce to the field of domestic tax and duty farms. King Mongkut composed several historical pamphlets and an English Grammar. He was a good mathematician and he calculated the occurrence of an eclipse. He abolished the custom which allowed everyone to keep indoors when the king went out. On every *uposatha* day he used to receive petitions from the public. He published edicts and he told the laity to give information to the religious authorities if they found anything wrong in the monasteries. He took steps for the edition of the annals of Thailand and he gave several orders on archaeological and literary questions,

> in which, though a good Pali scholar, he deprecated the affected use of Pali and enjoined the use of a terse and simple Siamese style, which he certainly wrote himself.

When Mongkut died, Chulalongkorn, his son, reached the age of sixteen. He took the throne and he became known in Thailand's history as Rama V. He got his early education under the guidance of Mrs. Loonowens. Then Robert Morant, an English tutor, took charge of his education. But due to Mongkut's death he trained him only about one year and a half.[33] He was a minor and for this reason his government come under a regency untill AD 1873. He visited India and Java and he studied the administrative systems of these countries. When he returned home he became a changed person and he gained experiences from these tours. He operated a series of reforms in his country and he made many changes into every department of the national life. He announced his coronation in AD 1873 and he abolished the practice of prostration in the royal presence. John F.Cady[34] says,

> The initial coronation ceremony was described as

33. *AHSEA*, p. 671.

34. *SEA*, pp. 351-2; *TSR*, I, pp. 1-2.

> something of a physical ordeal, especially in view of the Prince's feverish illness at the time. Brahman priests were much in evidence in the throwing of holy water on the white-garbed prince, at first from a golden bowl and then in a drenching shower of cold water released from an overhead canopy. This was followed by a procession on priests. Prime Minister and other high officials of government and high dignitaries of the Buddhist orders, all in turn pouring virtue-giving holy water on the shivering youth. Brahmans presented him with the magical flower-and-leaf symbols. The prince then discarded his wet clothing, donned the golden apparel of the king and ascended the octagonal dais to the throne, with Brahman priests crouching on every side, ostensibly instructing him in his duties and responsibilities. Following the administration of the formal oath of office, one of the priests proclaimed the new king as lord of his people, another as lord of the realm (land). The presentation of the insignia of royalty — golden sandals and chain sash, crown, ring and scepter — was followed by the discharge of a gun salute by both land and naval forces. High dignitaries prostrated themselves before the royal presence and foreign consuls stepped forward to great the new ruler. For Siam's first modern monarch, it was striking mingling of old and new. With the old predominating.

Rama V was a liberal reformer. He often used to drive about in public, used to mix with and used to talk with them informally. He was very young at the time of his accession to the throne and ministers who belonged to the previous reign played their great roles in his reign and they gave their directions in the affairs of the Thai government. He visited Singapore, Batavia and Samarang in AD 1871 and then went to Penang, Myanmar, Calcutta and Delhi. At each place he gave gifts to library and charitable causes. He met the leaders of the Myanmarese

Buddhist *saṁgha* at the Shew Dagon Pagoda in Rangoon and also he had a talk with the British chief commissioner there. At the time of his second and final coronation in AD 1873 he at the age of twenty became a monk and for a fortnight he lived in monastery which was situated within the boundary walls of the palace. This new king was mentioned as a dignified and an enlightened person. He in AD 1874 abolished slavery by a decree. It declared that all children of slave parents at the age of twenty-one would be free. King Mongkut laid down rules to mitigate the lot of the slaves, but Rama V declared that 'thenceforward no one could be born a slaves' and no one was allowed to sell himself for debt. He told that this was illegal. Under his patronage for the profit of the crown the compulsory services of the Prai and Sui classes in the army and police and in private labour were abolished. He appointed two councils of state to advise him in his government affairs. The king acted as president in the higher one and its members were princes and noble persons and they used to advise him on revenue measures and also on matters relating to the loyalty of his subjects. The lower-level Privy Council as a consultative semilegislative organ was established in AD 1874. It used to bring important matters and considerations for the attention of the court. A palace school for state support of secular education was established in AD 1878. There were also schools under the direction of several Buddhist monasteries and also Christian missionaries. A government printing office used to publish modern school textbooks and the Weekly Royal Gazette. On the European pattern the Thai Calendar was introduced in AD 1899 and Sunday was declared as a legal holiday. Free vaccination was given to the Thai people to stop the spread of Cholera. By a law Rama V announced the freedom of the press. An American ex-missionary became editor and several periodicals in English and in Thai were published under his direction. They were the Siam Repository, the Siam Weekly Register, the Siam Directory and the Sayahm Samai. An early royal declaration of religious toleration in AD 1871 was announced as a formal edict in AD 1878. A new royal palace in the European style was built between AD 1876 and 1880. The palace had the electric lights in AD 1894. Foreign advisors used to reside in European-style residences. There were a treasury, a custom-house, a museum, a post-and-telegraph centre, army barracks, hospitals, etc. French engineers surveyed Thailand's coaste. A German firm completed railway construction of about 200 miles in Thailand in AD 1900. It started from Paknam to Bangkok and then from the north-west to the Korat plateau. It first started with a German and an English engineers but afterwards the Thai government with its own engineers completed the Railway work. The railway to Lopburi which was about seventy miles north of Bangkok was completed in AD 1901. The northern line in AD 1909 saw its extension to Wtaradit and Sawankalok. In order to connect Bangkok with Singapore the Peninsula Railway began its work in AD 1900 and it completed its work up to Petchaburi in AD 1903. It wanted to extend up to the frontier of British Malay and for this reason an agreement was signed in AD 1909, with the Government of the Federated Malay States. Bangkok had telephones, electric lighting and a tramline and telegraph communications were connected with French Saigon. Steamboats were available on the river for the service of both freight and passengers. The Post and Telegraph Department became very efficient under a German advisor. A German and a British used to manage the Department of Mines. Danish drillmasters used to give training to the Thai armies and Navy and tried to bring discipline in them. The army was very busy to control and to maintain the Chinese population under control and helped the police very much. An experienced British settlement officer although faced many difficulties in his work, yet he gave very good service relating to land-survey programme for northern Thailand in AD 1880. Educational advisors tried to improve the superficial and dawdling methods of the wat schools. The Thai government spent very little money at that time for public education. John F. Cady says,

> Evaluation of government agencies during the nineties reflected the frustration of the foreign observers. A British education officer characterised the palace itself, paradoxically, as the object of popular loyalty and the cause of the absence of patriotism as the fountainhead of good laws and of bad rulers. In short, it was called a centre of thieving officialdom, idleness, frivolity and intrigue. Reverence for tradition condoned official corruption and injustice. Any overvigorous application of Westernised reforms threatened to revolutionise such a system, and the court as a whole was simply not radically inclined. Governors outside Bangkok followed traditional standards by 'eating' their provinces and resisting Western-sponsored innovations. Official speculation was accepted as the customary procedure if done in proper moderation. Salaried officials who eventually replaced the hereditary governors, were an improvement, but they usually lacked understanding of their duties and were not always honest. Siamese justice came in for particularly severe criticism, as follows: "The Minister of Justice . . . was beautifully impartial in the way he imprisoned the complainant, the defendant, and all the witnesses (he) could get, including the mothers and wives of those (he) could not get. . . . People . . . with remarkable selfishness . . . turn their backs and refuse to see or help innocent men."

King Rama V reformed the military system and also he introduced modern form of taxation. The power of aristocracy was limited. By his reforms he made a great change in the lives of the Prai and the Sui classes. He established a proper system of audit and accounts and he also reorganised the customs and the Inland Revenue.[35] For this purpose he in AD 1896 obtained the services of a financial advisor from the British government and after him

35. *AHSEA*, p. 673.

he got the services of a former Accountant-General of Myanmar. In AD 1901 the Thai government's first budget was published. Before this system was modernised, it was known that tax-gatherers and monopolists used to collect about five to six millions sterling annually from the people but the Treasury used to get from them only £ 1,200,000. Several tax collectors used to collect taxes without receipts and it was easy for them to collect taxes several times forcibly. But when the collection of taxes was improved in Rama V's reign, Thailand's people then lived in a better way 'then they had been ten years earlier'. The king in AD 1892 centralised the whole system of administration under the Ministry of the Interior and gave order to collect all the taxes to spend for the old farming system. Prince Damrong, his younger half brother, carried out the reformation of local administration under his instruction. He was a minister of the north and he played a vital role for the improvement of educational system. He had the capacity to organise the governmental system in a proper way and he was Rama V's principal advisor. He showed his great interest in matters connected with the French crisis of AD 1893 and he then engaged himself seriously to reorganise the governmental system. He reformed the local administration on the model of the British pattern adopted in Myanmar. There were circles in place of provinces and each circle had a commissioner as its head and he used to supervise the performance of non-hereditary governors. There were subdivisions of circles into districts, communes and ten-village units. Village headmen acted as the titular heads of these 'decade' units and they used to report crimes and to register the population. An elder took the charge of each hamlet of about twenty families and the elders together appointed the headman of the whole village. The commissioners had direct touch with the Ministry of Interior and they were responsible with the governors to select local officials for the districts and communes. Prince Damrong also established a Cabinet of Ministers in place of the older palace Senabodi. Rolin-Jaequemins with the help of several Belgian lawyers re-organised the administration of justice of Thailand during the reign of Rama V. They also made great improvement in Courts and prison reform. In this matter Prince Rabi helped them very much. In order to train the Thai lawyers and to modernise the country's legal system, the former with the help of the Belgian advisors played their great role to establish a legal school in AD 1897 in Bangkok. They also managed to bring provincial judges under centralised control in AD 1903. With the help of the French lawyers they revised the Penal Code in AD 1908. Rama V reformed the prison system and modernised the police force and he recruited officers for the police force from Imperial Police Service of India and Myanmar. He established the Department of Education and it later became known as the Ministry of Public Instruction. In AD 1899 the Thai government wanted to take the help of a British civil servant to re-organise its educational system and the Board of Education permitted Mr. J.G.D. Cambell to work as advisor to Prince Damrong for two years. But he was unable to do anything to improve the educational system. Secondary and higher education did not exist outside Bangkok and there were not many schools and their standard was very low and there were not many qualified teachers. Three government schools were established in Bangkok during the nineties under the control of several English teachers. Sunandalaya was a school for girls of the nobility. King's college was a boarding school for the children of the nobility and the other was a boys' day school for sons of middle class parents. Rama V took very initiative to introduce the English public-school system in Bangkok. In his days, Thailand had no university. But in specialist subjects the Thais used to get training in departmental schools. There were law and medical schools, a survey school and a military and naval cadet schools. But there was no technical schools and there was no institution to study art. There were great developments in education after the death of Rama V. R.L. Morant and W.G. Johnson played their great roles to reorganise primary education in Thailand. There were many British advisors in Bangkok in the reign of Rama V and they practically outnumbered advisors of any other nationality. They used to work in the fields of finance, police, education, land surveys and mining. Thailand's financial administration saw its great improvement from AD 1896 to 1903. All tax revenues were deposited with the treasury and the wasteful tax-farming system began its curtain after AD 1907. A substantial railway loan was raised in AD 1903 and 1909. Britain gave loan to Thailand for railways when the latter surrendered its claims to four Malay provinces. Jaquemyns of Belgium helped prince Devawongse for ten years in foreign affairs. Thailand had regular legations at Paris, London, Washington, St. Petersburg, Berlin and Tokyo. Jaquemyns acted as general advisor to Prince Damrong. The former tried to settle the crisis with the French in AD 1892-6 and he also took steps to reduce the abuses of extra-territorial privileges. Several American Protestant missionaries made their valuable contributions to the advancement of medical system in Thailand. Dr. James W. Mckean arrived in Bangkok in AD 1889. With the help of the Thai government Dr. Mckean introduced quinine pills, vaccination for smallpox and also established a leprosarium. A training school for doctors and nurses at Chiengmai in connection with a hospital was set up by Dr. Edwin C. Cort of John Hopkins in AD 1908. For their medical services in Thailand Dr. James W. Mckean, Dr. Edwin C. Cort and other doctor associates were decorated by the Thai government. The Ministry of Justice was established in AD 1892 in Thailand. In AD 1897 His Royal Highness, the late Prince Rabi of Rajaburi became minister of Justice. During his Ministry (AD 1897-1910), he gave valuable service to Thai law.

Thailand's principal exports were rice, teakwood, tin and also hides, cattle and forest products. British firms as traders showed their great interest in Thailand's trade and also in the timber field and tin mining. Thailand used to import British-made cotton cloth and hardware. Opium, which was regarded as second in importance to cloth, was also imported. The government did not stop its importation because it was powerless to do it and at the same time it did not want to sacrifice the revenues brought from the purchase by the Chinese of opium-farmer monopolies.[36] Several branches of the British banks were established in Bangkok from AD 1888 to 1894 and the French Banque de Indo-China operated there in AD 1897. The North German Lloyd started its service in AD 1900 in Bangkok.

In AD 1904 France made a treaty with Thailand.[37] The latter then did not claim its sovereignty over Luang Prabang and declared that the Cambodian frontier would be settled by a joint commission. France accepted its proposal and it was ready to evacuate Chantaban and it did not demand much in connection with its 'protégés' and the neutral zone. This helped the two countries to change their attitudes. By a further agreement Thailand in AD 1907 surrendered Battambang and Siamreap, the Cambodian provinces and France also returned some of the territories surrendered by Thailand in AD 1904 and declared that it renounced all its calims relating to jurisdiction over the Asian subjects. The Anglo-French Agreement of AD 1896 saved Thailand very much. Because this agreement did not allow the heartland of Thailand to fall into hands of France. "It inaugurated a new period of reform largely influenced by British ideas." In AD 1897 there was an Anglo-Thai convention and Thailand did not want to srrrender territory in the Thai Malay states and without the permission of the British it was not willing to grant special privileges in that region and in return Britain fully supported Thailand against any third power which tried to gain influence there. In AD 1899 there was an agreement over the frontier between the Pahang and Trengganu with Bangkok over the head of the Sultan of Trengganu. In AD 1900 Thailand also offered treaties with the rulers of Kalantan and Trengganu. There

36. *SEA*, p. 493.

37. *AHSEA*, p. 699.

treaties mentioned that they were dependencies of Thailand, their foreign relations would be conducted through Thailand, they would take the help of Thailand's advisors and their internal administration would not be interfered by Thailand. They needed to grant no concessions to foreigners without the consent of the Thais and they would pay one-tenth of their revenues to Thailand. These two states agreed, but in Trengganu's case Thailand did not assert its rights in practice. In March AD 1909 the new Anglo-Thai treaty was concluded. By this treaty Kedah, Perlis, Kalantan and Trengganu and the adjacent islands were transferred by Thailand to Britain. Britain also abolished consular jurisdiction in Thailand. The Federated Malay states in order to construct the railway and to establish a link between Thailand's railway system and Malay's railway gave the sum of four million pounds as loan to Thailand's government. We can conclude that Thailand's ninteenth-century rulers modernised the government, the army, education and transportation. They invited Western experts to help them in their efforts for modernisation. It lost much of its former territory, however, and was compelled to agree to a series of treaties that limited Thailand's control of foreign trade, taxes, customs collection and jurisdiction over foreigners.

Rama V had thirty-four sons and forty-three daughters. In his early days of his reign he sent his sons to England to study in public schools, universities and technical institutions.[38] Some princes became experts in the fields of law, agriculture and engineering. Others took their training in the British, German, Russian and Danish armies and in the British navy. Rama V's reign ended in AD 1910. His son named Maha Vajiravudh or Maha Vajrayudha or Wachirawut succeeded him and he became known as Rama VI. He was a British-educated prince. He got his education from Cambridge University and he worked in the British army for sometime. Shortly before his return to Thailand

38. *AHSEA*, p. 804.

in AD 1902, he received the title of heir-apparent. He stayed in England for a very long time and he had no contact with his family. After his accession to the throne he did not take the advice of the senior prominent members of his family. In this matter he discontinued his father's practice. Very rarely he took the help of his brothers and uncles. He appointed his favourites to important positions in the government. He established the 'Wild Tiger Scout Corps' and in which on a quasi-military basis he selected volunteers from civil servants and he was the chief Scout-General. He gave them club houses, a drill hall, uniforms and a rugby football team. He showed his favouritism to this personal bodyguard and for this reason he offended the regular army of his country. He was a person who enjoyed fine arts as pastime and he was a dramatic actor. He was a lover of art and he liked the theatre and in (polished) T'ai he composed or translated plays. He was very shy and he had not the capacity to lead and to govern a country. He did not like the heavy work in daily affairs of his governmental routine. He gave much of the detailed work to Prince Devawongse, his uncle. The latter was his father's closest companion and he was Minister of Foreign Affairs for about thirty years. He was regarded as the most powerful man in the country next to the king. He gave valuable services to the cause of Thailand's progress. He died in AD 1923. After his death Rama VI took the help of Chao P'ya Yomaraj and he depended very much upon him in various matters and he became Minister of the Interior. By extravagant expenditures on tours and state functions Rama VI practically emptied the privy purse of the palace and he did not try to impose curbs on corruption and inefficiency of his officers. His official conncillors wanted to advice him in many matters of his administration, but he did not encourage them and in many matters he completely ignored them. The influence of flatterers and a coterie of youthful courtiers had their important places in him and he always supported them very much. The extensive harem was abolished by him and he kept five selected wives. He was very much against the idea of constitutional democracy. There was very much corruption and discount existed in his country and he became very unpopular. Several army-officers tried to dethrone him in AD 1912 and AD 1917. The first was an assassination plot in AD 1912. Because of the establishment of the Wild Tiger Corps there by the king, the army and navy became very angry. The Bangkok troops became so much unhappy that they wanted to take march on the palace. About sixty army officers were arrested for this mutiny. The second was also mentioned as a military plot in AD 1917. This occurred because the king showed his favour to the pre-German section of the army. He wanted to tighten the royal absolutism. His behaviour gave much to discredit a capricious absolutism. He very rarely met the cabinet of ministers. He individually used to discuss with ministers and he took individual decisions. He understood the great value of the Boy Scout movement and he gave encouragement for its development. Thailand's schools were very much influenced by his ideas and they produced several companies of Tiger's Whelps and they were related to the Wild Tigers. King Rama VI brought few reforms in his administration. He wanted to recodify the law system and to modify the law of monogamy in his country. He also wished to abolish the extra-territoriality rules which affected Europeans in his country. He ordered all his subjects to adopt patronymics and he also introduced compulsory vaccination. Under his instruction and advice Thailand's women began to adopt European hair styles and the skirt. He also adopted the Gregorian calander. In AD 1917 he founded the Chulalongkorn University an Bangkok and it was named after King Chulalongkorn (Rama V). In AD 1921 he introduced compulsory primary education in his country. He also established the institution of the Red Cross Society. He showed his great love for football and atheletics. He was a great lover of sports and football became the most popular game in his country. He actively supported it. He on the model of the English public-school pattern founded a boarding-school — the famous Vajiravudh School in

Bangkok. Like his father Rama VI took the help of foreign advisors. British experts occupied important positions in various fields such as finance, judiciary, commerce, agriculture, health and irrigation. Frenchmen used to deal with legislative matters and the area of legal-code reform. Italians took part in public works and Americans gave their services in foreign policy. In AD 1914 the First World War broke out and Rama VI showed his sympathies towards the Allies. The Thai people were very much against French and the Thai army had a powerful pre-German section. Thailand showed its sympathy to the German side in AD 1914 because of losses of its territory to the British and French. Rama VI took the side of neutrality and after America's entrance in AD 1917 he joined the winning side. His government protested very much against Germany's methods of submarine warfare. The Thai government sent one thousand volunteer soldiers to France in AD 1918. Thailand obtained much from this war. Because it joined the winning side. It as booty got into its hands German shipping to the value of several millions sterling and its railway system became free from the control of the German people who used to manage it in the pre-war period. It became a member of the League of Nations. In AD 1922 a treaty was made between the United States and Thailand and the former abandoned all its extra-territorial rights in Thailand.

Rama VI died in AD 1925.[39] He had no son to ascend the throne of Bangkok. At first he was a bachelor but his marriage took place in AD 1922. He was unable to produce a male heir before his death. His youngest brother, prince Prajadhipok or Prachothipok succeeded him. He became known in Thailand's history as Rama VII. He never expected that he would become king of Thailand. He never thought of it for a moment. His father had seventy-six children and he was his last son. His uncle was Prince Vajirayan. He was the Supreme Patriarch of the Buddhist church. He requested him to spend his life to the cause of the

39. *AHSEA*, p. 807.

religion of the Buddha and to qualify himself to become his successor. Prajadhipak as a novice joined the monastory in AD 1917 and he stayed there for four months. But he left the monastery due to his ill-health, and he did not like to remain as a monk. He had liberal outlook and he was a responsible person. He gave his full support to the establishment of constitutional government and parliamentary procedures, but he allowed the High Council to become a virtual monopoly of princely incumbents who showed their attitude against any democratic reforms. He adopted a series of economic measures which practically offended the nobility, the army and the bureaucracy. His brother's many favourites were dismissed by him. He reduced the Civil List, the Royal Household expenditures, the Royal Corps of Pages from 3000 to 300 and also the number of circles from eighteen to ten. In this way he eliminated many high-level posts. His all these measures brought good results. Because they helped the Treasury to balance its budgets without taking risks to apply for foreign loans or to raise fresh taxation. He established a Supreme Council. Its five members were selected from the most important princes and it was mentioned as an advisory body and under his instruction the cabinet was revived. In AD 1927 he set-up a large Privy Council. It had its forty members. With an idea to receive advice from different types of advisors, he created it and its members used to give him information on many matters which he wanted to knew from them. The early years of his reign witnessed the establishment of a wireless service, the arrangement for the construcrtion of the Dom Muang airport for international air service and the erection of the Royal Institute of Literature, Architecture and Fine Arts with its National Library and Museum. A new Corrency Act in AD 1928 was introduced in connection with gold. Public Health Laws were introduced. It was not easy for the medical practioners to obtain their degrees and qualifications. For this purpose the rules became very strict. In AD 1928 Rama VII set-up a new Civil Service Law and the princely bureaucrats were not allowed to join it. The Department of Royal Pages was abolished by him. He took very stern attitude to reject the ancient theory of absolutist monarchy, but he was unable to get its support from the influential political-minded people. In order to establish governmental control over insurance and banking on act for the control of Commercial Undertakings of Public Utility was passed. In AD 1930 Dr. Karl Zimmerman of Harvard University surveyed the kingdom for the development of its economy. In AD 1931 the Thai government faced financial difficulties. The Minister of Finance in March AD 1931 announced a budget deficit of 11 million ticals. Thailand tried to get foreign loans in Paris and New York but it was unable to receive them. For this purpose it announced salary cuts which gave a blow to the junior official class and this class suffered very much. In AD 1931 Rama VII went abroad for medical treatment. In his absence a great rivalry grew up in the Supreme Council between Prince Bovaradej, the Minister of War and Prince Purachatra, the Minister of Commerce, over a matter relating to the field of economy. In AD 1931 it affected so much that there was a serious political crisis in Thailand and the Thai people lost confidence in them. This happened in the month of October, AD 1931. The official class and the army officers felt frustrated because the officers had lost their jobs due to Rama VII's 'drastic pruning of the Civil Service' and the army officers became very angry for the salary cuts. In AD 1932 Luang Pradist Manudharn or Pridi Banemyong became the leader of these people who were not al all happy to see that they were badly treated by Rama VII's government. This young man took his training as a lawyer in Paris and he was a Professor of Law at the Chulalongkorn University. He prepared a constitution and with the help of military he brought Bangkok under his control and made a bloodless revolution on June 24, AD 1932. Rama VII returned to Thailand after two days and the provisional constitution was accepted by him. The princes were not included in ministerial posts and the army and the People's Party, which was given its name by Pridi and his supporters, took the charge of the government. They announced a Senate which consisted of seventy members and it appointed an Executive Council which had the right to promulgate laws and had the power to control ministers. After a lapse of six months an elected Assembly took the place of the Senate. Pridi and his followers selected P'ya Manopakorn as President of the Executive Council. In December AD 1932 the new Constitution was adopted and a special committee was appointed. This committee performed its duty in close collaboration with the king. An Assembly of 156 members which had the capacity to deal with legislative matters, finance and constitution was formed as a temporary measure and the king appointed its half members. Every four years elections were conducted. Candidates who wanted to contest for seats were Thais of at least twenty-three years of age and they had their houses in their constituencies and they had to fulfil certain educational qualifications. The law of citizenship was modified and it also mentioned that among the privileges of the citizens the right to vote was the most important. The king had the right to dissolve the Assembly without the approval of the cabinet, but within three months a new election was held. He had the right to vote lagislation, but the Assembly by a second vote was able to overlook his vote. He had also the right to announce emergency decrees so long as the minister responsible countersigned them. The princes of the royal family were allowed to play their roles as advisors and also to take appointment in diplomatic posts. A political party was prohibited to give orders to any of its members with seats in the Assembly. In December AD 1932 Thailand's Constitution was finally drafted. It did not agree with some matters from the early Soviet pattern advocated by Pridi. It kept some measure of prestige to the crown and it referred to minor items for the king's prerogative. It transformed Thailand from an absolute to a limited monarchy. Today the king has considerable authority but he has very little political power. Princes were not allowed to become members in the State Council which became in course of time the Executive Committee.

Indirect suffrage would help to elect one-half of the membership of the Assembly and the ruling party would appoint the other half. Within ten years there would be an elective Assembly. The cabinet would occupy an important position in the Assembly. If new budgets were not voted then for application old budgets could be used. This constitution remained unchanged for about fourteen years and in AD 1946 Pridi's Free Thai Party altered it first and allowed Prince Soni Promoj, the former Ambassador to Washington, to occupy the post of Foreign Minister. The constitution was drafted by officers who were both civilian and military and the provincial members of the Assemly had a vested interest in it. It was unable to establish firm patterns of administration and it made no effective limitations to the application of power. The Prime Minister, who was assisted by a cabinet, the council of ministers, had executive power. The Parliament called the National Assembly included on upper house, the Senate, whose members were appointed by the king and a lower house, the House of Representatives, whose members were selected by the Thai citizens. At the king's request the People's Party as a political party was dissolved in AD 1933 and it became known as a social club. Several army officers and also high officers wanted to form a Nationalist Party and for this purpose they requested the king for his permission. But the king rejected their position. P'ya Manopakorn did not like to remain under the control of Pridi and his people and he wanted to free his government from their control. Pridi drafted an unpublished scheme of national economy and this was announced as communistic and by a coup he was allowed to go into exile. Pridi announced a planned economy. The economic system introduced by the government would bring and the Chinese monopoly in business, give scope for employment, capital needs and marketing facilities and play a great role to establish a friendly relation between employees and labourers. The government for the welfare of its subjects would purchase agricultural lands for redistribution by issuing state bonds. Party members would be candidates for election to the party Assembly and the president would be elected by the latter and the selection of the fourteen members executive committee would take place at the choice of the president and the ministers would be appointed by the committee and it would announce several laws. The government declared a national policy and arrangements were made to give vacant land to the unemployed people. The prime minister in another purge removed four army officers and their leader was Phaya or P'ya Bahal and the former asked them to resign. They were colleagues of Pridi. After their resignation they then made a plan for another *coup d'etat* and on 20 June AD 1933 they were successful. Then P'ya Manopakorn submitted his resignation and P'ya Bahal took his place. A new council was composed and his followers were its members. The government announced that it was anti-communist and it would do its best to defend the constitution. The king was not in the capital due to the *coup d'etat* and when he returned to the capital he told his people to remain calm and he wanted that peace and unity should be maintained in his kingdom. In September AD 1933 Pridi was allowed to return and a commission was made to investigate the charges of Communism against him. In March AD 1934 the report of the commission framed no charge against him and it cleared him. He became a free man from alleged communist affiliations in AD 1934. In October AD 1933 a serious military revolt took place and its leader was Rama VII's cousin, Prince Bovaradej and the Thai government was troubled by it. The Dom Muang airport was occupied by the rebel forces and they wanted the resignation of P'ya Bahal and his people. But when Colonel Luang P'ibun Songgram, the commander of the government forces, occupied the Dom Muang airport and suppressed the rebellion, then the leaders who revolted took shelter in Saigon and their revolt came to an end. The army officers did not allow the Chinese and Vietnamese communists to stay in Thailand and they were expelled from that country. Rama VII kept quiet through the crisis and he took a neutral attitude. He knew very well that most of the royal princes supported the rebels morally and financially and it was difficult for him to obtain the confidence of his people. He lost his control and in January AD 1934 he went to Europe for his eye surgery. A general election was held in November AD 1933. Very few voters voted and there were few candidates who took part in this election. Pridi's followers got a majority of the seats. Pridi returned to the cabinet and he from AD 1934 to 1938 became Minister of Interior, Foreign Minister and Finance Minister. He was a very popular person and can be mentioned as the ideal of the young intelligentsia. He announced a radical economic policy and Colonel Luang Pibun Songgram campaigned that there was the cammunistic element in the government. In September AD 1934 the Assembly took a step to ratify a rubber agrement with Britain. The cabinet then sibmitted its resignation. But P'ya Bahal was a popular person. He not only get a majority but also won a vote of confidence and he again occupied his office. From AD 1933 to 1938 He became the head of Thailand's government. He played a very vital role in his cabinet and he managed his rival factions so successfully that he got co-operation from them. Then there was a crisis in the Thai government. Rama VII voted a Bill which wanted "to abolish the need for his signature to be appended to death sentence". But the Assembly totally rejected it. Rama VII then wanted to abdicate and he also wished the resignation of the Assembly and a new general election. The Thai government tried to compromise but failed and in March AD 1935 the king announced his abdication. He gave statement that the emerging regime was undemocratic and militaristic. John F. Cady remarks,

> Monarchical government apparently lost out in Siam because the Western educated elite including the king himself lost faith in it. The fourscore 'promoters' who seized control of the government on June 24, 1932, were recruited from Westernised malcontents who denounced as unprogressive both royal absolutism and princely privilege. Worried at the outset over the possibility of

> British or French intervention to restore to power the firiendly monarchical faction, they devised a constitutional facade as a kind of shield and also espoused a number of liberal Western-type reforms. These included freedom of the press, social equality, education for all, graduated income tax, equalisation of bereaucratic salaries, a competitive civil service, lower postal rates and suspension of the unpopular land tax. In actuality, they preferred more direct means of control to constitution representative government. The economies of democratic nations were virtually paralysed by the world depression at the time, so that totalitarian patterns attracted attention in Siam as elsewhere.

Prince Ananda Mahidol, a nephew of Rama VII, became king of Thailand in AD 1935.[40] At that time he was a ten-year-old school boy in Switzerland. A Regency Council of three members was appointed to look after his affairs during his minority. At this time Prajadhipok and his wife were staying in England and he expressed his desire to stay there in future with the title of Prince of Sukhodaya. During Ananda Mahidol's time Colonel Luang Pibun Songgram became a very influential person and his influence grew very much when Pridi went to foreign tour in the middle of AD 1935. Owing to quarrels between its members, the State Council became bery weak and many army officers took the posts in the civil administration. This not only alarmed the Assembly but also gave indication that the govenment moved towards a military dictatorship. The army groups became very influential in the cabinet. Another general election was held in AD 1937. P'ya Bahal managed to remain as a head of his cabinet. The government did not tolerate the influence of the princes in politics. It sopposed it very much and it abolished the six traditional grades of hereditary titles officially. It also cancelled land and capitation taxes and it announced a nominal one per

40. *AHSEA*, pp. 812 and 937; *SEA*, p. 497.

cent tax on income and a two per cent tax on business. The treasury used to collect its principal sources of revenue from opium sales, customs and exercise levies, fees, licenses and fines. The Chinese people did not get good treatment from this government and they used to give discriminatory taxes on income, shops, banking operations and amusements. They were not able to take twenty-six designated professions which the Thais had the right to take these professions. In schools there was a prohibition to use the Chinese language for their instruction. In order to escape from these prohibitions they took Thai citizenship and the government also then began to raise naturalisation standards by mentioning literacy, wealth and army service requirements. The Assembly in December AD 1938 against the government brought a bill relating to an amendment to its procedure to give a detailed statement of the budget. This helped to bring the resignation of the council and P'ya Bahal took his retirement in AD 1938 because of his ill health. Colonel Luang Pibun Songgram was the head of the new government and Pridi was its Minister of Finance. The premilitarist Assembly accepted the former as Prime Minister. He was mentioned as the leader of a military faction hungry for glory, revenues and governorships. He was a political opportunist, ambitious personally, a jinge militarist and a moderniser. In March AD 1939 Pridi's new Revenue Code was passed and this helped to lighten the burden of the peasants and he became a free man from dependance upon the money-lender. The Chinese and the European people who had their commercial firms had to pay heavy taxes to the government. Several hundred Chinese schools were closed by the government. It suppressed Chinese newspapers, expelled several thousands opium addicts and arrested several Chinese leaders. Because the terrorist activities of the Chinese people brought a great danger to Thailand's society. These measures did not help the European people. They felt disturbed very much. Because in mining and forestry many Chinese people were engaged by them. The British used to manage the teak industry and these people did not get favourable terms at the time of the renewal of their leases and mere forest areas were kept for the business of the Thais. A state company wanted to manage local shipping and desired to operate it by buying vessels. The foreign shipping firms had to obey government's order and their capital was reserved 70 per cent for the Thais. Their all vessels were registered as Thais and about 75 per cent Thais were appointed as their crews. State subsidies were alloted to private Thai firms. Many technical, commercial and agricultural schools were established and in order to receive technical training many Thai students went abroad. In June AD 1939 the government under Colonel Luang Pibun Songgram changed the country's name from Siam to Thailand. The Thais mentioned their country as Muang Thai, 'the land of the free'. Colonel Luang Pibun Songgram campaigned to introduce Western manners and social practices in Thailand and he issued several government's order for these purposes. Both sexes had to wear European shoes and hats in public. A Westernised type of dress and family names were introduced for the people of Thailand by Colonel Luang Pibun Songgram. He also told them to use 'hello' in greetings. The practice of chewing betel was condemned and the government wanted to stop it. The education system became very strict and it came under the Ministry of Education. All schools rigidly followed the instructions and advices of the Ministry of Education and all teachers were registered. Colonel Luang Pibun Songgram's government tried to equate Buddhism with patriotism. Many Thai people were converted to Biddhism from Christianity and many non-Buddhists in government service lost their jobs as they had no chance of promotion. No official was allowed to marry an alien without special permission from the government. Colonel Luang Pibun Songgram's imperialist plans were the reannexation of several provinces on the Cambodian frontier and also the trans-Mekong region, several easternnmost Shan states of Myanmar, the Tanasserim coast, the lost Malay sultanates and Penang Island.

In AD 1931-41, he did not give much importance to foreign advisors and he spent one-third of the national revenues for military preparations. France collapsed in AD 1940, then Hanoi authorities accepted a minor revision of the 1926 boundary treaty. Colonel Luang Pibun Songgram then claimed all of Laos down to the Cambodian border and also three provinces of Cambodia. Under Japanese 'arbitration' awards these territories were captured during AD 1941. Thailand established a very close economic relation with Japan which was able to increase its trade with Thailand very much. In AD 1933 Thailand did not cast its vote in the 'League of Nations' censure of Japan over Manchuria. The Prime Minister of Thailand after AD 1938 established a militant youth organisation like Japanese type and he introduced a national code of honour called Wiratham which was adopted from Japanese bushide. This code gave emphasis on nationalist partisanship and loyalty and economic efficiency and industry, together with Buddhist principles of peace, gratitude, trustworthiness and respect for the young and infirm. Japan came very close to Thailand and their relations became very friendly after AD 1940 when Japan shouted for 'Asia for the Asiatics' and the 'Greater East Asia Co-prosperity Sphere' and both the countries professed Buddhism. Bangkok had a full-fledged Japanese Embassy and two new consulates were established at Saigon in the Malay south land and at Chiengmai in northern Thailand. Japanese 'fishing craft' with polished brass naval fixtures frequently visited the lower peninsular coasts. Japanese goods arrived in the Thai markets. Thailand demanded the restoration of the Cambodian and Laos territories which France in the earlier period had compelled Thailand to give. Britain and France were too busy in the Second World War in AD 1939 and this helped the Thai Prime Minister to recover territories and he got Japanese mediation in this matter. Until AD 1939, Thailand became known as the kingdom of Siam. At that time its rulers allied themselves with Japan and took the leading role to change the country's name to Thailand. They tried to enlarge the country's borders to include several areas which were inhabited by the Thai-speaking people and annexed border regions in Laos, Myanmar, Cambodia and Malay during the early years of Second World War. But when Japan lost its power, Thailand then made peace with Britain. After the arrival of the Japanese people in Indo-China in June AD 1940 Colonel Luang Pibun Songgram's government signed non-aggression treaties with Britain, France and Japan and in March AD 1941 the French people returned the Cambodian provinces of Battambang and Siemreap, together with the Laotian territory to the west of the river Mekong. The Thai Prime Minister fully co-operated with Japan and in January 25, AD 1942 Thailand declared war against Britain and the United States. The Thai government took active part in business ventures. Under its management there were paper factories, textile manufacture, distilleries, sugar and tobacco processing, oil refining and silk production. But because of mismanagement and inefficient administration these projects were unable to do their business well and they suffered very much. But some government projects were financially successful. After AD 1934 rubber production started to make profit. Government railways, telegraph and electric power installations were under the management of European advisors previously and they did their works very efficiently. Thailand took the help of western European and Americans to modernises its country's legal system and to esablish its political and economic independence it wanted 'nationalisation of industry and authoritarian political control on the fascist or Japanese model'. John F. Cady remarks that

> Thailand's 'promoters' thus followed the traditional bandwagon psychology. They 'bent with the wind' to get it on the winning side of World War II, batting at first on a Japanese victory and then shifting sides in 1944 when the odds swung the opposite way.

Colonel Luang Pibun Songgram's pro-Japanese policy was not very popular in Thailand.

> The Japanese flood of worthless currency used in payment for supplies produced an eventual tenfold increase in the cost of living measured in terms of the baht.

Under the encouragement of the Japanese the Thai government played an important role to persecute Thailand's Chinese population. The Thai anti-Japanese movement started in Thailand under the leadership of Pridi Banomyong who was Colonel Luang Pibun Songgram's arch-rival. At the time of the Japanese invasion Pridi was Finance Minister and he resigned and he stayed in northern Thailand for sometime. Later he was king's regent. He secretely supported Thailand's ambassador to Washington Prince Soni Promoj who refused to deliver his government's declaration of war against the United States. The ambassador told that this declaration was not the will of the Thai people. They never supported it. It can be mentioned as unrepresentative of the will of the Thai people. The Free Thai movement then began to appear. Several American agents came secretly in Thailand and stayed under Thai control in one European prisoner camp in Bangkok. Then by short-wave radio transmitters used to contact regularly with allied intelligence agencies in Colombo. The change of government took place at Bangkok in the summer of AD 1944. Colonel Luang Pibun Songgram wanted to erect an alternative capital at Pechabun in northern Thailand. This place was a detached centre from which his government would play a role to resist the continuance of the Japanese control. He distrusted the Japanese and their plans 'Asia for the Asiatics', 'Japan as leader, protector and light of Asia' and the 'Greater East Asia Co-prosperity Sphere'. He laid the foundation stones in April AD 1944 for the new Pechabun capital. But this was not possible because the place was infested with malaria. In the Assembly vote of August 2, AD 1944 Colonel Luang Pibun Songgram was defeated. "It was probably the result of military reverses suffered by the Japanese in the Pacific."

The Prime Minister resigned. It allowed Pridi's free Thai group to take the charge of the government and Nai Khuang Aphaiweng became Prime Minister of Thailand. After the end of the war Prince Soni Promoj returned to Bangkok and he became Prime Minister of Thailand for a short time and he stayed there up to January 1, AD 1945. At this time Thailand signed a treaty with Britain. America supported Thailand very much and for this reason the latter did not pay any penalty of its hostile policy toward England. Thailand's constitution needed to amend because to allow a prince to become Thailand's Prime Minister. Prince Soni Promoj was an incapable person and he did not like to occupy such a high office and he himself withdrew from his position. Pridi played a role as kingmaker until November AD 1947 when in a bloodless coup Colenel Luang Pibun Songgram again captured power. Since Second World War, the Thai government had to deal with small guerrilla movements which operated within Thailand's borders. During the Vietnam war it sent armies to support the South Vietnamese. After the War, the Thais and the Cambodians often clashed. Many people left their countries due to communist governments of Vietnam, Laos and Cambodia and lived in a refugee camps in Thailand. They gave much trouble in its internal law and administration.

Bhumibol Adulyadej or Bhumipol Adulet was a brother of Ananda Mahidol.[41] The former became king of Thailand in AD 1946. During the post-War period Thailand's political condition was not very stable and this instability helped Thailand to establish a military dictatorship. With the help of armies Colonel Luang Pibun Songgram not only maintained his control but also solidly built his own power and influence. In June AD 1951 he was kidnapped by the navy and marines. But the army and air force suppressed the revolt after three days. General P'ao Sriyanon, the director-general of police, and General Sarit Thamarat, Commander of the Bangkok army, were very close

41. *AHSEA*, p. 937.

friends of Colonel Luang Pibubn Songgram. The latter's opponent party was the Democrat Party and Khuang Aphaiweng was its leader. The party was established by him in AD 1948. A new 'permanent' constitution was drafted and this was introduced in January AD 1949. It allowed to function a bicameral parliament. Universal adult suffrage elected the lower house and the king appointed the upper house. Parliament was composed in such a way that Colonel Luang Pibun Songgram's party was unable to make its direct influence upon it. It had no direct role to control it. But in both houses the Democratic Party had several seats. In November AD 1951 there was another *coup d'etat* under the direction of Colonel Luang Pibun Songgram. Then the 1949 constitution was abolished by him and he declared that he played a role to revive the original constitution of 1932. This gave the opportunity for a unicameral parliament and its half of the seats were appointed by the executive appointment. There were about 123 appointed members of the new house and nearly all members were selected from army officers. The Chinese people in Thailand showed their appreciation very much when they heard the 'People's Liberation Army's' victory in China in AD 1949. The Chinese Communinst Party slowly but seadily established itself in Thailand and the Chinese labour unions, schools and press came under the influence of communism. Colonel Luang Pibun Songgram was very much against communism. The Thais were very much against the Chinese people. They were excluded from a long list of occupations, and their many schools were closed and the Thai government took several steps against their newspaper. In AD 1939 the annual registration free for aliens was four baht but in AD 1952 this was four hundred baht by a law. The nationality law of Thailand said that anyone born in this country became a national of Thailand but in AD 1953 this was amended with an idea to exclude children whose parents were Chinese. The Thai Police in November AD 1952 discovered a communist plot which wanted to overthrow the government and for this reason they raided several times in several times in several places of Bangkok, arrested several hundred Chinese people, suspended the activities of their associations temporarily and closed their schools. Then a law was passed in Thailand's Parliament and it prohibited communist activities in Thailand and General P'ao Sriyanon, the director-general of police, announced that the Chinese people, who did not behave properly and tried to violate the Thai law, were arrested by the Thai police. The rulers of Thailand felt insecured to see the communinst revolts in Vietnam, Laos, Myanmar and Malay and for this reason the anti-Chinese movement carried out in Thailand in AD 1953. In foreign affairs Colonel Luang Pibun Songgram adopted anti-communist policy. He did not recognise the Peking regime, opposed China's entry into the United Nations and supported the United Nations' cause in Korea in AD 1950. He fully co-operated with the United States. In AD 1954 when Dien Bien Phu was captured and Mr. Dulles, the United States' Foreign Minister, wanted action against the communist threat in South-East Asia, Thailand fully supported him. It took part in the formation of the South-East Asia Treaty Organisation (SEATO) at Manila and Bangkok was selected as its headquarters. Colonel Luang Pibun Songgram demanded stronger military guarantee which were included in the pact and in AD 1955 wanted SEATO bases in his country. Thailand established close diplomatic relations with the United States and a conference of senior American diplomats in the Far East was held at Bangkok in AD 1950 and American economic and military survey missions visited Thailand. These two countries signed agreements for economic and technical co-operation and for military assistance. Under the Mutual Security Act America in AD 1951 gave military aid to Thailand. The latter began to receive substantial aid from America. It got nearly 64 million dollers up to March AD 1955. Although this was used for military purpose but also through the Special Technical and Economic Mission in Bangkok aid was received to spend for irrigation works, railway rehabilitation and extension, port improvement, road construction, eclectricity generation and for many other projects. Several American technicians visited Thailand and worked there and gave various types of training to specialists there. Thailand also received special aid and malaria control and also to improve rice culture. It got various types of aid from America but there was no real co-operation from the Thai people and also from politicians. Certain Thai politicians for their own purposes used those funds. They were not interested to see the improvement and progress of their country. They selfishly misused these funds. Thailand was not only greatly benefitted by American aid but also with its help it was able to establish strongly its military dictatorship in power. Colonel Luang Pibun Songgram visited the United States and Britain in AD 1955. His return brought a great change in his policy. There was no political repression, there was no obstruction for the rise and the development of democracy, it began to bloom, political parties were allowed to register, like in London's Hyde Park Central Park in Bangkok was the place where politicians were permitted to discuss politics freely, the Thai Prime Minister regularly met pressmen and gave press conferences, the centre willingly transferred power to local authorities, the Chinese people were permitted to have rights approaching as near as possible to these of the Thai citizens and naturalisation was encouraged. Most probably, in order to receive popular support to establish his position frimly, Colonel Luang Pibun Songgram brought a great change in the policy. During his visit to the United States and Britain he saw the progress of democracy there, and it was very probable that he wanted to see and to develop the same political conditions and atmosphere in his own conutry. Thailand also attended the Bandung conference. When the Political restrictions were lifted by the government then about twenty-five political parties came into existence in Thailand. The Seri Manong Khasila Party was mentioned as the largest and the most influential party in Thailand. It had all the government's parliamentary supporters. A Socialist Front was formed by the leftist parties and they criticised the foreign policy of the Thai government. General P'ao Sriyanon spent many millions of baht for the propaganda of the Seri Manonghkhasila Party but the government at the general election which was held in February AD 1957, won but get only a bare majority. The Thai people did not like the government's policy and they bitterly citicised it. On seeing public dissatisfaction then a national emergency was declared by the government. The Thai people did not appreciate the government's move towards the path which led to democracy. The new government was formed after the general election of AD 1957 by Colonel Luang Pibun Songgram. But the government was weak. Because there were internal troubles and there was a bitter rivalry between General P'ao Sriyanon and General Sarit Thanarat. All these causes helped the Thai government to fall. General Sarit Thanarat did not take any leading part in the general election and afterwards he showed his dissatisfaction and he remained aloof from the Seri Manonghkhasila Party. He became the commander-in-chief of the army when the state of national emergency was declared by the government. He and his group occupied a very important position in the cabinet. He was regarded as the strongest person in it. General Sriyanon was not as influential as he was in it. The latter and his group in August AD 1957 gave their resignation as a body and on the night of September 16-17, AD 1967 he and the army took the leading part to overthrow the government by a bloodless coup. On seeing this political condition Colonel Luang Pibun Songgram went into exile and parliament was dissolved and there was a suspension of the constitution. Nai Pote Sarasin took the charge of a caretaker government. He was the Secretary-General of the South-East Asia Treaty Organisation (SEATO). A general election was held on December 15, AD 1957. But no party was able to get an overrall majority. Then a coalition which became known as the National Socialist Party took its birth. There were about 123 nominated members in it. The Unionist Party, a centre party, had forty-five members and the Seri Manonghkhasila Party had forty members and they were elected as independents. General Thanon Kittikachorn became new Prime Minister and Nai Pote Sarasin again joined the South-East Asia Traty Organisation as the Secretary-General on October 20, AD 1958 there was another bloodless *coup d'etat* in Thailand. General Sarit Thanarat went to the United States and England for several months for medical treatment. He arrived Bangkok secretly. He dismissed the Prime Minister and cabinet and became the head of a military junta called the 'Revolutionary Party'. He abolished all political parties and he arrested many people for alleged breaches of the Anti-Communism Law. According to foreign observers, no evidence was available for any communist danger. But owing to the shrinkage of its foreign exchange reserves and a cut of nearly 24 million dollars in American aid for AD 1958, the Thai government had to face serious troubles and it became bankrupt. Again the Thai government revived anti-Chinese discrimination and for this reason the Chinese community lost confidence in the government. About 80 per cent of the country's non-agrarian capital was under the control of the Chinese. The Revolutionary Party imposed in 'interim' constitution which made preparation for the appointment of a Constituent Assembly. This assembly would sketch a permanent constitution and exercise legislative powers. The Prime Minister would govern the decree and would impose emergency action if he would find anything necessary. General Sarit Thanarat became Prime Minister of Thailand on 9 February AD 1959.

From the facts mentioned above we can say that Thailand has failed to achieve political stability. The Thais and their political leaders were unable to understand the real meaning of constitutional democracy and it was for this reason there was no place for constitutional democracy in the political world of Thailand. The Thai people had no control over the government. For the spoils of government and for personal enrichment through corruption various bureaucratic cliques played active roles and remained busy in Thai politics. Corruption has occupied an important position in Thai life. Education was expanded very rapidly and compulsory primary education became very popular. But the standards at all levels were very low. Although population grew very rapidly, yet the Thais were able to maintain their standards very nicely. Thailand's economy was based on agriculture and it never witnessed the developement of the evils of landlordism and agricultural indebtedness. An American remarks,

> Thailand is a relatively well-to-do country. If much of its wealth consists in the opportunities provided by nature for the enjoyment of leisusre and a good life, it is not out of harmony with the temperament of the people.

An election was held on Sunday, November 17, AD 1986 in Bangkok. The Thai politicians made final efforts to influence and to woo voters. Mr. Chuan Leekpai, the former Prime Minister, was the leader of the Democrat Party. Mr. Chavalit Yongchaiyudh or Chaowalit Yongchaiyudh, the outgoing defence minister, was the leader of the New Aspiration Party.[42] They were top contenders and ran neck and neck in the fight for 393 seats in Parliament. The two front running parties themselves predicted that on November 17, AD 1996 that the margin will be thin, reading from five to ten seats. The democrats on Friday, November 15, AD 1996 rejected an Olive branch from the New Aspiration Party leader Mr. Chavalit Yongchaiyudh who had proposed that the two key parties would form a coalition government whatever the outcome of the polls. "There must be semeone to moniter the government and protect the interests of the people", Mr. Chuan Leekpai told in Bangkok. Mr. Chavalit Yongchaiyudh said in north-eastern Udon that he would keep the proposal upon despite the rejection of the Democrats. Traditionally, the party winning the most seats had the right to try to form a new government. But historically, Thailand has

42. *AA*, November 17, 1996, p. 5.

had coalition governments because no single party had won enough seats to held a government majority. There were 2,310 candidates from thirteen parties and they contested this election which was Thailand's second in sixteen months after Banharn Silpa-Archa, the outgoing Prime Minister, set snap polls in September AD 1996. Several Thai politicians in order to win this election had spent lots of money in it and at least eight people were killed by gunmen. Several political analysts mentioned it as one of the closest ever and the most violent and dirty in two decades. While campaigning about dozens were attacked. The Thamers Research Centre said that $ 800 million was spent by Thai politicians on this election and this centre reported further that this was 20 per cent more than the amount spent in the last polls. The Rajabhat Institute of teachers' training described that the poll was the most violent and dirty since the mid-1970s when student democracy groups toppled Thai military government. Poll Watch, the election watchdog, said that about 30 billion baht was spent on the election, including on vote-buying. The police told that two suspects were arrested and in north-eastern Udon Rachatani four million baht in fake banknotes were seized and they wanted to use these banknotes for vote-buying. Thailand's powerful military, which has lauched seventeen successful or attempted coups since AD 1932 when absolute monarchy ended, tried to maintain its neutrality in the polls. General Chetta Thanajara, the Army Commander-in-chief, expressed his opinion, "I urged soldiers to exercise their right by voting for politicians of their choice and ordered them to be strictly neutral." The business people heartily wanted to find a victory for the Democrats because the party had a strong economic team of qualified professionals and technocrats. The New Aspiration Party's members were defectors from other parties. Thailand prepared to ban the sale and consumption of alchol in public at the time of the general election. In order to ensure an orderly election, the ban required by law went into effect from 6 p.m. on Saturday until 6 a.m. on Monday (from 16

November to 18 November). The election commission official said that offenders faced jail terms of one to five years or a fine up to $ 2,000. In the July 1995 election, 68 people were arrested for prosecution for the offence. According to reliable sources most election officers and politicians "had already stocked their bars to tide them over the polling period into the early hours of Monday morning." Several thousand tourists who visited Thailand during the weekend were greatly affected by the ban. An election commission official told that the law only imposed ban to see the Thai people from drinking in public but when they wanted they drank in their houses. Foreign tourists were allowed to drink in their hotel rooms.

The New Aspiration Party of former army commander General Chavalit Yongchaiyudh was poised to form a new government after opposition Democrat Party leader Mr. Chuan Leekpai admitted that it apparently would gain the most seats in this general election.[43] which was held on November 17, AD 1996. Mr Chuan Leekpai spoke to supporters and journalists in his home province of Trang in the southern side of Thailand that

> The Aspiration Party has the right to form a new government whenever it wants to. We have no conditions but we are ready to be the opposition.

He was Prime Minister of Thailand from AD 1992 to 1995 and he told about six hours after the closing of the polls at 3 p.m. on Sunday, November 17, 1996. From unofficial results tabulated by a network formed by the *Nation* newspaper and a bank, two television channels, we learn that the New Aspiration Party and the Democrats each were leading in 124 races. But many of the remote areas that would report late were situated in northern province and everybody expected that these areas were in favour of the New Aspiration Party. Official results for most of the

43. *AA*, p. 5.

country were still not available and until Monday morning these results were not likely to be completed. Helicopters, boats and motorcycles were used to carry ballot boxes to provincial halls for vote counting in remote areas. In Bangkok on November 17, AD 1996. It was virtually certain that no Party would win a majority, and according to analysts, even if the Democrat Party established its position with a few more seats than its rivals, it might not be able to get enough partners to form a mojority coalition. There were smaller parties and their support could be essential to form a coalition government. The Chart Pattana (national development), a loose ally of the democrats, was in front in 51 races and the Chart Thai (Thai nation) Party of incumbent Prime Minister Banharn Silpa-Archa was in front in 36 races. About 2,310 candidates from 13 parties were condending for 393 seats in the Lower House of the Parliament. The Social Action Party, like the New Aspiration Party, a partner in Mr. Banharn's government, was ahead in 21 races. As had been expected, the Democrats showed overwhelming strength in Bangkok. According to official results from the city govenment, they were able to win 29 of the 37 seats in Bangkok proper. The right-wing the Prachakorn Thai (Thai citizens) Party, a member of the incumbent coalition party, captured four seats and four other parties, including Mr. Chavalit Yongchaiyudh got a seat apiece in Bangkok. The Thais wanted to elect a new government to replace one that collapsed under charges of corruption and incompetence. An election watchdog group told that a record of $ 800 million was spent on vote-buying and it was an increase of $ 200 million from the last election in July AD 1995. The city government announced that about 48.97 per cent voters voted in Bangkok and this per cent was higher than in the last general election. An interior ministry official said that he expected the average turnout nationwide to top the 62 per cent in AD 1995 election. Thailand had a population of about 60 million and it had more than 38.5 million voters and about 2.23 million voters voted for the first time. The largest concentrations of voters were in the provinces, where during elections vote-buying and gunplay were very cammon.

Former army chief Mr. Chavalit Yongchaiyudh was poised on Monday, November 18, AD 1996 to become Thailand's new Prime Minister after his New Aspiration Party won weekend elections and cobbled together a multi-party coalition.[44] He, who never concealed his prime ministerial designs, announced that the New Aspiration Party, which defeated the main opposition Democrats in election on Sunday, November 17, AD 1996, would lead a six-party coalition to form a new government. Six parties gave their consent to join and to form the government. Mr. Chavalit Yongchaiyudh spoke to the reporters at home of Mr. Chatichai Choonhavan, the head of the Chart Pattana Party, which left the opposition to join the New Aspiration Party-led coalition. He said,

> I asked Chatichai and other friends from these six parties to work together for the people and nation.

The new line-up would put the mainly rural based parties, which had their strongholds in the north and north-east, into power in Bangkok, where voters gave their votes in favour of the Democart Party of former Prime Minister Mr. Chuan Leekpai. Mr. Thanaporn Promyamyai and Philip McClelland from Bangkok wrote in the *Asian Age* on Tuesday, November 19, AD 1996 that Mr. Chavalit Yongchaiyudh should be named Prime Minister next week when the Thai Parliament will resume its activities and king Bhumibol Adulyadej will approve his nomination-normally, this was a formality. Most of the six parties were members of outgoing Prime Minister Mr. Banharn Silpa Archa's ill-fated coalition government which was collapsed under the weight of infighting and a poor public image. Mr. Chavalit Yongchaiyudh wanted to appoint experts and 'people of quality' for the cabinet of his government and he mentioned that the

---

44. *AA*, November 19, 1996, p. 5.

previous government did not appoint competent people to key postitions, and particularly economic ministries. Thailand's deputy Prime Minister elect Mr. Amnuay Virawan told in Hong Kong on November 18, AD 1996 that the new coalition government was not his first-choice line up. He mentioned further that he would have preferred to see the Democrat Party in the coalition ahead of the Chart Pattana Party. The Democrat Party was the second highest polling party in Sunday's election (November 17, 1996) with 123 seats behind the 125 for the New Aspiration Party. Despite his preference for the Democrats, Mr. Amnuay Virawan said that he had no strong reservations about the Chart Pattana Party and his main consideration was that the Chart Thai Party of former Prime Minister Mr. Banharn Silpa-Arch was not involved. New Prime Minister Mr. Chavalit Yongchaiyudh turned to the Chart Pattana Party after Mr. Banharn Silpa-Arch reportedly balked at the New Aspiration Party's plan for the new government. Mr. Amnuay Virawan confirmed that he was offered the position of deputy Prime Minister of the new government and he wanted to accept after talks with the coalition partners.

Mr. Chavalit Yongchaiyudh was the former army chief. His party narrowly won Thailand's general election which was held on Sunday, November 17, AD 1996. He on Tuesday, November 19, AD 1995 stepped up his drive for the Prime Ministership by pushing for the early convening of Parliament.[45] He talked with the leader of the second-largest group in his six-party coalition. Mr. Chatichai Choonhavan of the Chart Pattana Party told that he wanted Parliament to reconvene as soon as possible. "The situation rigtht now is not helpful, delays will only cause problems", and impatient Mr. Chavalit Yongchaiyudh spoke to reporters at the time of his meeting with Mr. Chatichai Choonhavan who served as Prime Minister from AD 1988 to 1990. Later a senior Chart Pattana Party official mentioned that despite

45. *AA*, November 20, 1996, p. 5.

reports about the beginning of horse-trading among the six parties in earnest, the allocation of portfolios in a new government had not yet started. Mr. Suwat Liptapallop, the secretary-general of the Chart Pattana Party, said that they discussed everything on Thursday evening (November 21, AD 1996). He told further that Mr. Chatichai Choonhavan had also asked Mr. Chavalit Yongchaiyudh to do something for the reconvening of Parliament as soon as possible. Then the leader of the New Aspiration Party can be nominated for Prime Minister and also the approval of him by king Bhumibel Adulyadej will take place. Mr. Banharn Silpa-Archa, the outgoing Minister, who showed his eagerness to meet to have a talk with Mr. Bill Clinton, the U.S. President, during his visit here next week, told earlier that he wanted to reconvene Parliament on December 6, AD 1996. Mr. Suwat Liptapallop gave his statement that the coalition would stay together and would work together despite reports that fractures were already appeared between the partners. There was a tension in the economic area. Because the outgoing deputy Prime Minister has given assurance for the post as finance minister and head of an economic 'dream team'. However, Mr. Chatichai Choonhavan, a headstrong former Prime Minister, has also been mentioned for a senior position in the government with an economic focus. Investors were happy to see the presence of both men in the expected government and they lifted the Bangkok bourse 2.3 per cent on Thursday (November 19, 1996), after a disastrous 5.4 drop the day before, and this was told by brokers. Much of Monday's (November 18, 1996) drop was attributed to news that Mr. Banharn Silpa-Archa took keen interest to join the coalition. However, the market recovered as it became clear that Mr. Banharn Silpa-Archa was bumped from the coalition in favour of Mr. Chatichai Choonhavan. Mr. Chavalit Yongchaiyudh's coalition, including four members of the last government will have to survive the fierce horse-trading as partners jockey for key ministers. All but two of the proposed coalition partners were members of Mr. Banharn Silpa-Archa's unpopular government.

Thailand's would-be government coalition showed signs of cracks amid a brewing struggle over key economic ministers on Wednesday, November 20, 1996.[46] Mr. Amnuay Virawan, the outgoing deputy Prime Minister, charged by Prime Minister-apparent Mr. Chavalit Yongchaiyudh with managing the economy, named controversial appointees to his five-man economic team. There was no immediate reaction from the Chart Pattana Party and former Prime Minister Mr. Chatichai Choonhavan, who also wanted broad responsibilities for the economy in the expected government of Mr. Chavalit Yongchaiyudh. Speaking to reporters at Bangkok's airport after returning from Hong Kong, Mr. Amnuay Virawan told that he would only join Mr. Chavalit Yongchaiyudh's government if the coalition agreed to support his economic plans and policies and allowed him to work freely to implement them. He said further,

> for the conditions to be acceptable, I would have to be both deputy Prime Minister and Finance Minister, if not I will be unable to carry out my work.

He mentioned further that he would like to appoint General Finance and Securities Plc. Chairman Mr. Narongchai Akrasorani and the former secretary general of the Securities Exchange Commission Mr. Ekkamel Kiriwat, as his deputies. He told further that appointing Mr. Ekkamel Kiriwat, who was asked from his post at the Securities Exchange Commission amid allegations of political interference last December as deputy Finance Minister, would help to restore investor confidence both here and abroad. However, according to analysts, the choice of Mr. Ekkamel Kiriwat could lead to tensions with the proposed government as he was dismissed from the Securities Exchange Commission by Mr. Surakirat Sathirathai, an advisor to the Chart Pattana Party, the second largest coalition partner. Mr. Surakirat Sathirathai most probably would become foreign minister in the

---

46. *AA*, November 21, 1996, p. 5.

prospective coalition government which was due to be installed next week following the narrow victory of Mr. Chavalit Yongchaiyudh's the New Aspiration Party in general election (Sunday, November 17, 1996). Mr. Kanaphan Nantasen of Deutsche Morgan Grenfell Securities (Thailand) said that it was controversial move which would be an obstacle to the unity of the government. Mr. Chatichai Choonhavan, who was the Prime Minister from AD 1998 to 1990 during a period of economic boom in Thailand, wanted key portfolios, including commerce, industry and communications for his Chart Pattana Party. Mr. Chavalit Yongchaiyudh met for lunch on Wednesday, November 20, 1996 with leaders of two smaller parties in his coalition and he reported that we came here to talk and to exchange views. We did not like to rush into everything and we would work step by step. Mr. Amnuay Virawan gave his indication that he also wanted to appoint to his economic team a number of leading figures from commercial Thai banks and finance and securities firms. He would be happy to work with the Chart Pattana People if they were qualified to perform the job. Mr. Kanaphan Nantasen of Deutsche Morgan Grenfall Securities (Thailand) said that the foreign investors and local retail investors wanted Mr. Amnuay Virawan that Mr. Chatichai Choonhavan, but local investors also looked back with nostalgia over the boom years of Mr. Chatichai Choonhavan's term. During the election campaign the New Aspiration Party mentioned Mr. Amnuay Virawan as the leader of the their economic 'dream team' and it described that he was a prefect preson to tackle the structural problems of the flagging Thai economy. The Chart Pattana Party had appeared more allied to the opposition Democrats which narrowly lost to the New Aspiration Party despite the popularity of the Democrats among the business community in Bangkok.

Mr. Chavalit Yongchaiyudh, the former army chief, took a step closer to becoming Thailand's next Prime Minister on Thursday, November 21, 1996 after King Bhumibol Adulyadej issued a royal course to reconvene the Thai Parliament. State-run Radio Thailand told that the Thai Parliament would reconvene on Saturday, November 23, 1996 with MPs elected in last weekend's general election (November 17, 1996) after the opening of the House of Representatives by the king of Thailand. MPs will then elect a House Speaker, probably from Mr. Chavalit Yongchaiyudh's New Aspiration Party, who will forward his nomination as Prime Minister to the king for approval. The King's approval was mentioned as a formality. Mr. Chavalit Yongchaiyudh waited impatiently to take the charge of his country as a Prime Minister since his party, the New Aspiration Party narrowly won on Sunday's election (November 17, 1996), while outgoing Prime Minister Mr. Banharn Silpa-Archa took his time in requesting the reconvening of the Thai Parliament. Meanwhile, the Thai press speculated that the coalition partners among themselves did not behave in a proper way and they were not in good terms for the possession of key portfolios, especially in the economic ministries, and that would bring the downfall of Mr. Chavalit Yongchaiyudh's ministry and his government. The executive committees of the six parties in a meeting on Thursday, November 21, 1996 discussed the joint policies of the new government rather than portfolio allocations. This was told by Mr. Suraporn Danaitangtrakul, who belonged to Mr. Chavalit Yongchaiyudh's group, the New Aspiration Party, in a news conference in Bangkok. Mr. Chavalit Yongchaiyudh told on television that his party never clashed with the second largest party in the present coalition, the Chart Pattana Party of former Prime Minister Mr. Chatichai Choonhavan. The Prime Minister apparent appointed Mr. Amnuay Virawan, an outgoing deputy Prime Minister and former banker, to head a team of experts to manage the economy. However, Mr. Chatichai Choonhavan also wanted to take the charge of broad economic responsibilities which no doubt complicated Mr. Amnuay Virawan's case because the latter wanted to control it fully and freely.

King Bhumibol Adulyadej of Thailand opened the Thai Parliament on Saturday, November 23, AD 1996 with a call to the nation's often-fractious parties to work together in the best interest of the people.[47] He is the longest-reigning monarch in Thailand. He officially opened the new session of the Thai Parliament and began the process to appoint the New Aspiration Party leader Mr. Chavalit Yongchaiyudh, the country's 22nd Prime Minister. The king in a brief five-minute speech told that

> it is your direct burden and responsibility to work together and be united to perform to the best of your ability for the prosperity of the nation and the people.

The Thai Parliament's first order of business on Saturday, November 23, AD 1996 was election of a Speaker of the Lower House, whose task was then to submit the name of the next Prime Minister to King Bhumibol Adulyadej for his approval. Mr. Chavalit Yongchaiyudh was visibly impatient, partly because of next week's visit by the US President Mr. Bill Clinton, but also, according to the Thai press reports, the soothsayers gave their warnings that the Prime Ministership may elude him if he did not grasp it quickly. Political sources said, however, that Mr. Chavalit Yongchaiyudh's rush to take office would have been a great blunder because he has not yet settled the distribution of cabinet portfolios among the six parties of his coalition. The Chart Pattana Party, member — two party in the coalition, issued a veiled threat on Friday, November 22, AD 1996 when it set a 7 p.m. deadline for the share out — the hour at which MPs went to vote for the new Speaker. Asked whether the Chart Pattana Party would back Mr. Wan-Muhammad-Noor Matha, the expected candidate of the New Aspiration Party, then Mr. Kern Dabbaransi, the Chart Pattana Party's deputy leader, told that if 'everything' was not settled by 7 p.m., reporters had the right to ask that question again. The Chart Pattana Party which demanded a very important and a preponderant role in managing economic affairs in the new government had in its command

47. *AA*, November 24, 1996, p. 5.

fifty-two (52) seats of the six-party alliance's two hundred twenty-one seats (221) in the Thai Parliament. The main opposition, the Democrat Party, which won one hundred twenty-three (123) of the three hundred ninety-three (393) seats in the Thai Parliament, against one hundred twenty-five (125) for the New Aspiration Party, indicated on Friday, November 22, AD 1996 that Mr. Bhichai Rattakul, the former party leader, would contest in Speaker's election as its candidate. The Chart Pattana Party wanted to take the full control of economic matters of the new government. But Mr. Chavalit yongchaiyudh while he campaigned promised that his long-time ally, Mr. Amnuay Virawan would head an economic 'dream team' in the next cabinet. The latter, who did not take part in the last election and suspended his Nam Thai Party, wanted to take the charge as the top leader of the economic affairs of the new government. But Mr. Chatichai Choonhavan, the former Prime Minister, was the leader of the Chart Pattana Party. He looked a more likely victor because his party's seats were very crucial in the coalition. Meanwhile, Mr. Chavalit Yongchaiyudh's own group the New Aspiration Party faced many problems. A large faction, composed of defectors from outgoing Prime Minister Mr. Banharn Silpa-Archa's the Chart Thai Party, demanded a large share of the cabinet spoils. The faction, headed by Mr. Sanoh Thientong, now became the secretary-general of the New Aspiration Party, argued that its members gave the New Aspiration Party a critical boost from fifty-seven (57) seats in the last Parliament to one hundred twenty-five (125) in the new Assembly and for this reason they should be rewarded in consequence. In order to solve their problems and to find a peaceful solution over their differences, several coalition parties met on Saturday, November 23, AD 1996 at Mr. Chatichai Choonhavan's home. From television reports it was learnt that there was no immediate agreement on the economic portfolios, and probably, later in the day on November 23, AD 1996 there was an expectance of a second meeting. The New Aspiration Party of Mr. Chavalit Yongchaiyudh formed the new government after the opposition Party, the Democrat Party conceded to take in the opposition benches though no party was able to win a majority.

From Bangkok we learn that an association of reporters has threatened to reveal the names of politicians who 'dump cash alongside their care' in an apparent attempt to buy loyalty. The *Bangkok Post* said it. The Reporters' Association of Thailand was quoted as saying that the politicians were 'furious'. The association mentioned that it would submit letters to the Prime Minister, and leaders of political parties on an attempt to stop such well-entrenched practices.

Uncertainly surrounded the fate of the Karen civilians escaping a Myanmarese military offensive amid reports on Saturday, March 1, AD 1997 that Thailand's Army Chief has called a halt to the repatriation of the Karen refugees.[48] From the *Nation* daily we learn that General Chettha Thanajare had stopped planned reallocations of the Karen refugees when the Thai military was criticised very much from the different parts of the world for sending back hundred of civilians into Myanmar. Informed a sources have confirmed that plans to shift about 4,000 Karen refugees from two camps in Kanchanaburi in Thailand had been put on held after the US and the UNA refugee agency voiced 'deep concern' to Thailand. About 900 women and children had already been forcibly repatriated. However, General Chettha Thanajare and the Thai officials said that there had never been any forced repatriation of the Karens. They told further that all the Karens who went back to Myanmar 'voluntarily wanted to return'. 'We have not done what to widely alleged'. General Mongkol stated in the *Bangkok Post*, 'Instead we are continuing with huminitarian aid to the Karen refugees'. He mentioned that

women and children fleeing the Myanmarese

48. *AA*, March 2, 1997, p. 4.

> government offensive would be given shelter and aid, but armed men would be pushed back unless they agreed to disarm.

Aid workers remained concerned about the safety of refugees,

> still believed to be filtering to the border of Kanchanaburi province during a lull in fighting in the Karen National Union's Fourth Brigade area, located in the Tenassarin division of southerm Myanmar.

From the *Asian Age*, Calcutta (Bangkok, March 25, AD 1997) It is known that around 5,000 ethnic Karen refugees are staying in Thailand in fear because the Thai army will use force to send them to Myanmar to the war zone they fled ahead of a Myanmar offensive. Some 2,500 Karens, including some 800 pushed back across the border earlier in March, were given refuge as troops overran Htaw Ma Pya Hta, where they took shelter on the Myanmarese side of the border. Food and medical assistance were arranged at Huay Sut in Ratchburi province, a few km from the border. But senior Thai Army officers did not like to sea the Karen refugees to stay in Thailand. They wanted their return to Myanmar. After their meetings with the Myanmarese officers, they told the refugees that Myanmar's army had promised to treat thaem well. Another 2,500 refugees at Pha Manng in Kanchanaburi province to the north of Huay Sut told the Thai army that they will return in the last week of March AD 1997. "The refugees are very afraid. They are sending us an SDS eveyday. Our fear is that they will to went back." A border source informed this. But the Thai officers, who belonged to the Ninth Army, was in charge of this area and they spoke to the refugees that the Myanmarese Junta had promissed to welcome them. Several guerrillas of the rebel Karen National Union (KNU) told on Thursday, March 20, 1997 that they were under pressure from the Thai Army to hold peace talks with Myanmar's military government. The Thai Army had pressured the Karen

National Union (KNU) to shut its liaison and other offices at the Thai-Myanmar border and searched for the commander of the group's Fourth Brigade to force him to meet the Myanmarese government. This was mentioned by a Thai Army officer. The Karen National Union with a view to find out greater autonomy for the eastern Myanmarese Karen state was formed and has declared a guerrilla was against Myanmar's ruling State Law and Order Restoration Council. The Thai authorities in the past practically ignored the activities of the Karen National Union on the Thai side of the border but when Mr. Chavalit Yongchaiyudh became Prime Minister of Thailand four months ago, their attitude towards the rebel group was completely changed. Thailand wanted order at the Karen refuges camps because about 90,000 refugees were living there. A Karen National Union Officer told us that the Thai Army officers came to us and told us that "since we are not in a position to fight Myanmar's ruling State Law and Order Restoration Council, we should surrender". Another said that the Thai Army had requested the landlords not to keep tenants who were members of the rebel groups. In order to force Colonel Oliver, the Karen National Union's Fourth Brigade Commander based in Myanmarese jungles opposite Thailand's Western Kanchanaburi province, to make a peaceful settlement with Rangoon separately from the mainstream the Karen National Union, several Thai officers were very busy in search of him. The Thai army told that the Karen National Union from other areas had already ceased their military operations and for this reason it was the duty of Commander Oliver to stop fighting. A Karen source mentioned it.

Thailand's national environment board has approved the petroleum authority of Thailand to construct its portion of a controversial gas pipeline from Myanmar.[49] Environmental activists in Thailand did not like this approval and they wanted

49. *AA*, March 26, 1997, p. 18.

to oppose the pipeline because they mentioned that 'it runs through forest reserves and along a fault line'. They accused the national environment board because they did not take notice of it and they totally ignored it. The Thai portion of the pipeline will go from the Myanmarese border through Kanchanaburi province to a power plant in Ratchaburi province, 95 km west of Bangkok. The owners of the Myanmarese part of the pipeline are France, Unocal of the United States, the Myanmarese government, etc. The human rights groups and democracy activists heavily criticised that portion of the project because it provided cash for the Myanmarese military regime.

Thailand has tried to strengthen its financial sector by unveiling a major fund raising plan to bailout the troubled property projects and telling small, shaky finance house to merge.[50] Mr. Rorngchai Marakanand, the central bank governer, told that the government would soon float up to 100 billion baht ($ 3.87 billion), seven year, zero-coupan bonds to raise funds to help the property sector. Most finance company executives welcomed the bail-out scheme, which would inject badly needed liquidity into non-bank financial institutions threatened by non-performing loans to the property sector. The governer told finance companies that proceeds from the bonds, expected to get cabinet approval this week, would be used for refinancing indebted property projects, giving developers more time to sell them while the market gradually improved. Mr. Nivas Homavachiravarakorn, senior executive vice-president of Nava Finance and Securities Plc. said, "This plan, comparing with other measures announced earlier, sounds the most practical in helping the whole industry." Mr. Rorngchai Marakanand mentioned that he hoped the planned zero-coupan bond issue to be a success as finance institutional buyers could use the bonds as reserves like other government debt instruments. The governer, backed by Finance Minister Mr. Amnuay Virawan also said Thailand's 91 finance companies

---

50. *ET*, March 10, 1997, p. 15.

to shape up, saying he expected many of them to merge in the next few years in preparation for greater competition from bigger foreign firms. The governer said,

> The Bank of Thailand will set guidelines encouraging as many mergers as possible. We will use carrot and stick to induce mergers, giving them incentives including as expanded scope of their liceaned business.

Mr. Krairit Uchukanondchai, the president of Thana One Plc. said,

> I fully support the merger policy. Finance firms need to be strengthened in order to complete in a globalised environment.

Months of market concern that the property slump would bankrupt troubled finance firms exploded last week when Finance One Plc. and Thai Danu Bank Plc announced a friendly merger, and the government ordered 10 finance houses to raise capital. The government action triggred public runs on about 15-20 billion baht of finance company deposits, but withdrawals eased after the Central Bank said that it would guarantee repayment of promissory notes issued by these firms. The Central Bank also instructed Thailand's 15 banks and 91 finance compenies to set aside 50 billion baht ($ 1.94 billion) as additional provisions for sub-standard assests within two years. A foreign analyst estimated that at least 8.8 per cent of bank and finance company loans were classified as doubtful or sub-standard assets and that their low quality would deteriorate further on the property sector slump dragged on. The Finance Minister of Thailand told that about 10 per cent of total bank loans are 25 per cent of finance lending went to the property sector but he stressed that only a portion of these had turned soured. On Monday, Mrach 3, AD 1997 the authorities ordered 10 finance companies, hard-hit by a liquidity crunch, to raise capital by a total of 8.25 billion baht ($ 3.17 million). They also toughened loan-loss reserve requirements for the country's 15 banks and 91 finance firms, many of which have huge exposure to the bloated and crisis-torn real estate market. The institutions' woes have been exacerbated by an economic showdown after a decade of almost double-digit annual growth and the Central Bank's high interest rate policy to deter attacks on the baht, which was hit by devaluation rumours last month (February, AD 1997). For good measure, the Central Bank governer Mr. Rorgchai Marakanand moved to reassure waverung foreign investors that currency stability remained a top policy priority.

During the reign of King Bhumibol Adulyadej India has established a very close diplomatic tie with Thailand. Mr. Chavalit Yongchaiyudh, the Prime Minister of Thailand, also made a great effort for India's close relation with his country. The Royal Thai Navy seized on the high seas on illegal arms shipment of a north-eastern rebel group of India recently and this clearly indicates that New Delhi's recent diplomatic initiative with Thailand has paid off. The external affairs ministry has appealed to the authorities in Bangkok not to allow north-eastern rebel leaders to use the country as a sanctuary for making arms and for holding strategy sessions. The latest issue of the Jane's *Defence Weekly* mentioned that the Royal Thai Navy captured an illegal arms shipment of the People's Liberation Army of Manipur in mid-March AD 1997. It stated that ten men were arrested when their 16-metre vessele was seized by a navy petrol boat and in the Andaman sea off the southern Thai seaport of Ramong it chased it.[51] The arrested persons, suspected to be PIA cadres were found holding Bangladesh passports. Among the two tonnes of weapons seized by the Thai Navy were the rocket propelled granade launchers, 20 American assault rifles, two recoillers guns, four M-79 granade launchers and more than 10,000 rounds of asserted ammunition. The *Weekly* described that an estimated quarter of the shipment was dumped into the sea by the PLA men before

51. *AA*, March 29, 1997, p. 3.

the vessel was boarded by the Thai Navy man. It was for the first time that the Thai authorities took action against north-eastern India rebels who for gunrunning have been using the particular sea route. There are several groups who have been using this Andaman sea route along southern Thailand to carry arms and ammunitions to their places. They are the banned Ulfa, both the Issac-Muivah and Khaplang factions of the National Socialist Council of Nagaland as well as the Sri Lankan Tamil Tigers. Thus, we conclude that arms seizure on high seas by the Royal Thai Navy indicates that Indo-Thai relations have improved very much and these two countries have come very close to each other when Mr. Chavalit Yongchaiyudh as Prime Minister took the charge of his country. Princess Maha Chakri Srindhorn of Thailand visited the Andaman and Nicobar Islands on Saturday, December 21, AD 1996 and she stayed there for five days. She saw the cellular Jail and laid a wreath at the national memorial.[52]

Mr. Chavalit Yongchaiyudh, the Thai Prime Minister, wanted a very close and friendly relation with Vietnam. During his two-day visit (March 29-30, AD 1997) there, he announced it. He left Hanoi on Monday, March 31, AD 1997.[53] He told that his government always looked forward for closer economic co-operation with Vietnam and in order to end fishing disputes with that country he pressed on with talks. On Sunday, March 31, AD 1997 he had a talk with his Vietnamese counterpart Mr. Ve Van Kiet to discuss stepping up co-operation in the banking sector as well as boosting air links and in order to establish Thailand's connection with Laos, Vietnam and Cambodia these two leaders agreed to help each other for the construction of two highways. Mr. Kiet was very much happy to receive the Thai Prime Minister in his country and he hoped to see more Thai investments in Vietnam. Several people, newspapers and allies of Mr. Chavalit

---

52. *TG*, December 22, 1996, p. 8.
53. *AA*, April 1, 1997, p. 4.

Yongchaiyudh assailed his decision and criticised bitterly on Tuesday, April 1, AD 1997 to grant a military pension to an army officer who gave his order to troops to fire on demonstrators, who had no arms in AD 1973. Mr. Chavalit Yongchaiyudh supported his case very much and he defended the $ 148-pension for the 64-year old army officer who was Colonel on the ground that he never faced criminal prosecution and no case was brought against him. The *Nation* daily in Bangkok reported on Tuesday, April 1, AD 1997 that health officials in northern Thailand warned consumers to stear clear of marijuana seasoning in their needle soup. The drug, which is traditionally used to give the food's taste, is still illegal even if it is dissolved into soup. Mr. Nisit Wattanachariya of Chiang Mai provincial health officer told it. he mentioned further that although only a small amount of marijuana was used in food, yet repeated use could creats a health problem.

The twentieth century witnesse an absolute monarchy in Thailand. But a bloodless coup in AD 1932 helped to change Thailand from an absolute to a limited monarchy. A revolution that occurred in AD 1932 overturned 700 years of absolute monarchy and it replaced it with a constitutional monarchy. To-day the king has considerable authority but he has very little political power in his hands. A recent constitution of Thailand has given executive power in the hands of the Thai Prime Minister, and the council of Ministers has helped him in many ways. Thailand's Parliament became known as the National Assembly. It has the Upper House, the Senate and the Lower House. There were many military coups in Thailand. The military rulers during their rule suspended various constitutions in several times and at the same time they also dissolved the legislature. But the king has occupied an important place in Thailand's constitution as head of state. During a coup attempt he publicly demonstrated for the support of the civilian government in Thailand and this no doubt indicated that he himself took part in Thailand's politics. Because he wanted to see the return of the civilian government in Thailand and he desired to find a great change in his country's political history. Thailand can be mentioned as the eldest independent state in South-East Asia. It has never been colonised. Since AD 1932 it has a constitutional monarchy. Various constitutional changes took place in various times. At present the executive power rests with the king and the cabinet and the legislative power is in the hands of the 246-member People's Assembly. Before AD 1962 the Assembly had two categories of members, viz., these elected by universal adult suffrage and these appointed by the ling on the advice of the government. With the improvement in the standard of education, the number of nominated seats gradually decreased. The Assembly by AD 1962 became a fully elective body.

More than 145 years after he died, the third ruler of Thailand's current dynasty is about to have 'The Great' added to his title. A newspaper in Bangkok mentioned it on Monday, April 14, AD 1997.[54] The rare honour came later in the fourth week of April AD 1997 when the government's cabinet changed the appellation of Phra Nangklao who reigned in Thailand from AD 1824 to 1851. This was told by the *Bangkok Post*. Only two of the nine kings of the Chakri dynasty were able to receive that honour proviously. They include the current king, Bhumibol Adulyadej, the world's largest-reigning monarch with 50 years on the throne and King Chulalongkorn, the fifth ruler, who reigned from AD 1868 to 1910 and contributed much to modernise his kingdom. Phra Nangklao was a conservative ruler who signed treatises with the British colonislists after they captured Myanmar. He also played a vital role to extend Thailand's sovereignty over Laos and Cambodia and the country's southern provinces. The son of a royal concubine, not a queen, Phra Nangklao was succeeded by Mongkut, who was his younger half-brother. The latter was loosely characterised in the Broadway musical and Hollywood film *The King And I*. It may be noted here that Thailand's rulers

54. *AA*, April 17, 1997, p. 5.

have been constitutional monarchs since AD 1932, even then, King Bhumibol Adulyadej is revered by the people of Thailand as semi-divine.

The Thai government took very stern attitude against smuggling of heroin in Thailand. The Thai police men have arrested two Europeans from Italy and Holland and charged them with heroin possession with intent to sell. This was told by the narcotics officers on Thursday, April 17, AD 1997.[55] The two Europeans were arrested along with two Thais on Wednesday, April 16, AD 1997 after the Thai police found 115 packets of heroin weighing a total of 940 gm in their car. A British woman who was sentenced to 25 years in prison for trying to smuggle heroin out of Thailand won approval on Thursday, April 17, AD 1997 to serve the remainder of her sentence in Britain. This was told by a Thai official of Mr. Chavalit Yongchaiyudh's government. A special team of Bangkok police was sent to Pattaya after Mr. Chavalit Yongchaiyudh, the Thai Prime Minister, described the country's leading seaside resort as a don of prostitution, drug-trafficking and money-laundering. Mr. Sanoh Thienthong, Thailand's Interior Minister, told on Sunday, April 20, AD 1997 that the Thai government took decision to move to restore the flagging reputation of the country's most seedy holiday spot. Despite being branded as Thailand's 'greatest source of evil' Most Bangkok residents rated the resort city of Pattaya as their first choice for a holiday.

Thousands of poor Thai villagers from impoverished north-east who have camped outside the Government House in Bangkok for three months seeking social justice ended their marathon protest on Friday, May 2, AD 1997.[56] A spokesman for the Assembly of Poor, as the protest organisers are called, said the 15,000 protestors who had demanded settlement of their land disputes with the government and better farm produce princes,

55. *AA*, April 18, 1997, p. 4.

56. *Ibid.*, May 3, 1997, p. 4.

were ready to trek home. The government had agreed to established a central fund valued at about two billion baht ($ 80 million) to compensate these protestors who could prove they had lost their farmland.

Thailand's Buddhist monks in a central Thai province followed the footsteps of the country's politicians by slinging mud and buying votes in an election for a temple abbot. The election for the abbot of the Phak Hai temple in Ayuthia, 70 km north of Bangkok has became so tainted that the Thai government's religious affairs department has been forced to intervene. This was reported in Bangkok's newspapers on Saturday, May 3, AD 1997.[57] "This election is dirtier than elections for village chiefs and headman." Mr. Somsak Soisup, a provincial councilman, told it, "It has defamed the religious institutions".

Myanmar's military leaders have imposed restrictions on visiting Thai afficials have warned them to stay clear of the street on which the opposition leader Aung San Sun Kyi's house. This was discussed by a Thai government official on Thursday, May 15, AD 643. The Thai foreign ministry received a warning letter from Myanmar's State Law and Order Restoration Council on Wednesday, May 14, AD 1997, two days before Mr. Chavalit Yongchaiyudh, the Thai Prime Minister, was due to make an official visit to Myanmar. The letter asked the Thai delegates travelling with Mr. Chavalit Yongchaiyudh not to go near University Avenue — the street on which Mrs. Sun Kyi's house. This Avenue has been barricated around Mrs. Sun Kyi's house since late last year to present people from visiting the Nobel Peace Laureate. The Thai official said that the letter specifically mentioned journalists who were coming with the Thai Prime Minister and requested them not to talk to Mrs. Sun Kyi to report her movements or actions. The letter has totally indicated that SLORC (Myanmar's State Law and Order Restoration

57. *AA*, May 23, 1997, p. 5.

Council) does not care at all about improving relations with its neighbour. The Thai official told:

> We know they will montior and follow us on every movement. I know they followed me when I visited Rangoon but there is no need to issue an official letter warning us, telling us where we should not go and whom we should not contact.

This was for the first time Myanmar's State Law and Order Restoration council has sent such a warning to state guests. But it is to be noted here that several delegates came with Indonesian President Mr. Suharto who visited Myanmar in February AD 1997 did not receive any such restrictions from the Myanmarese.

After a meeting with the Thai Prime Minister, Mr. Chavalit Yongchaiyudh, on April 12, AD 1997 most of the 20,000 people camped out in front of the Thai Parliament for three months, said that they were ready to end their protest. This was reported by local newspapers. Mr. Chavalit Yongchaiyudh gave the protestors his personal guarantee to do all in his power to solve their grievances. He promised to set-up a joint committee of the Government officials and protest leaders to remedy the 47 of 121 issues raised by the poor that were still unsolved. The protesters, who called themselves the Assembly of the Poor, have lived in a makeshift village on the pavement in front of the government house since early July AD 1996. Most leaders agreed to end the demonstration after their meeting with the Thai Prime Minister, but some people wanted to continue it to see Mr. Chavalit Yongchaiyudh's promises were adopted in a cabinet resolution.

Several Buddhist monks in the northern village of Thailand, right after reciting some chnats, wrapped a saffron robs around an old tree, the 50 millionth one to be 'ordained' in Thailand.[58] Then the villagers after watching the ceremony followed the

58. *AA*, p. 5.

monks' example, and covered the trunks of hundred of other trees in the forest with saffron robes. The ceremony went on for days and about 562,500 trees in the forested area of Nong Tao village in Chiang Mai province in northern Thailand were ordained into the monkhood. The ritual part of a new forestry conservation programme that combined traditional value for natural resources and involved local people in protecting Thailand's forest. The ordination of trees parallels a common practice among the Thai people in their early 20s, whose mark of maturity is gained after entering the monkhood for at least three months to live by the tenets of Buddhism. In the same way that the Thai people are ready to start life as an adult after going through monkhood, the ordained trees are expected to live to full mature age, their lives receive protection under Buddhism. Ma Patjana Suansri of the Thai Volunteer Service Foundation, a non-governmental organisation, involved in the forestry scheme told that

> the idea is to bring back the sense of belonging among villagers and to give them the feeling that they can have an active role in living with and protecting forest resources.

Dr. Pravej Wasee, a noted activist, described,

> in the midst of the destructive trend in modern society, it is necessary to reconnect people to the value they have deeply in their mind. To ordain the trees is to remind people about the value of nature.

Forest destruction in Thailand has continued through the decades, leaving only 20 per cent of the country forested. And as the crisis of deforestation became evident, tension also arose between the Thai government intent on its own forest conservation policies and villagers, who often lived in the highland areas that were the target of different forestry schemes. Indeed, villagers living in forested areas for generations are often accused of destroying trees and forests. It is pehaps, no wonder that 92 cases of land disputes were among the grips that rural demonstrators brought to the government's attention in protests in Bangkok recently. Likewise, instances where projects were supposed to reforest denuded areas turned out to be industrial schemes, they did little to help reforestation and alienated many villagers. Then King Bhumibol Adulyadej took interest in this matter and gave his advice that the best way to protect forest is to allow trees grow freely, without humans harming them. The King's suggestion for foerstry conservation was accepted by the non-governmental organisations and government agencies with financial support from private firms and on the occasion of the 50th anniversary of the king's accession to the throne this unique scheme began in AD 1996.

Top Thai policy-makers on Sunday, May 28, AD 1997 promised to take steps to help companies boost sagging exports but business people welcomed it very cautiously. At a government business exports Summit chaired by Mr. Chavalit Yongchaiyudh, the Prime Minister of Thailand in Pattaya, the resort town, the Thai government told clearly that it wanted to cut exporters' costs by speeding up tax rebates, cutting interest rates and reducing other infrastructural costs. But several measures belonged to them had no clear-cut timeframes. The government also wanted to waive an import cota system for raw materials used in making products for exports such as powdered milk. This was told by Mr. Narongchai Akrasorani, the Commerce Minister, after this summit. One leading Thai industrialist said,

> The spoonful of sugar the government promised to give makes bitter pills like the bearish economy much easier to swallow. But they can rest assured that their actions will be measured against their words. We will closely monitor whether the government does implement these plans.

Mr. Chekachai Aksaranand, president of the Federation of the

Thai industries, mentioned that in order to assess the government performance another meeting took place between the Thai authorities and the private sector. The Thai experts fell 0.2 per cent in AD 1996 against an increase of 23.6 per cent in AD 1995. Although the year AD 1996 witnessed a very slow start, yet the Thai Prime Minister was very confident and he told that the expert growth for AD 1997 will meet the target of 10 per cent as fixed by the Thai commerce Minister. He described,

> The April figures showed some sign of recovery in exports. I believe that with the scheme we announced on Monday, 26 May 1997, exports this year will meet the target. There are several potential products that we can develop and make Thailand a centre for these industries, such as foods, automobiles and parts, computers and electronics.

Several Thai exporters at a meeting mentioned that the biggest problem facing the country's hard-hit exports was none other than the Thai government itself. They bitterly criticised the authority for their failure to cut high interest rates, red tape to deal with corruption in the custom department and the absence of a focused export strategy. Mr. Kern Dabbaransi, the Thai industry minister, said that in order to help Thailand to connect with its South-East Asian neighbours in electronics, he was ready to submit measures for this purpose to the cabinet. It needed government support because in the next 20 years it would be regarded as the main export industry in every member country of the association of the South-East Nations. Mr. Kern Dabbaransi stated,

> Many neighbouring countries have had measures in place to support the electronics industry for a long time now. Fearing investors, would turn away from Thailand if action was not taken.

He submitted proposals including the creation of a customs free trade zone catering to the industry to the cabinet in the second week of June AD 1997. He also wanted permission for the state enterprises or the government to enter joint electronics ventures with the private sector and also for the provision of soft loans.

India and Thailand wanted to join a new formation economic group to promote trade and investment between South Asian and the South-East Asian countries. This was disclosed by a Thai minister on Thursday, May 29, AD 1997.[59] Mr. Pitak Intrawityanunt, the Thai deputy minister of foreign affairs, said that the Bangladesh-India-Sri Lanka-Thailand Economic Co-operation or Bistec has been urged by India's policy of going east and Thailand turning to west. This Bistec wanted to tap the potential for co-operation in agro-industries and in the fields of telecommunications, computer software, fisheries and tourism. Mr. Pitak told reporters at the end of his two-day visit to New Delhi. This Bistec wished to utilise $ 200 million earmarked by the United Nations Development fund for the development of the region. Mr. Pitak in order to take steps to boost trade, now $ 1 billion a year in both directions, and $ 800 million in investment by Thailand's companies in India, met Mr. P. Chidambaram, the then union finance minister, Mr. C.M. Ibrahim, the civil aviation minister and Mr. Beni Prasad Verma, the telecommunications minister in New Delhi. Thailand also hosted the launching of the Association of the South-East Asian Nations. It was regarded as biggest Asean investor in India. This Bistec could provide access to the South Asian countries to Asean which will become a free trade zone by the year AD 2003. Mr. Kobsak Chutikul, the director-general in the Thai foreign ministry, mentioned it. Investors from Thailand visited West Bengal in India in May AD 1997 and have expressed their desires to invest in infrastructure development projects in the state. There were about twenty-one members of this Thai group and their leader was Mr. Pitak Intrawityanunt. They met several senior state government

59. *AA*, May 30, 1997, p. 17.

leaders including Mr. Somnath Chatterjee, M.P. and Chairman, West Bengal Industrial Development Corporation Limited, Mr. S.K. Roy and had several discussions with them to identify areas of investment. The West Bengal State government wanted investment in sectors like tourism, electronics, software and construction of expressways from them. The state minister for industries and commerce expressed his satisfaction over the talks. The state governmet requested the Thai investors to invest in one of the three mega-growth centres approved by the centre for West Bengal and each of the proposed centres will be spread over an area of 1000 acres. Mr. Pitak Intrawityanunt gave his assurance to the state government to consider the matter. The Chairman of Webel requested the foreign team to erect a tower at 'infinity complex' at Salt Lake in Calcutta. The two sides explored possibilities of starting a jet air service on the Calcutta-Gaya-Phuket-and Nicobar route.

According to press reports, the wife of the Thai Prime Minister Mr. Chavalit Yongchaiyudh followed the advice of a fortune-teller and moved house to boost her husband's future.[60] An aide told in a telephone interview that Ms Khunying (Lady) Paṇkrua began moving out of the couple's spacious residence in suburban Bangkok on Monday, June 9, AD 1997. But Ms Pankura told that for its renovation she dicided to move out of their residence. "I fear the house may collapse. That is the sole reason for moving out." This was mentioned by Ms Pankrua on Sunday, June 8, AD 1997. The Thai press said that she believed moving house would lift Mr. Chavalit Yongchaiyudh's fortune and would extend the tenure of his six-month coalitish government which has been battered by its inability to turn around the country's faltering economy. No elected Thai Prime Minister has served a full fouryear term since AD 1932. When Thailand switched from absolute monarchy to its current British-style parliamentary system. The wife of the Thai Prime Minister Mr. Chavalit

60. *AA*, June 10, 1997, p. 5

Yongchaiyudh always depended on precious elephant for luck. She carried a jewel-studded elephant doll wherever she went for good luck. This was disclosed by a local media on Monday, June 23, AD 1997. Ms Pankrua Yongchaiyudh has clasped the doll publicly since she returned from a trip to Myanmar in March AD 1997. In order to bring good luck for her and her husband, she carried the doll on the advice of a fortune-teller. because her husband was facing an economic crisis in Thailand. She even took it to Cambodia and Laos when her husband made an official visit there.

Several Thailand and Singaporean firms on Monday, June 16, AD 1996 signed a $ 700 million joint venture in order to develop Thailand's largest industrial estate. At Bangkok's Government House the signing of the memorandum of understanding took place and the Thai Prime Minister and his visiting Singaporean counterpart Mr. Goh Chok Tong were present there. Thailand's Eastern Sugar Co. Ltd. and Singapore's JTC International Pvt. Ltd agreed to establish a joint venture firm. According to officials, the new firm, which will have an initial registered capital of $ 11.5 million witnessed the start of Bangkok's efforts to change the eastern seaboard into South-East Asia's biggest industrial hub. The 1.100 hectare Thai-Singapore 21 industrial estate would be able to attract $ 4.63 billion worth of investment after the completion of its four stages in AD 2003. Thailand's finance minister Mr. Amnuay Virawan and commerce minister Mr. Narongchai Akrasorani resigned on Thursday, June 19, AD 1997. The former was also a deputy premier in charge of economic affairs. He submitted his resignation letter to the Thai Prime Minister during a morning meeting at the Government House. He told reporters,

> I have submitted my resignation letter to the Prime Minister this morning (Thursday, October 19, 1997) and it is effective immediately. The reason behind my resignation is in order to show my political spirit and political manners.

It may be noted here that he was a technocrat and the Thai Prime Minister appointed him to head the economic 'dream team' six months ago. He resigned because he did not like to work amid political conflict and this no doubt have a very bad effect on the political world. He mentioned,

> my resignation will give the Prime Minister an opportunity to adjust his cabinet team — especially the economic team but it will not lead to any change in the Thai government's economic policy. Investors should not be worried as this is a personal change, not a policy change.

Mr. Narongchai Akrasorani, the commerce minister, quitted to show his sympathy with Mr. Virawan. Mr. Senchai Montriwat, the deputy secretary-general to the Thai Prime Minister, stated that Mr. Sempheb Amaetayakul will probably resign soon.

According to analysts, Thailand's banks suffered losses as cases of bad debts rocketted. Most of Thailand's once high-flying banks in earnings in AD 1997 could not do anything well because they were forced to make provisions to cover sour loans to the ailing property sector. This type of thing occurred when Thailand went through its worst economic downturn in over a decade, "with the troubled finance and cash-strapped property sectors particularly hard hit". Mr. Kasem Prunratanamala, a banking analyst at HSBC James Capel, told that Bank non-performing loan problems were quite serious because the economy has worsened more than earlier expected. Mr. Andrew Maule, an analyst at the Vickers Ballas described,

> We expect most of the country's 10 major banks to post negative earnings growth of about 10 to 11 per cent this year.

He stated further that Thailand's bank earnings affected very badly not only because of rising non-performing loans, but also due to tight liquidity, weaker non-interest rate income and narrowing profit margins. According to US investment bank Salomon Brothers, the net profits of the top eight banks of Thailand were expected to fall 22 per cent in AD 1997 and their failures were due to expected hikes in their provisions against possible loan loss. Mr. Kasem Prunratanamala said,

> The increase in non-performing loans of banks is quite worrisome. Banks might have to raise their capital to cover write-off of bad loans.

The Thai regulators shut down 16 ailing finance companies on Friday, June 27, AD 1997 and asked them to merge. These companies were Finance One, General Finance and Securities and Comic Finance and Securities. Mr. Thanong Bhidaya, the Finacne Minister, told,

> On Friday, June 27, AD 1997, all activities are supposed to stop, so there will be no withdrawals or anything. Within a few days, we will be proposing measures to protect depositors.

Mr. Rorngchai Marakanand, the Bank of Thailand governer at a press conference at the Government House in Bangkok, stated that the authorities in order to protect depositors, and creditors as well as borrowers, took these measures. Thailand's financing industry faced liquidity problems and many companies were about to collapse. According to the central bank officials, five healthy companies acted as core partners in the mergers. They were Nava Finance and Securities, Phatra Thanakit, Dhana Siam Finance and Securities, Krungthai Thanakit and National Finance and Securities. Mr. Rorngchai Marakanand mentioned that the sixteen finance companies were not forced to merge.

> If they have another option, if they have a major shareholder approved by the authorities who is willing to take over, then they can stay on their own, but they will have to raise their capital.

The Thai finance minister said,

> the problem is there are 91 institutions and that is too many to surmise. That is why we have to have a programme to get their institutions to merge and that is the only way to survival. The central bank will cut its credit lines to the 16 companies.

The other thirteen companies identified by the authorities were Gen Finance, Prime Finance and Securities, Dynamic Eastern Finance Thailand, Thai Fuji Finance and Securities, Thana One Finance and Securities, United Finance, Royal International Finance and Securities, ITF Finance, Country Finance, CI Sahaviya Finance and Securities, Thai Financial Trust, Finance House and Bangkok Metropolitan Trust. The Thai central bank has mentioned that it will force sixteen ailing finance firms to merge with healthy ones. Mr. Suraphel Thipvilai, assistant research manager at Vicker Ballas told,

> I think these moves could be quite positive in helping to restructure the industry in the longer term though in reality it is still likely to be a time consuming process.

The Bank of Thailand had discussions with the finance institutions to detail the workings of the latest steps and wanted their co-operation to soften the impact on nervous local depositors and the sector as a whole. The authorities gave assurance to the depositors of the 16 firms that their money was intact and the depositors could transfer their promissory notes to Krungthai Thanakit Plc. a unit of state-run Krung Thai Bank Plc. effective on Monday, June 30, AD 1997. Depositors with other finance firms in the 91-company sector also had the choice of moving their deposits to Krung Thai Bank if they were worried about the health of the sector but they would not be able to redeem their money immediately. The central bank mentioned that it would also establish controls on deposit rates fixed by finance firms on Monday, June 30, AD 1997 in a bid to ease the cost burdens of the companies. A manager of a level finance firm said,

> Depositors with the 16 finance firms have no choice but to turn to Krungthai Thanakit to protect their money. For others there is a choice but we don't see a big move from them out to Krungthai this week.

Depositors who moved their money to the two financial institutions would receive much lower interest rates than the double-digit figures offered in the past by finance companies scrambling to raise funds. But the central bank has not yet classified the fate to foreign loans to the companies. Mr. Graham Caterwell, the managing director of Deutsche Morgan Grenfell told,

> Foreign bank creditors are sweating as they await more clearer details from the central bank on the fate of their money to the 16-affected finance firms. Foreigners will be wary about lending in future to Thai institutions if they are not told precisely what will happen to their interests soon.

The local finance firm manager stated,

> The foreigners were the most exposed group to the 16 finance firms. The foreigners lent money to the firms under free market rules and now if they want to recover it looks as if they have no choice but to seek legal recourse.

The crises-ridden Thai finance sector was hit by overexposure to the depressed property sector. High interest rates have caused a severe liquidity crunch in the sector and Thailand's worst economic downturn in over a decade has given a blow to Thailand's business world. Thailand's finance firms stocks were dumped because of doubts over the quality of their assets and their non-performing loans. Their demise has badly dented the

Thai stock index which recently been lingering near eight year lows.

Thailand's top finance authorities on Monday, June 30, AD 1997 took active part to allay depositor fears about their money after launching a massive shake-up of the troubled finance sector. The authorities also told that there were no more critically troubled companies besides the 16 firms whose names were already announced on Friday, June 27, AD 1997 to get public sympathy and confidence. Thailand had earlier capped deposit rates for financial institutions to ease the burden of their interests. Commercial bank deposit rates were capped at 12 per cent, finance firms promissory note rates at 14 per cent finance firms call rates at 11 per cent. The finance ministry and the Bank of Thailand assured the depositors that their money would be protected but they did not know how they would help them. Mr. Rorngchai Marakanand, the Bank of Thailand governor told,

> We will do our best to help and be fair to the creditors of the 16 troubled finance companies.

On Friday, June 27, AD 1997 the Thai authorities forced the 16 ailing firms to bring plans to merge or have their licenses provoked and be merged with the healthy firms under purchase and assumption arrangements. They suspended the activities of the 16 ailing firms for 30 days and they gave them two weeks time to bring their plans for their future. The Bank of Thailand governor stated,

> I would like to ask depositors to understand and not be panicked as they will be fully protected. We expect the situation to return to normal soon.

The head of the Central Bank mentioned that depositors of 16 ailing companies could switch their promissory notes to negotiable certificates of deposit with Krungthanakit Plc. a branch of state-run Krung Thai Bank. Those who wanted to withdraw could do their promissory notes into NCDs.

Thailand's Prime Minister, Mr. Chavalit Yongchaiyudh told on Tuesday, July 1, AD 1997 that there would be no devaluation of the baht because of the country's worst economic slump in over a decade. The Thai people expected it very much. The Thai Prime Minister said in an address to the Thai nation on television to mark his six months in the office,

> We should not discuss currency in public but I can assure that we will not devalue the baht as the risk will outweigh the intial gain. If we wanted the baht devalued, why would we have defended it the way we did.

In mid-May AD 1997 Thailand's embattled baht came under foreign speculative attack. The Central Bank defended the currency very successfully and gave punishment to foreign speculators by cutting off their baht supply from local sources. The controls indicated a two-tier baht market — one offshore and the other onshore. Although the Thai government assured that the baht may not be devalued, yet several foreign analysts thought that the devaluation will take place soon or in order to allow depreciation the government will take action to change the baht system. Thailand's economy has fallen in such a way that the growth rate reached at around 5.6 per cent in AD 1997 as against 6.4 per cent mentioned in AD 1996. Experts have turned sluggish, the battered Thai bourse in eight years was at its lowest level and troubles have disturbed the ailing finance and the property sectors have suffered very much. The Thai Prime Minister told,

> The problems of Thailand were that we over borrowed and overspent and financed our spending with foreign debt. That's what we inherited when we took office. These woes had also affected sentiment in the baht. During the past six months we have been in office, we have had to defend the baht twice. As a soldier I can tell you that fighting on the battlefield does not cost as much as fighting in the money market.

Thailand rocketted markets with the floatation of the baht. It floated the baht and raised its key lending rate by two percentage points on Wednesday, July 2, AD 1997. Several currency analysts mentioned that they would like to wait and to watch how far the baht would be permitted to fall. On Wednesday, July 2, AD 1997, the baht was trading at 28.30/90 to the dollar. But analysts stated that the currency could weaken further to 30.00 to the dollar. Mr. Thanong Bhidaya, the finance Minister, told,

> The value of the baht will be determined by market forces to reflect fundamental economic forces. The ministry of finance and the Bank of Thailand believed that the managed float system will benefit Thailand's overall economic development.

Thailand's stock market gave a hearty thumbs-up to the news and investors for the bourse boosted the index by nearly eight per cent in busy trade and foreign institutions dominated the business. The Bank of Thailand tried its best to keep the baht from a meltdown and also played a great role to raise its key commercial bank lending rate by two percentage points to 12.5 per cent.

> The rate will replace the previous daily peg, which was fixed against a trade-weighted basket of currencies dominated by the US dollar.

Mr. Chaiyawat Wibulsawasdi, the Central Bank governor, said,

> However, it the baht goes beyond the appropriate rate the Central Bank will intervene in the market.

According to several Thai analysts, in the near-term, higher interest rates would give a blow to Thailand's economy,

> which is still grappling with a swollen current account dificit, slowing growth and troubled financial sector.

But at the same time they told that if the new moves brought confidence in the minds of the Thais, then there would be a chance for the Thai interest rates to fall in the coming months. The floatation will then permit the Bank of Thailand to avoid intervening to support the baht. The bank used up to $ 5 billion of its foreign reserves in May AD 1997 to defend the currency when it was under heavy attack.

> This exercise cut the country's foreign reserves to a two-year low of $ 33.3 billion at the end of May 1997 from around $ 37.3 billion a month earlier.

Several analysts wanted renewed near-term speculation against the baht because of negative sentiment over The Thai economy and recent activities to help its financial institutions. Thanong Bidaya, the finance minister, described

> Under the new system movements in the exchange rate are expected to be quite large at the initial stage. However, relative stability should be attained after a brief adjustment period.
>
> Here are details on the managed float of the baht announced by the Thai financial authorities on Wednesday, July 2, 1997.
>
> 1. The value of the baht would be set by market forces but the floatation would be managed by the authorities.
>
> 2. The baht's peg against a basket of currencies would be discontinued. Since 1984, the baht's mid rate against the dollar has been fixed on a daily basis by the central bank based on a trade-weighted basket of currencies denominated by the dollar.
>
> 3. The Bank of Thailand said it was raising its key bank rate to 12.5 per cent from 10.5 per cent, effective immediately. Bank rate is the rate the central bank charges on loans to commercial banks.

4. The Bank of Thailand said a baht-dollar reference rate would be set daily at the close of trade following the baht floatation. The reference rate would be based on the baht's trading average the day before.

5. The Bank of Thailand said it had an 'appropriate rate' in mind to which it expected the baht to move. If the rate went beyond the appropriate level the central bank said it would intervene in the market.

6. The central bank officials said that under the new baht system they would be following the Singapore model of managing the currency, without elaborating.

7. The Bank of Thailand governor Mr. Rorangachai Marakanand said Thailand had sought technical assistance from the International Monetary Fund and the Reserve Bank of Australia. The RBA has since agreed to provide technical advice to the Bank of Thailand in the managed float.

8. A two-tier baht market — one offshore and another onshore — that has been in place since the last speculative attack on the baht in May 1997 when the central bank imposed currency controls would remain for new but its future would be reviewed.

9. The Bank of Thailand said it expected the baht to remain volatile in the short-term after the floatation, but said the public need not panic. It would intervene in foreign exchange markets from time to time to achieve its baht floatation policy objectives and guard against excessive fluctuation. The Thai financial authorities will give business affected by the baht's floatation and volatile soft loans help to allow them to meet foreign debt re-payments. . . .

Myanmar and Thailand signed power treaty. Thailand agreed to buy up to 1,500 meagawatts of electric power from Myanmar by 2010 under a memorandum of understanding signed by the two countries on Friday, July 4, 1997.[61] The open agreement covered electricity generated from both hydropower plants and natural gas-fuelled power plants — the first time the hydropower was included in such an agreement. The Andaman Sea possesses vast natural gas resources and Myanmar had previously signed two gas supply agreements with Thailand to fire its power-hungry industrial zones in the Gulf of Siam. Thailand wanted to encourage the Electricity Generating Authority of Thailand or other designated agencies to buy up to 1,500 megawatts of electric power from 'feasible projects' in Myanmar by the year 2010 and it allowed the Thai investors to participate in implementation of power projects under the programme. Mr. Piyasvasti Amranand, the secretary-general of Thailand's national energy policy council, told at the signing ceremony that Myanmar had a technically hydropower potential estimated at 100,000 megawatts. He said that

> despite the enormous amount of hydropower resources in the union of Myanmar, there had been no dialogue specifically on the commercial arrangement for the purchase of power by Thailand from projects in Myanmar.

Under the memorandum of understanding, Myanmar and Thailand agreed to co-operate in interconnecting power transmission systems. The two nations also agreed to prepare a separete memorandum on the supply of water from Myanmar to Thailand. Mr. Sompong Amornvivat, the minister in the Thai Prime Minister's office and Mr. Khin Maung Thein, the energy minister of Myanmar, signed the power purchase agreement. The Association of South-East Asian Nations in Manila on Friday, July 4, 1997, wanted to complete a framework by 1998 for the

---

61. *AA*, July 5, 1997, p. 18.

creation of an Asean Investment Area to lure region-wide investors. Thailand was its member.

Mr. Anand Panyerachun, Thailand's interim Prime Minister after a successful military coup in AD 1991, for government service, received the Ramon Magsaysay award for 1997 from Manila. Mr. Panyerachun was cited for "sustaining the momentum for reform and democracy in Thailand in a time of crisis and military rule".[62] After relinquishing his temporary post, he was again asked to head the government in AD 1992 after soldiers killed demonstrators who demonstrated against the choice of the chief architect of the AD 1991 coup as Prime Minister.

Several South-East Asian Foreign Ministers decided on Thursday, July 10, 1997 in Kuala Lumpur to indefinitely postpone the entry of Cambodia into a regional trade group following a weekend coup.[63] Mr. Abdullah, the Asean's current chairman, said,

> The Asean stands ready to contribute their efforts to a peaceful solution in Cambodia and the Asean is sending a delegation to seek an audience with King Sihanouk and will also call on the two Prime Ministers.

He said further,

> We want to see the government in place, the coalition continue the constitution upheld.

An Indonesian foreign ministry spokesman told on Tuesday, July 15, 1997 that the foreign ministers of Indonesia, Thailand and Philippines met King Sihanouk in Beijing in China to discuss the political crisis in Cambodia. The Asean foreign Ministers held a special meeting in the second week of July AD 1997 and decided to postpone Cambodia's membership of the seven-nation

---

62. *AA*, July 5, 1997, p. 4.

63. *Ibid.*, July 11, 1997, p. 5.

organisation due to political turmoil in the country. Cambodia was about to join the Asean in July AD 1997 with Myanmar and Laos.

A buying spree of the Thai bourse continued in the first week of July AD 1997 although investors evaluated their purchases as they waited for the baht to stabilise. It pushed Thailand's bourses to all-time high. The Thai analysts and traders watched the Thai stock market, which was at eight-year lows, leap 130 points in three days to response to the Baht's managed float on Wednesday, July 2, AD 1997. The baht exchange rate against the dollar, which lost nearly 20 per cent of its value, was set daily against a weighted average of the previous day's trading levels. The Thai property market faced glut as foreign buyers lost their interest. An international property consultant said on Thursday, July 3, AD 1997 that local or foreign buyers had no interest in buying property outside Bangkok's central business district despite record low prices. Many developers could not sell their projects and they were not in a position to pay off their loans and this has given a great blow to the financial sectors. Bangkok unveiled reference rate as currency plunged 20 per cent. Thailand's central bank moved to shore up its economy on Thursday, July 3, AD 1997, a day after its currency plunged 20 per cent following the bank's decision to allow wider fluctuation against other currencies. In order to protect the value of the currency, the baht, Bank of Thailand introduced a 'reference rate' on Thursday, July 3, AD 1997. It did it with an idea to act as a guide for currency trading in Thailand. The move came a day after the bank permitted the first devaluation in its currency in 14 years by allowing the baht to trade in a broader range against other currencies. Owing to the weaker baht, the prices of imported goods became higher. Thailand's floatation of the baht may dampen investment in South-East Asia. Its central bank floated the baht on Wednesday, July 2, AD 1997 in a move that quickly through the establishment of a new, managed float regime pulled down 15 per cent its value.

South African President Mr. Nelson Mandela recently visited Thailand and he stayed there for two days.[64] On this occasion he toured the Grand Palace in Bangkok on Thursday, July 17, AD 1997 Mr. Chavalit Yongchaiyudh, the Thai Prime Minister, fell unconscious in a public meeting in Rai Ete which was about 210 km north-east from Bangkok. On the occasion of the Rice Festival of Thailand he was giving talk to the cultivators. Suddenly he felt unwell and fell down from dais. Immediately, his security guards took him to a shade and gave him medical aid and then he regained his sense. Due to excessive warm weather, he fell ill.

The baht sank to a record 30.10/30.30 baht per dollar late on Friday, July 11, AD 1997 against a central bank midrate of around 25.90 per dollar prior to the Thai action — a *de facto* depreciation of around 15 per cent. The Thai baht sank to new lows and several Bangkok dealers told that most of the selling was by companies and importers. The market was fairly thin actually, and there were virtually no buyers of the baht. So any small dollar buying can exaggerate the market. Some dealers thought that several foreign financial institutions had stopped rolling over their loans to Thai corporates and that was related to the high demand for dollars. The baht was quoted at 31.800/32.100 to the dollar at 0425 GMT. The baht had a subdued morning owing to a lack of interest after the Bank of Thailand (BOT) declared that it had intervened to support the currency on Monday, July 12, AD 1997. The Bank of Thailand mentioned that the baht had fallen about 15 per cent since it went towards a managed float on July 2, AD 1997 from the previous system of pegging the baht to a basket of currencies.

There were talks between Ranariddh, the prince and the members of the association of the South-East Asian nations in Bangkok,[65] and several political parties tried to establish peace

64. *AA*, July 18, 1997, p. 4.

65. *Ibid.*, July 19, 1997, p. 5.

in Cambodia. Prince Ranariddh met Mr. Prachuab Chaiyasarn, the Thai foreign minister, Mr. Ali Alatas, the Indonesian foreign minister and Mr. Domingo Saizon, the Philippines foreign minister. These three ministers arrived in Bangkok after their meeting with Cambodia's King Norodom Sihanouk in Beijing in China on Thursday July 17, AD 1997, where the ruler after his medical treatment was recovering. In the second week of July AD 1997 the Asean group wanted to delay Cambodia's entry into the group and to despatch ministers for talks with king Sihanouk, Prince Ranariddh and Mr. Hun Sen. The prince told three points to the envoys. There must be a peaceful solution, general election currently sheduled for May, 1998, must be held as soon as possible and the Asean should not recognise the current government in Phnom Penh. Mr. Hun Sen, the second Prime Minister of Cambodia, warned the Asean group not to interfere in Cambodia's affairs. He rejected the Asean group's offer to mediate in the dispute with Mr. Norodom Ranariddh, the ousted First Prime Minister, on Saturday, July 19, AD 1997. Mr. Norodom Ranariddh was ousted by Mr. Hun Sen in a coup and he told that Cambodia would solve the thorny problem on its own. The Association of the South-East Asian Nations sent the foreign ministers of Indonesia, the Philippines and Thailand on a mission to Cambodia to play an Asean role in the dispute with the two Prime Ministers — Mr. Norodom Ranariddh and Mr. Hun Sen and also King Norodom Sihanouk. The Indonesian foreign minister Mr. Ali Alatas said that

> at our meeting with Mr. Hun Sen, we were given quite a clear indication that (he) believed that the Asean at this stage should not contribute to finding a solution.

At the end of the team's shuttle diplomacy drive, Mr. Alatas told,

> they feel that themselves would find a solution in accordance with the constitution and other relevant laws.

He mentioned further,

> If these efforts do not yield results, then they (Cambodians) would ask for the intervention of His Majority the king as head of the state.

He added,

> The Asean will only assist in trying to contribute if all sides want that. That is why, as of this moment, our efforts stop and we will return and report to the Asean foreign ministers.

He said that the Asean must respect Mr. Hun Sen's position and did not like to interfere in the internal affairs of another state. The association of the South-East Asian Nations held its high profile annual meetings in the fourth week of July AD 1997 and in that meeting Myanmar and Laos joined the group and Cambodia has kept its place in waiting list. Myanmar under military rule and Laos were admitted as the newest members of the Association of the South-East Asian Nations on Wednesday, July 23, AD 1997. But due to political troubles Cambodia's case was not considered. At a ceremony during its 30th anniversary meetings, the foreign ministers of Myanmar and Laos signed documents of admission which were then turned over to the Asean secretariat. Prince Mohamad Bolkiah, the foreign minister of Brunei, Mr. Ali Alatas, the foreign minister of Indonesia, Mr. Abdullah Ahmed Badavi, the foreign minister of Malaysia, Mr. Domingo Saizon, the foreign minister of the Philippines, Mr. S. Jayakumar, the foreign minister of Singapore, Mr. Prachuab Chaiyasarn, the foreign minister of Thailand and Mr. Nguyen Nan-Cam, the foreign minister from Vietnam attended the signing ceremony at a hotel resort in Kuala Lumpur on Wednesday, July 23, AD 1997. The membership increased to nine and Brunei, Indonesia, Malaysia, the Philippines, Singapore, Thailand and Vietnam were its earlier members and they were admitted in AD 1995. On Tuesday, July 22, AD 1997, a senior

South-East Asian diplomat said that the Asean within this year (1997) will accept Cambodia's application for membership, despite Mr. Hun Sen's blunt rejection of the Asean efforts to mediate in his country's political crisis. He said,

> Mr. Hun Sen needs the Asean to attain legitimacy. The Asean is his only choice.

Cambodia's South-East Asian neighbours and business partners recognised Prince Norodom Ranariddh as the troubled country's first Prime Minister.

A senior Thai tourism official said on Thursday, August 14, AD 1997 that Thailand wanted to use its weak currency to win back foreign tourists in a two-year 'Amazing Thailand' promotion which the country would be able to earn one trillion baht ($ 32 billion).[66] Mr. Pradoch Phayakvichien, the deputy governor of the Tourism Authority of Thailand, told in an interview that he hoped more than 17 million foreign tourists would come to Thailand in AD 1998 and 1999 and from their visit the country would be able to earn 600 billion baht ($ 19 billion) in a much-needed foreign currency. Thailand always wanted to develop domestic tourism and hoped to earn 400 billion baht ($ 13 billion) during the same period. Mr. Pradoch Phayakvichien mentioned that the projects would help tremendously when the country was facing a sharp downturn. With the weaker baht, it would be very attractive to come to Thailand. In recent years Thailand's economy has gone from boom to bust, i.e., it has become bankrupt and by the fallout of mis-allocated resources and speculation the financial sector has fallen into turmoil and has faced a financial crisis. Since July 2, AD 1997 the Thai baht has dropped more than 20 per cent "after the authority scrapped a tightly controlled exchange regime and replaced it with a new managed float system". Tourism once was regarded as one of the countriy's biggest bread-winners but recently it lost its glamour because

66. *ET*, August 15, 1997, p. 7.

the Thai government did not pay any attention to it and showed its interest in export-oriented and lesser financial industries.

> From 1988, when the country launched 'visit Thailand year', until the Gulf war in 1991, tourism enjoyed double-digit growth figurs but tough competition from regional neighbours, the lack of proper promotion and concern over AIDS have taken their toll.

Last year (1996) in tourism the country mentioned growth of only 4 per cent. "Nevertheless, average revenue from tourism accounted for about 4.38 per cent of GDP during 1991-5". Mr. Pradoch Phayavichien told that not like other industries, which in order to remain in competition, require substantial investment on restructuring, but with an idea to make this tourism industry boom again, we have already all necessary resources. He mentioned further that the tourism authority would try to develop traditional events and cultures and as well as foods, handicrafts and harbal medicine as selling events and Thailand will give more importance on the visit of more women and family members as tourists to this country. He described that Thailand, of course, has some problems with prostitutes, both child and adult. But we are trying to solve that problem. He stated,

> Thailand has much more to offer than that. And it is not true that this country is not a place for female visitors. We will prove that to the world.

On Thursday, August 14, AD 1997 China, in order to help Thailand to overcome its current financial crisis, wanted to contribute $ 1 billion to an international package. Mr. Dai Xiapglong, the governor of the people's Bank of China (PBC), said,

> We have decided to provide $ 1 billion to Thailand as part of the package organised by the International Monetary Fund (IMF) to assist Thailand evercome its financial crisis.

He told in a press conference that the People's Bank of China (PBC) on Wednesday night, August 13, AD 1997 had informed the International Monetary Fund and the central bank of Thailand of its willingness to take part in the package finalised in Tokyo on Agust 11, AD 1997. The Chinese central government had already approved the decision of the People's Bank of China. Mr. Dai Xiapglong hoped that with the help of the International Monetary Fund and the financial circles of other Asian countries, Thailand would be able to solve its present financial crisis.

Several members of the Association of the South-East Asian Nations (Asean) discussed very seriously about the crisis of their currencies.

> The Thai baht, the Philippines peso, the Malaysian ringgit and the Indonesian rupiah have all come under intense speculative attack in recent weeks as investors question the health of these countries' investment-fuelled, high-growth economies.[67]

Thailand on Saturday, August 16, AD 1997 gave its proposal to establish a common fund which the members of the Asean countries could utilise it to defend their currencies. Mr. Prachuab Chaiyasarn, the Thai foreign minister, told that the Asean leaders discussed such a fund at their summit in December AD 1996 and included their currency crisis in their joint communique. He said that the proposed fund which he called the Asean Monetary Fund (AMF) would help the regional nations to stabilise their currencies in emergency cases. He told,

> We started the Asean because of the cold war to bring together countries which have grown stronger and stronger but now we are facing an economic war.

He mentioned further that

> the crisis had created opportunities as well, such as in

67. *AA*, August 19, 1997, p. 17.

> the form of closer co-operation within the Asean that he said could lead to earlier implementation of the Asean Free Trade Area of Afta. Under Afta, tarrifs within the Asean are to be cut to between zero and five per cent for most goods only in the next century.

The Thai foreign minister was very happy with Thailand's Asean neighbours and other countries as well as the International Monetary Fund and the World Bank for their contributions in helping the country over its current crisis. The international Monetary Fund (IMF) and Asia Pacific nations gave Thailand $ 16 billion "to share up its foreing reserves, which were depleted in recent efforts to defend the baht". Thailand received $ 1.6 billion in loans as the first instalment of the International Monetary Fund (IMF) assistance and pledged to meet the International Monetary Fund economic goals to receive further aid. The International Monetary Fund on Wednesday August 20, AD 1997 sanctioned $ 3.9 billion credit for Thailand,

> opening up the way for a $ 16.7 billion international bailout package — the biggest from global donors since $ 50 billion was made available to Mexico in 1995.

Mr Chaiyawat Wibulsawasdi, the governor of the Bank of Thailand, in a news conference told that the $ 3.9 billion International Monetary Fund loan was a three-year stand-by credit facility. He said,

> the extent of disbursement of the whole package depended on the amount of Thailand's foreign reserves. If they can remain high, Thailand would not have to tap the total amount of assistance. Thailand has $ 23.4 billion in forward swap contracts, which came due over the next 12 months.

He mentioned that $ 8.6 billion of contracts were onshore and $ 14.8 billion were offshore. Thailand has about $ 90 billion in foreign loans. According to analysts, the country would face problems if the short-term loans were not rolled over because Thailand has low levels of foreign reserves. The International Monetary Fund wanted to see Thailand to keep foreign reserves of at least $ 23 billion this year and $ 25 billion in AD 1998.

> Thailand, previously one of the world's fastest-grownig economies with gross domestic product growth averaging about nine per cent over the past decade, slowed sharply last year with 6.4 per cent growth.

According to Mr. Chaiyawat Wibulsawasdi,

> the current account deficit would narrow to about five per cent of gross domestic product in 1997, to about $ 9.10 billion — a sharp drop from the eight per cent of gross demestic product in 1996. The 1998 figure of about $ 5 billion would represent about three per cent of gross domestic product.

The Asian Development Bank (ADB) in order to improve the portable water supply in two north-eastern provinces of Thailand had sacntioned a $ 50 million loan to Thailand. The loan was mentioned as payable over 25 years and it included a grace period of five years. The Asian Development Bank loan covered 58 per cent of the total project cost.

> The interest rate will be determined in accordance with the bank's variable lending rate for US dollar loans which is currently at 6.82 per cent.

Thailand will use this loan to upgrade and to expand the distribution pipelines in Nong Khai and Udom Thani Water Supply Project and to instal new water distribution system in the 12 villages, and to construct a new water treatment plant and to introduce water transmission pipeline.

It may be noted here that currency turmoil in South-East Asia has wreaked havoc on local stock markets and brought the markets for initial Public Offerings (IPO) to a virtual standstill in some countries. At one point the Thai stocks shed more than five per cent. Mr. Thanathip Vidhayasirinun, the head of investment banking at Cathay Capital in Bangkok told,

> The Thai stocks plunged, shedding 5.09 per cent, or 28.51 points to 531.21 on Monday, after a more than five per cent fall on Friday.

Owing to the continued weakness in the baht and local political uncertainty, investors became nervous.

Mr. Chavalit Yongchaiyudh, the Thai Prime Minister, struggled hard to save his ministry from the economic turmoil. It is said that six-party coalition government struggled to survive several months amid mounting criticism of its handling of Thailand's economic crisis.[68] Several analysts questioned about the integrity of its cabinet ministers. Mr. Chavalit Yongchaiyudh faced his biggest leadership crisis since he assumed the charge of his office in December AD 1996. Last month (July AD 1997) a *de facto* devaluation of the baht took place with his government's permission and in August AD 1997 his government accepted a $ 16.7 million multi-national bailout package sanctioned by the International Monetary Fund (IMF). Everybody felt frustrated to see the financial crisis in Thailand. Mr. Suchit Bunbongkarn, the Political Science Professor at the Chulalongkorn University, said,

> I don't think the government will last very long. The baht, whose fall triggered a regional currency crisis over the past two weeks, tumbled torecord lows late last week. It has depreciated more than 25 per cent since Jyly 2, 1997. The Thai economy is projected to grow 2.5-3.0 per cent this year, its slowest rate in more than three decades and compared with 6.4 per cent in 1996.

---

68. *AA*, August 26, 1997, p. 5.

Mr. Chuan Leekpai was the former premier and he was the opposition leader. He and his party leaders bitterly criticised Mr. Chavalit Yongchaiyudh's government and told that his coalition government was unable to set-up an example for the Thais to accept austerity measures by its refusal to make sufficient cuts to next year's budget.

> A bigger spending cut would have spared the Thais higher inflation, stocked by a government decision to raise the value added tax to 10 per cent from seven per cent from mid-August 1997.

Mr. Chuan Leekpai and elder statesman Mr. Prem Tinsulananda on Monday August 25, AD 1997 requested Mr. Chavalit Yongchaiyudh, the The Thai Prime Minister, to do something for frugality for the Thais. The Thai Prime Minister in order to discuss his country's exonomy called a Parliamentary debate on August 28, AD 1997. Thailand's elder statesman and Privy Councillor, Mr. Prem Tinsulamonda on Monday, August 25, AD 1997 requested the Thai Prime Minister for more budget cuts and told that his government should play a great role to set an example of frugality for the Thais. He was Prime Minister of Thailand between 1981 and 1988 and he was regarded as a highly respected political figure. He was quite sure that Thailand would be able to solve its economic crisis but asked the government to lead the country in a national savings campaign. He said,

> I would like to tell Jiew (Mr. Chavalit Yongchaiyudh's nickname) that there is one example which you could easily and conveniently provide. When you talk about savings we should set an example. When you talk frugality, you should be frugal to set a model.

He described further that Mr. Chavalit Yongchaiyudh's six-party coalition government never became serious to cut its 1997-8 budget. The government has announced that it wanted to slash next years's budget by 59 billion baht ($ 1.84 billion), but its opponent criticised it and mentioned that the Prime Minister should have done "for a bigger spending reduction of at least 100 billion baht". The Thai Prime Minister accompanied by his wife Ms. Pankrua and three of his top officials attended a religious rite on Friday, August 29, AD 1997 and about eight brāhmaṇa priests from the Bureau of the Royal Household presided it. The religious ceremony witnessed the return of a brāhmaṇa statue in its original pedestal of the government House. This ceremony would brighten the star of the beleagured Prime Minister. In order to boost his luck to save his leadership the latter offered prayer to the god.

Thailand's central bank announced a $ 4.5 billion drop in foreign reserves from the end of June to mid-August AD 1997 which, according to analysts, was drastic but it was not unexpected. The Bank of Thailand in its monthly round up of key economic data mentioned that the country's foreign exchange reserves had dwindled to $ 27.9 billion as of August 14, AD 1997. The reserves at the end of July AD 1997 had fixed $ 30.4 billion and at the end of June AD 1997 the amount was $ 32.4 billion. The Bank of Thailand gave this report. Mr. Josh Andrews of the Thaimes Securities was an analyst and he said,

> It is a very drastic drop in two weeks and it is not a good sign. If reserves carry on dropping like that it won't take long to hit the Internatinonal Monetary Fund floor of $ 23 billion.[69]

In the third week of August AD 1997 the International Monetary Fund sanctined a financial rescue package for Thailand and it was about $ 17.2 billion. In order to solve its financial crisis the Sultan of Brunei gave $ 500 million to Thailand on Wednesday, August 27, AD 1997. In order to maintain Thailand's foreign reserves above $ 23 billion the package was contributed to Thailand. This was happened over the last few weeks at

69. *AA*, August 30, 1997, p. 18.

Thailand's market:

> It all began on July 2 when Thailand first devalued the baht. The region is witness to similar kind of exports to the rest of the world. With the devaluation of one currency, the neighbouring nations' exports became uncompetitive. They result: they devalued or tried to brow beat their own currencies. Soon foreign investors began to feel the pinch owing to new exchange rates and it spilled over to markets. In the last week alone the Malayaian stock market has lost some 11 per cent and the Thai stocks 10 per cent. In indonesia stocks fell by more that 14 per cent while in Philippines the markets lost 17 per cent over the week. . . . Except for the Thai baht, the other currencies were not officially pegged to the US dollar, but they did seem to follow the dollar in well-defined pattern.

According to leading business and political analysts, Thailand faced a worsening economy and increased social discontent and with an idea to restore confidence in the national government a proposal should adopt quickly for constitutional reforms. Many Thais believed that a period of political turbulance began to appear in Bangkok, and the government was responsible for it and the government should play a great role to reform the electoral system and to calm the economic storm. The Thais especially in the urban middle class knew very well that their political rulers, several senior civilians and military bureaucrats and businessmen have mismanaged and often have pillaged the country's economy. The opposition parties in the Thai Parliament blamed Mr. Chavalit Yongchaiyudh's government and the Prime Minister will have to answer for his government's failure to solve the economic crisis. The Democrat Party, the main opposition group in Thailand, said that it filed a no-confidence motion on Monday, September 1, AD 1997. After three weeks it would be debated. If the government survived the motion and does not talk about a snap election, then the Thai Parliament will vote on September 26, 1997 to draft a new constitution of Thailand. In order to curb vote buying, corruption, the governmental meddling with the civil service services and other forms of money politics, a government-mendated independent body has adopted a resolution and has drawn the charter. According to critics, these practices were major causes for the economic crisis in Thailand,

> The Thai stocks fell for the 10th straight day on Wednesday, August 27, 1997 while the baht remained weak, partly on fears of continued political instability.

Mr. Prem Tinsulananda was a former Prime Minister. He told that the country would be able to overcome the current crisis with "co-operation, unity and personal sacrifices for national interests". Mr. Chavalit Yongchaiyudh then made a public appeal for time to solve the economic problems. Mr. Surin Pitsuwan, a senior member of the Democrat Party, told that

> the Government's Mismanagement of the economy cannot be excused just like that. They will have to be made accountable and that is why there is a no-confidence motion.

The opposition members and other critics pointed out that if the government liked to put the Thai economy on a sound political base, then for the new draft constitution in the Thai Parliament, it should vote. Mr. Abhisit Vajajiva, a Democrat legislator, told that

> If we allow money-politics to grow, it is imposing greater and greater costs on economic and social development. Moreover, given the expectations that people have of this reform process, if they are frustrated, especially at a time when we are going through economic difficulties, these could be confrontation and a lot of public anger.

In order to end vote-buying and other electoral practices the draft constitution would establish an independent election commission. Several Thai politicians and their families would declare their assets before taking office. But many legislators may not accept their charter because they at the time of election in poor areas spend heavily on votes. They believe that there is a chance to grow rich if they hold offices.

Mr. Virabhongse Ramangkura, the newly-appointed Deputy Prime Minister for economic affairs of Thailand, blamed central bank for spending $ 12.6 billion to shore up the ailing finance sector.[70] The Bank of Thailand before the situation reached the crisis stage should have known the extent of the problems at finance companies. The Deputy Prime Minister for economic affairs said,

> if they adjusted policy in line with the country's economy earlier, since the economy was on the downtrend, the problem would not have happened.

A fortune-teller of Thailand said on Tuesday, September 9, AD 1997 that Ms. Pankrua Yongchaiyudh, the wife of the embattled Thai Prime Minister, Mr. Chavalit Yongchaiyudh sought help from Rāhu, 'the God of darkness' to allow him to maintain his six-party coalition government together. Mr. Attaviraj Sritula was regarded as Thailand's most popular soothsayer. He told that the Prime Minister's wife wanted to offer eight black objects to Rāhu at the temple which was located on the southern side of Bangkok. He mentioned that Ms. Pankrua Yongchaiyudh during the night of September 16, AD 1997 came to the temple and attended the ceremony for the welfare of his husband and his ministry. She offered a black chicken to a mythical 'God of Darkness', Rāhu in a bid to help and to save her husband's shaky government. Attaviraj Sritula told that the call on the 'God of Darkness' came as Mr. Chavalit Yongchaiyudh braced for an

70. *AA*, September 1, 1997, p. 18.

opposition-proposed no-confidence motion to be voted by the Thai Parliament at the end of September AD 1997. Ms. Pankrua Yongchaiyudh became famous for her faith in superstition. The *Nation* daily said, "Seeking the blessing of Rāhu to repel and jinx or bad luck is not uncommon among some suprsstitious Thais". By offering prayer and gifts she tried to bring stability and the prolong life of the coalition of her husband. Because of her faith in superstition and in superstitious ideas she has often become prominent in the nation's headlines. In order to drive away evil stars and to bring peaceful atmosphere at home, she had performed prolonged Buddhist ceremonies at her place. When her husband won the general elections nine months ago in AD 1996, she danced publicly at a temple to fulfil a religious promise. To bring her good luck she always carried a bejewelled stuffed elephant toy with her. In Thailand, an elephant is regarded as a symbol of power. When a Myanmarese fortune-teller told Mr. Chavalit Yongchaiyudh that the number 5 would bring him good luck, then he around the number 5 worked many political and personal events. The Prime Minister and his wife stayed in a house No.555 in central Bangkok street and he often arranged important meetings for five and fitteen minutes past the hour. The Thais believed that the Thai Parliment could be dissolved before a vote on key constitutional reforms. The coalition government won an early victory in a parliamentary vote to continue debate on the draft charter which mentioned for sweeping changes to the political system and an end to many politics. Several politicians wanted to end the debate and to held a quick vote on the charter. The opposition members of the Thai Parliament wished a quick vote because they thought that the government might dissolve the Thai Parliament in the 15-day lapse required between the end of debate and the vote on the constitution. Ms. Pankrua Yongchaiyudh believed that her husband's government would last if she offers prayer to appease Rāhu, a Hindu 'God of Darkness'. She wanted to sacrifice chickens and to make other offerings in a black magic ceremony to prolong the life of her husband's coalition government. She offered eight black foods and prayers to Rāhu. The offerings usually included black chickens, black beans and coca-cola. About 20,000 Thai people came to Nakhon Pathom from various places of Thailand to attend a lunar eclipse ceremony on Tuesday, September 16, AD 1997. They arrived there with a hope to change their luck. Rāhu, the Hindu God, was regarded as the god of darkness. He swallowed the moon during an eclipse. The Wat Srisathong Temple in Nakhon Pathom was situated about 50 km west of Bangkok and it was known as the Temple of Rāhu. It was adorned with the world's biggest Rāhu statue. The Thais believed that Rāhu had the power to bring good luck for them and for their country. Because the country's economy has worsened. Since AD 1996. Thailand has had an exceptional run of misfortune. Between AD 1985 and AD 1995, it acquired the world's highest average economic growth, but in AD 1997 it was forced to get a $ 17.2 billion international bailout package from the International Monetary Fund. Since July AD 1997, the baht came down to such a low position that it has lost a third of its value and Thailand's many financial institutions owing to non-performing loans closed their doors and the government in order to end corruption wanted to introduce constitutional reforms. In Thailand the purchasing power had gone down and the rates of the government's taxes were very high. Since Mr. Chavalit Yongchaiyudh, the Prime Minister, assumed power ten months ago, the position of Rāhu has grown, because under his leadership the country faced a very economic crisis and Ms. Pankrua Yongchaiyudh, his wife, had a faith in the powers of Rāhu to bring good luck for her husband and for her country. In order to prolong her husband's shaky government she attended Tuesday's (16.9.1985) lunar eclipse ceremony and offered prayer at the temple of Rāhu.

Thailand turned to the World Bank for the baht bailout. Mr. Thanong Bhidaya, the finance minister, told on Tuesday, September 2, AD 1997 that the World Bank will play a role as mediator between foreign creditors and Thailand's private-sector debtors.[71] In order to win back the support of investors and financial institutions, the finance minister wanted to increase the transparency of the Thai financial system. The foreign banks not only lost confidence in the government's economic management but also complained that in favour of domestic institutions in cases of default the foreign creditors have received second-class treatment. Mr. Thanong Bhidaya said that his government would play a great role to improve confidence in the government, including transparency. The economic crisis in Thailand has made the Thai currency plummet almost 25 per cent in value although Thailand had easy money and had almost 10 per cent annual economic growth for sometime. Several foreign institutions have lent $ 73 billion to the Thai private sectors and much of the money was used for constructing factories, real estate and consumerism. Thailand's export growth has fallen very miserably and the Thais and the foreign investors have lost confidence in the government's ability to solve the economic crisis. Owing to these factors, the foreign lenders did not like to keep open credit lines. In the meantime, the value of the baht has dropped very much and everything was very costly due to this and it was very difficult for borrowers to repay dollar-denominated loans. The industries like steel and petro-chemicals that were started with cheap capital began to face crisis very much. Mr. Santisuk Sanguanruang, the vice-president of finance and administration of the PVC producer Vinythai, said,

> in many cases, the construction capital for plants was borrowed, but operations were supposed to fund themselves through the continued fast growth in demand. His company was not facing such a problem.

It may be noted here that in AD 1997 the Thai PVC production capacity grew to 700,000 metric tons from 180,000 metric tons in AD 1991. But now there was not much construction in Bangkok

71. *AA*, September 4, 1997, p. 17.

and it was for this reason the annual growth of demand for PVC has dropped from 12 per cent in the boom years to about 2 per cent so far this year. A petro-chemical analyst mentioned a 200,000 metric ton surplus of PVC even if demand this year grew at 14 per cent. According to some leading business and political analysts, Thailand faced a worsening economy and increased social discontent. To restore confidence in the national government, a proposal for sweeping constitutional reform should be adopted by the government. Electoral reforms may help to calm the economic storm and the crisis. The baht plunged four cent to record low against the dollar in early domestic trading in Thailand. The Thai unit has dropped over 35 per cent of its value since it was floated in July AD 1997.

> In Thailand, the baht dived to a low of 38.00 on the dollar, fuelled domestic political concerns and regional instability. Dealers reported immense corporate selling pressure on shore due to tight dollar liquidity. The baht was quoted at 37.600/90 to the dollar onshore at 04 20 GMT against it early 38.000 level.

According to dealers,

> Commercial demand for dollars and uncertainty over a parliamentary debate on a controversial new draft constitution dented confidence that the economy would improve.

One US bank dealer told that under immense pressure the dollar/ baht stays and probably it will break 38 per cent dollar.

The Thais on Thursday, September 4, AD 1997 demonstrated outside Parliament as legislators began a two-day debate on a radical new draft constitution designated to clean up corrupt politics.[72] About 400 Thais dressed in bright green T-shirts and headbounds gathered near Thai Parliament and shouted for

72. *AA*, September 5, 1997, p. 5.

political reform and transparent government and they sopke in support of the proposed character. Just a little away from this place, there were about 30 people who shouted against the charter and they were yellow dresses. Mr. Sanam Ngophaiwan, a Bangkok businessman, said,

> I support the new constitution because it is better than the old one. It will help the country. It will make politics more transparent. It will help to solve corruption.

The Prime Minister of Thailand came under heavy criticism for his handling of a debate on a draft constitution designed to reduce corruption. Under mounting pressure from the public, newspapers and the military, he announced on Friday, September 5, AD 1997 that his coalition government would vote to pass the new charter when debate on it will be concluded on Monday, September 8, AD 1997. His government would amend it.

Mr. Kern Dabbaransi, the Deputy Prime Minister of Thailand, said on Sunday, September 7, AD 1997 that he hoped the Asean finance ministers would adopt a common stand on regional currency in the meeting of the International Monetary Fund — the World Bank in Hong Kong in the third week of September AD 1997.[73] He told,

> We will have our own meeting first in Bangkok and take a stand on the currency issue. We will decide on the Asean's position.

He as the minister of industries did not discuss the recent attacks on the region's currencies with Mr. Anwar Ibrahmin, Malayasia's Deputy Prime Minister and finance minister, and he invited him for the Bangkok meeting. Mr. Robin Cook, the British Foreign Secretary, told that Myanmar may not be allowed to attend the London Asean meeting. But the Deputy Prime Minister of Thailand, Mr. Kern Dabbaransi told that we do not want to isolate

73. *AA*, September 8, 1997, p. 18.

Myanmar. Mr. Mahathir Mohamad, the Prime Minister of Malaysia, stated that his country may boycott the meeting if Myanmar was not allowed to attend it. The Asean association in Bangkok in AD 1996 held its inaugural meeting. It was attended by the members of the Asean nations, the EU and South Korea, China and Japan. The United States opposed Myanmar's entry into the Asean group.

According to analysts, the Thai equity and currency markets gained in the first week of September AD 1997 but the baht faced pressure and political and economic matters played very much to unsettle both markets. The Bank of Thailand and the Monetary Authority of Singapore (MAS) signed a currency swap agreement worth $ 1 billion in Singapore on Saturday, September 6, AD 1997. The deal constitutes Singapore's contribution to the $ 16.7 billion assistance package co-ordinated by the International Monetary Fund (IMF) to help Thailand to solve its currency and liquidity crisis. The Monetary Authority of Singapore's spokesman told that there were two legs to the swap. If the Bank of Thailand likes to draw on the facility, we will extend US dollars in exchange of the Thai baht — at the end of the term we will get US dollars from them and they will receive the Thai baht. But on the facility no fixation of the rate of exchange would take place, but at the beginning there would forward rates. According to the Thai official reports, Thailand had an annual current deficit of $ 14.7 billion. Mr. Robert Rountree, the regional strategist at Nomura Research Institute, told,

> Regional currency turmoil, sparked by Thailand's *de facto* devaluation of the baht on July 2, will worsen over the next few months as the region's central bankers struggle to manage newly flexible exchange rates and more skeletons emerge from macro-economic closet. Even if currency speculators leave, these regional economies are still recording current-account deficits into 1998 that need to be financed. . . .

In order to prevent their currencies from falling too quickly in value against the dollar the South-East Asian monetary authorities have imposed high interest rates. But the local investment in stocks as well as the outlook for corporate earnings were curbed by the high interest rates. Thailand threw the entire South-East Asian region into economic crisis "with its July 2, 1997 managed float of the baht after months of currency speculation". Then the currencies fell and the rates had gone high througout the region. According to International Monetary Fund annual report, the International Monetary Fund gave an advanced alarm about Thailand, Malaysia and Indonesia's vulnerability to an economic turmoil. The South-East Asian nations, particularly Thailand were informed a year before the occurrence of the Thai baht crisis in July AD 1997. During regular consultations on the countries' economies the nation was informed about it. The recent increase in the current account deficit had pushed Thailand very much to its economic crisis. In the past years, the stability of the Thai baht did well in the world of the Thai economy. A greater degree of exchange rate would help to improve monetary autonomy and at the same time it would be good to reduce the incentive for short-term capital inflows. The banking sector should be supervised in a very efficient way. In July, the Thai authorities were forced to give up the 'peg' between the baht and the dollar, sending the Thai currency into free fall.

In Thailand, anxieties relating to the government's support for a new draft constitution boosted sentiment which helped the baht stage a rare rally. The Thai Prime Minister told on Friday, September 5, AD 1997 that his coalition supported the draft which helped in every way to the approval of the changes to the system and it also made an attempt to put an end to money politics. His earlier failure to take a step on the issue had given a chance of fears of public unrest. A Thai bank broker stated,

More dollar supply was soon in the market. I think the

> clearer picture of politics prompted exporters to be more willing to unwind their dollars.

The baht was at 36.20/45 to the dollar onshore at 04 30 GMT after rising to a high of 35.10 against 36.95/37.20 late on Friday, September 5, AD 1997. It was at 34.20/34.30 offshore against 35.20/35.50. Top industry leaders and analysts have warned that public confidence in the country's economy, the final bastion in any country's survival, is crumbling and urgent measures were very necessary for its restoration. At the same time they have requested the public not to loose faith as Thailand was passing through its most turbulent economic times and in order to prevent the economy from sinking further it was the duty of every citizen to do sacrifices. The Government stability, strong political will, determination to tackle current major problems with efficiency, transparency and consistency measures were needed solutions for the restoration of shaky public faith. Mr. Sangchai Ekkapatanapanit, a deputy secretary of the Federation of the Thai industries, told,

> It would be easier to convince foreign investors that Thailand is still a good place to invest in, which it is, if local people showed their faith. I believe our fundamentals are still O.K. especially for the export-related Industry. Political stability and sound government would help turn the situation.

Investors were still reluctant to hold the baht and they hesitated to put money in local financial institution and foreign creditors refused to roll over credit. Thailand faced its worst economic crisis in more than a decade since its economic bubble burst following years of highly leveraged growth. Many believed that the financial sector's over-exposure to non-productivity was the cause for the crisis.

The opposition members of the Thai Parliament and a large group of senators wished a quick vote because they thought the government might dissolve Parliament in the 15-day lapse required between the end of the debate and the vote on the constitution. Mr. Wallop Tangananurak, one of the senators, in favour of a quick vote told,

> We demanded to skip that rule and to vote on the constitution by this Friday (September 12 ,1997) because no body can assure us that an unwanted thing, like the dissolution of the House, might not happen during the period of waiting.

The Thai Prime Minister on Friday, September 12, AD 1997 bowed to pressure from the military and top finance officials and assured that his 222-seat coalition would play a great role to support the constitution. The opposition thought that the Prime Minister could dissolve the Thai Parliment and would anounce the date of elections if within the coalition rifts grew and if he thinks that he will not get support from his ministers. The charter supported by the coalition must be approved by a simple majority of the 393-seat elected Lower House and 262-member Senate, the opposition parties and the military senators. When the charter is passed and the king approved it, there must be 240 days of normal parliamentary proceedings before any dissolution could be taken. But before the constitution is approved, if the House is dissolved, then again the reform process must start. According to reliable sources, Mr. Chavalit Yongchaiyudh on Tuesday, September 9, AD 1997 made an attempt to dissolve the House but his plans were not materialised. Mr. Vittaya Thienthong, a legislator from the Prime Minister's party and brother of interior minister, said reporters that no dissolution will take place. He told reporters on Wednesday, September 10, 1997,

> I can reassure you that there will be no House dissolution. I can-not make a comment an any aborted attempt to dissolve the House.

Mr. Varathep Ratanakoon, the Thai goverment spokesman, told

that all six coalition parties in their support for a radical new draft constitution were united. Mr. Sanoh Thientong, the interior minister, said that there was no friction within the coalition. He mentioned further that the coalition parties still maintained their co-operation with each other and he hoped that although the government faced a no-confidence motion brought by the opposition party, yet, even then, it would not be disturbed and the coalition parties would remain intact. In order to solve the country's problems they would work together and would help each other.

According to analysts, the currency crisis of the South-East Asian region was discussed at the meetings of the International Monetary Fund and the World Bank in Hong-Kong. Mr. Stanley Fischer, the deputy managing director of the International Monetary Fund, said,

> The Thai crisis prompted the International Monetary Fund to spearhead a $ 17.2 billion rescue package to shore up the economy. The fund acted promptly in response to the situation in South-East Asia and issued warnings in the Thai crisis' early stage, unlike the Mexico peso debacle of late 1994 and early 1995 which caught everyone by surprise.

About 2,000 workers on Sunday, September 14, AD 1997 demonstrated and they demanded government's help because they were hard hit by Thailand's economic turmoil. The disgrantled workers from factories owned by the Thai government shouted for their demands and wanted to bring 'hundreds of thousands of labourers to the streets' if the government ignored their causes and did not take any notice of them. They requested the government

> to consider cutting the value-added tax from 10 per cent to 7 per cent, delaying the privatisation scheme for state enterprises, controlling the prices of goods, improving

welfare for workers and scrapping its plan to float wages.

Mr. Somsak Kaisook, the leader of the workers' committee, described that this demonstration not only warned the Thai government but also proved that the government did nothing for the poor people.

The Thai Brokers said that a no-confidence motion against the Prime Minister Mr. Chavalit Yongchaiyudh on September 24-25, AD 1997 and final vote on a new constitution on September 27, AD 1997 kept investors in a sideline. Four major banks of Thailand raised lending rates in the first week of September AD 1997. The Stock Exchange of Thailand index fell 1.1 per cent in the past week to 534.18 points. The Bank of Thailand told on Monday, September 15, AD 1997 that Thailand's foreign reserves fell to $ 25.90 billion at the end of Agust AD 1997, but it was $ 27.90 billion on August 14, AD 1997. But at the end of July 1997 — the foreign reserves stood at $ 30.40 billion. The International Monetary Fund which sanctioned a $ 17.2 billion bailout package to Thailand to solve its economic crisis mentioned that Thailand should keep a minimum foreign reserves of $ 23 billion in AD 1997 and $ 25.00 billion in AD 1998. The Thai finance minister said on Monday, September 15, AD 1997 that Thailand could boost its value-added tax again if the government revenue under its $ 17.2 billion bailout package of the Thai economy falls short of the International Monetary Fund targets.[74] The government will again think of a fresh increase of the tax on goods and services if it fails to achieve a budget surplus target imposed by the International Monetary Fund. Mr. Suppachai Pisitvanich, the finance minister's permanent secretary, stated the Bangkok is trying to maintain a surplus of around $ 1.14 billion in the budget for the fiscal year, ending September 30 next year. Owing to economic crisis, Thailand in August AD 1997 accepted a $ 17.2 billion International Monetary Fund rescue package. Several analysts and economists described on Monday, September 15,

74. *AA*, September16, 1997, p. 18.

AD 1997 that gasping Thai firms by a recent rise in lending rates were squeezed and were in trouble. Foreign Investors hesitated to invest money in Thailand. Mr. Songchai Ekkapatanapanit, a vice-president of the Federation of Thai Industries, told that the higher interest rate definitely created liquidity crunch problems. Several medium and small-sized businesses which had no across to foreign funding were the worst sufferers. A lot of companies faced problems, and many companies were forced to close their shops.

According to reports, an important member of Thailand's Prime Minister's embattled coalition made a plan to quit his government. The Prime Minister in the third week of September AD 1997 faced no-confidence motion and on constitutional reform he expected a crucial vote. Senior Army officers in the second week of September AD 1997 requested him to back down on his opposition to draft a constitution for the removal of political corruption which was responsible for Thailand's economic crisis. His embattled government faced a revenue short fall of $ 2.5 billion in fiscal AD 1998 "threatening targets set for Bangkok under the International Monetary Fund rescue deal". The *Nation* daily said that the possible short fall in official revenues has indicated a further tax rise to help to solve the country's fiscal position to enable to fulfil conditions given by the International Monetary Fund when it sanctioned a $ 17.2 billion financial rescue package.[75] According to analysts, the Thai government in order to solve the International Monetary Fund targets may possibly raise value-added tax for the second time. But a senior official of the revenue department told that the government had no intention to raise the value-added tax threshold of 10 per cent. Mr. Sachart Chaowisit, the revenue department's secretary general, told that any value-added tax hike after a cabinet meeting would need an amendment in the current law and it would require the approval of the cabinet. The *Nation* daily mentioned,

75. *AA*, September 17, 1997, p. 5.

> Among the options for achieving additional revenue is an increase in the value-added tax from the current 10 per cent, an oil tax hike or the introduction of a luxury tax.

Mr Sachart Chaowisit described,

> A value-added tax increase aimed at further curbing domestic consumption will probably be the most politically difficult as consumers have already complained loudly over the impact of the recent value-added tax rise from seven per cent.

The Thai government has already increased a value-added tax from seven per cent in August AD 1997 under the instruction of the International Monetary Fund for the rescue fund with an idea to establish its battered economy in a solid position. Under its bailout package which sanctioned in August 1997, Bangkok should keep a budget surplus in the 1998 financial year which began from October 1, AD 1997, of an amount which was an equivalent of one per cent of gross domestic product. The target of the surplus was at 48 billion baht. From the report of the revenue collection agencies it was known that the sharp economic downturn has brought a 10 per cent drop in the excise department's revenue target. The *Nation* daily reported that the total shortfall was 100 billion from the various agencies.

According to the International Monetary Fund, the reverberations of the foreign exchange crisis in Thailand on other South-East Asian countries' economies were excessive. The float of the Thai baht on July 2, AD 1997 gave its indication that how easily a crisis of one country affected confidence of other countries and influenced their activities. The semi-annual report mentioned that

> the economic fundamentals in Indonesia, Malaysia and the Philippines were generrally stronger than those in Thailand at the time of the crisis. While the Thai

> devaluation would imply a worsening of the competitive position of some of its neghbours in terms of economic fundamentals the extent of spillover effects would appear to be excessive.

The International Monetary Fund described that in gross domestic product Thailand's growth was forecast to slow to 2.5 per cent this year from 6.4 per cent last year. For this reason it gave a $ 17.2 billion loan to Thailand to improve its economy. The World Economic Outlook report mentioned,

> the pressures have been most acute in Thailand, where fraigilities in the banking system contributed to market concerns. The baht had dropped more than 30 per cent against the dollar since its float.

The baht was quoted onshore at 36.850/950 to the dollar against 36.55/56 late on Tuesday, September 16, AD 1997. The market was worried because in Thailand the political outlook was unclear and players continued to worry about a news report, denied by Bangkok that the International Monetary Fund might withhold rescue funds. Thailand has two crucial Parliamentary votes, one a no-confidence motion against the government and the other on a controversial draft constitution. The Internatinal Monetary Fund's semi-annual world economic outlook told,

> The problems surfaced in July 1997 in Thailand, when a strenghthening Thai currency and a large current account deficit heightened the perceived risk of a crisis.

Then a rescue package supported by the International Monetary Fund went to Thailand to improve its financial condition and to solve its crisis.

> The International Monetary Fund-sponsored $ 17.2 billion bailout, and a Thai commitment to 'a strong adjustment programme' means Thailand likely will gradually return to its characteristically strong economic performance.

The annual meeting of the International Monetary Fund began on Wednesday, September 17, AD 1997 at Hong-Kong. Some 16,000 people, including policy-makers from the International Monetary Fund's 181 member countries attended. The report said that the Thai growth rate was 6.4 per cent in AD 1996 but in AD 1997 the growth rate showed that it was so slow it came down to 2.5 per cent. The International Monetary Fund sanctioned a $ 17.2 billion loan package to Thailand in August AD 1997 after the fall of the baht currency and then huge problems began to appear in the week financial sector. The International Monetary Fund suggested that adequate measure should be taken to strengthen the financial sector and the balance of payments and confidence should be earned relatively quickly. Outside the Thai Parliament in Bangkok several protestors with banners demonstrated against the International Monetary Fund during an anti-government rally on Wednesday, September 17, AD 1997. Some 200 members of Thailand's 'Assembly of the Poor' protested and decried the impact of the country's economic crisis on urban and rural people and then marched towards the central bank of Thailand. Mr. Jonathan Thatcher from Hong-Kong stated,

> Thailand whose financial crisis has thrown Asia's booming economies into turmoil, is making amends but must quickly do more, the International Monetary Fund said on Thursday, 18 September 1997. After Thailand was forced to effectively devalue its currency in early July 1997, the International Monetary Fund rode to the rescue, putting together a $ 17.2 billion programme on condition that it put its crumbling economic house in order. . . . However the International Monetary Fund-led bailout, the largest since $ 50 billion was made available to Mexico to deal with its financial crisis, in 1995 has not restored confidence in the Thai economy as quickly as the Fund had hoped. Investors have fled the country in droves and the Thai has slumped around 40 per cent since July 1997.

Mr Michel Camdessus, the managing director of the International Monetary Fund, visited Thailand on Friday, September 19, 1997 to talk with the Thai Prime Minister, Mr. Chavalit Yongchaiyudh. The latter said that his government has taken plans for sweeping reforms of the troubled economy. The Thai officials told that they would be successful to meet the targets of the International Monetary Fund and would pass

> with flying colours the first quarterly review by the International Monetary Fund, set for September 30, 1996.

They found difficulties in the next year when the government met tough International Monetary Fund targets on the budgets, inflation and reserves. The International Monetary Fund's comment was that Thailand's economic reforms have satisfied it. A dealer with one US bank told,

> The International Monetary Fund's soothing comments helped smooth some ruffled feathers caused by an earlier report it might withhold rescue funds as it was unhappy with Thailand's progress.

Mr. Chavalit Yongchaiyudh's government had a majority in the Lower House and it survived the no-confidence motion. But the Thai investors nervously and cautiously watched for any sign of dissent within the ruling coalition and they also waited patiently to see any further weakness in regional currencies. On Friday, September 19, 1997 Stock Exchange of Thailand index lost 2.04 per cent on the week to close at 523.30 points. But when the no-confidence vote and a vote on key constitutional reforms were settled, the investors of Thailand returned to Thailand's market in a very energetic way and played their active roles there. Under the weight of the country's vicious economic turmoil, the Thai-language newspaper industry has fallen on hard times. Encouraged by the economic boom of the early 1990s and the rapid development of Thailand's financial markets, many newspapers appeared in recent years. But as the flourishing condition of the economy disappeared and the economy began to fall, then many newspapers found that it was very difficult for them to get circulation or advertisement for them. Mr. Prapan Bomyakiet, the vice-chairman of the Wattachak group, said,

> In terms of advertising revenue I think industry wide we are talking in terms of a 30-per cent drop in advertising revenue so far this year. At this time, it is necessary for us with most of the other publishing groups to streamline our operation, to rerestructure our organisation to try and . . . it as efficient and lean as possible.

He told further,

> We are prepared to survive this economic crisis through in the longer term. We are talking about an economic crisis which is very much here with us and I reckon will continue to be with us for another year or so.

The South-East Asian finance ministers met on Thursday, September 18, 1997 at Bangkok and they discussed an ambitious plan to set-up a regional fund, an 'Asean Monetary Fund' to rescue crisis-ridden economies of the countries of South-East Asia.[76] Mr Thanong Bhidaya, the Thai finance minister, told that the members of the association of the South-East Asian Nation would help each other in times of their financial crisis. Mr. Roberto de Ocampo, the Philippine finance secretary, mentioned that the regional fund would be a counterpart to the International Monetary Fund, as the Asian Development Bank was to the World Bank. Mr. Thanong Bhidaya stated that the proposed fund could be utilised to help regional currencies,

> which have come under a wave of speculative attacks since the float of the Thai baht on July 2. Japan will be a

76. *AA*, September 19, 1997, pp. 18-19.

> big brother to help us in this, particularly with the currency problems in the region.

In Bangkok several Asian and European finance ministers met on Friday, September 19, 1997 and they vowed to fight economic woes. The Thai finance minister at the opening ceremony of the first Asia Europe Meeting of the finance ministers said that new measures and initiatives from the discussion of the Asian and the European ministers had helped to establish a closer tie to strengthen the financial co-operation of Asia and Europe. He told further that the ministers from 25 Asian and European nation looked forward to co-operate in the financial sector and they discussed the macroeconomic and foreign exchange outlook, particularly the situation in Asia. Thailand's currency plunged by about 40 per cent since in July 1997 it was floated in Thailand's worst financial turmoil in decades. A $ 17.2 billion financial assistance package sanctioned by the International Monetary Fund was accepted by the Thai government in August 1997. The Thai crisis had a great effect upon regional markets and the ministers of the seven South-East Asia nations met on Thursday, September 18, 1997 in Bangkok. They had a talk on the region's economic woes. The Thai finance minister told that the ministers did not bring concrete measures in their discussions but they wanted to co-operate in times of their distress. The Thai Prime Minister said at the opening ceremony on Friday, September 19, 1997 that

> as the international financial market becomes increasingly complex, financial policy makers from Asia and Europe myst step up their co-operation on macroeconomic and financial policies. We need to join hands and together develop common strategies to deal with threats to our financial stability arising from systematic and contagious risks.

He met Mr. Michel Camdessus, the managing director of the

International Monetary Fund, and promised to reform his country's economic system to improve the image of Thailand's economic world. He told further that Mr. Camdessus with confidence stated that Thailand by its reforms and measures would be able to establish its financial position on a solid foundation. The meeting of the Group of Seven industrialised countries was held on Saturday, September 20, 1997 in Hong Kong. This meeting dominated by financial troubles in Thailand and other regions of South-East Asia allowed finance ministers from Great Britain, Canada, France, Germany, Italy, Japan and the United States their first chance as a group to debate the crisis. They said that they were very happy to see that Thailand after the collapse of the baht currency was helped by international efforts and they then requested Thailand to co-operate with the International Monetary Fund which sanctioned a $ 17.2 billion bailout package to improve its economic crisis. Financial markets were worried about the Thai government's "commitment to a reform programme under-pinning the bailout, and currencies and share markets across the regions remain under pressure". They stated that although they were satisfied with international efforts to help Thailand for the improvement of its economic crisis, yet they liked to watch the Asian markets very closely for any knock-on effects from the financial turmoils of Thailand.

Thailand's Prime Minister Mr. Chavalit Yongchaiyudh faced in the last week of September 1997 a no-confidence vote in the Thai Parliament for a new anti-corruption constitution. The opposition party aimed to target his handling of an economic turmoil in the no-confidence debate which started from Wednesday, September 24, 1997, but in business, media and urban cricles he has lost his credibility. Chanting and placard-waving Thai crowds surrounded the Thai Parliament to praise or condemn the Thai Prime Minister as he was busy in Parliament to play a gerat role to shave his shaky government. Bangkok's streets were crowded as three-day trust debate began in Thailand. According to the Thai policemen, a melee of around

3,000 people thronged the gate of the building, the Thai Parliament and shouted in loud voices and asked the Prime Minister to step down and to accept the responsibility for the country's chronic economic slump or sometimes they tried to boost his morale. In the House, the Prime Minister was very serious because he defended himself against allegations of economic mismanagement brought by the opposition party in a key debate on a no-confidence motion. Outside, the Thai people waved placards and banners and there were many students who asked the Prime Minister to step down immediately to give way for more competent leaders. Mr. Pakorn Saedan of Bangkok's Ramkambhaeng University told,

> The Prime Minister has to resign because his management of the economy has been ineffective and because there is corruption problem at high levels. We hope that he resigns and this will help heal the economic situation.

Others in the crowd were equally virulent and spoke agianst the Prime Minister's 10-month-old government and asked him to go. The latter on Friday, September 26, 1997 looked set to survive a crucial censure motion but immediately came under renewed pressure to push through a new anticraft constitution. The opposition members told that he was the root of all corruptions and economic mismanagement. The *Bangkok Post* announced the result of vote on the no-confidence motion a 'foregone conclusion' and in an editorial told,

> The side with the largest number of votes will prevail and go on to continue in mal-administration

and the no-confidence process was meaningless. Mr. Chavalit Yongchaiyudh, whose government was charged of costing the country over $ 50 billion, was forced into a cabinet reshuffle, but he was sure that his six-party coalition would support him in the censure debate. Saturday, September 27, 1997 was fixed as a key debate in Thai politics, because the Prime Minister faced two biggest challenges of his career as on the censure motion MPs vote early in the morning and on a new constitution afterwards. The Prime Minister survived no-trust vote. The Thai Parliament on Saturday, September 27, 1997 endorsed a new constitution which designed to clean up political corruption blamed for Thailand's economic turmoil, shortly after voting confidence in his unpopular governmet. Thus, the new constitution helped to ensure several more months of life for the government which was widely blamed for the sinking economy of the country and new laws for elections of Thailand under the new rules were passed. According to many Thais, under intense pressure from the Thai people Mr. Chavalit Yongchaiyudh changed his mind. At first he opposed the charter but seeing the public's attitude towards his government, he had to change his mind and he supported the charter. The official count indicated that in order to approve the charter, 578 to 16, in a vote of the Senate and the House of Representatives, the Prime Minister and his allies joined the opposition. About 17 members were absent.

The world's richest nations on Saturday, September 20, 1997 requested Thailand to implement reforms sanctioned by the International Monetary Fund because a currency crisis has made a very bad effect upon the regions of South-East Asia. Mr. Robert Rubin, the US treasury secretary, after the ministers' three-hour meeting said in a news conference that

> there was general satisfaction with the international efforts to assist Thailand. We discussed the critical importance. . . . Of Thai authorities implementing vigorously the programme they have entered into with the International Monetary Fund.[77]

Owing to flagging exports and real estate speculation, the Thai

77. *ET*, September 22, p. 5.

currency became very weak and it lost 30 per cent of its value agianst the dollar in July 1997. At the annual meeting of the World Bank and of the International Monetary Fund on Monday, September 22, 1997, the United States of America praised Thailand for its financial reforms after currency crisis. The US treasury secretary had a talk with Mr. Thanong Bhidaya, the finance minister of Thailand, and gave an optimistic note and he acknowledged for the first time that Thailand tried its best to do something to solve its economic crisis. The former after his meeting said,

> I think it is fair to say that they expressed real commitment to working with the International Monetary Fund and the World Bank.

Mr. Thanong Bhidaya on Monday, September 22, 1997 met the US treasury secretary and Mr. Alan Greenspan, the US Federal Reserve Chairman and the former said,

> We have no plan at all to seek now money. It is more important to tell them what we are doing and what is the government role in this.

He told further that the main purpose of his meeting with the top government official is to share up confidence in Thailand. The United States side mentioned,

> both nations share the view that rigorous and unambiguous actions to implement the International Monetary Fund programme, restore the health of the financial sector, and expand the disclosure of key economic and financial data are the best way to restore market confidence, stability and economic growth prospects.

Thailand's crrrency fell 30 per cent in value against the dollar and the financial markets of Indonesia, the Philippines and Singapore faced also the similar problem. Mr. Thanong Bhidaya, the finance minister of Thailand, said on Sunday, September 21, 1997 that his country has massive private sector debts and he assured his people that within two years he will be able to solve its financial crisis and will soon establish its former high levels of economic growth. Mr. Robert Rubin, who met Thailand's finance minister on Monday, September 22, 1997 at the time of the annual meeting of the International Monetary Fund told that Bangkok has promised a concerted move to keep its house in a proper order and has given assurance that it would co-operate closely with the efforts of the international community.

> They wanted to hear directly from us an affirmation of our commitment to the region. This puts us in a very constructive mode in dealing with South-East Asia's problems.

The United States did not give any cash to the Thai package but supported its efforts and played a great role to re-establish stability in Thailand and in other regions of South-East Asia. Mr. Lawrence Summars, a deputy of Mr. Robert Rubin, told that Thailand should follow strictly to the policy presctiptions of the International Monetary Fund. He said,

> To restore stability it is essential that the Thai government now follow through rigidly on its International Monetary Fund Programme.

The Thai Prime Minister said on Tuesday, September 23, 1997 that he instructed the government's budget bureau to identify a 50-60 billion baht ($ 1.4-1.6 billion) of possible cuts to the 1998 budget. The directions to shave more from the 923 billion baht budget approved last week (in the third week of September 1997) in the Tai Parliament came amid concerns that Thailand will not have enough revenue to attain a fiscal surplus in 1998. Accordinng to the terms of a $ 17.2 billion economic rescue package approved by the International Monetary Fund, Thailand was needed to have a fiscal surplus about one per cent for 1998.

The Prime Minister after a cabinet meeting told that he has introduced the budget bureau to submit necessary data at the next cabinet meeting on September 30, 1997 on how the cuts could be made on the budget for the year to September 1998 and the cuts should not disturb public health or welfare expenditure. He told further that the political budget cut would allay the need for any tax increase. The finance ministry of Thailand gave warning that if revenue was not sufficient to meet the revenue surplus target of the International Monetary Fund, then the government would impose a second hike to the value-added tax.[78] It may be noted here that in August 1997, the Thai government increased the value-added tax from seven to ten per cent, in a series of austerity measures needed to receive the International Monetary Fund bailout package which Thailand was in need to share up foreign reserves. Mr. Chaturon Chaisaeng, the deputy finance minister, told on Tuesday, September 23, 1997 that the budget cuts to be investigated by the budget bureau would help to avoid a further value-added tax increase. Mr. Aporn Chewakrieng, the chief economist at Deutsche Morgan Grenfell, told that the International Monetary Fund agreement would help the Thai government to maintain a surplus of about one per cent of gross domestic product about 60-70 billion baht in 1998. After three days of parliamentary debate the House of Representatives approved a budget of 923 billion baht for the year 1998. Although the finance ministry warned that a value-added tax would be imposed, even then, it predicted that the revenue of the government in fiscal year 1998 would reach 973 billion baht and this indicated a 50 billion baht surplus in its revenue. Mr. Michael Camdessus, the managing director of the International Monetary Fund, on Tuesday, September 23, 1997 mentioned that the market would take time to achieve its confidence in troubled Thailand. The International Monetary Fund and several countries in South-East Asia helped Thailand

---

78. *AA*, September 24, 1997, p. 18.

to recover from its economic turmoil with $ 17.2 billion in loans on condition that Thailand would reform the financial sector and would take action to curb its current account deficit. According to several Bangkok dealers, the baht was not likely to weaken beyond 37.30 to the dollar but its gains would be capped at 36.50. It was 36.95/37.05 onshore against 37.20/37.30.

Thailand's embattled Prime Minister has emerged victorious from a dramatic weekend in politics, evading censure and seeing a historic new charter adopted, but he was ready for survival for his next battle. The Prime Minister now again desperately tried to extend the life of his shaky government. He faced months of massive public pressure over the radical anti-sleeze constitution, despite the government's almost unanimous backing of the document during its cruicial parlimentary vote on Saturday, September 27, 1997. Mr. Varapol Sirivat, a businessman, told,

> people may have thought for a while that Saturday's double vote was going to settle the future of the country. But now that all the excitement is over and the dust has settled, it is clear that it is just the start of a new era of wrangling and political manoevring and that in reality little has changed so far.

Thailand's battered bourse and currency market were loosing value daily, and owing to the political uncertainty, the financial crisis went to the extreme. Mr. Chavalit Yongchaiyudh held talks with his key coalition patners on Saturday, September 27, 1997 on the reshuffle that appeared to be the price he must pay for narrowly surviving the censure vote. According to several analysts, the Prime Minister would have to drop some ministers and the *Nation* daily mentioned that about fifteen members would be replaced at the weekend. It said that he had

> given in to pressure from the Chart Pattana to overhaul his cabinet line-up by bringing in 15 technocrats to replace ministers with image problems in an effort to hang onto his position.

Until the changes were settled, the issue remained in the minds of the media and politicians.

It may be noted here that the Asian and Europeans economic ministers on Sunday, September 28, 1997 hold their one-day inaugural meeting at Chiba, Japan wanted to work together towards better ties and they wished more trade and investment between the two regions. Mr. Narongchai Akrasanee, the Thai commerce minister, said on Sunday, September 28, 1997 at Chiba in Japan that economic liberalisation was good despite the currency turmoil in Thailand.[79] He, however, mentioned the need for establishing shock-absorbing institutions. "You also have to put in institutional infrastructure to accommodate it." He told this on the sidelines of an econominc ministers' gathering of the Asia-Europe Meeting in Chiba near Tokyo. He acknowledged that the slow pace of financial liberalisation, however, had very bad effects in Thailand and he also mentioned a non-existent bend market in his country that could have worked when flooding comes as a reservoir of water. He stated that the debt issue was not very serious in Thailand because most debts were owned by 'foreign companies based in Thailand', particularly Japanese firms. According to him, these companies would help to solve private sector debts, if they played their great roles in the business world by doing more exports. During his meeting with Japan's trade and industry minister, the Thai commerce minister appreciated Japan's financial assistance in the currency woes of Thailand. He did not request further aid, but he wanted Japan's co-operation in boosting exports of shrimp, rice, automobile parts and other products. He also requested Japan to invest in real estate of his country.

The Thai baht closed weaker at 35.20 to the dollar offshore on Friday ahead of Saturday's vote in Bangkok on the constitution and the censure motion. Following the key Thai Parliamentary vote on Saturday, September 27, 1997, speculation shifted to

79. *AA*, September 29, 1997, p. 18.

whose heads will roll as premier Mr. Chavalit Yongchaiyudh, paying the price for political survival, negotiated with coalition partners on the make up his cabinet. After the Thai baht's *de facto* devaluation in early July 1997, currencies of the South-East Asian regions have fallen very sharply and these areas have faced an economic slowdown. Several analysts said on Sunday, September 28, 1997 in Bangkok that Mr. Chavalit Yongchaiyudh has survived a weekend no-confidence motion in Parliament and he was under pressure to take immediate and meaningful steps to help Thailand's stricken economy to establish itself on its feet, starting with a major cabinet reshuffle. Mr. Phaijit Sriverakarn,[80] an executive committee member of the premier's main New Asbpiration Party, told,

> A major cabinet reshuffle is needed for the administration to help to bring about economic recovery and regain public faith.

But ordinary Thais as well as economic and political analysts waited to see if his much-criticised six-party coalition had the capacity to pull the country out of its worst economic turmoil in decades. Several analysts mentioned that financial mrakets were likely to react nonchantly to Mr. Chavalit Yongchaiyudh's victory, and they waited patiently for the major cabinet reshuffle promised by a coalition spokesman on Saturday, September 27, 1997. Mr. Khanchit Assavasamvarn of broker Vickers Ballas & Co. Pvt. Ltd. said that the markets would watch to see if more respected economists and technocrats were appointed into the cabinet. The Thai analysts waited with a hope to hear the announcement on October 15, 1997 of more reform measures to bring order to the liquidity-squeezed finance sector where about 58 wakfinance firms were suspended. Mr. Khanchit Assavasamvarn told, "The markets will show muted reaction while waiting for these". According to political sources, in the reshuffle some senior

80. *ET*, September 29, 1997, p. 7.

ministers and politicians would allow several technocrats to take their places in the cabinet to help Mr. Chavalit Yongchaiyudh to stabilise the tottering economy. The analysts told that these ministers who were accused corruption, incompetence of economic mismanagement by the opposition party during the censure debate would be dropped from the cabinet. The Thai people expected that this reshuffle would take place before October 6, 1997 when the Thai Prime Minister would go to Japan. They welcomed the decision of the approval of a new reformist constitution on the weekend. Mr. Chavalit Yongchaiyudh told in the beginning of September 1997 that he might call an election in May 1998 but some senior coalition partners did not like this idea and they requested him not to do it because an early election could have a bad effect upon the battered economy. The Prime Minister's critics bitterly criticised him for his incompetency to handle Thailand's economic crisis which forced the country to accept a $ 17.2 billion rescue package which was approved by the International Monetary Fund to solve its financial problems. According to several analysts, with an idea to end decades of rampant money politics and political patronage, the new constitution was introduced in Thailand. Mr. Graham Catterwell, the country manager for Deutsche Morgan Grenfell said

> The constitution vote was positive. As for the no-confidence vote, it was expected and now markets will wait to see how it plays out.

The economic problems have very much influenced the public mood. The baht since it was floated on July 2, 1997 has plunged nearly 40 per cent against the dollar. The inflation rate has risen to a great extent and the authorities have closed in 1997 several finance firms where billions of the baht in public deposits were struck. Mr. Chira Hongladarom, the human resources consultant and academic, described,

> The new constitution gives Thais some expectation to

> look forward to in the next seven or eight months but. Mr. Chavalit Younchaiyudh faced a difficult task of restoring public faith in him. Thailand would feel more economic pains in the months ahead and Mr. Chavalit Yongchaiyudh could find it difficult to recruit quality technocrats to join his cabinet. The downturn momentum is still very strong except a small ray of hope in improving exports.

It was good news that the countries of Asia agreed to pool their resources to form a US $ 100 billion Bail Out Fund to help out economic under attack. But the USA did not think it was such a good idea.

> As the Thai crisis unfolded, most observers saw the difference that geography makes. They woulded why it was that the international financial community was sitting pretty and almost enjoying the Thais going through the special torture that financial collapse involved. There was none of the frantic hurry and anxiety which were in evidence when similar disaster had struck Mexico in 1994-1996. The explanation was obvious Mexico was, after all, in the US backyard.

USA's European partners were unable to see Thailand's problems as so serious. At first, the Thais went to Japan for help. Because in business the Japanese were involved in Thailand. They had a huge stake there. About 50 per cent of the Thai foreign debt was held by the Japanese banks. But the Japanese did not show any interest to help Thailand in their economic crisis. But Japan finally gave a help of an aid package of about $ 18 billion. Out of this, Japan's contribution was nearly 25 per cent, and China, Singapore and Taiwan gave $ 1 billion each. Other South-East Asian countries also contributed their shares to Thailand. But India did not help anything. The South-East Asian initiative to form a $ 100 billion bail-out fund was praised by Mr. Hiroshi Mitsuzuka, the Japanese finance minister, in the fourth week of

September 1997. Mr. Robert Rubin, the US secretary of the treasury, feared that the USA's role as the world's super power would be diminished and the International Monetary Fund's role would be diluted. It was very probable that the fear of Asia's self-sufficiency in reserve mangement was itself the reason for USA's trouncing the bail-out fund. One hopes that the Japanese and the South-East Asian countries will not be bullied into a trap of USA design and will not fall into its hands and will withdraw their proposal. Practically, the time has come for the establishment of the Asian Bail-Out Fund. It is quite true that a $ 100 billion bail-out fund run by professionals of Asia can difinetely help to bring greater stability of the Asian markets. Mr. Thanong Bhidaya, the Thai finance minister, told reporters in Tokyo on Thursday, October 9, 1997,

> The purpose of the Asia Fund it to round up the founding requirements and the contributions of Asian countries in case of a crisis and it is a good idea. But somehow it has been delayed. Why not put it in the APEC forum? Why just keep it within Asia? The IMF will not have enough to deal with any crisis by itself and (the Asian Fund) is an effort to prepare something more solid.

The Thai dealers said on Tuesday, September 30, 1997 that the renewed confidence over the Thai government boosted the baht. 'The government's survival of a no-confidence vote over the weekend was positive for the baht.' Gold bar price in Thailand have surged to 5,300 baht (US $ 148.50) per 15.24 grammes compared with 4,300 baht before the baht was floated in July, 1997. Thailand's worst economic crisis in decades had compelled the Thai people to sell gold and jewellery as a way to get cash. Because many people have lost their jobs. The manager of diamond shop in Bangkok's Ban Mor jewellery district told,

> Once client sold her diamond ring and earrings so she could pay her employees' salary. She just broke into toars when she took the ring off her finger.

Foreign ministers of South Korea, Singapore, the Philippines and Thailand took their cases to the United Nations on Monday, September 29, 1997 to address the General Assembly as its annual debate began its second week. Speakers from Brunei, Indonesia, Veitnam, Laos, North Korea, Australia, New Zealand, Japan, China, Myanmar and Malaysia also delivered their speeches in the General Assembly of the United Nations in the fourth week of September 1997 and also in the first week of October 1997.

In a bid to boost exports, Thailand's economic ministers on Monday, September 29, 1997 approved in principle a request for another $ 1.2 billion in loans to restructure the industrial sector and to improve technology. Mr. Kern Dabbaransi, the deputy Prime Minister and also the industry minister, told that in December 1997 through local banks a first tranche of $ 650 billion would be made available.[81] He did not say anything about the terms of the loan. The Export-Import Bank of Thailand in order to increase credit facilities for exporters also sought a $ 500 million loan from the Japanese creditors. In 1996 when the export growth collapsed, Thailand's financial woes came out in the open and the creditors and the investors were unable to decide whether Thailand could meet its obligations with sky-high foreign debt and a huge current account deficit. The central bank has closed 58 firms and requested them to produce rehabilitation plans. They would be stripped of their visible assets and their business licenses would be cancelled if they were not in a position to follow its instructions in a proper way. Mr. Suwat Liptapallop, the transportation and communication minister, on Monday September 29, 1997 told that the economic council from October 1, 1997 gave its approval an increase in the value-added tax on Port Authority of Thailand services to 10 per cent. The increase also applied to corporate users and mobile phone users of the Telephone Organisation of Thailand services, but until April 1, 1998 the increase for domestic fixed line users was postponed.

81. *AA*, October 1, 1997, p. 18.

The value-added tax on general consumer products rose from 7 per cent to 10 pre cent frrom August 16, 1997. Because the government wanted to make up for a drop in direct tax revenue with the recession so that the Thai government would be able to meet the International Monetary Fund targets. Several newspapers referred to the budget deficit for fiscal 1997-8 which began on Wednesday, October 1, 1998 reached 180 to 200 billion baht ($ 5-5.55 billion), despite the Thai government took steps to cut its expenditure. Such a dificit no doubt throw the country's commitments to the International Monetary Fund which asked the Thai government to follow its days in a very rigid way. The Finance One, Thailand's premier finance company, and also 58 other finance companies were shut down by the Thai government in 1997 because they faced financial difficulties owing to many bad loans to real estate firms. The Thai Government asked the companies to merge with stronger firms. But it was difficult for them to find partners.

Although Thailand got a $ 17.2 billion bail-out package from the International Monetary Fund, yet, Moody's investors service told on Thursday, October 2, 1997 that it had downgraded the ratings of all the country's corporate bonds and bank deposits.[82] According to Moody's, the downgrade reflected an erosion in Thailand's credit fundamentals as well as greater risk exposure for banks and business.

> The agency lowered the long-term ratings of all banks' deposits from a 3 to maximum of BAA 3 and they remain on review for a possible further downgrade. BAA 3 is one level above what is considered the equivalent of a junk bond rating. It also lowered the maximum long-term rating for corporate bonds from A3 to BAA 1, considered a medium grade as far as risk is concerned. The short-term rating for bank deposits and corporate bonds was slashed from prime-2 to prime-3 , with both

82. *AA*, October 2, 1997, p. 5.

> ceilings remaining on review for possible downgrade. While a number of domestic and international initiatives are likely to succeed in stabilising Thailand's external financial position, Moody's said the downgrades appear warranted.

The Thai banks and corporations in foreign currencies have borrowed large anounts of money. Since on July 2, 1997, the Thai government floated the Thai currency, the baht, it has lost of its value more than 30 per cent. It was because of this, the value of the debt owed by banks and corporations has risen very much.

> Bangkok Bank, the country's largest bank, had ratings, for deposits from A 3 to BAA 3 (long term) and from prime-2 to prime-3 (short term), and the bank's long-term debt rating from A 3 to BAA 1. The deposit ratings remain on review for possible downgrade. The outlook for the long-term debt ratings in negative. The Bank of Asia, long-term deposits were from BAA 2 to BAA 3. The bank's deposit ratings of BAA 3 and prime-3 and the bank's financial strength rating of D, remain on review for possible downgrade. In the export-import bank of Thailand, the rating of the bank's long-term debt was from A 3 to BAA 1. The outlook for the rating is negative. In the industrial finance corporation of Thailand the tong-term debt was from A 3 to BAA 1. The outlook for the long-term debt ratings is negative. The rating of the PTT Exploration International Ltd. was from A 3 to BAA 1.

The Thai baht traded sluggishly, sliding to 30/40 per dollar onshore against 36.20/34.40 late on Tuesday, October 2, 1997. It was at 35.60/70 offshore against 35.40/60.

Former Thailand's Prime Minister Mr. Chatichai Choonhavan, who was a key leader of the six-party governing coalition, on Thursday, October 2, 1997, demanded a swift cabinet reshuffle to boost the country's strruggling economy. He told the second largest coalition party, the Chart Pattana. He and Thailand's army chief wanted a re-allocation of ministerial positions at the time of a no-confidence debate. Mr. Chatichai Choonhavan[83] told,

> I think that there should be a reshuffle as soon as possible which could have a good effect on the economy. Whether it is this week or not I don't know . . . but if it is late it will damage the economy.

The Thai language daily *Matichon* referred to it. Mr. Chavalit Yongchaiyudh had survived an opposition censurs motion and he was under preasure to appoint more technocrats into his government, which under economic crisis had fallen into disgrace. Several local papers reported on Friday, October 3, 1997 that before leaving on a trip to Japan on October 8, 1997, he would conduct a minor cabinet reshuffle. A key party in the Thai government coalition has put pressure on the Thai Prime Minister for a major cabinet reshuffle to bring a good image of the government and to save the country from the economic turmoil. The seceratary-general of the Chart Pattana Party spoke to the *Bangkok Post* that a shake-up of ministers was the Prime Minister's last hope to win back public confidence. Mr. Suwat Liptapallop said,

> This is the last chance for the government. If there is to be reshuffle it must be a big one to improve the quality of the cabinet and solve national problems.

The currency turmoil in the South-East Asian countries has taken a severe toll on the petrochemical industry of this region. Several new petro-chemical producers in Thailand and in Indonesia found it very difficult to honour their dollar payments, both towards foodstocks (naphtha) as also important of capital equipment.[84]

---

83. *AA*, October 3, 1997, p. 5.
84. *ET*, October 10, 1997, p. 28.

Polyolefins producers were mentioned as the worst sufferers. The last four months have seen a depreciation of 30-40 per cent in the value of the baht and the rupiah, the currencies of Thailand and Indonesia, against the dollar, around the time massive capacities in poly-olefins went on stream. In both Thailand and Indonesia, the petro-chemical industry played a very significant role in the local economy but Thailand owing to the fall out of the currency crisis suffered very much. The Thai Olefins Co (TOC), the Thai Petro-chemical Industry (TPI) and the Thai Polyethylene (TPE) were doing business in Thailand's polymer industry and they faced many problems to do their business. According to industry reports, some Thai units faced bankruptcy. The International Monetary Fund felt frustrated to see the hopeless condition of the Thai petro-chemical industry and it refused to give fresh loan to it. The currency crisis brought a reversal of fortunes for poly-propylene (PP). Till a year back, the Asian region did not have enough poly-propylene, but during the first half of 1997 its supply was very good and Thailand, Malaysia, Indonesia and Korea produced very much. But now the petro-chemical producers in Thailand and Indonesia owing to a high-cost structure faced difficulty in its production and they stopped their production very much. From industry sources it is learnt that ploy-propylene prices have already moved up by about 10 per cent over the last two weeks to around $ 650 and everybody expected to see its further rise up to $ 750 short time.

Thailand took initiative to do something for its bank reforms. According to analysts, the Thai government did not want to miss the chance in satisfying overseas creditors and to create confidence in a nation that has fallen in difficulties from one financial crisis to another. It wanted to end an agonising wait for local markets. The officials of the Bank of Thailand, the International Monetary Fund and the World Bank have brought measures which aimed at reviving an industry hit by falling asset quality and a liquidity squeeze. About 58 of Thailand's 91 finance and securities companies were suspended by regulators in 1997.

The package was introduced in order to slove the problems of these firms and to strengthen the framework of surviving companies. The Thai stock market has dipped a pre-plan nerves, losing 2.5 per cent of its value in these days. Under the instruction of the package, the assets of the suspended finance firms come under the control of two new bodies — a Financial Restructuring Agency to look after good assets and an Asset Management Committee to examine the bad assets. In order to encourage capital inflows, foreign ownership rules were to be relaxed to give foreigners a great chance to hold majority stakes in local financial institutions for up to 10 years. With an idea to strengthen serviving firms, measures were taken and there were loan provisioning requirements and capital adequacy restrictions which allowed the banks to lift capital adequacy ratios to 12 per cent from 8.5 per cent. A top Thai official said on Sunday, October 12, 1997 that altogether 16 cash-strapped Thai finance firms were suspended from business earlier this year, i.e., 1997 and they all met a key deadline to submit rehabilitation or merger plans. Mr. Amaret Sila-on, the chairman of the government appointed merger committee, told that the foreign investors would be given permission to keep more than a 50 per cent stake for up to 10 years in any of 58 suspended finance firms. He was in his job for six weeks and political interferene was the main reason for his resignation. Thailand relaxed conditions for 58 suspended firms to resume business and increased the time and allowed them to repay a combined 430 billion baht borrowed from the central bank from three years to eight years. Most South-East Asian currencies became very steady on Tuesday, October 14, 1997 and everyone showed their keen interest on Thailand's financial reform package. The Thai baht slipped as players became steady for a much-awaited finance sector reform package. On Friday, October 10, 1997 the baht was at 35.50/60 per dollar onshore against 36.15/36.25. It was 35.80/90 offshore against 35.65/36.75. The market had a mixed response. The baht was at 35.36/42 to the dollar onshore at 0415 GMT against 36.45/55 on Monday,

October 13, 1997. The offshore rate was at 35.90/36.00. Mr. Somkid Jatusipitak, an advisor to Mr. Thanong Bhidaya, the Thai Finance minister,[85] told that Thailand announced the much-awaited financial reform package on October 15, 1997 which was one day earlier than previously scheduled. He said further that the details of the package were released after its approval by the weekly cabinet meeting on Thursday, October 14, 1997. At the time of the announcement of the package the presence of the deputy Prime Minister, the finance minister and the governor of the central bank were needed for its clarification. Thailand has accepted an International Monetary Fund sponsored rescue package worth $ 17.2 billion and it vowed to follow the International Monetary Fund-set austority measures. Its much awaited financial reforms were announced on Wednesday, October 15, 1997. According to several Thai dealers, its financial reform package punctured baht bubble. Practically, it left the baht mired in disappointment and in confusion. The International Monetary Fund and the World Bank endorsed the planned reforms which mentioned the appointment of two agencies to restructure and to look after 58 suspended Thai finance firms, the provisions for financial institutions to raise their capital and amendments to bankruptcy laws. Mr. Thanong Bhidaya, the finance minister, told that after a reshuffle he had no intention to remain as a finance minister in the cabinet of Mr. Chavalit Yongchaiyudh, the Prime Minister of Thailand. Mr. Bhidaya's decision came when Thailand's Prime Minister in order to boost dwindling state revenues reversed an unpopular hike in oil tax which Mr. Bhidaya supported and it also received the approval of the cabinet. According to a Thai analyst, Mr. Bhidaya's resignation could be mentioned as the 'death knell' for the Thai Prime Minister. He wanted the co-operation of the Thai people to help to implement the measures adopted by the cabinet and to solve the economic crisis of his country. The one baht oil tax

85. *AA*, October 14, 1997, p. 18.

increase was meant to help Thailand to receive one per cent budget surplus in the fiscal year till September 1998 as required under the International Monetary Fund rescue package. Mr. Bhidaya's resignation had a very bad effect upon the credibility of Mr. Chavalit Yongchaiyudh's ten-month old administration which wanted to appoint technocrats into the cabinet at the time of its reshuffle. Mr. Bhidaya told that he wanted to resign because he liked to see a new economic team. He get his appointment in the place of the former leader of Mr. Yongchaiyudh's economic 'dream team' Mr. Amnuay Virawan, who gave his resignation when ministers in the fractious coalition opposed a politically unpopular tax increase. About thousands took to the streets of Bangkok on Monday, October 20, 1997 and they demonstrated, protested and demanded the resignation of the Thai Prime Minister because he was unable to solve the country's worst economic crisis in decades. They blamed his very much and they indicated that he was responsible for it and he did nothing to solve its crisis. There were businessmen, academics, students and office workers in this procession and they marched in the financial district and they carried placards and shouted against rising food prices, job losses and the battered economy. Thousands of demonstrators blocked traffic on the usually traffic-clogged Silom Road and asked for Mr. Yongchaiyudh to quit following his shock decision to reverse key reforms. The Thai Prime Minister faced an embarassment when his coalition partners did not allow him a free hand in reshuffling his cabinet. After a meeting of the six-party coalition on Sunday, October 19, 1997, the party leaders told him that before selecting new ministers he should consult former Prime Minister Mr. Chatichai Choonhavan, the leader of the second largest party. It may be noted here that the Thai baht plunged to a record low of 38.15 against the dollar from Friday's (October 17, 1997) close of 37.15 after Mr. Bhidaya's announcemet was that he would resign. The beleaguered Thai currency had hit previous record low at 37.40 against the greenback on Friday, October 17, 1997. He was the second finance minister to resign from Mr. Yongchaiyudh's administration. Mr. Jimmy Koh, the regional economist with the British financial house IDEA, told,

> Despite what people may say, the market believes it is again political interference in economic policy.

During annual talks in Kuala Lumpur in October 19, 1997 several South-East Asian trade ministers have promised to speed up plans for a free trade area and to open up the region's lucrative services sector by 2020.[86] The association of the South-East Asian Nation's 29th economic ministers' meeting in Kuala Lumpur welcomed Myanmar and Laos which were its newcomers and told the positive aspects of the currency crisis besetting the region. The ministers mentioned that the financial storm had strengthened ideas for trade liberalisation and helped to create favourable conditions to develop exports and gave an opportunity to industries to improve their competitiveness. The group wanted to begin an introductory package for freeing up services in five fields — telecommunications, tourism, air and maritime transport services and business services from March 1998. Under a 1993 agreement, Brunei, Indonesia, Malaysia, the Philippines, Singapore and Thailand, who were six eldest Asean members, allowed to cut tariffs on most goods traded in the region to no more than 5 per cent by January 2003. The trade ministers in order to develop further and to promote the competitiveness of the region as an international production centre introduced guidelines for the establishment of an Asean investment area. In September 1998 a framework agreement on the investment scheme was completed.

The Thais kept pressure on the Thai Prime Minister to quit. The Thai cabinet ministers on Tuesday, October 21, 1997 handed in their resignations *en masse* to help the Prime Minister for a major reshuffle as pressure mounted on him to quit. This move

86. *AA*, October 21, 1997, p. 18.

did not indicate an immediate dissolution of the Thai cabinet. Mr. Sanoh Thientong, the interior minister, told on Tuesday, October 21, 1997 that the new ministerial list was ready for submission to the King.[87] According to the Thai Police and witnesses, about four thousand protestors gathered outside the Government House on Tuesday, October 21, 1997 and they demanded the resignation of the Prime Minister. Despite a massive protest outside his office, Mr. Yongchaiyudh managed to meet the German foreign minister, Mr. Klaus Kinkel, who was on a two-day visit to Bangkok. Mr. Prachuab Chaiyasarn, the Thai foreign minister, was with the Thai Prime Minister at the time of this meeting on Wednesday, October 22, 1997. Thailand's top army commander of the latter from imposing a state of emergency to retain power. The government faced the biggest outburst of middle class discontent and in 1992 street protest brought down the last military government. According to newspapers' reports, Gen. Chetta Thanajare, the army commander, on Tuesday, October 21, 1997 in a meeting of senior government leaders warned the Thai Prime Minister not to impose a state of emergency to stop protests by the demonstrators which so far were peaceful. The *Nation* newspaper mentioned that Mr. Chalerm Yubamrung, the interior minister, told the latter that in order to make a citywide sabotage campaign, an opposition leader-politician, a journalist and a political activist led these protests. The Prime Minister told,

> We realise the people are suffering from hardships. However, there are some groups of people who are trying to create cofusion, divisions which go beyond the freedom of liberty provided by the law.

The turmoil helped the Thai baht to plunge to new lows against the US dollar, which took its place to 39; 10 baht from 38.70 baht on Thursday, October 21, 1997. About thousand people from

---

87. *AA*, October 22, 1997, p. 5.

laid-off factory workers to middle class businessmen protested on Monday, October 20, and on Tuesday, October 21, 1997 in Bangkok's central business district and outside the Government House and they demanded the resignation of Mr. Yongchaiyudh. The demonstrations gave an indication about the government's inability to solve an economic crisis that has not only crippled Thailand but also has disturbed South-East Asia. Between 1985 and 1995 Thailand's growth rates were very high but in 1996 the country's half the financial institutions were closed owing to bad debt and since July 1997 the currency has lost 30 per cent of its value. About 100,000 people were without jobs. Mr. Yongchaiyudh was under pressure from the Thai public and the opposition party to reshuffle the cabinet. The Thai people on Tuesday, October 21, 1997 expected the announcement of the change because they heard from a report of the Thai television that the Prime Minister has set a late-night news conference on October 21, 1997 but they felt so sorry because no reshuffle was announced.

Thailand's political and financial uncertainties practically haunted South-East Asian currencies on Tuesday, October 21, 1997. A Thai dealer told, "The regionals are still gloomy, especially with the uncertainties in Thailand". Political chaes made an influence upon Thailand's financial markets after the risignation of Mr. Thanong Bhidaya as finance minister from the cabinet and the Thai people protested and asked the Thai Prime Minister to step down. A dealer with one US institution stated,

> The anti-Chavalit protests and demonstrations are coming at a bad time when the country is trying to regain investors'confidence. Any resignation is going to send the baht tumbling and regionals as well due to the close links South-East Asia has.

In early trade the Thai baht plunged to a new record low of 38.29 to a dollar. Offshore the baht was at 38.35/45 a dollar at 0430 GMT against 37.67/37.77 a dollar. Onshore the baht was quoted at 38.05/20 to the dollar compared to 37.63/37.73 on

Monday, October 20, 1997. Several onshore dealers mentioned that street protests against the government seemed to be followed mere closely by the offshore market but domestically these were less significant. Public dissatisfaction with Thailand's Prime Minister mounted so much that the Thai protestors demanded his resignation because they thought that he was responsible for an economic crisis of Thailand that has given a blow to South-East Asia. The Thai protestors carried placards of the revered monarch Bhumibol Adulyadej and shouted 'Chavalit, go away'. Mr. Montree Sornpaisarn, the leader of the protestors, told through a bullhorn that the Thai Prime Minister tried to get away with not changing anything. They said that it was the appropriate time for the Thai people to help their country. Mr. Kern Dabbaransi was a deputy Prime Minister and he was also a senior member of the Chart Pattana Party. He told that the Thai Prime Minister, who was the head of the New Aspiration Party, will mention the name of a new finance minister within 24 hours. A strong protest asking the resignation of the the Thai Prime Minister entered its third day on Wednesday, October 22, 1997 and as a result the Thai baht has plunged into record low. The Prime Minister met the leader of his government's second largest coalition partner and had talks for a cabinet reshuffle. Although the demonstration was peaceful, yet there was more bloodshed in the currency market, "with the crippled unit tumbling to a record low of 39.05 to the lollar in the domestic market". Since early July 1997 when it was devalued, the baht has fallen more than 40 per cent. The Thai Prime Minister met Mr. Chatichai Choonhavan of the Chart Pattana Party and discussed the reshuffle with them. The latter's house was very busy with activity on Thursday, October 23, 1997 as several Thai politicians gathered there for meetings with the former Prime Minister of Thailand. Mr. Sanoh Thientong, the interior minister, told,

> The Prime Minister is considering giving power back to the people to stabilise the economy, to stabilise the baht.

Mr. Suwat Liptapallop, the transport and communication minister and the Chart Pattana Party's general seceratary, told,

> the cabinet list will likely to be finalised in one or two days, but it depends on the Prime Minister.[88]

He said further that he had no idea about his party's withdrawal from the coalition. Mr. Kern Dabbaransi, the Deputy Prime Minister, stated that he requested the Prime Minister to form a new cabinet as soon as possible because the political uncertainty was so much that it hampered the progress and it give a blow to Thailand's economy. The baht fell to an all-time low of 39.60 to the dollar in Asian market on Wednesday, October 22, 1997. It was trading offshore at around 39.05 at midday on Thursday, October 23, 1997. The currency fell when the coalition partners began wrangling over the new cabinet. A government spokesman told on Friday, October 24, 1997 in Bangkok that the Thai Prime Minister reshuffled his cabinet and gave the key finance minister's post to banker Mr. Kosit Panpiemras. The reshuffle, mainly involving the economic portfolios, was announced after the Prime Minister had presented his new cabinet list to king Bhumibol Adulyadej for his approval. Mr. Panpiemras was an executive director of the Bangkok Bank. Another technocarat, the Siam City Bank, president, Mr. Som Jotusipitak's name was mentioned as commerce minister in place of Mr. Narongchai Akrasanee. The former was previously chief executive of Barli Jacker, a consumer and industrial company. Mr. Baruey Phadungsith, the former Stock Exchange of Thailand president, was mentioned as the deputy finance minister, and justice minister Mr. Suwit Hinkiti was named as deputy Prime Minister, in place of Mr. Montree Pongpanich. The reshuffle, which has made 20 changes of ministers and deputy ministers, was the second by Mr. Chavalit Yongchaiyudh since he assumed power as the Prime Minister of a six-party coalition government in last November 1996. In

88. *AA*, October 24, 1997, p. 7.

August 1997, he had reshuffled his cabinet to bring in two technocrats to oversee finance, fiscal, trade and economic matters. Mr. Panpiemras was mentioned as the third finance minister in Mr. Chavalit Yongchaiyudh's administration which had an economic crisis. The turmoil, stemming from major troubles in Thailand's debt-ridden finance sector, has seen the baht plunged more than 30 per cent since its *de facto* floatation in July 1997. Several qualified candidates did not accept the finance minister's portfolio because they were afraid to see the fate of Mr. Thanong Bhidaya and his predecessor Mr. Amnuay Virawan. They were ruined due to political interference and they knew that Mr. Chavalit Yongchaiyudh's government may not be able to rule for a very long time. It may be noted here that the country's many financial institutions were closed owing to bad loans and about 1000,000 jobs were lost because of business failures. Despite new cabinet, the Thai people expected early polla in Thailand. According to reports on Friday, October 24, 1997 in Bangkok, US oil giant the Enron Corporation has signed a three-year agreement to form a joint venture with a local partner to do work for power and water supply projects in troubled Thailand. The Enron Corporation was regarded as the world's third largest energy firm and it will take a 49-per cent stake in the venture with the EMC Group, a diversified engineering and construction company in Thailand. The Thai Prime Minister faced a revolt on Wednesday, October 29, 1997 within his own party over a cabinet reshuffle and about 31 MPs from his own New Aspiration Party, which occupied 125 Parliamentary seats, declared that they had formed a new faction to reassert themselves in the party after they lost out in the cabinet reshuffle. Mr. Chingchai Mongkoltham, the education minister, was the leader of the 'New Sunflower Group' and he became very unhappy to see Mr. Chavalit Yongchaiyudh's decision relating to cabinet reshuffle and he told that the latter did not consult his party's faithful followers. These MPs belonged to the north-eastern Thailand which was mentioned as the New Aspiration Party's major support base and this region was Thailand's poorest area. The Prime Minister tried to patch-up differences within his party and the six-party coalition he appointed 14 new ministers to receive confidence in the government. He offered an apology to Mr. Samak Sundaravej, the deputy prime minister, and the leader of the Prachakorn Thai Party, who threatened to quit the government after his party last out in the reshuffle. The Prachakorn Thai Party hold a meeting on Thursday, November 6, 1997 to take the decision to stay in the cabinet or not. The Prime Minister on Wednesday, October 29, 1997 had discussions with the MPs from the New Aspiration Party but he was unable to stop disillusioned Parliamentarians from their declaration of the formation of the 'New Sunflower Group'. The New Aspiration Party's symbol was the sunflower and Mr. Chavalit Yongchaiyudh founded this party about seven year ago when he resigned from his post as Thailand's military supreme commander and he began to take active part in Thailand's politics. He faced a very tough time now because he had to meet the various coalition demands. All the time he tried his best to satisfy them. The Thais felt frustrated to see his administrative ability to tackle the economic crisis of the country. They had no faith in his government. Under public and political pressure the Prime Minister reversed a tax hike proposed to help Thailand to meet fiscal requirements of the International Monetary Fund bailout package. Further uncertainty within the government areas on Wednesday, October 30, 1997 when there was a report that the leader of the second largest coalition party was about to resign.

About several hundred villagers, Buddhist monks and environmentalists on Sunday, November 2, 1997 protested against a multi-million dollar oil pipe-line which went through pristine forests in the western part of Thailand. Practically, the Thai Buddhist monks took the leading part in this demonstration and picked up cudgels against Thai-Myanmar pipeline project. The protestors gathered in Sai Yok National Park on the border with Myanmar and they shouted and condemned the Thai government to give premission to the 250 km (150 miles) Thai-Myanmar pipeline to run through the park. Several Thai Buddhist monks as part of the protest ordained dozens of trees on the land where the installation of the pipeline has taken place. Mr. Sor Sivalak, a prominent social critic and the main speaker at the rally, described

> with ordination, the trees will be sacred. Hopefully, the ruling elites will also respect our tradition, our culture . . . we will protect our trees.

About 20 Buddhist monks crossed a river and went into the dense jungle to ordain trees and they chanted sacred Buddhist *mantras*. They first prayed and then they blessed trees and wrapped a saffron robe around it. The demonstrators followed them and they helped them in their works and they wrapped robes around other trees of the area where the installation of the pipeline has taken place. The Thai cabinet decided on October 21, 1997 to construct the Sai Yok portion of the pipeline after the end of the rainy season. The petroleum Authority of Thailand (PAT), the sponsor of the 16.5 billion baht ($ 434.2 million) project, mentioned that about 110 km (70 miles) of the gas line has already been installed in the western Thai province of Kanchanaburi and Ratchaburi. It told that the installation of the pipeline will be completed by July 1998 as scheduled, despite the slight delay due to the demonstrations of the people and for this reason the Thai government required an environmental assessment before the installation of the pipeline in the park. According to the Thai activists, the Thai government made only a cursory environmental impact study and they told that the 8.4 km (5 miles) of pipelines which has covered about 42 acres (17 hectares) will have a very bad effect and will throw the wildlife in disorder in the area. Ms Soraida Salwala, the secretary-general of the friends of the Asuan elephant foundation, told,

> It will disturb of a lot of species, especially elephants. There is a salt lick (on the planned line) and if it goes

> through it will disturb the habitat of the wildlife. The salt lick is very important to all mammals.

But the Thai government officials mentioned that it will not disturb the forest and wildlife and its impact on them will be very minimal. Ms Soraida Salwala told,

> . . . the smell of the human beings around will drive all the wildlife away. They won't come back.

Several Myanmarese exiles also demonstrated on Sunday, Növember 2, 1997 and Myanmar's human rights groups and other activists very much opposed the Myanmar portion of the pipeline and Myanmar's military government by using force engaged workers to build roads and other infrastructure for the pipeline. The pipeline from the Yadana gas field in Myanmar's Gulf of Martaban to the state-run Electricity Generating Authority of Thailand's power plant in Ratchaburi will deliver natural gas. Under the 30-year contact with the Yadana developing group, led by French oil firm total SA, the Petroleum Authority of Thailand from the field will begin to take delivery of natural gas on July 1, 1998 at the rate of 525 million cubic feet per day.

Thailand's ruling coalition parties met on Monday, November 3, 1997 to restore the baht. The Thai skidded through the 41 baht to the US dollar mark on Friday, October 31, 1997 and several analysts predicted that it could drop as low as 50 baht to the dollar by year's end. Mr. Chavalit Yongchaiyudh on Monday, November 3, 1997 told that he would resign later this week to give way for a new leader of Thailand.[89] He was in power far about 11 months and he reported that he would seek an audience with king Bhumibol Adulyadej on Thursday, November 6, 1997 to tell him that he would resign. He stated further that

> On Wednesday, November 5, 1997 he would see through the Thai Parliament three key electoral laws under a

89. *AA*, November 4, 1997, p. 7; *ET*, November 4, 1997, p. 11.

> new anti-corruption constitution as well as six decrees on the restructuring of the crippled financial sector before he resigned.

Then he told,

> I will ask permission for an audience with the king because I think it is time to open the chance for another person to work. After that I will (continue to) work as an MP in Parliament so that the political situation will be normal and that the solving of economic problems can continue.

Earlier the Thai Prime Minister came under fresh pressure to resign because the baht hovered at record lows, the economy was in crisis and a prominent coalition leader resigned. He faced pressure from within his six-party coalition, opposition members and unhappy businessmen accused him for not taking a leading role to save Thailand from its economic problems which had disturbed its business world. He failed hopelessly to solve its economic woes. The beleaguered Prime Minister mentioned that he would resign because he had finished his work as a Prime Minister and "no-one has forced me to make an anouncement because I am not a person who can be forced." But he did not say anything about a person who, would take over the role of a caretaker Prime Minister or about the formation of the Thai government. In a letter to the Thai Prime Minister, the US President Mr. Bill Clinton told that the US would continue to work with Thailand and international financial institutions to try to help the economy which faced its worst downturn in decades. He was confident of the success of international efforts to help to solve the economic problems of Thailand. He stated in a letter,

> I want to assure you that the United States will continue to work with you and the international financial institutions to address Thailand's current financial

> difficulties. I am confident that this effort, combined with the dynamism and energy of Thailand, will ensure the success of this mutual endeavour.

The letter was released by the Thai government on Monday, November 3, 1997 in response to one wrote by Mr. Chavalit Yongchaiyudh to Mr. Bill Clinton and in it he stated his government's role to take the necessary steps to solve the country's economic crisis. Thailand in August 1997 was forced to negotiate a $ 17.2 billion international bailout package from the International Monetary Fund to help its economic problems. But the US contributed nothing to the package and for this reason it received criticism from the South-East Asian region. Mr. Chavalit Yongchaiyudh told on Tuesday, November 4, 1997 that he would resign as soon as the Thai Parliament announce its approval to pass the key financial bills and electoral reform laws. He said, "I will definitely resign after the council laws are passed". The controversial laws were presented to Parliament for approval during a special session beginning on November 5, 1997. The Thai Prime Minister said,

> My intention is to put an end to the political confusion and let the government focus on economic matters to implement the commitment the goverrment has made with the IMF.

The Thai people accused him very much because he failed to solve the country's economic crisis. He said that he would resign on Thursday, November 6, 1997. The six financial decrees were parts of the requirements mentioned by the International Monetary Fund in a $ 17.2 billion international bailout package given to Thailand in August 1997 to help to save its ailing economy. Members of Mr. Chavalit Yongchaiyudh's party and coalition made a demonstration on Wednesday, November 5, 1997 when for approval the decrees were presented to the Thai Parliament. According to several political analysts, the Prime Minister in order to ensure their approval by Parliament has submitted the passage of the laws ahead of his resignation. A new constitution which was introduced on October 11, 1997 mentioned that three key electoral laws must be passed before the dissolution of the Thai Parliament and also fresh elections must be announced originally, about six months were needed for this process. According to party sources, the Chart Pattana Party, the main opposition party, planned to form a new government. Although the Thai Prime Minister decided to go, yet the country was still in its crisis and its "shattered economy is far from being out of the weeds". Mr. Grahm Catterwell, an executive of European banking, told,

> But it is only a first step and will not mean that the country's fortunes will necessarily turn around. It will depends now on who emerges from the political wheeler-declering as the next leader. The most crucial problem facing the economy was the fate of the crippled financial sector, lumbering under the weight of more than $ 35 billion in bad debts. The really essential issue is the financial restructuring which must be carried out decisively and properly. Without action any successor to Mr. Chavalit Yongchaiyudh would labour under many of the same problems. The financial sector is the key problem plaguing the economy after institutions agreed to huge unsecured loans to entrepreneurs — mainly in the booming property sector — during Thailand's golden years in the 1980s and early 90s. The crunch came when a slowing in the world economy hit Thailand, all but killing the property industry and leaving the banks and finance companies on the brink of bankruptcy.

According to several analysts, the Thai authorities were unable to take action properly to wind them up and to limit the damage. Because they thought that their tough measures made them unpopular among business circles.

> The crisis has undermined confidence in the Thai economy, panicking its leaders who fumbled as they wondered how to tackle the scourge and sparking unrivalled protests and opposition to Mr. Chavalit Yongchaiyudh.

Several politicians in his government promised to remain together and wanted to work together without disturbing the government but they were unable to solve their problems. The Thai Prime Minister spoke to the cabinet on Tuesday, November 4, 1997 that he would present his resignation to king Bhumibol Adulyadej on Thursday, November 6, 1997 and it would be effective the following day. He stated,

> I will definitely resign after the crucial laws are passed. My intention is to put an end to the political confusion and let the government focus on economic matters to implement the commitment the goverment has made with the IMF.

During a special session which began on Wednesday, November 5, 1997 the controversial laws on finance and electoral reform were presented to Parliament. In response to Mr. Chavalit Yongchaiyudh's announcement, there was a sudden increase in the Thai stocks on Tuesday, November 4, 1997 and the baht currency jumped. Some Thai political analysts discussed his promise to resign and they opined, "the move might be a play to ease mounting pressure on the embattled premier so he could later return to job." Mr. Sukum Naunsakul, the political analyst at Ramkhamhaeng University, told,

> It is only a game for Chavalit to prolong his power. And I can bet that he will resign only to return to power.

Mr. Graham Catterwell, a country manager for Deutsche Morgan Grenfell, also commented. He described,

> Chavalit is still playing games. My guess is he wants to

> keep his coalition intact until it is time for the next general election.

Mr. Virabhongsa Ramangkura, Thailand's deputy Prime Minister, told,

> Thailand's changing politics will not effect its commitment to the IMF programme. Its implementation will not be delayed and everything will go according to schedule.

Just one day after Mr. Chavalit Yongchaiyudh's sruprise announcement, the Thai deputy Prime Minister made this comment.

King Bhumibol Adulyadej fell ill. His permanent physician told on Wednesday, November 5, 1997 that he was sickened by the political horse-trading over the will became Thailand's Prime Minister after Mr. Chavalit Yongchaiyudh.[90] Mr. Pradit Charoenthaitawee, the coronary specialist, said,

> His Majesty the king has fallen ill due to his concern over the current political situation. I therefore have drafted a statement appealing to every politician to stop political activities and to refrain form jostling for political position to the extent of delaying the formation of a government.

But a royal household official stated,

> If there is anything going on, the royal household would issue a statement as it did two years ago.

King Bhumibol Adulyadej had blood vessel surgery twice in 1995 for a heart problem. Mr. Pradit Charoenthaitawee commented at that moment when the Thai politicians were too busy and were very active over a replacement for Mr. Chavalit Yongchaiyudh because he has promised to submit his resignation to

90. *AA*, November 6, 1997, p. 1; *ibid.*, November 6, 1997, p. 6.

the Thai monarch by midnight on Thursday, November 6, 1997. King Bhumibol Adulyadej, the world's longest-reigning monarch, in times of trouble and distress in Thailand has always been a powerful force for country's unity. Although a constitutional monarch viewed as above politics, yet he has made a great influence upon Thailand's political world. On three different occasions over the past few decades, the Thai monarch has played a very significant role to make an end to bloody street demonstrations. According to several analysts, the statements by the doctor, who treated the 69-year old ruler in 1995, could help the Thai politicians to play their cautious roles in their political horse-trading. Mr. Sukhum Naunskul, a political analyst of Ramhamhaeng University, described,

> The statement may help lessen the intensity of the fighting for power. But the problem is that the Thai politicians never realise they are causing trouble.

Mr. Chavalit Yongchaiyudh made his resignation announcement on Monday, November 3, 1997, and, since then, several Thai politicians from his six-party coalition as well as the opposition members tried to agree on a new leader for Thailand. As political infighting and bargaining intensified in the wake of the Thai Prime Minister's decision to resign on Sunday, November 9, 1997, three candidates, who were all former Prime Minister of Thailand, were very active as the front runners to succeed him. They were :

1. Mr. Prem Tinsulananda was a privy councillor to constitutional monarch King Bhumibol Adulyadej. This 77-year old politician became an unelected Prime Minister from 1980 to 1988 and he guided Thailand through a deep recession in the early 1980s before its decade-long economic boom.
2. Mr. Chatichai Choonhavan was the leader of the Chart Pattana (National Development) Party. He succeeded

Mr. Prem Tinsulananda as the Prime Minister in a democratic election in 1988.

3. Mr. Chuan Leekpai was a lawyer and a leader of the Democrat Party. He was a soft-spoken person. He served as the Prime Minister from 1992 until 1995 when a land reform scandal brought down his coalition government. Despite the scandal, he is mentioned as an honest politician with a clean record. His party has skilled technocrats in economic management.

Mr. Chavalit Yongchaiyudh, the outgoing Thai Prime Minister, told, on Wednesday, November 5, 1997 that he would stay on as caretaker leader for up to nine days and the Thai politicians wrangled over the choice of a successor. He told,

> We will try to finalise a new government quickly. It should be finished in not more than seven days, or if it is slow it should not take more than eight-nine days.

It may be stated here that,

> the comments herald a longer-than-expected round of closed door political wheeler-dealing ahead of the unveling of a new leader and government to replace Mr. Chavalit Yongchaiyudh after his planned resignation on Thursday, November 6, 1997.[91]

Mr. Chavalit Yongchaiyudh said on Monday, November 3, 1997 that he would quit. Senior figure from his shaky six-party coalition then discussed to elect a new Prime Minister and to decide on the form of the next coalition government but from the discussion no new name was suggested as the new Prime Minister of Thailand. On Wednesday, November 5, 1997 the Thai opposition chief Mr. Chuan Leekpai denied a newspaper report that a deal had been struck under which he would became Prime Minister at the head of a new three-party coalition. He told that his

91. *AA*, November 7, 1997, p. 7.

Democrat Party was in contest with the party of outgoing Prime Minister Mr. Chavalit Yongchaiyudh but he mentioned that it was too early to say anything and he would see whether the current six-party coalition would work together. He told,

> We have to wait and see what happens with the six-party coalition. The six parties are still discussing their opinions and whether they can come to an arrangement to stay together, they can make a deal. He wanted to see a change in the form of the government.

According to the *Bangkok Post*, Mr. Chuan Leekpai would become Thailand's next Prime Minister after Mr. Chavalit Yongchaiyudh. The latter told on Monday, November 3, 1997 that he would submit his resignation on Thursday, November 6, 1997. He stated,

> On November 6, after my immediate duties are completed, I will inform the king to consider replacing me.

His announcement threw wide upon expectations about who might form a new government. Under-current rules, the Thai Parliament through a consensus among political parties can select any selected party representative to be the person who will become Thailand's new Prime Minister. Owing to political infighting and uncertainties, Thailand faced its economic crisis. But the Thais hoped that this new change in the political horizon would bring political stability in the progress of the economies. Mr. Somphob Manarangsan, a professor in the Economic Department of Chulalongkorn University, told,

> This will be an execellent option, if the new government is formed without political under-current. If the new government has some stability, economy will benefit from it tremendously, if not it will be put into a tailspin again. If the members of Parliament respect public sentiment

> and understand that economic stability also at this juncture depends on political stability, they will form an acceptable government to run the country.

South-East Asian currencies shed some of their gains on Wednesday, November 5, 1997 as early euphoria over Mr. Chavalit Yongchaiyudh's resignation gave way to worries about his successor. Practically, fresh worries assailed Asian currencies. In Thailand on Tuesday, November 4, 1997, the baht slipped to 39.40/66 to the dollar from 38.65/38.80. Because the political uncertainty played a role to unsettle the Thai market. There was a political horse-trading among the coalition parties of Thailand and the Chart Pattana Party's leader Mr. Chatichai Choonhavan's name apperead as Prime Minister to succeed Mr. Chavalit Yongchaiyudh. The offshore baht was at 39.60/60 against 38.40/38.50. Several suspended finance firms have lobbied Mr. Chatichai Choonhavan in his capacity as former advisor on economic affairs affairs to Mr. Chavalit Yongchaiyudh, in an effort to avoid closure. According to analysts, if he headed a new government, it no doubt would disturb the transparency of a financial reform process. Thailand's political troubles and the illness of its king brought the depression of its currency market on Thursday, November 6, 1977. In Thailand the baht lost its footing as the market awaited the outcome of talks between political parties to select a successor to Mr. Chavalit Yongchaiyudh. Former Prime Ministers Mr. Chuan Leekpai and Mr. Chatichai Choonhavan were mentioned as front-runners for the post of Thailand's Prime Minister, but conflicting Thai media reports allowed the market to act reluctantly. The head of regional currencies of one European bank in Singapore told, "At the moment, nobody even know who the actual Prime Minister is". According to the Bangkok dealers, the baht received some support from exporters with an idea that it would strengthen if the leader of the Democrat Mr. Chuan Leekpai became Thailand's Prime Minister. The baht was at 39.10/20 to the dollar onshore against 38.90/39.20 on Wednesday, November 5, 1997. Offshore the baht was at 39.20/40 agains 39.00/25. The Bangkok dealers mentioned that King Bhumibol Adulyadej's health also 'remained a source of concern'.

Mr. Chuan Leekpai, the opposition leader, on Friday, November 7, 1997, received enough votes for his appointment as Prime Minister of Thailand when defecting members of a government party supported him.[92] Several members of the Thai Citizens' Party decided to switch their allegiance to him and this came as a shock on Thursday night, November 6, 1997 to the members of the government coalition led by the New Aspiration Party of Mr. Chavalit Yongchaiyudh, the outgoing Prime Minister. The defectors played their vital roles to help the eight-party coalition led by Mr. Leekpai's Democrat Party control of at least 210 seats in the House of Representatives, where 197 seats were mentioned as a majority. Mr. Chuan Leekpai told that the Democrats on Sunday, November 9, 1997 submitted the lists of legislators in their coalition to Mr. Wan Muhammad Noor Matha, the Speaker of the House and from this the 59-year old Mr. Chuan Leekpai's name was suggested by him as the Prime Minister of Thailand. The former mentioned at a Friday's news conference (November 7, 1997) that "We now have a clear majority in the Thai Parliament". Previously, he was elected in 1992 as a Prime Minister and remained there until 1995 when a land scandal gave a blow to his coalition and his government collapsed. During his first term he was mentioned as an honest person. Mr. Chavalit Yongchaiyudh, the outgoing Prime Minister, resigned on Thursday, November 6, 1997 and this he had announced three days earlier. He was unable to play a significant role to tackle Thailand's worst economic crisis in decades and for this reason he had failed to win public confidence. While he was in his office the baht in the last week of October 1997 dropped in value from 25 to the dollar to a historic low of 41 to the dollar. Thailand's House of Representatives has approved

92. *AA*, November 8, 1997, p. 5.

three crucial laws which needed to pave the way for fresh elections. The *Bangkok Post* mentioned that the three crucial laws on Thursday, November 6, 1997 cleared their first reading but before returning to the House and the Senate for second and final readings they were scruitinised by Parliamentary Committee.

> The laws, fundamental to the process of political reform in Thailand following the adoption of a new anticraft constitution last month (October 1997), were rushed through an almost empty House of Representatives.

Most MPs were very busy in meetings at that time as political parties tried to form a new government after the resignation of Mr. Chavalit Yongchaiyudh. The opposition leader Mr. Chuan Leekpai and Mr. Chatichai Choonhavan, the leader of the second largest party in the old coalition, announced that they had enough support to form a government. Mr. Chavalit Yongchaiyudh promised new elections early next year but this will only be possible after the promulgation of the three laws.

> According to the new constitution, this process must be completed by February 7, 1998 — 120 days after the new constitution was formally adopted.

In order to stop vote-buying in the Thai general elections, the new laws were introduced.

> The three laws legislate on political parties, on the formation of a new independent commission to organise elections and on the regulations governing the election of MPs and senators.

Mr. Chavalit Yongchaiyudh told on Wednesday, November 26, 1997 that he will resign from the leadership of the New Aspiration Party which he founded and may retire from politics in the near future. Mr. Kuthep Saikrajang, a spokesman of the New Aspiration Party in a news conference disclosed,

> General Chavalit Yongchaiyudh will resign from the position of party leader on December 27, 1997. He is not willing to be reinstated because he wants to see the party to be led by younger generation.

The former Prime Minister gave his resignation on Friday, November 7, 1997 under pressure from the public, businessmen and his coalition partners because of his failure to solve Thailand's economic crisis.

Thailand's Democrat Party appeared to assume power on Saturday, November 8, 1997 as party leader Mr. Chuan Leekpai was a single stop away from royal approval for his appointment as Prime Minister. A majority of MPs gave indication to support him. A top Parliament official told that Mr. Chuan Leekpai's rival for the top post Mr. Chatichai Choonhavan had the support of less than half of legislature in the Lower House. Mr. Phaisit Phipatanakul, the secretary-general of the House of Representatives, said reporters in the Thai Parliament,

> The number of MPs supporting Mr. Chatichai Choonhavan is less than half.

After considering the lists, Mr. Wan Muhammad Noor Matha took the final decision and forwarded the lists to the Thai king for his approval on Saturday, November 8, 1997. Mr. Chuan Leekpai, 59, a former Prime Minister and a top leader of the Democrat Party, occupied his position on Friday, November 7, 1997 as the front-runner when several MPs from one party defected from the side of Mr. Chatichai Choonhavan. Both the leaders claimed their right to form a new government and this caused

> an unprecedented political stalemate in the scramble to succeed Mr. Chavalit Yongchaiyudh.

Several Thai dailies on Saturday, November 8, 1997 in their reports referred to Mr. Chuan Leekpai as victor in the political battle for the right he has captured to form a new government in Thailand. A front-page editorial in the *Bangkok Post* described,

> Mr. Chuan Leekpai may not be perfect but he is the best choice under the present circumstance and also under democratic rule.

According to a daily newspaper, the Thai public with 'hope and relief' became extremely happy to see Mr. Chuan Leekpai as the new leader and this reflected on Friday, November 7, 1997 in a 3.1 per cent gain on the bourse and the battered currency against the dollar became strong.

> The only debacle to Mr. Chuan Leekpai recapturing the post he hold from 1992 to 1995 came from the leader of the small Prachakorn Thai Party who refuses to formally acknowledge defections of his party's MPs from Mr. Chatichai Choonhavan's camp.

Mr. Samak Sundaravej, the leader of the Prachakorn Thai Party, announced his MPs support for Chatichai Choonhavan but at least fourteen of his party's eighteen MPs wrote a letter to the Speaker, Mr. Wan Muhammad Noor Matha, and they mentioned in it that they fully supported Mr. Chuan Leekpai. The support of the MPs of the Prachakorn Thai Party decided the fate of the candidates and it helped Mr. Chuan Leekpai to secure a majority and to obtain the right to form a government in Thailand. He has received the support of at least 210 parlimentarians including the Prachakorn Thai Party MPs in the 393-seat House. Mr. Samak Sundaravej in the nomination of a new Prime Minister declared strongly the right of a party leader to determins the allegiances. He met the Lower House Speaker and then said,

> I want to ask Mr. Chuan Leekpai how would he fool if twenty MPs of his party submit a letter to support Mr. Chatichai Choonhavan?

Mr. Phaisit Phipatanakul, the secretary-general of the House of

Representative, stated that the speaker first considered the lists prepared by the party leaders and afterwards he also considered the decision taken by individual MPs. Mr. Chuan Leekpai, the longest serving elected Prime Minister in Thailand's history, received full support from the financial community, because this community wanted a Democrat-led administration to play its great role to establish Thailand upon a solid foundation from its economic crisis. The Thai people became happy to see Mr. Chuan Leekpai as Thailand's new Prime Minister. Until a new leader took the charge of the Prime Minister, Mr. Chavalit Yongchaiyudh remained as caretaker Prime Minister of Thailand. The Thai monarch Mr. Bhumibol Adulyadej officially appointed Mr. Chuan Leekpai as Thailand's Prime Minister on Sunday, November 9, 1997 to lead Thailand out of the economic turmoil that forced his predecessor to resign. Mr. Chuan Leekpai, the leader of the opposition Democrat Party, was the Prime Minister of Thailand from September 1992 to July 1995. He, the leader of the main opposition Democrat Party, was regarded as an able person to solve Thailand's financial problems and on Sunday, November 9, 1997 he was named as the Prime Minister of Thailand. At party headquarters in front of hundreds of cheering supporters, a senior Parliamentary official presented him. He from a total of eight political parties led a new coalition government comprising about 210 members of the Thai Parliament. His own Democrat Party had 123 seats in Parliament. The Thai markets and the Thai investors wanted to see him as Thailand's Prime Minister because they thought that his significant role would save Thailand form its crisis. Mr. Archit Urairat, a senior Democrat MP, told,

> We really did not want it (get the government) this way and would have preferred to an election with a landslide victory. But it is a period of crisis and we have to do something for the country.

At first the Democrat Party hesitated to accept the task of

forming the government but on seeing the country's hopeless condition, it had to accept it. A new cabinet was formed and the most key economic portfolios were held by the Democrats. Mr. Chuan Leekpai vowed on Sunday, November 9, 1997 to the nation's woos but told that time and the people's co-operation were greatly needed to solve the country's crisis. He said,

> I realise that you have set high expectations. We will do our best not to let you down but I would like to say that all things leading to a better future cannot be achieved if we do not accept the reality and do not co-operate.

He mentioned it at a news conference on Sunday, November 9, 1997 at Bangkok. The Bangkok citizens showed their optimistic attitude towards new government. They were hopeful that Thailand's new Democrat-led government "means the beginning of the end of the country's worst financial and economic crisis in decades". A worker at US multi-national firm told,

> A new government means a new chance for us to get things right. The new Prime Minister has an excellent economic team and I hope that things will now start to improve.

Mr. Chuan Leekpai's appointment took place on Sunday, November 9, 1997 when he promised to do his best to solve his country's financial problems but at the same time he mentioned that he needed time and the co-operation of the Thai people to succeed. Many Thai people had great faith in the new government. A hotel receptionist mentioned,

> I am praying for Mr. Chuan Leekpai. He is a good and honest man. He must choose a cabinet that is above politics. Now is not the time to be arguing and fighting. She was hopeful for the future because the fall in the baht menat more people are coming to take a holiday in Bangkok.... The baht's fall is bad for sometime, but we

> have befefitted and I think this will continue.

But one office worker, however, pointed out that the baht's fall brought a very bad effect upon her company. She opined,

> We are a US firm and this baht decline has meant our prices have gone up by nearly a third. People are not buying.

A salesman at a British firm in Bangkok was very happy to see the new government in power. He hoped that Thailand's business would be prospered. According to several political analysts, Thailand's new government took shape on Monday, November 10, 1997 and it was just one day after the Democrat Party leader Mr. Chuan Leekpai assumed power as the new Prime Minister of Thailand. Mr. Sanan Kajornprasart, the secretary-general of the Democrat Party, stated,

> The forming of the new cabinet is about to be completed and the government will be able to start to work as soon as possible.

He took active part in the negotiations which brought all MPs from eight parties in the coalition to form a new government under the leadership of Mr. Chuan Leekpai. Thailand's new Prime Minister Mr. Chuan Leekpai and two members of his economic team, former finance minister Mr. Tarrin Nimmanahaeminda and former central banker Mr. Supachai Panitchapakdi in a news conference on Sunday, November 9, 1997 announced that the top priority of the new government was to revive the economy of Thailand.[93]

Mr. Michel Camdessus, the managing director of the International Monetary Fund, met Thailand's government on Friday, November 14, 1997 to secure a commitment that it will do its best to stick to the canditions of the International Monetary

---

93. *ET*, November 11, 1997, p.11.

Fund rescue deal. The new Thai government received the news of his arrival in Thailand after the appointment Mr. Chuan Leekpai as Thailand's Prime Minister by king Bhumibol Adulyadej. The leading *Nation* daily mentioned that the International Monetary Fund chief, in order to check progress on the bailout deals extended to the two limping Asian 'Tiger' economies, visited Bangkok and Indonesian capital Jakarta. Earlier Mr. Camdessus had mentioned his visit to South-East Asia to review the progress of Thailand and Indonesia in implementing the tough conditions imposed on them under the International Monetary Fund Programmes. He had met Mr. Chavalit Yongchaiyudh in September 1997 and announced his satisfaction with Thailand's adherence to the International Monetary Fund conditions for its rescue deal. The Thai people hoped that Mr. Chuan Leekpai's government would play a great role to help to stabilise Thailand's markets and to boost confidence in the Thai economy. Thailand must produce a budget surplus in 1998. Because it would help to keep its current account deficit in check and would give encouragement to move fast to restructure the crippled financial sector which was in a bad shape and was troubled by the weight of more than $ 35 billion in bad debts. According to several Thai analysts, Thailand should renegotiate with the International Monetary Fund for less stringent rescue package. Because it would need more money from the International Monetary Fund and its economy would be in trouble to face the tough budget cuts which the International Monetary Fund directed it to do it. According to reports on Tuesday, November 18, 1997, the International Monetary Fund, in order to help to establish its economy on solid foundation from its economic turmoil, has agreed to lift its foreign debt coiling from $ 5 billion to $ 9 billion. The *Bangkok Post* reported that the Thai government has made a plan to boost liquidity through more loans from foreign financial institutions and has tried to play a very cautious role to save the economy from contracting and sinking into recession. Mr. Tarrin Nimmanhaeminda told that the International Monetary Fund showed its sympathetic attitude towards the new Thai governmetn and in order to cover the necessary increase in borrowing, it has agreed to increase the debt coiling. It believed that without move, the economy registered no growth or shrink in 1997 and it have $ 17.2 billion dollar bail-out package to Thailand. The latter also borrowed $ 2.7 billion from the World Bank and the Asian Development Bank. It also wanted to borrow a further $ 6.3 billion. Mr. Supachai Panitchapakdi, one of the prominent figure of the new Thai government's economic team, mentioned that in order to boost growth and to tackle unemployment, money would be pumped into the economy through spending on essential projects. He described further that without increasing spending, the economy could fail heavily into a long recession. He also stated that the International Monetary Fund programme was finalised in August 1997 and under this agreement the economy was forecast to grew in 1997 by 2.5-3.5 per cent, but under the current conditions, the Thai economy would not be in a position to reach its target. In order to meet the International Monetary Fund's requirements for the bailout package, Thailand should move in a way to maintain a budget surplus in the fiscal year to Septimebr 1998 of one per cent or about 70 billion baht or $ 1.8 billion. The Thai Prime Minister and his economic team met Mr. Michel Camdessus and they promised him that they would play a constructive role to implement the programme of the International Monetary Fund and they would do their best to restore the confidence of the investors.

Mr. Chuan Leekpai, Thailand's Prime Minister, met Mr. Bhumibol Adulyadej, Thailand's monarch, on Monday, November 10, 1997 and he had a discussion with the coalition partners over a new cabinet line-up to solve his country's economic crisis. He received a royal appointment letter on Sunday, November 9, 1997 and it referred to him as Thailand's 23rd Prime Minister.[94]

---

94. *AA*, November 11, 1997, p. 7.

With an idea to complete the process he met face to face with the Thai king, the constitutional monarch of Thailand on Monday, November 10, 1997 and in his discussion with him he vowed that in order to cure Thailand's economic woes he would take quick and resolute action. According to several Thai analysts, his government could be more stable than Mr. Chavalit Yongchaiyudh's government, which was led by the New Aspiration Party. Mr. Suchit Boonbongkarn, the Dean of the Political Science Department of Chulalongkorn University in Bangkok, mentioned,

> This new coalition will no more stable because the Democrats are so much larger that the second largest party in it.

They had 123 MPs and the Chart Pattana Thai Party had just 39. Mr. Chuan Leekpai in his economic team has brought several prominent bankers. Mr. Tarrin Nimmanhaeminda was a minister of finance, Mr. Supachai Punitchapakdi was a minister of commerce and deputy Prime Minister and Gen Sanan Kajornprasart became a minister of interior and also the minister of defence. The Chart Pattana Thai Party wanted the portfolio of transport and communications, but it received the ministrry of education. According to senior party sources, Mr. Chuan Leekpai with his 123-seat Democrat Party on Tuesday, November 11, 1997 finalised on eight-party cabinet which on Wednesday, November 12, 1997 was sworn in by king Bhumibol Adulyadej and Friday, November 14, 1997 was fixed for its first meeting. In the first cabinet meeting Mr. Chuan Leekpai's policy statement was prepared and this was presented to the Thai Parliament and this was his first official job before his govenment began to work. After his policy speech in Parliament, he left for the Apec meeting and the summit was set for November 24 and 25 in Vancouver in Canada. The Democrat Party took the finance, foreign affairs and commerce portfolios. In Thailand the baht slipped to 37.40/60 to the dollar from 37.10/37.30 on Monday, November 10, 1997.

as initial euphoria over the appointment of the new Prime Minister Mr. Chuan Leekpai faded.

According to the Thai dealers, the market was awaiting to hear details of Mr. Chuan Leekpai's new cabinet and it considered steps for the rehabilitation of the financial sector. A foreign bank dealer in Bangkok told,

> Prime Minister Mr. Chuan Leekpai will have to move fast to capitalise on the positive sentiment the public has for him.

When he was appointed by king Bhumibel Adulyadej as Thailand's Prime Minister, the country offered a glimmer of hope to the Thai investors. He was a respected former Prime Minister and he emerged as the leader of Thailand's new government on Sunday, November 9, 1997 after the resignation of Mr. Chavalit Yongchaiyudh on Thursday, November 6, 1997. He then immediately vowed to work closely wity the International Monetary Fund, The foreign exchange market gave him the benefit of doubt as the bast became strong but other South-East Asian currencies showed their weakness. At 1510 EST-2010 GMT, the baht was quoted 37.30-60 to the dollar. Mr. Feroz Talyarkhan, the Managing Director of Asian fixed income research at Bear, Stearms and Co. Inc, told,

> Mr. Chuan Leekpai has to capitalise on renewed sentiment with a clear and bold economic restoration programme to get the country back on its feet.

Since the bailout package sanctioned by the International Monetary Fund was introduced in August 1997, the Thai government has failed to fulfil the conditions imposed by the International Monetary Fund to disburse the loan. For this reason, Mr. Chuan Leekpai has moved in very clever way and has acted in his administration according to the conditions of the International Monetary Fund to save his country from disgrace. In order to win confidence of his people, his government has tried its best to show its good performance. The Thai traders doubted as to whether he could have the courage to support to introduce a stringent austerity programme and to close fifty-eight troubled finance companies as directed by the International Monetary Fund. A currency dealer with a US bank described,

> Mr. Chuan Leekpai has a reputation of being a waffler. Because of his personal integrity, he may be the best choice, but his penchant for concialiation poses a danger of watering down any reform proposals.

He and his 'economic dream team' met top World Bank and the International Monetary Fund officials on Friday and Saturday, November 14 and 15, 1997. They reassured those visiting executives that politics would not play a role to interfere with efforts to rescue the economy. These officials have asked the Thai government to practise austerity measures to fulfil its conditions. But the Thais have doubted about the political will for their implementations.

Hundreds of disgruntled employees of fifty-eight suspended finance firms on Wednesday, November 12, 1997 outside the Bank of Thailand staged a noisy protest and shouted and accused the central bank for not doing its proper role to deal with the problems of their companies. The protestors, most of whom either had been laid off or about to lose their jobs, requested the central bank to take responsibility. There were placards with them and in them they mentioned,

> It is the Bank of Thailand's fault, but the finance firms are the ones to die. It is time to review the role and neutrality of the central bank.

The protestors submitted an open letter to the Bank of Thailand and in it they demanded it to set-up a committee to investigate fully and asked it to punish those who were fully responsible for not tackling the problems in a proper way in the finance sector.

It also urged the bank to review its supervisory role over financial institutions and to give more co-operation to foreign creditors of finance companies. About 1000 people took part in Thailand in this protest to show that owing to the fault of the Bank of Thailand they have lost everything, and in it they expressed their displeasure. The Bank of Thailand reported on Friday, November 14, 1997 that its foreign exchange reserves totalled $ 31.3 billion as of October 31, 1997, up from $ 30.7 billion mentioned as of October 15, 1997. The figure includes several billion dollars $ 17.2 bailout package approved by the International Monetary Fund. The Central Bank mentioned that total reseve money, cash in circulation plus deposits of financial institutions with the BOT, amounted to $ 11.4 billion. Mr. Michel Camdessus, the chief of the International Monetary Fund after his meeting with Mr. Chuan Leekpai hoped that if Thailand's new government properly observes austerity measure, sticks to the programme mentioned by the International Monetary Fund and restructures financial and industrial sectors, then its collapsing economy will be prospered and it will move in a proper way to find its renewed growth in the second half of 1998. From a Thai report it is learnt that Thailand's new foreign minister Mr. Surin Pitswan has promised that his ministry would help to boost the country's flagging export sector by not only giving co-operation to the finance ministry but also helping it in every way. He described,

> Together with economic-related assignments, the ministry will also campaign more to the outside world about our well-structural democracy, of which our political reform could be our best example.

Mr. Chuan Leekpai, Thailand's new Prime Minister, on Thursday, November 18, 1997 announced a two-track policy to beat the country's worst economic crisis in decades.[95] He, at the top of his economic agenda, wanted to restructure the financial sector.

---

95. *AA*, November 21, 1997, p. 18.

In the Thai Parliament he said that support from the international funds would not on its own restore faith in the Thai economy. In order to boost its foreign reserves, Thailand received a $ 17.2 billion bailout package from the International Monetary Fund. Tough austerity measures and a restructuring of the finance sector were mentioned as requirements of the package. Mr. Chuan Leekpai delivered a prepared policy statement at the opening of a two-day Parliamentary debate and he told that the Thai government would impose immediate steps to restore confidence and stabilise the Thai economy and within six months to one year medium-term policy would be effective. Since its floatation in July 1997, the currency has dropped sharply by over 30 per cent against the dollar and the cost of living became very high in Thailand. In investment and trade it also faced problem. The Thai government would appoint its Financial Restructuring Authority to allow those which can increase their capital to invest in Thailand to resume operations immediately, and to help these who have problems to seek mergers with local or foreign partners. He wanted to boost liquidity and to solve finance sectors' problems. It also mentioned that an issue relating to the problems of the fifty-eight suspended Thai finance companies has overhung the Thai financial markets for months. It would close the remaining troubled companies and its Asset Managment Corporation would manage their bad assets. Several Thai financial institutions have suffered very much owing to $ 33.3 billion in bad loans. The Thai Government in order to boost foreign exchange earnings took keen interest in the promotion of exports and the tourism trade. The Thai Prime Minister stated that medium-term measures would be used to restructure the company and to improve Thailand's competitiveness and also to develop efficiency in agriculture and industrial production. The Thai government in the capitalisation of state enteprises in the stock market tried to promote the private sector's role and also showed its interest to improve capital sources. In order to raise exports it would boost funds provided to the Export-Import Bank. Thailand's First Bangkok City Bank Plc. discussed with foreign financial institutions including the US-based City or Citi Bank about their participation in a planned capital increase. A Thaimex Finance and Securities analyst mentioned that if Citi Bank manages to acquire a controlling stake, then it would be great news for the medium-sized Thai Commercial bank. According to an official,

> With Citibank in the picture, Thailand's First Bangkok City Bank will be in the forefront of the banking industry and it will be one bank to keep an eye on 'as it moves from strength to strength'.

Thailand's Prime Minister attended an Apec summit in Vancouver in Canada. Several top Asia-Pacific leaders in Vancouver for an annual summit tried to calm markets disturbed by Asia's economic crisis on Sunday, November 23,1997. Mr. Bill Clinton, the US President, gave a news conference at the Asia Pacific Economic Co-operation forum, He stated,

> I think this is a time for confidence in the future of Asia. We have a few little glitches in the road here. We are working through them. Asia's ddifficulties were serious but he was confident they could be resolved. We need to approach this with determination, but with confidence. We need to take this very seriously.[96]

Here several summit leaders moved to discuss the fallout from Asia's fast-spreading economic crisis. In bilateral meetings, they did their best to hammer out their rsponse to the Asian crisis before the formal summit on Monday and Tuesday, November 24 and 25, 1997. On Sunday, November 23, 1998 several thousand leftist demonstrators demonstrated in Vancouver to protest the absence of human rights on the agenda of the Asia-Pacific Economic Co-operation summit which took place on Monday and

96. *AA*, November 25, 1997, p. 18.

Tuesday, November 24 and 25, 1997. Mr. Bill Clinton urged Beijing and Jakarta to release their political prisoners. He also criticised the summit for not focusing on the issue of the human rights. Mr. Mike Jondrzejezyk, the Washington director of Human Rights Watch, Asia, told on Monday, November 24,1997,

> President Clinton is meeting on Tuesday, November 25, 1997 with the leaders of China and Indonesia, two big emerging markets and even bigger human rights abusers.

He said further that both Chinese President Jiang Zemin and Indonesian President Suharto have

> tried to deflect domestic and international criticism of their human rights practices by hiding behind the 'Asian Miracle' of economic growth. But ironically, it is now a lack of open, accountable governance — a major cause of human rights problem — this is eroding confidence in many of Asia's leaders.

According to a draft summit communique, the Asia-Pacific leaders sent a bold message of confidence that Asia's troubled economies will soon recover from the economic turmoil. They kept faith in Asia and backed bailout plan for the countries hit by the crisis. They told that they would play a great role together to make sure the region was on the right path. The draft mentioned,

> Certain of the dynamism and resilience of the region, we underline our resolve to achieve sustainable growth and equitable development and to unload the full potential of the people who live here.

The leaders met on Tuesday, November 25, 1997 to finalise the draft communique at the end of their two-day summit. They also endorsed the Manila Plan which was attended by the deputy finance minister. The draft described,

> We believe it is critically important that we move quickly to enhance the capacity of the international system to prevent and respond to financial crisis of this kind. Therefore, we welcome and strongly endorse the framework agreed to in Manila as a constructive step to enhance co-operation and to promote financial stability.

The summit leaders also supported a proposal from their trade ministers to start liberalising trade in nine key sectors describing work in 1998 and implementing their plan in 1999. The draft stated,

> We find this package to be mutually beneficial and to represent a balance of interests.

The nine sectors were environment and services, medical, energy, forests, fish, toys, game and telecommunications. In 1998 several trade ministers for free trade in the region met and discussed six other sectors which were oilseeds, food products, rubber, fertilisers, automotive standards and civil aircraft. The Apec leaders wanted to open up financial service markets under the World Trade Organisation. The draft said that opening up financial service markets will improve competition and 'strongthen our economies' resilience in the face of external shocks". According to Western delegates, a strong showing of support by the eighteen-member organisation for free trade and open financial service markets would no doubt give a chance to restore investors' confidence in the faltering markets.

> Apec spelt out its vision for the next century. Included in its blueprint for the future was a commitment to expand electronic commerce in the entire region.

Mr. Bill Clinton saw really strong confidence in the future. His assessment came at the end of the eighteen-member Asia Pacific Economic Co-operation Forum which found its main task was dealing with the economic uncertainty sweeping through several

Asian capitals, including Thailand, South Korea and Japan. The US President told,

> We proved that our community is for good times and for challenging ones as well. Asia's financial difficulties could have made a turn inward, may be even to stay home. . . . But instead, we agreed to open trade in nine new areas totalling $ 1.5 trillion in goods and services. This is a really strong vote of confidence in our common future. We also supported an action plan to meet the financial challenges that we all face in Asia and I say that advisedly.

The summit leaders on Tuesday, November 25, 1997 met for more than three hours and discussed their concerns about the situation. Mr. Bill Clinton said,

> We all face them because Canada and the United States will not be unaffected unless we can restore confidence build and forward progress throughout the Asian area. We believe that the affected countries are doing the right thing, committing to take the right steps to remain strong. Last year, we set an agenda for more open trade. This year, we have set an agenda to help us meet the challenges of the international financial system in the 21st century, and to tackle other problems.

The Apec leaders endorsed an international rescue plan for countries disturbed by the economic crisis,

> putting the IMF and its strict reform requirements at the centre of any international bailout, with financing from individual countries as a backup.

The officials from the US mentioned that the financial crisis in the region did not disturb the accomplishemnts of the annual gathering. Mr. Daniel Tarulle, Mr. Clinton's international economic policy advisor, said

What is important is an effort to agree upon and implement the principle that are necessary for stabilising countries in East Asia and indeed around the world.

The Declaration :

We, Apec's leaders reaffirm our commitment to work together to meet the challenge of sustaining regional prosperity and stability. Certain of the dynamic and resilience of the region, to underline our resolve to achieve sustainable growth and equitable development and to unlock the full potential of the people who are here. We agree that the prospects for economic growth in the region are strong, and the Asia-Pacific will continue to play a leading role in the global economy. We take note of the rapid expansion of Apec's activities in recent years, and the increasing leadership role it plays in global economic affairs. Flowing from commitment embodied in the Osaka Agenda and the Manila Action Plan for Apec, we welcome the designation of 1997 as Apec's year of Action. We have reflected on the concrete results that Apec co-operation has generated throughout the year, and set out a vision of how, we may build upon these achievements in the years ahead. As the year draws to a close, we note with satisfaction that we have met and surpassed all that we set for ourselves at our last meeting. Addressing shared challenges : We have had a thorough discussion of recent financial developments in the regions. Our economic and the international community as a whole have a strong interest in seeing a quick and enduring restoration of financial stability and healthy and sustainable growth. These events reflect new challenges in the international financial system that requires new responses. The global dimensions of these problems suggest the need for a global response, with regional initiatives to complement and support therse

> efforts. We are resolved to work together to address these shared challenges. There is no doubt that the fundamentals for long-term growth and prospects for the region are exceptionally strong. We remain convinced that open market will bring significant benefits and we will continue to pursue trade and investment liberalisation to foster further growth.

Several Apec critics have criticised in Vancouver on Wednesday, November 26, 1997 that the economic globalisation proposed by the Asia-Pacific Economic Co-operation Forum was responsible for the recent havoc on regional financial markets. Mr. Walden Belle, director of the Bangkok-based Global Focus on the South, at a press conference told,

> The main culprit in the Asian collapse is the private sector, not the state sector. This is a crisis because of the abdication of government, not because of government. Throughout the west there was a consensus that the tigers of South-East Asia, the economic miracles, were the wave of the future and that Asia would be the engine of the world economy far into the 21st century. Asia is no longer seen as the source of miracles. It is seen as the most significant threat to the world economy. Financial liberalisation is the culprit of this crisis. This is a model of development that, despite a sort of trickle down effect in terms of ranking absolute incomes, was in fact marked by widening income disparities throughout the Asia-Pacific region. What we are seeing offered by the United States government, many of the countries here, and the IMF is that the answer to this crisis is more liberalisation. The prime force behind Asian liberalisation is the United States. The United States, the prime power within Apec has came here to pitch a programme of financial and full liberalisation.

It may be noted here that once Thailand was regarded as a model for other regional economies, but now it has received a $ 17.2 billion bailout package approved by the International Monetary Fund. When its currency collapsed, then Thailand appealed to the International Monetary Fund for its help. Mr. Walden Belle said,

> The IMF, driven by the theology of globalisastion, accompanied its aid with a set of policies for Thailand aimed at attracting foreign capital. As a result, the Thai government lost control of monetary policy. Thailand agreed to undergo structural adjustment, a formula for higher interest rates and local currency stabilisation. High interest rates shut out stable deomestic investment. This was the magic formula that was blessed by the World Bank, the International Monetary Fund and the US Treasury Department.

It may be mentioned here that organisers of Vancouver People's Summit, a group of human rights and labour activists, showed an anti-Apec massage to the city's streets on Sunday, November 23, 1997 and about 1000 people took part in this protest March. A protest against China's policy in Tibet was also planned. Mr. J. Argua, who co-ordinated the summit's working group on poverty, told,

> Apec does not deal with these issues. It is entirely focus on helping business to increase its own resources and trade and not with any social concerns.

Australia, Brunei, Canada, Chile, Malaysia, Mexico, New Zealand, Papua New Guinea, the Philippines, Singapore, Taiwan, Thailand and the United States of the Apec groups attended this summit.

According to the Asian Development Bank, the South-East Asian currencies grew by an average of 6.4 per cent between 1981 and 1990. Over the next six years this surged to 7.4 per cent with Thailand leading the way. Mr. Michel Camdessus, the

IMF chief, told,

> numerous sings of a gathering storm were found in Thailand : an appreciating currency amid slowing exports, a wide current-account deficit, financed by a substantial amount of short-term capital, rising external debt, inflated property prices and a weak and over-exposed banking system.

When Thailand's currency fell in July 1997, neighbours' exchange rates were under pressure and their less serious shortcomings were brought under a magnifying glass. Frantic efforts to improve markets controls only saw the hastening of a capital stampede. The crisis brought the downfall of Mr. Chavalit Yongchaiyudh's government and it also witnessed the return of Mr. Chuan Leekpai as the Prime Minister of Thailand. This gave him the inevitable task of implementing major reforms linked to a $ 17.2 billion dollar bailout package approved by the International Monetary Fund in August 1997. Investment houses referred to zero growth in Thailand in 1997 and negative figures in 1998 'with the situation easing in 1999 — if reforms take hold'. The Thai government itself has downgraded its 1997 forecast to 0.6 per cent from 2.5 per cent and the 1998 figures to zero to 1/2 per cent, from 3.5 per cent. Since July 2, when Thailand effectively devalued its currency and triggered the crisis, the dollar has gained an average of 38 per cent against the South-East Asian currencies.

Thailand's Buddhist monks were among the latest Thais who wanted to play a very prominent part to solve its economic woes. A group of monks in southern Thailand have started an appeal to help the government to repay loans from the International Monetary Fund. They took the decision to offer the money which was kept in common fund from their annual Thed Pha Pa fundraising campaign to the Thai government to repay loans. The money generally used for the maintenance of the Buddhist temples and also for the Buddhist monk's living expenses. Rev.

Phra Khru Prasrrnaawikhat, chief of the monks in the Sawi district of the Chumphon Province, told,

> When the economy of the country is good, people donate generously to the monks to build and maintain temples. Now the country is facing an economic crisis so the monks will organise Thed Pha Pa to rebuild the country.

In southern Thailand the campaign had already began and more than thousand people had already promised them to pay cash. The donations ranged from $ 1 to 100,000 baht.

The baht plunged to a new record low of 41.05 offshore amid strong corporate demand for dollar. Thailand's financial chiefs launched a bid on Wednesday, December 3, 1997 to allay fears over the collapsing currency. Mr. Tarrin Nimmanahaeminda, the finance minister, and Mr. Chaiyawat Wibulsawasdi, the governor of the Bank of Thailand, told that the baht would remain under pressure for 'a few days' because the market would stay for sometime to see the final conclusion of a rescue package which was negotiating at that time between South Korea and the International Monetary Fund. Both persons admitted that the baht's fall took place owing to external factors and there was no scope for intervention. The governor of the Bank of Thailand described that the baht along with other regional currencies would improve when South Korea would sign the programme of the International Monetary Fund. Then the rehabilitation plans for the 58 suspended finance companies would be announced and then the pressure will be relieved. Mr. Chaiyawat Wibulsawasdi mentioned further that the Bank of Thailand would continue to monitor the situation closely and may also 'direct the currency'. The Thai Commerce Ministry announced on Wednesday, December 3, 1997 that the Thai exports to the United States rose 24 per cent in the first nine months of 1997 compared with the same period in 1996 because of the plunging baht. Total Thai-US trade was up 15 per cent to $ 9.95 billion, with a surplus of 47.44 billion baht in favour of Thailand and this was an increase of 276 per cent on the same period, last year (1996). Mr. Manop Thongyen, the director of the ministry's trade statistics centre, opined that the depreciation in the Thai Unit since July 1997 had encouraged exports. Industrial goods valued at 194.78 billion baht made up 84 per cent of exports. Other goods included ready-to-wear garments worth 28.32 billion baht and computer and components worth 29.95 billion baht. In the first nine months of 1997 American imports had only increased by six per cent, valued, at 185.25 billion baht including integrated circuits and electrical machinery and cmoponents. But Mr. Manop Thongyen told that after September 1997 Thailand's export growth was not able to maintain the same high level as the value of currencies in competitor nations in South-East Asia had also plunged. Thailand's Central Bank in order to prevent further weakening on the local currency, has requested ten leading local companies to change US dollars into the baht. These companies were the CP Group, Siam City Cement Plc., Barli Jacker Plc., Thai Oil, Shinawatra Group, TPI Group, Total Access Communication Plc., Jasmine International Plc., Tripetch Isuzu and Tuntwx Plc. The English-language daily the *Nation* referred to it as an 'unprecedented move' because the Central Bank usually does not discuss such type of talks with the private companies. Some domestic exporters have also been told to change their dollars into the baht.

> The Thai Unit fell because of the regional economic turmoil and as the Thai companies rushed to buy the dollars to hedge their foreign borrowings, which are growing more difficult to service as the baht dives.

The finance minister and the Central Bank governor mentioned that the Thai government watched the currency very closely and announced that the baht would remain under pressure for a few days amid the latest regional anxieties. Mr. Supachai Panitchapakdi stated that the baht would stabilies in the second half of 1998 as capital inflows would begin to return because

Thailand has already imposed its own International Monetary Fund rescue programme. A Western analyst warned on Thursday, December 4, 1997,

> The markets are worried about mounting foreign debts caused by the fall of the baht and by the cost for exporters of buying dollars.

Thailand has over $ 100 billion of overseas debt and about $ 70 billion of it owed by the private sector. Many Thai firms with overseas loans have made profits but they were in great troubles by huge foreign exchange losses. Several Thai analysts told on Monday, December 1, 1997 that the fifty-eight (58) suspended Thai finance firms wanted a clear policy relating to their affairs from the Thai government. They mentioned that fewer than ten of the fifty-eight suspended finance companies would be allowed to re-open to function their companies when the Thai finance minister would disclose their fate. Mr. Thanawat Patchimkul, the vice-president of Sri Dhana DBS Securities, described,

> A major concern lies on how the government would handle on loans given by closed finance companies to their good customers. The government should solve this problem for them.

Mr. Vichien Tangadtaisak, the president of the suspended Thai Finance and Securities Co. Ltd., stated that the Thai Government must do something to solve the problems of overseas loans estimated as $ 16 billion for the suspended companies. He opined,

> I hope that the government could give equal treatment and in a transparent manner when making its decision. Also I hope that companies which are allowed to resume business could win back confidence from the public.

The Financial Restructuring Agency was set up to assess the status of the firms and to separate their good and bad status.

Thailand decided to take decision on the fate of the fifty-eight suspended finance companies in December 1997. Most players in the Thai financial markets resigned. Mr. Kavee Chukijkasem of the Capital Naemura Securities Plc. told,

> The mere that are closed down, the better in boosting market sentiment. Any signs of government wavering would weaken public faith in its resolve to clean up problems.

Several Thai analysts described,

> the kind of action the new government of premier Chuan Leekpai which came to power on November 15 with support from big businesses took against the suspended firms would measure its credibility and possible future in power.

Mr. Michel Camdessus, the managing director of the International Monetary Fund, disclosed in the first week of November 1997 that most of the suspended finance firms were insolvent and should be closed. Those firms before their suspension borrowed 430 billion baht ($ 11 billion) from the Central Bank's Financial Institutions Development Fund (FIDF) to meet public runs on their deposits. The Financial Restructuring Agency chief has completed the screening of rehabilitation plans from the firms and submitted the results to the finance minister. Top officials of the finance ministry and the Central Bank discussed the plan and the handling of the situation on Monday, December 8, 1997. Mr. Twatchai Yongkittikul, the Financial Restructuring Agency chief and Mr. Tarrin Nimmanahaeminda, the finance minister, disclosed the restructuring plan for the sector at a special news conference on Monday, December 8, 1997 and these activities practically helped to decide the economic future of the country. The Asian financial markets awaited and watched very closely Thailand's decision of fifty-eight ailing finance firms along with development in South Korea and Malaysia after another whiteknunkle week in the region's dealing rooms. Mr. Chuan Leekpai, the Thai Premier on Monday, December 8, 1997 announced his decision on the suspended firms. Thailand's new government tackled the country's most urgent ecomomic crisis in a long-awaited frontal assault and gave order to shut down all but two of the fifty-eight debt-ridden finance firms suspended earlier this year (1997). This move no doubt made thousands of workers jobless but it was one of the key measures referred to by the International Monetary Fund under a $ 17.2 billion bailout package. The Thai analysts opined in praise of the authorities' tough action in this matter. A Western banker told,

> At last, the government has taken the bull by the horns and done something positive and tough to help limit the damage to the economy and put Thailand on the road to an eventual recovery. But we have to wait and see exactly what will happen in practice as the process of winding up the firms and steadying the economy will take many months.

Mr. Twatchai Yongkittikul, the Financial Reatructuring Agency head, stated that the authorities has only allowed two of fifty-eight rehabilitation schemes. These were Kiatnakin Finance and Securities Co. Ltd. and Bangkok Investment Plc. He discussed further that fifty-six other companies, wallowing in billions of dollars of bad debt, will immediately be closed permanently. Thailand's finance minister mentioned that the decision has helped to

> restore confidence to the economy by eliminating the instability caused by the technically bankrupt firms and put Thailand back on the path to growth. The decision announced a clear signal that Thailand wanted to rebuild a strong and Viable financial sector. The sooner the financial system is restored to health, the quicker the economy will recover, making sustainable growth certain

in the future.

By mid-February 1998 the good assets, performing loans, will be stripped from the fifty-six closed firms and will be deposited to one or two commercial banks. The fifty-six firms have failed to receive approval from the authorities to re-open but some of them could be merged into one or two commercial banks by February 1998. The Thai government may have to absorb more than $ 5 billion in public deposits and debt held by these firms and for this reason a committee was established to work the credibility of the Bank of Thailand. The Thai finance minister stated,

> We hope very much that this will be enough to . . . signal that we are moving in the right direction in strengthening the total financial system. Next to be done, is to strengthen the overall (financial) system. Rules will become much stricter.

The closure of the fifty-six finance firms gave a blow to about six thousand Thai workers who had lost their jobs in addition to the estimated fourteen thousand workers who have already been laid off in the finance sector since the firms were closed earlier this year (1997). The finance minister mentioned that these six thousand workers would be allowed to work in the banks which will begin to work as new banks by the merger of some of the fifty-six finance firms. The announcement on the suspension of the finance firms helped the currency baht very much to recover in early dealings to 41.50/41.55 per dollar onshore. The stock market index jumped 3.65 per cent to 402.96 points by 0410 GMT. The Thai analysts welcomed Mr. Chuan Leekpai's government's action very much and told that it has taken the right step in the right direction. Mr. Jongkonee Wongphasukchet, the director of sales and research at Vickers Ballas, described,

> I would say that this is quite good news. The markets believe it is good that they can completely close so many

firms. We are going to the right direction.

According to several Thai analysts, the finance firms from foreign landers took around $ 16 billion as loans, and their total loans were about 800 billion baht ($ 190.5 billion). The Central Bank in the past has lent them over 430 billion baht to help them to solve when they faced liquidity problems.

The International Monetary Fund on Monday, December 8, 1997 in a vote of confidence over Thailand's economic reforms agreed to hand over $ 810 million to help Thailand to restore its economy and to solve its economic crisis and to establish itself on its economic feet. The decision, disclosed after several hours of debate by the board of the International Monetary Fund, indicated that the fund has made $ 2.4 billion available to Thailand since Agust 1997, when the International Monetary Fund in order to help Thailand to solve its economic turmoil sanctioned a $ 17.2 billion international rescue package to Thailand. It as loan has lent Thailand $ 3.9 billion over 34 months in the bailout package and it can be mentioned as its 13th largest single loan. But this was much less than it offered to Indonesia or to South Korea and these two countries were later recipients of the International Monetary Fund's emergency help. The Thai authorities have made solid progress over the past several weeks in implementing the IMF supported economic programme more forcefully, especially in the key area of restructuring Thailand's financial sector. The Thai government has approved a $ 300 million loan from the Asian Development Bank to help to restructure the country's battered financial markets. This was stated on Wednesday, December 10, 1997. The Thai government mentioned that the cabinet gave the go-ahead for the drawdown of the loan, which formed part of a $ 1.2 billion contribution from the Asian Development Bank to the International Monetary Fund rescue package. Thailand's embattled baht on Wednesday, December 3, 1997 dived into uncharted territory and the Thai analysts disclosed that the Thai currency was set to tumble further in the near term with no bottom in sight. The baht plunged to an all time low early as dollars quoted it at 42.90/ 43.10 against the dollar at 0355 GMT. According to the Thai dealers,

> the Thai unit was driven down by the dollar buying from companies which need to meet year-end debt repayments and on worries over South Korea's financial crisis and the battered won currency.

The stock-market managed to display some improvement by midday on Wednesday, December 3, 1997 despite the baht's skid. The Thai brokers opined that the market was oversold and players were treading water. The index was off 1.01 points to 377.13 at the midday break after hitting a day-low of 371.99 earlier. Mr. Chaiyawat Wibulswasdi, the Central Bank's governor, requested the Thai people to remain calm after the baht's plunge. He told that the Central Bank was monitoring the sliding Thai uhnit closely and would utilise its limited resources boldly to give new life into the Thai currency. The Thai finance minister stated that owing to the regional factors the Thai baht was plunged and there was not much Thailand could do because of limited financial resources. Thailand's depressed baht on Thursday, December 11, 1997 tumbled to another record low 'on regional currency blues' as the Korean won's continued collapse left Asian markets shaddering. The baht on Thursday morning December 11, 1997 dived to an all-time low in the onshore market of 43.25/ 43.35 per dollar. According to several local dealers, the baht was pressured by comments from Mr. Supachai Panitchapakdi, the Thai deputy Prime Minister, in Japan that druing the first quarter of 1998 Thailand might lower its high interest rates. Mr. Satien Tantanasarit, the vice-president at Thai Dnu Bank's treasury department, told,

> The baht was hit by regional plights. Basically, the market might look for reasons why the baht should be

> stronger than the won and the rupiah. . . .

Senior Central Bank official closely monitored the market but he was not worried as the Thai unit did not fluctuate worldly. Mr. Phitnu Pathanopas of Dhana Sia Finance described,

> The stock market was sluggish because of the weak baht which also made liquidity a bit high.

Several finance ministers, senior finance officials and central bank authorities from Brunei, Myanmar, Indonesia, Laos, Malaysia, the Philippines, Singapore, Thailand, Vietnam, Australia, China, Hong-Kong, Japan, and South Korea and the United States met for three days — November 30, and December 1 and 2, 1997 in Kuala Lumpur, the Malaysian capital to discuss and to tackle currency woes. It was regarded as the highest level meeting of officials who wanted to take action plan in the problems which have brought economic crisis in the South-East Asian region. The devaluation of the Thai baht not only brought the fall of share prices and currencies, but also forced Thai to receive help of the bailout package to save its currency termoil from the International Monetary Fund. Indonesia and South Korea also received monetary help from this fund. This meeting in Kuala Lumpur has brought together the nine members of the Association of the South-East Asian Nations and also several fianance ministers and senior officials of Australia, China, Hong-Kong, Japan. Mr. Lawrence Summors, the US deputy treasury secretary, represented Washington, The main purpose of the meeting was to regain confidence in the region. Solutions to the currency problems were also regarded as a main topic.

Thailand's baht currency which rallied after Mr. Chuan Leekpai's appointment as the Prime Minister in the second week of November 1997 has fallen again to more than 40 to the US dollar. Thailand's Central Bank governor requested the Thai exporter to sell their dollars to stabilise the Thai currency. At the close of trading Wednesday, the dollar was at 40.10 baht, up from 39.875 baht late on Tuesday, November 18, 1997. In the offshore market, the dollar was at 39.775 baht up from 39.10 baht late on Tuesday, 18 November 1997.

The Thai government officials told that Myanmar'smilitary government on Tuesday, December 9, 1997 promised to help Thailand to repatriate more than one million illegal Myanmarese workers.[97] Thailand wanted to repatriate Myanmarese who, as cheap labours, were working illegally, Mr. Chuan Leekpai, the Thai Prime Minister, and Mr. Ohn Gyaw, the Myanmarese foreign minister, discussed this matter and the latter vowed to help Thailand in this matter. In Bangkok he had talks with Mr. Surin Pitsuwan, the Thai foreign minister, and the two countries on border issues held talks at the Association of the South-East Asian Nations' summit in Kuala Lumpur. Mr. Surin Pitsuwan mentioned that they have border which is more than 2,400 km long. These two ministers discussed boundaries, displaced persons and illegal immigrants. The Thai foreign minister also spoke to the Thai reporters that the Association of the South-East Asian Nations was still in discussions with the European Union on the Myanmarese issue. An Asean-EU meeting scheduled in Bangkok in the first week of December 1997 was cancelled after a disagreement over whether Myanmar, as a new member of Association of the South-East Asian Nations, should join to take part in its activities. Thailand in particular had always insisted that Myanmar should be allowed to take part in its activities but the European Union stated that Myanmar had not signed up to take part in the forum and would not be allowed to invite to do so because of its human rights record. Thailand has signed an International Labour Organisation agreement on child labour. The *Nation* daily mentioned that Bangkok joined the International Labour Organisation (ILO) sponsered pact on the International Programme for the elimination of child labour at a meeting in

97. *AA*, December 10, 1997, p. 7.

Bangkok. Mr. Kasama Veravanna Ayutthaya, the primary education official, told that he signed an agreement on behalf of Thailand and it would give a grant of $ 86.000 for proper training of 164 primary school teachers.

The meeting of the Association of the South-East Asian Nations was held at the Palace of the Golden Horses Hotel in Kuala Lumpur from 14th to 16th December 1997.[98] The South-East Asian leaders on Monday, December 15, 1997 called on the United States, Europe and Japan to join an urgent international campaign to play a great role to end the region's financial turmoil. After the summit they issued a declaration. They told that all countries must remain united and must show their determination to face the challenge created by the currency problems. They exchanged their views on policies referred to by the leaders at the summit and they agreed on the following:

1. They strongly endorsed the Asean finance ministers' agreement on the early implementation of the Manila Framework to enhance regional surveillance, strengthen economic and technical co-operation, support measures to strengthen the International Monetary Fund's (IMF's) capacity to respond to financial crisis.

2. They strongly endorsed the Asean finance ministers' commitment to ensure sound economic fundamentals and strengthen the financial sector. Taking note of the recent establishment of Asean central bank forum, they supported the Asean finance ministers' decision to form a select committee with a permanent secretariat to develop a regional surveillance machanism that would emphasise preventive efforts to avoid the emergence of risks that would precipitate a crisis.

3. They emphasised the importance of the Asean finance

98. *AA*, December 16, 1997, p. 17.

minister's call upon the International Monetary Fund (IMF) to undertake in-depth analysis of the structure of global financial markets and short-term capital flows, including the on-going study of the operations of hedge funds and their impact on financial market activities as well as the implications of technology on capital flows.

4. Towards the end, while they agreed that it is important to have sound economic and financial policies and reforms to strengthen Asean's ability to cope effectively with the challenges associated with liberalisation, they stressed the importance of greater transparency of capital flows to ensure greater efficiency in the functioning of economies and financial markets. It is therefore urgent that global efforts be undertaken, including the central role of the International Monetary Fund (IMF), to find ways to arrest currency slide and restore stability to the currency markets.

5. They reaffirmed their commitment to maintain an open trade and investment environment in Asean including through accelerated implementation of the Asean free Trade Area, the Asean Investment Area and the Asean Industrial Corporation scheme. They agreed that in view of the present situation, every effort should be made to remove barriers to trade and to promete greater intra Asean trade and investment.

6. They called on Asean capital market authorities to expeditiously draw up measures to encourage the financing of infrastructure projects in Asean through the Asean capital markets and joint efforts to promote the attractiveness of the region's capital markets in international investors.

7. They reaffirmed the importance of co-operation on

economic and financial issue between the Asean finance ministers.

Several trade ministers of the Association of the South-East Asian nations signed documents on Monday, December 15, 1997 in Kuala Lumpur to implement an agreement to open the tourism industry and services sectors for member nations. Under the services protocal, all nine members — Brunei, Myanmar, Indonesia, Laos, Malaysia, the Philippines, Singapore, Thailand and Vietnam agreed to open up their tourism sector. In addition to tourism, Brunei, Indonesia, Malaysia and Thailand promised to introduce their maritime transport sector. Following were the leaders who attended the three-day Asean summit in Kuala Lumpur: (1) Brunian of Brunei : The Prime Minister, Senor General Than Shwe, (2) China : President Jiang Zemin, (3) Indonesia : Foreign Minister Ali Alatas, (4) Japan, Mr. Ryutare Hashimote, the Prime Minister, (5) Laos : Mr. Khamtay Siphandone, the Prime Minister, (6) Malaysia : Mr. Mahathir Mohamad, the Prime Minister, (7) Philippines : President Fidel Ramos, (8) Singapore : Mr. Goh Chok Tong, the Prime Minister, (9) South Korea: Mr. Kohkum, the Prime Minister, (10) Thailand: Mr. Chuan Leekpai, the Prime Minister, and (11) Vietnam : Mr. Phan Van Khai, the Prime Minister. At first Mr. Suharto, the Indonesian President, wanted to come to the summit to meet the leaders but his doctors advised him to take rest and so he decided not to attend the Asean meeting. Thailand on Monday, December 15, 1997 denied a report from a newspaper which mentioned that the Thai Prime Minister Mr. Chuan Leekpai stated that the International Monetary Fund aid package did not bring significant result and it was not fruitful and it might be too late to solve Thailand's economic crisis. A Thai government spokesman gave a statement ralating to it in Kuala Lumpur. He disclosed that the *New Straits Times* newspaper's report was 'factually erroneous and may be misleading'. The daily described that Mr. Chuan Leekpai, met the Malaysian Prime Minister Mr. Mahathir Mohamad on Sunday, December 14, 1997 in Kuala

Lumpur and had opined,

> the International Monetary Fund's assistance has not borne any significant result and it might be too late to rejuvenate Thailand's economy.

In August 1997 it received a $ 17.2 billion rescue package under an International Monetary Fund economic adjustment programme. The Thai government's statement mentioned that Mr. Chuan Leekpai agreed with Mr. Mahathir Mohamad at their meeting that for discussion at the three-day summit in Kuala Lumpur the prevailing currency situation in the South-East Asian region should be the main topic.

> In addition, the Thai Prime Minister agreed with the Malaysian Prime Minister that the IMF study currently being taken on the structure of the global financial market, and short-term capital flows should be speeded up and made available before its scheduled release in May of next year 1998.

It described that the Thai leader repeated again a statement he did at the Asia-Pacific Economic Co-operation Forum in November 1997

> for greater international efforts, including those by the major economies and international financial organisations, to address the current financial crisis in the region.

When Asia's markets spiral downward, several Asian business and political leaders warned that the International Monetary Fund bailout programmes have advised the wrong kind of medicine to help to save South-East Asia's economic turmoil but these solutions were useless and they would not be able to save the region from the economic crisis. These officials and executives criticised the International Monetary Fund for using force to implement measures — which they told

> were tailored to stop a government spending spree in Latin America a decade ago—, onto Asia's financial crisis, which has at its rest the overspending by corporations, not its governments. Relentless application of the agency's orthodox bailout, which includes increased taxes, high interest rates and budget cuts, will smoother the already fragile companies and economies of South Korea, Thailand, Indonesia and Malaysia, they warned.

> You smack a child for misbehaving so he learns a lesson, you don't beat him to death. While it is good to restrict unnecessary lending with high interest rates, the current tight liquidity is killing formerly viable companies,

told Mr. Chumipol Na Lamlieng, the president of Siam Cement PLC, a Thai Industrial Company. Recently Mr. Chuan Leekpai, the Thai Prime Minister, and the new South Korean finance minister mentioned,

> the IMF belt-tightening was cutting into their countries' real economies, rather than reining in spending.

But the official of the International Monetary Fund in Washington stated that the agency's Asian prescription was a necessary and it helped to stabilise Asia's financial markets so that recovery could be possible. He told,

> In these financial panics — and every time we go in, it is a financial panic — we see a need for tight monetary policy until confidence is restored. High interest rates were necessary to slow the rapid depreciation of Asia's economies. There has been a pervasive loss of confidence in the currency and we have to attract domestic residents and foreigners to hold the domestic currency. We ask interest rates to be raised to a level that will stop haemorrhaging of reserves.

Mr. Joffray Garton, a former American trade diplomat, described that the International Monertary Fund used the wrong medicine in Asia. He told further,

> It is a ligitimate question as to whether the International Monetary Fund is moving in with prescriptions that more relevant to Latin American-style crises than to Asian Crises. There is another difference between Mexico and the Asian crisis: Mexico is one country and the countries around it were not all succumbing to the same problem.

Mr. Mahathir Mohamad, the Prime Minister of Malaysia, was a good critic of the International Monetary Fund and he stated that his country would resist the agency's aid because its formula generally "helps guarrantee loan payments rather than rescue distraught economies". Mr. Chumpol Na Lamlieng, the president of Siam Cement PLC, mentioned that if interest rates did not ease by the end of the year (1997) from the current 20 per cent level, than one-third of Thailand's firms would be too short of cash for payment of interest on their debts. The International Monetary Fund official opined that a completely untonable situation was created by the crisis. He told,

> It has to be stabilised. The effects of continued depreciation are also devastating to all these companies that have large debts. The only reasonable way to confront these problems is to sharply raise interest rates and undertake a fiscal correction. Our view is, undertake these actions firmly, with conviction, and leave the markets in no doubt you are doing them, and you will stabilise the situation. Some Asian currencies had fallen between 30 per cent and 60 per cent in value. The way to stop it in the short term is to show that you are determined to defend the exchange rate, not at a particular level, but to defend it agianst continued depreciation. Once that period is over, interest rates can go down reasonably fast.

Mr. Chuan Leekpai, the Prime Minister of Thailand, and Mr. Supachai Panitchapakdi, the deputy Thai Prime Minister, told separately that the programme, which was recommended by the International Monetary Fund, "was harshly cutting into the country's real economy". The letter stated,

> The deflationary effect was stronger than the International Monetary Fund predicted, and I have to caution them. We have to accept that some assets are overpriced, but the current slowdown is strong, severe and exaggerated beyond what is necessary.

The three-day meeting of the Association of the South-East Asian Nations in Kuala Lumpur in the third week of December 1997 has dome little to stop flow from the region's financial wound. Practically, it has failed to put full stop to the Asian crisis. Several Thai analysts remarked that the markets were unimpressed with the activities of the Association of the South-East Asian Nations because they understood that it would not be able to do anything which would bring an immediate result. The Thai baht made gains after a poor start on Tuesday, December 16, 1997. According to several Thai dealers, it recovered from a deep dive to a record low after the intervention of the Central Bank. They told;

> The baht which sank to a record traded low of 49.35 earlier, was qieted up at 47.45-47.95 per dollar by the close after skidding to 49.0-49.50 briefly.

In order to pay off foreign loans, corporate dollar was bought against the baht. Mr Chaiyawat Wibulsawasdi, the Central Bank governor, said that the currency had stabilised after local market players took notice of their bank's advice to restrain from their damaging purchases. The Thai official and trade sources mentioned that the Thai authorities have given order to investigate into recent speculative attacks against the baht by local traders and they wanted to take up stern attitude against those who have bought dollars heavily. The Bank of Thailand tried to stop the slide of the local currency and showed its determination to check every major foreign exchange transaction which was made recently by local dealers, especially those who engaged themselves to buy dollars heavily. On Wednesday, November 17, 1997, the currency was quoted at 47.70/95 per dollar against a low of 49.00/49.50 on Tuesday, December 16, 1997.

> On Tuesday, December 16, 1997 it touched a record low of 49.35 hit by the contagion from regional currency falls and a corporate stampede to buy dollars to most foreign loan repayments.

The baht has new fallen by about 45 per cent since its flatation took place on July 1997. We can say here that the baht's fall has given a blow to Thailand very much because it struggled hard to save its economy from its worst economic crisis in decades. From a report we learn that the Petegrine Finance and Securities had been asked for clarification on its dollar buying. In order to prevent a wave of business closures as a result of Thailand's economic turmoil, Thailand's Parliament has passed new and more flexible bankruptcy laws. It relaxed bankruptcy rules to ward off crisis in Thailand. This was disclossed on Monday, December 22, 1997. It told that the amendments to the old Bankruptcy Act are expected to become law in January or February 1998. Everybody expected that the new bill will encourage creditors and debtors to restructure defaulting businesses rather than shut them down. At present the Bankruptcy Act only refers to liquidation in a very restricted manner. According to several Thai analysts, a mere far-reaching Thai law was very important because they thought that this necessary to restructure the Thai economy and to ensure smooth rehabilitation of the crippled and business sectors. The new legislation law was based on the US bankruptcy laws and it offered more flexibility to the creditors and debtors to renegotiate loan facilities to do for business restructuring. It also allowed the civil courts the right to appoint independent managers to supervise troubled businesses while rehabilitation plans were drawn up. At least three quarters of creditors' approval was needed for the plans and they will appoint their own representatives to see the implementations of these measures. If the plan failed to meet its target after five years, then the liquidation of assets took place. The Thai government stated,

> If the process fails to help the business the enterprise could be declared bankrupt by the court and liquidation under the bankruptcy law will follow.

About thousands of Thai companies faced bankruptcy as they fastened with buckle under the weight and heavy pressure of $ 72 billion in private debt. Many Thai companies with large offshore loans were very much disturbed by Thailand's plummeting currency, which has increased the costs of servicing dollar debts. Moody's Investors Service mentioned on Monday, December 22, 1997 that it had downgraded the foreign currency credit ratings of Indonesia, Malaysia, South Korea and Thailand in a fresh blow to the struggling economics of Asia. Thailand's foreign currency ceiling for bonds was dropped to Ba 1 from Baa 3 its B1 ceiling for bank deposits was also confirmed. Thailand's rating was cut owing to concern over credit and financial fundamentals. The agency described,

> The new government has started a long and difficult adjustment process. However, domestic political conditions may limit progress in this area.

Mr. Tarrin Nimmanahaeminda, the Thai finance minister, on Friday, December 19, 1997 demanded support from the Japanese banks and requested them for its foreign currency loan to be converted to Yen denomination.[99] The banking officials disclosed

99. *AA*, December 20, 1997, p. 18.

it in Tokyo on Friday, December 19, 1997. An official of one of the nine banks which had discussion with the Thai finance minister told,

> There was a request for converting our foreign currency loans to Yen-denominated loans as well as boosting yen-based payments for trade.

Thailand's finance minister met top banking officials of the nine banks which had branch offices in Thailand. In the earlier meeting with Japan's finance minister Hiroshi Mitsuzuka, the Thai finance minister stated that Thailand wished to increase Yen-denominated borrowings, but did not request additional funds from Tokyo. Thailand's dollar-denominated trade and borrowings played a great role in the Thai economic world before the financial crisis occurred and the devaluation of the baht in July 1997 took place. Mr. Tarrin Nimmanhaeminda went to Tokyo on Wednesday, December 17, 1997 with Mr. Olarn Chaiprawat, the president of the Thai Bankers' Association. The Thai finance minister and the bank officer tried to negotiate the roll-over of about half of Thailand's $ 72 billion private sector from foreign debt which was owed to the Japanese creditors. They told further that about $ 37 billion in short-term debt will be repaid soon. The Thai finance minister requested the Japanese finance minister to help his country in various ways to re-establish its economic world. The Asian Development Bank on Friday, December 19, 1997 approved a loan of $ 4 billion to South Korea and $ 300 million to Thailand. The loan to Thailand helped it very much to bring reforms in the country's financial markets. The amount was part of the Asian Development Bank's $ 1.2 billion contribution to a $ 17.2 billion rescue package approved by the International Monetary Fund in August 1997. Mr. Mitsu Sato, the president of the Asian Development Bank, told,

> This disbursement will have a major impact in dealing with the very important question of foreign exchange

> reserves. But it would take one or two years for South Korea and Thailand to put in place 'the institutional measures' needed to restore their economies and protect them from future crisis. These reforms will help to restore confidence in these economies and when fully implemented will help greatly reduce the risk of such events recurring in the future. We are confident that these reform programmes will do much to transform these sectors through increased reliance on market forces supported by independent regulatory agencies. The lesson that a country should learn from the currency turmoil is how to improve their policies and institutional capacities as such that it can take advantage of globalisation to better develop its economy rather than to avoid being integrated. In response to the Asian financial turmoil, the Asian Development Bank will focus its operations on the medium-term on helping developing member countries undertake the necessary reforms to help them withstand similar crises in the future.

The World Bank has given a $ 350 million loan to Thailand in the fourth week of December 1997 to help to restore the country's foreign reserves as it embarked on a major overhaul of its enfeebled financial system. The World Bank loan was a part of a $ 17.2 billion economic-bailout package approved by the International Monetary Fund which told that the Thai government must play a great role to show a budget surplus equal to one per cent of its gross domestic product in 1998. In order to help the Thai government to restructure the national financial sector, the World Bank agreed to give $ 350 million loan to Thailand. A bank statement issued on Tuesday, December 23, 1997,

> The structural measures supported by this loan will help restore confidence in Thailand's ailing financial sector. The funds will be used to enable the orderly closure of

> non-viable financial institutions and to strengthen the regulatory framework. The goal would be to create better incentives for creditors, depositors and debtors.

Mr. J Shivakumar, the World Bank's country manager for Thailand, also referred to it. He described,

> Strengthening regulation and supervision will increase the soundness of the remaining finance companies and will help prevent a similar crisis from happening again.

The funds were mentioned as part of the bank's $ 1.5 billion participation an International Monetary Fund-arranged rescue plan worth $ 17.2 billion. The World Bank's officials in the first week of December 1997 spoke highly of the Thai government for closing its fifty-six finance firms which were suspended in 1997. In order to help to support a national economy which by declining exports, heavy debt and a shaky currency had been nearly crippled, the Thai government was forced to suspend these financial firms. It permanently closed more than half of the country's finance companies in a bold move. Owing to this step by the government, about 6,000 Thai workers were jobless and gave the way for a 930 billion baht ($ 22.36 billion) asset acution. The Thai analysts mentioned it as the first step for Thailand to sort out its debt-burdened finance sector. Mr. Barry Yates, the head of regional research at Seamice Securities, described,

> This was medical amputation, now we have to see whether the cancer already spread to the rest of the system. It is critical for the remaining finance companies and commercial banks to increase their capital and hook up with strategic partners.

The Chairman of the Financial Restructuring Authority on Monday, December 22, 1997 described that the closed companies' assets would be auctioned off within a year to pay off depositors and creditors and this condition was mentioned by the

International Monetary Fund in its bailout package. The Thai finance minister disclosed that some of the high quality assets from the closed companies would be used for the establishment of one or two new banks. It may be noted here that the Orient Thai Airlines, one of the two privately-owned carriers in Thailand, owing to operating losses ceased operations from January 1998. Mr. Udon Tantiprasengchai, the airline's managing director, told that its regular operations would be shut down but the carrier might continue to provide charter flights. He criticised the Thai government for its failure to liberalise the airline industry and its policy of protecting the Thai Airways, which is regarded as the national carrier and about more than 90 per cent is owned by the Thai ministry of finance. It had a very good reputation but now the critics have criticised the company's management and they told that its service standards have declined. Several governments tried to privatise the Thai Airways but they were unable to materialise their plans. The Thai governments's policy of protection was unable to help Thailand's airline. An official from the aviation department of Thailand said that Bangkok would get another national carrier shortly. He told that the Angel Airlines was expected to apply for its licence at the beginning of the new year, 1998 and it would take off probably in June or July 1998. The Thai Airways International can be mentioned as Thailand's only national carrier.

Mr. Supachai Panitchapakdi, the Thai deputy Prime Minister, has criticised the United States for not giving help to Thailand to overcome its dire economic crisis.[100] He told it on Friday, December 26, 1997. He met many prominent Thai businessmen and politicians in Bangkok and he told that the US had been slow to help Thailand to the crisis and was not very serious to play a great role to offer assistance to Thailand in its troubled days. The Thai deputy Prime Minister said,

100. *AA*, December 27, 1997, p. 17.

> Ever since we have had the problem, the US has not seriously acted to help us at all. Japan showed high sympathy and understanding for our situation while the other countries just watched us fall indifferently. Washington's tardiness threatened to undermine its special status in Thailand and the region as a whole, while Japan's image improved. The US could help restore the confidence in the region by speaking with its private sector and fund managers by verbal, financial, trade or technological support. There are many ways that the US could help stabilise our currency. We don't want to specify how the US would help — they would step in and make decisions of their own. He praised Tokyo for its swift response to the crisis and urged Thai borrowers to negotiate Yen-denominated loans from now on. rather than seek US-currency loans. The Thai baht has lost more thatn 40 per cent of its value since it was floated in July amid the worst economic downturn the country has experienced in 50 years.

A $ 17.2 billion international bailout package was sanctioned in August 1997, with contributions from the International Monetary Fund, the World Bank and Asian Development Bank. Japan has given $ 4 billion, while Australia, Malaysia, Hong-Kong, Singapore contributed $ 1 billion each to Thailand and Brunei's contribution was $ 500 million. Many analysts thought that the rescue fund was not enough because Thailand wanted to create a new image of its wrecked finance sector and has paid more that $ 70 billion in private debt. According to the US ecnomists, the impact of Asia's economic crisis would have an effect upon several US companies which have large export markets in South-East Asia. Mr. Sempop Charoenkul, the Thai businessman, criticised the United States and told,

> the US should put its money where its mouth was. Now we knew who are our friends are. It was not enough for

> a friend to simply sit beside us and say I am sorry.

A major Thai bank was considered for purchase by the American giant Citibank and in a mangement shake-up it fired its president and chairman on Tuesday, December 23, 1997. Ms Tanya Sirivedhim, the assistant governer of the Bank of Thailand, told,

> First Bangkok City Bank was considered to be a more family-run bank. Credit-procedures at some family-run banks are not as professionally run as would be desired.

Mr. Chareen Siriwattanapakdi, who owned most of the country's licences to produce and distribute liquor, controlled the bank and about 40 per cent of the First Bangkok City Bank's shares were controlled by him. Although the region's banks showed their eagerness for capital from outside investors, yet they did not like to allow the foreigners to control them. A senior foreign banker in Thailand stated,

> These perverse lending practices combined with lax regulation and protectionist policies for local banks created the powerful connection that led to today's economic crisis. Every bank in this country needs more professional management.

The last six months of economic crisis gave an idea about the level of risky loans and this helped Moody's Investors Service Inc. on Monday, December 22, 1997 to lower the national credit ratings of Thailand, Indonesia and South Korea to junk status, "a rating normally assigned to risky corporate ventures". Several Thai banks and the Thai authorities have given resistance to allow foreign partners to take control of the bank. Mr. Sriyan Pietersz, a strategist at Soc Gen Crosby Securities, mentionet,

> This reluctance to give away control is ultimately going to work agaisnt them. Changes in the boardroom are a step to facilitating a takeover or merger that would in the end bring an infusion of new capital.

Mr. Tanya Sirivedhin told that

> the Central Bank, which holds a 15-per cent stake in First Bangkok City Bank, allowed the commercial bank's move and wanted that the installation of a mere professional management team would help to give confidence and this would no doubt stop the withdrawals from the bank.

Mr. Henry Ho, the Citibank's country manager, opined that he did not play a role in the changes and when the official announcement took place, he then only heard about these matters. He told,

> We are in the midst of conducting due diligence, with 30 people reviewing all components of the bank — we all decide the value of the bank when we have finished due diligence by the end of February, 1998.

Mr. Masatsugu Nagato, the general manager of the Industrial Bank of Japan, stated,

> The Thai officials are desperate to make the citibank deal happen. There have been many rumours about foreign takeovers, but not many have taken place. Now the authorities have shown they are willing to take action to make changes happen.

Thailand recently relaxed ownership rules which "had limited foreigners to a 25 per cent stake in the country's financial institutions". Thailand's second largest commercial bank closed representative offices in Vietnam and Myanmar in January 1998 to cut costs because the institution was battered by the regional slump. The Thai Farmer's Bank wanted to close the offices in Hanoi and Rangoon as "the number of Thais wanting to do business in both nations has dropped because of the economic crisis". *The Bangkok Post* told,

> Representative offices, which do not offer the full services offered by banking branches, do not directly generate income as their role is to advise customers in host countries. However, the offices can be expensive to set up and maintain. The bank's Burmese office costs an estimated $ 3,000 to 4,000 a month to run, not including staff salaries.

The Thai Military Bank and the Siam city Bank in order to lower operating costs reduced the number of staff in foreign offices and also recalled Thai personnel. The Thai Farmers' Bank and other banks were not quite sure about the approval of Myanmar's military government ralating to the opening of full brancehes by the foreign banks and the Thai Farmer's Bank opened a repersentative office in Rangoon in 1994. This bank in the future will apply for full branch licenses in Vietnam and in Myanmar when both nations will have a policy to give permission to commercial banks to operate as full branches. Its thirteen other representative offices are operating in different parts of Asia. The Citibank told that it did not want to purchase a major Thai bank.

Mr. Chuan Leekpai, Thailand's Prime Minister, told that Thailand may ask the International Monetary Fund to relax the terms of its rescue package as the economic crisis further eroded state revenue.[101] He told that the economic crisis which his government faced was worse than he had expected when he assumed power of Thailand. This was disclosed by the *Bangkok Post*. Thailand's Prime Minister in an extensive interview stated,

> The government might ask the International Monetary Fund to ease its bailout package requirements, particularly that there be a surplus for fiscal year 1997-98. Such a request could come after the fund releases the last instalment of its portion of the $ 17.2 billion

---

101. *AA*, December 29, 1997, p. 18.

> rescue package in February 1998. To make such demands before the money was handed over might lead to the IMF refusing to release it, damaging Thailand. It might also send the wrong messege to other Asian countries borrowing from the IMF.

Bangkok must maintain a budget surplus of one per cent of gross domestic product in fiscal 1997-98 under the International Monetary Fund bailout package and Mr. Chuan Leekpai and his economic team have promised to show their respect to it. Although the Thai Prime Minister told that Thailand would play its great role to meet the targets, yet he mentioned that it was very diffucult for them to meet the targets. He gave his warning to his countrymen that he was forced to introduce new taxes to make up for falling revenue. He described,

> My biggest concern is that we may not be able to collect enough revenue to meet expenditure.

The *Nation* newspaper reported on Monday, December 29, 1997 that Thailand's finance minister has requested three of the top five commercial banks to commit to a recapitalisation for greater liquidity in the financial system. Mr. Tarrin Nimmanahaeminda, the Thai finance minister, in his meeting with local newspaper editors, stated that the issues of liquidity, forex and the health of the financial sector were his great urgent tasks and these must be undertaken not only in a very efficient manner but also must be performed as soon as possible. He had discussions with top executives of the three banks — Bangkok Bank Plc., Thai Farmers Bank and Bank of Ayodhya and told them to declare their recapitalisation plans. He mentioned them that they should raise capital rather than intend to reduce their lending portifolios. Which in the financial system would help to tighten their liquidity. He said further that if the liquidity situation improved, then the foreign investors and creditors would be gained and they would get confidence in our economic world and this would help to improve the capital inflow. The state-owned Krung Thai

Bank in November 1997 disclosed that through an offer of two billion new shares it would try to raise its registered capital to 34.85 billion baht ($ 741:5 million) from 14.85 billion baht. Another bank, Siam Commercial Bank told in late October 1997 that through the offer of 600 million shares it would also try to raise registered capital by six billion baht. Japan's Sanwa Bank on Friday, December 26, 1997 mentioned that it would do its best to help its stake in Siam Commercial Bank to about 13 per cent from 0.6 per cent. Thailand's Bank of Ayudhya disclosed that its liquidity situation was very good and there was no need for a capital increase soon. In October 1997 Japan's Sanwa Bank declared a tie-up with the five Asian banks by sharing customers and consolidating transfers between their countries. Under the agreement, Sanwa Bank

> would have its cash management system connected with the five banks' 1000 offices in Thailand, Indonesia, Malaysia and the Philippines by March 1998.

The bank declared,

> Despite Thailand's stagnant economic outlook due to the devaluation of the currency and the dicline of the stock market, Sanwa is confident that Thailand remains an attractive market with high potential growth.

Siam Commercial Bank was founded in 1906 and it has about 400 branch offices in Thailand. Thailand's banks needed $ 19 billion or 900 billion baht to survive and without foreign capital it would impossible for Thailand's banks to survive. From Capital Nemura Securities Plc. it is known that Thailand's banks may need fresh capital of up to 899.60 billion baht. Of the country's 15 commercial banks, only four banks have so far declared that they did not want foreign capital.

Mr. Tarrin Nimmanahaeminda, Thailand's finance minister, told that the agencies — Moody's Investor Services and Standard and Poor's — should not group Bangkok with South Korea and

Indonesia, the two limping economies. Because these agencies downgraded Thailand's sovereign debt instruments to junk bond status. So the finance minister requested the world's top ratings agencies to give it a fairer hearing. He told the Thai newspaper editors on Tuesday, December 30, 1997,

> Moody's had declared Thailand's sovereign debt to be inferior to investment grade instruments despite his having briefed analysts for two hours by phone. We were badly damaged psychologically by Moody's downgrade. I lend considerable importance to the ratings given by these international ratings agencies. We have to separate ourselves from South Korea and Indonesia.

Top Thai officials and analysts described that although Thailand's economic atmosphere was deteriorating, yet the ratings downgrade did not fully give us a true picture of Thailand's fundamentals because the ratings were based on the information which was out of date. It may be noted here that Moody's Investor Services and Standard and Poor's have regularly downgraded Thailand's ratings since the occurrence of its economic crisis and the devaluation of the Thai currency, the baht in July 1997. An analyst told,

> December 1997's fourth week's sovereign ratings slash was however the most devastating to the damaged Thai economy in months, making Thai bonds difficult to sell abroad and heightening fears of worsening liquidity crunch. It is very bad news for the Thai economy.

Thailand's finance minister wished to go to the office of the International Monetary Fund when the completion of the recapitalisation of the battered Thai economy will take place by the end of January, 1998. Thailand in order to bolster Tourism tried to liberalise domestic and regional transport routes. Mr. Sithop Thangsuban, the Transport and Communications Minister, described that under the new policy beginning in 1998, private airlines would be allowed to operate on any domestic routes. He stated,

> We are trying to get rid of all the difficulties involved in liberalisation, including airfare control policies. This is expected to greatly support tourism. Thailand would also open up regional routes to private operators, beginning with regional markets such as Indonesia and Malaysia. Foreign airlines would be allowed to operate charter flights to any destination in Thailand with a custom's post.

Mr. Sam Rainsy, the leading Cambodian opposition figure, requested Thailand and the United Nations to protest deserters from either side of Cambodia's bloody civil war as a way of limiting the fighting. He gave a statement from France that most soldiers did not like to fight and would be happy to leave their posts if they could seek asylum in Thailand. He appealed to the Thai government and the United Nations for their shelter in Thailand. Thailand's Development Research Institute reported that the country will need an additional $ 8 billion in loans to increase its existing International Monetary Fund bailout package and also to give encouragement to foreign reserves. Mr. Chalengpheb Sussangkarn, the president of Thailand's Development Research Institute, disclosed that the Central Bank would need more money in 1998 to help foreign reserves, to give stability to the Thai bahts and to gain market confidence in Thailand's economy. He told further that although Thailand received the International Monetary Fund bailout package, yet the Bank of Thailand's reserves had fallen significantly and Thailand's foreign investors have sold the baht for the dollars because they feared that the foreign reserves were not enough for the country's huge debt obligations. He predicated that $ 8 billion in additional standing credit would help to raise foreign reserves by $ 3 billion. Mr. Philip Bowring of the International Harald Tribune referred to the International Monetary Fund's rescue package. He stated,

> There has never been a crisis like the one besetting Asian financial markets. It is international in origin and is a crisis of the private sector, not of government finances. Its nature explains why IMF rescue packages have had scant success. The currencies of South Korea, Indonesia and Thailand have all fallen faster after IMF intervention than they did before it. That is not surprising, the IMF is treating the crisis as a series of national events that require draconian local policies, rather than as an international liquidity domino event. This wrong-headed view will cause recession around Asia and perhaps the world. . . . The International Monetary Fund myopic view led to tumbling of the Asian currencies.

Several analysts warned that the economic turmoil which took its first step by July 2 devaluation of the Thai baht and peaked in October and November when panic selling reverberated across the globe, had not yet run its full course. More bad news was found when we find that regional economies became slow, the governments tried to tighten their belts, corporate earnings took a hit and foreign fund managers reduced their Asian allocations. As long as the currency turmoil was unable to settle down, the whole stock market prospects in the region would not move in proper way. A new report has warned that Asia has entered most difficult times in its recent history because political systems of nations disturbed by the regions' financial crisis have kept them to put to a serious test. A report on political risk in 1998 by Hong-Kong based Political and Economic Risk Consultancy Ltd (Perc) told that although the Philippines and Thailand were in a somewhat stronger political situation than Indonesia, yet much would depend on how effective the roles of the governments were to check financial turmoil which took its start on July 2, 1997 and then the Bangkok government decided to devalue its currency, the baht. It mentioned further that probably Thailand would like to keep its present government of Prime Minister Mr. Chuan Leekpai although the country was in great trouble by its economic crisis. But the real question will came when election will take place late in 1998 or in 1999. Thailand's finance minister requested the Thais to hand over their gold jewellery to help to bailout their nation. He had made this plan to allow the country to help itself out of economic crisis. He in an interview told that the armed forces would fan out across the country within two or three weeks to collect gold jewellery in exchange for interest-paying government bonds and treasury bills. He mentioned that the action would be the first part of an official policy of 'Chuay Thai' or 'Thais help Thais.' He stated that the country must do something to give emphasis on self-reliance. The gold contributions would play a gerat role on help Thailand's dwindling foreign currency reserves. The Thais, like many Asians, have tried their best to keep a large portion of their savings in gold and they generally used it in case of hard times. Thailand's finance minister was unable to say anything about how much gold the Thais have kept under their possessions and he did not say anything about the government's expectation of the collection of gold from the Thais. He wanted to strengthen the financial system by establilshing better management and he wished to increase the capital of commercial banks. He hoped that the country's largest bank will play its significant role in the capital increase. He expected that the Thai Farmer's Bank and Bangkok Bank would announce the capital-increase plans. He wanted to stabilise Thailand's external fianancial issues and also to discuss negotiations for the continuation of $ 92.9 billion in debt to foreign banks. He also made plans to pressure Japanese banks to convert their dollar-denominated loans to Yen. Japan was regarded as Thailand's leader in business affair but it itself faced a credit crunch in its own financial system. A team from the Japanese Export-Import Bank visited Bangkok to negotiate terms for Thailand's first Yen-denominated loan from Japan, worth $ 500 million to $ 600 million. Thailand's finance minister told that the third area of concentration will be on fiscal prudence. He stated his country would strictly adhere to the agreement and would try to follow the condition imposed upon it by the International Monetary Fund. He mentioned further that the fourth area of focus will be to strengthen Thailand's exports on a 'massive scale' through a soon-to-be announced comprehensive government initiative. He also described that the fifth sector of focus will be unemployment and other social issues. Mr. Surin Pitsuwan, Thailand's foreign minister, visited Malaysia to discuss increased Muslim terrorist activities in southern Thailand with the Malaysian government. He want to Malaysia on Monday, January 5, 1998 to say about closer co-operation from the Malaysian government in dealing with terrorism near the border. Even Thailand's Prime Minister Mr. Chuan Leekpai told that the Muslim guerrillas received their training in Malaysia and then after receiving training they come to southern Thailand to create disturbance and terrorism. A Thail police shot dead a suspected terrorist. The Bangkok Metropolitan administration in a statement announced that it has arranged free funerals for poor as part of the Chuay Thai (Thais Help Thais) scheme to give assistance to the less fortunate during the economic crisis. This was disclosed on Saturday, January 3, 1998 by several city officials.

Mr. Chuan Leekpai, Thailand's Prime Minister, on Monday January 5, 1998, told that the Thai government would renegotiate the terms of a $ 17.2 billion bailout package with the International Monetary Fund.[102] He talked with lawyers and Judges and he told them that the country was unlikely to meet a condition in the package requiring Thailand to produce a cash surplus equivalent of 1 per cent of its gross domestic product (GDP) in the 1997-98 fiscal year (September-October). Mr. Tarrin Nimmanahaeminda, the finance minister, went to the United States in mid-January 1998 to discuss with the IMF officials on

---

102. *ET*, January 6, 1998, p. 7.

this issue. Thailand's Chuan Leekpai's government planned to seek a review of its bailout package from the International Monetary Fund and this has raised questions over whether the bitter pill prescribed by the International Monetary Fund may be the right medicine for the ailing economy. Several Thai analysts mentioned on Tuesday, January 6, 1998 that the International Monetary Fund may be forced to become more flexible in its approach to Thailand, due to the changing circumstances surrounding the troubled Thailand's economic woes and a fretful in the value of its currency. Mr. David Riedel, the vice-president of equity research at Solomb Smith Barney in Bangkok told that the International Monetary Fund knew that it needed to be more flexible in its dealings with Thailand. Ms Allison Seng, an analyst with Standard & Poor's MMS International in Singapore mentioned that

> Thailand has done as best it can. At this point and time it's important for the IMF to be, may be a bit mere flexible.

Mr. Chuan Leekpai told that his country would ask the International Monetary Fund to review its conditions under a $ 17.2 billion multilateral bailout package approved by the International Monetary Fund for his country in August 1997. The request for a review same when the Thai government officials decided Thailand's economic problems would make it impossible for Thailand to meet targets, imposed by the International Monetary Fund as a condition for the aid. Mr. Sukhumbhand Paribatra, Thailand's deputy foreign minister, told on Tuesday, January 6, 1998 that Thailand wanted to discuss this matter with the International Monetary Fund because of the change in the circumstances since the sanction of the package by the International Monetary Fund in August 1997. He said that the discussion will be a review in good faith of the agreement which Thailand made with the International Monetary Fund last year, i.e., 1997. He described further that Thailand did not like to change in the package but wanted to review it. He visited Washington with the finance minister for this purpose in mid-January 1998.

The Thai government reacted to see the baht's latest record low on Tuesday, January 6, 1998 by tightening rule to prevent the Thai exporters from hoarding foreign currencies. The Thai cabinet moved in a definite way to stop hoarding foreign currencies and it gave its approval to introduce a new regulation on Wednesday, January 7, 1998 which would require exporters to transfer foreign currency earnings directly to Thailand upon receipt, rather than within 120 days as previously. Mr. Akapol Serasuchart, a government spokesman, told at a post-meeting news conference that when they will receive the payment, they will send the money back into Thailand immediately, and the exporters will deposit the funds in their bank acounts within seven days of arrival in the country and previously they were allowed fifteen days. The Thai currency dealers have mentioned that the baht's weakness was due to exporters' hesitance to sell the dollars they earned, because they feared the fall of the baht as it did for the last six months. The Thai baht was dragged to lows in the onshore market following a sharp decline in the rupiah. The baht was quoted at 53.00/53.10 to the dollar onshore after falling as low as 53.10 earlier. It was quoted at 62.05/52.35 on Wednesday, January 7, 1998. The Thai currency dealers told on Thursday, January 8, 1998 that the Thai government would have limited options in a new set of measures which were announced on Friday, January 9, 1998 to curb speculation in the battered baht. Mr. Tarrin Nimmanahaeminda, the Thai finance minister, stated that he wanted to take moves to restrain speculators from putting further pressure on the Thai unit which hit record lows in the second week of January 1998 and has lost 51.6 per cent of its value since its floatation in July 1997. The baht reached another record low of 53.30 to the dollar in early trade in the domestic market on Thursday, January 8, 1998. Thailand was very much hit by a severe liquidity crunch and faced troubles in its finance sector. Most Thai dealers had no clear idea about the Bank of Thailand's plan to take steps to share up the baht after it charged foreign exchange regulations on Thursday, January 6, 1998 to require exporters to more speedily convert their dollar holdings into the baht. The exporters were informed in the second week of January 1998 that they would keep dollars paid to them by foreign clients for up to seven days, against 15 days earlier, before their conversion into the baht took place. Many Thai dealers and businessmen appreciated the government's intention to take action on Thailand's exporters as logical move to help to boost the dollar supply in the market. A treasury official at a European bank opined that Thailand's Prime Minister Mr. Chuan Leekpai's economic team enjoyed confidence in the market because of the adoption of appropriate measures by his people in proper time.

Thailand told India to tread cautiously on reforms path. It on January 9, 1998 in Chennai, India cautioned India against plunging headlong into globalisation and it requested it to learn from the mistakes committed by some Asian countries which forced them to fall in a severe economic and financial crisis. Mr. Supachai Panitchapakdi, Thailand's deputy Prime Minister, at a special plenary at the partnership Summit organised by the Confederation of Indian Industry (CII) in Chennai, told,

> Avoid repeating the mistakes we made. We were expending our economies when we should have been consolidating and we were not forewarned of the dangers that lay ahead. The Asian economic crisis was not one of over-consumption but of over-investment and excessive reliance on external sources of borrowing as well as misallocation of short-term resources by the private sector in the region. India must put in place a 'water-tight' supervisory mechanism before it liberalised its financial sectors, as 'the speed of globalisation' was a crucial factor in sustaining the reforms process. India

> needed to liberalise and globalise, as it needed investments in excess of its domestic savings particularly to improve its infrastructure facilities. But — and this is a big but — you must have sound supervision system before you liberalise. Striking a note of sobriety and introspection, . . . fortunes had changed for the country in the last few months and leaders were wandering whether they could have been forewarned. The current crisis marked by an 'irrational unreasonable and illogical' meltdown in the values of east and south-east Asian currencies, besides sluggishness in economic growth, threatened to ballon into a global crisis soon.

He defended the Thai government's role in the problem of Thailand's financial crisis and he bitterly criticised the private sector in his country for borrowing from foreign countries too heavily and it did not properly allocate short-term resources in non-tradable assets like real estate. He stated,

> . . . The private sector had been overenthusiastic and committed themselves to high growth and profitability rates, leveraging accordingly and yielded to aspirations of placing their papers in the international capital markes. The government too had erred by allowing a free external borrowing regime to set in. As much as $ 90 billion were borrowed from overseas, with the private sector accounting for $70 billion. They tripped into financial mismatch when repayment commitments starred them in the face, even before their long-term projects became viable.

He requested India to take care of five factors in the efforts to liberalise its financial sector and to allow global capital — namely, stability of the government, management of overseas debts in a proper way, global competitiveness, sound macro-economic management and the speed of globalisation. He said,

> In the new situation, you can't afford to make any big mistake, for the margin for error can't be too large.

He mentioned this in reference to the Indian government's intention to give us interventionary rights in the financial system. He also opined that a coalition government would not do anything to affect economic reforms and coalitions were a fact of life, not just in India, by globally, and he spoke of a stable polilcy which would help to move a government a proper way.

In September 1997, Thailand, in order to reduce corruption and to increase transparency, passed a new constitution.[103] It wanted to move politicians to declare their wealth to the counter corruption commission. One commission investigator, when he spoke on condition of anonymity, referred to the Associated Press that Thailand's economic problems occurred due to its corruption. This was the main cause for it. In 1997, the speaker of the house of representatives mentioned that 50 per cent of the government budget was being siphoned off by graft. Mr. Chuan Leekpai, the Thai Prime Minister, on Monday, January 12, 1998 declared his wealth with only $ 71,400 in assets. The newspapers mentioned him as the poorest in his own cabinet. His cabinet was also poorer than that of his predecessor, Mr. Chavalit Yongchaiyudh. Its members' assets were announced in December 1997, a month after Mr. Chavalit Yongchaiyudh because of Thailand's economic crisis submitted his resignation. Mr. Chuan Leekpai's 49 ministers averaged $ 3.6 million in assets, while Mr. Chavalit Yongchaiyudh's ministers averaged $ 11.1 million. But as in Mr. Chavalit Yongchaiyudh's cabinet, the assets of the wives of Mr. Chuan Leekpai's ministers showed that they were frequently wealthier than their husbands. The Thai Prime Minister's wife had assets worth $ 121,000, nearly twice as much as the Prime Minister. According to several economists, Asia's economic problem was partly to a lack of transparency on debt levels and

---

103. *AA*, January 13, 1997, p. 17.

economic data. Greed was also an important factor. It may be noted here that Thailand's common people in order to boost foreign exchange reserves donated dollars in a campaign and Thailand requested the International Monetary Fund for bailout package, but the ministers and their families paid taxes which were extremely low. Mr. Chavalit Yongchaiyudh's wife with $ 2.5 million in assets paid no taxes on grounds that she was a housewife. According to investigators, the Thai ministers kept wealth in a spouses' name with an idea to hide wealth. Thailand's economists had great confidence in Mr. Chuan Leekpai's government and they stated that it had the capacity to revive the economy than Mr. Chavalit Yongchaiyudh's government which had a reputation for corruption. The former's ministers were also wealthy ministers. Topping the list was Mr. Petiphomg Lamsam, the deputy finance minister. He belonged to a banker's family, and declared $ 24 million in assets. Then Mr. Decha Sukaran, the deputy university affairs minister, with $ 24 million and Mr. Pradit Pataronpasit, the deputy minister of transport, with $ 17.4 million followed him. The latter's wife had $ 25 million in assets. But she paid $ 444 in taxes only. Mr. Chuan Leekpai's government will have to reveal its assets again when its government will leave office. At that time probes would be launched, if any unusual increases in wealth was found. But the counter corruption commission had no power to prosecute Thailand's politicians for wrongdoing. According to investigators, the new constitution played its vital role to strengthen the commission and the commission-members were very serious about their role to reduce graft.

Thailand's cabinet on Tuesday, January 13, 1998, approved a bond issue which it expected that it would help to woo millons of dollars in badly needed foreign currency from expatriate Thais. The state owned Government Savings Bank would issue the three-year bonds which will value at 10.00 baht ($ 180) to make them accessible to all income groups among the Thais living abroad. No limit was imposed on the size of the planned bond issue. But Mr. Chuan Leekpai, the Prime Minister, told on Sunday, January 11, 1998 that Bangkok hoped that the bonds would help to raise $ 500 million for cash-strapped Thailand. Mr. Akapol Serasuchart, the government spokesman, after the weekly meeting of the cabinet, told that the certificates from February 1, 1998 on the first of every month will be an offer. In order to meet the International Monetary Fund's cash surplus targets, which includes a requirement for budget surplus of 1 per cent of gross domestic product for fiscal year 1998, this issue was introduced to help Thailand. Mr. Akapol Serasuchart stated that these bonds would help to carry a coupon equivalent to GSB's (Government Savings Bank) one-year fixed deposit rate plus 1.5 to three percentage points which will be paid every six months. The Thais who are living outside the country will be able to buy the bonds through foreign branches of the Thai banks. The bonds will be exempted from tax and would help to raise cash but the government issues have faced very much by recent sovereign debt ratings downgrades. But the government hoped that individual bond sales will not be disturbed by the ratings cuts. In December 1997, Moody's Investor Services downgraded Thailand's sovereign debt rating to junk bond status, which limited Thailand's government's debt issues to sympathetic investors such as expatriate Thais. On Friday, January 9, 1998, Standard and Poor's rated Thailand's sovereign debt at one notch above junk status. According to several analysts and economists, Thailand did not like to follow Indonesia's path in freezing debt repayments. They told it on Wednesday, January 28, 1998. Although the webbly baht still remains under pressure and has lost more than 50 per cent of its value since last July 1998, yet the Thai currency has recently been more stable. They also mentioned that other positive factors were Thailand's sweeping financial reforms and strict adherence to an International Monetary Fund Programme linked to a $ 17.2 billion bailout package. Other key elements that would keep Thailand's path divergent from Indonesia were found such as a relatively more stable Thai political situation than in Indonesia and a healthier debt to foreign reserves ratio. Mr. Russel Kopp, head of research in Dresdner Kleinwort Benson in Bangkok, stated,

> It is far more unlikely for Thailand. One reason is that the currency has not gone as far as the rupiah has. There is much more stability in terms of the government here. To me, Indonesia is in a period of near anarchy. It is decidedly different. The other thing is, Thailand today has done reasonable well IMF-wise. And there is some hope or optimism that Thailand can be first in, first out (of the crisis).

The World Bank's president Mr. James Welfensehn visited Thailand on Friday, January 30, 1998 to see Thailand's financial situation and how Thailand has utilised the International Monetary Fund $ 17.2 bailout package to save itself from financial crisis and to restore investor's confidence. He announced that the bank would extend $ 300 million in new loans to Thailand to tackle unemployment. The Thai officials told that the loan would be in addition to the $ 1.5 billion pledged by the World Bank as part of the $ 17.2 billion International Monetary Fund's bailout package for Thailand. The World Bank Chief discussed this matter with Thailand's Prime Minister, who went to Davos, Switzerland in the last week of January 1998 to attend the World Economic Forum annual meeting. A team from the International Monetary Fund on Monday, February 2, 1998 arrived in Thailand and they met the officials of the Central Bank of Thailand. The Thai officials hoped that this will help to do a relaxation of some conditions of the International Monetary Fund's bailout package for Thailand. These representatives from the International Monetary Fund came to Thailand for their quarterly review of the country's progress under its $ 17.2 billion rescue fund. Their meetings with Thailand's top finance officials could bring a good result in relaxation of certain condition which have been blamed for unnecessarily strangling economic growth. Mr. Tarrin

Nimmanahaeminda, Thailand's finance minister, returned from the United States in the last week of January 1998 and he told that he had received assurances from the officials of the International Monetary Fund that the conditions imposed by it would be changed to reflect Thailand's new economic circumstances. The Thai finance officials stated that if the International Monetary Fund wished to relax certain budgetary conditions, then Thailand will be greatly benefitted by them and will be able to stand quickly on its feet from its economic turmoil.

> Economic growth could move into negative territory unless the government is given a reprieve from the International Monetary Fund conditions requiring a budget surplus in fiscal 1998 of about one per cent of GDP.

Thailand's government from its 1997-98 budget slashed about 180 billion baht ($ 3.5 billion) but even then, it would be impossible to meet the International Monetary Fund — targeted budget surplus of about 69 billion baht. All sectors of Thailand's economy were hard hit by the spending cuts and this would lead to massive unemployment unless the government is allowed to borrow more money to fund state investment. Mr. Mohamad Al Fayed, the owner of Harrods department store, told on Monday, February 1, 1998 that he met the Thai Prime Minister Mr. Chuan Leekpai and took keen interest to invest in several projects involving development of natural resources and minerals in Thailand. According to several analysts, glimpses of a mild turn-around in crisis-hit Thailand may be cause for encouragement, but the country still has to go a long way before it can be able to reach its target and to recover its lost prestige. Mr. Simon Flint, an analyst at Singapore-based reasearch house I.D.E.A., stated,

> Things are starting to look up for Thailand but it is not exactly out of woods yet. There is room for optimism but one should not be carried away.

The Thai government undertook financial reforms and for this reason Thailand's currency and stock market have brought good results. The Thai baht's abrupt drop on Wednesday, February 4, 1998 from highs near 46.00 to the dollar triggered falls in other South-East Asian currencies, which had been climbing steadily this week after Bangkok scrapped a two-tier trading system. The Thai dealers mentioned that the baht's fall took place owing to king Bhumibol Adulyadej's ill-health and a huge Thai corporate order for the dollars to settle debt payments. Local Thai companies had to buy about $ 300 million for a loan redemtion and the market was short. The US funds joined the selling when the dollar broke and that was the reason for the baht's fall. But the baht was back above the 50 per dollar on Thursday, February 5, 1998 when the matters relating to the king was hopeful after he gave a talk on television on Wednesday night (February 4, 1998). The Internataional Monetary Fund may relax the tough economic conditions imposed by it on Thailand and may allow the Thai government to run a budget deficit on 1-2 per cent of gross domestic product this fiscal year. According to the *Nation* daily, the International Monetary Fund and the World Bank understood that because of the regional economic crisis the Thai economy has slowed very much than expectd. Under the present International Monetary Fund conditions, in the present fiscal year the Thai government will have to show and to register a budget surplus of 1 per cent of gross domestic product to help to write off the bad debts of defunct financial institutions. But the rapid economic contraction since mid-1997 has destroyed tax revenue and for this reason the government has become helpless and was unable to balance the budget. If the International Monetary Fund approves the relaxation of its conditions in March 1998, then it would bring a great change in its bailout loans. The International Monetary Fund, the Thai finance ministry and the Bank of Thailand officials discussed the contents of the letter of intent which will be issued by the Thai government to qualify for a third International Monetary Fund loan installment of $ 1.7 -1.8

billion. Thailand has already received $ 4 billion and $ 3 billion as the first installment of its $ 17.2 billion multilateral bailout package in August 1997. Mr. Hubert Neiss, the International Monetary Fund Pacific chief, visited Thailand in the second week of February 1998 to finalise the contents of the third letter and a team from the International Monetary Fund arrived in Thailand in the first week of February 1998 and stayed for three weeks to review Thailand's economic progress and package terms. Mr. Tarrin Nimmanahaeminda, Thailand's finance minister, told that the International Monetary Fund would announce its revised terms by February 24, 1998 if the negotiations go well.

Thailand has donated 5,000 tonnes of rice and one million baht worth of medicine to Indonesia to help the nation when that country has faced severe economic crisis.[104] Mr. Surin Pitsuwan, Thailand's foreign minister, told on Tuesday, February 10, 1998 that he met President Suharto of Indonesia and he believed that the President "has a very, very firm grasp of all the issues that are facing all of us in South-East Asia". He mentioned further that it was a token donation of rice to ease any possible shortage of food. For victims of a drought in the eastern province of Irian Jaya Thailand gave one million baht worth of medicine. Japan has offered to loan Thailand money to help to ease rising unemployment because of the country's economic downturn. A meeting between Mr. Surin Pitsuwan, Thailand's foreign minister and a Japanese parliamentary delegation took place and they discussed a yen loan to support employment projects. The *Bangkok Post* mentioned,

> Discussion are at the initial stage. But the amount will not differ from the loan Japan extended to Indonesia, and depends on the projects Thailand proposes.

Mr. Hiroshi Ota, the Japanese ambassador to Thailand, initially made the offer to Mr. Surin Pitsuwan, Thailand's foreign minister

---

104. *AA*, February 11, 1998, p. 7.

and Mr. Tarrin Nimmanahaeminda, Thailand's finance minister, at a meeting in the first week of February 1998. Official estimate mentioned Thailand's unemployment at about 1.2 million people or 3.5 per cent of the workforce, but the number of jobless are expected to top two million later this year. The delegation of senior Japanese politicians from the ruling Liberal Democratic Party promised to recommend increased Japanese assistance for Thailand. Mr. Tara Nakayama, the delegation leader, and the former foreign minister, told that Japan would provide assistance to Thai students in Japan to help to ease their financial burden because of the weak baht. Japan's financial institutions threw a lifeline to Thailand's debt-ridden companies when the Thai government declared that up to 90 per cent of the country's private debts to Japan would be rolled over. The Overseas Economic Co-operation Fund of Japan meanwhile has made a plan to provide additional foreign currency loans to Thailand to boost its reserves and to ease domestic liquidity. Mr. Yugi Morimote, the chief representative of the Overseas Economic Co-operation Fund of Japan, told that the 'counterpart fund' was set to be introduced along with its 23rd Overseas Economic Co-operation Fund loan project for Thailand later this year. The dealer told,

> I have been waiting for a response from the finance ministry as to what we could do to help to solve the economic problems in Thailand.

In the second week of February 1998 the two-day meeting took place in Bali in Indonesia of the governors of South-East Asia's Central Banks — Indonesia, Malaysia, Philippines, Singapore, Thailand and Myanmar as well as Taiwan, South Korea, Nepal and Sri Lanka. Cambodia, Fuji and Tonga attended as observers. They, in order to resolve Asia's mounting debt problems, urged quick deals between creditors and lenders. They also requested the International Monetary Fund to be more flexible in imposing conditions for bailout funds and other aid to economies troubled by the regional currency crisis. On Friday, February 13, 1998 the governors wated to talk to the Group of Seven industrialised nations to help their countries to overcome financial turmoil as most regional currencies were hit by fresh weakness. They are Uninted States, Japan, Germany, France Canada, Italy and Britain.

Thailand wanted to abolish its decades-old anti-communism law which some politicians told that it could be used to suppress ordinary citizens. After the fall of the Berlin Wall and the collapse of the Soviet Union, Thailand has begun to think that its 1952 Anti Communism Act may no longer be necessary. Mr. Sanan Kajornprasart, Thailand's interior minister, stated,

> This anit-Communist law should be abolished because it can be used to restrict citizen's rights.

The Thai government has taken precautionary measures for cleaning up the banking and finance sectors, but looming mass bankruptcies and staff lay-offs were seen in the corporate sector. Mr. Bill Anderson, Seamice Securities analyst told,

> On the financial side they have actually been relatively decisive by shutting down some of the finance companies and taking over banks. I think, though, on the corporate side you are going to have nasty stories coming out over the next few months, including a huge number of bankruptcies. In the reasonably short term we are going to find out which companies are going to survive and which are not.

Although the International Monetary Fund was fully satisfied with Thailand's work, yet several Thai analysts in Bangkok have warned that more painful times lie ahead for Thailand on its long march to establish Thailand on its feet to regain confidence from its people and to save itself from its economic recovery. Mr. Tarrin Nimmanahaeminda, Thailand's finance minister, ruled out a currency beard regime for Thailand and distinguished between the Thai and Indonesian economies. Mr. Akapol Serasuchart, a government spokesman, mentioned the view of the finance minister, who referred to the government's economic council and said that despite speculation in the Thai markets in the first week of February 1998, a currency beard will not be introduced in Thailand. The baht's latest decline was tied to the rupiah's fall. But he was quite sure that the baht's improvement will take place because there was a great difference between Thailand's economy and Indonesia's economy.

Thailand's army on Monday, February 23, 1998 began to move 10,490 Karen rufugees from camps to place next to Salween national park in a bid to curb illegal begging trade.[105] They came from Myanmar. Thailand's army officers told the Karen refugees that you move either to a new refugee camp or you return to Myanmar. They said that the refugees were based at Ban-Au-Da-Na, Ban-Mae-Sakeeb, Ban-Ko-Ta and Ban-Seb-Jae in Mae-Sariang district of Mae-Hong-Song province in north-east Thailand. They were offered shelter at Mae-La-Luang refugee camp and also in Mae-Sariang district but further from the park's boundaries. The armey officer spoke on this occasion,

> We will move them out of the area to the Mae-La-Luang refugee camp or they can go to their country. It's their decision. Whatever they decide to do, it will be finished before the rainy season.

General Boonsak Kamhaengritthirong, the national security council secretary-general earlier requested non-government organisations to help the Thai government move the Karen refugees from the national park in Thailand's north-west border region. According to Thailand's forestry officials, Thailand's business people have engaged the Karen refugees to cut timber mostly teak to send it to Myanmar where it was stamped with Myanmarese seals and then, 'exported' back to Thailand. Mr.

---

105. *AA*, February 23, 1998, p. 5.

Chuan Leekpai, Thailand's Prime Minister, in the second week of February 1998 toured the forest-area and he felt frustrated to see that large areas of the park were severely damaged. Thailand's government officials told on Sunday, July 5, 1998 that it wanted to enlist United Nation's help to molve some 80,000 Kareon refugees to a camp considered very safe from cross-border raids by the guorrillas from Myanmar. Mr. Kobsak Chutikul, Thailand's foreign ministry spokesman stated that the refugees would be moved in July 1998 from Huay Kalek on the Thai-Myanmar border in north-western Tak province to Mae La camp further inside Thai region. The move followed months of deliberations on how the refugees will be protected from pre-Rangoon guerrillas's raids. Many Karen people were homeless and several people died in attacks on Huay Kalek camp by the Democratic Karen Buddhist Army earlier this year (1998).

According to Thailand's dealers, Thailand's stocks ended Friday, February 27, 1998 2.2 per cent as foreign players moved back into the market despite regional financial problem and fears of a Gulf conflict. A top regional analyst suggested that Thailand should take decision to implement a currency beard to control the volatile baht. He mentioned that Thailand should avoid politicians to give any kind of control over monetary policy in the future. Because there are many reasons to doubt their judgement on that issue. In order to keep monetary policy away from the politicians, Thailand should implement a currency beard foreign exchange system, Mr. Kobsak Chutikul, the director-general of the economic department in Thailand's foreign ministry, told that 80 per cent of Thailand's trade deficit was with Japan. "There is a general feeling in the region that Japan has to do more to shoulder the burden." Although few Japanese firms have left Thailand, some have reduced their instruments, especially in the auto-industry and several Japanese banks have made no big loans. Mr. Masatsube Ngate, the manager of Thai operation for industrial bank of Japan, stated,

> We have a saying that you should not weary if the night is dark because the dawn will come. But you have to survive the night first. How long will it be.

It may be mentioned here that Thai shares lost ground in morning trade on Tuesday, February 24, 1998 as investors remained sidelined before announcements of revised economic forecasts and possible tax rises. The Stock Exchange of Thailand composite index fell 9.08 points — or 1.7 per cent — to 512.74 in the morning session, while the Set 50 composits index shed 0.8 points to 38.32. According to Thailand's analysts, investors wanted to know the outcome of a crucial cabinet meeting which will consider the latest economic forecasts under the IMF-led bailout package as well as the possible implementation of higher taxes and a new duty on it.

> The latest economic forecasts to be included in the third 'letter of intent' with the IMF are expected to include negative GDP growth of minus three per cent in 1998.

The oil tax proposal would raise the price of petrol and this would lead to higher inflation as transport coss impacted on all levels of the economy. The poll of ten analysts in Thailand and Singapore mentioned an average forecast of 44.00 baht in the dollar in three months' time, compared with around 42.90/43.10 early on Friday, February 27, 1998. The Thai unit has lost around 40 per cent of its value, since it was floated on July 2, 1997. The poll indicated a wide range of expectations varying from a high of 37.50 per dollar to a low of 50. Several analysts described that positive export and current account data would underpin the baht in the coming three months.

Several South-East Asian finance ministers requested major industrial countries to help the region's battered economy by opening their markets more to the Asian imports. They wanted assistance from world's wealthy nations like the US, Japan and Europe to help Asia to recover from its economic crisis. They in

Jakarta for two-day meeting also launched a proposal to set-up surveillance system to keep a closer eye on the region's economies. They wanted to encourage trade among the countries in the region, but a proposal to use local currencies for local trade would have to be worked out between trading partners. Mr. Mahathir Mohamad, Malaysia's Prime Minister, referred to the local currency idea and President Fidel Ramos of the Philippines supported it but Thailand was skeptical about the plan. In a joint communique after a two-day Asean meeting, the finance ministers from the region told that they supported the use of bilateral payment arrangements as proposed by the special task force of the Asean Central Banks.

> The approach will initially be implemented on a voluntary basis, with a view to evolving this facility into a multilateral arrangement. . . . This regional Central Banks would act as clearing houses for trade payments and would offset each other's receivables and pay the differences in the US dollars. . . .

Thailand's opposition parties submitted a no-confidence motion against the government of Thailand's Prime Minister Mr. Chuan Leekpai on Monday, March 2, 1998 and they blamed the administration for incompetence and corruption.[106] Mr. Kuthep Saikrajang, a spokesman of the main opposition New Aspiration Party, told,

> The opposition has reached a common view and is set to submit the no-confidence motion against the government later on Monday.

After the submission of the motion, the president of the Lower House of Representatives will decide when it will be debated. Mr. Tarrin Nimmanahaeminda, Thailand's finance minister, has pledged direct support to cash-strapped banks and finance

106. *AA*, March 3, 1998, p. 7.

companies to raise new capital and a major reform of the Cental Bank. This was disclosed on Monday, March 2, 1998. He said that

> as the government's efforts to create macro-economic stability over the last three months had borne fruit, he would now be able to get down to that issues.

He stated the hands-on support for financial institutions looking for new capital and reform of the Bank of Thailand was very important for the restoration of investors' confidence in Thailand's shattered economy. He told further,

> the key issue was that banks had to recapitalise as quickly as possible to limit the damage cause by their massive bad debts and to reintroduce liquidity into the financial systems.

He also mentioned,

> If banks could not find local investors to buy new shares, they could always offer the shares of attractive prices to client depositors. That is why we have changed the regulations to international standards.

Thailand's Prime Minister Mr. Chuan Leekpai and President Suharto of Indonesia at the latter's Credana residence in Jakarta, Indonesia, on Monday, March 2, 1998 met to discuss the current economic crisis gripping South-East Asian nations,[107] and they were satisfied with their talks. They discussed many problems of their countries and they tried to find out the paths to solve these problems. France's banking giant Banque Paribas S.A. on Monday, March 2, 1998 mentioned that its exposure to Indonesia and other crisis-struck Asian countries was 'one of the lowest' among European banks. It described that it had a total outstanding credit of $ 2,712 billion to Indonesia, Thailand,

---

107. *AA*, March 3, 1998, p. 20.

Malaysia, South Korea and Philippines and that it created a general provision of $ 314 million 'against Asian risk'. Mr. Chavalit Yongchaiyudh's government was responsible for permitting around $ 30 billion in financial sector bailouts which brought the country's economy to its knees. A government committee which was set-up to probe the Central Bank's abortive bailouts of shattered financial institutions blamed Thailand's last government's policy and did not say anything against the bank's administration. It stated,

> There was no instance of corruption, yet the system needs improvement. Ultimately, however, responsibility rests with the last government.

Mr. Tarrin Nimmanahaeminda, Thailand's finance minister, in December 1997 gave his order to investigate into decisions to bailout finance firms and banks to the tune of around 800 billion baht ($ 30 billion) from 1996. Mr. Krirkkiat Pipathseritham, a probe committee member, told that Mr. Chavalit Yongchaiyudh's government had made law which helped to open the door for the rescue fund to lend billions of dollars. He described,

In the past, the fund required firms to place collateral against any loans, but the last government adjusted this law to allow loans without collateral. Mr. Nukul Prachuabmoh, the former Central Bank chief, was the leader of the probe committee and

> was charged with determining who was responsible for deploting the country's precious foreign reserves in events leading up to the country's collapse.

Mr. Chaiyawat Wibulsawasdi, Thailand's Central Banks's governor, met the cabinet and discussed on the status of the Central Bank rescue fund which "made the massive, and new largely irretrievable, loans". In August 1997 the International Monetary Fund sanctioned $ 17.2 bailout package to Thailand to solve its economic crisis and under its conditions, the central government over the next several years will repay the losses to the fund. The debt's interest alone will be more than 60 billion baht ($ 1.4 billion) a year. Mr. Chuan Leekpai cabinet received this report when the opposition parties led by Mr. Chavalit Youngchiyudh submitted a no-confidence motion against the government for its inefficiency and corruption. A report said on Wednesday, March 4, 1998 that the Thai premier Mr. Chuan Leekpai has given his approval on a British 'ASEM' trust fund initiative, and stated that it should cater to cash-strapped private-sector companies. He supported this idea which was proposed by Mr. Derek Fatchatt, the special European Union envoy and a British junior foreign minister, at meetings with Thailand's senior politicians and officials. The former mentioned that the fund which would be used primarily not only for technical assistance but also would deal with the social impact of the crisis. It would also give a guarantee facility for private flows. Mr. Na Htun, the United Nations' assistant secretary-general and the UNDP assistant administrator, attended the United Nations' conference 'On the Social Impact on the Asian Financial crisis' on Thursday, March 5, 1998 at the United Nations' Conference Centre in Bangkok. Mr. Chuan Leekpai, Thailand's Prime Minister, was present there and he warned that traditional social values might be affected by the ongoing crisis. A report mentione that the United States offered between $ 3 billion and $ 5 billion additional fund to Thailand to help its economic restructuring drive. This report arrived in Thailand after the United States' officials praised its efforts to implement reforms introduced by the International Monetary Fund and also stated that Washington was so pleased with its performance that it would play a great role to sanction additional International Monetary Fund's fund to help Thailand in its reforms and to revive its economy. The *Nation* daily quoted,

> the US administration would 'if Circumstances demand' contribute up to $ 5 billion more to Bangkok's $ 17.2 billion bailout.

The source described,

> The US would like to show its support for Thailand which has so far achieved stabilisation. Besides, Thailand's progress should further be distinguished from the rest of Asia's.

This was commented after the International Monetary Fund in Washington on Wednesday, March 4, 1998 sanctioned a further $ 270 million to Thailand to help to gain confidence and stability in Bangkok. The International Monetary Fund managing director Michel Camdessus stated that the fund approved the loan at a board meeting. He opined,

> Directors strongly commended the Thai authorities for resolutely implementing the economic programme in very diffucult circumstances and noted that this approach was increasingly being reflected in improved market sentiment.

Mr. Hikaru Matsunaga, Japan's finance minister, stated that Tokyo was ready to offer additional International Monetary Fund's to Thailand. Thailand's finance chiefs were very much happy to receive the news of the release of more funds of international rescue funds and Washington's assurance to support its case for more credit if necessary. Bangkok always tried to follow the conditions of the International Monetary Fund as far as possible. Mr. Tarrin Nimmanahaeminda, Thailand's finance minister, opined that the US treasury secretary Mr. Robert Rubin gave him encouragement and the latter stated that Washington would back his country for extra credit. He described,

> We are pleased that treasury secretary Rubin has expressed full support for additional IMF financing for Thailand in the forms of the supplementary rescue facility, if circumstances warrant. This is consistent with the IMF's understanding with Thailand and the IMF-supported economic programme.

A report stated on Friday, March 6, 1998 that about 1,500 angry Thai farmers with an idea to win government's help staged a rowdy and smelly protest outside the agriculture ministry in Bangkok. They bisieged it and polted it with plastic bags filled with urine and excrement.

A group of Thailand's activists staged a protest outside the US embassy in Bangkok on Tuesday, March 10, 1998 and they delivered a letter requesting Mr. Bill Clinton, the US President, to discuss human rights to Myanmar with Mr. Chuan Leekpai, Thailand's Prime Minister, during his visit to Washington. The Thai Action Committee for Democracy in Myanmar took part in this demonstration.

> They staged a play outside the embassy with a man dressed as member of an ethinic minority group from Myanmar. His legs were chained and he was beaten by a man dressed as a Myanmarese soldier.

A political officer of the US embassy received a letter from this group, which tried to draw attention to the human rights abuses in Myanmar and requested the US President to take interest in this matter and to do something for it. The letter mentioned about Thailand's Prime Minister's visit to the United States in the second week of March 1998.

> This will be a good opportunity for your Excellency to express strong concern on human rights violations in Myanmar.

The letter requested the US President to pressure the US businessmen to suspend their investments in Myanmar. Because he has already given permission for the approval of economic sanctions on this country. Thailand's Prime Minister, in order to cement the Thai-US relations and to boost investors' confidence in Thailand's battered economy, went to the United States. At the start of a visit to the country he addresed he Council of Foreign Relations in New York on Thursday, March 12, 1998 and appealed to the world's leading industrial powers to consider to reform the global financial system to ensure quitable growth.[108] He called for global economic reform. He told that Thailand would sincerely implement reforms prepared by the International Monetary Fund with an idea to revive its economy and to restore stability in Bangkok. His visit was billed as a major effort to convince investors that Thailand was committed to the International Monetary Fund-dictated reforms as part of the $ 17.2 billion bailout package. So he left Thailand for the United States on a trip which aimed at boosting investors's confidence in Thailand's battered economy. He described,

> We need all members of the international community and especially members of the G-7/8, who represent most of the world economic might, to look long and hard at the existing global system so that it can be reformed and rejuvenated where necessary to ensure that the new growth cycle will be equitable and sustained.

He referred to the Group of Seven nations plus Russia-Britain, Canada, France, Germany, Italy, Japan and the United States. He met the US President Mr. Bill Clinton on Friday, March 13, 1998 in Washington. He told that his government was 'going full-stream ahead' with a programme of Thailand's political reform that started in October 1997 with the introduction of a new constitution. He mentioned that Thailand's relationship with the International Monetary Fund was

> critical to the revival of market confidence and economic recovery. We commitment, consultation and transparency as the corner-stones of this relationship.

He thought that complacency was responsible for the recent economic crisis. He described,

---

108. *AA*, March 18, 1998, p. 18.

> During the period of rapid economic growth, we were too complacent. In the good times, we forget many important truths and neglected many important tasks. We created wealth but were perhaps negligent in creating competitiveness. We were successful in our economic performance, so much so that we did not examine the fundamentals of our politics and goverance, or tackle issues, such as bureaucratic inefficiency, lack of transparency and lack of accountability. Once the cracks appeared, we compounded the mistakes by committing much of our fiscal reserve to share up insolvent finance companies and our foreign reserve to defend the baht (the Thai currency). Naturally, we were quickly and severely disciplined by the market.

He talked with the US officials and he referred to Thailand's difficulty in honouring a 390-million-dollar contract with McDonnell Douglas in 1996 for the delivery of F/A-18 fighter jets. He felt sorry for this. He had no money with him for the F-18 fighter jets. He requested the United States' Politicians to understand the reality of the situation in Thailand and asked their businessmen to come to Thailand to invest there. The foreign creditors spoke highly of his government for its efficiency and praised it for carrying out painful reforms in exchange for bailouts from the International Monetary Fund. The United States announced on Friday, March 13, 1998 that it will buy-back eight F/A-18 fighter jets which Thailand gave its order in 1996 to help to relieve the country's financial woes. The declaration of this offer of assistance was made as Mr. Bill Clinton, the US President met Mr. Chuan Leekpai, Thailand's Prime Minister in the Oval office at the White House in Washington on Saturday, March 14,1998 to talk and to discuss the latter's country's economic turmoil. As a good will gesture to an old ally, the Clinton administration agreed to release the Thai government from a contract agreement to buy US-made jet fighters that it can no longer afford due to the battering its economy has received. Thailand's Prime Minister offered public apologies to the Wall Street while he sought support from the US governmennt and banks for his country's economic reforms. He confessed that Thailand's complacency was 'quickly and severaly disciplined by the market' and he became Prime Minister after the collapse of the Thai baht and his predecessor was forced to resign afger this incident. He told a gathering of bankers and academics at a reception on Wednesday night, March 11, 1998 hosted by the Council of Foreign Relations and the Asia Society-the two New York-based thinktanks,

> During the period of rapid economic growth, we were too complacent. We opened up our economy, but our stated plans to pursue discipline were not followed up. He acknowledged that the Thai government had not revamped its bureaucracy to make it more efficient and accountable, and had not created a competitive enough economy, noting mournfully that 'there is immunity in success'. He promised to meet the harsh targets recommended by the International Monerary Fund to close more than half of Thai finance companies, to cut state spending in the 1997-98 budget by 16 per cent and to raise taxes. Our relationship with the International Monetary Fund is key to the revival of market confidence and economic recovery. He would continue the political reforms the country has followed since the baht last nearly half its value last summer. He assured that the government would make 'substantial' progress in 1998 in enacting draft laws to implement the country's new constitution, passed last October (1997).

He also met top US state department and finance officials in Washington in the second week of March 1998. He needed the Wall Street's support to roll over much of the country's short-term debt, estimated to total some $ 3.6 billion by the end of 1998.

Bustered by the United States' help for his significant role to handle his country's financial crisis. Thailand's Prime Minister Mr. Chuan Leekpain faced a no-confidence debate on Wednesday, March 18, 1998 that proved more damaging to his opposition than his government and he survived the no-trust motion. Under his leadership the country has slowly but steadily emerged from the Asian economic turmoil and it established an example for other stricken nations on how to regain investors' confidence. The baht reached a 1998 high last Friday, March 13, 1998 as Mr. Bill Clinton, the US President, rewarded Mr. Chuan Leekpai's government for following a strict path for tough reforms mentioned by the International Monetary Fund in exchange for a $ 17.2 billion bailout in 1997. Mr. Bill Clinton sanctioned a new aid package for Thailand which was equal to 10 per cent of the bailout. It is pity to note here that the no-trust motion was moved by Mr. Chavalit Yongchaiyudh, the former general, who preceded Mr. Leekpai and led Thailand into last year's meltdown. Mr. Leekpai, a quiet lawyer, who served as Prime Minister between 1992 and 1995, made a governing alliance with eight parties led by the members of his own group, the Democrat Party. In three years this was the fourth Thai government and it contained several small parties from Mr. Yongchaiyudh's old coalition. Despite a narrow 207 to 185 majority, it was regarded as the most forceful in years.

> Mr. Leekpai is seen as corruption-bedeviled Thailand's most honest active politician. But the government's future is not as strong as Mr. Leekpai would like. Its majority could be reduced to just 10 seats if a rebel faction of the small Prachakorn Thai Party is forced out. A dozen Prachakorn Thai MPs joined Mr. Leekpai in forming the government, infuriating the party leader and avowed Leekpai enemy, Mr. Samak Sundaravej. He dubbed the rebels 'cobras' and is working to expel them from his party and their parliamentary seats. Mr. Sundaravej is leading the opposition attack in the two-day no-

> confidence debate. But the assault is more likely to target smalll parties with shady histories in previous governments. Expected accusations of corruption, however, may be blamed by the fact that the opposition parties levelling them have all in recent years served in the same governments as their targets. The opposition itself is far from united. The Chart Pattana Party, led by the former Prime Minister Mr. Chatichai Choonhavan, says it will not attack Mr. Leekpai head on, keeping open doors to eventually join his government. Rather Mr. Leekpai would probably be forced to seek a new ally in the Chart Pattana Party — an unstable combination that is likely to founder, or he could call for fresh elections.

The Thai baht remained the darling of the Asian currencies, briefly rising above the 40 per cent dollar level, and allowing Mr. Chaiyawat Wibulsawasdi, the Central Bank governor, to comment at the prospect of lower interest rates. He told, "The trend of a more stable baht could give rooms for lower interest rates." He mentioned further that the positive media reports relating to Thailand's Prime Minister's US visit had boosted market sentiment. We can say here that Thailand's fortune inspired tired Asian currencies. Several hundred poor Thai farmers in front of Thailand's government house demonstrated for more than a week and shouted and gave slogans and told that the Thai government did nothing to solve their problems. Mr. Alongkorn Palabut, Mr. Chuan Leekpai's personal secretary, suspected that the chief opposition party, the New Aspiration Party, took active part to help the Thai farmers to show this type of protest to raise tensions ahead of the no-confidence debate which began on Wednesday, March 18, 1998. But Mr. Chuan Leekpai was widely expected to survive the two-day censure debate. He returned from a successful trip to the US and there he received $ 1.7 billion in assistance as an endorsement for his significant role to handle the economic crisis of Thailand. Mr.

Alongkorn Palabut described that the farmers' leader Mr. Vaychai Matwa had good relations with Mr. Chingchai Mongkoitham, the New Aspiration's deputy leader and he was mentioned as 'one of the driving forces behind the censures debate'. He stated further,

> The gathering in front of the government house in the beginning was because people had problems, grievances.

But at this moment, he suspected the intentions of the leaders. Mr. Vaychai Matwa told that he did not play politics, and the farmers belonged to the poor, rural north-east and it was a stronghold of the New Aspiration Party and its leader was ex-Prime Minister Mr. Chavalit Yongchaiyudh. The farmers were very unhappy with unfulfilled promises to solve their problems and they felt frustrated to see the government's hopeless role to tackle their problem. Mr. Vaychai Matwa mentioned that the Thai government had promised to give the protestors 50 tents and 50 sacks of rice during the time of protest on the street outside the government house but they received only 10 tents and 3 sacks of rice. He opined that about 7,000 people took part in this demonstration but witnesses told that they numbered about 300. Thailand on Tuesday, March 17, 1998 announced that it would from April 1, 1998 double to 500 baht ($ 12.5) the exit tax for all International travellers leaving from its aiarports. A Thai government spokesman stated that despite the hike in the exit tax from 250 baht previously, it was much cheaper than that charged by other countries. The Thai cabinet at its weekly meeting took the decision to raise the exit tax. The Thai government hoped that it would earn 2 billion baht ($ 50 million) in revenue annually from the increase in this exit tax. The government spokesman announced,

> This should not affect the Thais too much because only 17 per cent of outbound travellers (from Thai airports) are the Thais.

A Thai censure debate against Mr. Chuan Leekpai's government was extended into a third day on Friday March 20, 1998, but he was still seen as certain of defeating the censure vote, scheduled for Saturday, March 21, 1998 which would help him to regain confidence in the economy by following strictly several measures of the International Monetary Fund. He survived a no-trust vote. On Saturday morning, March 21, 1998 he easily defeated a censure motion and won the vote in Thailand's Parliament by 208 to 177 after several days of attacks by the opposition. It may be noted here that he, who assumed power in November 1997 for the second time, was widely expected to win and to survive the no-confidence vote. Several economists and international leaders spoke highly of him and praised his leadership for guiding and inspiring Thailand in a proper way to achieve its goal. During the debate Thailand's interior and industry ministers were criticised by the opposition for their roles, but the Prime Minister did not want any cabinet reshuffle. His administartion has launched sweeping financial reforms under the guidance of the International Monetary Fund. Its activities and its movement in proper direction have established to some extent Thailand's position on solid foundation and have looked forward to lift its economic condition out of its crisis. Thailand was the first Asian country to ask the International Monetary Fund to sanction a bailout package and in August 1997 it received a $ 17.2 billion bailout package. According to the World Bank, Indonesia was not a major Thai export market and Thailand would not be badly affected by the former's economic crisis. On the baht's sharp recovery to a nearly four month high to around 40 per the US dollar on Monday, March 16, 1998, the World Bank official told that it was another boost for Thailand. The baht which at one point had lost over 50 per cent of its value since its floatation in July 1997 was down by about 36 per cent.

The Dutch banking giant ABN-Amro Holding NV has announced to purchase Thailand's 11th largest commercial bank, the Bank of Asia, on a buy-now, set the price-latter plan. It wanted to buy a majority stake in the Bank of Asia, but it would adjust the price later according to the value of the bank in two years. Mr. Ton De Beer, chief executive of ABN-Amro Asia-Pacific Plc stated,

> Basically the deal is a case of buy now and pay now, but adjust the price later when conditions are more normal.

Taiwan's China Development Corporation wished to spend $ 15 million to buy a 59 per cent stake in a unit of Bangkok Bank PCL. In preparation for a possible deal, Thailand's second largest bank, Thai Farmer's Bank declared that it would amend its articles of association to permit up to 49 per cent foreign ownership.

> Pending completion of due diligence, ABN-Amro will pay 7.5 billion baht ($187.3 million) for newly issued shares representing 75 pre cent of the Bank of Asia's enlarged capital. But in order to allow a 'fair valuation' of the Thai bank during calmer economic conditions, it was agreed that the Dutch bank would also pay a second instalment in two years. The amount of the second instalment will be calculated by an independent auditor using a formula the two sides have agreed. Prime concerns preventing a fair voluation of the bank new were currency volatility, the unknown number of non-performing loans and the general crisis environment affecting much of Asia. After the dollar soared from 25 baht in July 1997 to beyond 50 baht in January 1998, it has recently retreated to about 40 baht. This volatility combined with plunging stock values and deteriorating economic conditions, has made it hard to estimate how many of Thailand's heavily indebted companies will be able to repay their outstanding loans. 'In these conditions, an assessment of the fair value of the bank is extremely difficult. It is also a great carrot for management. I will be very happy to pay a great deal in the second tranche

because it means the bank is doing well and the economy is recovering.

Top leaders from ten Asian countries and fifteen members of the European nations met in London for the April 2-4 1998 second Asia-Europe Meeting with the Asian financial crisis wighing heavily on them. Mr. Tony Blair, the British Prime Minister, informally kicked off the twenty-five-nations Asia-Europe Meeting on Thursday, April 2, 1998. He addressed world leaders at the ASEM II Summit at the Queen Elizabeth II centre in London on Saturday, April 4, 1998. This was the second summit of ASEM and the first Asia Europe Meeting between leaders of 25 Asian and Eruropean nations was held in Bangkok in 1996. At the first meeting the Asian leaders requested the European leaders to pounce on the opportunities made by the vibrant tigers of East and South-East Asia. The Asian tigers showed their confidence with vigour and energy and the Europeans envied their strong economic growth. They were jealous of it. Now both sides were united by hopes by that Asia would recover before long from a crisis triggered by currency turmoil since mid-1997 and some Asian officials mentioned that the Eruopean Union (EU) might play a great role for greater trade liberalisation at an awkward time for Asia. Now some of the Asian countries were disturbed by social and economic problems and they wanted help from Europe. During the second ASEM summit, the leaders discussed the environmental and social issues. The European Union governments gave assurances on Thursday, April 2, 1998 that they would do their best to help Asia out of its financial turmoil as long as the governments there allowed to keep their markets open and follow economic reforms. When the leaders from the 15 European nations met the leaders from the ten Asian countries. Britain, the host country, pledged support to give all kinds of help to Asia to re-establish its position and to recover itself from its worst economic crisis. The European ministers declared that they have not done enough to solve a financial crisis that forced Indonesia, Thailand and South Korea to take help from the International Monetary Fund for bailout package totalling more than $ 100 billion. Mr. Jacques Chirac, the French President, told that he was sure that after a period of adjustment Asia

> would became back from the crisis which did not mean the end of the 'Asian Miracle'. Asia could expect a show of support from Europe at the summit.

Mr. Apinan Pavanarit, the director-general of the European Department of Thailand's ministry of foreign affairs, expressed,

> The second ASEM is quite timely in the sense that we are now facing this financial crisis.

In it Thailand's leaders referred to their financial sector crisis and the beginning of the regional turmoil in 1997 owing to currency crash and they spoke to the European leaders about several measures they have adopted to restore confidence. Mr. Chuan Leekpai, Thailand's Prime Minister, requested the European countries to move and to restructure corporate debts and to make preparation for export credits. Mr. Apinan Pavanarit, one of the main organisers of the first ASEM summit in Bangkok, told that we should not be friends just in times of prosperity, but we should be friends in time of need as well. Europe was interested in Asia's problems because it had a vested interest. The European banks alone have exposure of about $ 350 billion in Asia — more than the United States and Japan combined. He wanted Europe to help and support "for Asia's efforts to come to grips with its financial crisis". In addition to the regular chairman's statement, Thailand has appealed to the Asian and European leaders for a separate statement on Asia's economic crisis which dealt with Europe's efforts to help to tackle the problem. Host Britain has proposed to set-up the ASEM Trust Fund to give assistance to the ASEM countries, primarily in evaluating the 'poverty impact of the crisis'. For the Asians a multi-million dollar ASEM Trust Fund will be established and it will operate through the World Bank,

> harnessing European financial expertise on issue such as corporate governance company law and accounting standards.

In this summit the Asians were on the defensive and they were facing the series of financial crisis since mid-1997. Mr. Derek Fatchatt, the British foreign office minister, told that he does not believe the Tigers of 1997 have become the pussy cats of 1998. They sought more commitments from the European Union to help them to tackle their financial problems. Here they received a more sympathetic attitude than they found from Vancouver in Canada when they in the Asia Pacific Forum in November 1997 met their North American partners. At that time they were under the pressure of severe economic turmoil. In this ASEM summit the Europeans played their vital roles to do something for the Asians and they said that open markets and more open political systems will no doubt bring socio-economic stability in Asia. The second ASEM meeting came to an end on Saturday, April 4, 1998 and the leaders expressed their opinions in favours of open markets and they spoke against protectionism "as a response to Asia's economic ills". The European officials have expressed fears that the plunge in the value of some Asian currencies will lead to a wave of cheap exports and fuel protectionist pressures around the world. At the ASEM meeting it was decided that the Europeans did not want to offer major new financial assistance to the Asian countries but they made a plan to launch a trust fund at the World Bank to give grants to the Asian countries after judging the financial and social effects of the crisis and then they would receive the World Bank's loans. The meeting also proposed to set-up a network of the European financial exports to advise Asian countries to reform their banking and financial systems. The Asian leaders wanted to know from the European Union on how the bloc's single currency to be introduced in January 1999 would affect Asia.

Although Thailand suffered financial crisis, yet a number of encouraging signs began to appear there. Market confidence in its economies seemed to return. Since January 1998 the Thai baht by more than 40 per cent has strengthened and its stock market was up about 25 per cent. New foreign direct investment and portfolios investment again flowed back there. Gradually but steadily markets were recovering from the panic of several months ago and the investors very cautiously selected the places of their investment. Several Thai analysts indicated that economic output declined in 1998 by about 3 per cent in Thailand. Under continuous review the International Monetary Fund and the Thai authorities jointly introduced several programmes to cushion the downturn and its influence upon the poor and the unemployed and they were certain that the tough adjustments which were carried out were very important, helpful and necessary for Thailand. The economic adjustment can be mentioned as the basis for future growth. Thailand's trade position has improved remarkably, its foreign exchange reserves were good and stable and began to rise to a great extent and its domestic interest rates appeared to decline. It showed its determination to put itself on the right track by its reforms. Each programme was fixed to set to bring far-reaching changes to strengthen financial systems, increase transparancy, open markets and restore confidence. Several insolvent financial institutions wer closed down there and the Thai authorities asked other institutions to restructure and to follow within a very reasonable period certain practices relating to capital adequacy, prudential standards and accounting and disclosure rules. It has introduced other institutional changes to strengthen financial sector regulation and supervision, increase transparancy in the corporate and government sectors, create a more level playing field for private sector activity and expand competition. These reforms would help to bring a great change in domestic business practices, corporate culture and government behaviour. Mr. Chuan Leekpai's government has moved in a right way to implement these programmes in Thailand very forcefully. It has not

> shrunk from closing down more than half of all finance companies and intervening in the weakest banks. Markets have taken note of the government's determination in effectively wiping out the capital of politically powerful shareholders of these institutions. This same determination has been evident in the prudent manner in which interest rates have been raised to appropriate levels and budgetary discipline maintained.

Several Thai analysts on Wednesday, April 8, 1998 appreciated Thailand's austere fiscal budget for next year, i.e., 1998-99. It followed strictly the programmes and instructions adopted by the International Monetary Fund. Mr. Tarrin Nimmanahaeminda, Thailand's finance minister, on Tuesday, April 7, 1998 won cabinet approval for a proposed 800 billion baht budget for the 1998-1999 (October-September) fiscal year.

> The 1998-99 budget would not carry any deficit as government revenue would rise a projected 2.3 per cent next year along with expected 1.8 per cent of growth of the battered economy-Government revenue and gross domestic product are expected to decline 6.6 per cent and 3.0-3.5 per cent respectively this year.

Mr. Pan Puongsachart, the government spokesman, told reporters on Tuesday, April 7, 1998 that the government would introduce an extra mid-year budget, "its first in over a decade, if tax revenue exceeded expectation". The Thai finance minister expressed his opinion that we want to find ways of controlling normal mixed expenditure so that more funds would bring broad banking sector reforms, with a goal of regaining foreign confidence in the Thia baht and the economy. Several Thai analysts wanted heavy foreign investment in deeply discounted Thai assets, including property and equities in banks and financial institutions. Thailand lowered interest rates to bailout its industries. The plans were prepared in a meeting arranged by Mr. Chuan Leekpai, Thailand's Prime Minister, in response to looming disaster among Thailand's industries which were disturbed by high interest rates and banks' hesitations and unwillingness to make loans. The *Nation* newspaper mentioned that the Thai ministers worked hard to make the Bank of Thailand and commercial banks to work together to ensure control on loans to various industries to avoid problems that could create bad effect upon Thailand's economy. These ministers in order to help businesses agreed to speed up the released of loans from foreign sources and increase liquidity through the export-import banks and commercial banks and they gave priority to agriculture, manufacturing and services. Mr. Chuan Leekpai has done a very commendable job for his contribution to restore a measure of confidence in Thailand's economy since he assumed power about several months ago when the country was in trouble owing to economic crisis in this region but "problems still loom for businesses as the country grapples with recession". Many good firms owing to the reluctance of banks did not get access to fresh operating capital. On Wednesday, April 15, 1998 the Bank of Thailand cut repurchase rates and it announced that long-term bonds would be issued in a few months to ease competition by commercial banks for deposits keeping short-term interest rates dangerously high. The repurchase rate since March 9, 1998 has also dropped 3.375 percentage points from 23 per cent. The Central Bank also wanted to stop an interest rate war among commercial banks "competing for deposits by raising rates." The Thai government in order to rehabilitate has taken over four failing commercial banks.

From several newspapers it is known that Mr. Sanoh Thientong wanted to withdraw from the New Aspiration Party headed by Mr. Chavalit Yongchaiyudh, Thailand's former Prime Minister. He took this decision to depose the latter as the Party's secretary-general. This veteran Thai political leader has threatened to pull his faction out of the country's largest political party, now in opposition. Mr. Chavalit Yongchaiyudh planned to step down as leader of his party and the disturbance in the New Aspiration Party has helped to create problems in it and to divide the opposition and to strengthen Mr. Chuan Leekpai's government and his coalition. He had a thin 207-185 majority but for restoring a measure of confidence to Thailand's battered economy he was able to capture the hearts of the Thai people as the most popular Prime Minister of Thailand. He is now hailed in Thailand as a champion of his country's cause. The leader of one of Thailand's opposition political parties requested the leaders of small parties to form a united front to defeat the ruling democrats in the next election of Thailand. Thailand's opposition party sought united front to fight in the election.

Mr. Welfensehn of the World Bank told that the World Bank has worked on issues such as unemployment, healh care, social safety nets and the plight of migrant workers in Thailand. In this country $ 1.5 billion had been spent and about $ 300 million was used for direct social intervention. The World Bank always showed its keen interest in the Asian economic crisis and tried to do something for it. It started to work on things that are less important for the headline writers, things like the social impact of the crisis, like employment, poverty and food. It also equally went in on the restructuring of banking systems. According to the International Monetary Fund, the hedge funds brought Thailand's financial crisis and they moved in a way to build up large positions against the Thai baht and they were responsible for a devaluation that disturbed Asia's economies. These funds took up large positions against the baht two months before the *de facto* devaluation of the currency on July 2, 1997. Sources of evidence point to the fact that some macro hedge funds had large positions against the baht in summer of 1997. It appeared to us that hedge fund positions against the baht were built up gradually but they turned quite large only in the last two months prior to the Thai devaluation. Several Asian governments mentioned that the powerful hedge funds had a hand in the regional currency crisis. Just before its float, the Thai baht was pegged to a basket of currencies led by the US dollar. The International Monetary Fund stated that speculation against the baht helped to being devaluation and was responsible for Asia's economic crisis. Thailand's newspaper, the *Bangkok Post* described that Mr. Tarrin Nimmanahaeminda had talks with the International Monetary Fund's officials to prepare for the May review, the third since Thailand for its crisis-hit economy get a $ 17.2 billion bailout package in August 1997. After his meeting with them in May 1998 he wanted to submit a fourth letter of commitment to the International Monetary Fund-ordained reform drive. He opened that when the baht becomes more stable it will allow us to cut the short-term interest rate. He also met Mr. Michel Camdessus, the International Monetary Fund chief and Mr. James Welfensehn, the World Bank President in Washington and requested them for help from foreign exports to shake up the Central Bank of Thailand. The *Nation* daily told that he had talks with a number of ex-Central Bankers including Mr. Paul Volker, the former US Federal Reserve Bank Chairman, to join the advisory panel. Thailand's Prime Minister on Tuesday, April 21, 1998 asked the Central Bank of Thailand to play their active roles to help hundreds of Thailand's firms which faced a cash crisis. He asked Mr. Siri Garnjarenendee, the Central Bank's senior deputy governor, to explain why several Thai companies and exporters had been denied access to liquidity to keep their business going. The latter opined that the premier liquidity was tight because the Thai banks in order to recapitalise wanted more time to face new capital adequacy standards. Another problem appeared owing to a continued recall of loans by foreign creditors. Thailand's finance chiefs on Wednesday, April 22, 1998 mentioned that in order to ease a liquidity crisis, about 200 billion baht ($ 5.1 billion) of international rescue funds would be available into money market in 1998. They stated that in the middle of 1998 the funds would be introduced into the local money market and the government speculated that at that time the current cash crunch would be at its worst. Mr. Suppachai Pisitvanich, the Thai government's permanent secretary, described that the Asian Development Bank, the Japan Export and Import Bank and the World Bank would supply the money from rescue funds and the Thai government would raise funds through a Yankee bond issue of up to $ 3 billion. The Asian Development Bank told on Thursday, April 23, 1998 that Asia's developing countries must invest heavily in their rapidly growing labour force or in human resources if they want to recapture the growth momentum disturbed by the region's economic turmoil.

Growth Forecasts

GDP /	*1997*	*1998*	*1999*
Philippine	5.1	2.4	4.0
S. Korea	5.5	1.0	3.1
Singapore	7.8	3.0	4.5
Sri Lanka	6.3	5.6	6.0
Taiwan	6.8	5.8	6.2
Thailand	0.4	3.0	1.0
Vietnam	92	5.0	6.5

High skilled and flexible workers are sorely lacking to develop and to flourish the developing countries' own middle and high-technology products. The report mentioned the case of Thailand which produces less than half the number of engineers and scientists it actually needs.

Several analysts on Thursday, April 23, 1998 told that despite Standard and Poor's recent negative credit rating outlook Thailand's planned $ 1.0-1.5 billion international bond issue later this year will smoothly go ahead and rating may not likely to hit bonds. It won's really affect the bond issue, although there might be some slight import on pricing rather than demand. Thailand's few bonds have been issued in the international market. Cash-strapped Thailand most likely on the US market wanted to issue bonds $ 1.0-1.5 billion in May or June 1998. Most probably, it planned to issue additional bonds before the end of fiscal 1998 ending September. Standard and Poor's on Wednesday, April 22, 1998 mentioned its triple '8' minus long-term and 'A-3' short-term foreign currency ratings on Thailand. It also described Thailand's single 'A'- minus long-term and 'A-2' short-term local currency credit ratings. The Thai government has relaxed some of the controls on foreign investment in the financial sector. In October 1997, the Thai government told that foreign investors could held majority shareholdings in operating financial institutions for ten years, after which any further capital increases would have to be sold to local investors if more than 49 per cent was controlled by foreign investors. Taiwan's government has backed the investment drive

> as a way to counter a diplomatic embarge enforced by rival China, which accuses Taipei of exploiting South-East Asia's financial woes to win political points in the region.

China Development Corp and Chinatrust Commercial Bank have mentioned that they liked to buy new shares now being privately placed by Thailand's private lender, Bangkok Bank Plc. This no doubt highlighted a growing penchant for Thai financial assets. Among Taiwan-based investors who brought into Thai companies in March 1998 were China Development Corp., which spent about $ 20 million buying control of finance and securities from Bangkok First Investment, KG Investments Asia Ltd., part of Taiwan's KOOS Group, bought a major stake in Thai broker Securities One Plc and Yuanta Securities Asia Financial Services bought a 10 per cent stake in Nava Finance & Securities Plc. Thailand's agriculture ministry data indicated that Thailand's annual cotton output was at only 70,000-80,000 tonnes a year, although industry sources told that the actual output was much less. In Thailand cotton is not popular among farmers because of the amount of care and pesticide it requires. About 75 per cent of the production costs go to pesticides and that creates a lot of health problem to farmers along the way. Thailand's farmers prefer crops like soybeans or corn which they don't have to take care of much. Cotton's unpopularity is found in the Thai planting area which shrank to 50,226 hectares in 1997/1998 crop year (July-June) from 53,890 hectares in the previous year. The Thai government in order to boost the output decided to increased planting area. But the introduction of better strains or breeds was necessary to improve output. Several senior officials planned to introduce bio-engineered cotton known as BT cotton proposed by a US-based company. But local legislators and farm industry leaders opposed this move. The new breed was created by inserting genes of bacteria into the local Sriasamrong variety. But the transnational company which invented the new variety wanted to patent it. But the Thais told that if Thailand permitted foreign companies to patent plants, the transnational bio-engineering companies would do very little to modify local plant genes and varieties and patent it as their own invention.

A news report told on Thursday, April 30, 1998 that a new government report blamed a former finance minister and Central Bank officials for Thailand's baht meltdown. They practically mismanaged the defence of the currency. A government-appointed panel has sent this report to Mr. Chuan Leekpai, Thailand's Prime Minister, and the cabinet reviewed it on May 6, 1998. The report told that Mr. Amnuay Viravan, the finance minister, under Mr. Chavalit Yongchaiyudh, Thailand's former Prime Minister and two prominent Central Bank officials were unable to handle the baht properly. They have spoilt it by clumsiness. The bank officials were Mr. Rorngchai Marakanand, the governor of the Bank of Thailand under Mr. Chavalit Yongchaiyudh and Mr. Chaiyawat Wibulsawasdi, the current Central Bank governor. The governor of Thailand's Central Bank resigned on May 4, 1998

> following an investigation into his role in depleting the country's foreign reserves, a miscalculation that helped trigger the Asian economic crisis.

Mr. Chaiyawat Wibulsawasdi, the governor, told that he faced a direct criticism of his job and this has very much affected the bank's performance. Mr. Chatu Mongkol Sonakul, a respected former finance ministry official, who resigned in 1997 to protest the government policy, was selected for the new governor. Thailand's Prime Minister told on Sunday, April 26, 1998 that no deal was struck with Kuwait to buy a squadron of jet fighters F/A-18 from Thailand. The formal talks between the two countries had not taken place and it was difficult to say that the jets-ordered from the United States two years ago but now out of Thailand's budget — would go to Kuwait. The buyer has not yet agreed to our terms. Thailand liked to send a delegation to Kuwait to negotiate the re-sale of eight F/A-18 Hornet jets to that country. The Thai government wanted to relax its tough attitude against alien workers just two days before the palnned expulsion of thousands of illegal workers. Mr. Jongchai Thiangtham, Thailand's deputy labour minister, spoke to reporters on Wednesday, April 29, 1998 that the Thai cabinet agreed to accept the decision of the government committee which recommended some alien workers to allow to stay in designated industries and provinces for up to one year. The labour ministry asked for a relaxation of the policy for certain occupations and areas because it was unable to replace these people immediately with Thai workers. Fisheries and rice milling would suffer no doubt by the less of cheap foreign workers. The Thais did not like to work in these two industries. The Thai government wanted to expel the Myanmarese and the Cambodian workers from Thailand. But these alien workers were paid less than the minimum wage and were selected for dirty and low paid jobs and the Thais did not like there jobs. From the labour ministry it is known that illegal workers could be allowed to stay temporarily in 13 provinces bordering Laos, Cambodia and

Myanmar as well as a number of coastal provinces. In March 1998 it told that the repatritaion of about 300,000 illegal workers would begin from May 1, 1998.

Mr. Flemming Larsen, the International Monetary Fund deputy director for research, announced that there was clear evidence to show that the situation has improved very much and has begun to stabilise in the economies of Malaysia, Philippine, South Korea and Thailand. They suffered very much by the regional financial crisis. Against the US dollar, the Indonesia rupiah has depreciated by 62 per cent, the Malaysian ringgit by 22.4 per cent, the Philippines' money by 21.4 per cent, the South Korean won by 26.4 per cent and the Thai baht by 25.3 per cent since the appearance of the financial crisis in mid-1997. Several Asian finance ministers and Central Bank officials held meeting with the Asian Development Bank to find out the details of a mechanism to monitor each other's economy to discover early signs of a future crisis. At the opening of the Asian Development Bank's 31st annual meeting in Geneva, Mr. Mitsu Sato, the President of the Asian Development Bank, opined that the current event highlighted the importance of regional surveillance in preventing such a crisis from recurring. Regional surveillance could well be justified on the grounds of strong spillover effects within the region. According to media reports on Sunday, May 6, 1998, lack of exercise, narcotics addiction and pollution were mentioned as important factors for sharp drop in Thai life spans and they helped to shorten lives in Thailand by 15 years. A study by the Health Systems Research Institute mentioned that social and economic losses due to non-contagious diseases in Thailand had increased from 54 per cent in 1987 to 70 per cent in 1993 and were hoped to reach 81 per cent by 2020. Over past five years accidents, crimes, injuries and suicides had increased by 70 per cent.

The Thai government on Thursday, May 7, 1998 denied that the Myanmarese troops have set-up a base in North-west Thailand

and planned to launch attacks on the Shan ethnic guerrillas who have taken shelter near the border. The Thai district officials in the border province of Mae Hong Son stated that the Myanmarese soldiers have established their camps about 3 km inside Thailand because of shortage of water there. The Thai military officers want to the area in the Pang Mapha district but the troops, believed to be from Myanmar's 99th Battalion, did not like to leave the area. For a long time they stayed along the border and because of water they came to Thailand.

At the instruction of the International Monetary Fund, Thailand struggled hard towards updated bankruptcy code. It has a new bankruptcy law. As a foreigner, he can't be sure to get a fair hearing against a Thai. TheThai army reshuffled top officers in scandal on border with Myanmar. Mr. Chettha Thanajare, Thailand's army chief general, signed orders to reshuffle his regional commanders in the northern part of Thailand. He did it owing to a logging scandal along the Myanmar's border. Colonel Chaiyuth Bumpan, the commander of the 17th infantry regiment in the north-central province of Thailand, was transferred to lead the 4th infantry regiment in the Mae Sot district, in the north-western border province of Tak. The reshuffle has involved about 200 colonels. The Thai government in order to improve the protection of endangered teak forests in Salween National Park in the Mae Hong Son province, north of Tak and bordering Myanmar, gave order to the Thai army to reshuffle its top officers. Because the Thai army has the responsibility to protect Thailand's forests.

Mr. Tarrin Nimmanahaeminda, the finance minister, said that Thailand has secured more financial aid from the International Monetary Fund to stabilise the baht crrrency. He mentioned that talks with the International Monetary Fund on a fourth letter of intent on economic reforms had thrown flood of light on regional currency stability and stated that the worsening condition of the Asian crisis could help to grant the further credit. The Thai-language Wattachak business daily described that the Thai government sought eight to ten billion dollars in further credit. Dr. Thaksin Shinawatra, the leading economist and the former deputy Prime Minister of Thailand, on Tuesday, May 12, 1998 referred to the South-East Asian economy which will hit the bottom in 1998 before its recovery.[109] Business will be hit hardest by a liquidity squeeze caused by the closing of financial institutions and tightening of credit to face the IMF requirement. Consumer prices are expected to rise 15 per cent this year and nine per cent in 1999. Merchandise exports are expected to return, rising by five per cent and eight per cent in 1999. Thailand's current deficit would no doubt receive a 3.4 per cent surplus in 1998 and two per cent in 1999. A combination of high private foreign debt exposure, a current account deficit that approached eight per cent, stagnating exports, inflated asset prices in the finance and real estate sectors and an exchange rate which stayed obstinately pegged to the US dollar left Thailand vulnerable to repeated speculative attacks on the baht. Since August last (1997), Thailand tried to follow the conditions of the IMF's economic stabilisation programme after it requested the global lending agency for emergency assistance. It may be noted here that Thailand's economic system was outwardly market-oriented, but it was still designed by socio-political forces and institutions that did not go to adapt well to the rigorous demands of a highly competitive global market place. Mr. Tarrin Nimmanahaeminda, the Thai finance minister, told on Tuesday, May 12, 1998 that the Asian currency instability could re-appear owing to the developments in some South-East Asian countries which have disturbed their efforts to revive their economies. Thailand's finance ministry officials opined that Indonesia's growing public and student protests had an effect upon the Thai baht. Mr. Andrew Houston has given an account of Thailand's economic crisis. He described that in many parts of Asia interest

---

109. *AA*, May 13, 1998, p. 19.

rates have started to fall, as a wave of portfolio inflows have pushed up stock prices and boosted local money suppllies. Thailand's banks underperformed the market during 1986-9 because of huge capital raising. At the end of 1985, Thailand's banks had total capital of Bt 40 bn. Between 1985 and 1989 they increased an additional Bt 38 bn of new capital, most of which was assimilated by loan loss provision expenses. Now Thailand's banks again appear to give another similar underperformance. At the end of 1997, they had Bt 434 bn of equity. But they will want to raise at least Bt 425 bn over the next four years to do their business with non-performing loans. Mr. Marc Levine[110] describes,

> Thailand's economic crunch forced a sharp narrowing in the country's ballooning current account deficit last year (1997), while the indicator went into surplus in December (1997) amid a contraction of the economy.
>
> However, the latest figures released on Friday (February 27, 1998) while showing Thailand is sticking to its International Monetary Fund prescribed austerity regime, also warn certain basic economic problems still need to be tackled.
>
> The current account deficit, once one of the most vivid warning signs the economy was overheating and set to spin out of control, eased to $ 3 billion in 1997 from $ 14.4 billion a year earlier.
>
> The country turned the screws on imports as cash flow dried up and as the falling baht made them unaffordable, while its need to boost exports grew dramatically, a Socgon Crosby analyst said.
>
> Thailand recorded a trade deficit of 84.4 billion baht last

---

110. *AA*, February 28, 1998, p. 18.

> year (1997), with exports rising 29.8 per cent to 1.79 trillion baht, and imports up 4.3 per cent to 1.87 trillion baht, officials said. The figures were released by the Central Bank of Thailand on Friday (February 27, 1998) during its monthly unveiling of key economic data under a transparency drive urged by the International Monetary Fund's bailout scheme.
>
> However, while Bangkok posted a current account deficit for the whole of 1997, it boasted large current account and trade surpluses for the third straight month in December (1997) as the economy showed signs of moving out of the red.
>
> The Central Bank said the current account surplus rose sharply to $ 1.18 billion in December (1997) from $ 997 million in November (1997), while the trade surplus was $ 1.03 billion, up from $ 844 million. The indicators showed Thailand was trying to adhere strictly to its IMF package in a bid to dig itself out of its financial hole.

Thailand's Prime Minister Mr. Chuan Leekpai spoke at the Asian Development conference on Thailand in Hong-Kong on Monday, May 18, 1998. He told that the country in order to restore the confidence of investors has devoted its full attentions to financial reforms. The Bank of Thailand on Monday, May 18, 1998 took over the management central of seven finance companies after they were unable to meet recapitalisation deadlines. The bank has asked the seven finance companies to mention their capital and raise fresh funds in line with the Central Bank capital adequacy requirement after the write-offs. These companies were Nava Finance Public Co. Ltd., Union Asia Finance Public Co. Ltd., Erawan Trust Co. Ltd., Bangkok Asia Finance Co. Ltd., Mahatun Finance Co. Ltd., Progressive Finance Co. Ltd., and Ksit Finance and Securities Co. Ltd. They came under the direct supervision of the Bank of Thailand and they will continue to operate normally, to keep their corporte names and creditors and depositors will be protected. The Central Bank will replace the boards of directors of each of the seven companies. The Central Bank's Financial Institutions Development Fund (FIDF) will give liquidity support to these companies if needed. The Krungthai Thanakit Plc., a finance and securities subsidiary of state owned Krung Thai Bank Plc., had been told to look after the firms and it will receive a full commercial banking licence. The Central Bank's Financial Institutions Development Fund will purchase shares for recapitalisation of Krungthai Thanakit and these shares will be converted into shares of the proposed new commercial bank. Mr. Tarrin Nimmanhaeminda, the Thai finance minister, told that the Thai baht had been fairly stable around the 39-to-the dollar mark in these days because the investors and financiers had understood that the Thai problems were quite different from these of other regional economies. The International Monetary Fund's officials were in Thailand to prepare Bangkok's fourth letter of intent, a quarterly commitment to reforms under the International Monetary Fund's bailout package. The reforms were mentioned in details in the letter and when it was ready, then it was sent to the Thai cabinet for approval and afterwards it was despatched to the International Monetary Fund in Washington on June 10, 1998 before the arrival of a further $ 800 million of international funds in Bangkok. Thailand's inflation target for 1998 was referred to 10 per cent instead of 11.6 per cent as mentioned in the third letter of intent. The finance ministry in order to stimulate economic growth and to help to lower interest rates sought the International Monetary Fund's permission to allow a wider deficit in the year to September 1998 Budget. The Thai government wanted to ratify four controversial financial decrees in the Thai Parliament. The Lower House of Representative met on Monday, May 25, 1998 for a special sitting to ratify the urgent decrees following a constitutional court ruling on Saturday, May 23, 1998 that the Thai cabinet of the Prime Minister Mr. Chuan Leekpai in April

1998 approved the decrees which were legal. The ratification has given power to the Thai government to raise $ 18 billion in foreign and domestic bonds, to raise its foreign borrowing ceiling, to help it to perform much-needed financial reforms and to destroy a severe domestic liquidity squeeze. The government wanted the ratification as early as possible because the Thai cabinet at its weekly meeting on Tuesday, May 26, 1998 included them in its fourth letter of intent which was sent to the board of the International Monetary Fund in Washington on June 10, 1998, and this helped to disburse another $ 800 million from the $ 17.2 billion bailout package. The decrees were voted on Monday, May 25, 1998. The Thai opposition told that the business people at the expense of the taxpayers and the poor communities were benefitted by the decrees. Several Thai analysts mentioned that the government faced problems to ratify the decrees and this indicated the beginning of an uphill battle in coming months as the economic turmoil deepened and this helped to bring higher unemployment and corporate bankruptcies. The Thai cabinet approved Bangkok's quarterly commitment to the International Monetary Fund and Thailand's finance minister told that it was extremely difficult to say with certainty about the speed of the economic recovery. The letter itself mentioned,

> While important progress has been made conditions in the real economy are still deteriorating as the economic decline during the first half of 1998 is proving to be deeper than previously anticipated. It described that the Thai government had given a new look on Bangkok's reforms which were shifted from setting appropriate short-term monetary and fiscal targets to broader micro-economics strategies in areas such as social welfare, privatisation and corporate law.

Mr. Jacques Bouchery, the chief executive officer of Societe Gansrale's Thai Unit, SG Asia Credit Plc., wanted the implementation of these ligislative changes as early as possible. There are still many structural reforms that need to be undertaken and if they are done very quickly there will be a turn-around. The Thai government in order to restore the shattered confidence of foreign investors must concentrates on reforms such as bankruptcy, foreclosures and property ownership. Most people said that the range for Thailand's recovery was between one year and three years and Thailand was somewhere in the middle. The Thai baht slid through the 40 point mark against the dollar over the week to close on Friday (29.5.1998) at 40.35-38 compared to its previous close at 39.25-30 units a week earlier. According to the Thai analysts, owing to regional pressure the currency became weak and its fall took place. The currency traders told that the baht had slipped to 40.65-75 against the US dollar in morning trade — from 40.35-38 at the close on Friday, May 29, 1998 and this gave an indication of uncertainty about regional currencies. The Stock Exchange of Thailand corporate index fell 11.35 points to 314.24 during morning session with the banking index down 10.23 points at 185.51 and the finance sector 88.30 weaker at 918.53. The Central Bank governor said on Friday, June 5, 1998 that he was happy with baht's range of 42-43 per dollar. The baht's limited market supply has helped to restrain foreign speculation against the currency. The Thai Stocks plummeted 5 per cent by 08.44 GMT on Wednesday, June 10, 1998 as investors sold out on concerns over the weaknesses of the Japanese Yen and sharp declines in regional markets. The Intrernational Monetary Fund gave Thailand $ 133 million from a $ 3.9 billion loan on Wednesday, June 10, 1998 but disclosed that the Thai economy remained 'weaker than anticipated' and the whole region faced a very difficult time. Mr. Michel Camdessus, the International Monetary Fund's managing director, mentioned the latest payment and told that Thailand's economic preference was very bad and it forced the authorities to re-assess their economic targets. He opined,

> considerable risks lie ahead, as shown by the recent turbulance in financial markets. The complex task of financial and corporate restructuring has yet to be completed and regional economic prospects remain diffcult.

The Thai stocks fell 5.24 per cent on Wednesday, June 10, 1998 to their lowest level for 10-1/2 years amid a downturn in prices across the region. Several Thai investors were anxious to see that the baht currency, trading at around 43.40 to the US dollar, faced a new pressure. But Mr. Michel Camdessus told that the Thai balance of payments had improved, reserves had been replenished and since the beginning of the year the exchange rate had improved very much. Under the economic programme Thailand has achieved very much and has done good progress and this has helped to regain the confidence of financial markets in its economy. The Thai government in its structural reform and economic stabilisation had done very well. Thailand expected to receive a $ 400 million World Bank loan for the improvement of its banking sector. The loan will form part of the international rescue package. Mr. Michel Camdessus told that the International Monetary Fund's Wednesday's (10.6.98) payment showed that this fund as loan gave $ 2.8 billion to Thailand. Thailand's shares staged strong rallies in early trade. Its beleaguered Stock Exchange of Thailand (SET) index went 2.04 per cent in early trade on regional gains and the Yen. It reached 2.58 per cent to 264.07 at 0530 GMT, a gain of 6.63 points. The Yen has helped the Thai market very much. The Thai stock market index on Friday, June 19, 1998 closed 10.83 points lower at 284.32, down 3.67 per cent on the day, after a stormy week in which composite SET index gained 1.77 per cent or 4.95 points. According to the Thai dealers, the baht will remain at the 40-42 per the US dollar level this week and was not likely to strengthen beyond 40 as at this level there will be strong resistance, although it should rally with the Yen. Mr. Tarrin Nimmanahaeminda told that in

Thailand short-term interest rates were likely to dip further in the near term after the Thai government by issuing bonds turned its attention to ease a severe liquidity crunch.

The Sultan of Brunei, Haji Hassanai Buikiah held talks with the Thai Prime Minister at the Government House in Bangkok on Saturday, May 16, 1998. The two leaders discussed the current unrest in Indonesia as well as the financial crisis in the region. The Sultan was on a three-day official visit to Thailand and he returned to Brunei on Saturday, May 16, 1998. The communication ministers of the 18-member Asia-Pacific Economic Co-operation Forum met for three days from Wednesday, June 3, 1998 at Singapore. Several senior officials of the Asia-Pacific Economic Co-operation in a statement on Tuesday, June 2, 1998 agreed to a framework for action to priorities the use of electronic commerce (E-commerce) by businesses and consumers, harmonise E-commerce policies, promote the development of E-commerce infrastructure, the delivery of the government services via Internet and to take important steps towards the development of free and open trade in the Asia-Pacific Economic Co-operation region by 2020. Australia, Brunei, Canada, Chile, China, Hong-Kong, Indonesia, Japan, South Korea, Malaysia, Mexico, New Zealand, Papoa New Guinea, Philippine, Singapore, Taiwan, Thailand and the United States belong to the Asia-Pacific Economic Co-operation group. In order to honour Thailand's queen and to improve the image of the Thai women, a Thai Buddhist sact has planned a mase ordination of 100.00 nuns. This was disclosed on Tuesday, July 21, 1998. The Dhammakāya foundation mentioned that the 'Upasika-Kaew' or pure ladies project has taken place on August 12, 1998 on the occasion of the 66th birthday of Queen Sirikit, the wife of Thailand's constitutional monarch Bhumibol Adulyadej. Thailand for the first time had organised this kind of event to honour the fairer gender. Thailand's men by custom spend a few months of their lives in the Buddhist monasteries as Buddhist monks. In Thailand very few Thai women have taken their ordinationas as nun and the majority of the Thai Buddhist clergy has never encouraged Thailand's women to join the Buddhist Saṁgha and to lead their lives as nuns. The ordinatioan would no doubt allow them to transfer their merits to the queen, elevate and appreciate the role of the mother in the society and to raise the awareness.

Thailand's cash-strapped ministry of defence sold mosquito repellent to Malaysia and made a profit of more than $ 4.8 million in 1998. Owing to Thailand's economic crisis, its defence ministry has looked for alternate source of income and it has accepted budget cuts. Thailand and Malaysia have forests where Malaria, a mosquito-borne disease, has threatened the health of these regions. The Thai military's pharmaceutical plant has made the repellent. The Thai defence ministry told on Thursday, July 23, 1998 that a Website set for Thailand's Prime Minister was flooded with messages. The ministry designed the Website, addressed WWW. Chuan TH. Org. to receive the public opinion on the performance of the Prime Minister, the armed forces and the government. Thailand's common people through this channel were able to reach the Prime Minister. The ministry mentioned that a programme to delete obscene language was installed on the site. Thailand's chief government whip has requested the wives of the members of the Parliament to see that in order to ensure quorums their husbands must attend house sessions. Because Mr. Chuan Leekpai's six-party coalition government had a slim 12-seat majority in the Lower House of 389 seats. For this reason it was necessary for all the members of the Thai Parliament to come and to show their presence in its every business to attain quorums and to win votes. Mr. Charoen Kantawong, the chief whip, described that the members of the Thai Parliament regularly disappeared from the House sessions and for this reason he has informed thier wives and has appealed to them to discipline their husbands. Absent government MPs have made delays in voting on key bills. The South-East Asian foreign ministers on Friday, July 24, 1998 in Manila strongly criticised the nuclear tests done by India and Pakistan and they agreed to a wider fight against drug trafficking. They wanted a regional early warning system to check the regions' economic problem. The nine-member ASEAN sought to make South-East Asia a nuclear weapon free zone including a ban on nuclear arms on ships crossing international waters in the region. These members met the foreign ministers from the United States, China, Russia, Britain and India and they discussed security matters. In the draft communique, the Asean foreign ministers appealed to all countries which have not yet signed the nuclear Non-Proliferation Treaty and Comprehensie Test Ban Treaty for the safety of the whole world and to establish a nuclear free world. The draft communique strongly endorsed the finance ministers' earlier decision to introduce an Asean surveillance mechanism to monitor regional economic and financial indicators to solve the future cases at an early stage. The foreign ministers agreed to proposals to use regional currencies in trade among the Asean countries to help them not to depend on the US dollars in their businesses. Mr. Chuan Leekpai's cabinet gave permission to a sweeping cleanup package for the country's 'rotten financial sector'. Thailand's finance minister told that the Thai government issued three executive decrees to push through its restructuring programme. It will help the entire nation to rehabilitate their businesses, leading to job creation. These were very important because it had become very difficult to attract overseas investors. Thailand's severest economic crisis in decades has crippled much of the formerly profitable bank sector which the rating agency Fitch IBCA mentioned that Thailand needed about $ 16 billion to $ 20 billion in new funding for its survival. It would probably move its attention to model its bank sector package on Chile's 1982 reforms. The Chilean reforms included a separation of banks' good and bad assets and a bad-loans-for-government-bond swap which left the vast majority of commercial banks in the hands of the Chileans. In contrast, Mexico's banking system reforms of 1996 witnessed that the foreigners bought its entire financial system. Mr. Thawatchai Yongkittikul, the secretary-general of the Thai Bankers Association, stated in the first week of August 1998 that he thought 'write-downs' were necessary to encourage foreign investment in the Thai banks. Write-down involve a bank reducing the par value of its shares, or the number of its shares to reflect a fall in the value of its assets. The Thai bankers stated that write-downs will probably be directed only at the elements of Thailand's 15 listed banks from which the political fallout could be contained. The Krung Thai Bank official, told on Thursday, September 24, 1998 that Thailand's Central Bank has decided to invest $ 4.5 billion in state-run Krung Thai Bank Plc. to rebuild the financial sector. The Cental Bank's Financial Institutions Development Fund (FIDF) has planned to invest 18.5 billion baht ($ 4.5 billion) in a private share placement by Krung Thai Bank. The placement of 18.5 billion new shares at 10 baht will no doubt help to boost Krung Thai Bank's registered capital to 219.85 billion baht. Under comprehensive banking reforms announced in August 1998, Krung Thai Bank will swallow First Bangkok City Bank Plc. and the performing assets of Bangkok Bank of Commerce Plc. with the FIDF swaping dent in the troubled banks for equity in Krung Thai Bank. Following a capital increase and co-operative restructuring, Krung Thai Bank will then be placed for sale to private investors as one of Asia's biggest commercial banks outside Japan. At the end of 1997 Krung Thai Bank's total assets were fixed at 792.7 billion baht and it has became the third biggest institution in Thailand after Bangkok Bank Plc. and Thai Farmers Bank Plc. The Thai government currently owned 73.6 per cent of Krung Thai Bank through the FIDF (59 per cent), the ministry of finance (12.1 per cent) and the Government Savings Bank (2.5 per cent). In order to help to stabilise Thailand's battered banking and finance sectors the FIDF was created in 1997. It has already given more than one trillion baht into ailing institutions and also gave one hundred thirty billion baht to First Bangkok City Bank Plc. and also to Bangkok Bank of Commerce Plc.

The Thai security forces arrested six members of a rebel

Karen army when they illegally arrived in north-eastern Thailand. Thailand's soldiers and rangers during a regular patrol of the Salween river in the Sop Moci district of the Mae Hong Son province, captured six rebels from the Democratic Karen Buddhist Army. These six men were arrested when they found in their possession of two 9 mm pistols, a shotgun, an M16 assault rifle and two M26 grenades. The arrests prompted residents of the Ban Mae Sam Laeb village to leave their homes in fear of reprisal attacks from the Democratic Karen Buddhist Army. Which to steel supplies attacked the Thai village from Myanmar. An armed group of Karen ethnic rebels on Wednesday morning, March 11, 1998 entered northern Thailand and attacked a refugee camp in Thailand and they set fire to over 1,000 refugee huts in a Karen camp in Thailand. The Democratic Karen Buddhist Army fighters, after crossing the Moci river into the Mae Sot district about 423 km north of Thailand, attacked a Karen refugee camp with heavy weapons and killed several people there. During the attack, the raiders looted dwellings in the Hua Kolok refugee camp, killed many refugees, injured several persons and then returned to their place. About 1,000 Myanmarese troops attacked a key Karen insurgent base on Saturday, March 14, 1998 and raised tensions along the frontier with Thailand where the Karen refugees feared cross-border raids. A raiding party allied with Myanmar's military government fired more than 10 mortar rounds on Sunday, March 16, 1998 into a refugee camp in Thailand where about 30,000 refugees have taken their shelter. Major Chamlong Phetong, chief of staff of the 3rd Army told that Thailand's soldiers returned artillery rounds and drove off the attackers who attacked the Mae Hla refugee camp. The raiders, belonged to the Democratic Karen Buddhist Army, a faction of the Karen ethnic minority allied with the government of Myanmar against the Karen National Union, which for fifty years has fought for Karen autonomy. The Democratic Karen Buddhist Army attacked another refugee camp, Huay Kalek on Wednesday, March 11, 1998 and many people were killed and baout 9,000 people have lost their homes. This army group, an allay of the Myanmar government, has attacked several Karen refugee camps inside Thailand. The refugees in Thailand faced a wave of cross-border raids from Myanmar and for this reason thousand refugees became homeless. The Myanmar-backed forces several times attacked Karen refugee camps, close to the frontier and the refugees sheltering in Thailand were loyal to the Karen National Union and the attacks were made to sever contacts between the camps and the Karen National Military units. The Thai armed forces opened fire on Myanmr-backed rebels who on Monday, March 23, 1998 attacked a refugee camp in Thailand. The Thai armed forces have deployed reinforcements at the border area because the Democratic Karen Buddhist Army wanted to destroy all the refugee capms in Thailand. The Democratic Karen Buddhist Army was separated from the predominantly Christian Karen National Union in 1994 when the former Karen National Union fighters turned against their leaders and claimed religious discrimination and joined forces with the Myanmarese government forces. Soon after its establishment the Democratic Karen Buddhist Army turned its attention to attack refugee capms in Thailand. They have raided and attacked camps several times, burnt many houses, destroyed properties and killed many refugees in Thailand. The Thai army has been ordered to use its force to protect the ethinic Karen refugee camps in Thailand from the cross-border raids by the Myanmarese troops. General Chettha Thanajare, Thailand's army chief, gave order to protect the refugee camps when the Mawkar refugee camp in northern Thailand's Tak province was attacked by the Myanmarese troops. He became very angry with the latest cross-border assault and has ordered the army to use all means in countering the aggression.

Thailand in order to revive the battered economy might close at least three of 15 commercial banks in a much-awaited financial sector shake up. Thailand's people expected the merger of the three state-run banks — Siam City Bank, First Bangkok City

Bank and Bangkok Metropolitan Bank. But Bangkok Bank of Commerce may ask the foreign investors to buy it. Mr. Tarrin Nimmanahaeminda, the finance minister, told that the Thai economy should start to bottom out in the beginning of 1999 provided by outside developments the government's efforts are not neutralised. Japan's sluggish enonomy and a devaluation of the Chinese currency could have a bad effect upon Thailand's crisis. They may help to prolong its crisis. It may be noted here that the Thai government will try its best to move forward with reforms.

Mr. Prem Tinsulananda, Thailand's former Prime Minister, celebrated his 78th birthday on Monday, August 24, 1998 and he praised the leadership of the interior minister who tried to topple him in 1981 *coup d'etat*. Mr. Sanan Kachomprasart, Thailand's interior minister, on behalf of the government of Thailand's Prime Minister Mr. Chuan Leekpai, presented Mr. Tinsulananda with the traditional gift of floral banquets at his home. The latter was a former general and in now privy councillor to King Bhumibol Adulyadej of Thailand. He remained as Prime Minister of Thailand from 1980 to 1988. Mr. Somchai Khunpluem, known widely as Kamnan Poh, said that he would remain loyal to the Chart Thai (Thai Nation) Party as long as his son Mr. Sonthaya would remain as one of the top five candidates for a cabinet post after the next election. The former has become quite well-known as Thailand's top crime boss. His son as a member of the Chart Thai Party has already become deputy communication minister. The Party's leaders was Mr. Banharn Silpa-Archa, Thailand's former Prime Minister. Most probably, this party would be included in the next coalition government and Mr. Sonthaya would be a full minister. Thailand's police director on Thursday, September 3, 1998 accused Myanmar and Laos of allowing large numbers of illicit amphetamine factories to operate on their soil. General Pracha Prommok after attending a high-level anti-narcotics meeting cahired by Mr. Chuan Leekpai, the Prime Minister, told that Myanmar and Laos have no problems because they are getting money and their laws are permitting them to do so. He said that Thailand would depend on bilateral meetings with officials of these countries to request them to close those factories of Myanmar and Laos. A foreign ministry spokesman stated on Friday, September 18, 1998 that Thailand has applied for membership in the conference on disarmament ot heighten its bargaining power in lobbying nuclear states to sign a test ban treaty for South-East Asia. Mr. Kobsak Chutikul, the Thai foreign ministry spokesman, told that membership in the international group would provide Thailand and the Association of South-East Asian Nations with a new channel to lobby nuclear powers to sign the South-East Asian Nuclear Weapon Free Zone Treaty. In 1995 about nine South-East Asian countries signed the treaty in Bangkok. Mr. Hubert Neiss, the director of the Fund's Asia-Pacific department, told that Thailand's recovery was important to the International Monetary Fund as Bangkok had "by and large implemented the strategy of the International Monetary Fund's programme in Asia". He said further that if Thailand wanted additional funding. The International Monetary Fund would look into 'augmenting' its existing $ 17.2 billion rescue package, but it did not foresee Thailand wanting more money. The Thai baht on Monday, September 7, 1998 moved gradually in late trade but dealings were thin and the rate was almost unchanged because the foreign parties were not present in the market. The baht was quoted at 40.63/40.73 per dollar against 40.70/40.75 in the morning.

King Bhumibol Adulyadej on Monday, October 5, 1998 approved a new cabinet. He gave his consent for the new line up and he allowed Mr. Chuan Leekpai to get a healthy parliamentary majority in his government. The new cabinet was the first reshuffle from the latter's 11-month-old coalition government. The seven-Party coalition will have now 256 members in the 388-seat Lower House and the Prime Minister has included 51 from the Chart Pattana Party. Many Thai analysts warned that the inclusion of the Chart Pattana Party MPs from the opposition may bring disaster and this may also help to undermine stability and to move towards an election sooner rather than later. Representatives of Thailand's Muslims community visited Malaysia's embassy on Thursday, October 8, 1998 to call for the release of Mr. Anwar Ibrahim, the former deputy Prime Minister of Malaysia, and his supporters, who were detained in the prison for some-times. In an open latter to Mr. Mahathir Mohamad, the Prime Minister of Malaysia, the three Thai Muslim organisations — the Muslim Law Society, the Muslim Institute for Consumer Protection and the Young Muslim Association of Thailand — told that the law under which they are being held — is unjust. They doubted very much that they would not get a fair trial. They bitterly criticised Malaysia's International Security Act which without trial keeps people indefinite imprisonment. Mr. Supat Thamphet, a member of Parliament from the ruling Democrat Party, admitted to reporters that he had raised money from the private sector to finance a Thai Kickboxing in Australia. He did it for the promotion of the Thai martial art. He resigned from his post. Princess Galayani Vadhana Kromluang Narathiwat Rajanakarin, the elder sister of Thailand's King Bhumibol Adulyadej, accompanied by 70 Buddhist monks, attended a robe-presentation ceremony at the Wat Chatawan temple in Malaysia on Wednesday, October 7, 1998. The Thot Krathin ceremony involving visits to several Buddhist temples in South-East Asia was held to commemorate the 72nd birthday of king Bhumibol Adulyadej. During the ceremony, robes were presented to Buddhist monks for gaining merits by the lay people. About 1,000 people on Wednesday, October 14, 1998, in central Bangkok watched the unveiling of the first official monument to those slain in a 1973 pre-democracy uprising which helped to topple a military dictatorship. But former activities and relatives felt sorry at the state of modern Thai democracy, political corruption and the lack of students's active role in politics. About 73 activists were killed and many hundreds were injured in the student-led revolt on October 14, 1973 in Bangkok. Mr. Sombat Thamrongtanyawong, one of the key activists, in the uprising told that he was very much disappointed by the materialism and lack of political consciousness amongst modern Thai students. Many Thai Buddhist monks led a march in Bangkok on Wednesday to mark the 25th anniversary of the October 14, 1973 popular uprising against the military dictatorship of Field Marshall Thanon Kittikachorn and Prapass Charueethiara.

Officials from Indonesia, South Korea, Malaysia, Philippines, Singapore and Thailand attended the meeting of the finance ministers and Central Bank governors of the Group of Seven (G-7) rich industrial nations in Washington and began talk on how to spend the $ 30-billion aid package offered by Japan on October 3, 1998. In the global rice trade Thailand is expected to export at least 5.8 million tonnes rice in 1999. Queen Fabiola of Belgium as the guest of King Bhumibol Adulyadej and Queen Sirikit arrived in Bangkok on Saturday, October 17, 1998 and attended church at the University campus in Bangkok on Sunday and visited several places in the capital and dined with the Thai royal family in the evening. Mr. Tarrin Nimmanahaeminda, the Thai finance minister, won a promise for some of the Japanese funds and has received praise from the International Monetary Fund for following strictly the reform referred to by it. Mr. Kiichi Miyazawa, the Japanese finance minister, mentioned his 'firm commitment' to support Thailand, stating its progress in implementing reform. An International Monetary Fund report of October 1998 spoke highly of Thailand, recipient of its $ 17.2 billion aid package, for its reforms but told that it requested 'steadfast implementation' of the programmes to consolidate gains. Mr. Chatu Mongkul Sonakul, the governor of the Bank of Thailand, hoped to see gross domestic product (GDP) to grow 1 per cent in 1999. Thailand's Central Bank chief on Wednesday, October 21, 1998 indicated that inflation and interest rates would fall by the year and the economy would start growing again in 1999. A recent survey by the Thai Farmers Bank found that

Thai Buddhism has fallen victim to the crippling economic crisis which has forced devotees to curb participation in religious activities and cut back their spending on religious artefacts. Shops and neighbouring temples were mostly empty customers while people have also declined to spend their average donations to monks from between 100-200 bahts to 50 bahts. Thailand's film board has refused to allow 20th Century Fox to shoot a new non-musical version of the King and I in the country because it has insulted the Thai monarchy. The film was banned in Thailand and the Thais thought that the depiction of the Fourth King of the country's Chakri dynasty was inaccurate and insulting. About ten dealers, economists and research houses gave an average forecast of 37.07 baht per dollar at the end of 1998, although most players were sure that the baht could rise in the short term. They expected that it would climb towards 35 per dollar in the short term. The leaders of the twenty-one members of the Asia-Pacific Economic Co-operation Forum (APEC) which grouped Australia, Brunei, Canada, Chile, Hong-Kong, Indonesia, Japan, Malaysia, Mexico, New Zealand, Papua New Guinea, Philippines, Russia, Singapore, South Korea, Taiwan, Thailand, the United States and Vietnam attended the APEC summit on Tuesday and Wednesday, November 17 and 18, 1998 at Kuala Lumpur in Malaysia. They declared at the end of their summit that they vowed to meet the challenge of easing not only the Asian financial crisis but also they wanted to do something for the global economic crisis. The US embassy in Bangkok re-opened on Monday, November 23, 1998 because it was closed on Friday, November 20, 1998 as a precaution against terrorism. The mission was closed due to fears of potential attacks on the US interests around the world. Mr. Michel Camdessus, the International Monetary Fund managing director, praised efforts by Thailand to improve its economy and stated that recovery should begin this nation by next year, i.e., 1999. It may be noted here that financial strains have pushed up Thailand's suicide rate. Its economic collapse was blamed for the doubling of the suicide rate. Two suicides are reported each day in Bangkok usually by poisoning, shooting, hanging or leaping from a building. King Bhumibol Adulyadej lighted the 13th Asian flame on Thursday, December 3, 1998 during a ceremony at Chitrlada Palace, his official residence, in Bangkok. The flame was carried in a miniature golden carriage from the palace to Sanam Luang Park, where it was kept until the opening of the Games on Sunday, December 6, 1998 and the Asian Games ended on Sunday, December 20, 1998 in Bangkok. Several foreign and trade ministers from Brunei, Indonesia, Laos, Malaysia, Myanmar, Philippines, Singapore, Thailand and Vietnam attended the Asean ministers' summit on Tuesday and Wednesday December 15 and 16, 1998 in Hanoi, Vietnam and they discussed the regions's economic woes and also the issue of Cambodia's admission into Asean group. During the summit the Asean leaders approved further cuts in tariffs, promoted measures to boost investment, considered the feasibility of a regional currency, aimed to develop an Asean bond market by 2010 and requested continued financial assistance from industrial economies and international institutions. Four of the nine heads of government took part in the two-day Asean meeting in Hanoi. Mr. Chuan Leekpai, Thailand's Prime Minister, told that the economic crisis had raised questions about whether the association of the South-East Asian Nations could regain its vitality and he added further that the group needed to develop "new approaches and new thinking to keep up with the rapid pace of developments, both regionally and internationally". On Wednesday, December 16, 1998 the Asean leaders met Mr. Keize Obachi, the Prime Minister of Japan, Mr. Hu Jinato, the Vice-President of China and Mr. Kim Dae Jung, the President of South Korea to discuss closer co-operation between South-East Asia and North-East Asia in relating to aid and monetary policy. Many of the Asean leaders acknowledged the need to revamp their economies and institutions to make them more open and competitive. Vietnam wanted to treat Cambodia as a full member but Singapore stated that the strife-torn country must complete promised political reforms before it can join the group. Cambodia had been expected to join the Asean group in mid-1997 along with Laos and Myanmar but its entry was delayed when Prince Norodom Ramariddh, the co-Prime Minister, was ousted by Mr. Hun Sen. As a group, the major industrial countries were projected to grow by 2.0 per cent in 1998 and by 1.6 per cent in 1999. The International Monetary Fund said that,

> in the emerging markets — Indonesia, Malaysia, Philippines and Thailand — are forecast to contract by 10.6 per cent in 1998, then by 1.4 per cent in 1999. Asia as a group is projected to grow by 2.6 per cent in 1998 and 4.3 per cent in 1999.

Thailand's Crown Prince Maha Vajiralongkorn and Princess Bhajrakitiyabha arrived in India on Wednesday, December 23, 1998 and they were welcomed by the Vice-President of India Mr. Krishna Kant. They met the Rashtrapati and the Prime Minister of India. Their visit would help to establish better co-operation between the two countries. The prince was accompanied by a 60-member high-powered delegation. His visit may resurrect Indo-Thai trade ties. It may bring result in a trade, economic and scientific agreement that can herald the return of a more profitable trading relationship between the two countries.

The Thai economy until 1995 had an average annual growth rate in excess of seven per cent, moderate inflation and a stable exchange rate, accompanied by high savings rate and a tradition of very conservative monetary and fiscal policy. But owing to the high investment ratio there was the large account deficit in it. But in 1996 its weakness began to appear very prominently. Too much dependence on cheap foreign capital following the liberalisation of the financial sector and capital account had helped very much to execessive investment and consumption and for this reason there appeared high current account deficit. Thailand opened up many economies which had lower production costs and then it began to lose its competitive edge in low-end products. It depended very much on extenal funding to finance the savings-investment gap and for this reason external debt relative to GDP appeared from 32 per cent at the end of 1989 to 50 per cent in 1996. In favour of short-term loans the relative risks and term structure of interest rates gave an indication to significant shortening of the average maturity of its external debt. The share of short-term debt rose from 26 per cent in 1989 to 50 per cent in 1995. The deterioration of the Thai economy brought a great change in many foreign investor confidence and the economic and financial system became subject to increasingly volatile capital movements. The Thai government became very much worried to see its economic condition and in order to save its economy from its fall, to give new life into it and to move it out of the economic and financial crisis, the Thai government under the International Monetary Fund's economic adjustment programme introduced economic measures which mentioned primarily on macro-economic stability and financial sector reform. On the macro-economic front, strong monetary and fiscal discipline were introduced at the beginning to inspire investor confidence in the authorities' ability and willingness to address problems. When macro-economic conditions showed its improvement and confidence appeared in ivestors' mind, then the monetary and fiscal policy system played its vital role to support economic recovery as specified since the Fourth Letter of Intent (LOI of May 1998). In order to recognise a sharp economic recession monetary targets were relaxed. The International Monetary Fund programme in its fiscal policy mentioned that the public sector will have to achieve a surplus of one per cent of fiscal year GDP to give way partially for the fiscalisation of financial restructuring costs. Successive programmes, however, indicated the need to do fiscal help to protect against rapidly contracting economic activities, particularly domestic demand, and to give protection against adverse social impacts appearing from increased unemployment as well as in response to declining revenue intakes in line with the economic trend. The target for the public sector balance was changed from a surplus to a deficit of two per cent of GDP in the Third Letter of Intent, three per cent of GDP in the Fourth Letter of Intent and 3.5 per cent in the Fifth Letter of Intent. In order to reform and to restructure the financial system the operation of 58 finance companies was suspended by the Thai government. The Thai authorities took measures to prevent further back runs and systematic risks as well as to gain public confidence and the Financial Institutions Development Fund was given charge by them to give a guarantee of the deposits and liabilities of the financial institutions. The Financial Restructuring Authority (FRA), Radhanasin Bank (RAB) and the Asset Management Corporation (AMC) were created in October 1997. The Restructuring Authority looked after the rehabilitation plans of the 58 suspended finance companies and after examining their liquidation process allowed to re-open only two of the fifty-sight suspended companies. The Asset Management Corporation has taken the charge of the responsibility of bidding for the lowest quality assets as a buyer of last resort to help to stop fire sale of assets of the fifty-six closed finance companies, which in turn in the total financial system could undermine underlying collateral values. For other domestic financial institutions, several steps have been taken to strengthen their capital bases through a combination of internationally accepted loan classification and provisioning (LCP) standards and private sector-led recapitalisation. The Bank of Thailand and several commercial banks signed a series of Memoranda and the banks had to maintain their BIS capital adequacy ratio at a minimum of 8.5 per cent. Foreign investors were allowed to acquire majority shareholding in local financial institutions for up to 10 years. The Thai government with an idea to facilitate corporate and financial sector restructuring showed their interest to guide and facilitate the process of corporate debt restructuring. The Bankruptcy Act (1940) was amended to help the process of corporate reorganisation, increase the scope for out-of-court workouts, and ensure fair treatment of both creditors and debtors. In order to revive the economy, give opportunities for future growth, ease hardships on the poor members of the society and upgrade competitiveness, many structural reform measures were introduced. Domestic and external stability has improved very considerably, inflation rate has gone from over 10 per cent to below six per cent, the bank within the 36-38 range for a somewhat prolonged period has remained stable and the current account continued to remain surplus. Foreign reserves have also improved to comfortable levels at US $ 28.2 billion on October 22, 1998. The short-term interest rates from the peak of over 20 per cent to less than five per cent have declined. The bank lending rates have also declined and this would no doubt help to solve problems in the real and financial sectors. When a sign of renewed confidence has appeared in the Thai economic and financial system, then foreign direct investments have begun, the stock exchange index has occupied some ground and bank deposits have started to increase. Leading indicators such as investment and manufacturing indices gave their indication that Thailand has now arrived in the bottom. The Thai government and the International Monetary Fund in their latest review have visualised that the Thai economy has started to recover in 1999. The Thai government has taken steps to improve domestic industry, to use Thailand's own products and this has helped to sustain the country's own industry also. For the first time Thailand had participated in the Industrial India Trade Fair in Calcutta in December 1998. The Thai government has played a very important part to improve the country's economy and has closed down over the last two-three years about several banks and financial institutions which were mentioned as bad sector. The backbone of the Thai economy is its agriculture, service and tourism sector. As a means of producing national income mainly through foreign exchange, tourism has contributed very much to the national economy of Thailand. The figures for 1996 record that the numbers of visitors were 7,192,145 which was an increase of 3.46 per cent with the country earning over 219,364 billion baht in tourism revenue. The overall development and marketing strategies, very efficiently planned, researched and implemented, clearly gave the clear picture of the vision and determination of Thailand's tourism authorities to achieve a truly sustainable, market-oriented, environment-friendly industry. The Thai Consul General in Calcutta Mr. Supoto Isarankura na Ayudhya said that India being one of the neighouring countries will have to play a significant role in Thailand's economic reconstruction. At a time when the Thai government was taking initiative to carry out the confidence building exercise, it was in dire need of co-operation from the neighbouring countries like India. After the recessionary trend that Thailand had faced very much, the Thai economy then slowly but steadily has looked up now. At this point of time, the Thai business community has turned their attentions towards India. In fact, Thailand and India for a long time have been traditionally continuing a brisk trade relationship with each other. Many Thai companies took part in the Industrial India Trade Fair 98 in Calcutta in December 1998. The present two-way trade between the two countreis have been fixed consistently at $ one billion and never it had crossed the $ 0.5 billion mark. Tadao Chino, the president elect of the Asian Development Bank (ADB) told that he expected crisis-hit Asian economies to start picking up in 2000, with a sign of stabilisation already detected in Thailand. In that country where drastic economic reforms have taken place, currency rates had already hit the floor and are now stabilising and its foreign reserves have picked up. Definitely it has a great chance to do well in 1999. The International Monetary Fund's report mentioned that Thailand, the first country, which was disturbed by the economc crisis, would emerge first from recession with 1.0 per cent growth in 1999 after contracting by 8.0 per cent in 1998. The International Monetary Fund chief became very happy on seeing Bangkok's pace of reform and he in the third week of December

1998 approved a $ 140 million payout from the country's $ 17.2 billion bailout package. Thailand's recovery might also gain speed, has given courage and stability to currency and lower interest rates. In terms of the phase of its cycle, Thailand is a few months ahead of other South-East Asian countries. Thailand is a good example of how a stronger currency pushed it to second place in Asian rankings in US dollar terms. The Thai stock index rose 25 for the year, surpassing Wall Street, where the Dow Jones Industrial Index rose some 17 per cent over the same period. However, in local terms, the Thai index ended the year down 4.5 per cent at 385.82.

Capital Inflows of Asean Economies
Average

1989-1995	*1991-94*		*1995*	*1996*	*1997*
Indonesia					
Net Private capital flows	4.2	3.5	6.2	6.3	1.6
Other net in investments	2.6	1.9	3.1	2.7	0.1
Malaysia					
Net Private Capital flows	8.8	11.3	8.8	9.6	4.7
Other net investments	2.3	3.7	4.1	4.5	- 0.6
Thailand					
Net Private capital flows	10.2	9.1	12.7	9.3	-10.9
Other net investments	7.4	6.8	10.0	7.7	-12.6

It will be seen that Indonesia, Malaysia and Thailand have undergone proportionately large net private capital inflows during the entire decade, until the crisis erupted in 1997.

A senior Thai official told on Wednesday, December 30, 1998 that Dr. Supachai Panitchapakdi, the Thai deputy prime minister, has the backing of 40 World Trade Organisation members for the top job at the World Trade Organisation. Thailand has campaigned here for him and expectations are high in Thailand that he has a great chance of succeeding Mr. Renato Ruggiero when his term will expire in April 1999. Even though an indication of the result is not expected until January 1999 at the earliest, but the Thai politicians have already started battling to capture cabinet portfolios of Mr. Supachai Panitchapakdi — which include the trade ministry. Mr. Ruggiero's term officially expires next April 1999 but he has told that he may retire earlier if a consensus candidate emerges. At the invitation of CII Dr. Supachai Panitchapakdi came to Calcutta in the first week of January 1999 and visited the Nicco Park. He was accompanied by Mr. Rajib Kaul, the chairman of the Nicco company and Mr. Arijit Sengupta, the Park's security officer. He was very much happy to eat Thai food of the Food Park of the China town. Sri Lanka's foreign minister Mr. Lakshman Kadirgamar said that Tamil Tiger rebels have used bases in Thailand to funnel weapons to their comrades in northern Sri Lanka. He told that the issue had been raised with Thailand in 1996 and 1997 but our government has not received any reply from the Thai authorities. Thailand's *Nation* newspaper on Monday, January 11, 1999 reported it.

Asia, Europe: trade heavy weights[111]
Economic crisis tops ASEM agenda April 2-4, 1998 in London

1996 figures	*Exports to EU*	*Imports from EU:*	*Eu trade balance*
Brunei	524	1,333	809
Indonesia	8,997	8,827	-170
Malaysia	11,884	9,502	- 2,382
Philippines	4,220	4,081	-139
Singapore	11,663	15,459	3,796
Thailand	9,427	10,679	1,252
Vietnam	1,813	1,631	-182
ASEAN total	48,528	51,512	2,984
China	37,796	18,549	19,247
Japan	66,159	46,199	-19,960
South Korea	14,042	18,069	4,027

Exposed in Asia

EU lending blashed at Asia-Europe Meeting in London

EU outstanding bank loans

Singapore	133.3
South Korea	37.8
China	28.1
Indonesia	23.1
Thailand	20.0
Malaysia	12.7

---

111. *AA*, April 6, 1998, p. 18.

Philippines	7.0
Vietnam	1.0
Brunei	0.5

Outstanding bank loans to Asia (ASEM)

243 European Union	181 Japan	31 United States

Trade in the balance

EU-Asia	
US $ 489 billion	EU-US
	US $ 271 billion

Total trade 1996

Thailand

Political History
and
Buddhist Cultural Influences

To

The People of Thailand

Thailand

Political History and Buddhist Cultural Influences

by

Kanai Lal Hazra

Vol 2: Buddhism and its Influence on Thai Culture

Decent Books
New Delhi

Published and Printed by:
Decent Books
D-36/A-1, Mohan Garden
Najafgarh Road
New Delhi - 110 059

Distributed by:
D.K. Printworld (P) Ltd.
Regd. office : 'Sri Kunj', F-52, Bali Nagar
New Delhi - 110 015
Phones : (011) 545-3975, 546-6019; *Fax* : (011) 546-5926
E-mail: dkprint@4mis.com

ISBN 81-86921-12-5 (Set)
ISBN 81-86921-13-3 (Vol. I)
ISBN 81-86921-14-1 (Vol. II)

First Published in India in 2000

Contents

Volume I

Political History

	Preface	v
	Abbreviations	ix
1.	Thailand's Political History	1

Volume II

Buddhism and its Influence on Thai Culture

	Abbreviations	vii
2.	An Account of Thailand's Buddhism : Its Introduction, Rise and Development	339
3.	Thailand's Buddhist Art	407
4.	A Survey of Thaland's Buddhist Literature	485
5.	Conclusion	531
	Bibliography	551
	Index	559

Abbreviations

AA	:	*The Asian Age*, Calcutta.
AAT	:	*Art and Archaeology in Thailand*, Published by the Fine Arts Department. In Commemoration of the 100th Anniversary of the National Museum, Thailand.
AB	:	*Ananda Bazar Patrika*, Calcutta.
ABGPN	:	*A.B. Griswold and Prasart na Nagara*, A Pali Inscription from Vat Sri Ratnamahadhatu, Subarnapuri.
ACHBAS	:	*A Concise History of Buddhist Art in Siam*, Reginald Le May.
AHS	:	*A History of Siam*, W.A.R. Wood.
AHSEA	:	*A History of South-East Asia*, D.G.E. Hall.
ANAEI	:	*A New Account of the East Indies*, Alexander Hamilton.
ASEAW	:	*Ancient South-East Asian Warfare*, H.G.Q. Wales.
Baa	:	*Buddhist art and architecture*, Robert E. Fisher.
BACSEA	:	*The Buddhist Annals and Chronicles of South-East Asia*, K.L. Hazra.

Bapat	:	*2500 years of Buddhism*, P.W. Bapat.
BEA	:	*Buddhism in East Asia*, Sukumar Dutt.
BEFED	:	*Bulletin l'Ecele Francaise d'Extreme Orient*, Hanoi.
BEFEO	:	*Bulletin do l'Ecole Francaise d'Extreme Orient*, Hanoi.
BM	:	*British Malaya*, A Lennex Mills.
CDSEA	:	*Collective Defence in South-East Asia*, Chatham House Report, London.
Chdv	:	*The Chamadevivamsa, G. Coedes, Documents sur l'histoire politique at religiouse du Laos Occidental, Bulletin de l'Ecole Francaise d'Extreme Orient, XXV*, Hanoi.
Damrong	:	*Prince Damrong,'The story of the records of Siamese history'*, The Siam Society, Fiftieth Anniversary Commemorative publication, *The Siam Society Journal*, vol. I.
DRTS	:	*Description du Royaume Thai au Siam*, Jean Baptiste Pallegeix.
DSEA	:	*The Diplomacy of South-East Asia*, Russel H. Fifield.
DVP	:	*Dīpavaṁsa*, ed. H. Oldenberg.
ECT	:	*Economic Change in Thailand since 1850*, James C. Ingram.
ET	:	*The Economic Times*, Calcutta.
FYS	:	*Five Years in Siam*, H.W. Smyth.

GRAHAM	:	*Siam*, W. A. Graham.
HB	:	*Hinduism and Buddhism*, Sir Charles Eliot.
HPWT	:	*History of Protestant work in Thailand*, Kenneth E. Wells.
HTBSEA	:	*History of Theravāda Buddhism in South-East Asia*, K.L. Hazra.
ICS	:	*The Indian Colony of Siam*, P.N. Bose.
IICSEA	:	*Influence of Indian culture in South-East Asia*, R.C. Mazumdar.
ISEA	:	*India and South-East Asia*, R.C. Majumdar.
IWGS	:	*The Impact of the West on the Government of Siam*, Walter F. Vella.
JECSCC	:	*Journal of an Embassy to the Courts of Siam and Cochin China*, John Crawford.
JKM	:	*Jinakālamalī*, G. Coedes, BEFEO,Vol. XXV, Hanoi, 1925.
KM	:	*King Mongkut*, Frankfurter, O, Journal of Siam Society.
LBS	:	*Le bouddhisme a Siam*, Lean Feer. Memoire de la Societe Academique Indo-Chineise de France I.
LEHII	:	*Les Estate Hindouises d'Indochina at d'Indonesia*, G. Coedes.
LV	:	*Locust Valley*, Augustin.
LVRRM	:	*La Vie religiouse du Roi Mongkut*, R. Lingat.

Mahabodhi	:	*Buddhism in Thailand*, Ven. P. Amara Thera, *The Mahabodhi*, Nov-Dec, 2521-1997, Vol. 85, Nos. 11-12.
Mhv	:	*Mahāvaṁsa*, W. Geiger.
MKS	:	*Mongkut, King of Siam*, Abbot Low Moffat.
MTI	:	*Mangalartha Temple Inscription.*
PLC	:	*The Pali Literature of Ceylon*, G.P. Malalasekera.
Sas	:	*Sāsanavaṁsa*, M. Bode.
SASP	:	*Some Aspects of Siamese Politics*, John Coast.
SC	:	*Siam and Combodia*, Rachel Wheatcroft.
SCR	:	*Some Siam, the crossriads*, Josiah Crosby.
SEA	:	*South-East Asia*, John F. Cady.
SGEC	:	*The Sheaf of Garlands of the Epoch of the Conqueror*, N.A. Jayawickrema, Being a translation of the Jina Jina-kalamalipakaranam of Ratanapanna Thera of Thailand, PTS, Translation Series.
SGEC	:	'*The Sheaf of Garlands of the Epochs of the Conqueror*', Pali Text Society, Translation Series, no. 36, N.A. Jayawickrema.
SSJ	:	*The Siam Society Journal*, Vol. II.
STC	:	*Siam in the Twentieth Century*, John Garden Drummond Campbell.

SUR	:	*Siam under Rama III*, Walter F. Vella.
TAII	:	*Thai Art with Indian Influences*, Premsak Jermswatdi.
TAIL	:	*Thai Art with Indian Influences*, Premsak Jermswatdi.
TAKE	:	*The Ancient Khmer Empire*, L.P. Bridggs.
TAT	:	*The Arts of Thailand*, S.V. Beek and L.D. Jettoni.
TCICSCL	:	*Travels in the central parts of Indo-China, Siam, Combodia and Laos during 1859-60*, Henry Mouhet.
TDMKJS	:	*A True Description of the Mighty Kingdom of Japan and Siam*, Joest Schouten.
TESG	:	*Thailand, Economic Survey Group, Report on Economic Development Plans*, Bangkok.
THRAF	:	*Thailand, Human Relations Area Files*, Thomas Fitzsimmons.
TG	:	*The Telegraph*, Calcutta.
Thailand	:	*Thailand*, Swami Sadananda.
TKHAAT	:	*The Kingdom of Haripunjaya, Art and Architecture-Thailand*, Srisakara Vallibhotana.
TLP	:	*Thailand: Land and Peoples*, Prachoem Chomchai.
TMGI	:	*The Making of Greater India*, H.G.Q. Walas.

TMSEA	:	*The Making of South-East Asia*, G. Coedes, tr. by H.M. Wright.
TPSCHRAF	:	*Thailand: Its People, Its Society, Its Culture, Human Relations Areas Files*, Wondell Blanchard.
TSM	:	*The Statesman*, Calcutta.
TSR	:	*The Siam Repository*, Sannel J. Smith.
TSRWR	:	*The Siam Rath Weekly Review*, August 29, Bangkok.
URPAA	:	*Une Recension Palie Des Annales d'Ayuthia*, G. Coedes, *Bulletin de l'Ecole Francaise d'Extreme Orient*, XIV, Hanoi,
Wyatt	:	David K. Wyatt, Chronicle Tradition in Thai Historiography, South-East Asian History and historiography, ed. C.D. Cowan and O.W. Walter.

2

An Account of Thailand's Buddhism Its Rise and Development

BUDDHISM, which is the state religion of Thailand, has played a great role in Thailand's political, religious, social and cultural history. The Hīnayāna and the Mahāyāna, the two important schools of Buddhism, have flourished from the earliest period till the present day in Thailand. It is regarded as one of the greatest important Buddhist centres of the world. About ninety (90) per cent of the Thai people are Budhists. The Hīnayāna or the Tharavāda sect of Buddhism, which was introduced into Thailand long before the Christian era, has became the major creed and the religious faith of the Thais. They have accepted its philosophy very much and have tried to follow it with great devotion. Taoism and Confucianism, the two religions, also have taken their growth in Thailand from China. The people of Southern Thailand tried to follow the religion of Islam and the hill-tribesmen were animists, i.e., they had faith in the spirits of nature or ancestors. Brāhmaṇism or Hinduism as well as Christianity also flourished in Thailand. Ancient Thailand became known as 'the Land of Yellow Robes' which are the sacred garments or the Buddhist monks and it can be mentioned as the only country in the world where "the king is constitutionally stipulated to be a Buddhist".[1] Buddhism still exists and plays

1. *TAII*, p. 15.

its vital role in Thailand. It exerts tremendous influence still on the life of its people and contributes very much to its history.

From the *Mahāvaṁsa*, a chronicle of Sri Lanka as well as the Rock Edict XIII of the Maurya emperor Aśoka, it is known that after the Third Buddhist Council Aśoka had sent nine groups of Buddhist missionaries to different countries outside India for the propagation of the Buddha's doctrine. The Thais believed that Sona Thera and Uttara Thera, Aśoka's missionaries, visited Suvarṇabhūmi to preach the Buddhist faith there. According to them, the name Suvarṇabhūmi was closely associated with the first phase of the introduction of Buddhism in Thailand. But its identification is still shrouded in mystery. The Thai scholars mentioned that this region was located in Central Thailand and its capital was at Nakon Pathom, but others states that Suvarṇabhūmi was in Myanmar and Thaton, which was situated near the Gulf of Martaban, was its capital. The Laotian and the Cambodian scholars stated that the area of Suvarṇabhūmi was in their lands while some other people claimed that the area of Suvarṇabhūmi represented the Malay Peninsula. The Kalyāṇī inscriptions of Myanmar and the *Sāsanavaṁsa*, a Myanmarese chronicle, described that the location of Suvarṇabhūmi was in lower Myanmar. According to several British scholars, Suvarṇabhūmi was Sudhammanagara or the city of Thaton. Many people also claimed that it was the city of Pegu in Myanmar. Both European and Indian scholars suggested that Suvarṇabhūmi represented the territory of lower Myanmar of Sudhammanagara. Although they believed that Aśoka sent two Buddhist missionaries named Sona and Uttara Theras for the propagation of Buddhism to Suvarṇabhūmi which corresponded to Myanmar, yet, no archaeological evidence was available to support the introduction and development of Buddhism there at that time. Apart from the Sri Lankan chronicle, there was no other source which referred to the flourishing condition of Buddhism in Myanmar before the fifth century AD. The Thai scholars also supported this view. H.R.H. Prince Damrong Rajanubhab claimed that central Thailand was the place where the introduction of Buddhism took place and this was the city of Nakon Pathom. In Thailand many archaeological artifacts were found which had great similarity with the religious materials of India during the days of Aśoka. In order to commemorate the arrival of Aśoka's missionaries, a huge *stūpa* or *pagoḍā* named Pathom Chedi or Pathama Chetiya was erected in Nakon or Nakorn Pathom. The archaeological objects such as the Stone Wheel of the Law bearing the Buddhist crede 'Ye Dhamma hetuppabhavā . . .' were found. H. H. Prince Dhanivat opined,

> The Siamese, basing their claims on the extensive finds, on the site of Nakorn Pathom of antiquities of the Mauryan pattern such as Deer and wheel motifs and the questions of 'ye dhamma hatuppabhavā' are inclined to believe that this was an old part on the Gulf of Siam (Thailand). They therefore claimed its identity with the centre of Suvarṇabhūmi, specially on account of the prevalence of placenames bearing a similar meaning such as U-Thong (the cradle of Gold), and Supanburi (the City of Gold) an equivalent to Suvarṇabhūmi in a Siamese translation.[2]

He described further,

> In any case it seems certain that the type of Buddhism introduced was once known to most by the name of Hīnayānism or Theravāda Buddhism, the type in fact prevailed in the days of Aśoka.

John F. Cady in his book *South-East: Its Historical Development* has mentioned that the land of Suvarṇabhūmi

2. *Mahabodhi*, pp. 351-5.

was situated in the area to the north of the Gulf of Siam.[3] It indicated that Suvarṇabhūmi represented the whole area from the valley of the Menam river up to the Malay Peninsula. Other scholars referred to the border of Suvarṇbhūmi from the Mon or Rāmññadesa country up to Champa or Vietnam and from Myanmar up to the Malay Peninsula. One authority claimed that Suvarṇabhūmi was in the Sumatra island because over 1,000 years ago, the people described Sumatra as Golden Island. On the basis of positive archaeological evidences, the Thais claimed that the exact location of Suvarṇabhūmi should be traced to central Thailand and north of the Malay Peninsula. Several Thai scholars mentioned that Suvarṇabhūmi was in the area of Thailand lying in the western parts of the Menam river. In Thailand there were several towns whose names were closely associated with gold or *súvarṇa* and these cities were Angthong (the basin of gold), U-Thong (the cradle of gold), Supanburi (the city of gold), Kanchanaburi, the north of the Malay Peninsula at Surathani whose original name was Muang Thathong (the port city of gold), etc. All these names informed us that they had received their names from the name of Suvarṇabhūmi. Formerly, these towns were same as the region lying in the valley of the Menam river which was called Suvarṇabhūmi. It may be noted here that not only in Thailand but also the word 'gold' was closely associated with some of the place-names, such as the name 'Sunāparanta' in Myanmar which suggested 'the border-city of gold' and also 'Thathong', the original name of the city of Thaton, the Mon country, which referred to 'the land or area of gold'. If the identification of Suvarṇabhūmi with lower Myanmar is accepted, Buddhism would have been introduced to that country during the reign of Aśoka. But no archaeological evidence prevailed in lower Myanmar which showed the existence of Buddhism there as early as the third

3. *TAII*, p. 18.

century BC. Therefore, the identification of Suvarṇabhūmi with lower Myanmar is not conclusive. The Thais claimed that the whole area of central Thailand, north of the Gulf of Siam and the Malay Peninsula represented Suvarṇabhūmi. In course of archaeological excavations, several Buddhist antiquities were found at Nakon Pathom or Nagara Pathama which then represented the central capital of Suvarṇabhūmi. From the authority of the literary sources and Thai traditions, many Thai historians argued that Nakon Pathom was the region or the first place in South-East Asia where Sona Thera and Uttara Thera, Aśoka's missionaries, arrived for the propagation of Buddhism because many archaeological objects were discovered there. They believed that Suvarṇabhūmi was located in Central Thailand, north of the Gulf of Siam. Its capital was Nakon Pathom and the whole area of Suvarṇabhūmi comprised the central, north-eastern and southern parts of Thailand. Suvarṇabhūmi was not situated in lower Myanmar, Thaton of the Mon country or Sumatra or the Malay Peninsula as several scholars had claimed for a long time.

According to the traditional belief in Thailand, Buddhism was introduced in Thailand during the reign of the Maurya ruler Aśoka. The Sri Lankan chronicles, the *Dīpavaṁsa* and the *Mahāvaṁsa* say that Mahādhammarakkhita and Mahārakkhita introduced Buddhism to Mahāraṭṭha and the Yona region during the reign of Aśoka.[4] The chronicle of Myanmar the *Sāsanavaṁsa*'s author has identified Mahāraṭṭha with Thailand.[5] He told that Mahāraṭṭha was Mahānagararaṭṭha in Thailand. He stated further that the Yonaka country extended along the valleys of the Menam and the Mae Phing rivers and also the Shan states to the north of these. According to several scholars, Mahāraṭṭha

4. *DPV*, ch. VIII, vv. 8-9; *Mhv*, ch. XII, vv. 5-6.

5. *Sas*, p. 8.

was the region of the Upper Godāvarī. It is Mahārāṣṭra in western India. The Yena region was located in the north-west region of India where many Indo-Greek people used to live there. But the traditions relating to the identification of Mahāraṭṭha and the Yona region with the regions of Thailand was rather late. There was no archaeological evidence which gave us information of the existence of Buddhism in Thailand as early as the third century BC. Thus, from it we conclude that it is very difficult to accept the location of Mahāraṭṭha and the Yona region where Aśoka sent his Buddhist missionaries to preach Buddhism there.

From the archaeological finds excavated at the Menam valley, it was known that this region was an important centre of Theravāda Buddhism from the sixth or seventh century AD onwards. The Dvāravatī kingdom in the lower Menam valley in lower-central Thailand was an important centre of Buddhism. Hiuen Tsang, the Chinese traveller, mentioned a Buddhist kingdom named To-lo-po-ti which was located between the Pyu kingdom of Sirikhetta (Prome) in lower Myanmar and the Khmer kingdom.[6] According to E.J. Eitel, To-lo-po-ti was Dvārapatī or Dvāravatī, the lord of the gate. G. Coedes and other scholars mentioned it as Dvāravatī. Its archaeological remains gave us an idea that the foundation of this kingdom took place in the sixth or seventh century AD. The Mon people belonged to the kingdom of Dvāravatī and their capital was at first at Nagarama Patha or Nagara Prathama or Nakon Pathom or Nakorn Patom or Phra Pathom and later at Lavo or Lopburi. The political influence of the Dvāravatī kingdom reached up to Haripuñjaya (Lampoon) in northern Thailand. From the literary sources and the Thai traditions, the Thai historians opined that Nakon Pathom was the place or the first region in South-East Asia where Buddhist missionaries or Aśoka arrived to

6. *HTBSEA*, p. 69.

preach and to propagate Buddhism there because many archaeological objects were discovered in the area surrounding this town. A large and varied number of ancient Buddhist antiquities were found at Nakon Pathom.[7] Prominent among the Buddhist antiquities at this region was the huge Buddhist *stūpa* which the Thais referred to it as the Phra Pathom Chedi (Pathama Chetiya) which was most probably erected in commemoration of the arrival of Aśoka's missionaries to preach Buddhism there. According to scholars, this great *stūpa* was built in the third or in the fourth century BC. Nakon Pathom was an important town in ancient times and the great *stūpa* of the Phra Pathom Chedi threw flood of light on the introduction and development of Buddhism there. This great Chedi was no doubt a great sanctuary where the introduction of Buddhism first took place in Thailand and from it began to flourish in neighbouring countries. This Chedi was restored several times. In the reign of King Mongkut or Rama IV of the Chakri dynasty of the Bangkok period the original form of this structure of this *stūpa* in course of its restoration was replaced by the new one. Under this ruler's patronage, this *stūpa* was restored. Most probably in 1853 a great Chedi was build to cover the original one. But the first construction was unable to complete it and the new construction began in 1860 and four chapels were built to keep four images of the Buddha in different attitudes at the four cardinal points with a circular gallery to connect them. This can be mentioned as the new form of the *stūpa*. The original *stūpa* had a great similarity with the Indian *stūpa* of Sāñcī which was built during the reign of Aśoka. The lower portion of the *stūpa* in the form of dome or *aṇḍa* resembled the dome of the great *stūpa* at Sāñcī. Like an inverted basin or cup, the dome of the Phra Pathom Chedi had its shapd circular. A square altar or *harmika* which was crowned with

---

7. *TAII*, pp. 20-1.

a parasol (*chattra*) was placed at the top. The base which had a circumambient gallery was also square and there was an enclosure outside. Many Buddhist antiquities were found at Nakon Pathom and in neighbouring places, but all these antiquities had the same style as was prevalent in the reign of the Maurya ruler Aśoka. Several Buddhist sculptural objects were unearthed at Nakon Pathom and its neighbouring regions. A fragment of an inscription in archaic Mon of the sixth century was found at Phra Pathom.[8] Another Mon inscription was found in a monument called San Sung at Lavo or Lopburi in Thailand and it mentions various gifts offered to a Buddhist monastery. It was without date. G. Ceedés referred to it in the seventh century AD. C. Duroiselle described it in the sixth and seventh centuries AD. According to D.G.E. Hall, it can be described to the eighth century AD. C. Duroiselle opined that its few letters were closely related to the Pallava script of south India, which was in the fourth and fifth centuries AD was a great centre of the Theravāda form of Buddhism. The *dharmackra* (the Wheel of the Law) associated with a figure of deer, foot-prints of the Buddha, the *vajrāsana*, seated Buddhist images and votive tablets bearing inscriptions '*ye dhamma hetuppabhavā* . . . ' in Pāli were discovered at Phra Pathom. Recently, several archaeologists from the Department of Fine Arts, Bangkok and the staff of Pennsylvania University (USA) had excavated the ancient town-site at the Nakon Sawan and Nakon Pathom provinces. They found ivory combs with the design of Indian style and Indian seals along with the Stone Wheel of the Law. All these antiquities showed that they belonged to the objects which were used for worship before the introduction of image-worship by the Indian people. Several images of the Buddha in bronze or bluish limestone not later than sixth century AD were found at P'ong Tuk in the province of Rajapuri (Ratburi)

8. *HTBSEA*, p. 69.

in lower Thailand. Among several ruined buildings discovered at P'ong Tuk, one had the remains of a platform and fragment of columns. The appearance of this platform closely resembled a similar platform at Anurādhapura in Sri Lanka. The archaeological finds, the architectural and sculptural remains and Pāli inscriptions gave an impression that from the sixth century AD onwards the Theravāda sect took its firm rests in the lower Menam valley and soon it became the most prominent religion there. But when the Khmer rulers, who were great patrons of Brāhmaṇism and the Mahāyāna form of Buddhism, controlled this region, even then, the Theravāda sect existed there. The Buddhist monuments and antiquities of the Theravāda school belonged to the Dvāravatī school of art. The Dvāravatī kingdom which represented the name of the ancient empire was located in central and north of the Gulf of Siam. The Thai scholars opined that its capital Nakon Pathom was able to extend its development to such extent that not only Buddhism but also Buddhist art and culture flourished. The Buddhist objects were found in this kingdom and they indicated that they belonged to several periods and Buddhism also took its growth in different stages here. The Dvāravatī people came in close contact with India and Sri Lanka and the Buddhist antiquities were found there in large numbers. Thus, the Dvāravatī kingdom was regarded as the first place where from the earliest period Buddhism prospered.

The Haripuñjaya kingdom of the upper Menam valley was an important kingdom in northern Thailand. The *Jinakālamālī*,[9] a text of the first half of the sixteenth century AD, mentioned a political alliance between the kingdoms of Haripuñjaya, Rāmaññanagara and Lopburi. The sage named Vāsudeva in the year 1204 of the *mahāparinibbāna* of the Buddha, founded the city of Haripuñjaya. Then the princess

---

9. *JKM, BEFEO*, XXV, 1925; *SGEC*, pp. 36-7.

Cammadevi, the daughter of the king of the city of Lavo or Lopburi and the wife of the provincial ruler of Rāmañña-nagara, occupied the throne in AD 663 and began to rule there. She came to Haripuñjaya with soldiers and five hundred great elders versed in the three *piṭaka*s. Lopburi was an important centre of the Theravāda sect and Rāmaññanagara in the lower Menam valley was also its great centre. The middle of the seventh century AD witnessed the introduction of the Mon culture and the Theravāda form of Buddhism in the Haripuñjaya kingdom. This Mon kingdom played a vigorous role in the establishment of Theravāda Buddhism in the upper Menam valley in northern Thailand.

In the beginning of the seventh century AD the rulers of the Śailendra dynasty brought under their control most of the areas of Sumatra, Java, Borneo and some parts of the Malay Peninsula and Palembang became their capital in the Sumatra island.[10] These kings consolidated their empire soon and it became known as the Śrī-Vijaya empire. They rose to power in a short period. They conquered several territories including the Malay Peninsula and the archipelago part of southern Thailand. All these regions became the vassal states of the Śrī-Vijaya rulers, who were the followers of the Mahāyāna form of Buddhism. Under their patronage it became the accepted religion in the Malay Peninsula and several places in the south of modern Thailand. In the beginning of the seventh century AD this event occurred. Several scholars stated that the Śrī-Vijaya rulers became the paramount power in the whole of the island-country of South-East Asia in the beginning of the seventh century AD and from that time they contributed very much to the progress of the Mahāyāna form of Buddhism in southern Thailand. Thus, this form of Buddhism became very popular in southern Thailand, but other parts of Thailand, i.e., the central and

10. *TAII*, p. 25.

the north-eastern parts of Thailand and also the northern portion of the Gulf of Siam followed the Hīnayāna form of Buddhism. From archaeological evidence it was clear that the Mahāyāna sect prospered in southern Thailand. The great *stūpa* which the Thais called the Phra Mahadhatu (Maha-Tat) indicated the propagation of Mahāyānism there. The location of the great *stūpa* was in the modern province of Nakon Śrī-Tammarat in southern Thailand. There was another *stūpa* in Chaiya, a modern sub-district in the province of Surathani. These two Buddhist *stūpa*s belonged to the Mahāyāna style of art. Their architectural features had great similarity with the Mahāyāna Buddhist *stūpa*s in Java and Sumatra. According to the Thai archaeo-logists, the Mahāyānists, who converted the Thai people into their own faith under the patronage of the Śrī-Vijaya rulers, erected the Buddhist *stūpa*s in both southern Thailand and also Java and Sumatra islands. The Buddhist antiquities found at the southern side of Thailand indicated that Mahāyānism played its great role there. Several Buddha and *bodhisattva* images were found in many caves of the Nakon Śrī-Tammarat, Trang, Patalung and Patani provinces and the discovery of these images helped very much to prove the existence of the Mahāyāna form of Buddhism there. The image of *bodhisattava* Avalokiteśvara was found at Chaiya, a sub-district of the Surathani province. The images of other deities in the Mahāyāna pantheon on large numbers were also unearthed there. The Mahāyāna was known as the cult of the *bodhisattva* worship and the Mahāyānists regarded the *bodhisattva*, their deity besides the Buddha. The discovery of Mahāyāna Buddhist images gave a clear indication that the people of this region were worshippers of the Mahāyāna sect. The images of the *bodhisattva* were found in southern Thailand and also in Java, Sumatra and the Malay Peninsula, and their style had grat similarity with the style of Indian art. Thus, from the basis of the archaeological evidence it was clear that the seventh century AD saw the growth and progress of the Mahāyāna sect in the religious life of the people in southern Thailand. Not only the image of the Mahāyāna deities but also the votive tablets in large numbers were discovered in southern part of Thailand. The Thais referred to the votive tablet as Phra Pim, 'an object made of raw-clay bearing the figure of the *bodhisattva* and the Buddha on its surface'. The Buddhist votive tablets were unearthed in the caves of the provinces of Nakon Śrī-Tammarat, Trang and Patalung and they had the alphabet and date which looked like the Mahāyāna style of the Śrī-Vijaya period. These votive tablets with the date AD 657-757 informed us that the Śrī-Vijaya empire of the Śailendra dynasty flourished during this period. Thus, the archaeological evidence found in southern Thailand clearly helped to suggest the introduction and development of Mahāyānism in southern Thailand in the first half of the seventh century AD under the patronage of the Śrī-Vijaya rulers. The Buddhist antiquities and monuments which found in this region during the time of the development of Mahāyānism belonged to the Śrī-Vijaya school of art and architecture.

The Lopburi period witnessed the second phase of the introduction and the development of the Mahāyāna sect in Thailand. The Kambuja or the Khmer empire was one of the powerful kingdom of South-East Asia after the seventh century AD. This country is located in the east and south-east direction of modern Thailand. The reign of Sūryavarman I marked a turning point in the history of Kambuja or Cambodia. Because this Khmer ruler and his successors played their aggressive roles to extend the boundaries of the Khmer kingdom far and wide. They brought Champa and Annam, and also the lands of the north of the Menam valley in modern Thailand under their control. The Khmer inscription of the reign of Sūryavarman I informed that this king despatched armies to capture lands comprising north of the Gulf of Siam and around the valley of the Menam river in AD 1002. The eleventh century AD witnessed the rise and growth of the Khmer rule over several regions of the Menam valley.[11] An inscription dated Śaka AD 944-1002 was found at Lavo or Lopburi in southern Thailand and it referred to king Sūryavarman I (AD 1002-50) of Cambodia. Another inscription was found at Sal Cau or San Chao in Lopburi.[12] It had no date but it showed the Khmer rule at Lopburi in the eleventh century AD. The archaeological evidence also throw light on the Khmer rule over Sukhodaya and Sri Sachanlai (Svargalok) in north central Thailand in the eleventh century AD.[13] The Khmer power under the rule of Sūryavarman II (AD 1133-50) reached the peak of its political and cultural development and the Khmer rule existed at Lopburi during this period. Jayavarman VII occupied the Khmer throne towards the end of the twelfth century AD and he included the entire Menam valley except the Mon kingdom of Haripuñjaya under rule.[14] Towards the middle of the thirteenth century AD when Śrī Indrāditya became the ruler of the kingdom of Sukhodaya, the political supremacy of the Khmer kingdom of Cambodia over this region came to an end. For the administrative facilities, the Khmer rulers had established several headquarters of the Khmer dominion and Lopburi was the chief Khmer headquarter in Thailand and it became an important centre of the Khmer outline and civilisation. Each headquarter was governed by a Khmer general or Viceroy who controlled power on behalf of the Khmer rulers. The Khmer viceroy of Lopburi managed the whole of the south Dvāravatī kingdom. The town or Sukhodaya controlled the north Dvāravatī empire. Other

11. *AHSEA*, p. 105; *TMSEA*, p. 100.
12. *TAKE*, p. 160.
13. *HTDSEA*, p. 131.
14. *TAKE*, p. 237.

headquarters were the town of Śrī Top or Śrī Deva, the town of Pimai and Sakon-Nakorn. From AD 1017 onwards the Khmer art and culture were able to establish themselves in the Menam valley, and the Khmer civilisation continued to maintain its influence over the north of modern Thailand as far as Sukhodaya and Sawankhalok towns.

From the seventh to the thirteenth centuries AD the Mahāyāna form of Buddhism developed in Southern Thailand, while western, northern and central Thailand witnessed the progress of the Theravāda sect. Several Buddhist *stūpa*s or *pagoḍā*s at the Mahādhātu monastery indicate that those were erected after the Śrī-Vijaya style. The same style of the *stūpa*s or *pagoḍā*s was also found at Chaiya. In the province of southern Thailand many images of Avalokiteśvara and other Mahāyāna deities were found. Under the patronage of the Khmer ruler the Mahāyāna sect began to flourish in several parts of central and eastern Thailand. Many Mahāyāna temples and images of the Buddha, *bodhisattva*s and of other Mahāyāna gods and goddesses were discovered in the provinces of Sakon-Nakorn, Nakorn-Rajasima and Lopburi.

Under the patronage of the rulers of the Dvāravatī kingdom the Theravāda form of Buddhism flourished in the lower Menam valley. But in the eleventh century AD when the lower Menam valley came under the control of the Khmer empire. Mahāyānism and Brāhmaṇism prospered, because the Khmer rulers were their patrons. A Khmer inscription dated Śaka 944-AD 1022-25 found at Lopburi mentioned certain religious edicts issued by Sūryavarman I, the Khmer King of Cambodia.[15] It was decreed that in all holy places, temples, monasteries and hermitages, the assetics, the *sthavira*s, and the Mahāyāna *bhikkhu*s should offer to the king the merits of their piety. People who disturb the prayers

15. *HTBSEA*, p. 133.

or the sacred duties of the pious should be handed over to tribunals for trial and punishment. From the above inscription it was clear that not only the Mahāyāna sect but also the Theravāda form of Budhism folurished at Lopburi during this time. This period also witnessed the progress of Brāhmaṇism there. Sūryavarman I was an ardent follower of Mahāyānism, but, even then, he patronised Brāhmaṇism, which was the religion of his ancestors. It is to be noted here that in the beginning of the eleventh-century AD Mahāyānism did not prosper very much in the region which comprised central and noth of modern Thailand because king Sūryavarman I and his successors as well as their vassal rulers helped Brāhmaṇism to flourish. No outstanding achievement of Mahāyānism took place there during this period. According to several scholars, the introduction of the Mahāyāna sect in Thailand took place after the end of the reign of Sūryavarman I of Cambodia.[16] In AD 1180 Śrī-Vijaya ruler who came to power in Nakon-Śrī-Tammarat was a devout follower of Mahāyānism and this form of Buddhism became very popular during this time in Śrī-Vijaya. This king under the Khmer influence became the viceroy of Lopburi and one of his sons was able to capture the throne of the Cambodian empire. The Mahāyāna sect prospered in Thailand and it contributed very much to the religious life of the Thai people. The stone inscription with the Khmer script of AD 1007 was found and it mentioned the erection of religious monuments under the Khmer patronage in Lavo or Lopburi. Most of these monuments were offered to the Mahāyāna deities and they belonged to the Khmer school of art. Several stone temples were built and these were dedicated to *bodhisattva* Avalokiteśvara and other Mahāyāna deities. These monuments were found in some provinces of Thailand and from them one guessed that the Mahāyāna sect was

16. *TAII*, p. 28.

introduced in Thailand during the eleventh century AD and from this period onwards this sect became very popular in Thailand. The remains of the stone temple in the province of Lopburi informed us about the strong Khmer influence on its architectural design. The stone temple in the town of Pimai and the stone temple on the top of the mountain named Khao Banomrung in the province of Buriram in north-eastern Thailand gave an impression of the growth and progress of the Mahāyāna sect in Thailand. The style and technique of these stone temple helped to indicate that they belonged to the Khmer school of art of the Pre-Angkor Vat period. A large number of sculptural objects were found at Lopburi, Pimai, Śrī-Top, Buriram and other provinces in north-eastern Thailand. The discovery of these sculptural objects gave information on the development of the Mahāyānism in these regions. The images of the Buddha, the *bodhisattvas*, Lokeśvara and other Mahāyāna deities were found in these provinces and one concluded from them that the Mahāyāna sect was able to make a great influence upon the religious and cultural life of Thailand. These images showed that they belonged to the Lopburi school of Khmer art. These epigraphical and archaeological evidences helped very much to remark that the arrival of the Mahāyāna sect took place in Thailand in two different periods. Under the patronage of the Śrī-Vijaya rulers it was introduced in the seventh century AD in south Thailand, and the Khmer rulers of Cambodia played their prominent roles to introduce it in central and northern Thailand in the eleventh century AD. The Buddhist art found in these regions (during this period belonged to the Śrī-Vijaya and the Lopburi schools of art. From the Buddha image, which were unearthed in north, eastern, southern and central Thailand, gave a clear indication of the properity of the Mahāyāna sect there. The Buddha images from the town of Pimai near Korat in central-eastern Thailand showed the influence of the Khmer art. It may be mentioned here that although various religions were practised at Lopburi under the Khmer rule, the discovery of the Buddha images and the Buddhist monuments signified the importance of the Mahāyāna and the Hīnayāna sects at Lopburi during this period. Although the Mahāyāna sect under the Khmer rule maintained its importance and pre-eminence, yet the Hīnayāna sect also prospered there as it had flourished in this region under the role of the Dvāravatī rulers.

The Haripuñjaya kingdom in the thirteenth century AD was a great centre of the Mon culture and the Theravāda sect prospered to a great extent there. Several inscriptions in the Mon language and mixed with Pāli were found at Haripuñjaya. The use of Pāli in these inscriptions showed that before the arrival of the Thais, the Theravāda form of Buddhism took its growth very firmly in the upper Menam valley under the patronage of the Mon rulers and this region became its great centre. The Wat Don inscription of king Sabbādhisiddhi (or Sabbasiddhi) mentions the construction of a monastery called the Jetavana and a Uposatha hall by the ruler who reigned at Haripuñjaya in the beginning of the thirteenth century AD.[17] It describes the gifts of lands, slaves and cattle to this monastery by the king and he also erected there *cetiya*s in its precincts. It also says that the king and his two sons Mahanam and Kaccay had left the world in order to enter the monastic life at the Jetavana for sometime. In this monastery the Rājaguru and about two hundred disciples used to live. Two inscriptions were found at the Wat Kukut at Haripuñjaya. The inscription no.1 discusses a *pagoḍā* called the Ratanacetiya and the re-establishment of a monastery. King Sabhādhisiddhi was a donor. The inscription no.2 mentions the Buddhist Saṁgha and a monastery. An inscription was found at the Wat Sen Khaot-to or Khao Ho at Haripuñjaya. It reveals the erection of a hall, the

17. *JKM, BEFEO*, XXV, pp. 189-92; *SGEC*, p. 110.

establishment of ten statues of the Buddha and several donations. Tju Mahāthera of the city of Haripuñjaya was its author. Another undated inscription was discovered at the Wat Ban Hlui and it speaks of the Jetavana monastery.[18] All these inscriptions informed the flourishing condition of the Theravāda sect under the patronage of the Mon people at Haripuñjaya during this period. It may be noted here that before the Thais established their contact with Sri Lanka, the Mon people contributed to its progress in Thailand.

According to scholars, the history of the introduction of the Theravāda form of Buddhism in Thailand had colse relation with the history of Myanmar's ruler King Aniruddha's reign becasue it was during his time the Pukam (Pagan) Theravāda form of Buddhism flourished in Thailand from AD 1057 onwards.[19] King Aniruddha wanted to reorganise the Buddhist Saṁgha with the help of Shin Arahan, a competent monk from Thaton, the capital of the Mon country in lower Myanmar. According to his advice, the former sent the envoy to the Mon kingdom for the Buddhist monks and the sacred Buddhist texts. But the Mon king refused to give them. The Myanmarese king became furious and he captured Thaton and brought many learned Buddhist monks and the sacred Buddhist texts to Pagan, his capital in AD 1057. Then under his patronage and with the active help of Shin Arahan, the Myanmarese Buddhist Saṁgha was reformed. The king then propagated this new form of Buddhism, the Pukam (Pagan) Theravāda form of Buddhism throughout his kingdom and outside. It is generally accepted by scholars that Thaton, the capital of the Mon country in lower Myanmar, was conquered by him and it was regarded then as the most prominent centre of the Theravāda form of Buddhism. Several territories were conquered by him and these became his vassal

---

18. *HTBSEA*, p. 134.
19. *TAII*, p. 29.

states. He not only captured north Arakan, Shan states, etc., but he also extended his suzerainty over the lands, now comprising modern Thailand. His kingdom reached up to the regions in northern Thailand — the old Lan-nathai kingdom and the Haripuñjaya kingdom. The western and the central parts of Lopburi and the Dvāravatī kingdom of the Menam valley were occupied by him. He also brought Chiengmai, Lopburi and Nakon Pathom under his control. He then introduced the Pukam (Pagan) Theravāda sect in these regions. These territories under his patronage were greatly influenced by this new sect of Buddhism. His religious policy had helped to establish the firm foundation of the Theravāda sect in these areas of Thailand which came to be settled by the Thais who arrived from Yunan in China. As soon as the new settlors reached there, they came under the influence of this form of Buddhism which became known as Pukam (Pagan) Theravāda Buddhism and it prospered from the second half of the eleventh century AD to the thirteenth century AD. The architectural features of the Seven Pagodas (Chedi Jet Yod) in the town of Chiengmai, north of Thailand had great similarity with the Seven Pagodas in Pagan in upper Myanmar. Most propably, Aniruddha, the Pagan King, erected both Buddhist monuments. Several scholars accepted this view of the introduction of the Theravāda form of Buddhism in Thailand in the eleventh century AD. But according to Premsak Jermsawatdi,

> this view does not seem to be correct. Aniruddha never conquered and brought the pure Theravāda form of Buddhism from Thaton, the capital of the Mon country in lower Burma. This sect came from some other place, not from Thaton city. This sect of Buddhism which later on became the official religion of Pagan during Aniruddha's reign came from Nakon Pathom. . . . It is also probable that this sect of Buddhism came from

the place situated in the Menam valley of modern Thailand. The reasons may be stated as follows: From the Burmese tradition as well as the recent archaeological researches we learn that the effects of war between Pagan and Thaton were responsible for the progress and prosperity of Burma in many respects. First of all, there was complete transformation of Burmese cultures under the influence of the Mons. The Burnmese adopted their religion, script and sacred literature and while the Mon kingdom was destroyed, the Mon culture started on a new career in Pagan. . . . Henceforth the king of Pagan became great champion of the Hīnayāna form of Buddhism hitherto current in lower Burma and it has flourished in the whole country down to our time. In the field of art, the architectural style bearing Mon influence took deep roots in Burma during this time. . . . But the question arises: where is the Mon town which was captured by Aniruddha ? In those day, there were several Mon towns in South-East Asia, not only Thaton, the capital of Mon Sudhammavatī kingdom in lower Burma. Other Mon towns were Haripuñjaya in north of Thailand, Talaing of Ramaññadesa country and Nakon Pathom, the capital of the Dvāravatī kingdom in the Menam valley, in modern central Thailand. As regards Thaton, archaeological researches have revealed that this town had new fortifications. There are no remains of monuments and fortifications and the archaeologists have concluded that it was not Thaton of the Mon country which was occupied by Aniruddha. Further, Nakon Pathom, the capital of the Dvāravatī kingdom in central Thailand, was one of the ancient Mon towns. Here, we have an old fortification and the remaining monuments and antiquities are exactly the same as unearthed in

Burma and in India also. One important evidence in support of Nakon Pathom being the Mon town conquered by the Burmese king is the inscription bearing the Mon script which is carved on the pedestal of the Buddha image and stone altar, which have been discovered in several towns of Thailand such as Nakon Pathom, Lopburi up to Haripuñjaya in north Thailand. The style of the Buddha image and the architectural features of monuments indicate clearly the Mon influence. Yet other supporting evidences are the votive tablet, the Buddhist credo stone-slab and the silver coins found in Pagan of lower Burma and the Nakon Pathom, their style and materials being the same. All these Buddhist antiquities were never found in other places such as in Thaton. Besides this, the Mon inscriptions in the Mon script, found both in Pagan and Nakon Pathom, bear close resemblance to each other. Thus, on the basis of archaeological researches it can be said that Nakon Pathom was the Mon town which came under Aniruddha's dominion. A look at the map of Burma will also convince the reader that Pagan and Thaton are situated closely. Also Thaton being a border town it was no difficult for Aniruddha to conquer and annex it to his kingdom. On the other hand, Pagan and Nakon Pathom were situated at a far distance, and the latter was an old kingdom having culture and civilisation. Pagan was just a new city which had became a powerful state within a short period. It was therefore natural on the part of the ruler of Nakon Pathom to have turned down the request of Aniruddha for sending the Buddhist scriptures and monks, which ultimately resulted in the outbreak of war between the two countries. From all accounts, therefore, it seems safe to suggest that the Mon town which under

> Aniruddha's dominion was Nakon Pathom, and not Thaton of lower Burma. According to Buddhist tradition, for about AD 1157 onwards there was no strong base of Theravāda Buddhism in Thaton. The Buddhist Saṁgha in the Mon country owes its origin to upper Burma, and Buddhist Saṁgha and the Buddhist teachers in Thaton had descended from the line of the elder Theras (learned monks) of Pagan in upper Burma. Thus, the Mons of Thaton were indebted in many respects to Pagan in their religious development. This being the case, it is difficult to understand why Aniruddha should have invaded Thaton for the purpose of carrying the Buddhist order from Thaton to Pagan, which was already a seat of Buddhist religion since early times. In fact, Aniruddha did not bring Theravāda Buddhism from the city of Thaton, but from Nakon Pathom city, the central authority of the Dvāravatī empire in Menam valley, central Thailand. This being so, the question of the introduction of Pukam (Pagan) Theravāda Buddhism in Thailand (known as the third phase of Buddhism) does not arise at all.

The foundation of the Sukhodaya kingdom in AD 1257 marked an important landmark not only in the political history but also in the world of Buddhism in Thailand. Sukhodaya in north of modern Thailand became the capital of the first independent kingdom of the Thais and it began to flourish from the thirteenth century onwards. The Thais came from Nanchao in southern China and settled down over the northern plains of Thailand under the suzerainty of the Khmer empire. At an unknown date perhaps about AD 1220, the Thais threw off the Khmer influence and founded the Thai kingdom at Sukhodaya. They were followerrs of the Mahāyāna sect of Buddhism. But after their arrival in

Thailand, they were influenced by the Mon culture and they accepted Theravāda Buddhism which under the patronage of the Mons prospered in Thailand during this period. The date of Indrāditya, the founder of the Thai kingdom of Sukhodaya, cannot be determined with certainty. G. Ceedés referred to his coronation provisionally around AD 1220 and suggested that Rama Khamheng ascended the throne before 1283, Śrī Indrāditya was succeeded by his second son Ban Muang who reigned for a very short period. After his death Rama Khamheng, his brother, captured the throne.

Rama Khamheng, a son of Indrāditya, was a capable ruler. He extended his dominion in all the four directions and established his friendly relation with China. During his reign the Thai kingdom included not only several states in Thailand but also Pegu (Hamsavatī) in lower Myanmar and Nakon Śrī Thammarat (Ligor) in the Malay Peninsula. He was an ardent follower of Buddhism and decorated his capital Sukhodaya with a number of temples, images of the Buddha and monasteries. He was the first monarch in Thailand who raised Buddhism to the status of state religion in the kingdom of Sukhodaya. His stone inscription gave an account of the happy religious life of the people and the practice of the religion that were in vogue in the kingdom during his reign. He tried to help his people to follow the way of the Buddha. The king himself and all his people, irrespective of rank or sex, practised Buddhism and he celebrated the Kaṭhin festival or 'presenting robes to the monks' with pomp and grandeur at the end of the rainy season retreat. The inscription says,

> People in this state of Sukhodaya are inclined towards charity and to observe the precepts. King Rama Khamheng of Sukhodaya as well as his houshold and his court . . . men or women, they all have faith in the religion of the Buddha; they observe the precepts through the duration of the rains, after which they

> present the Kaṭhin during the stipulated month thereafter. In this ceremony they present by way of offerings, moulds of cowries, of betels, of flowers, also sustain seats and beds, as well as the usual accessories of the Kaṭhin amounting to two millions each year. For the presentation of the Kaṭhin they go out to the park (on the hill); and on their return to the city the cortege stretches from the park right up to he edge of the plain, which becomes resonant with the sound of music and chariots. Everybody is free to play, to laugh and to sign.

King Rama Khamheng played his great role to impress the Gospel of Truth as preached by the Lord Buddha on the minds of the people with an idea to create a religious atmosphere in his kingdom. He ordered to build a stone-throne on the ground surrounded by palm trees at the central place of the capital and requested the monks to sit on it and to preach the sermons to the people on holidays. Sometimes the king used to sit on it in order to show himself to his subjects. The inscription describes,

> King Rama Khamheng of this state of Sukhodaya had, in 1214 (1292) year of the dragon, planted palms for 14 harvests and ordered workers to fashion this stone alab and place it in the midst of the palms. Venerable monks were invited to sit and deliver sermons on holydays to public congregations. On other days King Rama Khamheng sat giving official audiences.

In the epilogue to his inscription he mentioned,

> Rama Khamheng sought to be ruler and lord over all the Thais, to be preceptor and instructor to all the Thais, to know true virtue and righteousness. Among men that live in the realm of the Thais, for knowledge and insight, for bravery and daring, for energy and

> force, there cannot be found a man equal to him, — one able to subdue hosts of enemies, owing cities wide and elephants many.

He built a monastery called Wat Araññika (Forest Monastery) on the west of the city where he allowed a learned Patriarch from Nakon Sri Dharmaraj (modern Ligor in the Malay Peninsula) to stay there. His inscription reveals,

> There are reverend teachers, there are venerable monks; there is a Mahāthera. Toward sunset from this city of Sukhodaya is a forest monastery. Prince Khun Ram Khamheng made of it an offering unto Phra Mahathen (Mahāthera), the Archpriest, the scholar who studied the Tripitaka unto its end, the head of his order and above every other teacher in his realm. He came here from Sithammarat. In the midst of that forest monastery is a temple-building that is large, lefty and exceedingly fair. It has an enlighten cubit image standing erect.

The king very often used to visit this temple attached to the Forest Monastery on the days of the New Moon and Full Moon to worship the Buddha image. The Sukhodaya inscription threw flood of light on the state of the country, condition of the people and the system of the government during his reign. The king himself mentioned his own government in his inscription of 1292,

> During the life-time of King Rama Khamheng the city of Sukhodaya has prospered. There are fish in its water and rice in its rice-fields. The lord of the country does not tax his subjects, who throng the roads leading to cattle market and ride horses on their way to sell them. Whosoever wishes to trade in elephants or horses does so, whosoever wishes to trade in gold and silver does so. When a commoner, a noble, or a chief

> falls ill and dies, or disappears, his ancestral home, his clothes, his elephants, his family, his rice granaries, his slaves, the plantation of areca and betel inherited from his ancestors, all are transmitted to his children. If commoners, nobles or chiefs have a dispute, the king makes a proper inquiry and decides the matter with complete imparatiality. He does not enter into agreements with thieves and receivers. If he sees rice belonging to others he does not covet it and if he sees the riches of others he is not envious. To whomsoever comes on elephant-back to seek him and put his own country under his protection, he will extend his support and assistance. If the stranger has neither elephants nor horses nor servants nor wives nor silver nor gold, he will give them to him and invite him to regard himself as being in his own country. If the king captures warriors or enemy soldiers, he neither kills them nor beats them.

The king always wanted to keep personal cantact with his subjects. He could be approached even by the meanest of his subjects for royal protection. His inscription describes,

> In the gateway of the palace a bell is hung; if anybody in the kingdom has some grievance or some matter that is ulcerating his entails and troubling his mind, and wishes to lay it before the king, the way is easy: he has only to strike the bell hung there. Every time King Rama Khamheng hears this appeal; he interrogates the plaintiff about the matter and gives an entirely impartial decision.

The Sukhodaya inscription has given a description of Buddhism in Rama Khamheng's reign which was the Theravāda or Pāli Buddhism. The testimony of several inscriptions of his successors indicates Sri Lanka's prominent role in the subsequent religious history of Sukhodaya. An inscription found in the Wat Sri Chun refers to Sukhodaya's religious ties with Sri Lanka during the reign of Rama Khamheng's son and immediate successor Lo Thai. But the Sukhodaya inscription does not say anything about any religious intercourse between Sukhodaya and Sri Lanka. According to several scholars, Pāli Buddhism may have arrived in Thailand from Cambodia. But this type of Buddhism was quite unknown then to the people of Cambodia, who were followers of the Mahāyāna form of Buddhism. Sir Charles Eliot states,

> Whilst they were subject to Camboja, they must have felt the influence of Sivaism and probably of Mahāyānist Sanskrit Buddhism but no Pāli Buddhism can have come from this quarter (Camboja).

Most probably, it was Rama Khamheng who was responsible for the introduction and the development of the Theravāda doctrine of Sri Lankan Buddhism into his kingdom from Nakon Śrī Dharmaraja (Ligor) where several Buddhist relices were found and Hīnayāna Buddhism prevailed there. The Sukhodaya inscription says that the king invited a learned Buddhist monk from Liger for the propagation of the Theravāda form of Buddhism in Thailand. This inscription of his reign refers to the visit of a Mahāthera from Siridhammanagara or Śrīdharmanagara to Sukhodaya in his reign and the construction of the monastery of the Araññikas for this Mahāthera by the king.[20] Siridhammanagara has been identified with modern Ligor and it is known in Thai as Nakorn Śrī Dharmarāja 'City of the king of the Law (Dhamma)' and in Malay as Nakhon Si Thammarat and in Pāli writings as Tambaraṭṭha and Tambaliṅga and in the Sri Lankan texts as Thambalinga and Tamaliṅgamu. Rama Khamheng's inscription mentions,

20. *HTCSEA*, pp. 141-2.

> To the west of this city of Sukhodaya there is a monastery of the Forest Monks. King Rama Khamheng built and offered it to the venerable preceptor, learned in all the Three Baskets, in erudition excelling all other monks in the whole island. He hailed from Nakorn Śrī Dharmaraja.

This venerable preceptor belonged to the Laṅkā Theravāda form of Buddhism. A sect of Pāli *Tipiṭaka* in Sri Lankan script was also brought from Nakorn Śrī Dharmarāja to Sukhodaya. Thus, king Rama Khamheng played a very vital role for the propagation of the Laṅkā Theravāda form of Buddhism in Sukhodaya and he was the first monarch who proclaimed Buddhism as the official religion of his kingdom. The *Jinakālamālī*'s accounts show that Siridhammanagara contributed very much to establish close contact between Sri Lanka and Thailand and from this it may be concluded that Thailand established its religious and cultural contact with Sri Lanka through the medium of Siridhammanagara in the middle of the thirteenth century.

In Thailand Nakon Śī-Thammarat (now a province in the south of modern Thailand) was regarded as the first region, where the Lankavong monks visited and propagated and preached the doctrine of the Lankavong sect there. This region late on became one of the important centres of the Lankavong sect of the Hīnayāna Theravāda sect of Buddhism. After Nakon Śī-Thammarat, the activities of the Lankavong monks soon reached Sukhodaya. King Rama Khamheng, who reigned in Sukhodaya at that time, became very happy to know about the deep learning and strict discipline of the Lankavong monks of Nakon Śī-Thammarat. So he invited some of them to propagate the Lankavong doctrine and discipline in Sukhodaya, and under his patronage the Lankavong monks there propagated the doctrine.[21] This fact is proved by King

21. *TAII*, p. 33.

Rama Khamheng's stone inscription, dated about AD 1277 which mentions that several monks from the town of Nakon Śī-Thammarat arrived in Sukhodaya. Thus, from this time onwards this new form of Buddhism was introduced in the Sukhodaya kingdom under his patronage. The architectural buildings such as *stūpas*, *vihāras*, monasteries, *cedis* as well as sculptural production on the fashion of the Lankavong design and style witnessed an important landmark in the world of Thailand's Buddhist art. The archaeological remains of Buddhist art and architecture of this period gave us an idea about the existence of the Lankavong sect in Thailand. At the Wat Chang Lom in the Sawankhalok province a Buddhist *stūpa* with Sri Lanka's influence was found. King Rama Khamheng built this *stūpa* in AD 1288. Its architectural features were the elephant's half-body which was placed around the pedestal and base of the dome of the *stūpa*. This style was taken from the *stūpa* named Chedi Chaikong which was built by King Duttagamini of Sri Lanka. The replica of the Buddha's foot-print was found on the top of Khao Prabat Yai in Sukhodaya and it had a great similarity with the foot-print at the Sumana Kūṭa (Adam's Peak) mountain in Sri Lanka. Later on this Khao Prabat Yai received the name of Sumana Kūṭa mountain according to Sri Lanka's tradition. The rest of the Bodhi-Tree from Sri Lanka was planted in Sukhodaya during the reign of Rama Khamheng. Thus, the tradition of the worship of Sri Lanka's Bodhi-Tree began from his reign to the Bangkok period in the reign of King Mongkut or Rama IV of Bangkok. The Buddha image with strong influence of Sri Lanka's art of sculpture was found in Sukhodaya. The prosecution of Buddha image of the Lankavong sect of Buddhism was found and it indicated the introduction of this sect of Buddhism in the Sukhodaya kingdom. It may be noted here that the main styles of the sculpture of the Buddha image in the Sukhodaya period were copied from Sri Lanka's art and sculpture. Thus, it may be concluded that the Lankavong Theravāda sect of Buddhism from Sri Lanka was introduced in Thailand from the thirteenth century onwards. It was first introduced at Nakon Śī-Thammarat, south of Thailand and then from where it arrived in the Sukhodaya kingdom during the reign of King Rama Khamheng, who not only gave his patronage to propagate it but he also gave help to make this Buddhist sect his state religion.

Although Rama Khamheng was a devout Buddhist and he played his great role for the progress of Theravāda Buddhism, yet he could not do anything to stop the animistic beliefs and practices of the ancient Thai people. His inscription says,

> (To the south of Sukhodaya) a spring gushes forth from the hillside. Brama Khamheng is the spirit (p'i) and get (*devatā*) of this hill and he is above all the other spirits of the land. If whatever prince who happens to be ruling over the country of Sukhodaya faithfully continues to worship him and to present him with the ritual offerings, then the country will remain stable and prosperous, but if he does not carry out the prescribed worship and does not present him with the ritual offerings, then the spirit of the hill will not longer protect, nor respect this country which will then decline.

This inscription was enough to prove that the Sri Lankan or the Theravāda form of Buddhism which had made a great influence upon the life of the Sukhodaya people under the royal patronage in the second half of the thirteenth century was unable to suppress the traditional animism of the Thais. It lingered also in the succeeding ages until it was finally incorporated within Buddhism. But these animistic ideas of the Thais did not practically disturb Buddhism's prosperity because King Rama Khamheng

> who had established and maintained all the inhabitants of these countries (i.e., in the whole of his kingdom) in the observance of the Law, without execption,

always tried to follow the wise policy. The king himself, noblemen, members of the royal household, and his subjects showed their inclinations more and more towards the practice of Theravāda Buddhism, which during the reign of his successors flourished all over the kingdom of Sukhodaya. The Lankavong monks used to reside in the forest hermitages erected by the king himself. They used the Pāli language to perform their religious ceremonies. They din not stay with the local Sukhodaya monks in the same monastery and they did not perform Saṁghakamma and other religious ceremonies with them. Later on, the Lankaveng monks and the Sukhodaya monks lived peacefully by the wise policy of King Rama Khamheng. When the unification of the Buddhist Saṁgha took place in the Sukhodaya kingdom, then the monks were divided into two sections called the Araññavāsī or the Vanavāsī and the Gāmavāsī. The Araññavāsīs represented these monks who stayed in forest hermitages and showed their keen interest in Vipasanadhura or meditation, while the Gāmavāsis took their attentions to Ganthadhura or they devoted themselves to the study and teaching of the scriptures and these monks stayed in villages and towns. King Rama Khamheng was a religious person and he tried to follow the doctrines of the Theravāda form of Buddhism as far as possible. Under his patronage this sect prospered in his kingdom. He adopted several measures for better organisation and administration of the Buddhist Saṁgha in his kingdom.

Rama Khamheng was succeeded by his son Lothai or Lodaiya (AD 1317-47). During his rule the power of Sukhodaya declined almost as rapidly as it had arisen. He appointed his son Luthai as viceroy at Satchanalai (Sawankhalok) in AD 1340 and he died probably in AD 1347. He took keen interest in works of Buddhist merit. He acquired the title of Dhammarāja or Dhammikarāja or Dharmarāja or Dharmikarāja, pious king for his contribution to the development of Buddhism. He founded several Buddapādas or footprints of the Buddha in imitation of the one worshipped in Sri Lanka on the summit of Sumana Kūṭa or Adam's Peak. The *Jinakālamālī* a chronicle of Thailand, refers to the establishment of Sri Lanka's Buddhist Saṁgha in Sukhodaya during his reign. A famous Mahāthera from Sri Lanka named Udumbara Mahāsāmi 'Great Sage' came to the Rāmañña country, i.e., lower Myanmar from Sri Lanka.[22] At that time a Thai monk named Sumana went to lower Myanmar to receive the Upasampadā ordination at the hands of Udumbara Mahāsāmi and to study religious texts under his guidance. The Mahāthera's arrival indicated mutual ties between the Budhist Saṁghas of Sri Lanka and lower Myanmar as well as of lower Myanmar and Sukhodaya and Sri Lanka's significant contribution to its neighbouring countries for the progress of Buddhism. Lo Thai, the king of Sukhodaya, on hearing of Udumbara Mahāsāmi sent an envoy requesting him to send a monk who would be able to perform all religious works of the Buddhist Saṁgha in Sukhodaya. The Mahāthera sent Sumana to Sukhodaya. His arrival in Sukhodaya helped to introduce the Sīhala Saṁgha or the Buddhist Order from Sri Lanka in Sukhodaya. He stayed at the Ambavanārāma or the Mango Grove monastery to the east of Sukhodaya and worked hard for the progress of the Sri Lankan form of the monastic discipline there. Thus, Udumbara Mahāsāmi, who belonged to Sri Lanka, helped to introduce the Sīhala Saṁgha in Sukhodaya and to propagate Theravāda Buddhism in that country through Sumana, a monk from Sukhodaya. Sumana was an important figure in the religious history of Thailand.

22. *HTBSEA*, p. 142.

He gave valuable services to the cause of Buddhism in Sukhodaya in the reign of king Lothai, who was a great patron of Buddhism. When he was in Sajjanālaya, he heard the wondrous nature of a miraculous relic of the Buddha which was sent by Aśoka from India in the third century BC. At the request of king Lothai Sumana brought the relic to Sukhodaya and the former received it with great honour.

The fame of Udumbara Mahāsāmi also reached Nabbisipura (Xieng Mai) in northern Thailand. The king of Nabbisipura at this time was Kilanā or Kuenā or Phra Chao Kuena. The *Jinakālamālī* mentions that he was born in AD 1339 and at the age of sixteen he was consecrated ruler in AD 1335. He sent an envoy to Udumbara Mahāsāmi in the Rāmañña country and he requested him to send a competent monk to perform all religious acts in Nabbisipura. He sent Ānanda Thera to Ḳing Kilanā. Sumana Thera also went to Nabbisipura at the request of the king of Nabbisipura. He went there to play an important role for the establishment of Theravāda Buddhism and the Sīhala Saṁgha in northern Thailand.

The next ruler of the Sukhodaya kingdom was Luthai or Lithai (AD 1347-76), who was Lothai's son. He was a devout Buddhist. He showed mercy towards all beings. During his rule Buddhism became very popular in Thailand. An inscription describes,

> This king observes the ten royal precepts. He showed mercy towards all subjects. When he saw another man's rice he did not covet it, and when he saw another's wealth he did not behave unworthily. If he arrested people guilty of cheating or insolence, those who put poison in his food so as to cause him illness or death, he never killed or beat them, but forgave those who behaved evilly towards him. The reason why he repressed his heart and restrained his temper,

> and did not give way to anger when he might have done, was that he desired to become a Buddha and to take every creature beyond the ocean of the affliction of transmigration.

He gave his full support to the establishment of several Buddhist centres and temples in his kingdom. He studied the *Abhidhammapiṭaka*, the *Vinaya*, the Vedas, the *Śāstra*s, the *Dharmnāya*s, the *Jyotiśāstra* (astronomy) and other Brāhmaṇical texts. The *Traibhūmikathā*, a large treatise on Buddhist Cosmology, now known as the *Traiphum P'a Ruang* was composed by him. Thus, in his reign Sukhodaya became a great centre of Buddhist studies as well as Buddhist activities. He gave his full support to the development of the Sīhala Saṁgha in Thailand. The Nagara Jum inscription dated Śakjarāja 1279, i.e., AD 1357 written in the Thai language and belonging to the reign of Luthai mentions that a sacred and authentic relic of the Buddha 'Śrī Ratanamahādhātu' was brought from Śrī Lanka and was installed by the king in AD 1357 at Nagara Jum. It also states that a branch of the sacred Bo-Tree was brought to Thailand from Sri Lanka and was planted near this sacred relic at Nagara Jum. The second part of the inscription refers to the establishment of several Buddhapādas in Thailand on the model of the Buddhapāda of the Sumana Kūṭa *parvata* in Sri Lanka by King Luthai. Two inscriptions, one in the Khmer language and the other in the Thai language found at Sukhodaya were installed by king Luthai. They refer to the invitation sent by king Luthai to Mahāsāmi Saṁgharāja who has been identified with the Saṁgharāja Medhaṅkara and with Udumbara Mahāsāmi. These inscriptions were composed to commemorate the arrival of the Saṁgharāja from Sri Lanka, his installation at the monastery of the Mango Grove and the ordaining of King Luthai. The Khmer inscription gives details of the arrangements made by the king of Sukhodaya in honour of the Mahāthera. Most probably, these arrangements were extremely elaborate and on levish scale. The king then invited the Mahāsāmi Saṁgharāja as well as the *theras*, *anutheras* and the whole assembly of monks to ascend the Golden Tower in the Royal Palace and then entered the Buddhist Saṁgha as a novice. When he had pronounced his vows and had received ordination, he descended from the Golden Tower and took a walk to go to the Mango Grove. His subjects felt frustrated to see their king's ordination as a monk and they requested him to leave the Buddhist Saṁgha but the monks told him to remain in the Buddhist Saṁgha. At the request of the Mahāsāmī Saṁgharāja, King Luthai left the Buddhist Saṁgha and reassumed the royal power. He was the first Thai monarch who left the throne temporarily and entered the monastic life of a Buddhist monk. The Araññavāsī and the Gāmavāsī, the two sections of the Buddhist monks, had improved their administration. A feagmentary inscription in the Thai script at the Vat Mahādhātu of Sukhodaya refers to a monk named Mahāthera Śrī Sraddhārājacūlāmuni Śrīratanalaṅkādīpa Mahāsāmī, the grandson of Pha Muang, the chief of Mo'an Rat,who helped the father of Rama Khamheng to establish the independent Thai kingdom of Sukhodaya. He had given up his royal robes and he accepted the life of a monk. He visited Sri Lanka and obtained two sacred relics and several layman from Sri Lanka came with him to Thailand. These laymen resided in five villages in Thailand. Thus, the evidence of the Buddhist inscriptions in Thailand amply proved that the monks of Sri Lanka were held in high esteem in Thailand and the Thai Buddhist turned their attention to Sri Lanka for religious inspiration and a close religious tie existed between the two countries at that time. Thus, from the accounts stated above we conclude that Theravāda Buddhism under the patronage of the Thai rulers flourished in the kingdom of Sukhodaya. The Sukhodaya rulers devoted themselves to the progress of Buddhism.

During the reign of King Rama Khamheng and King Luthai, the Sukhodaya kingdom reached the zenith of political glory. But after their death, their successors were weak rulers and they were unable to protect their kingdom from the rulers of Ayuthia. As a result, Ayuthia captured the Sukhodaya kingdom and in AD 1378 it became Thailand's new capital. The second half of the fourteenth century AD witnessed the rise and growth of the kingdom of Ayuthia in southern Thailand. This new kingdom was founded in AD 1350 by a Thai prince who belonged to the rulers of Jayasenapura (Xieng Saen) in northern Thailand and the capital of the kingdom was known as Dvāravatī Śrī Ayudhya (Ayuthia). He ruled over the central and lower Menam valley (Lopburi), Suvarnapuri (Suphan), Rājaburi (Ratburi), Pojrāpuri (Phetburi), Candraburi (Canthaburi) and a greater part of the Malay Peninsula including Tenasserim, Tavoy (now in Myanmar), Ligor and Singora. His rule even extended over Sukhodaya in the north and Malacca in the south. He was succeeded by his son Ramasuen and after one year he abdicated in favour of Boromorāja or Paramarāja or Paramarājādhirāja, his uncle. He was Boromorāja I. The establishment of the new kingdom at Ayuthia and the changing of the political centre of Thai power from Sukhodaya to Ayuthia marked the beginning of a new era of great cultural prosperity. Owing to this transformation, Ayuthia became an important Buddhist centre and Buddhism flourished in Ayuthia. All the Ayuthian kings from king U-Thong or Rama Tibodi I, the founder of this kingdom up to kings who ruled in the fourteenth century AD were pious rulers and were followeres of the Lankavong Theravāda form of Buddhism and several Buddhist monasteries were constructed and Buddhism flourished in Thailand during this time. During the reign of king Rama VI (AD 1910-25) Mr. Brayā Sundarapuri (I Karnasūta), the Governor of Suvarṇapurī, presented an inscribed gold sheet to Prince Damrong

Rajanubhāb.[23] It was discovered in the *navaśūa* at the top of Subarnapuri's principal monument, the Prāng of Vat Śrīratnamahādhātu. The inscription consists of a salutation in Sanskrit and three stanzas of the Pāli verse written in Khmer characters. The late Mahā Chām Doṅgaṁvarṇa, the learned epigraphist of the Royal Institute, translated it into Siamese. The gold sheet was later lost and no photographs or rubbings of it were available. Maha Cham Doṅgaṁvarṇa's transcription and translation were printed in *Prajum Śīlā-carik*, vol. III (Bangkok B.E. 2508. Inscription no. 47, pp. 75 f). Prof. Kamaleswar Bhattacharya of Paris and Professor Visuddhi Puṣyakula of Bangkok translated the Pāli into English.

Text

Siddhirastu

Yoyujjharaja	*paramorucakka*
vattitināmavidite	*imametha thūpaṁ*
Kacapayaṁ thapayi mā-	*rajidhātuy'ante*
assāpi kālavikale	*ayam āsi thūpe II*
tass'orase sakalabhū	*talarājarājo*
rājādhirājapavare	*pana kārayāne*
thūpaṁ purādhikataraṁ	*imam asea c'anto*
gabbhe ṭhapeti munine	*varadhātuyomā II*
thūpa pasanne	*vararājarājā*
hemādipūjā	*hi'bhipūjiyoti*
punnena me te-	*na anāgate'ham*
buddho bhavoyyan-	*ti varaṅ karoti II*

23. *ABGPN*, pp. 1-6.

Translation

May there be success.

The king of Ayojjha known by the name of Paramorucakkavatti caused this *stūpa* to be built, and deposited some relics of the conqueror of Māra inside, but later on, this *stūpa* fell into decay from (the passage of) time.

His son Rājādhirājapavare, who is king over the kings of the whole earth, causing the *stūpa* to be rebuilt larger than before, deposits these relics of the Sage in the inner chamber.

Havining faith in the *stūpa*. His Majesty does homage with offerings of gold and other things, and makes this wish: "As a result of this meritorious deed of mine, may I became a Buddha in the future."

Ayojjhā is the Pāli form of Ayodhyā, the old name of Ayudhyā. The text commemorates the rebuilding of a *stūpa* (Pāli : *thupa*) which had been founded by a king of Ayodhyā called Paramorucakkavatti, who deposited some relics of the Buddha inside it. Later on, when it had fallen into decay, it was rebuilt, 'larger than before', by his son Rājādhirājapavaro, who was 'king over the kings of the whole earth', and who deposited some more relics of the Buddha inside it. The rebuilt monument is presumbly the Prāng where the inscription was discovered and the statement that it was made 'larger than before' means that, in accordance with a well-known practice, the old monument was allowed to remain standing, but was completely encased inside the new one. We have no means of knowing the architectural form of the original monument; it too may have been Prāng, though smaller than the present one; but it could equally well have been a monument of a different type. When an old monument is encased in a new one, the architecture of the new one may or may not imitate that of the original.

As the inscription gives no dates, the identity of these two kings of Ayudhyā, father and son, is uncertain. The question was discussed in 1957 in a learned article by Luang Boribal Buribhand (Hlvan Poripala Puribhanda), from which we have borrowed freely in preparing the present paper.

The title of the father, Paramoruckkavatti, looks like a slightly expanded Pāli rendering of Paramacakrabarti. As *cakkavatti* is the Pāli form of *cakrabartī* (Sanskrit *cakravartin*), it might be thought that the father was king Mahācakrabarti was died while Ayudhyā was being besieged by the Burmese, but that it is impossible: his son and successor Mahindra cannot have rebuilt the monument because he reigned only a few months before being captured, and died while he was being taken to Burma.

In fact the titles of Ayudhyan kings are seldom distinctive. They tend to be both repetitive and shifting; various kings use the same elements of titulature again and again, in different permutations, and any one king may permute them differently at different times. The title Cakrabarti was borne by most of the kings of Ayudhya, perhaps all of them, ever since it was adopted by the founder of the kingdom. Rāmādhipati (1351-69), who was likely inherited from the kings of Lavo.

The architecture of the Prāng suggests the fifteenth century. Luang Boribal aptly compares it to the Prāng of Vat Rājapūraṇaḥ at Ayudhyā, which was built in 1424 and with the Mahādhātu at Biṣṇuloka, built in 1482.

It is regarded as the most important monument at Suvarṇapurī. Its name Śrīratnamahādhātu, 'precious great relic', shows that it was built to contain one or more major relics of the Buddha and, like the monuments with similar names in several other old cities of Siam, was intended to be the magico-religious centre of the principality in which it stood. We may therefore assume that the founder was one of the kings of Ayudhyā who belonged to the House of Suvarṇapurī.

In the second half of the fourteenth century and the early fifteenth century, the House of Subarṇapurī waged a bitter struggle against the House of Rāmādhipati to the throne of Ayudhyā. The first member of the Subarṇapuri family to reign over Ayudhyā was Paramarājādhirāja I (1370-88), who seized the throne from Rāmādhipati's son and successor Rāmeśvara, sending the latter to rule over the province of Labapuri as his vassal. Paramarājādhirāja I, whatever he may have built at Subarṇapurī, cannot be the 'father' in the gold-leaf inscription, because the son who succeeded him on the throne of Ayudhyā did not live long enough to rebuild anything; in 1388, a week after his accession, he was killed by the ex-king Rāmeśvara who came down from Labapuri with an army and made himself king of Ayudhyā for the second time. Rāmeśvara died in 1395, and was succeeded by his son Rāmarāja. Meanwhile Indarāja, a nephew of Paramarājādhirāja I, became prince of Subarṇapurī, nominally as a vassal of Ayudhyā, but in fact ruling his territories almost like an independent monarch, and at the same time plotting to seize control of Ayudhyā for the House of Subarṇapurī. In 1409, by means of a *coup d'etat*, he made himself king of Ayudhyā.

Nothing would be more natural than for Indarāja to build a reliquary monument to mark the magico-religious centre of the principality of Subarṇapurī either before or after he became king of Ayudhyā. As we have suggested, the title of the 'father' who founded the monument commemorated in the gold-leaf inscription is equivalent to Paramacakrabarti. There can be no objection to identifying him with Indarāja, who is called Paramarājādhipati-Śrī-Mahā-Cakrabarti in a stone inscription dating from 1418. Indarāja died in 1424. He was succeeded by his son Paramarājādhirāja II (424-48). This monarch, in the year of his accession, built the Prāng of Vāt Rājapūraṇaḥ. It is entirely reasonable to believe that he rebuilt the monument founded by his father at Subarṇpurī, giving it the form of a Prāng which it now has, and which is strikingly similar to that of Vāt Rājapūraṇaḥ. There is thus no difficulty in identifying him with the 'son' in the gold-leaf inscription. The title Rājādhirājapavaro is evidently a metrical equivalent of Pavararājādhirāja, which is close enough to Paramarājādhirāja to make the identification fit easily. Even his claim to be 'king over all the kings of the Earth' though it reflects the hyperbole common in the titles of the day, is not without some measure of justification. At least during part of his reign he was suzerain over a larger territory than any of his predecessors, for he not only inherited their possessions, including his father's suzerainty over the old kingdom of Sukhodaya, but also invaded Cambodia in 1431 and captured the city of Angkor.

Boromorāja (AD 1370-88) I constructed a residence named the Laṅkārāma at Ayuthia for the monks of Thailand.[24] Dhammakitti Mahāsāmi, who received the Upasampadā ordination in Sri Lnaka, returned to Ayuthia and stayed at the Laṅkārāma and composed the Saddhammasaṁgaha. An inscription dated 750 of the small Siamese era, i.e., AD 1388 written in the Thai language and belonging to the reign of Boromorāja I mentions several monks who occupied important positions in the religious history of Thailand during this period. Tanhaṅkāra Mahāthera became the chief monk after the death of Padumuttara Mahāthera. After him Vassabhu Mahāthera occupied his place. Then Mantrisāviṇṇanaka Mahāthera succeeded him. Many monks used to live in Ayuthia at that time. Among them prominent were

24. *HTBSEA*, p. 152.

Sumaṅgala Mahāthera, Khemamaṅgala Mahāthera, Dharmaghosa Mahāthera. Ñāṇagambhira Mahāthera, Sumanadeva Mahāthera, Buddhavamsa Mahāthera, Surya Mahāthera, Rāmavasi Mahāthera, Dharmasenāpati Mahāthera, Ānanda Mahāthera and Dharmakitti Mahāthera. It indicated that Ayuthia was a great centre of Buddhist culture during the rule of the Ayuthian ruler Boromarāja I. The Buddhist Saṁgha had a very good administration and the monks followed the rules of the Buddhist discipline faithfully. After Boromorāja I, Rāmasuen, Rāma Rāja, Boromorāja II, Boromo Trailokanāth, Boromorāja III, Rāmādhipati, Boromorāja IV, Mahā Chakrapat. Mahim, Mahā Dharmarāja, Narasuen, Indrarāja II, Śrīsudhammarāja and Narai ascended the throne of Ayuthia. Some of these rulers tried to follow the policy of expansion within Thailand and into Cambodia. During the period AD 1448-88 the religious history of Thailand gave an account of the glorious days of the Lankavong Theravāda form of Buddhism under the patronage of king Boromotrailokanātha or Trailok. He reigned for forty years and during his rule the development of this sect took place in several respects. The king became a Buddhist monk and was ordained at the Wat Chulamani in Pisanulok. The Thai chronicles mention that about 2,388 men were ordained also on this memorable occasion. The kings of several neighbouring kingdoms sent royal gifts of robes, bowls, etc., to the king of Thailand on this occasion. It was an important event in the history of Buddhism in the Ayuthian period. King Trailok became monk for a period of eight months and was ordained in the presence of many monks under the presidentship of venerable Mahāsāmi Saṁgharāja. On this occasion the interpretation and the re-organisation of the Buddhist doctrine was also discussed and planned and this no doubt indicated the religious activities of his region. He was the first Thai king who offered his own palace to the

Buddhist Saṁgha.[25] He built monasteries and *vihāra*s within the boundary of his palace. He adorned the image of the Bodhisattva's 500 incarnations in AD 1458. The production of these images showed his great love and faith in Buddhism. A new sect of Buddhism named the Vanaratnavong or the Pakaee sect which differed from the Lankavoṇg Theravāda form of Buddhism was established. This sect was introduced in the reign of king Indrarāja I in AD 1422.

The fifteenth century was an age of great devotional activity in Thailand and it witnessed strong influx of Buddhism from Sri Lanka. In AD 1423, twenty-five from Nabbisipura (Xieng Mai) in northern Thailand together with eight monks from Cambodia went to Sri Lanka to receive the Upasampadā ordination and there they were joined by six Mon monks from Myanmar.[26] The king of Nabbisipura was Tissarāja (AD 1401-42) or Sam Fang Ken, who was Sen-Muong Ma's son. He was a heretic without faith. He honoured demons and worshipped wooded groves, trees, rocks, forests, spirits, etc., with cattle and buffaloes. In his kingdom many people worshipped demons. It is possible that the Thai monks from Nabbisipura came to Sri Lanka to get the help of the Buddhist order in Sri Lanka to put an end to this state of religious affairs and to establish the Theravāda form of Buddhism and higher ordination in Thailand. Thirty-nine monks studied the sacred texts thoroughly and also learnt the correct manner of recital of the sacred texts from the Buddhist monks of Sri Lanka. They were ordained in AD 1224 at Yāpāpaṭṭana in Kalyāṇi (Kelaniya) in Sri Lanka. Then they returned home accompanied by two monks Mahāvikkamabāhu and Mahāuttamapañña from Sri Lanka in AD 1425. They stopped awhile at Ayuthia, Sukhodaya and Sawankhalok on their way home and finally reached Nabbisipura in AD 1430. The

25. *TAII*, p. 35.

26. *HTBSEA*, p. 155.

Jinakālamālī says that after spending the second, third, fourth and fifth *vassa* seasons at Ayuthia and other places, they reached Sawankhalok and from there they arrived in Sukhodaya in AD 1429. Then they came to Nabbisipura in AD 1430. There they spent the seventh and eighth *vassa* seasons. Then they toured throughout northern Thailand and they visited Śrī Sachanlai (Svargalok), Haripuñjaya (Lampoon), Khelaṅganagara (Lampang), Jaṁrayapura (Xieng Rai) and even Jayasenapura (Xieng Saen) and they ordained the local monks and established the Theravāda form of Buddhism and the Sīhala Saṁgha in Thailand. They founded the Rattavanamahāvihāra at the north-west of Jayasenapura. Afterwards many monks in Nabbisipura from them received the Upasampadā Ordination in the reign of Tissarāja. After their arrival in Thailand from Sri Lanka they introduced a new sect in Ayuthia. It can be mentioned as a sub-division sect of the Lankavong sect. It became known as the Vanaratanavong or the Pa-Kaee sect and it had flourished in the province of Nakon Śī-Thammarat and Patalung of South Thailand before its introduction took place in Ayuthia.[27] The Ayuthian people had mentioned this sect in South Thailand as 'Southern Sect' or 'Southern Vanaratnavong'. The monks who belonged to this sect practised the doctrine very rigidly than the Lankavong monks. The Vanaratnavong sect received its prominence in the reign of King Trailok, who died in AD 1488. He was a patron of this sect. But the Lankavong Theravāda form of Buddhism flourished period by period under the patronage of the later Thai kings.

Tissarāja's son Tilakarāja played a great role in the development of the Sīhala Saṁgha or the Buddhist Saṁgha from Sri Lanka in northern Thailand. He was a devout Buddhist.

He was ended with heroism, valour, prowess and

27. *TAII*, p. 36.

> splandour, was capable of discerning what is beneficent to one's and others, was prudent, faithful and pious and was possessed of profound wisdom.

He became known as the Universal Monarch Siridhamma, the Emperor Tilaka. His reign has been described as golden age of art, literature and religion in Nabbisipura. The *Jinakālamālī* refers to the higher ordination of 500 men or the banks of the river Binganadi by the elders Medhaṅkarañāna and Maṅgala-sīlavaṁsa under the patronage of the king. He then conferred upon the elder Medhaṅkara the title of Atulasaktyādhikaraṇa Mahāsāmi. In AD 1447 the king entered the Buddhist order for sometime and then with the permission of his teacher he assumed office again as a king.[28] He built one Uposatha hall at the Rattavanamahāvihāra or the Wat Pa Daeng Luang in AD 1451. A seedling grown from a seed from the southern branch of the Mahābodhi tree at Anurādhapura in Sri Lanka in AD 1455 was planted at the Mahābodhārāma (Wat Cedi Cet Yod) at Nabbisipura. In AD 1475 a great Buddhist council was held at Nabbisipura for the revision of the Pāli scriptures. This council was held in the Mahābodhārāma and it continued for a year. All the learned monks in Thailand took part in this council. In the history of Buddhism in Thailand this council became known as the eighth Buddhist council. After the death of Tilakarāja, his grandson ascended the throne of Nabbisipura in AD 1487. He built the Tapodārāma in AD 1492. He also purified a Khaṇḍasīmā at the Upari-ārāma monastery or the Wat Bon in northern Thailand in AD 1493.

The next ruler of Nabbisipura was Tilakapanattu, "Greatgrandson of Tilaka". He occupied the throne at the age of thirteen in AD 1495. He was regarded as one of the greatest kings of Thailand. He played a vital role in the history of Buddhism in Nabbisipura and his efforts were largely

28. *HTBSEA*, p. 161.

responsible for the expansion of Buddhism and the development of the Buddhist Saṁgha in Thailand at that time. He was a devout Buddhist and under his patronage not only Nabbisipura but whole northern Thailand became the centre of Buddhist activities. He built many Buddhist temples and monasteries and he established many Buddhist images there. He constructed the Pubbārāma, 'the Eastern Monastery' in AD 1497 in the village where his grandfather and father lived earlier. He also built a great Buddha statue in the Uposatha hall at the Pubbārāma. At the time of its installation he gave *dāna* to several thousand Buddhist monks who belonged the Sīhala sect, the Nagaravāsīgaṇa and the Pupphārāmavāsīgaṇa. He in AD 1515 visited the city of Jayasena in northern Thailand and he met the Buddhist monks who belonged to these fraternities. He conferred the title of Rājaguru on the Mahāsāmi of the Sīhala sect and it indicated the importance of the Sīhala sect in Thailand in the sixteenth century AD. He enclosed the Mahādhātu *cetiya* with a wall of silver and with pure gold. He built the Mahādhātu *cetiya* in Haripuñjaya and he fortified the city with a solid stone wall. He patronised the Buddhist scholars and religious institutions very much. The flourishing condition of Buddhism and the existence of several well-organised education and religious institutions in the country gave an impetus to scholastic activities in Thailand during his reign. He died at the age of forty-three in AD 1525. Then his son Jeṭṭhādhipati ascended the throne of Nabbisipura in AD 1526. He gave valuable services to the cause of Buddhism. Under his patronage the Sīhala sect performed the Upasampadā Ordination in AD 1527.

In the sixteenth century AD Theravāda Buddhism and the Sīhala Saṁgha flourished in Thailand. The *Jinakālamālī* refers to the existence of three sects in Thailand: the Sīhala Saṁgha or the Sīhala sect, the Nagaravāsīgaṇa, the native sect and the Pupphārāmavāsīgaṇa, the Rāmañña sect. Of these sects, the Sīhala sect occupied a very prominent place in the religious history of Thailand. In all ecclesiastical acts this sect took the leading part and performed the religious acts first and afterwards the Nagaravāsīgaṇa and the Pupphārāmavāsigaṇa took part in them. In AD 1548 the king of Nabbisipiura conferred the title of Rājaguru 'Royal Teacher' on the Mahāsāmi of the Sīhala Saṁgha. It indicated the prominence and importance of the Sīhala Saṁgha in the religious history of Thailand in the sixteenth century AD. An eighteenth-century document discovered in Sri Lanka described that a sapling of the Bodhi tree from Anurādhapura in Sri Lanka was planted at Muan Lakon (Nakhon Si Thammarat) (modern Ligor) during the reign of the Thai King Dhammāśoka who can be assigned to the sixteenth century AD.

In the middle of the sixteenth century AD King Tabinshwehti (AD 1534-50) of the Toungee dynasty of Myanmar with a large Myanmarese army invaded Ayuthia and King Maha Chakrap'at (AD 1549-64) of Ayuthia tried to resist this invasion and fought bravely to protect his kingdom from enemy's attack. Bayinnaung became king of Pegu in Myanmar (AD 1551-81) after Tabinshwehti and attacked Ayuthia twice. This Myanmarese king invaded the kingdom of Maha Chakrap'at for the possession of white elephants. In AD 1564 Ayuthia surrendered and the former brought Mahā Chakrap'at, his queen and his younger son to Pegu as hostages and a son of Mahā Chakrap'at occupied the throne of Ayuthia as a vassal ruler under the control of a Myanmarese garrison. Mahā Chakrap'at became a Buddhist monk in Myanmar and in AD 1567 he with the permission of Bayinnaung returned to Ayuthia. But the ruler of Myanmar again invaded Ayuthia in 1569 for Mahā Chakrap'at's anti-Myanmarese activities and the latter's death took place during this invasion. After the war Mahā Dhammarāj became the ruler of Ayuthia in AD 1569 as vassal ruler with the permission of Bayinnaung and he ruled for twenty-two years. Ayuthia's war with the neighbouring countries did not allow this country to do something for the progress of Buddhism. The Myanmarese king, Bayinnaung not only made a great influence upon Ayuthia, but also he carried his prowess as a conqueror to Nabbisipura. Although he was extremely busy in war with Ayuthia, Nabbisipura and other neighouring countries, yet, he contributed very much to the establishment of Buddhism in these countries. He repaired the damage that had been inflicted upon Buddhism during his wars with Ayuthia. He reformed Thailand's Buddhist Saṁgha and for its development he introduced new rules in it. He restored monasteries and he erected new religious buildings there. He showed his great devotion to Buddhism and he played a prominent role to help Buddhism in every matter to regain its lost glory. Pra Naret, who ascended the throne of Ayuthia in AD 1590 or 91, was Maha Dhammarāja's son. In Thailand's history he was known as Narasuen. The Myanmarese king, Nanda Bayin attacked Ayuthia for five times. But he was not successful. Narasuen attacked Pegu, invaded Cambodia and captured its capital Lovek in AD 1594. He not only saved his country from his enemy's invasion but he established Buddhism and repaired all religious buildings. Ayuthia established its contact with the Western world in the sixteenth century AD. The Dutch, the British and the Portuguese arrived in Ayuthia to make trade with that country. King Phra Narai (1657-68), the younger son of Prasat T'ong, welcomed them in Ayuthia. He also established his contact with Louis XIV of France. The seventeenth century was an important period in Thailand for trade and commerce. But from the religious history of the country nothing is known in Thailand about the development of Buddhism during this period.

The reign of king Boromokot of Ayuthia marked a turning point in the history of Buddhism in Thailand. He ruled over

Ayuthia from AD 1732 and it was at this time Sri Lanka received the Buddhist faith and doctrine from Thailand, although it was the country from where Thailand had received Buddhism in early years. Thus, the eighteenth century AD witnessed Thailand's religious intercourse with Sri Lanka. Uparat, the younger brother of T'ai Sra, ascended the throne of Ayuthia in AD 1733. He took the title of Maha T'ammaraja II or Mahā Dhammarāja II. In Thailand's history he was known as king Boromokot also. His relations with Myanmar was very friendly. His reign was peaceful and prosperous. He was a pious Buddhist and he was personally introduced in the welfare of Buddhism. He erected many monasteries throughout his kingdom. During his rule, Ayuthia became a great centre of Buddhism and religious mission from Sri Lanka came there to get help and assistance from the monks of Ayuthia. Śrī Vijaya Rājasiṁha of Sri Lanka sent the ministers and monks to the court of king of Ayuthia for Buddhist monks. He saw that there were not many good monks in Sri Lanka and its Buddhist Saṁgha was declining. In order to purify it he wanted to invite monks from foreign countries where Buddhism existed in a flourishing condition. At the request of his ministers and Saranaṁkara, a Buddhist monk, he sent two religious missions to Thailand where the Buddhist Saṁgha existed in its purity. Two high officials of the royal court and five pupils if Saranaṁkara went with this mission. But this attempt was disastrous. The ship on its first journey was wrecked. Before the arrival of the second mission in Sri Lanka from Thailand Śrī Vijaya Rājasiṁha died. On hearing of his death the king of Ayuthia did not send any monk to Sri Lanka. Śrī Vijaya Rājasiṁha's successor king Kirti Śrī Rājasiṁha for the purification on the Buddhist Saṁgha in Sri Lanka sent a religious mission to king Beromokot. Sri Lanka's chronicle, the *Cūlavaṁsa* mentions that the king of Thailand was a pious ruler and he fulfilled the ten *pāramis* (or *pāramitās* or perfections are *dāna*, 'giving of alms', *sīla* 'leading a moral life', *nekkhamma* 'renunciation', *paññā* 'knowledge', *viriya* 'manliness', *khanti* 'patience', *sacca* 'uprightness', *adhitthāna* 'will power', *metta* 'love' and *upekkhā* 'serenity'). During his rule the Buddhist Saṁgha flourished. He gave his full support for the progress of Buddhism. When he knows from Sri Lanka's envoys that Buddhism was in a miserable state in Sri Lanka he at once announced that 'I will be helper in order to achieve there the furtherance of the order of the Enlightened One'. He then discussed with the Saṁgharāja of Ayuthia and many other learned monks and selected monks who were 'an abode of virtues, easily satisfied, and content, and powerful with the virtues of life of piety and discipline' for Sri Lanka. He gladly sent a chapter of more than ten monks to Sri Lanka. Three Ayuthian ambassadors also came with them. The leader of this group was Upali Mahāthera. The Thai king sent a golden image of the Buddha, a superb golden book, a magnificent royal letter in Pāli and also gifts of various kinds to king Kirti Śrī Rājasiṁha. They were received with great honour by the king of Sri Lanka and under royal patronage the Upasampadā Ordination was held in Kandy in Sri Lanka in AD 1756. The *Cūlavaṁsa* also says that the king of Thailand again sent a group of ten monks to Sri Lanka for the progress of its religion and for the furtherance of its Buddhist Saṁgha. Their leaders were Visuddhācariya and Varanañāmuni. King Kirti Śrī Rājasiṁha was greatly moved by the timely help of the king of Ayuthia who not only sent monks to Sri Lanka twice but also gave valuable books which were not available in Sri Lanka. The King of Sri Lanka in return sent also valuable presents to the king of Ayuthia. King Bokomokot received the envoys with great honour. He also gave over to the ambassadors of Sri Lanka many costly books, model of the sacerd foot-print, gifts for the Tooth Relic, costly presents to the king of Sri Lanka and a royal letter. They brought with them from Thailand ninety-seven copies of the Pāli texts to Sri Lanka. Visuddhācariya Mahāthera from Ayuthia lived in Sri Lanka for four years and he returned to Ayuthia in AD 1758. Thus, King Kirti Śrī Rājasiṁha purified the Buddhist Saṁgha in Sri Lanka with the help of the Buddhist monks from Ayuthia. A sect known as the Siyām sect or the Siyāmagāma sect or the Siyāmavaṁsa or the Upālivaṁsa Nikāya after the name of the venerable Upāli Mahāthera or the Siyāmopāli sect was established in Sri Lanka at that time. This was no doubt a notable event in Sri Lanka-Thailand relations. The Ayuthian Buddhist missionaries were successful in their religious propagation. They gave helpful services to re-introduce the higher ordination and to re-organise the Buddhist Saṁgha in the island. In order to ensure the correctness of the ordination they performed a ceremony of rectification of the boundary of its Uposatha. They performed about 700 ordinations for monks and 3,000 for novices. Thus, the Buddhist monks and novices of Sri Lanka who were ordained by them became known as Syama Vaṁsa (Syamabong) or Upāli Vaṁsa — the Siam or the Thai sect of the Buddhist Saṁgha. Its history known as the Syamapasampadavat was written in Sri Lanka by a Sri Lankan Thera named Buddharakkhita of the monastery of the Pubbārāma in Kandy in Sri Lanka.[29] The Syama Vaṁsa or the Siama sect of the Hīnayāna form of Buddhism is a major sect in Sri Lanka even today. King Boromokot died in AD 1758. His son Boromorāja VI ascended the throne of Ayuthia (AD 1758-67). He was the last king who ruled in Ayuthia. The Myanmarese king Alaungpaya attacked and destroyed the kingdom of Ayuthia in AD 1767 and the whole kingdom lost its independence and became his vassal states. But it may be mentioned here that even after its destruction, the Lankavong Theravāda form of Buddhism flourished and played its prominent role as the national religion of the Thai people. In

---

29. *TAII*, p. 36.

the midst of such unsettled state of affairs, a Thai leader of the Chinese origin, General Phaya Tak Sin fought against the Myanmarese invaders and defeated them and drove them away from the regions of Thailand and established his capital at Ratburi (Dhonburi) near Bangkok in AD 1767. He re-united Thailand and restored order in his country. He then showed his keen interest in the affairs of Buddhism in Thailand. He tried to restore and to improve the religious condition there. Because of war and of the destruction of Ayuthia, the organisation of the Buddhist Saṁgha suffered very much there. King Phaya Tak Sin tried to restore Buddhism in its purity. He invited many senoir Buddhist monks to his capital and he appointed the seniormost as the Saṁgharāja and other monks were also honoured according to their qualifications. Thus, the Buddhist Saṁgha was again organised and purified as it was during the Ayuthia and the Sukhodaya period. But King Phaya Tak Sin after his fifteen years of reign sufferd very much from mental disorder and he was executed in AD 1782. His death brought the end of the Dhonburi period.

The fall of Ayuthia took place in AD 1767. The Dhonburi period came to an end in AD 1782. The repeated invasions of the Myanmarese armies had forced the Thai rulers to establish a new capital at Bangkok. It opened a new era in the history of Thailand. General Chao Phaya Chakri, who was known as Rama I (AD 1782-1809), was the founder of the Chakri dynasty at Bangkok. King P'ra P'utt'a Yot Fa Chulalok was also known as Rama I. He ascended the throne in AD 1782 and was the founder of modern Bangkok. His reign saw a great struggle with Myanmar. He made attempt to restore Buddhism in perfect form. In his reign the Lankavong Theravāda form of Buddhism played a role in the religious history of Thailand as the national religion. He took several important steps to promote this sect. He financed from his own privy purse a new and complete edition, written on palm-leaves which was the Buddhist canon of the *Tipiṭaka*. But this *Tipiṭaka* edition was made in a hurry from unreliable texts. The king occupied an important position in the religious history of Thailand for his close association with the Ninth Buddhist Council which was held at the Monastery of Nirvāṇa at Bangkok. For the reformation of the Buddhist Saṁgha and for the revision of the texts of the *Tipiṭaka* he convoked this council. Thus, this Chakri dynasty or the Bangkok dynasty began its rule by the refromation of the Buddhist Saṁgha.When the Myanmarese army capatured Ayuthia in AD 1767, the city was destroyed by fire and many Buddhist texts and manuscripts of the *Tipiṭaka* stored in the monastic libraries were reduced to ashes. The political disturbances greatly hampered the progress of Buddhism. As a result it was on the decline. The Buddhist Saṁgha had sunk to a very level of degeneracy. Phaya Tak or P'ya Taksin came to the throne in 1767 and he was great leader. He saw the unsatisfactory condition of the Buddhist Saṁgha and he dedicated himself to the service of the religion. He was its great benefactor. He wanted to form a new collection of the canonical texts. For this reason he sent monks to the provinces and even to Cambodia to collect the best copies of the *Tipiṭaka* in existence and he asked them to bring them to the capital. Before he did anything with these copies, he was driven from the throne due to political reason and he was executed. His successor Rāma I, after his accession to the throne, followed up the policy of his predecessor and with great effort and devotion he tried to do something for the advancement of the religion of the Buddha in his kingdom. He turned his mind to the noble task of repairing the damage that had been inflicted upon the religion by the foreign invaders during Thailand's war with its neighbouring countries. The king himself played a significant part in the great reformation that took place during his reign. Frankly speaking, the initiative came from him but not from the Buddhist Saṁgha of monks. But the monks loyally and faithfully lent their support to his work and their activities showed that they even allowed themselves to be guided and protected by the king, who for the establishment and purification of the religion, played a significant role in the country's religious history. He distributed the collected copies of the *Tipiṭaka* to the royal monasteries. But these copies were not in perfect form. Then the king and his brother felt disturbed not only at the laxity in the rules of discipline of the Buddhist Saṁgha but were horrified to see that the country had no single true copy of the sacred texts. All the members of the Buddhist Saṁgha warned them that there was danger for the future of the religion because the sacred texts were not available in the country. Without their proper help the monks were not in a position to do any ecclesiastical act. The king investigated the matter and invited the leading monks and asked them to come to a decision on the problems he set forth before them. They, therefore, at the advice of the king, held an assembly of a hundred high dignitaries of the Buddhist Saṁgha in the hall of the Royal palace where they all agreed that for the restoration of the sacred texts in their original form they wanted a revision and recitation of these texts in a 'Sangāyana' or 'council'. The king requested the learned Buddhist monks to go to the monastery of Bang Va Jai (now called the Monastery of Ra: Khang of the right bank of river), the residence of the Saṁgharāja for discussion with him in this matter. There they selected 218 Buddhist monks and 32 lay scholars to constitute the important council which was known as the Ninth Buddhist Council. From the point of view of the history of Buddhism in Thailand it was of immense value. Under the royal patronage many new monasteries and *pagoḍās* were constructed and the king with the help of the Buddhist monks was able to purge the Buddhist Saṁgha of all impurities and corruption that had crept into it. After this council Buddhism received a new impetus and flourished to great extent. An immediate consequence of the king's earnestness and devotion was that the religion was zealously practised not only by the royal people and the court but also by the common people.

King Rāma I and his brother were great patrons of Buddism. The Monastery of Nirvāṇa was selected as the place of the council because of its position between the palaces of the king and his brother. At this time the monastery was renamed as the Monastery of Sri Sarvajña. On the 12th November 1788, the king and his brother went in a procession to that monastery where at the instance of the king himself a great assembly of 250 learned Buddhist monks and lay scholars in the kingdom was summoned with the idea of making a new redaction of the three *piṭaka*s. Vimala Dhamma, the Saṁghrāja of the Monastery of Pho, who was one of the leading members of the council and who wrote the *Saṅgītivaṁsa*, a history of the nine councils in Pāli, before the commencement of the meeting, read a supplication to the gods, who had heard the actual words of the Buddha. He prayed to the gods that they would hole them in their efforts and would protect them against the evil powers which would try to disturb their minds and work. After this prayer the members of the council decided to divide the assembly into four groups and each group was alloted a portion of the sacred scriptures. Si, the Saṅgharāja, was the president of the first group. At his advice, the *Suttantapiṭaka* was revised and the place of the meeting was at the Monastery of Bot. The second group under the leadership of Vanaratana Sukh, the Saṁgharāja of the Monastery of Sri Sarvajña, dealt with the *Vinayapiṭaka*. The president of the third group was Vimala Dhamma, the Saṁgharāja of the Monastery of Pho. This group charged with the production of the true text of the Saddavisesana. The fourth and the last group did work on the Paramatthapiṭaka and its president was Buddhācārya Pao, the Saṁgharāja of the Monastery of the Indārāma.

During the session of the council, King Rāma I and his brother used to come everyday, morning and evening, to the monastery. They used to distribute food in the morning to the monks in the council and at the time of prayer in the evening they again came to offer candles and liquid refreshment. The recitation and the revision of the *Tipiṭaka* continued for a period of about five months, from the 12th November 1788 to the 10th April 1789. It is known that 288 manuscripts in not loss than 3,568 bundles of palm-leaf were arranged as the revised collection. King Rāma I had prepared a copy of these manuscripts which is called 'Council Edition' or 'Edition of the old Masters'. It consisted of 354 texts. The king built a special hall to keep the texts of the holy *Tipiṭaka* as settled by the members of the council. At the end of the council, he distributed yellow robes to the monks and garments to the laity. Then the *Tipiṭaka* manuscripts were taken in a royal procession and were kept in the Monastery of Phra Kao. The magnitude of this council may be examined by the latest edition of 1925-8, consisting of 45 volumes of an average of 500 octave pages. The revision on this occasion resulted in what became known as the *Tipiṭaka Chabab Tongyei* — the Great Gilt Edition written on palm-leaves. It is still preserved and kept in the library in the precincts of the Chapel Royal of the Emerald Buddha in the royal palace in Bangkok. All the Buddhist countries of the world referred to this council as the Ninth Buddhist Council. King Rāma I took several measures for the purity of the Buddhist order. He issued several decrees governing the conduct and behaviour of the Buddhist monks and under his instruction and guidance the ecclesiastical authorities used to deal with the monastic administration. The royal decrees proclaimed by the king became known as Kotmai Phrasough or Decrees for Monks. One decree mentioned that every monk or novice on leaving his preceptor should have an identity card. Another decree stated that every abbot under his jurisdiction had to maintain a register of all monks and he was responsible for their conduct. This new form of the development of the Buddhist Saṁgha took place in Bangkok and King Rāma I played a great part in it. Many Pāli texts of his country depicted him as a pious monarch. Under his patronage Buddhism became prominent and many learned Buddhist monks flourished in his reign. His youngest brother Mahāsurasiṁhanāda founded the Monastery of the Great Relic, the Wat Mahādhātu in the second half of the eithteenth century AD in Thailand. This monastery occupied an important place in the religious history of Thailand and it contributed very much to the progress of Buddhism there. Its first Saṁgharāja was Sukh, who was not only a prominent figure in Thailand's religious world but also gave valuable services for its popularity. King Rāma I died in 1809.

The next ruler of the Bangkok dynasty was Rama Tibodi or Rāma II (AD1809-24), who was Rāma I's son. In AD 1810 the Myanmarese invaded Thailand and captured Xumphon (Jump'ern) and Thalang. King Rāma II sent his brother prince Senānurakṣa to fight against the Myanmarese army and he drove them out without any difficulty. The prince had a serious attack of Malaria during the campaign and he took a vow that after his recovery from illness he would become a monk. As soon as he arrived in Bangkok from the battlefield he took the yellow robe and became a monk and stayed at the Monastery of the Great Relic for some days. King Rāma II during his reign introduced a well-organised ecclesiastical educational system and the teaching of the sacred texts and under his instruction the relevant Pāli literature was properly re-organised to suit the present requirements.

> The traditional education of monks and novices in Thailand centres mainly on the studies of the Buddhist Doctrine and Pāli language. For the study of the doctrine, there are three grades. The monks or

> novices passing such examination are termed Nak Dharma, literally meaning one who knows the Dhamma. On the other hand, the study of Pāli has seven grades, starting with the third and ending with the ninth grade. Students passing Pāli examination are called Parian or Maha or Phra Maha meaning an academic degree. For example, monks and novices (Samanera) passing the first Pāli examination are entitled to write 'p.3' after their names. Generally the study of Dhamma and the Pāli literature goes hand in hand and takes at least seven years to complete. This system of ecclesiastical has been the basis of the monastic education even today.

During the reign of Rāma II Sri Lanka came under the British domination. So the king was much worried about the condition of Buddhism under the British rule in Sri Lanka. He in AD 1814 wanted to send a religious mission in Sri Lanka to study the religious condition under the rule of the British and to establish religious and cultural ties which were interrupted since the fall of Ayuthia in AD 1767. According to the advice of the Saṁgharāja of the Monastery of the Great Relic, the king selected four monks from this monastery and four monks from the Monastery of Rajapuraṇa. They left Bangkok in AD 1814 with gifts from the king for the principal shrines and high priests of the Buddhist Saṁgha in Sri Lanka. But this journey proved disastrous due to shipwreck. They after two years reached Anurādhapura in Sri Lanka. They were well-received by the monks, the Sri Lankan people and also by the British officials who were ruling the country at that time. They visited all the sacred places of Sri Lanka and after spending a year there they returned to Bangkok in AD 1818 with six cuttings from the Bodhi Tree of Anurādhapura. The Saṁgharāja of the Monastery of the Great Relic received one of them and it was planted in the north-east corner of the monastery. During this time Prince Mongkut, a son of King

Rāma II, as a Sāmaṇera joined this monastery. It is to be noted here that King Rāma II for the progress of the religion of Sri Lanka sent several religious missions there. For his religious activities the two countreis — Sri Lanka and Thailand established their close religious ties between them. During his reign there was a scandal in the Buddhist Saṁgha in Bangkok. Three well-known Buddhist monks led scandalous lives. They had their families and produced several children. Buddhaghoṣācārya, who belonged to the Monastery of the Great Relic, was one of them. King Rāma II felt sorry for it and he sas with grave concern that the Saṁgha was gradually drifting from its age-old and vigilantly preserved orthodoxy towards a way of life that was totally contrary to the disciplinary code of the monks. These three monks were found guilty before a special court and were imprisoned. The king had a talk relating to this matter with the Saṁgharāja. Mi of the Monestery of the Great Relic and request him to write a book, viz., the *Dvādānusāsani* on the observance of the vows of the Buddhist monks in collaboration with Āt, the Saṁgharāja of the Monastery of Sa: Ket. This text was introduced to all monasteries and king Rāma II gave order that it was to be studied by each and every monk of the country. The Saṁgharāja with the permission of the king of Thailand revived the festival of Visākha or Vaisākha, the anniversary of the birth of the Buddha, of his enlightenment and of his Mahāparinibbāna. King Rāma II died in AD 1824.

The next ruler of the Bangkok dynasty was Rāma III or Phra Nang Klao (AD 1824-51). Under his patronage the Lankavong Theravāda form of Buddhism prospered in Thailand. The monastic administration was reorganised. King Rāma III for his administration created four jurisdictions: northern, southern, central and Araññavāsī. The first three jurisdictions were brought under the control of Gāmavāsī. The head of the ecclesiastical hierarchy was Somdet Phra Saṁgharāja or the Patriarch who was appointed by King

Rāma III. The four wings of the Saṁgharāja had each a chief at the head, who occupied the position of Somdet Phrarajagana and king Rama III appointed them. Under the patronage of the king the Pavaranivesa monastery or the Wat Pavaranivesa in Thailand was established by a Thai Prince named Śakti in AD 1826. At first it was known as the 'New Wat' but afterwards it received the name of Pavaranivesa "an expression very similar to that by which the Palace of the Sacred kings was designated". King Rāma III not only patronised it but he appointed in AD 1837 as its Abbot or Saṁgharāja his own brother Prince Mongkut who had obtained his early education in several other monasteries. Within a very short time it became a well-known centre of the Theravāda form of Buddhism and it remained pre-eminent throughout the religious history of Thailand. King Rāma III in his religious activities was always guided by his brother Mongkut. The farmer took steps to restore the Monastery of the Great Relic in its original form. In AD 1844 or 1845 he started its restoration but he could not see its completion. Because he died suddenly in AD 1851.

After a reign of twenty-six and a half years, king Rāma III passed away. His successor was his half brother Mongkut who had spent for more than fourteen years as an abbot of the Pavaranivesa monastery.

> His long monastic probation had enabled him to acquire a much greater experience of the needs of the country and to set free an individuality much more original that if he had received in the Royal Palace. Thanks to him, Siam was quick to come out of her deadly isolation and to enter steadily into a way that was to make her a modern state.

Mongkut ascended the throne at the age of forty-seven years. He assumed the title of Rama IV and he ruled from AD 1851 to 1868. His reign proved to be one of the most inspiring periods for the cause of Buddhism. King Rama III appointed him as the Saṁgharāja of the Monastery of the Pavaranivesa in 1837 AD Mongkut made efforts to the progress of Buddhism and contributed significantly to its development. At first he joined the Wat Samorai or the Monastery of Samorai. But he was not happy with the method of teaching of the members of the monastery and the practices observed by them. He then joined another monastery and he studied the Pāli texts very seriously. He palyed a vital role to the cause of Pāli studies. He then met one monk from Pegu in lower Myanmar and his timely help and guidance inspired him very much and he joined the Wat Samorai at his request. He remained there for seven years and he tries to propagate the teachings of the Buddha. As a monk, he led a very simple and pure life. In order to beg his food daily, he used to go everyday from village to village and he was happy whatever he used to get from it. In summer and winter seasons he visited many sacred places, met many people and discussed many religious problems with them. He in January 1837 became abbot of the Wat Pavaranivesa at the advice of King Rama III. He stayed there for fourteen years. He worked hard for this monastery and within a very short time it became a famous centre of Pāli learners in Thailand. As a monk he founded a new sect the Dhammayuttika or the Shammayutta in 1837 in the reign of Rama III. The followers if this sect

> rejected all practices that had not authority other than custom. They accepted all canonical regulations, not merely following them mechanically, but endeavouring to keep their significance over present in their consciousness. They were expected to understand the formulas they recited, the reasons for the rules they were subject to and the meaning of the acts they performed.

Although the Thais never accepted the Dhammayutta

doctrines fully, yet they had a great influence upon the life of the Thais. By his vigorous religious activities and by his judicious selections and rejections Mongkut revived the original doctrine of the Buddha. He created a new Buddhism and popularised it in Thailand. He was able to establish his contact with Sri Lanka and with the permission of King Rama III he sent a religious mission to the king of Kandy in Sri Lanka and from there he brought many Pāli texts which were not available in Thailand at that time. In AD 1840 five monks from Sri Lanka came to Thailand and stayed at the monastery of Mongkut. Afterwards the latter sent five monks to Sri Lanka to study Pāli and Buddhism.

King Rāma III was succeeded by mongkut who took the title of Phra Chom Klao or His Majesty Phra Baht Somdech Phra Paramedr Maha Mongkut Phra Cham Klao Yu Hua and he was also known as Rāma IV. He was a very remarkable person. He was one Thai king whose fame travelled beyond the frontiers of his kingdom, not only as an able king and statesman, but also as one of these few heroes who by their piety and reforming zeal carved out a place for themselves in the history of Buddhism. He worked hard for the moral, intellectual and social improvement of the Thai people. He as a Monk lived in the monastery for twenty-six years. His pilgrimages, preaching and his simple monastic life of twenty-six years had a great effect in his mind and he made him not only an accomplished person but also helped him to rule the country efficiently as an enlightened ruler. Under his personal care and observation, his subjects were always dutiful to their parents, offered gifts and charities to the poor and deserving and practised non-injury and led a pious life. He always encouraged his people to do works of social value. The greatest service he rendered to the religion was the reformation of the Buddhist Saṁgha and the introduction of the pure form of Buddhism in Thailand. In order that men might follow the path and reach fruition in Nibbāna he created several religious monuments in his kingdom. He sincerely devoted his life to the cause of Buddhism. His reign was peaceful and prosperous, and was one of the brightest periods of religious scholarship in Thailand. He was regarded as a great patron and protector of all Buddhist coremonials and activities. He patronised the *kaṭhin* ceremony and took a prominent part in it and he raised it to an even conspicuous place. He was an enthusiast in the cause of the religion and he personally took interest in the development of the religion of the Buddha and also in the welfare of his subjects. He erected four monasteries viz., the Somanassa (AD 1853), Padumavana (AD 857), Rājapratiṣṭha (AD 1564) and Mahākūṭasatriya, (AD 1866) and he placed them under the authority of Pavaret, an abbot of the Pavaranivesa monastery. They belonged to the Dhammayuttika sect which was founded by Mongkut while he was the Abbot of the Pavaranivesa Monastery. When he assumed the royal power after the death of his brother he then appointed prince Rikṣa, better known under the title of Somdet Krom Phaja Pavaret (Pavaresvariyālaṅkaraṇa) as an Abbot of the Pavaranivesa monastery. He remained there from AD 1851 to 1892. King Mongkut sent all his sons to the monastery of Pavaranivesa. Even Chulalongkorn, the immediate successor of Mongkut, remained there as a novice for six months. With great effort and devotion, Mongkut preached the religion of the Buddha and he encouraged others to rise up for its welfare. He induced many young persons to join the Buddhist Saṁgha and to lead a pious and noble life. For its genuineness and austere practices and for its famous monks, the Pavaranivesa monastery under his guidance and patronage attained great prominence and several branches were established to play vigorous role for the development of Buddhism in Thialand. Pious people gradually took keen interest in its affairs and at each *vassa* season more and more ordinations were conferred by its monks. Owing to Mongkut's important role as its abbot and also as a king of Thailand, this monastery became very prominent in the religious history of Thailand. About one hundered and fifty monks used to reside there at that time. Thus, Mongkut was successful in bringing the reformation of the rules of the discipline of the Buddhist Saṁgha. But its result divided the Buddhist Saṁgha into two sects: one, the Mahānikāya or the old orthodox sect or the unreformed sect and the other, the Dhammayuttika sect, or the reformed sect. In the second half of the nineteenth century AD Sri Lanka again established its contact with Thailand. This time Sri Lanka's public wanted to establish a printing press of their own and for reason they sent an envoy to the king of Thailand for financial assistance from the king. King Mongkut gladly gave a heavy amount for this purpose. A printing press at Galle in southern Sri Lanka under the name of the Lankapakāra Press came into existence in AD 1862 with his help. The king died in AD 1868.

Chulanongkorn occupied the throne in AD 1868 after the death of his father king Mongkut. He took the title of Rāma V (AD 1868-1910). Like his father he was a devout follower of Buddhism and he patronised the Monastery of the Great Relic. During his rule it recovered its lost prestige and importance. He appointed Phra: Devamoli Dit, a renowned Pāli scholar of the Monastery of Aruna as its Saṁgharāja. He also conferred on him the title of Somdet Phra: Vanaratana in AD 1910. Under his patronage the new Saṁgharāja prepared the first printed edition of the *Tipiṭaka*. He also received from the king a sum of 80,000 from the estate of Prince Mahāvajruṇhisa who died in AD 1890 for the complete restoration or the Great Relic Monastery. During the reign of Rama V Prince Vajirañāṇavararasa, a son of king Mongkut, became the third abbot of the Pavaranivesa Monastery after the death of Pavaret in AD 1892. Under the king's patronage the Mahāmakutarājavidyālaya, a kind of university, was established in AD 1893 and it received its name after king Mongkut. The king gave his help to its development and he took keen interest in the affairs of the religion. He gave money for the publication of the Thai *Tipiṭaka* and he requested the abbot of the Pavaranivesa to distribute the copies of the *Tipiṭaka* to prominent Buddhist scholars of the various parts of the world. The Thai king also gave his patronage to publish in AD 1902 a text known as the Law Code on the administration of the Buddhist Saṁgha of Thailand and the abbot of the Pavaranevesa Monastery helped very much in this matter. It is now the Constitutional Law of the Thai Buddhists and was the source and model of all later Pāli and Thai Law texts written in Thailand. King Rāma V in AD 1905 built the Candra building after the name of his daughter Candrāsavadvāra.

The next ruler was Prince Vajiravudh. He was known as Rāma VI (AD 1910-25). In AD 1904 he as a novice joined the Pavaranivesa Monastery and he stayed there for sometime. In AD 1914 he erected the Diamond building. He brought the Rāmasisuddhavāsa Monastery which was nearly abandoned for a very long time under the administration of the Pavaranivesa Monastery in AD 1905. He was a great patron of Buddhism. During his reign Vajirañāṇavararasa was an abbot of the Pavaranivesa Monastery. His deep knowledge of the Dhamma and the Vinaya and his reformation of the Buddhist Saṁgha attracted the notice of the king, who, on seeing his good performance, conferred on him the title of Mahāsamaṇa. In his reign Phra: Dhammatrailokācārya Hong took the charge of a Pāli school in AD 1912. He was appointed as the Saṁgharāja of the Monastery of the Great Relic after the death of Somdet Phra: Vanaratana Dit in AD 1923. In Thailand Theravāda Buddhism flourished under the patronage of king Rāma VI.

Prince Prajadhipok ascended the throne of the Bangkok dynasty in AD 1925. He became known in Thailand's history as Rāma VII (AD 1925-35). He was a zealous Buddhist. Vajrañānavararasa, the abbot of the Pavaranivesa Monastery, always guided him, advised him and inspired him in his religious works. He contributed a valuable service to the progress of Buddhism in Thailand in his reign. He received his ordination in AD 1917 from the Monastery of Pavaranivesa. The Saṁgharāja of the Monastery of the Great Relic recceived the title of Phra: Vimaladhamma from the king. Under the proper guidance of the new Saṁghrāja of the Monastery of the Great Relic the school of Pāli became an important centre of religious teaching in Thailand in the reign of King Rama VII. It should be mentioned here that the Monastery of the Great Relic belonged to the Mahānikāya sect of Thailand but its followers began to clothe themselves after the style of the monks of the Dhammayuttika sect which was founded by king Mongkut while he was the Saṁgharāja of the Monastery of Pavaranivesa. The Monastery of the Great Relic played a significant role in the history of Buddhism of Thailand and played a very prominent part for the progress of the religion and its language. The Pavaranivesa Monastery too occupied an important place in the history of Buddhism in Thailand. Under royal patronage it remained pre-eminent as the main centre of Theravāda Buddhism and its abbots gave their valuable services for the development of Buddhism in Thailand. In the reign of Rāma VII a Buddhist council was held in Bangkok. It tried to restore and to interpret the *Tipiṭaka* and then a 1500-volume edition of the *Tipiṭaka* was published. King Rāma VII offered these complete *Tipiṭaka* to several monasteries in Thailand. He patronised this council and it revealed his great faith in Buddhism and his contribution to the progress of Buddhism in Thailand.

Prince Anandamahidol who became known as King Rāma VIII occupied the throne of the Bangkok dynasty after King Rāma VII. He was also a pious ruler and Theravāda Buddhism flourished in his reign. Under his patronage the translation of the Pāli *Tipiṭaka* was completed into the Thai language. This great religious work in Thai script became known as

Phra Tripitaka Chabab Thai or the *Tripitaka of Thai* edition. It no doubt marked a landmark in the history of Buddhism in Thailand.

Prince Bhumibol Adulyadej succeeded his brother King Rāma VIII in AD 1846. He became known in Thailand's history as Rāma IX. This present king became a Buddhist monk like his predecessors. His reign celebrated the Buddha Jayanti, the 2500th Anniversary of the Buddha's *mahāparinibbāna* and Thailand remembered this day with great celebration in Bangkok and also in other parts of the country. King Rāma IX restored and erected several Buddhist monuments in Thailand for the glorification of Buddhism. Under his patronage the two Buddhist universities which were founded during the reign of Rāma V flourished and gave their valuable services for the development of Theravāda Buddhism and its language in Thailand. These universities contributed very much to the progress of Buddhist education in Thailand. King Rāma IX's reign witnessed the meeting of the council of World Buddhist Association V in Bangkok and it was sponsored by Thailand. Many delegates from Buddhist countries took part in this meeting. This was aslo an important Buddhist event which marked the development of Buddhism in Thailand. Under King Rāma IX's patronage Buddhism prospered in Thailand and it is now the state religion of Thailand.

The Lanka Theravāda form of Buddhism has occupied the highest position in Thailand's religious history and it has become the national religion in Thailand. Beginning from the Sukhodaya period right up to the present Bangkok period Buddhism has been mentioned as the prominent religion of the Thai people with the Thai kings as its chief patrons for over 700 years without any disturbance. About fifty Thai kings of the eight dyanasties have reigned successively in Thailand and Sukhodaya, Ayuthia, Dhonburi and Bangkok have acted as their capitals for more than seven centuries and they were all Buddhists. The king, the supreme head of the country, is regarded as the defender and protector of Buddhism, which, from the time of the foundation of the Sukhodaya kingdom to the present day, has played its role as Thailand's state religion. Out of forty-two millions of population about 94 per cent are Buddhists and others are Hindus, Muslims, Christians, etc. In Thailand there are about 25,322 monasteries and more than 200,000 monks and novice live there. The ecclesiastical authority of the Buddhist Saṁgha acts as its administrative body and it looks after its administration but the Thai government is also responsible for the affairs of the Buddhist Saṁgha and its responsibility relates to the matters connected with the state and the laity. Its duty is to strengthen unity and joint action between the Saṁgha and the state and good relation exists between them. There are three organs of the state; the Saṁgha as the legislature, the Saṁgha Mantri as the executive and the Vinayadhara as the judiciary. By the Saṁgha Act of 1962 which came into force on the 1st January 1963, a great change took place in Thailand's Buddhist Saṁgha and then the Mahāthera Samagam, the Supreme Council of the Buddhist Saṁgha, was established.

3

Thailand's Buddhist Art

THAILAND has seen the rise and extinction of a number of various art styles. These were brought from foreign lands and from a fusion of several modes, alien and native, the local people under the patronage tried to create a style which was entirely new. Until the thirteenth century AD, India, Sri Lanka and Cambodia (Kampuchea) made a great influence upon Thailand's art. The establishment of the Sukhodaya kingdom in the middle of the thirteenth century AD saw the rise and the development of the Thai art. Thailand's architecture is an admixture of various ideas which were borrowed from India, Sri Lanka and Cambodia. But the Thai architects from these ideas produced their own expression and crearted their own imaginations. Every decorative piece or painting in a Thai religious structure tried to symbolise a particular aspect of Thai Theravāda Buddhism. A Thai Buddhist religious complex became known as a 'Wat'. It can be used to mean a temple or monastery. It indicates a place of worship, of meeting or of education. After King Mengrai of Chieng Mai defeated the Mon king of Pagan in AD 1288 he built Wat Kathom in Chiengmai and he named it for the architect who gave its design. Thailand's wats were often received their names for their important image — Wat Phra Singh in Chieng Mai and Wat Phra Keo in Bangkok. The word 'Phra' is an honorific for Buddha image. The word 'Phra' in Wat Phra Chedi Si Samphat is used as an honorific for the word *chedi* which follows it.

Thailand's Buddhist art can be divided into two distinct periods.[1] The first period became known as the Mon or the Dvāravatī period. The Mons made their valuable contributions to shape it. It took its origin from the fifth century AD and maintained its existence until the Khmer invasions took place five hundred years later. For the next two hundred years the Khmers played their vital roles in this region. From south China and owing to Mongol pressure from the north, people took their migration and finally a new Thai state was formed and its capital was Sukhodaya or Sukhothai.

The sculpture of Thailand was originated around religion,

> Whether of Indian orgin, Mon-Indian, Mon-Khmer, Khmer, Khmer-Thai, or of pure Thai source, only divinities or the symbolical representations of doctrines were sculptured; in one word *mūrtis* always were chiselled so that the populace might adore and revers.[2]

Practically, Thailand's sculpture was undertaken from the point of view of religion. Whether the origin of a figure was purely Indian, Mon, Khmer or Thai or it was originated from hybrid influence such as Mon-Indian, Mon-Khmer or Khmer-Thai, primarily for devotional purpose it was done. The Khmers dominated the Menam valley for sometime and they were responsible for the development of Cambodian ideas into Thailand. But during the thirteenth-fifteenth century AD when the Khmers came under the control of Thailand, then the Cambodian ideas were transformed into Thai conception. Frescoes, mural paintings and architectural designs were all kept but a Thai outlook was introduced in them. Certain details were added by the Thais. Swami Sadananda says,

> It resulted in a monotonous rigidity based on inflexible Siamese canons, almost boresome in its innumerable

1. *Baa*, p. 172
2. Thailand, p. 42.

details. This movement which cannot be claimed as a happy augury is noticed in minor crafts like wood carvings and lacquor work. But in spite of these hide-bound monotonous conceptions none of the arts were allowed to be extinct. The only branch that escaped the hand and past rules of theory were the immaculate bronze images.

Dvāravatī was regarded as the cradle of the first Mon-Indian sculpture, but it also can be mentioned as the place of the primitive Khmer art. The specimen was found at Sri Deva.[3] The Dvāravatī kingdom established a close cultural link with Sri Lanka and South India and this was proved form the discovery of Indian motif in suclpture and architecture. The Wheel of Law and other symbolical representations arrived in Dvāravatī from Sri Lanka via Ligor. At the time when Dvāravatī was part of Fou-nan in Cambodia, the images of Dvārapālas, Ardhanārīs, Yakkhas and Viṣṇus were brought directly from India. These were found at P'ra Pat'om and Pong T'uk and these were mentioned as the evidence of the earliest speciment of sculpture in Thailand. These two places indicate the areas where the Aryan first established their colony. Dvāravatī established its identity as Hindu region as long as Chaiya and Nakon Śī Thammarat remained as important places of Brāhmaṇism. In course of time these regions became well-known Buddhist centres. It is known from records that Dharmarāja, the Thai ruler of Chiengmai (Xieng Mai) who, reforming Buddhism in his country, invited Sumana, the pupil of the famous Udumbara Swāmī, established the images of Śiva and Viṣṇu. Although Sukhodaya was a Hīnayānist place, yet the Vaiṣṇava influence was still existing there. Because the wheel and fish motifs on its ceramics were available there.

Thailand's traditional arts not only had their inspiration but also borrowed and adopted many of their features from Indian,

3. Thailand, p. 13.

Mon-Khmer, Sinhalese, Chinese, etc. Practically, Buddhism played a great role for the rise, development and growth of Thai art and the former had a close connection with it. For this reason, Thai art became known as the Buddhist art. The Thais were devout Buddhists. They were great patrons of Buddhism and they contributed largely to its propagation. They showed their great devotion to it by making, sculpting or casting beautiful images of the Buddha and for the establishment of these images they constructed many buildings.[4] Although India made a great influence upon the Classical Thai Buddhist art, yet it was unable to get its help directly from there. In Thailand Indian art and craftemanship were mentioned as the prototype of the Buddhist art. It is known that from the first quarter of the beginning of the Christian era adaptation and imitation from India began in Thailand. Several schools of Indian art established their close contact with Thai art at a very early period. From stylistic evidence it is learnt that the Amarāvatī school of Indian art was able to inspire the Buddhist art in Thailand in the early centuries of the Christian era. Afterwards, Thai art was greatly influenced by the Gupta, the Pallava and the Pāla-Sena art from India. In the field of architecture, Thailand was influenced by the Cālukyas of Bādāmī in the Deccan, the Pallavas of Kāñcī on the cost and the Pāṇḍyas of Madurai in the far south. These three south Indian empires helped Thailand to receive the modelled type of the architectural art from them. India sculptors and painters contributed largely to the development of sculpture and painting of Thailand. The Gāndhāra, Mathurā, Amarāvatī and the classical art of the Gupta period had their significant role for the rise and the development of the Buddhist art in Thailand. The Orissan art and architecture and also art from Bengal were mentioned as the main prototype of art in Thailand. In the early period when the Buddhist art in Thailand was originated, at that time it had a close relationship with Indian art. The Dvāravatī kingdom, the early powerful kingdom of central

4. *TAII*, p. 59.

Thailand, for the growth and progerss of the primitive art in Thailand took the help of Indian artists, sculptors and painters. In this kingdom the artistic activities in art, architecture and sculpture took place very much and this was happened under its patronage one for this reason it became known as the Dvāravatī school of art. It was the first and the earliest Buddhist school of art in Thailand. Several archaeological sources mention that the Buddha images, bas-relief and the *dharmacakra* were discovered and they trace the influence of the Gupta period and also the work of Indian artists. Śrī-Vijaya's art also occupied an important place in Thailand. This Śrī-Vijaya kingdom was able to extend its influence over several regions of Indonesia, Cambodia and some parts of south and central Thailand. Several monuments of the Śrī-Vijayan art in Thailand had close similarity with the monuments found in Java and Sumatra islands. They had Mahāyāna influence because this sect of Buddhism became very popular in Java, Sumatra, Malay Peninsula, southern Thailand also in Cambodia. This Śrī-Vijaya school of art took its rest very strongly in Thailand. It also became very popular like the Dvāravatī school of art. It took its origin after the Dvāravatī school of art. Then appeared the art of the Lopburi period (eleventh-fifteenth centuries AD). It became also known as Khmer art because this region was occupied by the Khmers, the Mahāyāna form of the Buddhism made a great influence upon this period of arts. Then the Thais rose to power and they became the ruler of Thailand.

The rise and the development of art during the Dvāravatī period (sixth or seventh-eleveenth centuries AD)

The Dvāravatī school of art was regarded as the earliest school of Buddhist art in Thailand. It can be mentioned as the art of pre-Thai period. The Mon people founded the Dvāravatī kingdom in central Thailand. Under their guidance and inspiration this kingdom became well-known in the seventh and eighth centuries AD and the rule of this dynasty came to an end in the late tenth or in the beginning of the eleventh century AD.[5] In the central part of Thailand many of the Theravāda Buddhist objects were found and they belonged to the seventh century AD. According to scholars, the style of art of these objects belonged to the Dvāravatī school of art. Most probably, the capital city of this kingdom was at the town of Nakon Pathom, at an ancient site at Ku-Bua, the Ratburi province or at U-Tong in the Supanburi province. Nakon Pathom, and U-Tong or U-Thong in the provinces of Supanburi and Ratburi and at Muang Fa Dae Sung Yang at Kalasan in north were the great centres of the Dvāravatī art. It flourished very much there. Even in south Thailand sculptures belonged to the Dvāravatī school were found. It may be noted here that early Buddha images in Cambodia had great similarity with the style of the early Dvāravatī school of art. In the second half of the seventh century AD the people of the town of Lavo or Lopburi founded the Haripuñjaya kingdom in northern Thailand. In that kingdom the Dvāravatī art flourished. The monuments belonged to this art were the earliest Buddhist religious buildings in Thailand. But the pure Indian structure was found and this may trace Indian influence in the field of architecture in Thailand before the beginning of the seventh century AD. In order to commemorate Theravāda Buddhism in Thailand, later Dvāravatī religious buildings were constructed and they belonged to the different styles of architecture. In the Dvāravatī period many *stūpa*s were built and these *stūpa*-structures had different styles. Here is given an account of these types:

1. The five-storeyed stupa or chedi with terrace in each story. The basements of the stupa were decorated with the frieze of stucco and burnt-clay illustrating the narrative story of Buddhist texts.

2. The stupa with a square base, with the central part in a hemispheric shape and a painted final.

5. *TAII*, p. 61.

3. The stupa with the square base, has a central part in the form of an inverted alms-bowl and a final part divided into many superimposed flat rings terminated by a bulb. This style of stupa might belong to art of Mahāyāna Buddhism.

4. Stupa with square base and five terraces, the lowest being the biggest and the smallest terraces at the top. Each terraces has niches, three in number in each of the four directions. Inside these three niches standing Buddha image are housed.[6]

In the Haripuñjaya kingdom the Wat Kukut in Lamphun was Dvāravatī's architectural building. It had five successive terraces. In north-eastern part of Thailand there were religious buildings which had the architecture of the Dvāravatī school of art. In each corner of basement there were pillars and each pillar had the lotus-shape on the capital. In the Dvāravatī period the roofs of the architectural buildings followed the style of Indian architecture. In this period brick and lime, masonary and stucco were used. The Gupta art of India made a great influence upon these works. The Pathom Chedi was the great temple which was erected at the province of Nakon Pathom. The Thais referred to it as the first sanctuary of this land. It had a vast circular Pra-Chedi or Phra Chedi or *stūpa* with four *vihāra*s and a terrace platform. The shape of the dome of circular form of this *stūpa* was like a cup or an inverted basin. The base of this *stūpa* was square and it had a circumambient gallery and there was also an enclosure. According to scholars, the Mons constructed this great *stūpa* at Nakon Pathom. But after sometime it was destroyed. Then in 1860, King Mongkut or Rama IV of the Bangkok dynasty built it in the form of Phra Chedi. He constructed four new *vihāra*s and also the circular gallery which surrounded the *stūpa*. The work was completed in the reign of

6. *TAII*, p. 62.

King Chulalengkorn or Rāma V. This great *stūpa* or Phra Pathom Chedi was erected beautifully by the artists of the Dvāravatī school in Thailand. This great *stūpa* was regarded as

> the greatest and most perfect example of religious buildings in the Dvāravatī school of art in Thailand from remote times up to the present day.

It may be noted here that the Dvāravatī school of art had its beautiful and excellent sculpture and also stucco decoration. From the sixth or the seventh century AD sculpture began to appear there. The art of Amarāvatī from south India gave artistic inspiration to the artists of the Dvāravatī school of art to produce their sculpture. The Dvāravatī sculptors were inspired very much by the farmer's style and workmanship and also they received help in the field of iconography and sculptural style from the Gupta and the Post-Gupta art of India. They tried to follow faithfully the artistic style of Indian cave temples. They introduced nothing new. In Indian art of Amarāvatī and also in the Gupta art the right hand of Buddha image did the gesture while the left hand held part of the robe, but in the Dvāravatī art the left hand of the image did the same gesture as the right. The Dvāravatī sculptors produced the Buddha images of different gestures and character. They totally followed the Gupta style but in their forms they brought towards a greater simplification. Apart from stone carving, the stone Wheel of Law and Grouching Dear which were found from Nakon Pathom, Ratburi, U-Tong and other regions, were their productions. The Dvāravatī images in stone and in bronze were greatly influenced not only by the Gupta and the post-Gupta styles which developed in central and western India from the fourth to the eighth centuries AD but also by the Pāla style of north-eastern India. In sculptural field stone played a great role no doubt and most of the Dvāravatī Buddha images were carved by the sculptors in stone and very few images were cast by them in bronze. The early style of the Buddha image had great similarity with the style of the Gupta and the post-Gupta. The Dvāravatī sculptors had done very well with the stone seated Buddhas. The seated images were made in the Indian mode with the knees for apart and the soles of the feet were placed upwards in the *vīrāsana* position. The Dvāravatī sculptors introduced the Indian concept of seating Buddha on the throne and his feet in the European fashion were palced solidly on the ground. His right hand was in the *vitarka mudrā* while his left hand was slightly above the knee in the same position. The Buddha image had

> the small ushnisha, the distended ear-lobes, the spiral curis of the hair and their abnormal size, the elliptical form of the face, the bulzing upper eyelids, the lightly outlined eyebrows in the form of a swallow springing from the top of the nose-bridge, the long eyebrows, unsmoothed forehead, the broad mouth, big hands and feet and the modelling of the torse, where the limbs appeared from under the robs like a nude sexless body under a fine diaphanous cloth.

Thus, the style of the Dvāravatī Buddha image had great similarity with that of the Buddha image from Sārnāth and the cave-temple of Ajantā of the Gupta period. The body of the early Buddha image of the Dvāravatī school of art was covered by the thin robe very closely. The robe had both the short and long forms. The short form came to an end over the chest and nipple and the long form was able to cover the body up to the navel. The image pedestal was an expanded lotus-flower with the large petal and in the middle of the lotus petal there was the prominent axis, which was surrounded by small lotus-petals. The pedestal had both up and down lotus designs of a row of lotus petals. There was the halo behind the head of the standing Buddha image of the early period of the Dvāravatī school of art. The halo was in the form of carving the curved line around the head of the Buddha and it appeared in a pointed end on the tompost of halo itself. The early Buddha image was made in the attitude of benediction. The Dvāravatī Buddha image of the later period had large hair-curls, a flat face, curved and connected eyebrows, prominent eyes, a flat nose, thick, the *uṣṇīṣa* or protuberance of the skull and the distended ear-lobes. In several bas-reliefs, the Buddha in a standing pose was on the back of a mythical creature with the body of a bull, the wings of a swan and a hawk like beak. Indra and Brahmā or two Bodhisattvas attended him. The large *dharmachakra* (or Wheel of the Law) in stone was found in Thailand.

The Dvāravatī school of art produced many terracotta sculptures and these were found at Nakon Pathom. The heads of the Buddha and also the heads of the Hindu gods, called Devatā Heads were found. In order to decorate the base of the Dvāravatī temple, the ordination hall, *vihāras* and *stūpas*, the Dvāravatī school of art produced many stucco-sculptures and their moulding took place in many ways such as the Buddha head, dwarfs and Devatā gods or divinities. Many Buddhist votive tablets of the Dvāravatī school of art were discovered at Nakon Pathom, Ratburi, Supanburi, etc. The earliest, dating from the fourth to seventh centuries, depicted the miracle of Sāvatthi when the Buddha confounded the heretics. The influence of the style of the Gupta and the Pāla art was felt very much in some of Dvāravatī's votive tablets. The bas-reliefs depicting the life of the Buddha were also carved by the artists of the Dvāravatī school of art. In the sculptural field of this school of art several stucco animal figures such as lion, elephant, deer and the stone pedestal in different decorative styles were made by the Dvāravatī sculptors.

Traditionally, Thailand depended very much upon wooden materials and these have prevented the survival of most Dvāravatī structure.[7] But excavations have given an idea about foundations of laterite

7. *Baa*, p. 174.

a material that was clay-like when freshly dug but altered to near stone hardness upon exposure to the air.

Stūpas and temples were constructed with laterite, brick and vegetables glue mortar and stucco and carved stone were used in them for decoration. Dvāravatī's stone foundations indicates their great similarity with the temples of Myanmar and had simple, square stone-structures, with a porch on one side and a pyramidal roof. Indian Hindu sanctuaries followed this style. From excavations it is known that wood or brick was used for the *vihāras* and the Buddhist assembly halls. In style the Dvāravatī period had great similarity with Sri Lanka. The later Thai architectural styles received their great inspiration from Sri Lanka which was regarded as the primary source for most of its works. The first Dvāravatī images were the earliest original Buddhist sculptures of South-East Asia. Boisselier, the French art historian, mentions it. Their facial structures indicates a Mon ethinc type. It may be stated here that the most popular Dvāravatī subjects were selected from these events which took place within a succinct period of time in the story related to the life of the Buddha, and it began with his final meditation just before his enlightenment and it ended with his first sermon in the Deer Park at Sārnāth. Thailand's later sculpture favoured bronze over stone. It used thin surface. It tried to follow the Sukhodaya model and it attained 'increased delicacy and greater stylisation'. Sukhodaya maintained intact the earlier Dvāravatī use of brick construction, stucco niches and terracotta figures. The former established its contact with Sri Lanka and it received great support from it for the development of its religion, literature, art, sculpture and architecture. Sri Lanka made a great influence upon the Sukhodaya style and its many works were produced from its close contact with Sri Lanka. In Dvāravatī stone images, wheel occupied an important place. Although it originated from the Aśokan wheel-topped pillars, yet, this theme became very popular in the Dvāravatī period. This emblem was adopted by Buddhist artists in different cultures. The Dvāravatī artists showed thier great interest in terracotta and stucco, and used moulds and constructed figures and architectural elements for the decoration of the outside walls of temples and *stūpa*s. Their remains give us a clear idea about skill, artistic sense and imagination of Buddhist artists and sculptors of the Dvāravatī period. In later Thai art the malleable nature of clay was widely used. The Buddha's Enlightenment was regarded as the favourite subject of the Dvāravatī artists and sculptors of Thailand. They very frequently portrayed the *māravijaya* pose with the seated Buddha in the *bhūmi-sparśa-mudrā*. This Thai pose created by them became very popular in Thailand during the Dvāravatī period. Another popular Dvāravatī type image was the standing Buddha, with both hands held chest-high, with palms forward in the *vitarka-mudrā*. Alexander Griswold remarks,

> the particular image and gesture is actually a variation of the gesture of teaching or exposition, dharma-chakramudra, as soon in the famous Gupta Buddha from Sarnath. If so, the Thai figure would refer to the First Sermon, following the Enlightenment, for despite the significance of the teaching gesture, a mudra unique to Buddhism, images in the Dharamachakramudra are not found in Thailand or Cambodia.

The Buddhist art of the Śrī-Vijaya period (from the eighth to the thirteenth centuries AD)

The Śrī-Vijaya kingdom was regarded as the most powerful maritime kingdom of South-East Asia in the eighth century AD. Its capital was in Sumatra and it extended its dominions up to Java and Malay Archipelago, as well as Nakon Śī-Tammarat (Tamaliṅga) and Chaiya (Corahi) in the south of Thailand.[8] During the Śri-Vijaya period the Buddhist art flourished in Thailand and it became known as the Śrī-Vijaya school of art. This school had its artistic activities in south Thailand. Like the Dvāravatī

8. *TAII*, p. 64.

school of art, it not only get its inspiration but also borrowed the style from India. Mahāyāna Buddhism flourished in this kingdom and the art that developed here belonged to the Mahāyāna school. It is very difficult to say when the art of the Śrī-Vijaya period took the help of the style of art from India. But it is known that the people from southern India founded an empier called Champā Nagara or Champā near south Vietnam. The art of this empire was very similar to the art of the Śrī-Vijaya period. From it we conclude that both art styles were Indian in origin and these were guided and inspired by the style of art from India. The people, who belonged to the Śrī-Vijaya kingdom, were the followers of the Mahāyāna Buddhist sect. In South-East Asia the Śrī-Vijaya art occupied an important place and it may be mentioned as one of the perfect early Buddhist arts in South-East Asia. In south Thailand it made a valuable contribution in the field of architecture and sculpture and it had its great influence in Chaiya sub-district of the Surathani province, the Songkha province, at the Ra-Not and Cha-Ting-Pra sub-districts of the Nakon Śī Tammarat province and at Ta-Kua-Pa and its remains were discovered in U-Tong of the Supannaburi province and at Sukhodaya of north and central Thailand. The Gupta, the post-Gupta, the Amarāvatī and the Pāla-Sena schools of art, architecture and sculpture gave their artistic inspiration and workmanship to it. Apart from Buddhist elements, several objects relating to Brāhmaṇism of this period were discovered in some provinces which belonged to south Thailand. It can be noted without any doubt that during the Śrī-Vijaya period Chaiya and Surathani became well-known as very prominent centres of the Śrī-Vijayan architecture. Several monuments were constructed during this period and they were dedicated to Mahāyāna Buddhism. There were *maṇḍapas* or cell-chambers for the Buddha images and the summit of structure was built in the form of *stūpa* with terraces at Pra Borom That Chaiya. Another famous *stūpa* was the Phra Mahathat *stūpa* at Chaiya. In the Buddha image the *uṣṇīṣa* was like that of the Dvāravatī art.

Between the eye-brow or middle of the forehead, there was a *ūrṇa*. In front of the *uṣṇīṣa* of the Buddha there was always a Bodhi leaf. Apart from all these things, there were the smoothed forehead, the arched and curved eyebrows, flat face and soft lips. The short robe covered the chest and the big robe came down up to the navel. In the pedestal large lotus petal with three small lotus petals were found. The hands and feet of the Buddha image were very mild and slim along with the body. In the artistic style of the Śrī-Vijayan Buddha image we get an idea about the advanced stage of the art of the Buddha images in the pre-Thai Buddhist art. During the Śrī-Vijaya period the statue of the *Bodhisattva* Avalokiteśvara, the supreme deity of Mahāyāna Buddhism was produced. The images of this god were found at Chaiya, in the Surathani province and in other regions of south Thailand. Their style indicate a very strong influence of the Gupta and the Pāla-Sena schools of art. One image of the Boddhisattva Avalokiteśvara was found in Chaiya and this was mentioned as the masterpiece of sculpture of this period. Its style traced the influence of the Pāla-Sena school of art. In this statue there was the cord or the sacred thread which was placed from the left shoulder and from there it reached below the waist. In other statues there were the crowns, the jewelled ornaments on the neck and arms and there were robes. In the north-eastern part of Thailand the Mahāyāna figure of Maitreya Bodhisattva was found. Under the Nāga image the Buddha images was discovered. This image was not in the attitude of meditation but in the attitude of defeating the Māra, the Evil. Many bronze images of the Śrī-Vijaya period were found. A bronze Buddha in the posture of Māravijaya or victory over Māra with an inscription in 1185 was found. There were the figures of Lord Śiva, Kubera, etc. Several terracotta elements and Buddhist votive tablets in slay were also found. They depicted the Mahāyāna themes and they were found with Sanskrit inscription. The Śrī-Vijaya school of art gradually disappeared from Thailand when the rule of the Śrī-Vijaya kingdom come to an end.

The Buddhist art of the Lopburi period (from the eleventh to the thirteenth centuries AD)

The art of the Lopburi period was influenced very strongly by the Khmer art.[9] A new style of early Buddhist art in the central, eastern and north-eastern parts of Thailand flourished and it had close affinity with the Khmer art of Cambodia (Kambuja). During the Lopburi period the Khmers expended their dominions over central Thailand in the valley of the Menam river and their chief centre was at Lopburi or Lavo. Not only the Khmers established themselves there politically, but they also remained very busy there for their artistic activities. For nearly three centuries the Khmers extended their dominions and also they contributed very much to the field of art, architecture and sculpture. Apart from the Khmers' dominions over the Menam valley of central Thailand, the ancient Mon kingdom of Dvāravatī and some regions of north Thailand were ruled by the Khmers. The Dvāravatī kingdom was divided by the Khmer king into two separate provinces which became the headquarters of the Khmer principalities. Sukhodaya became the capital of the northern province and Lavo or Lopburi was selected as the headquarter of southern province by the Khmer viceroy. From one of the Khmer incriptions as well as the remains of the Khmer temples with Buddhist elements found in several towns in central and north-eastern parts of modern Thai territory we learn that king Jayavarman VII (AD 1181-1220) of Cambodia at the beginning of the twelfth century AD played a great role to extend his political influence in the north-eastern and central parts of modern Thailand. Till the close of the twelfth century AD the Khmers maintained thier supremacy in central and north-eastern parts of modern Thailand. The Thai people who migrated from southern China moved towards the Indo-Chinese Peninsula after the end of the twelfth century AD and began to settle in the region which became known as Thailand. Then the Khmers were involved in wars with the Thais who defeated them and took the control of

9. *TAII*, p. 67.

these areas from the Khmers towards the close of the thirteenth century AD. The Thais established their independent kingdom which became known as Sukhodaya. In the middle of the fifteenth century AD the Khmers were totally defeated by the Thais and they lost their power and influence and in course of time Cambodia became a vassal state of Thailand. The Lopburi school of art flourished from the eleventh century AD and it continued to play its role up to the latter part of the thirteenth century AD. Most of the objects and monuments which belonged to the Lopburi school of art were dated from the eleventh century onwards and they were carved from stone and were made in bronze also. They belonged to the Mahāyāna school. The early Lopburi sculptors created many Mahāyāna Buddha images including. *Bodhisattva* Avalokiteśvara and Maitreya *bodhisattva*. The standing Avalokiteśvara were found with the *vitarka-mudrā* like Mon statues. The standing Maitreya *bodhisattvas* were also found. They had thin mustaches; there were no ornaments and there were very short robes. The chignon was high and full. Not only Lopburi, but also several areas in central and north-eastern parts of Thailand witnessed the rise and the development of art, architecture and sculpture of the Lopburi school of art and the Khmer art made a great influence upon this field. During this period both Brāhmaṇical as well as Buddhist monuments belonged to the Mahāyana sect were erected by the Lopburi artists in Thailand. The Prasad Hin or the Prasat Hin or the Stone temple at Lopburi was regarded as the outstanding monument of this period. The stone temple of this period at Pimai (the Nakon Ratchasima Province) reminded us of the Khmer architecture in Thailand. The carved lintels over the doors of the main sanctuary indicate that this temple was erected for the Mahāyāna sect and it was surrounded by a rectangular wall. According to archaeological sources, originally, this temple was constructed during the time of Jayavarman II who belonged to the ninth century AD. It had a rectangular form and had a one-side door entrance. The other three door entrances was small in size.

There was the portico in front of the main sanctuary. The Wat Maha-Tat and the Phra or Pra Prang Sam Yot (the temple of the three *stūpas* or the temple of three towers) were two important Khmer temples of Lopburi. The Wat Maha-Tat had a sanctuary-tower with a *maṇḍapa* which was attached to the whole in a walled enclosure. To the west of the main tower there was a *stūpa*. The base was octagonal in shape; the measuring of each face was 16 yards in length and there was a circumference of about 130 yards. The height was between 45 and 50 feet and by a stoop and a narrow stairway one was able to reach the summit. The *stūpa* was built of laterite blocks and there was no ornamentation. It was composed of a series of terraces leading up to the chamber above and a pinnacle surmounted it. The entrance gateway was formed of three enormous, round, equidistant laterite blocks and were surmounted by two more enormous blocks joined together and laid horizontally with pointed gable ends and a pinnacle showing a four-faced figure of either Brahmā or Civa (Śiva) appeared from the centre. A long, low wall of laterite blocks enclosed the temple grounds. There was a stone pillar round the capital and in front of this pillar was a small shrine which contained an image of the Buddha seated on the Nāga king. The temple of Maha-Tat there were hundred and eighty-nine different structures and a *stūpa* was in the centre. There was a huge Assembly Hall to the east of the building. The style of the Pra Prang Sam Yet showed that this waas a brāhmaṇa temple. The three towers of this temple indicated the Hindu Trinity of Brahmā, Śiva and Viṣṇu. Several bearded figures with clubs in their hands were found on the towers. The peculiar form of the Khmer architecture was found in three of these towers called the Prāng which appeared for the first time in Thailand. Afterwards, this style of architecture became very popular in Thailand and it was found in many religious buildings of Thailand. The Prāng shape had close affinity with the Prāng or tower of the Angkor Vat or the Bayon temple and other Khmer towers of the eleventh century AD. Stone or brick was used for the Prāng and it was decorated with jackfruit petal. Indian architecture made a great influence upon this style. The Indian *śikhara* can be mentioned as the prototype of the Khmer Prāng and the Thai architects, who got inspiration from this style, took the hlep of it for their architectural works. It may be noted here that the architectural buildings of Lopburi were not constructed on the high platform but usually they had a low basement of foundation. The temple had no window and the *stūpa* was there in the form of a square. In every square terrace there were the niches for keeping the standing Buddha images. There was the miniature small *stūpa* in the corner of each *stūpa*-terrace. In plan the town-planning of this period was square. The centre of the town space was there to construct the main and large temples. There were temples for the gods of Buddhism, Śaivism and Vaiṣṇavism. The town had gate-entrances and fort with same laterite enclosures. The style of town-planning was same like the town-planning of the city of Angkor Thom which was constructed by King Jayavarman VII of Cambodia and the Bayon temple was the central shrine in the centre of Angkor Thom. We can say that the town-planning of Lopburi was miniature replica of Angkor Thom. In bronze and stone there were several sculptures which were produced by the Lopburi school of art. Several styles and gestures of the *Bodhisattva* Avalokiteśvara, Maitreya *bodhisattva* and the Prajñāpāramitā, the Mahāyāna goddess, were found. The Lopburi art in style took its inspiration and guidance from the Śrī-Vijaya art, the Kamboja art and the Dvāravatī art. Several Buddha images in different *mudrās* were found. The Nāga motif was closely associated with the Buddha image in the Lopburi school of art and it was also mentioned as the important motif of super-structure of later Thai religious buildings such as the bet. The gable of the bet in Thailand had the triangular wooden framing which was decorated with the design of the Nāga. The seated Buddha image under the Nāga called Pra Nag Prok 'The Buddha seated under the head of the Nāga's head'. This was regarded as the most popular style of the

Buddha image of the Lopburi school of art. The decorated Buddha images with ornaments of this period were also found. The Lopburi artists also produced both Śiva, Viṣṇu and Viśvakarmā images. The Khmer Angkor Vat style and the Bayon style made their great influence upon them. Sandstone and bronze were used for these images. The style of the Buddha images of the Lobpuri school of art had a single image seated or standing on a pedestal or seated under the Nāga. The later part of the twelfth century AD saw the appearance of a group of the Buddhas on the same pedestal for the first time. Sometimes, the Buddha image under the Nāga in the middle, the image of the *Bodhisattva* Avalokiteśvara on the right and the Prajñāpāramitā, the Mahāyāna goddess, on the left. In the early style of the Buddha images of the Lopburi school of art there was the *uṣṇīṣa* on the skull in the shape of low glund but the shape had different forms they were the coil of shell or shape of small cone, the shape of crown with lotus flowers and petals. The styles of hair had the fold hair and the curls of hair and there were the head-dress and low crown of the Buddha's head. The Buddha had broad and square face and large and thick mouth and lips, very prominent eyebrows, long nose and square chin. In the case of the standing Buddha the whole body was covered by the robe and in the case of the seated Buddha image there was no robe in the right shoulder. The end of the robe came down up to the navel. The rim of a skirt-like lower robe was found in a very prominent position. The ear was very long. There were neck-bracelets, arm-bracelets and necklaces round the neck and the upper part of the Buddha's body. The form of lotus-flowers in both forms of up and down lotus-petal was made as the Buddha's pedestal. The petal of lotus was made in the form of rim line at the end of each petal. The Buddha image of the late Lopburi school of art had the head in oval shape, a line or rim at the mouth of the Buddha, the style of *uṣṇīṣa* in the form of up long-lotus petal and the small halo in the form of cone in the middle of lotus *uṣṇīṣa*. In the Buddha image with the Nāga the eyes were sunk in the face, and it had the beard and mustache. The skirt like lower robe had the prominent rim at the waist and ankle of the Buddha image. The image of this robe was arranged in the form of rectangular cloth and it was placed in front of girdle. The seven-headed uncrowned Nāga which was placed over the head of the Buddha was the halo of the Buddha. The coil of the Nāga's body had three parts. The Buddha had very sensitive face and his attitude looked like a kind-hearted person and had a smiling face. A status of the small Dhyānī Buddha which was placed in front of the *uṣṇīṣa* of the statue was found. The statue's head was square and the forehead was straight and the jaw was square and firm and the eyebrows were very straight. The nose was rather flattened but the mouth was long with full lips. The eyes were placed in a downward fashion. The hair never formed of spiral curls, but looked like scales divided by partition lines. The Buddhist votive tablets in terracotta and in metal were found. Several architectural elements on various votive tablets with the Buddha images or other Buddhist saints seated within a Prāng or a Khmer tower during this period were discovered. The stone portrait or King Jayavarman VII of Cambodia was found at the Pimai temple in Nakhon Ratchasima. The Lopburi school of art also produced brown glazed ceramics which in Thai became known as 'Khmer jars'.

The rise and growth of the Buddhist art in Thailand from the late thirteenth century to the present day

The Thais established themselves in Thailand and the art which was developed by the Thai people had close connection with Thailand's history and culture. The Thais gave their valuable services but also their artistic activities contributed very much to the development of this art which flourished from the beginning of the Thai history, i.e., from the latter part of the thirteenth century to the present day.[10] Some elements of art from the primitive Buddhist art of Thailand were adapted by

10. *Ibid.*, p. 70.

this real Thai art for its growth. But the Mon, the Khmer and the Śrī-Vijaya arts were regarded as the prototype of the new Thai Buddhist art. Thus, in the history of the real Thai Buddhist art five different schools of the Buddhist art in successive periods flourished and they were the Chiengsaen school of the Buddhist art, the Sukhodaya school of the Buddhist art, the U-Tong school of the Buddhist art, the Ayudhyā or the Ayuthia school of the Buddhist art and the Bangkok school of the Buddhist art in Thailand. The first three Pre-Thai Buddhist schools of art which flourished in the Dvāravatī, the Śrī-Vijaya and the Lopburi periods played their roles in the development of the new Thai Buddhist art. The real Thai Buddhist art made a great change in their artistic activities, and it moved independently in sculptural and architectural fields. The Thais erected new styles of architectural buildings which were dedicated by them to the Hīnayāna sect. The Pra *chedi*, the Bot and *vihāra*, the Phra Prāng, the Mondop and the Prasat were mentioned as the principal religious buildings in Thailand. The *kuṭi*, the Ho-trai, the Sala Kan Parian, the Salas and the Ho Rakhang were other structures of Thailand. The Wat or monastery was always rectangular and in size it was of greater length than width. The enclosure walls were about 3 ft thick and were high from about 12 to 14 ft. There was the enclosing wall with its gateways in every wat. The Thai gateways had a variety of designs and each Wat had its own architectural style. The Bot was one type of Thai religious building and it was like an Indian *caitya* hall where the Buddhist monks used to go to offer their prayers. It had a rectangular plan and a large gilded seated Buddha image in stucco or in bronze was kept upon a high pedestal at its end. It had sloping roofs which were covered with glazed files in colour. Originally, the idea of the Bot came from the old Indonesian-Thai house of thatchid material. The Cho-Fa (bunch of sky) or the horn-like finial was found at both ends of the ridge of each roof of the religious or royal building. Most probably, it got its idea from the horned-mask which kept in the same point of the buildings for magic and animistic purposes. This type of thing was very popular in Indonesia and other parts of the Pacific Islands. The Thai Bot or temple had its roof and it was erected over a basement which was about 50 cm. to 1.50 m. high. It had some gate-like openings and it had one, two or three front or rear doors on both sides. It had porches in front and rear or porches and pillars around it. Its interior was decorated with a simple ample nave or a nave and two aisles with pillars. The doors and windows of the Thai Bot had decorations with ornamental flames in stucco and also with glass mosaic. The panels of the windows and doors were decorated beautifully outside with gilded lacquor ornaments but the interiors were painted in vivid colours with mythical figure of guardians. In Thailand there were some Bots which had ornaments in inlaid mother of pearl and the style of the ornaments was very elaborate. The pillars of the interior and the exterior of the Bot were octagonal of round and their capitals were in the form of lotus flowers. There was no abacus in the pillar's capital. The Bot had eight Somas (Sima) which were placed over some basement. In the Thai Bot there was the huge Buddha image. The interior corner-end of the Bot had large gilded sitting Buddha image either in bronze or in stucco. The walls of some Bots were plain, but the walls of many Bots were decorated with paintings. The window-panels externally had decoration with lacquor-work which in Thai called Loi Rot Nam. The Tha *vihāra* was constructed in the centre of the courtyard which was enclosed by a gallery and there were boundary-walls and there were square pillars to support the roof. Alnog the gallery there were many Buddha images which were made in bronze or in stucco. There were four or more gateways in the Thai *vihāra* and glazed tiles in bright colours were used to cover the roof of the galleries and gateways and white colour was always used to paint the walls. In Thailand the *stūpa* became known as the Chedi or the Phra Chedi. In one Wat or monastery there was one Chedi of a large size or there were several Chedis of various sizes. The meaning of the word Phra was 'exalted' and it took its derivation from the Sanskrit *vara*. The name Chedi was the Thai equivalent of the Pāli *cetiya* and the Sanskrit *caitya*. This kind of monument was constructed in order to keep the ashes of the dead. In Thailand the Phra Chedi was meant for a sacred monument or a reliquary. A Thai Phra Chedi had four parts : the plinth, the dome-shaped structure called the 'bell', the platform and the spire. The *aṇḍa* or round tumulus which surrounded the balustrade in the *stūpa* of Sāñcī in India was the bell or dome-shaped structure of the Thai Chedi. After sometime Thailand witnessed a rectangular form, with or without reduced angles or corners and other decorations in place of the bell or dome-shaped structure. Above the bell or dome-shaped structure, at the 'neck of the bell' there was a small quadrangular platform and in Thailand it became known as Banlang (in Pāli, *pallaṅka*) with a number of colonnades above it. The spire was placed above the platform. The lower part of this latter section had circles which were arranged one upon the other and they became known in Thailand as Plong Chanai. Sometimes the circles took the shape of lotus flowers which became known in Thailand as the Bua Klum and the meaning was lotus clusters. The Pli or plantain bud was placed above the circle. Then the Pli had the upper and lower divisions with a round ball in between. There was another round ball at the highest point of the upper Pli and in Thailand it became known as Yadnam-Khang or dew-drop. Another structure of the Phra Chedi was the Hom which was

> a number of flat pieces with pointed top arranged round the axis of spire of sturcture.

Its upper part went up to three diminishing tiers of lotus-clusters. Most probably, these pointed tops or hem of these flat pieces took their derivation from the Sanskrit word *hema* meaning gold or *hima* meaning snow. In the Phra Chedi of the northern type there was a cubical solid mass with four niches at its sides and there were images of the Buddha in high relief or round relief. This cubical mass had one or more storeys and there was the domed *stūpa* at the crown. When the *stūpa* was hollow, then one of the niches took the shape of the entrance door. In the north of Thailand there was another type of the Phra Chedi which had "many receding cubical storeys enriched with horizontal rows of standing Buddha images in high relief". The Phra Prāng was mentioned as the second type of the Thai *stūpa*. It took its origin from the corner tower of the Khmer temple and in course of time it became well-known as a new form of the Thai *stūpa*. It was square in plan and domical in roofing. It appeared from a large base to an elliptical shape and its outline was very beautiful. It had three niches and one entrance door. There were images of the Buddha in its inner part. It had four cells. One was the small chapel and the other three had the images of the Buddha. The end of the seventeenth century AD onwards witnessed the development stage of the Thai Phra Prāng. The Thai Mondop looked like the *maṇḍapa* of the Indian temples. Most probably, it took its idea from the *moṇḍapas* of Indian temples. It was the planned square cubical structure and there were several pillars around it. Its structure was a curved pyramidal mass which was formed by many low domical roofs and had a slendour pinnacle as finial which became known as Yot in Thailand. Each layer of the roof had its decorations with the ornaments and these were known in Thailand as Song Ben Talong. The Mondop's wooden superstructure was always beautifully decorated with wooden carvings gilded and enriched with glass mosaic and there were two or three different coloured glasses with designs. It used to enshrine holy Buddhist objects. Sometimes it was mentioned as a library and a store-room for objects for the purpose of religious ceremonies. The Pra Sat or castle was the Thai building which was used for religious or secular purposes. This structure was composed of a square sanctuary with its domical *śikhara* and there were the four porch-like ante-chambers. One form of timber superstructure of the Thai Pra Sat kept the traditional *śikhara* of Hindu temple at the finial of the roofs. The other superstructure maintained the same form and style and same ornaments as the forms of the Mondop. It was used for the royal throne hall and for some venerated objects. The Ho Trai was the Thai architectural building which served as the library for the Buddhist sacred books. It had a basement which was constructed with brick but the wood was used in order to build the room. There were some Ho Trais which had the ground rooms with bricks and wooden rooms were constructed over the ground rooms. There was no interior decoration in them and there were paintings on the walls, windows and door panels of some of them. They were constructed by three parallel attached rooms and watch room had its proper roof. The slopes of the central room were joined by the inner sides of the roofs of the right and left rooms and two gutters received the water of the four slopes. Two or three rooms were constructed but they were attached to each other and their roofs had no connection with each other. The Sala was an open pavilion. It was rectangular in plan. In order to support the architrave over which the roof was placed, four wooden or brick pillars were used for its construction. Generally, the Salas had no pyramidal superstructure, but the Salas at the royal summer residence of Bang Pa In Palace near Bangkok, had the pyramidal roof. They were erected for secular purpose, and they were constructed along roads or canals, where people used to go there for taking rest. The Ho Rakhang was found in every Wat or monastery in Thailand. Its roof was covered with a coat of plaster of with glazed tiles. It was built of brick and had a high platform with steps in one or four sides. There was a four-pillared pyramidal roofed small building over this platform. Inside there was the ball to announce the time in the morning or evening. Wood was also used to construct its four pillars and there was a small temple on the top. The Kuti or the Sangarama was found in every Wat or monastery. It was used for the residence of the Buddhist monks only. It had several buildings or a long building with many cells in a row for the purpose of their residence.

Sometimes, in front of it, there was a varandah. A wall or a fence or a canal was there it separate it from the monastery or the Wat.

Cambodia invaded Thailand in the tenth century AD and this was the end of the Dvāravatī period. Then the Khmers modified the art styles in their own way and the Khmer styles continued to play a role in Thailand's art world for sometime. Then an independent Thai kingdom was established at Sukhodaya in AD 1240 and it remained in power up to AD 1438. The rise of the Sukhodaya-style Buddha, the most distinctive of Thai images, took place in Thailand in the thirteenth century AD and it became very popular as Thailand's best-known style. There were two types — one image was the seated Buddha and the other was the walking Buddha or the Buddha in walking style. The seated Buddha in the *māravijaya* pose was found first in Dvāravatī. But in Sukhodaya it was in a more distinctive Thai manner,

> with greater stylisation of the hands and proportions of the body and the addition of the flame ushnisha on top of the head. A remarkable image, which combines Thai ethnic features with yogic tranquillity and inner power, it records the auspicious moment in a unifield blend of grace and abstraction. The extended proportions and high level of abstraction derive from Indian written descriptions of the Buddha, in similes that describe the physical forms of the gods by relating the various parts of the human body to chracteristic aspects of nature. . . . The Sukhothai Buddha is the most abstract of the image of the Buddha, a tribute to the Thai ability to blend religious meaning and literary descriptions with a sophisticated artistic sensibility to produce a remarkable and original creation of transcendent spirituality in himan form.

The walking Buddha of Sukhodaya was made beautifully and it showed "the delicacy and grace of the dance rather than the typically iconic frontality of most Buddha images". During the Myanmarese wars nearly all Thai architecture was destroyed but several *stūpas* were reconstructed in Ayuthia and this throws flood of light on the stylistic directions that maintained throughout late Thai art. Now-a-days, the Thais mention the lotus bud spire and say that this was the contribution of the Sukhodaya builders. The Khmer tower or Prāng, a gently curved shape which ended in a point, but it had no connection with the main Thai tradition. When the Myanmarese attacked and destroyed Ayuthia in AD 1767, then Buddhist architecture of Thailand depended mainly on more decorative elements, especially exquisite surface patterns. When Bangkok became capital of Thailand, then Chinese influence was felt very much and there apperead a combination of delicacy and surface decoration in wood in art and architecture of Thailand. Although there were Chinese and Islamic elements, yet the style of Thai paintings maintained a distinctly Thai flavour in their delicate, linear drawing, bright colours, textile patterns and ethnic features. These took place after the thirteenth century AD. There was a great differences from Indian models in their greater size.

According to H. G. Quaritch Wales,[11] from AD 550 until about AD 1000 central Thailand became well known as the Dvāravatī kingdom. From the remains discovered in this region we learn that they belonged to the Hīnayāna Buddhist art. They were closely related to the Gupta or Post-Gupta tradition. From Lopburi, Nakon Pathom and P'ong Tuk and from other regions round the head of the Gulf of Siam, several archaeological remains were discovered and they were *stūpa* bases and monastic platforms like those of Anurādhapura in Sri Lanka, architectural fragments ornamented with simple motifs of the Gupta style, sculptured panels with the Buddha's first sermon, votive tablets, 'Wheels of the Law' and stone images of the Buddha, either standing, with the robe which covered both shoulders in north

---

11. *TMGI*, p. 40.

Indian fashion or the seated Buddha in the European posture or 'turning the Wheel of the Law.' According to P. Dupont, the Dvāravatī standing Buddha took shape from Indian prototypes in the sixth century AD. It became famous for its following features —

> joined eyebrows, both forearms extended forwards with hands in the same mudra and skirt or robe formerly held- one hand now suppressed.

All these features gave the image complete symmetry. Early bronze figures of the Dvāravatī period were not at all impressive. They were small in size. But G. Ceedés mentions one rather larger than usual (16.5 inches high). It was a standing figure and tis both hands were in the gesture of instruction and as a work of art it had no value. From the bronze figure of the Dvāravatī artists it is clear that during the Dvāravatī period the artists were unable to show thier artistic skill in creating beautiful bronze images and from this it can be said that it was in a very elementary stage.

The development of Buddhist sculpture in Thailand

The dress of the Buddha images and of other Buddhist divinities as well as the monastic robe were regarded as the main features of the developed stage of the Thai sculpture.[12] The robe was used to cover both shoulders or was used in such a way to leave the right shoulder expressed. There were four postures — walking, standing, sitting and reclining. If the Buddha was in the sitting posture, then the legs of the Buddha was kept in three different ways. The ordinary pose of a person sitting in a chair was mentioned as the European fashion (*paralambanāsana*). The other was the 'Hero' posture (*vīrāsana*) with legs folded and one leg was kept on the top of the other. The other was the adamantine posture (*vajrāsana*) with the legs crossed in such a

---

12. *TAII*, p. 76.

way that each foot took rest on the opposite thigh and the soles turned upward. The most common hand positions for standing or walking figure of the Buddha of Thai Buddhist sculpture in its developed stage were *abhaya-mudrā* or dispelling fear 'with the palm of hand forward and the fingers pointing upward' and *vitarka-mudrā* or giving instruction 'which was similar but with the thumb and forefinger joined'. For the seated Buddha image, the position of meditation became very popular and this meditation *mudrā* became known as *samādhi* or *jñāna*, both hands were placed in the lap and palms were kept upward. The other was the *bhūmi-sparśa mudrā*, 'calling the Earth to witness'. These features were developed in the field of sculpture of Thailand.

A note on the style, technique, characteristics and subject-matter of the Thai paintings

During the first three pre-Thai periods of Dvāravatī, Śrī-Vijaya and Lopburi, painting was not available much in Thailand. But in the real Thai Buddhist art of the period, not only art, architecture and sculpture developed, but the Thai painters also took active part to produce their activities in the field of painting. In order to use painting for religious purposes and to decorate the Bets, *vihāras* and temples, the Thai painters painted their paintings in Thailand. In this country there were several different forms of paintings. The dry fresco mural found in one or more of the buildings was regarded as the most important type. Another type of painting was introduced in Thailand and this was a long cloth banner and Khoi paper. On special occasion these were found in the monasteries. An important category of the Thai paintings was the manuscript—illustrations and their materials were the long and narrow palm leaf books. Not only from palm-leaf but also from Khoi paper in its one continuous sheet folded like an accordien the manuscript was taken. This type of painting was available before the Bangkok period. In the middle of the page it had a large illustration and sometimes it covered the double unfolded section. During the Bangkok period the manuscript of Khoi paper had one or two smaller illustrations at the end of the page with the text between them. They were religious works no doubt, but several manuscripts discussed treatises on the real or legendary worlds of human beings and animals and other secular texts. Thus, the above-mentioned facts traces the important roles played by the mural wall-painting, the painting on cloth and the manuscript painting on Khoi paper in the development of the Thai paintings. In the earliest period the remains of the paintings were very few in number but, even then, they sruvived. Most probably, they were paintings of the Dvāravatī period, which had close connection with the paintings in India and in Sri Lanka. Some remains of the paintings of the Śrī-Vijaya period in southern Thailand were found. Their styles indicate that they were an admixture of the Sri Lankan and Śrī-Vijaya styles of painting. For technical purpose the Thai painters made aprearance with some unusual painting materials. For the mural painting they generally prepared the wall of the Bot, *vihāra* and other religious buildings by washing it several times with water and ki-lok leaves were given in it to remove any trace of salt.[13] Then white chalk mixed with a binder of tamarind seeds was boiled and then a coating of plaster was applied. Cloth and paper were used for a thin application of the same mixture. From the beginning of the eighteenth century the paints were imported from China in powder form. The duller and more limited colours of the earliest painting were local pigments and for the preliminary outline the red ochre was always used. A tree gum named *ma-kwit* in Thai language was mixed with the points and another gum from *madua* tree was also used as a glue for the gold leaf. The paint was applied to the dry paster. This cannot be mentioned as a true fresco technique. The Thai painters used brushes made of tree roots and bark with silver handles. The brush of the *lamjiek* root, the brush of the *gradangaga* flower, etc., were used by the Thai artists and before using them they

13. *TAII*, p. 78.

kept these brushes very much in water to make them pliable. In Thailand there were brushes which were made of cow's hair. For a fine work the Thai paintings used special brushes which were made of hair taken from the inner part of a cow's ear. Owing to the wooden brushes they painted their works in a very nice way. The colours, which were taken from earth and earth powder as well as colours from different plants, were used by the Thai painters in their paintings. Nam Ya or painted water was mixed with gum or paste. The cocount shell of the pottery bowl was used as the utensil for the mixture of gum and colour. Yellow colour taken from the gum of a plant, red colour taken from the red ochre earth from the cliff or the road, white colour taken from white earth-powder, green colour taken from green-stone, blue colour taken from the boiled leavers of Cram tree and the black colour taken from the lamp black were used in the Thai paintings. In these paintings the religious subjects and stories, scenes from the life of the Buddha and the narrative story of Buddhist divinity called the Jātaka stories (Chadok in Thai) were able to occupy important places as subject-matters of the Thai painters. The Thai painting as well as the Khon or classical Thai dramatic art took their subject-matters from the stories of the *Rāmāyaṇa*, called the *Ramakien* in Thailand. Landscape, trees, citadels, palaces and other structures as also scenes of celestial and other mythological beings — Yakṣas, Yakṣiṇīs, *deva*, goddess, Kinnara, etc., were other subjects of the Thai paintings. These paintings were similar to the paintings found at the Ajantā cave in India and the latter was regarded as the prototype of the Thai paintings. Thailand's painters also showed their interest in groups on arhcitectural structures, human and animal figures wandering amidst forests and groves which depicted the very Thai life in its natural order. They painted the human fugures on a small scale, about 25-30 cm. in hight. Buddhism also played a great role as the subject of these paintings. In Thailand's paintings human figures according to their ranks were represented by three kinds of style. The first style illustrated royal and celestial beings and in classic style they were painted. Several Thai artists tried their best to focus all their talents. These figures' dresses, crowns and jewellery were the same as those were used by the royal people of the past. The dignitaries and other royal attendants belonged to the second type. They were painted by the Thai artists according to thier ranks. In the third type they painted the common people in a very realistic style. The artistic value of these paintings contributed very much to the field of painting of Thailand for its development. It gave an idea about Thailand's social, religious and cultural life. The style and technique of the Thai painting possessed the basic elements of all Asian paintings. A combination of mass and line was an important factor for the composition of the Thai painting. The figures were drawn first and then colours were used in them. The details and ornaments were introduced in a way which was similar to the Indian and early Islamic technique. The figures, furnitures, chariots, etc., were drawn in the same fashion but a group of rocks or a clump of flowers gave an indication about the influence of the Chinese people in the style.

Thailand's Buddhist art of the Chiengsaen period

North Thailand's art began from the Chiengsaen school of art, i.e., from the latter part of the eleventh century and it continued to flourish up to the fifteenth century AD. The Thai people who moved southwards from their ancient home in south China established their kingdom in the northern region of Thailand. It became known as Chiengsaen and also as the Lan-na-thai kingdom. The monuments and antiquities of this period belonged to the Chiengsaen school of art. Chiengsaen was the name of an ancient town of Thailand. The location of the town was on the right bank of the Mekong river in the vicinity of modern Chiengsaen province of north Thailand.[14] Afterwards, Chiengsaen became one of the sub-districts of the Chiengsaen province.

14. *TAII*, p. 80.

Thailand's Buddhist art which took its origin in this ancient town later flourished in the whole region of the ancient kingdom of Lan-na-thai or Yonok. This new school of art was able to extend its influence in Chiengmai, Chiengrai, Lamphun and Lamphang. It took its firm root in the northern part of Thailand in the kingdom of Lan-na-thai and its capital was the city of Chiengsaen. Gradually, it extended its influence in the valley of the Mekong river up to the region which is now known as the kingdom of Laos and also in the north-eastern part of Thailand. In the early centuries of the Christian era the Thais took shelter in the valley of the Menam river and absorbed the culture of the Mon-Khmer races at that time when they settled in several regions of modern Thailand. Afterwards, they established themselves into several Thai areas and all these states came under the control of their own people. After sometime, the independent Thai kingdom of Lan-na-thai or Yonok was established by a new Thai chief who was King Prohm of the Singapore dynasty. His father was king Kuñjaraj and he became well-known in Thailand's political history as the first powerful Thai ruler. Not only the dominions but also the sezerainty of the Khmers in north Thailand were also destroyed by him. Under his able leadership his kingdom's border was extended from the Laos kingdom to Luang Prabang and several other regions. His new capital was at Chaiprakarn (now a district in the province of Chiengrai, north Thailand). Then King Mengrai (AD 1258-1237) ascended the throne after him. Under his patronage the Chiengsaen school of art developed in Thailand. Not only the Myanmarese art and culture but also Indian Buddhist art of the Pāla period made an influence upon it. Their artistic activities and workmanship helped the artists of this school to develop their art. The Pāla rulers of Bihar and Bengal extended their political and cultural influence in Japan, China, Korea, Java, Sumatra, Malay Peninsula, Myanmar and north Thailand. They patronised the Tantric or the Vajrayāna Mahāyāna sect of Buddhism and they took active part to propagate this form of Buddhism of several places of Far East and South-

East Asia. The inscriptional evidence of the Nalanda Copper Plate of Devapāla, the Pāla King, traces that through Java the Chiengsaen school of art got the influence of the Pāla art from India. At that time a close cultural relation was established between Devapāla, the Pāla king and the Śailendra king, Bālaputra Deva of Java or modern Indonesia. Most probably, from this time this island and other neighbouring regions were not only influenced by the Pāla art and culture but the Malay Peninsula, southern Thailand and the Lan-na-thai kingdom of north Thailand were able to receive the artistic influence of the Pāla art. This art from Java arrived in south and north of Thailand and the monuments and antiquities of several regions in south of Thailand gave an indication of the influence of the Pāla art. Some sculptures of Nakon Śī-Thammarat of South Thailand reminded that both the Pāla and Khmer art made a great influence upon them. Some had pure Khmer influence but the influence of the Pāla art was not found in others. King Aniruddha or Anuruddha, the Pagan ruler of north Myanmar, extended his political influence in north Thailand and Myanmar at that time received the Pāla school of the Tantric Mahāyāna art. Thus, it indicated that from north Myanmar the Pāla influence arrived in Chiengsaen of north Thailand. Archaeological evidence gave an idea about the influence of the Pāla art on the Myanmarese art. The Buddha images became quite well-known and popular in Pagan, king Aniruddha's capital. These Buddha images in many ways were influenced by the Pāla-Buddha images. Thus, the Myanmarese sculptures of the early Buddha images were closely related to the early Buddha images of the Buddhist art of the Chiengsaen school of north Thailand. Most probably, through the activities of the Buddhist missionaries under the patronage of the Pāla rulers, the Pāla Buddhist art and culture reached upper Myanmar and north of Thailand was invaded by King Aniruddha of Pagan in the middle of the eleventh century AD. Thus, the Mahāyāna sect, the Myanmarese art and the Pāla art flourished in these regions for sometime. It is very probable that the Pāla art which made a great influence upon the artistic activities of the Myanmarese art played a great role in the north of Thailand for the development of its artistic activities in the field of art. Some scholars say that it came through the ancient land-route which was used by the Indian settlors to go to various countries of South-East Asia. The Chiengsaen style of architecture and sculpture flourished after the foundation of the town of Chiengmai by King Mengrai in AD 1297. The Wat Chot Yot (Seven-spired Temple) at Chiengmai was erected in imitation of the Mahāvihāra or the Mahābodhi Temple at Pagan in upper Myanmar. This Pagan temple was constructed in the beginning of the thieteenth centurty AD by the Myanmarese king Htilominle, who was Aniruddha's successor. This temple was built in imitation of the Mahābodhi Vihāra at Bodh-Gayā in Bihar in India. Thus, from it we conclude that there existed a close religious ties not only between India during the time of the Pālas and Myanmar but also Thailand established its link with them. The Buddhist art of the Chiengsaen school of Thailand came very close with the artistic activities of these countries.

In the Chiengsaen style of architecture a *chedi* or a *stūpa* had a large and high dome or body of structure. Above the body of temple decorated by bell-shaped dome of *stūpa*, there were square-shaped corners, and in front of the structure there was the arch or bower at the basement. The body of structure was exactly like the body of a bet or a *vihāra* in the style of the Chiengsaen school. There were the two or three storeyed roofs of structure which separated the body of a bet or a *vihāra* in two parts and there was no window. There was the uppermost roof which was decorated by the Cho-Fa or decorative designs. These designs in the form of the Nāga head were made of stucco. The lower part of these designs which was placed on the tomost of the roof was known as Bai Raka in Thai. The pediment of monument was made in the form of undecorated design. There were timber tiles on the roof of structure and in front of the structure there was no gallery or covered roof. A coiling body and a raised hood of the Nāga head were the designs of the staircase of a temple or a bet. There was no coiling inside the body of structure and there was the inner wooden structure. The row of pillars was arranged on both sides of the structure. In order to support the beam the row of pillars was arranged on both sides of the structure. In northern Thai language the Mondop of the Chiengsaen style of architecture became known as the Ku which had successive superimpesed storey-roofs. It was built in order to keep a Buddha image. In Chiengsaen's architectural building at the Wat Pra Yuen (monastery of the Standing Buddha) in the provinced of Chiengmai in northern Thailand the Myanmarese art of architecture was found. It was built in the imitation of the structure of the Ānanda temple in Pagan in upper Myanmar. It had four niches in four directions and the standing Buddha images were kept in the niches. According to its characteristics, the sculpture of the Buddha image was divided into two types — the early Buddha image and the late Chiengsaen or the Chiengmai style. The Pāla school of sculpture from India played a great role in the early period and the late period witnessed the importance and the influence of the Buddhist art and sculpture of the Sukhodaya period which prospered from the thirteenth to the fourteenth centuries AD in north and central Thailand. The style of the Buddha image of the early Chiengsaen school took its sculptural features from the image of the Pāla school of India. The early Chiengsaen style called the lion type had close resemblance with the Pāla sculpture. It produced the Buddha images in black stone slabs carved in half relief as the lion of the Śākyas. The Buddha's body was fat and its shape was round and not only his head was round but also his face was round and short. The protuberance or Ketumala on the head was in the style of lotus-bud (*uṣṇīṣa*). The eyes were half-closed, the lips and eye-brows were very prominent and had a sensitive nose. The pedestal of the Buddha image was made in the style of a lotus-pedestal. The petals of the lotus were large and flat in size and there were also lotus petals. The robe was arranged in such a way that there was no robe on the right nipple and the short upper fold of robe came down over the left shoulder and it ended above the left nipple. The hair was arranged in a style of spiral curls. The Ketumala in the fashion of knob-like took its rise "from the centre of the head in lotus-bud covered with similar curls". The legs of the Buddha were crossed. The Thais mentioned the *bhūmi-sparśa-mudrā* of this image as Sa dung Mara or also as Māra Vijaya *mudrā* which showed that the right hand was kept over the foreleg, the arrangement of the finger was in the fashion of pointing downward to the north and the left hand was kept on the lap of crossed legs. Several of the early Chiengsaen Buddha images had an ornamentation which no doubt served as their background. The Sukhodaya style of art made its great influence upon the Buddha images of the later Chiengsaen school which was regarded as cotemporary with the farmer. The Buddha images of the later Chiengsaen school had smaller spiral curls of the hair, with the parting line round the topknot. Other features of the Buddha images were the same as was referred to in the early group. But the robe of the Buddha images after keeping the right nipple bare came down over the left shoulder and the style of its arrangement was much lower than in the Buddha image of the early Chiengsaen school. The posture of the legs of the latter school was not crossed like the style of the early group. The right foreleg was kept on the left one and in Thai it was known as Samadhi Rab and this gave an indication of the influence of the Sukhodaya art. In the style of flickering fame the *uṣṇiṣa* was kept on the top of the protuberance of the Buddha's head and it never arranged in the style of the lotus-bud as was found in the early Chiengsaen school. In the Chiengsaen period there were many seated Buddha images but very few images of the standing Buddha were found during this period . Metal and stucco were used as materials for this purpose. Stone was not used very much but bronze images belonged to this period were found. About nine different type of *mudrā*s of the Buddha images were available in this period. Crowned

Buddha images of the later Chiengsaen style were not discovered. Many Budha images of this period were carved from crystal and semi-precious stones. Many Buddhist votive tablets in metal in the Māra Vijaya *mudrā* were found and they belonged to the period. Other images of the Brāhmaṇical delitise as well as portraits of laymen of this period were discovered. During the later Chiengsaen period some ceramic productions were found at Wieng Kalong Kiln in the district of Wieng Pa Pao, Chiengrai and at San Kampaeng in the province of Chiengmai. In the Chiengsaen period the coinage in the Lan-na-thai kingdom and Langchang witnessed the beginning of the first Thai coinage which was used as currency in the Thai Market. These coins were slender and long, some coins were like fish and some coins had the shape of a ship. These coins were used in the Lan-na-thai kingdom, Luang Prabang, Vientiane and in several towns of the north-eastern region of Thailand. The paintings of the Chiengsaen period were greatly influenced by the Myanmarese paintings. The drawing of the northern murals was less sensitive and the colour was not very bright and the general effect was 'dry and crisp'. At the Wat Pra Sing in the province of Chiengmai a wall mural painting was found and this episode was from the Sang Thong, which was a classic of Thai literature. In the murals there were figures of royal people in traditional Thai royal dresses. There were also other paintings of legal life and these were discovered in Payao in the province of Chiengrai of north Thailand. The earliest painting on cloth was found at Amphur or sub-district, near Chiengmai. This painting was a long banner of cloth and its measurement was about 7' by 4½' and it was folded into clay jar and was kept in the crypt of the Chedi Wat Dok-ngoen (Silver Flower). In this painting the Buddha was descending from heaven in a shower of flower, jewellery and silver nuggets and musicians from heaven, several disciples, royal people and several other people were with him. It belonged to the fifteenth century AD.

Thailand's Buddhist art of the Sukhodaya period (from the thirteenth to the fifteenth centuries AD)

The first powerful Thai kingdom was Sukhodaya and its capital also became known as Sukhodaya or Sukhothai (happiness of the Thais). The Sukhodaya period was regarded as the golden age of Thailand. The cultural activities prospered during this period. Not only Buddhism flourished but also the Buddhist art developed very much. Sukhodaya became an important province of upper central part of modern Thailand. The period of the Sukhodaya kingdom (AD 1238-1439) witnessed the introduction of the Theravāda sect from Sri Lnaka. In Thai it became known as the Lankavong Nikāya or the sect. The Lankavong at the Hīnayāna sect of Buddhism from Sri Lanka was first introduced in this kingdom and it still remains as the state religion of Thailand. The Thai artists of the Sukhodaya period in their artistic activities were greatly influenced by Sri Lanka's Buddhist art. The Lankavong Theravāda sect of Buddhism was regarded as the main source for the construction of several Buddhist monuments in the Sukhodaya period. They were wat or monastery, *vihāras*, temples, *stūpas* or Chedi Phra Prāng, bot, etc., The architectural designs from Sri Lanka as well as the architectural features of the early Thai Buddhist art, the Khmer art of Lopburi and the Śrī Vijaya art of the southern Thailand made their great influence upon them. One can see octagonal-based Mon monuments *chedis* whose bases have the support of Sri Lankan elephants and thick Khmer Prāngs in brick and stucco but there is no stone in it.

> Sukhothai's own architects, however, were responsible for the lotus bud filiables on the slendor chedis which are the hallmark of Sukhothai architecture.

The original Sukhodaya *chedi* had three superimposed rectangular pedestals which supported a small and redented central part on the top of which was a filial in the design of a lotus-bud (Phum-Kha-Bin in Thai language).[15] These types of *chedis* were found at the Wat Mahatat in the old town of Sukhodaya and at the Wat Chedi Chot Thaew (the seven-rows of *stūpa*) in the town of Si Satchanalai in Thailand. There was a great controversy relating to the origin of this style of the Sukhodaya *stūpa*. According to scholars, it was the pure Thai workmanship but others mentioned that other countries made their influence upon this style. Prince Damrong Rajanubhab, a great Thai scholar, on the basis of the figure of an ancient Chinese *stūpa*, stated that there was a great similarity in style between this ancient Chinese *stūpa* and the original Sukhodaya *chedi*. King Intradit, Sukhodaya's founder, began the Wat Mahathat (Great Relic Wat) and Ram Khamhaeng continued it and king Lu Thai in AD 1345 completed it. There were about 200 *chedis* and 10 *vihāras* and also other numerous structures. In it the Śrī-Vijayan and Sri Lankan styles were found. The Sukhodaya *chedi* or *stūpa* was a copy of ancient Chinese *stūpa*. Most probably, this style was introduced by king Ramakhamheng,[16] who visited China and was very much impressed by the style and design of the Chinese *stūpa* and the art of ceramic were in China. He was so much happy with the artistic styles, activities and workmanship of China that not only he took keen interest in them but also he played a great role for their introduction in his country. Thus, the original style of the *stūpa* in Thailand first took its imitation from the original Chinese source, but, afterwards, this was influenced by the style and artistic activities of the Thai artists who brougtht its perfection and erected it in thier own way. The round *stūpa* indicated an influence of Sri Lanka's architecture which took its root in the Sukhodaya period when the Lankavong Theravāda Buddhist sect began to prosper in the kingdom of Sukhodaya. In this *stūpa* there was a square or rectangular basement. It had alms bowl-shaped dome or *aṇḍa*,

15. *TAII*, p. 85.
16. *Ibid.*

the square box or banlang in Thai and there was the successive superimposed spire above the square box. Practically, this style very much imitated the style and architecture of the Thupārāma *stūpa* of Anurādhapura in Sri Lanka. The *stūpa* at the Chedi Wat Chang Lom followed the same style. The *stūpa* was round in plan with beautiful decoration at the basement in the style of basement which was surrounded by rows of half-body and head of elephant caryatids.[17] In it there were the rectangular basement, the lotus pedestal, the bell-shaped dome, the platform or banglang above the dome, the Pleng Chanai or circles which were imposed one upon the other and the spire of *stūpa* or the *pli* (plantain-bud). King Rama Khamheng erected this *stūpa* because he wanted to keep the Sri Lankan art in his kingdom. The style of the Śrī-Vijaya *stūpa* was found in the Sukhodaya period. It had a rectangular basement which was decorated by the niches to keep the Buddha image with the upper portion of tall rectangular basement and this was crowned with a round *stūpa* and was srrounded by the smaller *stūpa* of the same type at the four corners. The lotus-bud *chedi* was used in several other monuments which were erected by King Lu Thai. Other important wats with lotus-bud *chedis* were the Wat Trapang Ngaen (Silver Pond Wat) and the Wat Om Rob in Sukhodaya, the Wat Chedi Chet Thaew and the Wat Suan Kaew Utayan Noi in Si Satchanalai and the Wat Wang Phra That near Kamphaeng Phet and Chiang Moi's Suan Dok in the Lanna kingdom. The Phra Prāng or a new type of Thai *stūpa* was found at the Wat Pra Śrī-Ratana Mahathat Chalieng in the city of Si Satchanalai in Thailand.[18] This type of *stūpa* in the Ayudhyā period was restored. Its whole structure was constructed on the single basement. Its portico or the front porch was erected by the side of structure and it had no lintel or door-jambs and in it the niches were built to keep the walking Buddha image. The *vihāra* of this

17. *TAII.*
18. *Ibid.*

period was larger in size than the bet or the ubeseth and there were no large windows in it, and the walls were decorated with small rectangular cavities. The architecture and sculpture of the Buddhist monuments of the Polonnaruva period in Sri Lanka made an influence upon some of the *vihāras* of the Sukhodaya period. The roofs of the bet and the *vihāras* of the Sukhodaya period were curved for beautification. There were two or three rows of pillars and the wall of the structure was constructed by the side of the third pillar-row. There was the large door-entrance with wind-cavity in front of the bet or the *vihāra*. There was no ceiling and two kinds of tiles were found on roof. One type was up and down-tiles and the other type was cutted-end tiles which were bathed with green gum-colour. There were the Cho-Fa and decorative extension of the apox of the gable and also Bai Raka on the roof of the building.[19] It may be noted here that all the religious buildings of the Sukhodaya kingdom were constructed in the centre of the town which was surrounded by three large and high ranging walls. The bet which belonged to the later Sukhodaya period had galleries which surrounded the Phra Prāng or *chedi*. Afterwards, the temple-planning totally followed the style, design and architecture of the Ayuthia period. The pillars were constructed from laterite. The capital of the pillars was made in the style and design of Bua Klum or lotus cluster and there was not abacus of pillar and there was the hole. In the *vihāra* of the Wat Sri Chum in the city of Sukhodaya there was a double wall and it had a small tunnel inside and through which one was able to take a walk up to the roof. Most probably, this idea was borrowed from the *vihāras* of the city of Polonnaruva in Sri Lanka. Because some *vihāras* of that city had a narrow passage inside the double wall and the people in order to worship the image of the Buddha used to take walk around the image. Afterwards, the Thai artists modified this technique at the Wat Si or Śrī Chum. The elephant fromed an integral part of many Sukhodaya's Wats. They were the Wat

19. *TAII*, p. 86.

Chedi Si Hong, the Wat Chang Rob and the Wat Chang Lom in Sukhodaya, the Wat Chedi Chang Lom in Si Satchanalai, and the Wat Chang in Kamphaeng Phet. They were built in brick and stucco and groups of elephants were found in bases. Other important wats and monuments of Sukhodaya were the Wat Trakuan, the Wat Chetupon, the Wat Si Pichit Kiti Kalayaram in Sukhodaya, the Wat Mongkon, the Wat Chedi Sung Phra Bhat Yai and Wat Chanasengkram.

The Sukhodaya period witnessed the development of the sculpture in Thailand. It reached the zenith of its glory during this period. In the field of sculpture the earliest Thai art of Dvāravatī made an influence upon the activities of the Thai artists of the Sukhodaya period. The Sukhodaya sculpture had a close link with the Dvāravatī sculpture. In the former the body of the Buddha was in complete rest, the muscles were relaxed, and the face was calm and quiet and there was a smile in face which reflected a state of deep inward contentment.[20] The Thai sculpture made the image of the Buddha in a perfect state where the Buddha after his enlightenment reahced the state of Nirvāṇa. They get this idea and realised it very much and brought this heavenly atmosphere in the Buddha's image in a very nice way. There were four categories of the Sukhodaya Buddha images. In the first category there was a tall flickering flame-like motif of the hole on the *uṣṇīṣa* of the Buddha's head, the size of hair-curls was very well-proportioned, the face was like an oval with arched eyebrows and a smiling expression was there, had a hooked nose, there was no parting line round the topknot of head, had pointed chin, the nipples were very prominent, there were large shoulders and the waist was small. The lobes of the ears were curved upward to give the angle form by the attachment of the neck with the shoulders. The robe which was hanging on the left shoulder was quite long and it came up to the navel. Usually, the Buddha took his seat in a folded-leg fashion (Samadhi

20. *TAII.*

Rab in Thai) and he was in the posture of subduing Māra (Māra Vijaya Mudrā). The image had the plain pedestal and there was the form of concave shape in the middle of the pedestal. This category had five different postures of the Buddha image. The Sukhodaya Buddha image of the Kampaengphet group had long face, bread forehead and a pointed chin. The Sukhodaya Buddha image of the Pra Puttha Chinasat group belonged to the reign of king Luthai (AD 1347-68) and his successors. This image had round face, plumb cheeks, a corpulent body and four equal fingers. The high flickering flame of the halo on the uṣṇīṣa of the Buddha's head was longer and higher than that of the first category. The image of this group was found in the Wat Pra Śrī Ratna Mahatat in the province of Pitsanulok of Thailand. The Buddha image of the Wat Trakuan group was found first at the Wat Trakuan in the old city of Sukhodaya and the Buddha image received its name and group after that wat or monastery or temple. An early Chiengsaen influence was felt very much upon the image of this group. The seated Buddha image had crossed-legs with the sole of feet upwards, bread and flat face and short nose. Some images of this group showed the influence of Sri Lanka. The Phra or Pra Putthe Sihing which belonged to this group was regarded as one of the most venerated Buddha images in Thailand. Most probably, it arrived in Thailand from Sri Lanka either in the reign of King Śrī Indrāditya, the founder of the Sukhodaya empire, or in the reign of his son, king Rama Khamheng in the middle of the thirteenth century AD. It may be noted here that the Thai workmanship was found in this image but the Sri Lankan characteristics were also there. The Buddha images in the Sukhodaya period were found in four postures: seated, reclining, standing and walking. The walking Buddha called the Lila (in Thai and yātrā in Sanskrit) posture was mentioned as the masterpiece of the Sukhodaya sculpture. In this posture, the Buddha raised his one heel and he kept his other feet firmly on the ground, and in order to dispel fear he lifted his one hand in the gesture of giving instruction and he kept his other hand by the side of the body as if it was moving naturally while he was walking. The figure were in the graceful posture which symbolised the turning of the Wheel of the Law. A graceful undulation was found in the body of this image. The head was like a lotus-bud and the outline of the lobes of ears curved a little upwards and it gave to emphasise the harmony of the whole structure. The toes on the walking images showed that they were of equal length, the soles were flat and the projection of the heels took place very firmly. Early Sukhodaya statuary began with the reign of king Rama Khamheng. Classical Sukhodaya Buddha images belonged to the early fourteenth century AD. "The Buddha of these images is an other worldly, almost surrealistic figure." The statues of the Hindu gods of the Sukhodaya period were also found. They were statues of Śiva, Umā, Viṣṇu and Harihara. Not only the bronze and metal Buddha images, but the stucco image of this period were also available. In order to decorate religious architecture the Thai architects took the help of the stucco bas-reliefs. Lime, sand and juice of sugar-cane were used to compose the stucce and in a few hours it became very hard and it was for this reason the Thai artists very skillfully and quickly used to perform their works. A beautiful stucco bas-relief was found at Wat Trapang Tong Lang which was situated outside the old town of Sukhodaya. In it the Buddha descended from the Tavatimsa heaven. This relief was very similar to a mural painting which was found in the Northern Temple of Polonnaruva in Sri Lanka. It belonged to the twelfth century AD. Most probably, the Sri Lankan mural made an influence upon it. The Sukhodaya period also produced the Buddhist votive tablets in terracotta and metal. The walking Buddha under a frame called the Phra Khampaeng Khayong in Thai was found. It became quite well-known for its workmanship. The Buddha's foot-print was carved in stone and in bronze during the Sukhodaya period. The Buddha's foot-print in bronze was found in the Wat Sadet in the province of Kampaengphet in Thailand. This period also witnessed the fabrication of the ceramic ware in glazed stoneware and this became known as the Sankalok or the Sangalok in Thai. It was an abbreviated form of Sawankhalok. The Chinese artists influenced the pottery and ceramic works of Thailand. King Rama Khamheng visited China twice. During his second visit to China several Chinese artists who were experts in the pottery and ceramic works came to Thailand with him form China. The Thai potters learnt very well the style and techinque of the ceramic were production from the Chinese potters and they used to export their productions to Japan, Indonesia, Bornee, etc. They not only produced the vessels, domestic utensils, dolls and receptacles from them but the heads of the Nāgas, the door-guardians, etc., were also made by them during the Sukhodaya period to decorate the religious architecture. During the Sukhodaya period the style of the Thai painting was the two-dimensional art. There were mural paintings at the ceiling of a narrow stairway at the Wat Si or Śrī Chum in Sukhodaya. Several stone slabs with the *Jātaka* scenes and several inscriptions in the Sukhodaya script were found. The Indian style made a great influence upon these mural paintings. The fragments of murals were found at the Wat Chedi Chot or Jot Thaew in Si Satchanalai of Thailand. In the murals, among his disciples and adoring devotees the Buddha occupied his seat. The colour scheme of the Sukhodaya painting was monochromatic red, white and black, and it was for this reason the sculptural reliefs have got some of the charactersitics. It is interesting to note here that the brāhmaṇas performed the royal and civil ceremonies in the courts. This was the custom in the Buddhist kingdom of South-East Asia from ancient times to lthe present day. This suggested that besides the Buddha images, several statues of the Hindu deities were available in the Sukhodaya kingdom. The middle of the fourteenth century AD witnessed the fall of the political power of the Sukhodaya kingdom. The new Thai chief then founded the new kingdom of Ayuthia as the capital city of Thailand. Sukhodaya then occupied the position of the vassal city of the new kingdom of Thailand.

Although it lost its independence, yet its Buddhist school of art never came to an end. It played its glorious role what it did before and it prospered in the field of art, architecture and sculpture up to the sixteenth century AD.

Thailand's Buddhist art of the Haripuñjaya period

The Haripuñjaya *stūpas* for their distinctive style can be divided into four types — pyramidal-storied structure, an octagonal-shaped *stūpa*, the Śrī-Vijaya-like Chetiya and an octagonal storied *stūpa*.[21] The first type became very popular and many *stūpas* of the later period were built like the style of the first type. The early type of the image of the Buddha has a rather round and smooth face and the Dvāravatī school has influenced some of its facial characteristics. The later type of the images of the Buddha has a long face and buldging eyes which indicate the indigenous character of its locality. Stucco decorations of the *stūpas* and the printed Buddha gives us an idea about the influence of art from the Śrī-Vijaya, Pāla and Lopburi schools. Mortuary bowls and pots incised with symbolic designs refer to a funeral cult and the magico-religious belief of the indigenous people.

The Wat Chamatewi also known as the Wat Kukut lies about three-quarters of a kilometer to the north-west of the western gate to Lamphun. It was built numerous times over the centuries and king Athitarāja (AD 1120-50) of Haripuñjaya reconstructed it to commemorate his victory over Lopburi. The Wat Phra That of Haripuñjaya dates from the ninth century AD. There was a large gold-clad *stūpa* in it and it was restored many times over the years.

No images of Hindu deities were produced in Haripuñjaya. The Buddha images were of stone figures. The heads of several Buddha images were found at the Wat Phra That Haripuñjaya. They were cast in bronze. The Haripuñjaya sculptors preferred

---

21. *TKHAAT*, p. 282.

standing Buddha images to seated Buddha images and most often they wanted to work in stucco and terracotta rather than less malleable materials. Three statues at the Wat Phra That Haripuñjaya were typical of these from a later period of the Haripuñjaya art. They were influenced by the Pāla-Sena mode of dress. These seated Buddha images were in meditating pose and they placed their hands in their lap and they kept their feet in the *vajrāsana* position and they covered their both shoulders with robes. Their heads were covered with large curl hair and there was a low *uṣṇīṣa* at the top. Some of the best sculpture is seen in the standing Buddhas which were found in the niches of the octagonal *chedi* at the Wat Chamatewi. Both shoulders were covered by the robe and its symmetrical pleats indicate the influence of both Dvāravatī and Lopburi. The Haripuñjaya artists showed their great skill in terracotta. The praying disciples are regarded as some of the most splendid statuary in Thailand's art. Terracotta and baked clay were also used in small, solid votive tablets.

Thailand's Buddhist art of the U-Tong or U-Thong period (from the twelfth to the fifteenth centuries AD)

The U-Tong or U-Thong Buddhist art flourished in the central part of Thailand.

> The name of U-Tong has been chosen to disignate the period to which certain images appear to belong which show a strong Khmer influence allied with various features of a true Siamese art. The greater number of images of this type so far found come from Ayudhya and Lopburi, but they have also been at Supanburi and as far north as Muang Sau, in short, throughout the territority which formed the nucleus of the kingdom of Ayudhya. If people were sure that these images were all posterior to the foundation of this kingdom in 1350, they might be naturally classed under the title 'School of Ayudhya, early style'. But it is quite possible that these

which came from Supanburi and its neighbourhood are interior to the foundation of Ayudhya, and it seemed that the name of U-T'ong corresponding to the name of the capital of the principality which was the cradle of the realm of Ayudhya, would be a suitable one for this mixed or transition style, which doubtless reflected the judicial vicissitudes of the country.' (G.Ceedés, La Museo National de Bangkok, *Ars Asiatic*, vol. XII, p. 34, Paris, 1928. Reginald La May, *A Concise History of Buddhist Art in Siam*, Tokyo, Japan, 1962, p. 137).

U-Tong was regarded as a great centre of the Khmer culture in Thailand and its Buddhist art tried to follow strictly the Khmer style and design. The school of art was mentioned as the art of the early Ayudhyā period.[22] It was very difficult to say anything about the name U-Tong and the region where it was located. Some scholars say that its area corresponded to the capital of the Thai principality before its rise took place as the capital of the Ayudhyā or the Ayuthia kingdom, and it was regarded as the second capital of Thailand. U-Tong, who belonged to the royal family of the Chiengsaen dynasty or the old estern Chiengrai family of King Prohm of Chaiprakarn in the ancient Lan-na-thai empire in the extreme north of Thailand, was a Thai Prince. Later on, he established the Ayuthia kingdom and he became known as king Rama Tibodi I. The ancient city, which was situated in the lower part of the Menam valley in central Thailand, received the name U-Tong. Supannaphum was its another name. Literally, the name U-Tong means 'a Golden Cradle'. Because, according to Thai traditions and legends, a father of a Thai prince gave him a cradle of gold. In Pāli, the name Supannaphum or Suvarṇabhūmi indicates the land of gold or source of gold also. Now the old city of U-Tong or Supannaphum has lost all its glories and practically, it is in ruins and it is in the west of the modern province of Supanburi in

22. *TAII*, p. 90.

Thailand. It is now one of the sub-districts in that province. In the north the border of the city U-Tong was able to spread up to Saranburi, in the east up to the mouth of the Chao Pya or the Menam river, in the south up to the province of Ratburi and in the west up to Pegu in lower Myanmar. This city was regarded as the meeting place of several cultures and civilizations such as the ancient Mon cultlure, the culture of the Dvāravatī kingdom, the Khmer culture from the Lopburi region and the Thai Hīnayāna or the Theravāda Buddhistic culture with the influence of Sri Lanka from the capital of the Sukhodaya kingdom. Thus, the U-Tong school represented art which received influence, guidances and inspirations from various activities of artists of several regions of Thailand.

In the history of the Buddhist art in Thailand the sculpture and the architecture of the U-Tomg period occupied an important place. This period produced the Buddha images which were a combination of the Mon, Khmer and Thai elements.[23] The Pra Mahathat of Chainat in the province of Chainat was an example of architecture of this period. The *stūpa* of the Wat Pra or Phra Boromothat indicated the mixure of influences of the Sukhodaya and the Śrī-Vijaya styles. The two superimposed rectangular basements shortened at four corners (called Yor Mum in Thai) or the bent rectangular plan were its architectural characteristics. The style of the Śrī-Vijaya architecture influenced very much to erect the body of structure. In four directions there were four porticos or niches in the body of structure. The porticos had decorations with pediment and door-jambs. The design of the seated Buddha image in high relief was found on the pediment. A round *stūpa* of the Sukhodaya style decorated the body of structure. The small *stūpa*s in imitation of the main *stūpa* surrounded the main round *stūpa*. The Phra Prāng of the Wat Phra Śrī Ratana Mahathat in the province of Lopburi in Thailand was another religious building of this period. The Wat's *prāng*

23. *TAII.*

dating from the thirteenth century AD was a prototype for Ayuthia style *prāngs*. The Buddha images of this period were rigid, austere and pensive. The shape of the head was cubical and the curls of the hair were very small. A filet was there to separate the hair from the forehead. The eyebrows were very prominent and the nose was flat. The other characteristics were the long robe which came down from the left shoulder and ended in a straight line, a folded-leg posture, the attitude of the Buddha when Māra was subdued and the pedestal concave in outline. There were three different types of the U-Tong Buddha images. The style of the Buddha images of the first group was the result of the mixture of the Dvāravatī art with the Khmer or the Lopburi art. This group belonged to the twelfth and the thirteenth centuries AD and was the earliest of the three groups. The Buddha images of the second group gave an indication of the Khmer or the Lopburi influence in style. It belonged to the thirteenth and the fourteenth centuries AD. In this group there was the great transformation of halo or skull protuberance of the Buddha image and from the small knot or flower-bud it changed into a flame-like motif. The square face and jaw and the long mouth indicated the Khmer influence. The straight forehead, thick lips and mouth, half-closed eyes and a long and of the robe over the navel which fell down from the left shoulder were the characteristics of the Buddha images of this group. The third group suggested that the Sukhodaya art was able to influence the Buddha images of this group. But the large mouth, the flat nose and the dot-like curl of hair gave an indication of the influence of the style of the Khmer or the Lopburi art. The face of the Buddha was oval in shape and this traced the Sukhodaya style in it. The eyebrow were arched and the incised lines were there to mark sharply. The hair was arranged in the fashion of dot-like curl. The halo took the form of flickering flame-like motif on the tall Ketumala or skull protuberance. The waist was small, the shoulders were large, the fingers were slender and the long end of the robe was placed over the navel. All these features gave a clear indication of

Sukhodaya's influence. The U-Tong sculptors made many seated Buddha images and they wanted to work in bronze but also they produced several terracotta, sandstone and gold images. The Mon and the Khmer influences played their vital roles in the U-Tong sculpture.

Thailand's Buddhist art of the Ayuthia period (from the fourteenth to the eighteenth centuries AD)

According to historians, scholars and art critics, the Ayudhyā or the Ayuthia school of art was the national art of Thailand.[24] The artistic activities progressed and flourished to a great extent during the reign of the rulers of the Ayuthia kingdom. Its capital was Ayudhyā or Ayuthia which was regarded as the second capital of Thailand. This dynasty ruled for four hundred years (AD 1350-1767) and it came to an end when the Ayuthia kingdom fell at the hands of the Myanmarese. They completely destroyed the capital city. King U-Tong established the new kingdom of Ayuthia on an island of the Menam or the Chao Pya River, which was about forty-miles north of Bangkok and was about thirty-one miles south of Lopburi or the city of Lavo. In AD 1350 the capital Dvāravatī Śrī Ayudhyā or Ayuthia was established. Here the influence of Vaiṣṇavism was found. It is said that the name Ayudhyā was derived from the town of Oudh in Uttar Pradesh in India, which was regarded as the city of Lord Rāma, one of the ten *avatāra*s or incarnations of Lord Viṣṇu. King U-Tong became known in Thailand's history as king Rama Tibodi I after the foundation of the Ayudhyā or the Ayuthia kingdom. The Buddhist art developed very well during the reign of the Ayuthia rulers. The Ayuthian or the Ayuthayan sculptors mainly devoted themselves to create the images of the Buddha. They depicted a wider range of incidents in which the Buddha was involved. They selected to portray events in his life other than the standard meditation or the Māravijaya modes. Bronze was very much used and in its casting the Ayuthian sculptors did very well.

24. *TAII*, p.92.

Thus, we find in the colossal seated Buddha in the Vihan Phra Mongkon Bopit adjacent to the Wat Phra Si Sanphet. Gold, wood and stucco-covered brick were used by the Ayuthian sculptors. According to the cultural progress and the activities of Thailand's artists in the reigns of different rulers of this dynasty, the Ayuthia periods were divided into four sub-periods.[25] These were: (1) The development of the art of the first period when King U-Tong (King Rama Tebodi I) established Ayuthia as an independent kingdom in AD 1350 and it came to an end when king Borom or Boromo Trailoknath or King Trailok reigned from AD 1448 to 1488. These reigns covered the period of one hundred thirty-eitht years (138 years) which witnessed the growth and progress of the Buddhist art in this kingdom. (2) The development of the art of the second period began from the last part of the reign of King Borom Trailoknath to the end of the rule of King Tong Dham (AD 1628). These reigns covered the period of the Buddhist art of one hundred thirty-seven years (137 years). (3) The growth of the art of the third period started with the reign of King Prasat Thong in AD 1630 and it ended in the last years of the reign of King Trai Sra in AD 1732. It covered a period of one hundred two years (102 years). (4) The art of the fourth or the last period not only witnessed the reign of King Boromokot in AD 1732 but up to the rule of the Ayuthia kingdom's last ruler King Ekatat who was dethroned because the Myanmarese invaded the kingdom in AD 1767. It covered the period of the activities of Thailand's artists of thirty-five years (35 years). The Ayuthia art tried to imitate the art of the Sukhodaya, U-Tong, Lopburi or Khmer periods.

THE FIRST PERIOD (AD 1350-1488)

In the first period or in the early period of the Ayuthia art, the Lopburi and the U-Tong schools of art contributed very much to the development of its artistic activities and workmanship. The style of architecture of these two schools became very popular

25. *TAII.*

in this period. In the design of the Phra Prāng or the Pra Prāng or Prah Kham the central monuments of many Buddhist monasteries were erected and this design totally followed the Lopburi or the U-Tong style.[26] Although the Phra Prāng of this period followed the design of the structure of Khmer school, yet there were some characteristics in it which differed from the Khmer art. The Phra Prāng was higher than the Khmer Prāng of Lopburi or U-Tong and the higher basement occupied the same level with the body of the structure. The porch was attached to the body of the Phra Prāng and the most prominent porch was in the front side of the Prāng. King Boromoraja I (AD 1370-88) built the Wat Phra Mahathat in AD 1384 in the city centre. Its centre was a 38 meter high laterite *prāng* surrounded by a six meter tall spire. In AD 1633 King Prasat Tong rebuilt it. In order to increase its height to 50 meters, bricks and plaster were used. King Boromoraja II the Wat Ṛathburana in AD 1424. The Wat Na Phramāna was built in mid-fifteenth century AD. The Wat Phra Si Samphet was erected in AD 1491 at the place of Ramatibodi's first palace. King Ramasuen constructed the Wat Phra Ram in AD 1368. The Sukhodaya style made an influence upon the round *chedi* of this piriod. The body of the structure was made with the four porches in four directions. A bot of this period had no window but there was a hole for the purpose of wind on the upper part of its wall. A porch or portico was made in front side of the bot (known as Mukhasan in Thai). There were rows of pillars in the interior part of the bot (called Saewharn in Thai) and the wall of sturcture had no decoration of painting. Only on outline of lotus-line was found in the four sides of wall. The sculpture of the first period followed the style and design of the U-Tong sculpture. The type of sculpture became very popular at Ayuthia. The style of the Buddha image of the U-Tong period took its firm rest at Ayuthia even before its foundation by king U-Tong as his capital and it flourished not only in his kingdom but it continued to prosper during te reign

26. *TAII*, p. 93.

of king Borom Trailokanath or king Trailok (AD 1448-88). There were some sculptural characteristics of the Buddha image of this period. In the form of lotus-bud or frame-like motif there was the halo on the skull-protuberance or *uṣṇīṣa*. The head of the Buddha image had the small spiral-curl hair and there was the Raiprasok or the parting line round the topknot. There was the square chin in the shape of human chin and from the left shoulder the long end of robe fell down. The Buddha image had the square-shaped folded legs and there was the pedestal with concave outline. In AD 1458 king Borom made several bronze Buddha images which represented various previous lives of the Buddha (Pra Bodhisattva Horoi Prachat of 500 incarnations in Thai). In these images there was the pure style of the Ayuthia sculpture which practically began to flourish from the middle of the fifteenth century AD. The Ayuthia sculptures erected seated Buddha in the Māravijaya fashion with the feet in the *vīrāsana* position and also in the *samādhi* or meditating position. They alos produced many standing Buddhas with alms bowls or with their hands in the *vitarka-mudrā* or the *abhaya-mudrā* gesture. They also created a number of walking Buddhas and their weight rested on the right rather than the left foot and the right rather than the left hand displayed the *abhaya-mudrā*. In the early period of the Ayuthia kingdom the style of the Ayuthian painting gave an indication about the influences of the Khmer and the Sukhodaya paintings. Black, white and red colours were used and several spots were covered in gold in the Ayuthia paintings. The figures were rather stiff and heavy. In the mural paingings the use of polychrome composition or mixed colour composition took place. The mural painting in the crypt of the main Prāng of the Wat Ratburama in Ayuthia of AD 1424 was found. There were hieratic rows of seated Buddha and standing disciples in the lower part of crypt and *Jātaka* scenes decorated the four niches. The painters painted these figures on the fresco surface. The style of the use of colour and sketching of outline suggested that this painting did not imitate old mural paintings. The wood-carving objects such as carvẹd doors, carved windows of the bet and the *vihāras*, book-cabinets and boxes for palm-leaf manuscripts were mentioned as the minor arts of the first period of the Ayuthia art. The Ayuthian painters in their mural depicted the Tesachat, the life of the Buddha, the Ramakien and also a few local stories.

THE SECOND PERIOD (AD 1491-1628)

King Borom Trailokanath in AD 1463 reigned in Pitsanulok in northern Thailand. At that time an influence of the Sukhodaya style was found in Thailand's art which belonged to the second period.[27] The round *stūpa* or *chedi* of bell-shaped dome of the Sukhodaya style became very popular in Thailand. Although the Thai artists of this period followed the general architectural characteristics of the *stūpa* from the Sukhodaya *chedi*, yet they introduced new designs of architecture in their works. They adapted bell-shaped dome or body or structure of the *chedi* which was higher than that of the style of the Sukhodaya dome. A new form of low rows of pillars also decorated the *chedi* or the *stūpa*. These rows of pillars became known in Thailand as Saewharn. The great *stūpa* at the Wat Yai Chaimonkol and three large *stūpa* at the Wat Phra Sri Sanpot in the province of Ayuthia were built during this period. There were bell-shaped domes and porches in all the four directions. The walls of the *bet* or the *vihāras* were not decorated with designs. The real Ayuthia sculpture began to take its shape from the reign of King Rama Tibodi II (AD 1491) and this type of sculpture was found in the production of the Buddha images. The artists of this period were very much influenced by the Sukhodaya style when they produced the halo and outline of the Buddha's face in their sculptural works. There was a small parting line round the topknot on the head and the big and of the robe came down from the left shoulder of the Buddha image and it was arranged in the design of a straight line or it fell down in such a manner as two pointed

27. *TAII*, p. 94.

ends of robe. The facial expression showed that there was no life in it but the pedestal of the image was decorated with designs. The gesture of the *māra vijaya-mudrā* occupied the very prominent place in most of the Buddha images of this period. The seated Buddha images with disciples on both sides and the decorations of the pedestal with the figures of the Yakṣas or the demons in some images were found. This period did not produce many walking Buddha images and the Buddha images in meditation *mudrā*. The second period of the Ayuthia painting showed the gradual development of the influence of the Sukhodaya painting in it. The painters not only used monochrome colour in composition of thier paintings but they also used many colours. The figures were rather heavy and stiff and were lifeless. Red ochre, black and yellow were mentioned as the main colours for the Ayuthia paintings. The minor religious arts of this period were the wood-carving objects. Besides the wooden domestic furnitures there were minor religious arts in this period and they were the carved temple door-panels and carved door-panels of the *vihāra*s decorated with the figures of the gods. King Rama Tibodi II in AD 1492 erected the large *chedi* of the Wat Pra Sanpot to keep the ashes of his father, king Borom Trailokanath. The Wat Pra Śrī Ratana Mahathat was another important reliquary in Ayuthia. A gold Buddha image, several Buddhist votive tablets, precious ornaments and numerous gold objects were found in these reliquaries.

THE THIRD PERIOD (AD 1630-1732)

The third period began with the reign of King Prasat Tong and it ended in the reign of King Trai Sra in AD 1732. It covered a period of one hundred two years (102 years). The Lobpuri or the Khmer style, the Chinese art and the Western or the European art helped to make a great influence upon the development of the Ayuthia art of this period. France under the rule of King Louis XIV established diplomatic relations with king Narai of

Ayuthia and it was for this reason the Ayuthia art was influenced by the arrival of the French art in Ayuthia.[28] King Prasat Tong subjugated the Khmers and owing to this reason the Prāng and the Khmer architecture became very popular in Ayuthia in the middle of the seventeenth century AD. The Prāng at the Wat Chai Watena Ram in Ayuthia belonged to this period and was in the Khmer style. This was regarded as an imitation of the Angkor Vat temple in Kamboja. There was a main central Prāng with four small *chedi*s and the row of gallery was able to connect the four corners. This period also witnessed the appearance of the redented *chedi*. "It was the *chedi* with reduced corner from the basement up to the portion of neck of the boll-shaped dome." This style of the *chedi* differed completely from the *chedi* which belonged to the first and second periods of the Ayuthia art. The Sri Lankan *stūpa*, the Sukhodaya *chedi* and the Śrī-Vijaya architecture played their great roles for the formation of the new style of the *chedi* in this period. France helped very much to build several religious houses and also structures which had the style of Western art and these were found at the city of Lopburi in the reign of King Narai. The royal palace of King Narai in Lopburi was erected in the style of Western architecture. In Thai this Western style became known as the 'Gothic Porch'. There were Western decorative designs in the interior wall of the royal palace and the decoration of ceiling followed the style of Roccoso art of Europe. There were no porch and gallery in some *bet*s or monasteries. The windows which were decorated by porches began to appear again. During the reigns of King Prasat Tong (AD 1629-56) and his son King Narai (AD 1656-88) the sandstone Buddha images became very popular. Cambodia became a vassal state of Thailand in the former's reign and the Thai artists tried to follow the Khmer works of art very much and because of its popularity many sandstone Buddha images were produced by them. In this period of the Ayuthian art the

---

28. *TAII*, p. 96.

Thai artists who belonged to the middle and southern parts of Thailand made the red sandstone Buddha images. There were double lips or there was a faint moustache over the mouth of the sandstone Buddha images and sometimes there was a double line around the eyes of the Buddha image. Towards the end of the sixteenth century AD the crowned Buddha images began to appear in Thailand and gradually, they became very popular in the third and the fourth Ayuthian periods. In Thai they became known as Pra Song Khrueng. The third period witnessed the development of the Thai paintings in a far-advanced stage. The Thai painters used many colours and they applied gold on figures and ornamental designs. Apart from the use of black, red and yellow colours, the Thai painters took keen interest to use green, blue and violet colours in their paintings. Mural paintings on the walls of religious buildings, Lai Red Nam designs of book cases and the boxes for the Buddhist scriptures and also the paintings in manuscripts were found in this period. The minor arts in this period were the carved doors, pulpits, book-cabinets and boxes for palm-leaf manuscripts. In the reign of King Narai there was an influence of Christianity in Thailand and several minor arts of Christianity were found at the Lopburi town. These objects were basement of silver cross-post, silver mixed with gold glass, one pair of silver candlesticks, etc. Different domestic utensils made of metal and pottery were introduced in this period. The currency in the form of coinage became known in Thai as Nguenpodduang and it had designs of Garuḍa, crown, castle, etc.

THE FOURTH PERIOD (AD 1732-67)

The Ayuthia art of the fourth period began with the reign of king Boromkot (AD 1732) and it ended when the Ayuthian kingdom fell at the hand of the Myanmarese in AD 1767.[29] It covered a period of about thirty-five years. The *bet*s and the *vihāra*s of the fourth period had curved basement and roofs and the brick pillars

29. *TAII*, p. 98.

for the inner parts of the structures were also used. The capitals of these brick pillars were made in the form of lotus-buds and the Thai artists adopted this style from the Sukhodaya architecture. Some of the capital pillars of the Ayuthia art were made in the form of stylised blooming lotus. In the late Ayuthia period the brick walls with narrow rectangular cavities began to appear in Thailand. At first plain terracotta tiles were used as roofs for the religious buildings in this period. The reign of King Petracha (AD 1688-1702) saw the introduction of the glazed tiles. He covered his monastery and *bet* with these tiles. It became very popular in Thailand as the Wat Krabuang Khluab and in Thai it was the Glazed-Tile Monastery. The crowned or the decorated Buddha images called the Pra-Song Khrueng in Thai became well-known during this period. Sometimes they were found with ornaments in a very lavish way (known in Thai as Pra Song Khrueng) and they were decorated also only with a diadem and earrings. The main characteristic of the latter type was lateral protrusions of the diadem above the ears. The crowned Buddha images of this period had the long-shaped heads with diadems. The heads were crowned by high conical masses and these were formed by two, three or more plain rings and the lotus-buds were always placed at the top. The lobs of the ears had pointed earrings. This type of thing was found in the Khmer art. The girth was decorated with ornaments and this was found in the Lopburi art. The Sukhodaya art made an influence upon the facial lineaments and the forms of the figure. The figures were very stiff. The arrangements of the robes of the Buddha images were made in such a fashion which helped very much to give the statues a bell-shaped outline. Most of the standing crowned Buddha images had either one or two hands raised. This style was introduced in sculpture in Thailand in the fourth period. The Buddha images were shapeless and they were decorated all over with ornaments. In this period there was an existence of another type of the Buddha images which belonged to the Nakon Śī Thammarat style. The style, design and pattern of the Buddha images of this school took their imitations from the Pra Puttha Sihing at the province of Nakon Śī Thammarat in southern Thailand. They looked exactly like the Buddha images which belonged to the early Chiengsaen school. But the face of the Buddha was rounder in shape, the robe-end was placed above the left nipple and the image of the Buddha showed that it had a fat body. Most probably, the Buddha images which belonged to the early Chiengsaen school and the Nakon Śī Thammarat school were influenced by the Pāla art from India and this influence came to Nakon Śī Thammarat through Java which had close cultural link with the Pāla kingdom. In this period many Buddhist votive tablets were discovered and they represented many small seated Buddhas on the same plaque, the crowned standing Buddha image under a frame, etc. The image of the Future Buddha Maitreya Bodhisattva, the Buddha's Foot Print, the figures of the Buddha's disciples and the images of the Hindu gods were also found. In the reign of King Boromokot the Thai painters produced many mural paintings and their works from the paintings of the previous periods differed very much in composition and the use of colours. They very skilfully did the sketched outline of figures and they used colour which was polychrome. They were wooden works and wood-carving objects of the late Ayuthia period. These were regarded as minor arts. The art of mother-of-pearl inland work was the new production of Thailand's minor arts. The Thai artists were inspired by the Chinese people to produce this type of work but after aquiring this skill from them they made it in their own way. Other minor arts of this period were glass decoration, the production relating to polychromatic ceramic ware (Bencharong in Thai) which was decorated with pure Thia designs and the production of Nielleware. The black Nielloware and the Ta Tong Nielloware 'decorated designs with the piece of gilded gold' were mentined as two types. Under the patronage of the Ayuthia rulers the Buddhist art flourished in their kingdom for more than four centuries. In about AD 1767 a great change took place in the political affairs of the kingdom. The Myanmarese soldiers defeated the Thai rulers of the Ayuthia kingdom and destroyed the capital of the kingdom and it camd under their rule. But King Taksin the Great not only defeated them but also founded his new capital at Dhonburi or Danaburi. Thailand's Buddist art began to flourish there and this period lasted only for fifteen years. It came to an end when the death of king Taksin the Great took place. Dhonburi's art was based on the art of the Ayuthia period and its characteristics were like these of the Ayuthia art.

Thailand's Buddhist art of the Bangkok period or the Ratanakesin period (from late eighteenth century to the present day)

The period from AD 1782 to the present day is called the 'Bangkok' or 'Ratanakesin' or 'Ratnakesin' period, and the latter was the formal name for the city which became known as 'the city of the Emerald Buddha'. Thailand's Buddhist art which prospered in the present capital of Thailand became known as the Bangkok art. It received its name from that city. The art of this period began form that time when Bangkok was founded as the capital of Thailand. At first it was a small town. It began to expand very rapidly when the people from Ayuthia came and settled in the Dhonburi-Bangkok area. It then established itself as the capital of the Chakri dynasty. With its establishment its development took place in a very rapid way. The Bangkok school of art began to flourish in Thailand from AD 1782, and it continues to flourish up to the present day. King Rāma I constructed Bangkok as the third or the present capital of Thailand and he founded the Chakri dynasty to rule over there. The art of this period can be mentioned as the mixture of several styles of art which are the India art, the Chinese art, the Western art and also the long series of adaptations of former Thai art. This period marked the turning point in the history of Buddhist art in Thailand. In every respect it was regarded as the age of re-imitation of Indian art.

For sometime the Thai artists did not reproduce the style of the Indian art but again during this period this style played a very vital role in the field of Thailand's Buddhist art. The style of the art of the Bangkok period was based on the style of the art of the Sukhodaya or the Ayuthia period. The second phase of the Bangkok art began in the second half of the nineteenth century AD when King Mongkut or Rāma IV ascended the throne of the Bangkok dynasty. This period witnessed many changes in Thailand's art. Soon new style, new technique and new ideas were introduced for its development. The architectural characteristics of the religious buildings of the Bangkok period were found in the syle of the *bet* and the *vihāra*, the *chedi*, the *stūpa*, the *pra prāng*, the *prasat*, the *mondop*, etc. The *bot* or the *viḥāra* was "the building stucco covered with brick in plan and rectangular in form with a large nave". Sometimes it had lateral aisles and a porch of peristyle. The main entrance of the building was kept in the east. On the back and front of the building there were one, two or three doors. The roofs were covered with glazed tiles, there were decorations of the Nāgas, the rearing heads of the Nāgas were placed at the corners and the combined tails were kept at the top. The tympanum at the gable ends was of carved wood with cental motif which was decorated with the images of Lord Śiva on the bull or Viṣṇu with Garuḍa. The doors and windows of the *bot*s or the *vihāra*s were found with miniature world mountains, and the doors and windows were decorated with carving, lacquer or inlay. In north Thailand the monasteries or the *bot*s had brackets from the top of the wall to the caves and these were carved with figures of animals, *nāga*s and human beings. The *mondop* was constructed in a cubic form with stepped pyramidal roof. King Rama I reconstructed the Phra Buddha Patha at the province of Saraburi. Another *mondop* was the Wat Phra Kaew (the temple of the Emerald Buddha) which was used as library. The *prasat* was in the form of a miniature palace. It was cruciform in shape with a *prāng* at the intersection of the roofs. The Ho Trai or the Ho

Traipiṭaka was the library of the Bangkok period. In order to prevent rats, white ants and insects from destroying the manuscripts this was constructed on stilts over a pond. The styles of the architecture of the *prāng* and the rodented *chedi* or *stūpa* became very popular during the first three reigns of the Bangkok rulers (AD 1782-1851). The construction of the Pra *prāng* at the Wat Arun or the Temple or Dawn began in the reign of king Rāma II and it came to an end in the reign of king Rāma III. During the reigns of the first three Chakri rulers the body of the *prāng* was erected on the lotus-basement and lion basement, and the four porches which were attached with structure took their shapes in four directions. There was no front porch and the spire of the *prāng* was beautifully decorated with the motif of petal of the jack-fruit. The round *stūpa* or the *chedi* became very popular in the reign of king Rāma III. This style was originated from Sri Lanka. King Rāma III built four wats and restored in the Chinese style — the Wat Chalerm Phra Kiat, the Wat Raja Oros, the Wat Thong Nophakhum in Thon Buri and the Sala Gong in Bangkok's Wat Bovornivet. The deputy king of Rāma III founded the Wat Bovornivet in AD 1827. Later king Rāma III built the Phra Panya Vihan for his half brother, the future king Rāma IV, who was its abbot and stayed several years there to revise the Buddhist scriptures. The wat was used by subsequent kings. Rāma VI and Rāma VII were ordained at the Wat Phra Kaew but they used to reside at the Wat Bovornivet. The present monarch, king Rāma IX (Buddhist Adulyadej) took his ordination there and used to reside in its monks' quarters. King Rāma III constructed the Lohaprasad in the courtyard of the Wat Thoptidaram. The round *stūpa* of this period was the Pra Pathom Chedi of the province of Nakon Pathom. Its construction started in the reign of King Mongkut or Rāma IV and its completion took place in the reign of King Chulalongkern or Rāma V. The Marble Temple or the Wat Benchamabopit was built in the reign of king Rāma VI or in early twentieth century AD it was designed by Prince Naris. In the Bangkok Period there were not many changes in the architectural designs and styles. The carved base roof architecture of the *bet* or the *vihāra* was kept in some of the buildings of king Rāma I and Rāma II. Although the old Thai wooden houses were usually kept, yet from the reign of the third ruler of the Bangkok dynasty brick structures began to appear in Thailand. These were built in Thai style and also in Chinese style. Because the influence of the Chinese art was felt very much in the reign of king Rāma III. But king Rāma IV was influenced by the Western architecture and it was for this reason many seculer religious buildings were built in Western style. King Rāma IV constructed the Wat Rajapradit, a small but charming *bot* in white and grey Chinese marble. The Western architecture became very popular during the reign of king Rāma V. He built the Wat Rajabopit in AD 1870 and also the Wat Benchamabopit. Originally, the Chakri Mansion in the Grand Palace in Bangkok was built by king Rāma V in a Western style, but afterwards, its roof was constructed in Thai style. The architectural designs of the Bangkok period were very good. It made a little change in the style of the older models. The Prāng of the Bangkok period became higher and taller. The outer decoration had a glittering surface of coloured tiles, mosasic, gilt and figured porcelain. In the reign of Rāma I not many Buddha images were made. He did not allow his artists to make new Buddha images. But he asked his people to bring 1200 Buddha images, which were left in northern Thailand because of Thailand's wars with Myanmar, to Bangkok. He told then the Thai sculptors to restore them and he distributed them to many Buddhist monasteries in Bangkok and it its neighbouring areas. These images belonged to the style of art of Sukhodaya, U-Tong and Ayuthia. There were some images which were produced in the Bangkok period and the Bangkok sculpture followed the styles of sculpture of Ayuthia and U-Tong. But their facial expression were even more lifeless. The reigns of king Rāma II (AD 1809-24) and king Rāma III (AD 1824-51) witnessed the creation of the

Buddha images which had the same style. The Thai sculptors showed their keen interest to decorate these images beautifully but they did nothing for their facial expression. Under the patronage of king Rāma III about forty different attitudes of the Buddha images were created. The sculptors tried to follow the traditional style for some Buddha images and also for some Buddha images they introduced new attitudes and styles. These statuettes were regarded as the origin of 'the Bangkok Buddha images'. King Rāma III's reign witnessed the creations of two standing Buddha images, each three meters tall and clad in 84 kg of gold. They were dedicated to the king's father and grandfather and were kept in the *bet* of the Wat Phra Kaew. King Rāma III's sculptors also produced 33 small bronzes which depicted the main events of the Buddha's life. King Rāma IV (AD 1851-68) showed his great love for the development of Western culture in Thailand. He was determined to take steps to modernise Thailand and he wanted to make it to the level of development enjoyed by the Western world. New political ideas were introduced and a new scientific approach was approved to take to cure social problems which Thailand faced these days. In art there was an attempt to imitate the spirit of Western art. New subjects and themes were introduced and many new artists appeared in the field of Thailand's art. So in Rāma IV's reign the Buddha images were made under the influence of the Western art. His period witnessed the invention of a more realistic Buddha images. They had a folded robe and had no skull-protuberance or *uṣṇīṣa* on the head. Several Buddha images became known as the Pra Samputthapanni or the Sambuddhabarni or Pra Niran Tarai or the Phra Nirantaraya — "the Buddha seated in the crossed-leg posture" and in the *samādhi* position and were a very realistic looking robe. This new type of the Buddha image never became popular in Thailand. The Thai sculptors then began to create the *uṣṇīṣa* and the traditional robe of the Buddha image in the reign of king Rāma V (AD 1868-1910). The rise of the influence of Indian art took place again in Thailand's Buddhist art of the Bangkok period. In the reigns of king Rāma V or Chulalongkorn and king Rāma VI the Buddha images of Bangkok were very much influenced by the Buddha images of the Gandhāra style of India. During the reign of king Rāma V the old forms of the Buddha images with the skull-protuberance (*uṣṇīṣa*), the transparent robe and the folded-leg posture were again found in Bangkok. The Buddha images became more human. The Bangkok artists followed the style of the Gāndhāra school of the Buddha image of India and they introduced it in their field as far as possible. The Buddha images had wave-line hair on the head and *uṣṇīṣa* and the whole body was covered with wavy folded robe. These styles of the Gāndhāra school were imitated by the Bangkok artists in their field in king Rāma V's reign. From the reign of king Rāma VI onwards although the Buddha images had still some important characteristics such as the flame-like halo on the skull-protuberance, *uṣṇīṣa*, long ear-lobes and the monastic dress, yet they were more and more humanised. In order to create new type of the Buddha image, the Thai artists fully copied and imitated all the features of the Gāndhāra Buddha image. It can be told as the re-birth of Indian art in the creation of the sculpture in Buddhist art in Thailand in the Bangkok period. The Buddha images began to appear in a human form. In order to celebrate the 2500th anniversary of Buddhism Professor Silpa Bhirasri, the famous contemporary Thai artist, created the large standing Buddha image in this style in 1957. Besides the Buddha images, several Buddhist statues and the images of the Hindu gods were found in Bangkok during this period. Many new Buddhist images in traditional style were created for the wats or monasteries. The Bangkok painters created the mural paintings very nicely. They took their themes from the life of the Buddha, the *Jātaka* scenes, the Buddhist cosmology, etc. The painters did very carefully the flowering trees and rocks in their mural paintings and they borrowed this style from the Chinese paingings. The colours of the mural paintings during the Bangkok period became very rich and deep and they were even richer and deeper than the mural paintings of the Ayuthia period. The painters in their colours used gold leaf in a very lavish style. The pictorial art and several sets of smaller paintings on cloth of this period were found. The painters in them used the same technique and style of the mural paintings. The Bangkok period witnessed the introduction and the development of Western artists' ideas, technique and novalties into Thai paintings. The foreigners in their native costumes — figures of Moslems, Portuguese, Dutch, French, etc., began to appear in many mural paingings of this period. The painters like the Chinese flowering trees copied them very carefully and they used them like visiting actors in Thailand's traditional scenes. They painted these figures very flatly like other figures in the story. But too much Western influence in the field of art did not impress. It did not help to create ideas, imagination and inspiration.

> The brilliance of chemical colours and the instability of some of the 19th century ones throw the traditional colour harmony of the composition out of balance. And aesthetically, the natural solidity and flat plane quality of the wall is lost when it is seemingly pierced by deep vistas. Only a few exceptional artists in the West managed to find the right combination of naturalism and stylisation.

During this period two types of manuscripts one made of strips of palm-leaves and the other of paper appeared. Thus, there were two kinds of materials on which Thai characters were written — palm-leaf and Khoi. Like the monks of medieval Europe 'Khoi' manuscript copyists and their patrons mentioned their work as a holy task which would gain them merit. The Khoi manuscripts received their name from the materials on which they were written. The palm-leaf manuscript was used for religious purpose and the help of the paper manuscript was taken for a wide variety of subjects. The page of a manuscript of palm-leaf during this period was a strip about 18" x 3" cut from the leaf of the corypha palm. The individual palm leaves were dried and trimmad to flat sheets between 35 and 45 cm long and 5 to 7.5 cm wide. In order to make a smooth surface for the purpose of writing, these strips were then pressed in bundles, trimmed and sanded. The text was inscribed with the help of a needle-pointed stylus and the soot was rubbed over the pages which were tied together through two holes in the middle of each leaf. Two hard covers were used to keep the pages of the manuscript in a nice way. Then the whole volume in a piece of cloth was wrapped and was tied with a cord which helped to fix a knife-shaped object inscribed with the title. There was no illustration or ornamentation in any fashion in the palm-leaf manuscripts which were used by the Buddhist monks. The paper of the paper manuscripts was made from the bark of a tree, streolus aspera. The paper thin bark was taken from the Khoi tree and then soaked in water. After boiling it in lime water until it became a pulp, then a thin layer of the pulp cameout in a stream into a framed tray of heavy cloth. When there was no water in it, then the pulp layer was rolled smooth and dried. The yellowish gray paper was coated with size or blackened with lacquer and polished.

> The edges were trimmed and the sheet folded accordien like into 70 to 80 panels, 30 to 60 cm wide to form a book which, when opened, could be up to 50 meters but was usually around 18 meters.

The illustrations were pointed on the sized paper with the same dry pigments which were mixed with a binder and these were used on the murals or they were mixed with lacquer and were applied on a sized or lacquered background. In several manuscripts which dated from before the seventeeth century AD, the illustration occupied the centre of the panel. Other manuscripts of this period tried to cover an entire panel or even a double spread. In some manuscripts of the later period the illustrations were arranged along one or both edges of each panel with the next separating them. The illustrations were important parts of the manuscripts. The words were written with the ink which was made from lampblack 'which coated the ceiling above a cooking fire'. The soot of a burnt pine tree can be used for the best quality lempblack. The Khoi manuscript managed to survive themselves from the Ayuthian period and they discussed only religious topics such as the Traiphum and the Tesachat. Two Khoi manuscripts were commissioned in AD 1776 by king Taksin. One is 50.9 m of 272 leaves including 109 illustrations and it is kept in the Berlin Museum. Another one is in Bangkok's National Museum and it is 34.7 m long. Its half is dealt with the Traiphum and the rest is devoted to the events relating to the Buddha's life, the Tesachat. The manuscripts of the Bangkok period discussed various subjects on the military strategy, elephants, horses, etc., and in order to help astrologers, they were also used. The Khoi manuscripts which were iconographical treatises were known as the Tamra Thopharup (Devarupa). In the middle of the nineteenth century AD the traditional Thai painting began to disappear in Bangkok. In its place the Western oil paintings appeared and the Thai painters then devoted their time and energy to deal with the Western paintings. In order to preserve the traditional Thai paintings some painters took training in the old technique under the instruction of the Fine Arts Department of the Silpakorn University in Bangkok and also the Arts and Crafts Secondary School in Bangkok and they were able to preserve copies of some of the vanishing murals. School children began to learn to sketch some of the decorative motifs, but in the remote village of Thailand the traditional Thai painting did not survive. Painting can be mentioned as one of the Thailand's greatest cultural achievements. Classical painting always dealt with religion and morality. Only the paintings of the Ayuthia and the Bangkok periods have survived to the present day. The murals of Ayuthia and Bangkok used the Tesachat, the life of the Buddha, the Ramakien and the Traiphum

(Three worlds) to decorate the walls of a single *bet* or *vihan*. The backgrounds of the Ayuthian murals were generally painted in light hues and there was no attempt to create landscapes. But the Bangkok artists tried to paint every available space with figures, buildings and foliage.

> The period divides roughly into the years of adherence to past art styles during the reigns of King Rama I and II followed by a delving into new, principally Chinese themes during the reign of King Rama III and succeeded under the leadership of Rama IV and V by a determined attempt to look westward and adopt a European aproach to art. Thai art after the death of King Rama V in 1910 was to take a radically different turn. . . .[30]

King Rāma III's reign can be mentioned as the high point of classical Thai painting. The Bangkok artists in his time tried to introduce new ideas and they depicted "traditional subjects in manners reflecting Bangkok aesthetics and times rather than these of eras long dead". They borrowed Chinese ideas and in the Chinese style they created the entire scene. The second half of the nineteenth century AD witnessed the occurrence of the final stage of Classical Thai painting and the introduction of Western ideas took place in it. An artist, who represented a most radical departure from the classical norm both in theme and treatment, was patronised by king Rāma IV. In the Bangkok period the wood-carving objects were found. They were the carved thrones, chariots, the large royal barges, book cabinets, pulpits, furnitures, the moulding carved doors, roof brackets and gables of temples and also the Buddha images and other figures in the round or in relief. Besides the wood-carving objects, the silverworks in the form of bowls and caskets with beautiful designs were regarded as other forms of minor arts. Early Bangkok sculptors used bronze, wood and stucco to produce their

---

30. *TAT*, pp. 184 & 186.

works. It was very difficult to find stone images in the Bangkok period, but numerous marble bas-reliefs were found. Several Thai sculptors produced numerous images of the trinity of Hindu deities. Although there were not many images of Brahmā, the creator, but there were many statues of Viṣṇu, the preserver and of Śiva, the destroyer. Viṣṇu was very popular in Thailand becasue his *avatāra*, Rāma was the hero of the literary classic, the *Ramakien*. Several rulers of Sukhothai (Rāma Khamheng) and Ayuthia (Ramatibodi and Ramasuen) included his name into their own and the kings of the present dynasty have all adopted his name (Rāma I, Rāma II, Rāma III, Rāma IV, Rāma V, Rāma VI, Rāma VII, Rāma VIII, and Rāma IX). Nārāyaṇa (Phra Narai in Thai), another *avatāra* of Viṣṇu had its great popularity in Thailand. Śiva was portrayed in the standing position with his unadorned body and had several arms. Several Thai sculptors have created images in stone, wood, gold, silver, ivory, gemstones, stucco, terracotta and ceramics, but the bronze was regarded as the most popular material and many Thai artists produced many bronze images in Thailand.

> Since ancient times the technique used to cast images has been the 'lost wax' process. Solid bronze pieces were created but it was more common to cast hollow core images.

The largest known bronze Buddha image was the fourteenth century AD eight-meter-tall seated Phra Śrī Śākyamuni Buddha image. It was made in Sukhodaya. It was tranferred to Bangkok's Wat Suthat by king Rāma I from Sukhodaya's Wat Mahathat. Terracotta has been used in Thailand since Neolithic times for figures and also for architectural decoration. Many Thai sculptors have done very well in shaping it for various purposes. During the Sukhodaya period many ceramic decorative figures were created by several Thai sculptors. The modern crowned Buddha images made in Thailand, Laos and Cambodia were greatly influenced by the Myanmarese models. But they also took ideas from the Khmers who ruled over Thailand and Laos between the eleventh and the thirteenth centuries AD. The earliest crowned Buddha in Khmer art were these on the Pimai lintels of north-east Thailand of the twelfth century AD. A crowned Buddha seated on *nāga* was also found. Later in the twelfth century AD a crowned Buddha appeared on a lintel at the Preah Khan of Kampeng Svai. A crowned Buddha seated on a *nāga* and bronze and wooden standing crowned Buddha images of the twelfth century AD were found.

Thailand's modern art

King Rāma V (AD 1869-1910) was a great patron of Western arts. During his time he moved towards Westernisation and it made a great influence upon Thailand's arts. The Western modes of architecture became so popular in Thailand in his reign that a British architect was employed by him to design his palace in Italian Renissance style.[31] With the object of transforming Thailand into a first-rate modern country, he brought many foreigners to work in different departments of his administration. This trend continued into the twentieth century. Thailand's leaders were very much fond of European-style buildings in Thailand and for this reason they brought many Europeans to construct houses in European style. Many bridges of Bangkok got Italian decorations.[32] German architects trained many Thai architects and they designed many buildings in Thailand. When the Ananda Phiman Hall, which until the 1970s served as the national Parliament building, was constructed, Thailand then got the services of the Italian artists to paint the interior of its dome in neo-Renaissaance scenes. The bronze statue of king Rāma I which can be found at the foot of the Buddha Yodfah (memorial) Bridge was cast by Mr. Corrade Fereci, an Italian sculptor, in Italy. This Italian artist occupied an important place

31. *TAT*, p. 205.

32. *Ibid.*

in Thailand's art and he gave valuable services to its development and several sculptures were created by him to place at various points around the city, Bangkok. His contribution to Thailand's art was so much that he was regarded as the Father of Modern Art in Thailand. He came to Thailand in 1924 at the invitation of king Rāma VI (AD 1910-25) and he produced several bronze statues to celebrate the exploits of Thailand's past heroes. The year 1933 witnessed the establishment of a constitutional monarchy in Thailand by the revolution and in this year he under the royal patronage founded the institute of Fine Art within the Department of Fine Arts in Thailand. Its aim was to instruct and to guide Thailand's young sculptors in modern art and he played a very vital role in it. He served as its head up to the time of his death in 1962. In course of time this institute received the status of Thailand's University and it became known as Silpakorn (Fine Arts).

The period between 1932 and mid-1950 saw the progress of European ideals and its rapid growth and also the exclusion of Thai subjects or themes in Thailand's art. It "was characterised by a pursuit of European ideals to the exclusion of Thai subjects or themes".[33] After the Second World War Thailand's artists began to seek their own norms. During the pre-War period two major works of sculpture were created and these were designed by Feroci — the Democracy Monument in 1939 and the Victory Monument in 1941.[34] Two fine sculptors, Mr. Piman Mulapramuk and Mr. Sitthidot Saenghiran and a painter Mr. Fua Haripitak flourished during this period. In the 1950s Mr. Sawaeng Songmangmae and Mr. Sitthidot Saenghiran introduced nude design in their sculptural works and Mr. Paitoon Maongsemboon created bronze statues of animals. The eminent sculptor of this period was Mr. Khien Yimsiri. Another sculptor of this period was Mr. Chit Riengpra cha who crearted many wooden figures

33. *TAT*, p. 206.

34. *Ibid.*

of young village boys. Another painter of this period was Mr. Prayoon Ulushata. During this time Mr. Angkarn Kaiyanapongsa became well-known for his poetry as well as his paintings. Another painter of this period was Misiem Yipintsoi. She was an accomplished painter in the 1950s and she then showed her interest in sculpture and in 1963 she produced many welded metal statues. She can be mentioned as the first Thai lady sculptor. Mr. Damrong Wong-Uparaj became famous in the 1960s and he selected rural and seaside village life as his subjects in his paintings. In the 1970s, Mr. Pichai Nirand became very well-known as a powerful painter of Buddhist themes.[35] Like him, Mr. Thawan Duchanee and Mr. Prateung Emjaroen tried to express their ideas through Buddhist themes. During this period many artists used acrylics to produce hard-colour and hard-edged works with a great deal of force. Several Thai artists who had studied in art schools in the West produced their works in their own style. During this period Thailand's sculpture for the first time received no attention. Practically, it was neglected. Thailand's painting began to move in new directions. Mr. Chakrabhand Pesayakrit was an outstanding painter during this period.[36] He was a superb portraitist and he interpreted classical themes in soft colours and he introduced new life in them. He also portrayed characters from the literary and dramitic classics. Mr. Cheewa Komelmalai showed his interest to work in stone and papier muche.[37] Mr. Prinya Tantisuk tried to pursue graphic art. In the 1980s Thailand's painting has entered a new phase and new artists tried to reinterpret Buddhism and its iconography to find a more mature understanding of man's role in the cosmos. In this process they for the first time produced a new style of modern art "that in unique to Thailand and one which is begining to attract widespread interest from outside country". Mr. Thawan

---

35. *TAT.*

36. *Ibid.*

37. *Ibid.*

Duchanee belonged to a school of representational art called 'Visual Dhamma'.[38] He trained abroad but he returned to his native place Chiengrai where produced a spirit village of 10 houses built in his version of northern style architecture and decorated with wood panels. He inspired many new painters to move in their own way. Another artist of this period was Mr. Prateung Emjaroen. He was a fine painter. Mr. Pichai Nirand was also a famous painter. Mr. Surasit Sonakong was painter and he belonged to the north-eastern town of Rai Et and he depicted wats and the temple in them in the dim light of dawn or the glow of candlelight. Mr. Preecha Thaothong was another painter who depicted wat interiors but 'his delight is in playing with contrasts between light and shadow'.[39] Mr. Arunothai Somsakul was another painter whose works are filled with hidden images. Mr. Chalermchai Kesitpipat from Chiengrai and Mr. Pany Vijinthanasarn from Prachuap Khiri Khan were two young painters who in their works offered an alternative path through Buddhist contempletion.[40] The former's works

> convey both a sense of philosophical insight and of peace which resonates, rather than a static serenity devoid of movement of life.

But the latter's works showed that he used red and midnight blue colour. Although there was a great difference in their technique, yet these two painters "have joined their talents in an endeavour which links them to the artists of ancient Thailand".

Thailand's three theatrical arts were Khon (masked), Puppet and Nang Hai (giant hide figures). The Khon or masked drama can be mentioned as one of Thailand's supreme classical art. It

---

38. *TAT.*
39. *Ibid.*, p. 211.
40. *Ibid.*, p. 212.

appeared during the Ayuthia period. In the royal courts it was a very popular entertainment. It took its theme from the Ramakien. The Thai puppets became well known as a form of drama as well as an art form. The puppet theatre took its shape from the Ayuthia period. It was regarded as a palce art, but it made its way into popular theatre in much simplified form. It became very popular in the reigns of Rāma II, Rāma III, Rāma IV, Rāma V and Rāma VI. The Hun Luang or the Hun Yai (Royal or Large) puppets performed up to the reign of King Rāma II. The Hun Lok (small) puppets dated from the reign of king Rāma V. Around AD 1870 the second or the deputy king adopted one set of puppets from the Chinese theatre and performed Chinese drama. Later, a second set appeared to perform the Ramakien. The Bangkok National Museum is now keeping the second set and 51 of the Chinese puppets. The Hun Lekhon puppets dated from the end of the reign of king Rāma V and it was regarded as a modification of the Hun Lok. The beginning of this century witnessed the appearance of the Hun Krabok puppets which were used by Thailand's several troupes. Mr. Chakrabhand Pesayakrit, one of Thailand's foremost artists, in the past decade, has given new ideas in his puppets "whose expression and costumes have been rendered in exequisite detail that rival the finest puppets over created". The Nang Hai or the giant hide figures or the shadow puppet theatre arrived in Thailand and in Cambodia (Kampuchea) from India. In the fifteenth century AD the Nang Hai (Giant Hide) figure which were as tall as men took their appearances to perform the Ramakien and in the royal courts they were regarded as a popular night time entertainment. In the creation of the Nang Hai puppets, magic played its significant role. From the skins of water buffaloes or cows, the figure were carved. They were soaked in salty or challey water for two weeks and then they dried and scrapped clean of hair. Then charcoal was used to darken them. Then they were carved in such a way to represent a character or group of characters. Several ancient traditions refer to three key actors who were Phra Ram, the hero, his brother Lak and the Rusi or *ṛṣi* or holy hermit. The figures of Ram and Lak were made from the skin of buffaloes, but the figure of Rusi, who possessed magical powers to protect the troupe to help the success of the performance, was made from a tiger's skin.

4

A Survey of Thailand's Buddhist Literature

THERE are many local chronicles in Thailand which are generally *tamnān*, 'stories, legends', connected with the localities, principalities of northern Thailand. These works were written by several Thai Buddhist monks, who have composed them within the frameworks of Buddhist chronology and geography. They have narrated the legendary story of the time of Gotama Buddha or earlier Buddhas, the spread of Buddhism in several places, etc. These stories may be divided into three groups, the *tamnān* of the distant past in extreme northern Thailand, the universal histories written in Pāli and in Thai in the fifteenth and sixteenth centuries and the monumental *tamnān* of Buddhist images, relics and institutions.

Tamnān of the distant past

The various *tamnān* texts of the distant past of uncertain data and authorship in northern Thai script (Tai Yuan) discuss the early states of extreme northern Thailand before the establishment of such states as Lanna Thai and Nan. These texts mention miraculous legends, a long list or rulers and Buddhist establishment. The *Tamnān Muang Suwannakham*[1] gives the origin and history of a state in the

1. Wyatt, p. 111

extreme north-central region of the Indo-Chinese Peninsula in the Mekong valley. This text has its historical value. The Singhanawati chronicle and several other texts refer to Suwannakomkham as a historical antecedent of the kingdoms of Chiangsaen, Bhiangmi and Phaya in northern Thailand.

Most probably, the *Muang Ngoen Yang Chiangsaen*[2] is a late work and it deals with the history of a state of the same region mentioned above from its beginnings down to the establishment of Chiengmai by Mengrai in AD 1296. It also gives an account of Phayo, King Ngam Muang and his successors.

The *Tamnān of Singhanawatieuman*[3] discusses the Chiangsaen region and gives accounts of several local states and sacred shrines by relating their foundation to Buddhist prophecies and mythology. The Suwannakomkham chronicle has connection with its latter part.

The *Tamnān Chiengmai* or the chronicle of Chiengmai[4] was written the first half of the nineteenth century AD. It is a history of the Chiengmai region. The first portion of the text refers to the history of the country from the Buddha's predecessors to the reign of Aśoka and its second portion mentions the reign of King Mengrai (AD 1259-1327). This work also gives king Tilokarāt's reign (AD 1442-87) and his relation with the Myanmarese people.

Universal histories

The *Cāmadevīvaṁsa* and the *Jīnakālamālī* are two major Pāli historical works of Thailand which were composed by the Thai Buddhist monks at Chiengmai. They help to study northern Thailand's Buddhism. Prince Damrong states,

2. Wyatt, p. 112.
3. *Ibid.*
4. *Ibid.*, p. 113.

The first example we have is that by Mahānāma, who wrote the history of Buddhism in Ceylon in Pali. When our priests went for the purposes of study to Ceylon, and when priests from Ceylon came to this country, the latter were considered teachers as from the time of Sukhothai and from the time when Chiengmai was still a sovereign state. The priests of Ceylon showed the way of writing history after the manner of the Mahawongse; they composed religious histories of religious monuments. This was done in Pali and so Phra Bodhirangsi composed the Chamadevivongs, the history of Haribhunjai; Phra Ratana Paññānāna wrote the history of the Jinkālamāli; and Phra Brahma Rājapañña wrote the Ratana Bimbawongs, the history of the emerald Buddha.

Some of these histories were written in Siamese, like the history of the Mahadhat of Nakon Śrī Dharmarāj.

These histories, although having to do in part with foreign countries, are also the foundation of Siamese history.[5]

The Cāmadevīvaṁsa or the Chamadevivongs

Ven. Phra Bodhirangsi or the Mahāthera Bodhiramsi, whose centre of activities was either in Nabbisipura (Chiengmai or Xieng Mai) or in Haripuñjaya (Lampoon or Lamphun) in northern Thailand wrote the *Cāmadevīvaṁsa* or the history of Cāmadevī in Pāli.[6] It is a mixture of prose and verse. It is not dated. Prince Damrong mentions the composition of this text between AD 1460 and 1530 because at this period the kingdom of Nabbisipura became a great centre of Pāli culture. From this period onwards Sri Lanka came into close contact

5. Damrong. pp. 94-5.

6. *Chdv, BEFEO*, XXV, pp. 2 ff and pp. 141-77.

with Nabbisipura and other regions of northern Thailand. The former contributed very much to the introduction and the development of Theravāda Buddhism and its language Pāli there. Under royal patronage and with the help of the Buddhist Saṁgha in Sri Lanka Nabbisipura as an important centre of Buddhism and its language Pāli became well known in Thailand. G. Coedès refers to the date of the *Cāmadevīvaṁsa* in the first quarter of the fifteenth century AD. Dr. Saeng Manavidura opines that Bodhiraṁsī, the author of the *Cāmadevīvaṁsa* and Ratanapañña, the author of the *Jinakālamālī* belonged to this period. The *Cāmadevīvaṁsa* begins with an account of the Buddha's visit to the northern part of Thailand where he prophesied that his religion would prosper there. It gives an account of Haripuñjaya in northern Thailand, Cāmadevī's arrival there with the help of the sages, Vāsudeva and Sukkadanta, her consecration as a queen to the three of the Haripuñjaya kingdom, the introduction and the development of Buddhism there with the help of 500 Buddhist monks from Lopburi, the establishment of the Buddha's relics at its shrine and a list of several kings who occupied its throne after Cāmadevī. Its first section deals with the Buddha's visit to the future site of Haripuñjaya, his prediction relating to this city and king Ādityarāja. The second section describes the history of five *ṛsis* — Vāsudeva, Sukkadanta, Anusissa, Buddhajaṭila and Surahma and the foundation of the town of Migasaṅgha or Migasaṅgara. The third section discusses Vāsudeva's message to his friend Sukkadanta of Lopburi who visited the city of Haripuñjaya for its foundation. The fourth section narrates the latter's arrival in Lopburi in search of Cāmadevī. The fifth and the sixth sections mention Cāmadevī's arrival in Hariphuñjaya and her consecration as a ruler there by Vāsudeva and Sukkadanta. The seventh section gives a description of war between the ruler of Hariphuñjaya and Milakkarāja or Bilaṅkarāja, the barbarian king. The eighth section accounts the marriage and consecration of Cāmadevī's son Mahantayasa as a king there. The ninth section commences the foundation of Khelāṅganagara by Mahantayasa. The tenth section refers to Cāmadevī's arrival at Khelanganagara and the foundation of Ālambaṅganagara. The eleventh section speaks of Cāmadevī's reign at Ālambaṅganagara, her return to Hariphuñjaya and her death. The twelfth, thirteenth and fourteenth sections inform us about several rulers who reigned up to Ādityarāja of the eleventh century AD. Its account is a queer admixture of facts and legends but sometimes it throws light on some political and religious events of the country. But "it is not of great historical value and in many respects inferior to the *Jinakālamālī*". Its author is discursive in his style and much of his narrative is legendary. His language is always very clumsy. His work cannot rank as a literary performance of the first order. But the *Cāmadevīvaṁsa* is a sort epic poem intermingled with moral reflections and these are also there in its 'inexhaustible talkativeness'.

The Jinakālamālī

Ven. Phra Ratanapañña Thera of Chiengmai of northern Thailand wrote the *Jinakālamālī* in the first half of the sixteenth century AD.[7] Saeng Manavidura states,

> The original manuscript of the Jinakālamālīpakaraṇa is found nowhere new. Nor is the copy written in Chiengmai on any kind of material found now a days. Only a few people now living in Chiengmai know about the book.
>
> In Thailand there is only one manuscript copy of the Jinakālamālīpakaraṇa, and it was written on palm leaves consisting of 5 bundles (Phuk, in Thai) and 14

7. *SGEC*, p. xxxii.

leaves. Each bundle consists of 24 leaves, and as there are altogether 134 leaves. The letters are written on both sides of the leaves, and thus there are altogether 268 pages of palm leaves. It was written in Cambodian characters during the Ayudhya period probably before 2300 BE. It might have been copied or transliterated from elder manuscripts by many generations. But the third bundle of the Ayudhya MS was last after it had been copied.

Later in the Bangkok period, Phrabad Somdet Phra Buddha Yod Fa Chulalok, the first king of Bangkok (otherwise called Krung Ratanakesin), who upheld Buddhism, asked 218 Elders and 32 lay people, all well-versed in the Tripiṭaka, to work together in order to revise the Pali canon, the Atthakathās, the Tīkās, the Yonanās and the Dipanis. The Jinakālamālīpakaraṇa was then revised and copied from the Ayudhya manuscripts. The revised copy consisting of five bundles and fourteen more leaves — 268 pages of palm leaves in all, is called the First Reign's copy (Thai, Chabap Ratchakan Thinung). The king had it copied in duplicate in 2332 BE. The First Reign's edition is complete in itself, because it was copied from the original Ayudhya manuscript.

Next, in the reign of King Rama III, the third king of Bangkok (2367-2394 BE) who was greatly interested in Buddhism and who improved, built and renovated Buddhist temples, and had many Buddhist books written, the Jinakālamālīpakaraṇa was again revised and copied, this time in Cambodian characters on palm leaves, consisting of six bundles.

Again in the reign of King Mongkut (2394-2411 BE) which was the fourth reign of Bangkok, the

Jinakālamālīpakaraṇa was once more revised and written in Cambodian characters on palm leaves, consisting of eight bundles.

It should be noticed that the text of the Jinakāla-mālīpakaraṇa written in the first reign of Bangkok, was revised according to the Ayudhya manuscript, and the later revised copies were based on the copy written in the first reign of Bangkok, because it was understood to have been well revised. So, from the first to the fourth reign of Bangkok, there were copies to the Jinakālamālīpakaraṇa in addition to the one written in the Ayudhya period.

In 2337 BE the first king of Bangkok, Phrabad Somdet Phra Buddha Yod Fa Chulalok, asked five learned men of his time, namely: Phra Vichien Preschā Phrayā Potchanapinon (Vacanavimala), Luanag Udom Chindā, Luang Rāchāpirom (Rājābhiramya) and Luang Thammapinion (Dhammābhimanda) to translate the Jinakālamālīpakaraṇa into Thai. The translated book was written on Thai black paper in Cambodian characters, and then named Jinakāla-mālīnī, consisting of 12 volumes.

The reason for its being called 'Jinakālamālīnī' is that on the last covering leaf of the First Reign's Copy there is found written in Cambodian script the following Thai passage: 'Phra Jinakālamālīnīmī hā phūk kap sipsi lān' which means 'The Jinakālamālīnī consists of five bundles and fourteen were leaves'. The term Jinakālamālinī, must be read in Thai as 'Jinakāla-mālīni', because in Thai, the letter 'N' with the vowel 'I' is generally read as 'ni', but, according to the ancient Thai pronunciation it is read as 'ni'. The Ancient Thai people did not use the intonation signs such as Mai-

> Ek and Mai-To but they had to add such signs for themselves. So, when the word 'ni' meaning 'This' is added to the word 'Jinakālamālīni, which is the Pali term, it has to be understood as if it were a Pali term, i.e., that it forms the Pali term 'Jinakālamālīnī'. This is wrong. The correct form is 'Jinakālamālīnī' which means 'The Jinakālamālī'.
>
> In 2451 BE King Chulalongkorn, the fifth sovereign of Bangkok had both the Pali copy and the Thai translated copy published and called it, 'Jinakālamālīnī', according to the translated copy.
>
> Later in 2482 BE Nai (Mr) Sathien Pandharangsī translated the Jinakālāmālī into Thai.[8]

The Phonsavadan Yonok, another Thai chronicle, refers to Ratanapañña as the chief of the Bodhārāma monastery of Xieng Mai.[9] P. N. Bose describes,

> In the preface of the Jinakālamālīnī, published in 1908 from Bangkok, the prince Damrong supposes that Ratnanapañña in question on one of the two monks, of the same name, one of whom belonged to Lampang and the other to Phujao (1511).

But from the colophon it is clear that Ratanapañña composed the *Jinakālamālī* while he was residing in the Ratana Mahāvihāra of Chiengmai. Saeng Manavidura mentions,

> The manuscript of this book written in Pali by Van. Phra Ratanapañña Thera of Chiengmai city is called '*Jinakālapālīpakaraṇam*'. Some say that author was from the town Phayao in the present Chiengmai province. They go on the evidence that at the

8. *SGEC*, pp. xxxiv-xxxvi.
9. *ICS*, p. 131.

ceremony of the setting up of the Buddhist Boundry (Sima, in Pali) of Wat Maha Bodhārāma there were two Buddhist monks from Phayao taking part, and they were Ven. Phra Candaramsī and Ven. Phra Ratanapañña. This evidence has led them to conclude that it is the Ven. Phra Ratana-pañña who wrote the Jinakālamālīpakarana and the book was completed in 2071 BE.

As a matter of fact, at the end of this book (p. 129. PTS ed.) one can find the following passage:

'Iccovam sattha parinibbānate vassānaṁ saṭṭhi-adhike dvisahassaparimāṇa aṭṭhasattati-adhika ca aṭṭhasata-sakarāja Mūsika-saññite saṁvacchare Jinasasānassa ciraṭṭhitattham viracite'yam jantho Jinakālamālī nāme paripuṇṇo' which would imply that the Jinakālamālī was completed 2060 years after the death of the Buddha.

But shortly before the end of this book (p. 128, PTS, ed.), there occurs the following passage:

'Ekūnanavutyādhike atthasata-Sakkarāja Jaṭṭhādhi-patirājā visakhamāsassa sukkapakkha dutiyatithiyā condavāra Sīhalagaṇam upasampādesi' which can be freely rendered as 'In 889 Lesser Era the ruling king who was the elder son made the order of monks belonging to the Sīhala sect perform the ordination ceremony on Monday, the second day of the sixth month of the year (i.e., May). Here the year 889 of the Lesser Era is qual to the year 2071 BE by adding 899 to 1182.'

Although the concluding sentence of the book states that it was completed in 2060 BE the passage just quoted refers to the king's patronage in the conduct

> of the higher ordination in the Sīhala sect in 2071 BE. The passage relating to the events appearing in this book should, therefore, be authoritatively taken into account, rather than the passage which mentions the time when the book was completed, So it is reasonable to hold that the Jinakālamālīpakaraṇa was completed in 2071 BE and 2060 BE.[10]

The *Jinakālamālī*, which speaks of the Buddha's religion and the Buddha Saṁgha, is historically interesting. In it we find some passing reference relating to the religion of Kamboja (Cambodia), Yonaraṭṭha (the Yonaka country extends along the village of the Menam and the Mae Phing rivers and includes the Shen states to the north of these), Sukhothai (Sukhodaya), Sajjanalaya (Śrī Sachanlai), Ayojjhapura (Ayuthia), Khelāṅgapura (the city of Lampang, the present Lampang province), Jāmrayapura (Xieng Rai), Jayasenapura (Xieng Saen), and some other regions of the neighbouring Buddhist kingdom, but as a chronicle of religious history of Haripuñjaya (Lampoon) and Nabbisipura (Chiengmai), it is of great value. Like other Thai chronicles as well as Sri Lankan and Myanmarese chronicles, it is a standard chronicle. N. A. Jayawickrema opines,

> It falls into the same category of literature as the Pali chronicles, Vamsakavya of Ceylon, of the later avadāna of Thaialnd. It also shares the properties of a praśasti-kāvya in that some of the chapters towards the end of the book are intended as an exaltation of King Tilok and his great-grandson Phra Muang Keo as well as the Mengrai dynasty in general to which they belonged.

N.A. Jayawickrema says,

---

10. *SGEC*, pp. xxxii-xxxiii.

> Yonarattha, the highland region north of Lampoon with capital Chiengrai and Bingaraṭṭha, the kingdom of Mae Phing including Lampoon and Chiengmai. The Yona country, the Yonaraṭṭha or the Yonaka kingdom or the Yona kingdom the highland region north of Lampoon with capital at Chiengrai called Yonak in Thai.[11]

The *Jinakālamālī* opens with an account of Buddhism in India, the introduction and the development of Buddhism in Sri Lanka, and the spread of Sīhala Buddhism and the Sīhala Saṁgha in different places of northern Thailand. Its subject-matter can be divided under six main headings, viz., Chabbidhanidāna, Saṅgītikālakathā, Laṅkāsāsanapavatti, Haripuñjayapavatti, Lāvavaṁsakathā and Sīhala-sāsanāgamana Sīhalasāsana Jotanakathā. The first chapter which is known as the Chabbidhanidāna discusses 'the sixfold antecedent' of Gotama Buddha's life beginning from the mental resolve (*manopaṇidhāna*) of the Bodhisattva up to the Mahāparinibbāna of the Buddha. It also gives a description of the relics of the Buddha and it refers to the twenty-five Buddhas including Gotama Buddha. The second chapter is called the Saṅgītikālakathā and it mentions the three Recitals or the Buddhist Councils held during the reigns of three Indian kings Ajātaśatru, Kālāśoka and Aśoka. The third chapter which is called the Laṅkāsāsanapavatti describes the history of Buddhism in Sri Lanka from its introduction in the reign of Devānaṁpiya Tissa of Sri Lanka after the Third Buddhist Council up to the arrival of the Tooth-Relic in Sri Lanka in the reign of Kittisirimeghavaṇṇa. The fourth chapter which is known as the Haripuñjayapavatti provides us with information regarding the political as well as the religious history of Haripuñjaya, the foundation of the Haripuñjaya kingdom, the arrival of Cāmadevī, the daughter

---

11. *SGEC*, p. 39, fn.2. *BACSEA*, p. 39, fn. 2.

of the king of Lava or Lopburi in Haripuñjaya, her installation as a queen there, the erection of the great *cetiya* (the Haripuñjaya-mahādhātu) and the reigns of Āditya and Nīpā. The fifth chapter or the Lāvavaṁsakathā speaks of the Lava dynasty, the names of several kings, the foundation of Nabbisipura, its significant role as an important centre of Buddhism, the Elder Sumana's account, the introduction and development of Sīhala Buddhism in several places of Thailand and the arrival of the Sīhala image there. The sixth chapter which is called the Sīhala-sāsanāgamana and the Sīhalasāsanajotanakathā reveals the spread of Sīhala Buddhism in Thailand.

The *Jinakālamālī* is an important source for a religious history of Thailand. It presents a valuable information in religious intercourse between Sri Lanka and the Buddhist countries in South-East Asia. It also gives an accouts of the introduction and the development of Sīhala Buddhism in northern Thailand and in some parts of South-East Asia. It may be noted here that the author of the *Jinakālamālī* had no fair knowledge of the history of the foreign countries. But the account of the religion of the author's own country shows more knowledge of the subject than these of Myanmar and Sri Lanka and it is far more complete. N.A. Jayawickrema remarks,

> Prince Dhannivat observes that Ratanapañña's knowledge of the political history of the dynasty of Sukhodaya-Sajjanālaya kingdoms in rather meagre compared with his greater familiarity with the events connected with the Ayudhyā kingdom. The narration of events in his own country of Lanna appears to be the most trustworthy of them all. Apart from this, the abundant information on the religious intercourse between Ceylon and South-East Asia, particularly these references prior to the establishment of the

> Kalyāṇī-Upasampadā in lower Burma in Dhammaceti's reign, provides useful data, if properly sifted and analysed in reconstructing a phase of history of South-East Asia that has so far not received much attention. Since the author has extracted his information from a wide range of sources both reliable and not, one has to exercise the utmost caution in accepting his statements in toto.[12]

The *Jinakālamālī* is very often corroborated by other sources. Although the confused nature of some of the events stated in it threws a great deal of doubt on its historicity, yet the value of the *Jinakālamālī* lies in it that it enables us to present a brief but connected account of the religion of the Buddha in northern Thailand. Saeng Manavidura says,

> to write his book in Pali the Ven. Ratanapanna Thera must also have been very learned, and if there were difficulties he could consult the scholars of the time. So the language he used in his book (Jinakālamālīpakaraṇa) is entirely correct and sweet.
>
> He tells us many interesting events and authoritative facts including the names of the people and the places, the condition of Buddhism, the faith, the mindfulness, the wisdom and the ability of the people in these days, so explicitly that his book should be regarded as one of the best ancient history books of Thailand; especially with regard to the Lanna Thai kingdom.

The Saṅgītivaṁsa

A Bangkok monk named Somdet Phra Wannarat (Phonnarat) wrote the *Saṅgītivaṁsa* or the *Saṅgītiyavamsa* or the 'History of the Recitals' in the year of the Buddha 2332 in the month

12. *SGEC*, pp. xv-xvi.

of Citta-27 March-10 April, 1789 in Pali.[13] G.Ceedés thinks that the author was Vimaladhamma, the Thai Royal Teacher (Rājaguru). In the introduction of his work the author remarks,

Visuddhivaṁsam pavarañ ca Buddhaṁ
Visesakhemaṁ Vimalañ ca Dhammam
Visuddhisilaṁ abhivandiya Samghaṁ
Karomi Sangītiyavaṇsānamaṁ.[14]

From the above verse several scholars refer to Vimaladhamma as the author of the *Saṅgītivaṁsa*. It was written immediately after the revision of the Pāli canon under the patronage of Chao Phaya Chakri or Rama I (AD 1782-1809), the founder of the Chakri dynasty of Bangkok. In order to commemorate the cremation ceremony of H.R.H. Prince Chudhadhajadharitiloka Kromkhum Hojboon Indra Iaya, a son of King Rama V, Maha Vajirāvudh or King Rama VI gave permission to publish it in AD 1923.[15]

The *Saṅgītivaṁsa* is a valuable source for the study of both political and religious history of the kingdom of Ayuthia in Thailand. It mentions the establishment of the kingdom of Ayuthia, its rulers, its fall, its political importance in Thailand and its relation with the neighbouring countries. It also describes the important contributions made by the king of Ayuthia to the progress of Buddhism in Thailand. It has its importance in the history of Buddhism in South-East Asia. It refers to valuable information on the religious intercourse between Thailand and Sri Lanka and the development of Buddhism in the regions of South and South-East Asia. Its first chapter which is known as the Jambudīpasaṅgītiniddesa discusses the prediction of Dīpaṁkara, the birth and the early

13. *URPAA*, *BEFEO*, XIV, pp. 1 ff.
14. *ICS*, pp. 55-6.
15. Bapat, p. 44, fn. 1.

life of the Bodhisattva, the first and the second Buddhist councils in India, Aśoka's conversion to Buddhism, the third Buddhist Council and Mahinda's visit to Sri Lanka. The second chapter which is called the Laṅkādīpa-catuṭṭhavārasaṅghaniddesa deals with the fourth Buddhist Council, the history of Buddhism in Sri Lanka, a genealogy of the Maurya Emperor Aśoka and several rulers of Sri Lanka. The third chapter which is known as the Laṅkādīpa-rājavaṁsaniddesa or the Great Dynasty of the kings of the island of Sri Lanka speaks of the arrival of the collar-bone and the Great Bodhi, the passing away of the Elder Mahinda in perfect Nibbāna, the establishment of the relic of the right eye-tooth, the arrival of the relic of the frontal bone, the erection of the Mahinyangana Thupa, the Maricavatti *cetiya*, the Lohapāsāda, the raising of the Suvaṇṇamalī *cetiya* and the progress of Buddhism in Sri Lanka. The fourth chapter which is called the Dantadhātāvatāraniddesa gives an account of the arrival of the Tooth-Relic in Sri Lanka and the city of Haripuñjaya. The fifth chapter which is known as the Samaññāsārājaniddesa mentions the foundation of Haripuñjaya, the rise of Cāmadevī, the emergence of the Great Relic at Haripuñjaya and the dynasty of King Ādityarāja (Ādiccarāja). The sixth chapter which is called the Lāvavaṁsarājaniddesa or the account of the kings of the Lava dynasty provides us with information on king Mengrai's rule, the Thera Sumana's possession of the sacred relic, his arrival in Nabbisipura, the arrival of the Sīhala image in Sukhothai, the construction of a *cetiya* at Pupphārāma in Nabbisipura, the account of the Mahādhātu *cetiya*, the description of the Tilakabaddhasīmā, the arrival of the Jewel-image in northern Thailand, king Tilaka's reign, the origin of the Buddha statue at Pupphārāma, the origin of the Buddha image Sikkhi, the episode of the Sandalwood image and the construction of a stone rampart at the city of Haripuñjaya. The seventh chapter which is known as the Anukkamachatiṁasarājaniddesa describes the history of thirty-six kings of Ayuthia who were Rāmādhipati Suvaṇṇadola (AD 1350-69), Rāmessura (AD 1369-70). Paramarājādhirāja (Banu-Maha-nāyaka) (AD 1370-88), Suvaṇṇacanda (AD 1388), Rāmessura (2nd time) (AD 1388-94), Rāmarāja (AD 1394-7), Nagarainda (AD 1397), Paramarājādhirāja, Paramatilokanātha, Indarāja, Rāmādhipati (AD 1529), Buddhaṅkura, Raṭṭhādhirājakumāra Jayarājāsi, Bayatta and Jinarāja (Vaṁsādhirāja) Dirarāja Mahāmahinda, Mahādhammarāja, Sidviratna, Narissa, Ramessara, Indarāja (AD 1610-28), Jeṭṭharāja, Ādiccavaṁsa, Sudhammarāja (AD 1630), Diyara, Suvaṇṇapāsāda, Anujadhirāja, Narāya (AD 1664), Bijjarāja, Mahāupāda, Sarasakka, Mahācora (AD 1732), Mahākālarājādhirāja, Rāmādhipati, Udumbarapuppha (AD 1758) and Jeṭṭhadhirāja (AD 1758-66). The eighth chapter which is known as the Navadhamasṅghaniddesa opens with an account of the ninth Buddhist Council in Bangkok during the reign of Rama I in AD 1788. The ninth or the last chapter is Nānāanisamsacetiyathānapañcantaradhānaniddesa and it states about the good results of various works and also refers to the modes of dispersion of the religion.

The Mūlasāsana

The *Mūlasāsana*, the origin of Buddhism, was written in the dialect of the Lanna Thai kingdom in the northern part of Thailand.[16] It was written in the Tai Yuan language in Chiengmai in the fifteenth century AD.[17] David K. Wyatt opines that it was compiled just before the composition of the *Cāmadevīvaṁsa* and the *Jinakālamālī* and it acted as a source for them. Saeng Manavidura remarks,

> Mūlasāsana deals with the history of the Lanna Thai kingdom and the origin of Buddhism in that kingdom.

16. *SGEC*, p. xliii.
17. Wyatt, p. 116.

> The Ven. Ratanapañña bases the part of his Jinakālamālīpakaraṇa dealing with Buddhism in the Lanna Thai kingdom mostly on this book and writes out in Pali what is connected with Buddhism in the Lanna Thai Kingdom. It can also be said that at this point he translates the Mūlasāsana into Pali.[18]

The first edition of the *Mūlasāsana* was published in Bangkok in 1939. The second edition was published in Chiengmai in 1970. Based on a very defective manuscript the first edition was published. The second is exactly a reprint of the first. For this reason we find many defects in it. In some places the narration of events is not very clear and it is confused. But, even then, it is an important chronicle for the study of northern Thailand's religious history. It gives an account of the religion of Sukhodaya in Lodaiya's (Luthai's) reign (AD 1317-47).

The colophon to the *Mūlasāsana* mentions Brah Buddhañāna and Brah Buddhabukāma, as its two authors. Buddhañāna was the fourth abbot or the Saṁgharāja of the Flower-Garden Monastery at Nabbisipura. He occupied his post from AD 1418 to 1429. He composed some portions of the *Mūlasāsana* while he was holding the office of the Saṁgharāja. He was the main author who wrote it first and continued it up to AD 1429. Buddhabukāma, the second author, composed the last portion of the *Mūlasāsana*. Some scholars refer to him as the twelfth Saṁgharāja of the Flower Garden Monastery. He was identified with Mahākukāmañānasāra, the twelfth Saṁgharāja in Thai history. He held his office from AD 1489 to 1499. Most probably, Buddhañāna wrote the chapter dealing with the religious events in the reign of King Lodaiya in the first half of the fifteenth century AD and Buddhabukāma after him engaged himself to wrịte this work. They were well-known figures in the fifteenth century AD and

18. *SGEC*, pp. xliii-xliv.

most probably they used to live in the Flower Garden monastery. Because the *Mūlasāsana* was mentioned by many Thai scholars as the chronicles of the Flower Garden Monastery. Saeng Manavidura states that identity of the author of the *Mūlasāsana* is not yet established.

The *Mūlasāsana* begins with the Bodhisattva's resolution to become a Buddha. It gives an account of the introduction and the establishment if Buddhism in northern Thailand in the fifteenth century AD. Although there is a gap of about a century between this event and the date assigned to the writing of the *Mūlasāsana*, yet, the information stated in the *Mūlasāsana* is authentic.

'Monumental' tamnān

The *tamnān* of Buddhist images, monuments and institutions in northern Thailand as well as in other parts of Thailand are known as the 'Monumental Tamnān'. They threw flood of light on Buddhism and Thailand's religious intercourse with neighbouring countries.

E.W. Hutchinson[19] in his article 'Sacred images in Chiengmai' states,

> It is common knowledge that in the fifteenth-century Chiengmai possessed both the Enerald Buddha now in Bangkok, also the Ceylon Buddha (P'ra Sihing) which is sometimes identical with the mutilated image still at Wat P'ra Sihing. It is not so well known that Chiengmai still possesses two small figures to which great sanctity, if not magic powers, are attributed namely the P'ra Keo Se Tang Kamani (Literal translation from the Lao. In Siamese, it should be literally whity body, crystal) and the P'ra Sila, both of which are kept locked up at Wat Chiengmai.

19. *BACSEA*, p. 48.

Wat Chiengmai was founded by Mengrai, the T'ai conqueror of Lamp'un, who established the city of Chiengmai on its present site at the end of the thirteenth century : he is said to have spent his last days in residence at this temple. Wat Chiengmai lies in the north-east corner of the city wall, and is notable for the row of life size elephants projecting from each of the four sides of the Chetiya at its base.

Palm-leaf chronicles relating to both images have been transcribed, and in the case of P'ra Sīlā translated from Pali into Lao by P'ra Maha Mun of Wat Ho T'am who is the leading scholar at present in Chiengmai.

P'ra Keo Se Tang Kamani is a small crystal figurine on a hollow gold base. The lower surface of the base bears an inscription in Lao characters to the effect that it was made in CS 1235 (AD 1874) by order of Chao Int'anon, the reigning chief of Chiengmai at that time and that it contains 303 Baht and 3 Sik of pure gold.

The crystal viewed at some angles appears black, especially the head : at other angles it appears to have greenish tinge in the transparent white substance. The workmanship is not particularly fine. The head is crowned with a cap of thin gold.

The chronicle concerning this image is a long rambling narrative with little pretence to historical precision. Its main interest lies in its association of the image with the wisaka ceremonies in the month of May, when the rains on which the former depends for his crops are about to break.

P'ra Maha Mun states that his version of the Tamnan was copied from a MS Lao at Wat Ram P'oeng on the

7th August, 1920 for these interested in the history of Chiengmai.

Tamnān P'ra P'ut't'arup Se Tang Kamani[20]

E.W. Hutchinson in his article 'Sacred Images in Chiengmai' gives an account of the Tamnan P'ra P'ut't'arup Se Tang Kamani.

A short summary of it is as follows,

When the Lord Buddha had given 25 years in the ministry at Wat Khotawanaram (Wat Pa Tan), he went round begging one day along the banks of the Raming (Me Ping) to the south-east of mount Ussu (Doi Sut'ep) as far as the grove of the Mai Yang Trees where he sat under a chump of five trees to rest after his pilgrimage.

Khun Sen Tong brought five maidens and offered them with himself as slaves, but our lord refused the offer and preached to him that he should enter his niece of seven years old as a nun.

Our Lord prophesied that 837 years after his death a city named Chimai would be founded there. He then returned to Wat Pa Tan.

Khun Sen Tong had the likeness and the prophesy of our Lord engraved upon stone and buried at the source of Mo Kha, west of Doi Sut'ep.

Later P'ra Indra brought a crystal from the Second Heaven and gave it to P'ya Rām, king of the Lawa country, ordering a figure of the Buddha to be carved in the month of May on 8th day of the waxing mean.

---

20. *BACSEA*, pp. 49-50.

Subsequently, Nang Cham T'evi brought the crystal from Muang Lawa and deposited it at Lamp'un.

When P'ya Mangrai conquered Chiengmai, he invited the Crystal Buddha to be placed in Chiengmai, where it remained until P'ya Suriyawong removed it by stealth to Ayut'ya.

Afterwards, P'ra Muang Yot brought it back and placed it again in the sacred sanctuary, where it was preserved until P'ra Muang Sam P'ya established the ceremonial which has been handed down from one generation to another and performed each year between the eighth day of the waxing mean to the full moon in the month of May from the year CS 741 onwards. During the festival the image is bathed in water from Wieng Lhet Lin.

This image with the P'ra Sihing and P'ra Sīlā, is associated with the prosperity of Chiengmai. The city which possesses these three images will thrive.

The date CS 741 (AD 1380) serves to associate this image with the Ceylon Buddha — an association actually admitted in the last part of the chronicle — since it was about the same date that King Muang Ma brought back the P'ra Sihing or Ceylong Buddha to Chiengmai.

An examination of the features of the P'ra Kae Se Tang Kamanī confirms the impression made by the chronicle that this image had its origin in this country.

P'ra Sīlā

The *Journal of the Siam Society*, vol. II, refers to the P'ra Sīlā. It mentions,

It is far otherwise with the small stone tablet which may be called the Stone Buddha. The features of the central figure are not of this country : its complete nudity is foreign to religious art here: an enlarged navel compensates apparently for complete absence of sex attributes finally, the posture of the hips calls for comment.

The attitude and the posture of the hips are clearly the same as that depicted in the sculptural reliefs of the second century AD at Bharhut. If the Bharhut relief is the earliest known representation of this attitude, it would appear that the P'ra Sīlā at Chiengmai follows a later, and possibly Ceylonese development of this tradition.

The three figures in relief on the face of the tablet are glided over with a gold covering. It is however possibly to see the raw stone of the tablet in places where the wooden frame does not completely cover the sides, and it is a dark 'pepper and salt shade'. In the text of the chronicle the stone is called P'imp'akan. Some suggest that this word, which can be used to denote a certain sea-shell, implies that the substance of the tablet is fossilised shell; others translate it as stone capable of taking an impress, i.e., soft stone.[21]

Tamnān of P'ra Sīlā

The *Journal of the Siam Society*, vol. II, discusses the Tamnan of P'ra Sīla. It says,[22]

> P'ra Maha Mun has transcribed the Pali in Lao characters side by side with his Lao translation. He concludes his translation with the following note:

21. *BACSEA*, p. 50.
22. *Ibid.*, pp. 51-2.

The Tamnān was written in the year CS 1146 (AD 1785) on the 14th day of the waxing moon in the 11th month a wieng Pa Sang, by order of P'ra Maha P'ot'a Lang-ka. It was translated by P'ra Wutinyan (P'ra Maha Mun) on the 13th day of the waxing moon in the 5th (northern) month at 1 pm in the year CS 383 BS 2465 (AD 1922). He first discovered it with the stone Buddha at Wat Chiengmai and found the image to correspond in every respect with the description of it in the Tamnān.

Following the discovery, several replicas of the images were made by the faithful that same year. P'ya San Lan, a Chiengmai Grandee, had a wax model made from which three bronze images were cast. In CS 1284, P'ya Dok Chai, another Grandee of Chiengmai, had a stone copy made only differing from the original in being mixed with brick instead of pure stone. In the same year merit-makers had another copy made of the same colour. There were thus three images in all of stone and three in bronzes representing the Lord Buddha begging for alms in Rachakrut.

Regarding the replicas of the image, it appears that the plaster statue of Buddha in the northern nitch of the Chetya Wat Siri Kot was, as the Bronzes of that Wat maintain, copied from the central figure of the group comprising the P'ra Sīlā. The figure in the southern nitch of the Chetya of Wat Mun San suggests a similar inspiration. The narrative, briefly summarised, is as follows :

The first portion describes the circumstances under which the P'ra Sīlā was created at Rachakrut seven years after the Buddha's death by Achatasatru, one of the eight recipients of the relics of the Buddha.

> (The extent and nature of the relics are described in detail and seven of them are said to have been embodied in the Stone Buddha, thereby endowing it with miraculous powers). . . .
>
> The second part of the chronicle relates the removal of the Stone Buddha from Rachakrut to Ceylon by there Theras and the invitation they were received from P'ya Anutat'a to remain in his kingdom. They decided however to bring the Stone Buddha to Harip'unchai (Lamp'un).
>
> The miraculous power of the Stone Buddha to produce rain was manifested during a shortage of fresh water on the sea journey from Ceylon to La-Khung, where an attempt by the Prince of that place to detain the Stone Buddha was not successful. After passing through Sawankalok the three Theras brought the Stone Buddha to Nakon (Lampang) where it remained for a long time.
>
> The third portion of the chronicle relates the removal of the Stone Buddha from Lampang to Chiengmai by king Tilok *c.* AD 1840. Its first abode was Wat Mun San, until Tilok brought it into his royal Sanctuary.

The chronicle of the stone Buddha

The *Journal of the Siam Society*, vol. II, discusses the chronicle of the Stone Buddha.[23] It states,

> The funeral of our Lord was celebrated by eight princes in Kusinarai, the prince of which laid claim to the remains. His claim was resisted by the remaining seven Princes who sent a letter to say they were building a stūpa to contain the bones which they

23. *BACSEA*, pp. 52-5.

asked should be delivered over to them.

A Brāhmaṇa who was the teacher of all the eight princes proclaimed it unseemly for them to wrangle over the Master's Bones. He had a measure made from a golden coconut shell which contained 32 handfulls. He then called for the Bones of our Lord and distributed them equally in eight portions among the eight princes.

They were all delightful and took back each his own share to his own country where it was deposited in Chetya made for the purpose.

Each of the eight portions of our Lord's relics was what could be contained in sixteen coconut shells — being five shells of large bones, five of medium and six of small bones. They were thus in all forty shells of large bones, the same of medium bones and forty-eight of small bones. The size of the large bones was equal to that of a bean; of the medium ones to that of half a gram of rice; of the small ones to that of a cabbage seed. The radiance of the large bones was as of gold; that of the medium ones as of pearl; that of the small ebes as of a white flower. These eight portions of the relics spread their radiance over all four quarters of the compass. . . . The portion allotted by the Brahmin to P'ya Achatasatru was conveyed by him to his kingdom of Rachakrut (Rachakana). Seven years seven months and seven days after our Lord Buddha's death he invited all the Bronze to venerate the relics of our Lord's Bones and he distributed alms.

P'ya Achatasatru, who was wise in all the eyes of his people formes the pious design of fashioning a statue of Buddha and sent to the sea for stone for engraving.

He had the master depicted in the action of begging in the city accompanied by the Lord Ananda with a begging bowl on his left, with the elephant Narakiri behind him on his right — all three figures on the same stone surface a span and four inches in height and a span in breadth.

P'ya Achatasatru and the Bonzes placed the image above the altar, after willing seven of the sacred relics in a gold receptacle to enter into the stone through a recess in the face of the Stone Buddha, one entered into the head; one into the forehead; one into the breast; two into the shoulders; and two between the knees. The Stone Buddha forthwith rose into the open air to show its power; it then returned to its place above the altar.

P'ya Achatasatru had a shrine made for the Stone Buddha on an eminence upon a high mountain out of reach of the covetous. Down below to set up a platform for the worshippers.

Silawangso, Revatta, Nyanakamip'on three Theras who were travelling from land to land worshipping the images and relics of Buddha came in the course of their travels to Rachakrut and did reverence to the Stone Buddha on the Mountain Shrine.

Becoming desirous to obtain possession of the Stone Buddha, they spread out three yellow robes one upon another, and besought the Stone Buddha to come down to them. The Stone Buddha rose up in the air and descended upon the yellow robes out by the three Theras. They were overjoyed and sent ward of the happening by letter is P'ya Achatasatru — He, on recipts thereof, declared that if the will of the Stone

Buddha was for sharing life in common with them, its departure was well; and he gave them permission to take away the Stone Buddha, if they had the power to do so.

The three Theras replied that they had thes power. P'ya Achatasatru did homage to the Stone Buddha and to the three Theras; he then put them on board a ship in which they reached Ceylon. There they rested.

P'ya Anurata, knowing how the three Theras had carried off the Stone Buddha, caused an invitation to be sent to them. When he had done homage to the Stone Buddha and to Theras and had lustrated the Stone Buddha with perfumed water, a great shower of rain fell. He was overjoyed and desired that the Stone Buddha and the three Theras should remain in his land of Anurata. They replied that since the will of the Stone Buddha was to share life in common with them, they would take it to Harip'unchai to be of service to a great number of merit makers. Having heard their words and having done homage to the Stone Buddha, P'ya Anurata took the three Theras down to the best in which he despatched them.

When they reached mid-ocean their drinking water gave out. Whereupon they poured water upon the Stone Buddha, and straightway a heavy shower of rain fell supplying drinking water for those in the boat until they reached shore.

On disembarking, Silawangso, the elder Thera, placed the Stone Buddha in his begging bowl, and carried it in turn with the younger Thera.

Upon reaching Lakhung, the three Theras bathed the Stone Buddha, following which there was a great downpour of rain. The worthy prince of Lakhung greatly desired the Stone Buddha and invited it to take up its abode in his kingdom. The three Theras met the request in the same way as they had already met a similar one. They spread out their robes on the ground and uttered an invitation to the Stone Buddha who soared up into the air and descended upon the robes.

Seeing that the decision was against him, the Prince of Lakhung gladly sent the three Theras upon their way. Silawangso took the Stone Buddha in his begging bowl and proceeded to Sachanalai which is Chalieng or Sawaikalok.

The Prince of Chalieng did homage to the Stone Buddha and to the three Theras and sent them on their way. They arrived at Muang Nakon and deposited the Stone Buddha there, where it remained for a long time.

When Mun Dong came and took over the goverance of Muang Nakon he sent to tell P'ya Tilok (Tilokrat) of the Stone Buddha. Tilok then sent and brought the Stone Buddha to Wat Padeng Mang in which it was deposited at that time when P'ra Mahayanap'ote was Abbot. The Abbot bathed the Stone Buddha; and straightway a great shower of rain came down.

A certain leader, Mun Nangsu Vimala Kitit had a shrine built as a dwelling for the Stone Buddha in Wat Mun San. He brought the Stone Buddha to that temple to be a shining light to the Faithful for 5000 years.

Put't'agan, the Abbot of Wat Mun San on being translated to Wat Suan Dok, took the Stone Buddha

> with him, but subsequently had it restored to Wat Mun San, where it was to remain as a shining beacon to the Faithful.
>
> Tilok, the righteous, having vanquished all his enemies, became king of Chiengmai in the Lannat'ai. He had illuminations set up on banana and sugar-cane stems all the way between his palace and Wat Mun San. He then went and took the Stone Buddha and placed it in the sanctuary at his palace in the year Kat Met. His great grandchildren descendants up to the present day have venerated the Stone Buddha.
>
> From the beginning onwards, in any year when there was a shortage of water, the ruler had the Stone Buddha lustrated, and rain then fell in abundance.

The chronicle of the Stone Buddha refers to the religious history of Thailand and it also gives names of several rulers of northern Thailand and their contributions to the development of Buddhism there.

The P'ra Sihing or the Sihinganidāna

The *P'ra Sihing* or the *Phra Sihing* or the *Sihinganidāna* 'the history of the statue of the Buddha named Phra Sihing'[24] was written in Pāli by Bodhiraṅgsī or Bodhiraṁsī between the years 2000 BC and 2070 BC. He wrote it in the fifteenth century AD. He was also the author of the *Cāmadevīvaṁsa*. It is now available in Pali. Phraya Pariyattidharmadhātā first translated it into Thai about forty years ago. Again it was translated into Thai by Dhanit Yupha, the Director-General of Fine Arts Department, Bangkok and this translation was published by the Fine Arts Department in AD 1963. This work discusses the history of the statue of the Buddha named 'Phra

24. *SGEC*, pp. 130-1.

Sihing' which was originally cast in Sri Lanka. When King Phra Ruang (Ram Khamheng, 'Rama the Brave') knew the miraculous power of this statue, he then requested the prince of Nakhon Śrī Dharmarāj or Dhammarāj or Nakhon Śī Thammarat to go there to take permission to bring it to Sukhodaya. The text also mentions the wanderings of the image to different places in Thailand from Sri Lanka. In the reign of Rama Khamheng this image was brought from Sri Lanka to Sukhodaya via Nakhon Śrī Thammarat or Nakhon Sithammarat. From there it was brought to Ayudhyā in AD 1378. During Thailand's internal troubles it was removed to Kamphaengphet in AD 1382, Chiengrai in AD 1388 and Chiengmai in AD 1407. Most probably, Bodhiraṁsī, in order to celebrate its arrival in Chiengmai, wrote the *P'ra Sihing* or the *Sihinganidāna*. To study Thailand's political and religious history, this text has its great value.

The *Journal of the Siam Society*, vol. II, describes the *P'ra Sihing* or the *Sihinganidāna*.[25] It mentions,

> At Nakhon Śrī-Thammarat, in a chapel in the precinct of the former palace of the Chao, there is a famous bronze statue of the Buddha, known as Phra Phutta Sihing 'Sinhalese Buddha'. It is locally believed to be the authentic claiment of that title as against two other statues bearing the same name, one now in the national Museum at Bangkok, and one in Wat Phra Sing at Chiengmai. The legendary history of the Phra Phutta Sihing is as follows: 'In the year of the Buddha 700 (AD 156) the Sinhalese king, wishing to see a likeness of the Buddha, went to a monastery and said to the monks, 'When he was upon earth, the Buddha came three times to this island of Ceylon. Is there anyone now alive who saw Him ?' The king of the

25. *BACSEA*, pp. 56-63.

Nāgas suddenly appeared in the likeness of a young man, and created an image of the Buddha. The Sinhalese king summoned the finest artist and commanded them to make an image in beeswax, identical to that created by the king of the Nāgas. From it they cast a statue, in an alloy of gold, silver and tin. When it had been rubbed and polished, the image was glooming and brilliant like that of the living Buddha.... In the year of the Buddha 1800 (AD 1256), Recarāja, king of Sukhothai, sailed down the Menam and came to Nakhon Śī-Thammarat. The king of that city told him of the miracles reported concerning the Sinhalese statue. Rocarāja asked 'Could I go there ?' 'No' replied the king of Nakhon, 'it is quite impossible, since four powerful divinities guard the island of Ceylon'. The two kings therefore sent a messanger to Ceylon, and the Sinhalese king gave him the statue, after worshipping it for seven days and nights. The messenger put the statue on beard a junk. The junk, tossed about by the winds, struck a roof and was destroyed; but the statue floated away on a ship's plank. Through the power of the king of the Nāgas, the plank floated for three days and came to shore near Nakhon Śī-Thammarat. The king of Nakhon found it, brought it home, and worshipped it. Then he sent a message to Rocarāja, announcing that the statue had been received. Rocarāja went ot Nakhon Śrī Thammarat and took the states back with him to Sukhothai where he worshipped it.

The image remained there until the foundation of the Ayudhyā dynasty in southern Thailand. "Its removal to the north of Siam was due to the action of King Mahabrahma of Chiengrai, who hearing of its merits brought an army south to carry away the image.

Mahabrahma, after depositing it for a while at Chiengrai, took the P'ra Sihing to Chiengsen. He then placed it in the sanctuary of the great Buddha at Chiengrai. His nephew, Sen Muang Ma of Chiengmai, attacked him and brought him as prisoner with the Statue to Chiengrai. It was placed in Wat P'ra Sing towards the end of the sixteenth century."

The Jinakālamālī refers to the Sihala image. It says, "It is said that 700 years after the teacher had passed away in perfect Nibbāna there twenty canker-waned Arahanta in the Island of the Sihalas. At that time the king of the Sīhalas wishing to see a likeness of the Buddha went to the monastery and asked the leading Elder of the order. 'It is said that our Enlightened One visited the island of Lanka thrice during his lifetime. Is there any one even new who has seen Him ?' At that very instant on account of the (supernormal) power of the canker-waned Arhants the king of the Nāgas appeared before him in the guise of a youth and created likeness of the Buddha in order to dispel the doubt of the Sīhalas. For seven days and nights the king paid homage to the image of the Buddha. The king then had master sculptors summoned before him and having had an images of the Buddha (first) made of beeswax similar to that created by the king of the Nāgas and having had the outer mould carefully finished, had an alloy consisting of molten tin, gold and silver poured within. When the rest of the work such as filing and buffing was over it became dazzling and resplendent liking the living Buddha himself. And the king of the Sīhalas diligently worshipped it according to divers forms of ministration and honour. His sons, grandsons and great-grandsons too, in lineal descent, paid homage to the Sīhala image.

And at a subsequent period 1800 years after the passing away of the Perfectly Enlightened One in perfect Nibbāna, in the year 618 of the Royal Śaka Era, a king named Roca was reigning in the city of Sukhodaya in the Syama country which is situated in the fringe of the south-eastern sector of Jambudīpa. It is said that a handsome and strong man of the village of Go was (one day) wandering in the forest. A female divinity seeing him and wishing to cohabit with him tried her womanly wiles on him, and he cohabited with her. And as a result of their union a son was born. He too was strong and handsome; hence all the inhabitants of the village, united consecrated him ruler. He reigned there. At that time he was known as king Roca, but at a later date he was also referred to as king Radra.

It is said that king Roca who was eager to see the great ocean, one day, went down river along the course of the river Nan accompanied by an army of many tons of thousands and went as far as the city of Siridhamma. It is said that king Siridhamma was reigning there. He heard of king Roca's arrival, went forward to meet him, showed him great honour and narrated to king Roca in the manner he had come to hear of it the wondrous nature of the Sīhala, image of the island of Lanka. Hearing this King Roca said thus, 'Is it possible for us to go there ?'King Siridhamma replied, It is not possible.' Why ?

'It is said that four divinities, the divine king Sumana and these named Rama, Lakkhana and Khettagama of great majesty and supernatural power guard the island of Lanka diligently. Then both kings despatched an envoy. And having despatched it king Roca returned to Sukhodaya. The royal emissary went to the island of the Sīhalas and narrated to the king of the Sīhalas that entire episodes, Hearing this, the king of the Sīhalas paid homage to the Sīhala-image for seven days and nights and handed it over to the envoy. The royal emissary placed the Sīhala-image upon a ship and set sail.

And that ship driven forward by the fury of a severe gale hit a rock in the sea and became wrecked. But the Sīhala-image remained (aflot) on a single plank. This plank drifted along for three days and reached, by the power of the Nāga kings, the vicinity of the city of Siridhamma. At that time King Siridhamma saw at night in a dream revealed to him by the deities, the arrival of the Buddha image as though he had seen it with his very eyes, and despatched ships in all directions early in the morning. And he himself went in a ship looking for the Sīhala-image behold that plank by the resolution of will of the king of the deities, brought it with him and paid homage to it. Thereupon King Siridhamma sent a message to king Roca of his Having found the Sīhala-image. Hearing this king Roca went to the city of Siridhamma, conducted the Sīhala-image to Sukhodaya and honoured it.

The lord of earth caused to be erected, in the city of Sajjanālaya, a mighty and magnificent thūpa built of stone and brick and wall plastered over with mortar (and also an image-house) of solid bronze gilded all over and resembling a celestial abode.

And having had it erected he conducted a magnificent ceremony in honour of the dedication of the great monastery in the company of the large multitude that had gathered together from the cities of Sajjanālaya, Vajrapākāra, Sukhodaya, Jayanāda and so forth. And King Roca having accumulated numerous meritorious deeds entered the mouth of death.

In succession to him his offspring King Rama reigned at Sukhodaya. He too honoured the Sīhala-image in the self-same manner. King Pala who ascended the throne there in succession to him (also) honoured the Sīhala-image. In succession to him his own begotton son king Udakajjotthata ascended the throne there and paid homage to the Sīhala-image. In succession to him king Liddyya reigned there. And he who had studied the word of the Buddha contained in the three Piṭakas became widely known as Dhammarāja 'the Righteous monarch'. It is said that once there was a famine in the city of Jayanāda. Rāmādhipati, the king of Ayojjha, came from Kamboja and under the pretext of selling grain seized it. And when he had seized it he stationed in the city of Jayanāda his chief minister Vattiteja who was ruling (as viceroy) in Suvaṇṇabhūmi and himself returned to the city of Ayojjha itself. Thereafter Dhammarāja sent many gifts to Rāmādhipati and had a request made from him for the city of Jayanāda, and so did king Rama gave it to Dhammarāja. Vattiteja again went back to Suvaṇṇabhūmi and having received it he installed his younger sister Mahādevī in the city of Sukhodaya and the minister Tipañña at Vajirapakara and he himself conducted the Sīhala-image to the city of Jayanāda and honoured it.

When King Rāmādhipati, the paramount lord of the Kamboja kingdom and the city of Ayojjha, was lying in his death-bed, Vattiteja came from Suvaṇṇabhūmi and seized the kingdom. Next, when king Dhammarāja of the city of Jayanāda reached heaven Vattiteja came from the city of Ayojjha, captured the city of Jayanāda, took the Sīhala-image to the city of Ayojjha itself and honoured it. And the chief minister Brahmajeyya seized Sukhodaya. The minister Tipañña was governing from the city of Vajirapākāra. He sent his mother to the king of Ayojjha. And she was dear to and beloved of the king of Ayojjha. One day speaking pleasant words to the king and on the pretext of requesting him for a bronze image of the Buddha, she took the Sīhala-image and losing no time despatched it in a ship to the city of Vajirapākāra. And King Tipañña who was pleased and overjoyed honoured well the Sīhala-image with great ministrations of divers nature.

Then one day, Mahābrahma, the everlord on the city of Jamrāya heard of the wonderous nature of the Sīhala Buddha-image from a monk who had come from the southern kingdom and, seeing a replica of the Sīhala-image made by him with beeswax, was greatly pleased and overcome with religious fervour and setting forth as he was anxious to see the Sīhala-image, he equipped a fighting force and reached the city of Nabbisi. He requested his elder brother king Kilanā (Kuena) for forces, and, taking with him an army of 80,000 marched forth in due course, and arriving in the vicinity of the city of Vajirapākāra he encamped there and sent an emissary to king Tipañña. Thereupon, king Tipañña sent an envoy to the paramount lord of the city of Ayojjha. Hearing this, Vattiteja equipped a fighting force in no time and marching along reached the entrance to the Great River. Mahābrahma sent a minister as envoy with tribute together with the Great Elder Sugandha. They entered the city and deliberated (with the king) in pleasant conversation. And the great Elder Sugandha for the purpose of being the arbitrator for both of them stood in the middle of a ship, and both kings stationed themselves on either side of the ship. In order to bring about a reconciliation of the two of them, the Elder Sugandha uttered these words:

Both of you are of great fortune, of great wisdom and of great power, are established in truth, united with truth and hold the Dispensation of the Buddha in great esteem.

You are mainstay of the inhabitants of the kingdom, and are virtuous and beloved of your subjects; may both of you be reconciled with no enmity towards each other.

Here is Vajirapākāra and yonder the city of Nabbisi; let what is bound with the cord of amity be one and not separate.

Hearing his words both kings accepted them deligently. King Tipañña bestowed upon the sub-king Mahābrahma such gifts as lordly elephants as presents. Mahābrahma bestowed upon King Tipañña horses and other such gifts and a royal consecration. And having made these gifts Mahābrahma begged of King Tipañña for the Sihala-image. King Tipañña gave him the Sīhala-image as desired. And now Vattiteja sent an emissary to Tipñña saying, 'Whether Mahābrahma now retreats or not I shall advance upon him and engage him in battle'. Hearing this, king Tipañña said to the great Elder Sugandha, 'Sir, both these kings are heroic and are highly powerful, it is not possible to dissuade them. Do you make Mahābrahama withdraw to a distance and establish him in the city of Takka ?' The great Elder sent a message and had Mahābrahma apprised of that matter. Learning this he thought 'let Vattarāja follow me; I shall rejoin him in battle' and retreating from the city of Vajirapākāra he remained at the city of Takka ready for battle. King Tipañña had the news of the retreat of Mahābrahma conveyed to Vattiteja. And further, Tipñña speaking kindly words to the Elder Sugandha entrusted the Sīhala-image to him. The Elder had it placed on board a ship and reached the city of Takka sailing upstream. And Mahābrahma too, who felt as thogh anointed with nectar, in due course arrived at the city of Nabbisi carrying the Sīhala-iamge in a golden palanquin and placed the Sīhala-image in the Great Monastery inside the inner city. Thereupon, the king (Kuenā) who was his elder brother began towards the south-western corner of the great Thūpa of the self-same Great Monastery, the construction of a new niche for the Sīhala-image to repose. Even before the niche was completed Mahābrahma took the Sīhala-image to the city of Jamrāya for the purpose of making another image of bronze, its exact replica, and next to the city of Jayasena and consecrated it at Pallaṅkadīpaka. With great ceremony and honour. Bringing it back to the city of Jamrāya he kept it at the Monastery of Mahābuddharūpa 'The Great Buddha Statue' and a Buddha statue resembling the Sīhala-image in dimensions and appearance, cast from the alloy of bronze, lead, gold and silver and held a great ceremony in honour of the dedication of the Buddha statue.

The Ratana Bimbawongs or the Ratana Bimbavaṁsa

Phra Brahma Rajapañña, a young Chiengmai monk in Pāli wrote the *Ratana Bimbavaṁsa*, 'the history of the Emerald Buddha' in the Mahadhammarājabbata Monastery at

Sajjanālaya.[26] There is no date in it. But we know its existence during the reign of Rāma I. This Emerald Buddha became very famous in Thailand and it was kept in the Temple of the Emerald Buddha within the walls of the Grand Palace. The *Ratana Bimbavaṁsa* discusses the history of this image. Before its installation in Bangkok in AD 1782, it visited several places of Thailand, Cambodia and Laos. In the religious history of Thailand this chronicle has its importance. It is very probable that the author wrote it in the last quarter of the fifteenth century AD from an Indian source.

The *Journal of the Sian Society*, vol. II, refers to the *Ratana Bimbavaṁsa*. It describes,[27]

> The Emerald Buddha was made by Nāgasena, the master of Milinda, 500 years after Buddha's death. It is one cubit and one inch high, and contains seven relics of Buddha.
>
> In the year AD 256 it was removed from India to Ceylon and remained there until Anuruddha, king of Pagan, came to Ceylon in search of a correct copy of the scriptures. He took the image away with him; but the boat in which he placed it was carried out of its course by a storm, and its contents found their way to Angkor. Anuruddha came to Angkor on his magic horse to rescue them, but overlooked the image with he returned to Pagan. The Emerald Buddha thus remained at Angkor until the Siamese invasion, when it was carried off to Kampeng P'et. Eventually Mahābrahma took it to Chiengrai with the P'ra Sihing. When Sen Muang Ma restored the latter to Chiengmai, the Emerald Buddha escaped attention, having been disguised under a coating of lime. In the

26. Wyatt, p. 177; *BACSEA*, pp. 64-5; *SSJ*, II, pp. 62-5.
27. *BACSEA*, pp. 64-5.

> fifteenth century Tilok, king of Chiengmai, sent for it, but it proved to be too heavy to be carried over the hills. A more sucessful attempt was then made to carry it by cart to Lampang where it remained until Tilok collected it and placed it in the great Chetya at Chiengmai.

The Emerald Buddha Image is 19 inch high and 17 inch from knee to knee. The base is about 2 inch high.

The Phoṅsāvadān Yonok

The *Pheṅsāvadān Yonok* or the 'chronicle of Yonok' or 'the History of Yonaka' or 'the Annals of Yonaka' was written by Phya Prajākich Korachakr or Phaga Prachakitch Korachakr (Jem Bunnak) in AD 1906 in Thai.[28] It is known that he compiled it from many Laotine chronicles. It discusses a history of several regions now included in Bayap circle. Prince Damrong describes,

> The author was at pains to collect and collate all the material available, land as he did so with perspicacity and a profound knowledge of antiquity, his book is a very good one. It is one fact one of the best works in the field of Siamese history, and it is much to be regarded that Phaya Prajākich Korachakr died so young, as he gave promise of great things as a historian.

The Phoṅsāvadān nu'a

The *Pheṅsāvadān nu'a* or the 'Annals of the North' or the 'Northern Annals' is a collection of popular Thai traditions.[29] It was compiled under the patronage of king Phra Buddha Yotfa Chulalok. The king for the compilation of the annals

28. *BACSEA*, pp. 65-6.

29. *Ibid.*, p. 66; Damrong, pp. 81-2.

requested his brother Prince Surasinghananda to collect all the documents. The prince then told Phra Vichien Pricha or Preecha, the chief of the royal teachers, to do necessary arrangements for the collection of materials. Prince Damrong says,

> It appears that the method adopted by Phra Vichion Prichā was to collect all the old manusctipts he could find which he believed to relate events that happened before the building of Ayudhya. And sometimes he simply noted down what he heard from old people in the North who remembered the old tradition. All this material he arranged in order just as he thought it would fit in, his purpose being to make it a consecutive whole like the history of Ayudhya. The result is that in the Northern Annals we have combination of many narrations, and sometimes one story is repeated twice. The chronology is thus entirely unrealiable, and breaks down if any attempt is made to compare one date with another. None the less, there is a solid substratum of fact to be obtained in the incidents narrated in this history; only one must not put credence in their sequence as set down by Phra Vichien Prichā.

The Phoṅsāvadān Krun Kao Chabāb Prasot Aksaranīti or the Phra Rajaphongsavadan Krung Kao Chabab Hluang Prasot

Hluang Prasot Aksornit (Pho Barion) (Phra Pariyati Dharmadhātā) or Luan Prasot saw the manuscript of the Annals known as the Phonsvadan Krun Kao Chabāb Prasot Aksaranīti or Phra Rajaphonsavadan Krung Kao Chabab Hluang Prasot in AD 1907 and Prince Damrong published it from Bangkok in the same year.[30] According to George Ceedés,

30. *BACSEA*, pp. 66-7; *ICS*, pp. 7 and 54.

"it is the eldest recension of the Annals of Ayuthia". This Pāli record mentions the history of Thailand or rather Ayuthia from Chulasakaraj 686-966 (AD 1304-1604). At the request of a king of Thailand this Pāli history of Ayuthia was written.

The Phoṅsāvadān Krun Kao

Prince Vasukri who was Known as Krom Somdet Phra Paramanujit or Prince Paramanuxit Xinnorot wrote the *Phoṅsāvadān Krun Kao* or the Annals of Ayudhyā in AD 1840 in reign or Phra Nang: Klao.[31] Prince Damrong states,[32]

> In composing it he made use of the history of Somdet Phra Wannaratna in Pali. One part which was walled Mahayuddhakar and the other Chulayuddhakar. The two volumes were thus ascribed to Krom Somdet Phra Paramanujit and were generally considered the only books in existence relating to the history of the Ayudhya period.

It refers to the history of Thailand from the foundation of Ayudhyā. The capital to its destruction by the pupil from Myanmar in AD 1767. The author discusses the reign of the first king of the Chakri dynasty of Bangkok. King Chulalongkorn (AD 1868 -1911), the fourth king of this dynasty, requested Chao Phya Dibakara Wongs (Kham Bunnak) to continue this history up to the end of his reign.

The Pathamasambodhi

The *Pathamasambodhi* in Pāli was written in Thailand.[33] From it we do not get the name of its author and its date. It refers to the life of the Buddha. Most probably, it was written before the seventeenth century AD because the *Gandhavaṁsa*,

---

31. *BACSEA.*, p. 67; *Ibid.*, pp. 7 and 55.
32. *BAESEA*, p. 67.
33. *Ibid.*, p. 68; *ICS*, pp. 129-30.

the Myanmarese work, mentions it. Phra Nang Klao, the king of Thailand in AD 1844 requested Prince Paramanuxit Xinnorot who was then known as Suvaṇṇaraṁsī to collect fragments of this work. At this time he was the leading thera of the monastery Vat Xetuphon at Bangkok. The prince collected all the documents and in AD 1845 he compiled the present recension of the *Pathamasambodhi*. It has thirty chapters.

The Uppātasanti

The Myanmarese chronicle the *Sāsanavaṁsa*, refers to the names of some Pāli works of the Thai Buddhist monks. It mentions the *Uppātasanti*, but there is no reference to the name of its author and its date in it.[34] There are seven *śloka*s in it in honour of the Buddha, Dhamma and the Saṁgha. To save themselves from any harm and to avoid accidents, people generally recite these *śloka*s.

The Saddhamma-Saṁgaha

Dhammakitti, who probably belonged to the last quarter of the fourteenth century AD wrote in Pāli the *Saddhamma-Saṁgaha* which is a history of Buddhism in Sri Lanka from the earliest times down to the end of the reign of Parākramabāhu the Great (AD 1164 -97).[35] In the colophon the author says,

> There is a Thera named Dhammakitti who shines like the moon in Sīhala in the sky of religion, causing to blossom by his rays of wisdom the lotuses, the people of Ceylon. He is a mine of good conduct and virtue and is famed in the land of the Sīhalas like the moon in the sky; thoroughly versed in the Piṭakas and in all sciences, a man of wisdom, delighting the Island

34. *BACSEA*, p. 68.
35. *Ibid.*, pp. 69-71; *ICS*, p. 130; *PLC*, p. 10.

> of Lanka. His pupil, known as Dhammakitti Mahāsāmi, desirous of coming to Lanka, having come to great beautiful country, amassed much merit. After receiving the higher ordination of an elder, he went back to his own land and there, having reached the city of Yadaya (Ayodhya ?) while living in the great abode of Lankarama, built by the king named Paramarāja, by him, Dhammakitti Mahāsāmi, well-controlled and wise, composed this Saddhamma-Saṁgaha, complete in every way.[36]

According to G.P. Malalasekera, Dhammakitti, the author, belonged to India and wrote the *Saddhamma-Saṁgaha* in that country.

The Thai people mentioned that Dhammakitti, who was a native of Ayodhyā or Ayuthia in Southern Thailand, wrote the *Saddhamma-Saṁgaha* in Thailand. The colophon refers to a king named Paramarāja who constructed the Laṅkārāma, the monastery of Lanka in the city of Yodaya (Ayodhyā). There was a king named Paramarājādhirāja (Borommaraxathirat) who ascended the throne of the kingdom of Ayuthia in AD 1370 and he reigned up to AD 1388. The Pāli *Annals of Thailand* describe him as Banumahānāyaka, the maternal uncle of Ramessura, the second king of the kingdom of Ayuthia.[37] There is a reference to the city of Yodaya in the colophon. According to G.P. Malalasekera, the city of Ayudhyā is in India. No Buddhist text mentions the name of the Laṅkāramā which was erected by Paramarāja in the city of Yodaya (Ayodhyā) in India as referred to by G.P. Malalasekera. It is very difficult to find the name of an Indian king in the fourteenth century who was known as Paramarāja. There are references to fifteen monks in the kingdom of

36. *PLC*, p. 245.

37. *ICS*, p. 58.

Ayuthia in the reign of Paramarāja and Dhammakitti Thera.[38] The Buddhist texts of Thailand describes the name of the Laṅkārāma in that country. Most probably, Dhammakitti Thera was a prominent figure in the religious world of Thailand and he contributed very much to the progress of Buddhism and to the development of Pāli literature of Thailand. Although we do not get a definite account about the author's country, yet, from the above facts we conclude that the author was the prominent monk of the city of Ayuthia and settled at the Laṅkārāma and wrote the *Saddhamma-Saṁgaha*.

The *Saddamma-Saṅgaha* contains eleven chapters. It opens with the events of three convocations. It mentions a fourth convocation at the presence of the Maurya ruler Aśoka's son, Mahinda and Mahāriṭṭha, the first Thera from Sri Lanka, who acted as its president and gave the recital of the Vinaya. It then refers to the reign of Duṭṭhagāminī, the beginning of the writing of scriptures under Valagam-aba's patronage, the activities of Buddhaghoṣa in Sri Lanka for the progress of Pāli literature and it continues it accounts up to the reign of Parākramabāhu the Great who took keen interest in the activities of Kassapa and his colleagues for the writing of Pāli commentaries. Then it describes the authors and the principal works from the earliest times down to the reign of Parākramabāhu the Great. The next two earliest chapters reveal the merits from the writing of the Piṭakas and from listening to the doctrine. It is to be noted here that the *Saddhamma-Saṁgaha* does not say anything about Thailand, its history and its religion. Naturally, for this reason, it throws doubt about the author's country and the place where he wrote it. Owing to the paucity of evidence, it may not be possible to say anything definitely.

---

38. *ICS*, p. 60.

5

Conclusion

ACCORDING to historians the Thais about several thousand years ago took their origin in north-western Szechwan in China. They believed that the Thai race originated in southern provinces of China at about the same time when the formation of the Chinese race took place. Then they were compelled to migrate south when their conflict with the Chinese began. In AD 650 they took their migration from their original home in southern China for livelihood and to save themselves from the Chinese invasion and they established a new kingdom called Nanchao situated in north and north-west of Yunnan. But they faced many problems with the Chinese and the Tibetans and in AD 1253 under the attack of the Mongol chief, Kublai Khan and his powerful army, the Thai kingdom was in great trouble. This was the reason for the Thais to move into South-East Asia. It is generally believed that the Thais migrated from China but recent research has mentioned that from early times they used to stay along both sides of the border with China and in the thirteeenth century AD they asserted their independence. Frankly speaking, Thai history began from that time. Then the Thais arrived in the Indo-China Peninsula and they from the region around the Chao Phraya River drove away the Lao and the Khmer people. In the thirteenth century AD they founded in north central Thailand the new Thai kingdom Sukhodaya which literally means 'Happiness of the Thai people'. King Rama Khamhaeng who was regarded as the greatest king of this dynasty, made several reforms, gave judgements, directly supervised the chief administrators of the kingdom and he himself led his armies in times of war. The Thai alphabet which was of Indian origin was instituted in AD 1283 by this great ruler. Although it was modelled on the Sanskrit language, yet it showed the Cambodian influence. During the period of the Ayuthia kingdom (AD 1350-1767) in south Thailand the country was able to extend its territories and conquered all the regions formally ruled by Sukhodaya and it established its political tie with Holland, Portugal and Great Britain and it became South-East Asia's prominent nation for its development. The establishment of the new kingdom at Ayuthia and the changing of the political centre of the Thai power from Sukhodaya to Ayuthia marked the beginning of a new era of great cultural prosperity. For 400 years Ayuthia reigned gloriously in Thailand's political world and it was able to establish its power on a solid foundation there. It became rich on trade and decorated its capital with beautiful monuments to show its development in political, religious and cultural history of Thailand. But in 1767 the Myanmarese army destroyed it. For about 400 years an absolute monarchy existed in Thailand. The Thonburi or the Dhonburi dynasty (AD 1767-82) did not rule for a very long time. Then came the Chakri dynasty of Bangkok in AD 1782 which was established by the Thai general Chao Phya Chakri. Ever since this dynasty ruled in Thailand and it faced many problems from Western imperialism. The two kings of this dynasty, king Mongkut or Rama IV (AD 1851-68) and king Chulalongkorn or Rāma V (AD 1868-1910) played their vital roles to introduce several reforms to modernise their country. Under their patronage slavery was abolished, outmoded royal customs were done away with and a great change took place in them and the power of the aristocracy was curtailed. Thailand's nineteenth-century rulers tried their best to modernise the government and they took the help of the Western advisors to assist in the modernisation efforts of the army, education and transport system. Under the leadership of King Mongkut and King Chulalongkorn, Thailand became the only country in South-East Asia that never became a colony of the European powers and it was able to retain its independence during the colonial era. Because their ability, skill, personality and statesmanship helped Thailand very much to maintain its position. But it lost much of its former territory and it agreed to a series of treaties that forced to curtail its power to control of foreign trade, taxes, customs collections and jurisdiction over foreigners. Until 1939 Thailand was known as the kingdom of Siam. But at that time its rulers established their close contact with Japan and they showed their great efforts to change their country's name to Thailand 'land of the free people'. The title is justified in this sense that Thailand is the only country in South-East Asia that never came under the rule of the European powers. Although the Thais were free of foreign domination, yet they were very keen to accept modern ideas from foreign countries. The Thai rulers expanded their country's borders and they captured several border regions in Laos, Myanmar, Cambodia and Malay during the early years of Second World War. Thailand established peace with Britain when Japan lost its great power. It despatched an army division to support the south Vietnam during the Vietnam war. After the end of the war, the Thai and the Cambodian forces many times clashed each other along their border. Many people took shelter in refugee camps in Thailand and their presence sometimes threatened Thailand's internal stability. Into the twentieth century Thailand remained an absolute monarchy. But in 1932 a bloodless coup occurred and this compelled Thailand to transform from an absolute to a limited monarchy or a constitutional monarchy. In 1932 in Thailand the bureaucratic and the top military officers played their prominent parts to bring a successful revolution and the king was 'shorn of all his powers'. Since then Thailand faced many bloodless coups, practically, the revolution of 1932 overturned 700 years of absolute monarchy and replaced it with a constitutional monarchy. From 1832 until 1947 it was governed by the civilian bureaucrats, the Thai politicians and the military officers. Since 1947 the military officers with the help of the Thai civilians have taken the power of the government of Thailand. In 1975 it had a temporary constitution. It referred to a limited monarchy. Today the king has very little political power. By its most recent constitution a Prime Minister of Thailand, who is helped by a cabinet, the council of ministers, receives executive power. Cabinet members appointed by the Prime Minister take responsibility for policy docisions and individually they are responsible for their respective ministries. There were several military coups in Thailand since it became a constitutional monarchy. During the periods of military rule, various constitutions were suspended and the king as the head of the state has stayed there. In 1981 during a coup attempt the king demonstrated in support of the civilian government and he for the first time took active part to show his dissatisfaction in Thailand's military rule and he wanted to see the return of the civilian government in Thailand. He felt frustrated for Thailand's political leaders' role in its political world and he liked to find a great change in his country's political history. The king is regarded as the ceremonial head of state and all state activities are performed in his name. He must move on the advice of his ministers. In times of distress and trouble in Thailand, he has always been a powerful force for the country's unity. Although he is a constitutional monarch and he is above politics, yet he has made a great influence upon Thailand's political world. Because on three different occasions over the past few decades, the Thai monarch helped the country for his significant role to make an end to bloody street demonstrations.

The Prime Minister and his cabinet control everything. The present king Mr. Bhumibol Adulyadej has ascended the throne of Thailand in 1946 and is the longest reigning monarch in Thailand. During the post-war period Thailand's political condition was not very stable and for this reason it came under a military dictatorship for sometime. The Thais and their political leaders did not realise the real meaning of constitutional democracy and corruption has occupied an important place in the lives of the Thais. Former army chief Mr. Chavalit Yongchaiyudh became Thailand's Prime Minister in November 1996. He defeated his main opposition the Democrats in election and he belonged to the New Aspiration Party. He formed the new government when his opposition party the Democrat Party took its seat in the opposition benches though no party was able to win a majority. He was disturbed by many problems and the struggled hard to save his country from economic turmoil. His six-party coalition government faced bitter criticism of its handling of Thailand's economic crisis from the opposition members and the country's financial companies have suffiered very much due to financial problems. A period of political disturbance appeared in Bangkok and his government was responsible for it and it failed to reform the electoral system and to calm the economic storm. The Thais blamed him for his government's mismanagement of the economy, and his inefficiency and his poor role could not do anything to put the Thai economy on a sound political basis. Thailand's baht currency on May 14-15, 1997 was hit by a massive attack by speculators. Not only Thailand but also Singapore jointly tried to defend the baht. Mr. Amnuay Viravan stood against its devaluation and he resigned as Thailand's finance minister on June 19, 1997. The Bank of Thailand declared a managed float of the baht and called on the International Monetary Fund for 'technical assistance'. The declaration effiectively devalued it by 15-20 per cent on July 2, 1997. Practically, it ended a record low of 28.80 to the dollar. The International Monetary Fund approved a rescue package for Thailand including loans on August 1, 1997. Thailand on August 5, 1997 unveiled an austerity plan to complete revamp of its finance sector as part of the International Monetary Fund — suggested policies for a rescue package. The International Monetary Fund on August 20, 1997 sanctioned $ 3.9 billion caredit for Thailand. The package totalled $ 16.7 billion. Brunei late gave $ 500 million to the bailout package and thus brought it to a total of $ 17.2 billion. Thailand received a $ 17.2 billion international rescue package from the International Monetary Fund to solve its economic turmoil. The regional currency crisis began on July 2, 1997 when the baht was devalued in Thailand and the baht since then has lost more than a third of its value. The Thai Prime Minister faced a no-confidence vote in Parliament for a new anti-corruption constitution and his opposition party criticised his because he has lost his credibility and has abused the people's confidence. In September 1997 Thailand's Parliament endorsed a new constitution which designed to clean up political corruption blamed for Thailand's economic turmoil and his unpopular government has survived a no-confidence motion in Parliament. Mr. Chavalit Yongchaiyudh wanted to take meaningful steps to help Thailand's stricken economy to establish itself on its feet and he started with a major cabinet reshuffle which was needed for the administration to move to bring about economic recovery and to regain public faith and he reshuffled the cabinet in October 1997. The world's richest nations in September 1997 requested Thailand to implement reforms sanctioned by the International Monetary Fund because its currency crisis has a very bad effect upon the regions of South-East Asia.Thailand took initiative to do something for its bank reforms and the Thai government did not want to miss the chance in satisfying overseas creditors and to create confidence in a nation that has fallen in difficulties from one financial crisis to another. In October 1997 the Thais protested and demanded the resignation of Mr. Chavalit Yongchaiyudh because he was unable to solve the country's worst economic crisis in decades and they abused him very much. They thought that he was responsible for it and he did nothing to solve its crisis. The Thai government in order to protect depositors and creditors as well as borrowers, took the measures to close down 16 ailing finance companies and asked them to merge in June 1997. Thailand's worst economic turmoil in decades and political pressure from within his ruling six-party coalition and also in business circles were so much that Mr. Chavalit Yongchaiyudh was forced to resign as the Prime Minister of Thailand on November 4, 1997. The baht rose to 38.75 from 40.15 on the unpopular Prime Minister's departure. He was unable to play a significant role to tackle Thailand's worst economic crisis in decades and for this reason he failed to win public confidence. While he was in his office the baht in the last week of October 1997 dropped in value from 25 to the dollar to a historic low of 41 to the dollar. The fall of the baht gave him a signal to make way for his government's fall. Because its fall made him so unpopular that he was forced to resign. He did a great blunder not only in the political world but also in the business world. His eleven-month old administration did not go very well to handle Thailand's economy and its inefficiency brought disaster and crisis in its economic world. On November 7, 1997 the opposition leader Mr. Chuan Leekpai announced his plan to form the new government. He became Thailand's Prime Minister on November 9, 1997. He is regarded as the longest serving elected Prime Minister in Thailand's history. He has received full support and co-operation from the financial community who wanted a Democrat-led administration to play its great role to establish Thailand upon a solid foundation from its economic crisis. He from a total of eight political parties has led a new coalition government comprising about 210 members of Parliament. At first the Democrats did not want to get the government this way and they indicated an elction with a landslide victory. They hesitated to accept the task of forming the government but on seeing the country's helpless condition, they had no option, but had to accept it. A new cabinet was formed and most key economic portfolios were held by the Democrats. The Thai people became very happy to see Mr. Chuan Leekpai as their Prime Minister. At the time of his appointment he promised to do his best to solve the country's financial problems but at the same time he mentioned that he needed time and the co-operation of the people to succeed. He was mentioned as the 23rd Prime Minister of Thailand.

Thailand which is known as 'the Land of Yellow Robes' is the only country in the world where the king, the head of the state, is 'constitutionally stipulated to be a Buddhist' and where Buddhism has prospered and in all respects has fulfilled the life of the Thais. Buddhism still maintains its existence as a living force there. The traditional belief in Thailand is that Aśoka, the Maurya ruler of India, sent Buddhist missionaries after the Third Buddhist Council in India to introduce Buddhism in Thailand. The Dvāravatī kingdom in the lower Menam valley in lower central Thailand occupied a prominent place in the political and religious history of Thailand from the sixth or seventh century AD to the first half of the eleventh century AD. It was a well-known centre of Theravāda Buddhism. The Mon people were the inhabitants of the Dvāravatī kingdom and their capital was at first at Nagarama Patha or Phra Pathom and later at Lavo or Lopburi. The Mahāyāna sect made considerable progress under the patronage and full support of the Śailendra rulers of the Śrī-Vijaya empire in several regions in the south of modern Thailand and this occurred in the beginning of the seventh century AD. The Buddhist antiquities and monuments were found in these places when Mahāyānism prospered and they belonged to the Śrī-Vijaya school of art and architecture. The Lopburi period marked the second phase of the introduction and the development of Mahāyānism in Thailand. Lopburi, the chief Khmer headquarter in Thailand, became an important centre of the Khmer culture and civilisation. The Khmer empire of Cambodia maintained its control over several lands of the Menam valley in lower Thailand in the eleventh century AD and it brought Mahāyānism and Brāhmaṇism there. From AD 1017 onwards the Khmer art and culture developed in the Menam valley and the Khmer civilisation influenced the north of modern Thailand as far as Sukhodaya and Sawankalok towns. Under the patronage of the Dvāravatī rulers Theravāda Buddhism flourished in the lower Menam valley but in the eleventh century AD when it came under the control of the Khmer empire not only Mahāyānism and Brāhmaṇism, but also Theravāda Buddhism existed side by side in the religious history of Thailand as indicated by a Khmer inscription dated Śaka 944. Although the Mahāyāna sect under the Khmer rule maintained its importance and pre-eminence, yet the Hīnayāna sect also prospered there as it had existed in this region under the rule of the Dvāravatī kingdom. The Dvāravatī rulers were able to extend their political influence up to the Haripuñjaya kingdom in northern Thailand. This kingdom in the upper Menam valley was a centre of Theravāda Buddhism and the Mon people, who were its great followers, were its inhabitants. They helped very much for the progress of Theravāda Buddhism in Thailand. The characters of several Mon inscriptions of the thirteenth century AD discovered at Haripuñjaya which were identical with those of the Mon inscriptions of Myanmar between the eleventh and thirteenth centuries AD threw flood of lights on close religious and cultural links between northern Thailand and Myanmar. Southern Thailand witnessed the prosperity of Mahāyāna Buddhism from the seventh to the thirteenth centuries AD, while Theravāda sect played its great role in western, northern and in central Thailand. Several Buddhist *stūpa* in the Śrī-Vijayan style at the Mahādhātu monastery and many images of the Buddha, Bodhisattvas, Avalokiteśvara and of the Mahāyāna gods and goddesses in the provinces of southern Thailand indicated the existence of Mahāyānism in these regions. The establishment of the Sukhodaya kingdom in AD 1257 witnessed an important event not only in the political history but also in the history of Buddhism in Thailand. The Sukhodaya rulers were great patrons of Theravāda Buddhism. King Rama Khamhaeng who became prominent for his services to Buddhism was responsible for the introduction and the development of the Theravāda doctrine of Sri Lankan Buddhism into his kingdom, Sukhodaya from Nakon Śrī Dharmarāja (Ligor) where several Buddhist relics were found and the Hīnayāna form of Buddhism prevailed there. The Sukhodaya period saw Thailand's contact with Sri Lanka through the medium of Śrī Dharmarāja or Siridhammanagara (Ligor) in the Malay Peninsula and Myanmar. The arrival of a Mahāthera from Sri Lanka in the Rāmañña country, the coming of a Sukhodaya monk to the Rāmañña country for ordination at the hands of the Mahāthera from Sri Lanka, the request of the Sukhodaya king for a Buddhist monk from the Mahāthera of Sri Lanka then in the Rāmañña country. The return of Thailand's monk to his native country from the Rāmañña country with the permission of Sri Lanka's Mahāthera, the latter's important role for the establishment and the development of the Buddhist Saṁgha from Sri Lanka in Thailand, King Rama Khamhaeng's patronage for the introduction of the Theravāda doctrine of Sri Lankan Buddhism in Sukhodaya and for the establishment of the Lankavong sect as his state religion, the plantation of the Bodhi-Tree in Thailand from Sri Lanka, the strong influence of Sri Lanka's design and style upon the architectural buildings such as *stūpas*, *vihāras*, monasteries, *chedis* as well as sculptural productions of Sukhodaya and the discovery of Sukhodaya's Buddha image with strong influence of Sri Lanka's art of sculpture indicated Sukhodaya's close religious ties with the Buddhist Saṁghas of Sri Lanka and Rāmañña (Myanmar) in the first half of the fourteenth century AD. The second half of the fourteenth century AD witnessed direct religious intercourse between Thailand and Sri Lanka and the establishment of the Buddhist Saṁgha from Sri Lanka in Thailand. The rise and growth of the kingdom of Ayuthia in southern Thailand in AD 1350 marked the beginning of an era of great cultural prosperity. All the Ayuthian kings who reigned in the fourteenth century AD were devout followers of the Lankavong Theravāda form of Buddhism and under their patronage not only Buddhism flourished but also several Buddhist monasteries were erected there which gave inspiration for the progress of Theravāda Buddhism in Thailand and the presence of many Buddhist monks helped Ayuthia very much to become a great centre of Buddhist culture during this time. The fifteenth century AD was an age of great devotional activity in Thailand and it witnessed strong influx of Buddhism from Sri Lanka, the arrival of the Buddhist monks in Sri Lanka from Thailand to study the religious texts and to receive the Upasampadā ordination from the Mahātheras of Lanka and the introduction and the development of the Buddhist Saṁgha from Sri Lanka in Thailand with the help of the Mahātheras from Sri Lanka. During the period AD 1448-88 the Lankavong Theravāda form of Buddhism flourished in a glorious way under the patronage of King Boromotrailokanath or Trailok in Thailand. The ordination of the king and also of 2,388 men as monks in Thailand, sending of royal gifts of robes, bowls, etc., to king Trailok from kings of several neighbouring kingdoms on this occasion, the discussion of the interpretation and reorganisation of the Buddhist doctrine on this occasion, the construction of monasteries and *vihāras* within the boundary of the king's palace, the decoration of the images of Bodhisattva's 500 incarnations and the establishment of a new sect of Buddhism named the Vanaratnavong or Pa-kaew marked the religious activities of the kingdom of Ayuthia in the fifteenth century AD. Theravāda Buddhism and the Buddhist Saṁgha from Sri Lanka flourished in Thailand in the sixteenth century AD. This century witnessed Ayuthia's war with Myanmar, its political turmoil and its rulers' devotion to Buddhism and their great role for the progress of Buddhism in thier kingdom. The seventeenth century was not only an important period in Thailand for trade and commerce but also for Thailand's contact with the Western world. But from the religious history of the country nothing is known in Thailand about the progress of Buddhism during this period. The eighteenth century saw Thailand's religious intercourse with Sri Lanka and the reign of King Boromokot (AD 1732) marked a turning point in the history of Buddhism in Thailand. This century opened a new chapter in relations between the two countries. The purification of the Buddhist Saṁgha in Sri Lanka with the help of the Buddhist monks from Thailand sent by King Boromokot of Thailand in the reign of king Kirti Śrī Rājasaṁha of Sri Lanka, the performance of the Upasampadā ordination in Kandy in Sri Lanka in AD 1756, the arrival of the Thai Buddhist monks in Sri Lanka for the progress of religion and the establishment of the Siyama sect or the Siyamagama sect in Sri Lanka in the eighteenth century showed Thailand's religious activities and the prosperity of its religion. In the second half of the eighteenth century the foundation of Dhonburi by Phya Tak Sin took place. It saw the re-unification and consolidation of Thailand and the restoration, the improvement, and purification of the Buddhist Saṁgha in the Dhonburi kingdom. The fall of Ayuthia took place in AD 1767 and the

Dhonburi kingdom came to an end in AD 1782. The Chakri dynasty took its appearance at Bangkok in AD 1782 and it opened a new era in the political and religious history of Thailand. The popularity of the Lankavong Theravāda form of Buddhism as Thailand's national religion, important steps for its promotion, writing of a new and complete edition of the Tipiṭaka on palm-leaves, convocation of the Ninth Buddhist Council at Bangkok under king Rāma I's patronage, adoption of several measures for the purity of the Buddhist Saṁgha in Thailand, issuing of several decrees to govern the conduct and the behaviour of the Buddhist monks, and to deal with monastic administration and its reorganisation, the foundation of the Dhammayuttika Nikāya, the celebration of the 2500th Anniversary of the Buddha's Mahāparinibbāna under the patronage of king Rāma IX, the construction and the restoration of several Buddhist monasteries and the progress of the two Buddhist Universities in Thailand under personal care and ovservation clearly gave an impression of the development of the Lankavong Theravāda form of Buddhism during the reigns of the Chakri dynasty rulers. All these above events helped us to know that the rulers were zealous Buddhists and Buddhism reached the zenith of its glory during this time. The present king Rāma IX like his predecessors to playing his vital role for the growth and progress of Buddhism in his kingdom.

Sukhodaya's glory rested on its sculptures. Most art historians have spoken highly of its artistic activities for wonderful creations. Rama Khamhaeng, who reigned in the latter part of the thirteenth AD, saw the beginning of the early Sukhodaya statuary. Classical Sukhodaya Buddha image were produced form the early fourteenth century AD. The Sukhodaya kingdom sculptors were mentioned as the first to make Buddha in all four positions — standing, walking, seated and reclining. Several artists, who belonged to the Haripuñjaya kingdom, created an art which showed their leanings towards contemporary arts of other cities in the region but under these influences they produced an art which was as individualistic as the sculptors themselves. For the first time in Thailand's art no images of Hindu deities were created by the sculptors during the Haripuñjaya period. They liked to produce standing Buddha images than seated Buddha images and most oftern they engaged themselves to work in stucco and terracotta rather than less malleable materials. They displayed their true genius in terraccota sculpture. The U-Thong sculptors devoted themselves to create Buddha images which were usually seated but on some occasions standing or walking. They generally loved to work in bronze but sometimes they created a few terracotta, sandstone and gold images and they were influenced by Mon and Khmer. The Ayuthian sculptors created many Buddha images and their primary aim was to produce a wilder range of incidents relating to the Buddha's life. Their principal medium was bronze and they showed their great skill in its casting. The Sukhodaya school and the school of Lopburi Via U-Thong made their influences upon the early Ayuthian sculptors. During the Ayuthian period standing Buddha became very popular, and showed a great variety of poses than before. The early Ayuthian sculptors produced a number of walking Buddha but their weight rested on the right rather than the left foot and the right rather than the left hand gave the *abhaya-mudrā* pose and the Ayuthian images' faces were usually broad. The Buddha footprints of the Ayuthian period became very popular but they were little different from these of previous periods. During this period the huge brick Buddha image were covered by stucco and word carvers used to decorate doors, windwos and ceilings. The Ayuthian potters produced not only Buddha images but also human and animal figures. Phetburi, Uttaradit and Nonthaburi were the places where the finest examples of the Ayuthian period's paintings were found. The Ayuthian murals painted the Tasachat, the life of the Buddha, the Ramakien and also several local stories. The Ayuthian artists created excellent lacquer and gold art objecs as well as beautiful manuscripts of religious themes. In the Bangkok period under the patronage of the Thai rulers western modes and styles were adopted and were introduced into the Thai art. Bangkok Wat architecture plans were exactly like these of Ayuthia. The styles of Chinese architects and artists were also taken by the Bangkok architects to build and to testore several wats during the reign of Rāma III. Western ideas and styles made their great influence upon the art world of Bangkok in the nineteenth century AD. It is said that in the annals of Thai art Bangkok period sculpture was not mentioned as a shining star. Between 1782 and 1851 sculptors of this period searched intensively into old literary and Hindu texts to discover new ideas, themes and ways in which they wanted to create the Buddha and without precedent they produced various pieces in their imaginations. Early Bangkok sculptors worked in bronze, wood and stucco. No stone images were available but many marble bas-reliefs were found. King Rāma III was an active patron of the arts. Under the patronage two standing Buddhas, each three meters tall and clad in 84 kg of gold, were created. They were dedicated to the king's father and grandfather and were placed in the bet of the Wat Phra Kaew. There were 33 small bronzes, one for each of Ayuthia's 33 kings and depicted the main events of the Buddha's life and these were the most remarkable creations of king Rāma III's sculptors. In 1836 the king commissioned statues of 80 *r̥ṣis* to show all the *yoga* exercises. After 1851 the Bangkok government supported new ideals based an modern thought. During the reign of Rāma IV a new rationalism undressed art of its other worldliness. Under his patronage the Bangkok sculptor created the Sambuddhabarni, the image, which had a simplified robe and had a flame upon his head. The second image of his reign was Nirantaraya which was without *uṣṇīṣa* and it was in the *samādhi* position and had a very realistic looking robe. But these style did not last for a very long time and they began to disappear after the death of king Rāma IV. King Rāma V took keen interest to create several images of the Buddha and Hindu deities in bronze. Of the many decorative works in sculpture during the reign of Rāma III the most outstanding were the 152 marble bas-reliefs of scenes from the Ramakien which were produced to decorate the base of the Wat Chetupon's bot. The Bangkok sculptors did not show their interest in wood carving. It may be noted here that Sukhodaya was regarded as an age of sculpture and Ayuthia was mentioned as an era of architecture, but Bangkok witnessed the flourishing condition on painting. Thus, it was an age of painting. During this period painting flourished very much and pain ters showed their creative talents on the murals which helped to decorates the inner walls of *vihāns* and the bots of the wats. The medium of painting was murals, manuscripts, lacquer and gold works which were used to decorate manuscripts, cabinets, wat doors and windows and some utensils. In the reigns of king Rāma I and king Rāma II past art styles played their great roles in the art world of Bangkok. During the reign of king Rāma III Chinese themes occupied an important place in artists' mind to create their ideas. But kings Rāma IV and Rāma V were Western-minded persons and they wanted to adopt European approaches and ideas to art. After the death of Rāma V in 1910 that art radically took a different turn. According to many art historians, king Rāma III's period marked the high point of classical Thai painting. The artists began to look toward a wider world beyond the horizon. They created figures, ships, costumes, architecture and accoutrements of the Chinese, Europeans and Arabs into their paintings and also borrowed Chinese motifs and in the Chinese style they created the entire scenes. The drive toward Westernisation that started in earnest in the reign of Rāma V continued to move in a vigorous way and it was able to exercise a great influence upon Bangkok's art world. In the twentieth century the Thais were in great love for Western style of architecture and it went up to such an extreme point that king Rāma V himself had appointed a British architect to build his palace in Italian Renaissance style. Many European-style buildings and bridges were constructed in Thailand under the management of European architects and engineers. German architects were employed to train the Thai architects and this trend continued into the twentieth century. Corrado Feroci was a man with a passionate interest in modern art and he was mentioned as the Father of Modern Art in Thailand. King Rāma VI invited him from Italy to Thailand in 1924 and the latter produced bronze statuary to celebrate the exploits of Thailand's past heroes. In 1933 he founded an institute of fine arts within the Department of Fine Arts in Thailand. European ideals, themes, designs and styles became very popular in Thailand between 1932 and the mid-1950s. During this period Thai subjects and themes were execluded from Thailand's art world. The Thais became very mcuh fond of European styles and designs. In the 1950s Sawaeng Songmangmee and Sitthidet Seenghiram occupied prominent places in Thailand's art world by sculpting nudes and Paiteen Maungsomboon produced crafted bronze statues of animals. In the 1970s Pichai Nirand was a powerful painter of Buddhist themes. During this period the Thai artists used acrylics to create hard-colour and hard-edged works with a great deal of force. At this time the Thai painting began to move in new directions. There were political and social disturbances in Thailand and the Thai artists created paintings of social protest which informed society's downtrodden. The 1970s witnessed a resurgence of interest in sculpture but this time abstract forms took the place of the realism of the 1850s. The Thai painting turned its attention to the religious art in the 1980s. Prinya Tantisuk followed graphic art and Kiettisak

Chaenonart took interest in social protest. For the first time they introduced a style of modern art that was really unique to Thailand and gradually it began to attract attention from outside the country: Thawan Duchanee was a master of line and iconography of all religions and was mentioned as one of the doyens of a school of representational art called 'Visual Dhamma'. According to the Khoi manuscript copysists and their patrons, their works were holy works which helped them to gain merit. The Khoi manuscripts received their name from the paper on which they were written. The Thai puppets were a form of drama as well as an art form. The shadow Puppet Theatre which became very popular in Thailand came to this country and Cambodia (Kampuchea) from India.

Buddhism has inspired the life of the Thai people and has played an important role in Thailand's social, religious and cultural life. Many local chronicles which are generally the *tamnān* 'stories, legends' connected with the localities, principalities of northern Thailand were written by the Buddhist monks within the frameworks of Buddhist chronology and geography, and they guide the readers to study the country's religious history. The Tamnān Muang Suwannakham, the Muang Ngoen Yang Chiengsaen, the Tamnān of Singhanawatieuman and the Tamnān of Chiengmai are the *tamnān* texts of the distant past. The *Cāmadevīvaṁsa*, the *Jinakālamāli*, the *Saṅgītivaṁsa*, and the *Mūlasāsana* are the universal histories written in Pāli and Thai in the fifteenth and in the sixteenth centuries AD and are very helpful to study Thailand's Buddhism. The period between the second half of the fifteenth century AD and the first half of the sixteenth century AD was very significant from the religious, literary and cultural history of northern Thailand. Under royal patronage and with the help of the Buddhist Saṁgha in Sri Lanka, Chiengmai and other regions in northen Thailand became famous as important Buddhist centres and Pāli literature flourished there during this time. The Tamnān P'ra P'ut't'arup Se Tang Kamani, the Tamnān of P'ra Sīlā, the story of the Stone Buddha, the *P'ra Sihing* or the *Sihinganidāna*, the *Ratana Bimbawongs*, or the *Ratana Bimbavaṁsa*, the *Phoṅsāvadān Yonok*, the *Phonsavadan nu'a*, the *Phonsavadan Krun Kao* or the *Phongsavadan Krung Kao* are the *tamnān* texts of buddhist images, monuments and institutioins in northern Thailand as well as in other parts of Thailand and they are known as the 'Monumental Tamnān'. They are works of outstanding value to the readers because they throw flood of light on Buddhism and Thailand's religious intercourse with neighbouring countries.

Bibliography

Amara Thera, Ven. P., Buddhism in Thailand, *The Maha Bodhi*, vol. 85, B. E. 2521, November-December, C. E. 1977, Nos. 11-12, Calcutta, 1977.

Ananda Bazar Patrika, Calcutta, Prafulla Sarkar Street, Calcutta.

Art And Archaeology in Thailand Published by Fine Arts Department in Commemoration of the 100th Anniversary of the National Museum, September, 19, 1974.

(a) Forward by Capt. Sompop Piromya R. T. N., Director General.

(b) A Pali Inscription from Vat Sri Ratnamahadhatu, Subarnapuri.

(c) The Technique of Thai Traditional Painting by Elizabeth Lyons.

(d) Buddhist votive Tablets and Caves in Peninsular Thailand by Stanley J. D. Corner.

(e) Crowned Buddha Images in South-East Asia by Dorothy H. Fickle.

(f) The Kingdom of Haripunjaya by Srisakra Vallibhetma.

The Art of Indian Asia, vol. I, Bellingen Series XXXIX by Heinrich Zimmer and completed and edited by Joseph Cambell, Bellingen Foundation Inc., New York, 1955.

The Arts of Thailand by Steve Van Beek and Luca Invernizzi Tetteini, London, 1961.

The Asian Age, Calcutta, Prafulla Sarkar Street, Calcutta.

Backus, Mary, ed., *Siam and Laos as seen by our American Missionaries*, Philadelphia, 1884.

Bapat, P. V., *2500 years of Buddhism*, Publication Division, Ministry of Information and Broadcasting, Government of India, New Delhi, 1971.

Blanchard, Wendell and others, *Thailand : Its People, Its Society, Its Culture, Human Relations Area Files*, New Haven. Conn., 1958.

Book, S.V & Jottoni, L. A., *The Arts of Thailand*, revised and updated edition, London, 1991.

Boribal, Luang, *Ancient Monuments in Siam*, Part I, Bangkok, 1933.

Bose, Phanindra Nath, *The Indian Colony of Siam*, Lahore, 1927.

———, *The Indian Colony of Siam*, Lahore, 1927.

Briggs, Lawrence Palmer, 'Dvaravati, Most Ancient Kingdom of Siam', *JAOS*, LXIII, 1945.

———, *The Ancient Khmer Empire*, Philadelphia, 1951.

———, Dvaravati, the most ancient kingdom of Siam, *Journal of the American Oriental Society*, LXV, New Haven 1945.

Buribhand, Luang Beribal and Grisweld, A. B., *Sculpture of the Peninsular Siam in the Ayuthia Period*, The Siam Society Fiftieth Anniversary Commemorative Publication, Bangkok, 1954, vol. II, 1929-53.

———, and Griswold, A. B., *Thai Images of the Buddha*, Bangkok, 1972.

———, 'Ruang Phra Phutta Sihing' (in Siames), reviewed in *Journal of the Siam Society*, vol. XXIV, Bangkok, 1937.

Burney, Henry, *The Burney Papers*, Vajirnana Library, Bangkok, 5 vols., 1910-14.

Cady, John F., *South-East Asia, Its Historical Development*, New Delhi, 1976.

Campbell, John Gordon Drummond, *Siam in the Twentieth century : Being the Expreiences and Impressions of a British Official*, London, 1902.

Claeys, J. A. V., L'archaeologie du Siam, *BEFEO*, XXXI, Hanoi, 1931.

Coast, John, *Some Aspects of Siamese Politics*, Institute of Pacific Relations, New York, 1953.

Collective Defence in South-East Asia, Chatham House Report, London, 1956.

Coodes, G., *Les Etats Hindouises d'Indochina et d'Indonesia, E. de Boccard*, Paris, 1948.

———, *The Making of South-East Asia*, tr. A. M. Wright, London, 1966.

———, *Bulletin de L'Ecole Francaise d'Extreme Orient*, vol. XXV, Hanoi, 1923.

———, *Recueil des Inscriptions du Siam*, vol. I, Bangkok, 1924.

———, *The Empire of the South Seas (Sri Vijaya from the VII to the XIIIth centuries)*, The Siam Society Fifteenth Anniversary Commemorative Publication, vol. II, 1929-53, Bangkok, 1954.

———, One Recension Palie Des Annales d'Ayuthia, *Bulletin De L'Ecole Francaise D'Extreme Orient*, vol. XIV, Hanoi, 1914.

———, "Le Musee National de Bangkok", *Ars Asiatica*, vol. XII, Paris, 1972.

———, *Recueil des Inscription du Siam* (Part II), Royal Institute, Bangkok, 1929.

———, Une Recension Palies Des Annales d'Ayuthis, *Bulletin de l'Ecole Francaise d'Extreme Orient*, XIV, Hanoi, 1914.

———, The Camadevivamsa, Documents sur l'histoire politique at religious du Laos Occidental, *Bulletin de l'Ecole Francaise d'Extreme Orient*, XXV, Hanoi, 1925.

Crawfurd, John, *Journal of an Embassy from the Governor of India to the Courts of Siam and Cochin China*, H. Colburn, London, 1828.

Crosby, *Jesiah, Siam : The Crossroads*, London, 1945.

Damreng, Prince, 'The story of the records of Siamese history', The Siam Society, Fiftieth Anniversary Commemorative Publication, *The Siam Society Journal*, vol. I, 1904-29, Bangkok, 1984.

Damrong, Rajanubhab, H. R. H. Prince, History of Siam prior to the Ayudhya Period, *Journal of Siam Society*, vol. XIII, Bangkok, 1920.

———, *History of Buddhist Stupas in Siam*, Bangkok, 1926.

Dhaninivat, Prince, *A History of Buddhism in Siam*, Bangkok, 1960.

Dhanit Yupha, in the foreword to a new addition of the text, translated from Pāli by Saeng Mobwithun, Nithan Phraphutthasihing, Bangkok, 1953; C. Notton, *P'ra Buddha Sihinga*, Bangkok, 1933.

Dipavamsa, H. Oldenberg, London, 1879.

Dupont, P., *L'Archaeoligis Mons de Dvaravati*, Pub. Ecole Francaise Extreme Orient, XLI, Paris, 1959.

Dutta, Sukumar, *Buddhism in East Asia*, Indian Council for Cultural Relations, New Delhi.

The Economic Times, Calcutta.

Eliot, Sir Charles, *Hinduism and Buddhism*, vol. III, London, 1971.

Fickle, D. H., *Images of the Buddha in Thailand*, Singapore, 1989.

Fifield, Russel H., *The Diplomacy in South-East Asia, 945-58*, New York, 1958.

Fisher, Robert E., *Buddhist Art and Architecture*, London 1993.

Fitzsinnons, Thomas, *Thailand, Human Relations Area Files*, New Haven, Conn. 1957.

Frankfurter, O., "King Mongkut", *Journal of Siam Society, Bangkok*, vol. 1, 1904.

Ganguly, O.C., *A Group of Buddhist Sculpture from Siam*, Calcutta, 1929.

Graham, W. A., *Siam*, 2 Vols., London, 1924.

———, *Siam : A Handbook of Practical Commercial and Political Information*, London, 1912 and 1924, 2 vols.

Greslier, G., 'Nete sur la sculpture Khmers ancienne", *Etudes Asiatiques*, Paris, 1925.

Griswold, A. B., *King Mongkut of Siam*, New York. 1961.

Griswold, A. B., and Prasat, na Nagara, 'King Lodaiya of Sukhodaya and his contemporaries', *Journal of the Siam Society*, January 1972, vol. 60, part I, Bangkok.

Hall, D. G. E., *A History of South-East Asia*, London, 1964.

———, "From Mergui to Singapore, 1686-1819", *Journal of Siam Society*, XLI, part 1, July, 1953, Bangkok.

Hamilton, Alexander, *A New Account of East Indies (1688 to 1723)*, 2 vols., Edinburgh, 1727.

Hazra, Kanai Lal, *History of Theravda Buddhism in South-East Asia*, Calcutta, 1982.

———, *The Buddhist Annals and Chronicles of South-East Asia*, New Delhi, 1986.

———, *Pali Language and Literature*, vols I & II, New Delhi, 1994.

Hutchinson, E. W., *Adventures in Siam in the Seventeenth Century*, London,

1940.

Ingram, James C., *Economic Change in Thailand since 1850*, Stanford, California, 1955.

Jayawickrema, N. A., Pali Text Society Translation Series, No. 36, 'The Sheaf of Garlands of the Epochs of the Conqueror' London, 1967, being a translation of *Jinakalamalipakaranam* of Ratanapanna Thera of Thailand.

Jeremias Van Vliet, *Revolutions arrivees au Siam on 1647*, Paris, 1663.

Jermsawatdi, Premsak, *Thai Art with Indian Influence*, New Delhi, 1979.

Jinakalamali, ed., Aggapanahapandita, A. P. Buddhadatta Mahathera, Pāli Text Society, London, 1962. G. Coodes, *Bulletin de l'Ecole Francaise d'Extreme Orient*, XXV, Hanoi, 1925.

Jinakalamali, ed. G. Coodes, *BEFEO*, vol., XXV, Hanoi, 1925. Tr. by N. A. Jayawickrama, PTS, Translation Series, No. 36, "The Sheaf of Garland of the Epoch of the Conqueror", Being a translation of the Jinakalamalipakaranam of Ratanapanna Thera of Thailand with an introductory essay by Saeng Manavidura, London, 1967.

Joost Schouton, *A True Description of Mighty Kingdom of Japan and Siam*, Roger Manley's translation, London, 1663.

La May, Reginald, *A Concise History of Buddhist Art in Siam*, Tokyo, Japan, 1963.

Landon, Kenneth Parry, *Siam in Transition*, London, 1939.

Lands And Peoples : *Asia-Australia New Zealand - Occania*, vol. 2, U.S., 1983 : Thailand by Pracheem Chemchai, Chulalongkorn University, Bangkok.

Le May, Reginald, *A Concise History of Buddhist Art in Siam*, Cambridge, 1938.

Levy, Paul, Les traces de l'Introduction du Boudhisms a Luang Prabang, *BEFEO*, XL, Hanoi, 1940.

Lingat, R., La vie religious du Roi Mongkut, *Journal of Siam Society*, XX, Bangkok, 1926.

———, History of Wat Mahadhatu, *Journal of the Siam Society*, vol. XXIV, Bangkok, 1931.

———, History of Wat Pavaranivesa, *Journal of Siam Society*, vol. XXVI, Bangkok, 1932.

———, 'The Cult of the Emerald Buddha', *Journal of the Siam Society*, vol. XXVII, I, Bangkok, 1934.

Mahavamsa, W. Geiger, PTS, London, 1908.

Majumdar, R. C., *India and South-East Asia*, Delhi, 1979.

———, *Influence of Indian Culture in South-East Asia* (three lectures), Ahmedabad, 1969.

Malalasekera, G. P., *The Pali Literature of Ceylon*, Colombo, 1958.

Maung Tin, Pe, and C. H. Luce, *The Glass Palace Chronicle of the kings of Burma*, London, 1923.

Mills, Lennex A., *British Malaya, 1824-1867*, Singapore, 1925.

Mills, Lennex A and Associates, *The New World of South-East Asia*, Minneapolis, 1949.

Moffat, Abbot Low, *Mongkut, the King of Siam*, New York, 1962.

Mongkut, King : "English Correspondence of King Mongkut", *Journal of Siam Society*, XXI, Bangkok, 1927.

Mookherji, Sudhansu Bimal, *South-East Asia : A Study of Socio-Economic, Political & Cultural Problems and Prospects*, Calcutta, 1966.

Mouhot, Henri, *Travels in the central parts of Indo-China, Siam, Cambodia and Laos during 1859-90*, 2 vols, London, 1864.

Notton, C., *P'ra Buddha Sihinga*, Bangkok, 1933.

———, *The Chronicle of Emerald Buddha*, Bangkok, 1932.

———, Annales du Siam I : chroniques de Suvanna Khamdeng Suvanna K'em Kham Sinhanavati, Paris, 1926, In Prachum Phengsawadan, Bangkok, 959; reprinted Bangkok Khurusapha, 1969, XLV; Annales du Siam, III : chroniques de Xieng Mao, Paris, 1932; Tamnan Phun Muang Chiengmai, ed. Rong Sayamanon, Bangkok, 1971 : a Thai version; Annales du Siam II: chronique de la p'un Histoire de la Dyanastie Chamttori, Paris, 1930.

Pallegeix, Jean Baptiste, *Description du Reyaume Thai au Siam*, 2 vols., Paris, 1854.

Paranavitana, S., "Religious Intercourse between Ceylon and Siam in the 13th-15th centuries", *Journal of th Royal Asiatic Society*, Ceylon Branch, vol. XXXII, no. 85. Colombo, Ceylon.

Prachun tamnan Phrathat, phak thi I las phak thi 2, Bangkok, w1970.

Pramoj, Seni, and Kukrit, *The King of Siam speaks*, Typewritten Manuscript, Bangkok, 1948.

Prince Dhaninibat, *History of Buddhism in Siam*, Bangkok, 1960.

Rachel Wheatcroft, *Siam and Cambodia*, Delhi, 1986.

Riggs, Fred W., *Thailand*, Honolulu, 1967.

Ruang Chammathewiwang, Phengsawadan Muang Hariphunchai, Bangkok, 1921; reprinted with Thai translation only, 1930 and 1967; partial romanised Pāli text and French translation, G. Coodes, Documents sur l'histoire politique at religiouse du Laos Occidental, *Bullentin de l'Ecole Francaise d'Extreme Orient*, XXV, 1925, Hanoi; C. Natton, Chronique de La p'un Histoire de la Dyanastie cham t'evi, Paris, 1930.

Saddhammasangaha, ed., Nedimel Saddhunanda of the Asokarama vihara at Kalutara in Ceylon, *Journal of the Pali Text Society*, Ceylon Branch,. 1890.

Saddhamma-Sangaha, ed., N. Saddhananda, *Journal of the Pali Text Society*, London, 1890.

The Siam Rath Weekly, Review, August 29, Bangkok, 1957.

Sangkhitiyawong, phengsawadan ruang Sankhayana prathammawinai, Bangkok, 1923.

Sasanavamsa, M. Bode, PTS, London, 1952.

The Siam Society Fiftieth Anniversary Commemorative Publication, Selected Articles from the *Siam Society Journal*, vol., I, 1904-29, vol. II, 1929-53, Bangkok, 1954.

Smith, Samuel J., The Siam Repositery, Bangkok, 1869-74, 6 vols.

———, *History of Siam, Reign of H. M. Somdetch P'ra Narai, 1651-1682*, Bangkok, 1880.

Smyth, H. W., *Five Years in Siam*, London, 1898.

Thai Art with Indian Influence, Premsak Jermsawatdi, New Delhi, 1979.

Thailand, Swami Sadananda, Calcutta, 1941.

Thailand, Economic Survey Group, Report on Economic Development Plans, Bangkok, 1957.

Tamnan Mulasasana, Bangkok, 1939; King Lodaiya of Sukhodaya and his contemporaries. by A. B. Griswold and Prasart na Nagara, *Journal of the Siam Society*, January 1972, Part I, Bangkok.

Tamnan Phra Kaen Morakut Chabap sombun, The Fine Arts Department, Bangkok, 1961; Ratnabimvavamsa by Saeng Monwithun, Tamnan Phra Kae Morakot in Thai, Bangkok, 1967.

The Telegraph, Calcutta, Prafulla Sarkar Street, Calcutta.

Thompson, Virginia and Richard Adloff, *The Left Wing in South-East Asia*, New York, 1950.

Turpin, M., *History of the Kingdom of Siam and the Revolutions that have caused the overthrow of the Empire up to AD 1770*, Bangkok, 1908. Tr. by B.O. Cartwright from the original Paris edition of 1771.

University of Ceylon, *History of Ceylon*, vol. I, Part II, Colombo, 1960.

Vella, Walter F., *Siam under Rama III, 1824-1851*, New York, 1957.

———, *The Impact of the West on the Government of Siam*, Berkelay, California, 1955.

Wales, H. G. Quaritch, *Ancient South-east Asian Warfare*, London, 1952.

———, *Siamese State Ceremonies, Their History and Function*, London, 1931.

———, Dvaravati in South-East Asian Cultural History, *Journal of the Royal Asiatic Society of Great Britain and Ireland*, Parts 1 7 2, London, 1966.

———, *The Making of Greater India*, London, 1961.

Wyatt, David K., *Chronicle Traditions in Thai Historiography, South-East Asian History and Historiography*, ed., C.W. Cowan and O. W. Wolters, Cornell University Press, Ithaca and London, 1976.

———, *The Crystal Sands : Nagara Sri Dharmaraja in Early Thai History*, Ithaca, 1975.

Wells, Kenneth E., *History of Protestant work in Thailand, 1828-1858, Church of Christ in Thailand*, Bangkok, 1958.

Wheatcroft, Rachel, *Siam And Cambodia*, New Delhi, 1986.

Wheatley, P., *The Golden Khersenese*, University of Malay Press, Kuala Lumpur, 1961.

Wood, W. A. R., *A History of Siam to AD 1781*, with Supplement, London, 1929; revised ed., The Siam Barnakich Press, 1933.

Index

Abdullah Ahmed Badavi, 142
Abdullah, 138
Abhaya-mudrā, 435, 461
Abhidhammapiṭaka, 372
Abhisit Vajajiva, 152
ABN-AMRO Asia-Pacific Plc., 295
ABN-AMRO Holding NV, 294-5
Aceh, 32
Achatasatru, 507, 509-11
Adam's Peak, 367, 370
Adhitthana, 388
Adiccaraja, 497
Adiccavamsa, 500
Aditya, 496
Adityaraj, 8
Adityaraja, 488-9, 499
AIDS, 144
Ajantā, 415, 437
Ajātaśatru, 495
Akapol Serasuchart, 267, 272, 279
Alambanganagara, 489
Alan Greenspan, 175
Alaungpaya, 44, 389
Alongkern Palabut, 292-3
Alexander Griswold, 418
Ali Alatas, 141-2, 244
Allisen Song, 266
Amarāvatī school, 410, 414, 419
Amaret Sila, 189
Ambavānarāma, 370
Amnuay Viravan, 535
Amnuay Virawan, 103, 105-7, 109, 113, 127-8, 191, 197, 306
Anand Panyorachun, 138
Ananda Mahāthera, 380
Ananda Phiman Hall, 479
Ananda, 371, 442, 510
Anandamahidol, 86, 92, 404
Anda, 429, 446
Andaman and Nicobar Island, 116
Andaman, 115-16, 137
Andrew Houston, 310
Andrew Maule, 128
Ang Chan, 53
Ang Duong, 53-4
Ang May, 53
Ang Non, 47
Ang Tong, 47
Ang Votey, 53
Angkarn Kaiyanapengsa, 481
Angkor Them, 424
Angkor Vat, 423, 425, 464
Angkor Wat, 4
Angkor, 13, 25-6, 49, 379, 523

Anh Eng, 49
Aniruddha, 356-60, 440-1
Anna Loonowens, 66
Annals of Ayudhya, 526
Annals of the North, 524
Annals of Yonaka, 524
Annam, 350
Anthong, 342
Anthony Weltdon or Weldton, 39, 41
Anujadhiraja, 500
Anukkamachatimsarajaniddesa, 499
Anurādhapura, 347, 383, 385, 396
Anuradjapura, 433, 447
Anuruddha, 440, 523
Anusisusa, 488
Anwar Ibrahmin, 158, 325
Ap'ai, 43
Apec Summit, 24, 226-30
Apinan Pavanarit, 297
Aporn Chewakrieng, 177
Arahanta, 526
Arakan, 357
Araññakas, 365
Araññavāsi, 369, 373, 397
Archit Urairat, 214
Archpriest, 367
Ardhanaris, 409
Arijit Sengupta, 335
Arts and Crafts Secondary School, 476
Arunothai Somsakul, 482
Asean Monetary Fund, 170
ASEM, 285, 296-8
Asia-Europe Meeting, 179, 296
Asia-Pacific Economic Co-operation Summit (Apec), 224, 226-30, 245, 298, 317, 327
Asian Age, 102, 111
Asian Development Bank (ADB), 147, 170, 218, 230, 238, 251-2, 255, 304, 308, 333
Asian Games, 328
Aśoka, 340, 346, 371, 417, 486, 495, 499, 529, 538
Assam, 1
Assembly Hall, 423
Assembly of Poor, 119
Asset Management Corporation (AMC), 223, 331
Association of South-East Asian Nations (ASEAN), 137, 143, 145-6, 159, 170, 192, 240-4, 248, 266, 282, 319, 324, 328-9, 336
Ataran, 36
Athitaraja, 458
At'ityawong, 34
Attaviraj Sritula, 153
Atthakathas, 490
Atulasaktyadhikarana Mahasami, 383
August, 504
Aung San Sun Kyi, 120
Australia, 184, 230, 240, 255, 317, 327
Ava, 36, 44, 47
Avalokiteśvara, 349, 352-3, 420, 422, 424, 540
Avatāras, 458

Ayodhia, 25
Ayodhya, 376, 528
Ayojjha, 376, 519, 520
Ayojjhapura, 494
Ayudhya, 5, 24, 376-9, 427, 447, 454-5, 458, 490-1, 496, 514-15, 525
Ayuthia, 4, 5, 24, 26, 28, 38, 40-8, 120, 374, 375-82, 386-91, 396, 405, 427, 433, 448, 455, 457-69, 471, 474, 476-9, 483, 496, 498, 500, 526, 528-9, 532, 541-2, 544-5
Ayut'in, 24-5
Ayut'ya, 505

Ba Thammarat, 14
Bachay, 22
Badami, 410
Badawpaya, 48
Bai Raka, 441, 448
Baiteen Maonembeen, 480
Balaputradeva, 440
Bali, 277
Ban Mae Sam Saeb village, 321
Ban Muang, 361
Ban-Au-Da-Na, 279
Ban-Ko-Ta, 279
Ban-Mae-Sakeeb, 279
Ban-Sob-Jae, 279
Bandung Conference, 95
Bang Klang Thao, 17
Bang Pa In Palace, 431
Bangkok, 4, 39, 45-56, 59, 63-6, 70-1, 73-5, 78-9, 81, 84-5, 91-2, 97-8, 101-02, 104-7, 110-11, 113, 115, 117-20, 123, 126-7, 129, 139-40, 148, 153, 155, 158-9, 166-7, 171-2, 176, 178-80, 183, 186, 191, 193-4, 196-7, 209-10, 215, 217, 219-20, 224, 229, 241-2, 254, 259, 263, 265-6, 273, 278, 286-8, 297, 305, 312-14, 317, 324-8, 333, 345, 346, 367, 375, 390-1, 394-7, 404-5, 407, 413, 427, 431, 435-6, 455, 458, 468-9, 471, 474, 476-8, 480, 489-92, 497-8, 500-2, 513, 523, 525-7, 532, 535, 543, 545-7
Bangkok Bank Plc., 259
Bangkok Post, 110, 118, 173, 187, 208, 211, 213, 276, 303
Bangkok dynasty, 397, 403-4
Bangkok Investment Plc., 230
Bangkok Metropolitan Bank, 323
Bangkok Metropolitan Trust, 130
Bangkok National Museum, 483
Bangladesh, 115, 125
Bangladesh-India-Srilanka-Thailand Economic Co-operatin (Bistec), 125
Banharn Silpa-Archa, 99, 101-4, 107-8, 323
Bank of Ayodhya, 259-60
Bankruptcy Act, 331
Banlang, 429, 447
Bantam, 36-7
Bantoi Srei Inscription, 16
Banu-Maha-nayaka, 500, 528
Barli Jacker Plc., 196, 233

Barry Yatus, 253
Baruey Phadungsith, 196
Batavia, 68
Battambang, 46, 49, 65, 75, 90
Bayap Circle, 524
Bayatta, 500
Bayinnaung, 30, 31, 385-6
Bayon, 423-4
Bearm Stearms and Co. Inc., 220
Beijing, 138, 141, 225
Belgian, 73-4
Bengal, 410, 435, 439
Beni Prasad Verma, 125
Berlin, 74
Berlin Museum, 476
Berlin Wall, 278
Bhajira Kitiyabha, 329
Bharhut, 506
Bhiangmi, 486
Bhichai Rattakul, 109
Bhumibol Adulyadej, 92, 102, 104, 106, 108, 115, 118-19, 123, 196, 200, 204-6, 210, 214, 217-19, 275, 323-6, 328, 405, 535
Bhumipol Adulet, 92
Bhūmi-sparśa-mudrā, 418, 435, 443
Bihar, 439, 441
Bijjaraja, 500
Bilankaraja, 488
Bill Anderson, 278
Bill Clinton, 104, 108, 201-2, 224-6, 287-9, 291
Binganadi, 383
Bingarattha, 495
Bishop Linean, 40
Bishop Lambert de la Motto of the French Society, 36-7
Bishop of Heliopolis, 36
Bishop Pallegeix, 61, 63
Bisnuloka, 377
Bodharama, 492-3
Bodh-Gayā, 441
Bodhi, 499
Bodhirangsi, 487, 513
Bodhiramsi, 487, 488, 513-14
Bodhisattva, 349, 352, 354, 381, 416, 420, 422, 424, 495, 499, 502, 540, 542
Bodhisattva Avalokiteśvara, 420, 422, 224-5
Bodhi leaf, 420
Bodhi-Tree, 367, 385, 396, 540
Boisselier, 417
Bon, 49
Boonsak Kamhaengritthirang, 279
Borneo, 348, 452
Borom, 459, 461
Boromo Trailoknath, 459, 461-3, 541
Borommaraxaathirat, 528
Borome Trailokanatha, 26, 380, 541
Boromokot, 44, 46, 386-89, 459, 465, 467, 542
Boromeraja, 25-6, 28-9, 44-5, 374, 379, 380, 389, 460
Bot, 427-28, 445, 469
Bo-Tree, 372

Bovaradej, 81, 84
Brahma Rajapanna, 487
Brahma, 416, 423, 478
Brahmajeyya, 520
Brāhmaṇism, 339, 347, 352-3
Braya Sundarapuri, 374
Brest, 38-9
Britain, 95, 119, 278, 288, 319, 326, 328, 533
British, 479
Broadway, 118
Brunei, 142, 150, 184, 192, 230, 240, 244, 255, 317, 327-8, 335, 337
Bua Klum, 429, 448
Buddha, 354-5, 359, 361-2, 367, 372, 376-7, 391, 397, 399-401, 407, 410-20, 423-9, 432-5, 437, 440, 442-4, 447-54, 456-67, 469-73, 476-9, 485, 488, 494-5, 497, 499, 502, 504, 507, 509-10, 513-14, 516, 518, 523, 526-7, 540-1, 543-6
Buddha Jayanti, 405
Buddha Yodfah Bridge, 479
Buddharakhita, 389
Buddhabukama, 501
Buddhacaraya Pao, 393
Buddhaghoṣa, 529
Buddhaghoṣācārya, 397
Buddhajatila, 488
Buddhanama, 501
Buddhankura, 500
Buddhapadas, 370, 372
Buddhavamsa Cosmology, 372
Buddhavamsa Mahathera, 380
Buddhist Cosmology, 372
Buddhist Council, 495, 499-500
Buriram, 354
Burma, 357-60, 377, 496
Burmese, 22
Burney treaty, 54

C. Duroisell, 346
C.M. Ibrahim, 125
CI Sahaviya Finance and Securities, 130
C.P. Group, 233
Calcutta, 68
Calcutta-Gaya-Phuket and Nicobar route, 126
Cālūkyas, 410
Camadevi, 487-9, 495, 499
Camadevivamsa, 486-9, 500, 513, 548
Cambodia, 1, 3-4, 21, 25-7, 31-2, 34, 43, 47-50, 53-5, 59, 61, 65, 75, 88-90, 92, 116, 118, 127, 138, 141, 143, 262, 277, 307, 328-9, 340, 350-4, 365, 379-81, 391, 407, 409, 411-12, 418, 421, 424, 426, 432, 464, 478, 483, 490-1, 494, 523, 532-3, 548
Camboja, 1, 19, 365
Cambridge University, 76
Cammadevi, 5, 348
Canada, 172, 219, 224, 227, 230, 278, 298, 317, 327
Candaramsi, 493
Candra, 403
Candraburi, 374

Candrasavadvara, 403
Canthaburi, 374
Canton, 55, 63
Capital Namura Securities Plc.. 235
Carl Gutzlaff, 55
Carlos Manuel Silveria, 50
Cathay Capital, 148
Cetiya, 429, 453
Ceylon Buddha, 502, 505
Ceylon, 21, 487, 494, 496, 506, 508, 511, 514-15, 523, 527
Chabap Ratchakan-Thinung, 490
Chabbidhanidana, 495
Chadok, 439
Chainat, 456
Chaiprakarn, 439, 455
Chaiya, 349, 352, 409, 418, 420
Chaiyawat Wibulsawasdi, 134, 146-7, 232, 239, 248, 284, 292, 306-7
Chakrabhand Pasayakrit, 481, 483
Chakri, 47-8, 118, 327
Chakri dynasty, 345, 390-1, 468, 470, 498, 526, 532, 543
Chakri mansion, 471
Chalengpheb Sussangkarn, 262
Chalermchai Kesitpipat, 482
Chalieng, 512
Chalorm Yubamrung, 193
Chamadevivongsa, 6, 487
Chamdevi, 7
Chamlong Phetong, 321
Champa, 342, 350, 419
Chandec, 53
Chantabun, 45
Chao, 514
Chao Fa Jai, 35
Chao Int'anon, 503
Chao Phaya Chakri, 47-8, 390, 498, 532
Chao Phray river, 2
Chao P'ya Yomaraj, 77
Chao Phya Dibakara Wongs Bunnak, 526
Chao Pya, 456, 458
Chaowalit Yongchaiyudh, 98
Chapel Rotal of the Emerald Buddha, 394
Chareen Kantawong, 318
Chareen Siriwattanapakdi, 250
Charles Eliot, 2, 19, 365
Chart Pattana Party, 101-9, 178, 187, 195, 203, 206, 209, 219, 292, 324
Chart Thai Party, 101, 109, 323
Chatichai Choonhavan, 102-7, 109, 167, 191, 195, 206, 209, 211-13, 292
Cha-Ting-Pra, 419
Chatu Mongkal Sohanuk, 307, 326
Chaturon Chaisaeng, 177
Chau Fa Mongkut Sammatt Wongs, 60
Chava, 22
Chavalier de Chaument, 37, 38
Chavalit Yongchaiyudh, 98, 100, 109, 112, 115-17, 119-23, 126-7, 133, 140, 148-9, 151-5, 162, 164, 169, 172-4, 178, 180-2,

186-7, 190-8, 210-12, 214, 217, 219, 220, 231, 270-1, 284-5, 291, 293, 301-2, 306, 534, 536-7
Chedi, 345, 428-9, 469-70
Chedi Chaikong, 374
Chedi Jet Yad, 357
Chedi Phra Prang, 445
Chedi Wat Dok-ngoen, 444
Cheewa Komelmalai, 481
Chekachai Aksaranand, 123
Chen Ta-Kuan, 12-13, 15
Chennai, 268
Chetiya, 503
Chetta Thanajara, 99, 110, 193, 309, 322
Chetya, 509, 524
Chiangmai, 357
Chiba, 179
Chieng Mai, 407, 409, 441, 442, 444, 447, 459
Chieng Rai, 6, 8-9
Chiengmai, 6, 24-32, 34-6, 44-5, 47, 63, 74, 89, 117, 122, 486-7, 489, 492, 494-5, 500-8, 513-14, 516, 523-4, 548
Chiengrai, 439, 444, 455, 482, 495, 515-16, 523
Chiengsen, 24, 47, 427, 438-44, 450, 455, 467, 516
Chihili, 18
Chile, 230, 317, 319, 327
China, 2, 11, 18, 93, 141, 159, 182, 184, 225, 230, 240, 244, 305, 317, 319, 323, 328, 336, 339, 357, 360-1, 408, 410, 421, 433, 436, 438-9, 446, 452, 463, 467-8, 470-1, 473-4, 477, 483, 531, 545-6
China Development Corporation, 295
Chinese Communist Party, 93
Chingchai Mongkol Sonahuk, 307, 326
Chingchai Mongkoitham, 197, 293
Chira Hongladarom, 181
Chit Riengpra, 480
Cho-Fa, 427, 441, 447
Chorahi, 418
Christian era, 339, 410
Christian Karen National Union, 322
Christianity, 339
Chuan Leekpai, 98, 100, 102, 149, 207-23, 231, 235, 237, 240-1, 244-6, 248, 258-9, 264-6, 268, 270-2, 274, 280, 282-3, 285, 287, 289, 291-2, 294, 297, 299, 301-2, 306, 312-13, 318-19, 323-4, 328, 537-8
Chuay Thai, 264-5
Chudhadhajadharitiloka Kromkhum Hojboon Indra Iaya, 498
Chula Sakarat, 31
Chulalongkern, 25, 31, 40, 67, 81, 118, 148, 208, 219, 401-2, 414, 470, 473, 492, 526, 533
Chulalongkern University, 78
Chulasakaraj, 526
Chulayuddhakar, 526
Chumipol Na Lamlieng, 246-7

Chumphon Province, 232
Citi Bank, 224, 256, 258
City of Gold, 341
Civa, 423
Claude Cooret de Boullay, 38
Cochin China, 65
Colombo, 91
Colonel Chaiyuth Bumpan, 309
Colonel Luang Pibun Songgram, 84-96
Colonel Oliver, 112
Comprehensive Test Ban Treaty, 319
Confederation of Indian Industry (CII), 268
Confucianism, 339
Constance Phaulkon, 4
Constantin Hierachy, 37
Constantine Phaulkon, 37
Constitutional Law, 405
Coromandal Coast, 36, 39, 54
Corrado Foreci, 479, 547
Country Finance, 130
Cradle of Gods, 341
Culavaṁsa, 387, 388
Curtana, 39

D.G.E. Hall, 29, 346
Dai Xiapglong, 144-5
Damrong, 14, 72-4, 486-7, 492, 524, 526
Damrong Rajanubhab, 341, 374-5, 446
Damrong Wong-Uearaja, 481
Danaburi, 468
Dangrok, 50
Daniel Tarulle, 227
Dantadhatavataraniddesa, 499
David K. Wyatt, 500
David Riedel, 266
Deccan, 410
Decha Sukaran, 271
Decrees for Monks, 394
Deer Park, 417
Deer, 341, 346
Defebce Weekly, 115
Delhi, 68
Democracy Monument, 480
Democrat Party, 93, 98, 100-3, 109-10, 151-2, 207-8, 210, 212, 214, 216, 219, 291, 325, 535
Democratic Karen Buddhist Army, 321-2
Denmark, 64
Department of Fine Arts, 346
Derek Fatchatt, 285, 296
Deutsche Morgan Grenfell Securities (Thailand), 106, 131, 177, 181, 204
Devanampiya Tissa, 495
Devapāla, 440
Devarūpa, 476
Devatā, 416
Devavengsa, 74, 77
Dhammabhimanda, 491
Dhammaceti, 497
Dhammakaya Foundation, 317
Dhammakitti Mahasami, 379, 528-9
Dhammakitti 527-8

Dhammaraja, 370, 519-20
Dhammaśoka, 385
Dhammayutta, 62
Dhammayuttika, 62, 399, 401-2, 404
Dhammayuttika Nikaya, 543
Dhammikaraja, 370
Dhana Siam Finance, 240
Dhana Siam Finance and Securities, 129
Dhanit Yupha, 513
Dhanivat, 341
Dhannivat, 496
Dharmacakra, 346, 411, 416
Dharmacakramudrā, 418
Dharmaghoṣa Mahāthera, 380
Dharmakitti Mahathera, 380
Dharmanayas, 372
Dharmarāja, 24, 370, 409
Dharmasenapati Mahathera, 380
Dharmikaraja, 370
Dhonburi, 46, 390, 405, 468, 532, 542, 545
Dhyānī Buddha, 426
Diamond building, 403
Dien Bien Phu, 94
Dipanis, 490
Dipankara, 498
Dīpavaṁsa, 343
Diyara, 500
Doi Ba, 28
Doi Suthep, 6, 9
Doi Sut'op, 504
Dom Muang airport, 80, 84
Dominge Saizon, 141-2
Dow Jones Industrial Index, 334
Dresdner Kleinwort Benson, 273
Duarto Fernandez, 28
Dubruant, 40
Dulles, 94
Dutch, 474
Duttagamini, 367, 529
Dvadanusasami, 397
Dvārapāla, 409
Dvarapti, 344
Dvaravati, 3-4, 10, 408-19, 421, 424, 432-6, 449, 453-8, 538-9
Dvaravati Sri Ayudhya, 24, 374
Dvaravati kingdom, 344, 347, 351-2, 355, 357-8, 368
Dynamic Eastern Finance Thailand, 130

E.J. Eitel, 344
E.W. Hutchinson, 502
East India Company, 33-4, 36-7, 40-1, 50
Eastern Sugar Co. Ltd., 127
Edwin C. Cert of John Hopkins, 74
Ekat'at, 44
Ekatat, 459
Ekat'etsarat, 32-3
Ekkamel Kiriwat, 105
Electricity Generating Authority of Thailand, 200
Elihu Yale, 39
Emerald Buddha, 468-9, 502, 522-4
England, 39, 56, 76-7, 97

Enron Corporation, 197
Export-Import Bank, 224

Fang, 46-7
Far East, 84
Feroz Talyarkhan, 220
Festival of Visakha or Vaisakha, 397
Fidel Rames, 244, 282
Finance House, 130
Financial Restructuring Authority (FRA), 331
Fine Arts Department, 470, 513
First Bangkok City Bank, 224, 256-7, 320, 322
Flemming Larsen, 308
Flower-Garden Monsatery, 501-2
Forest Monastery, 363
Fort St. George, 36
Fou-nan, 409
France, 75, 278, 283, 288, 386, 463-4
Frederick Henry of the Netherlands, 34
Free Thai movement, 91
Fre Thai Party, 83
French, 474
Fua Haripitak, 480
Fuji, 227
Fullerton, 51, 52

G. Coedes, 344, 346, 361, 434-5, 488, 498, 525
G.P. Malalasekera, 528
Galle, 402
Gāmavāsī, 369, 373, 397
Gandhara, 410, 473
Gandhavamsa, 526
Ganthadhura, 369
Garuḍa, 465, 469
Gen Finance, 130
George Burnaby, 37
George Coedes, 15, 21
George White, 37
German, 479
Germany, 172, 278, 288
Gia Long, 49
Glazed Tile Monastery, 466
Global Fovus, 229
GO, 517
Goh Chok Tong, 127, 244
Golden Island, 342
Gotama Buddha, 485, 495
Gradabgaga, 436
Graham Caterwell, 131, 181, 203-4
Great Britain, 172, 532
Great Relic Wat, 446
Great Relic, 499
Group of Seven, 172
Gulf of Martaban, 340-2
Gulf of Siam, 343, 347, 349, 351, 433
Gupta, 410-11, 413-16, 418-20, 433

H.G.Q. Wales, 433
Haṁsāvatī, 5, 22, 361
Hangsavati, 22
Hansa, 64

Hansi, 89, 116, 257, 328
Hanoi, 89, 116, 257, 328
Haribhunjai, 487
Harihara, 451
Haripuñjaya, 4-11, 344, 347, 348, 351, 355, 359, 382, 384, 412, 413, 453-4, 487-9, 494-5, 499, 539, 543-4
Haripunjayapavatthi, 495
Harip'unchai, 508, 511
Harold Tribune, 262
Harrods, 274
Ha-tien, 47
Henry Burney, 51-3
Henry Ho, 257
Hikarn Matsunaga, 9, 286
Hīnayāna, 339, 341, 349, 355, 358, 365-6, 409, 433, 445, 456, 539, 540
Hīnayāna Buddhism, 7
Hindu, 408
Hinduism, 339
Hiroshi Mitsuzuka, 182, 251
Hiroshi Ota, 276
History of Siam, 29
History of Yonaka, 524
History of the Recitals, 497
Hiuen Tsang, 344
Hluang Presot Aksornit, 525
Hlvan Peripala Puribhanda, 377
Ho Rakhang, 427, 431
Ho Traipitaka, 469
Holland, 119, 532
Hom, 429
Hong Kong, 64, 103, 105, 158, 168, 172, 240, 255, 263, 312, 317, 327
Ho-trai, 427, 431, 469
Hsinvyushin, 45-7
Htaw Ma Pya Hta, 111
Htilominle, 441
Hu Jinato, 328
Hua Kolek, 321
Huat Sut, 111
Huay Kalek, 280, 321
Hubert Noise, 276, 324
Hue, 43
Hun Krabok, 483
Hun Lekhen, 483
Hun Lok, 483
Hun Luang, 483
Hun Sen, 141-3, 329
Hun Yai, 483
Hyde Park, 95

Indarāja, 378, 379, 500
India, 73, 115, 125, 318-19, 329, 333, 341, 344, 346-7, 349, 359, 371, 407, 409-10, 414, 417, 427, 434, 436, 440-2, 452, 458, 467, 468, 472, 483, 495, 499, 523, 528, 532, 538, 548
Indo-Chinese Peninsula, 421, 486
Indo-Greek, 344
Indonesia, 138, 141-2, 145, 160, 166, 184, 188, 192, 217, 225, 238, 240, 244, 246, 250, 256, 260-3, 272-3, 276-7, 283, 294, 296, 310, 317, 326-9, 334, 336, 411, 427-8, 452

Indra, 416
Indrabhupati, 15
Indrāditya, 13-15, 17, 361
Indrapatindraditya, 15, 17
Indraraja, 380-1, 500
Industrial India Trade Fare in Calcutta, 332-3
Int'araja, 26, 33
Interadit, 446
International Monetary Fund, 136, 144-8, 150, 155, 158-60, 163-9, 172, 174-7, 181, 183, 185, 188, 190-1, 198, 202, 216-18, 220-2, 227, 229-36, 238, 240-3, 245-8, 251-5, 258-9, 261-6, 271-9, 281, 284, 286, 288-91, 294, 297, 299-300, 302-3, 308-16, 324, 326, 329-30, 332-3, 535-6
Inthamon Peak, 2
Inthavern, 7
Irian Jaya, 276
Issac-Muiwah and Khaplang factions of the National Socialist Council of Nagaland, 116
Italian, 479
Italian Renaissance style, 479
Italy, 64, 119, 172, 278, 288
ITF Finance, 130

J. Argua, 230
J. Shivakumar, 253
J.G.D. Cambell, 73
Jacques Bouchery, 314
Jacques Chirac, 297
Jai Jott'a, 28
Jakarta, 217, 225, 282-3
Jam Sunnak, 524
Jambudipa, 517
Jambudipasangitiniddesa, 498
James Brooke, 54, 56
James Capel, 128
James I of England, 34
James II, 39
James W. Mckean, 74
James Welfenschn, 273, 302-3
Jamrayapura, 382, 494, 522
Japan, 89-90, 159, 170, 172, 179, 181-4, 227, 239, 240, 242, 244, 251, 255, 260, 276-8, 280-1, 286, 288, 297, 304, 315, 317, 323, 326-8, 336, 439, 452, 485, 533
Jaquenyus of Belgium, 74
Jasmine International Olc, 233
Jātaka, 437, 452, 461, 473
Java, 67, 348-9, 411, 418, 439, 440
Jayakumar, 142
Jayananda, 519-20
Jayasenapura, 374, 382, 494, 522
Jayavarman II, 422, 424, 426
Jayavarman, VII, 351, 421
Jayavarman VIII, 12-16
Jengkonee Wongphasukchet, 237
Jesse Caswell, 61
Jesuit Pere Tachard, 38
Jetavana, 355-6
Jetthadhipati, 384
Jetthadhiraja, 500
Jettharaja, 500

Jewel image, 499
Jiang Zenin, 225, 244
Jimmy Koh, 192
Jinakālamālī, 4-6, 14, 347, 366, 370-1, 382-4, 486-9, 492-7, 500, 516, 548
Jinakalamalini, 491, 492
Jinakalamalipakarana, 489-4, 497, 501
Jinaraja (Vamsadhiraja) Diraraja, 500
Jñāna, 435
Joffray Garton, 246
John Crawfurd, 51, 69
John F. Cady, 43, 67, 70, 85, 90, 341
John Hunter, 50
Jonathan Thatcher, 168
Jongchai Thiangtham, 307
Joot'a, 28, 34
Josh Andrews of the Thaimes Securities, 150
Journal of the Siam Society, 505-6, 508, 514, 523
JTC International Pvt. Ltd., 127
Jump'orn, 395
Jun Lekhen, 483
Junk Ceylon, 41

Kaccay, 355
Kalantan, 52, 75, 78
Kalasan, 412
Kalasoka, 495
Kalyāṇī inscription, 340
Kalyāṇī, 381
Kalyāṇī Upasampada, 497
Kambala, 5
Kamboja, 11-12, 15, 421, 424, 464, 494, 519
Kambuja, 12-16, 350
Kamleswar Bhattacharya, 375
Kamnan Poh, 323
Kampeng Svai, 479
Kampengchhnang, 53
Kamp'engp'et, 22, 29
Kamphaeng Phet, 447, 449-50, 514
Kamphaung alphabet, 21
Kampeng P'et, 523
Kampuchea, 1, 407, 483, 548
Kamratan An Pha Muang, 12
Kanaphan Nantasen, 106
Kanburi, 36
Kanchanaburi, 110-13, 199, 342
Kandy, 388, 389, 400, 542
Karen, 110, 112, 279, 280, 321-2
Karen National Union, 111-12, 322
Karl Zimmerman of Harvard University, 81
Karnasutra, 374
Kasama Veravanna Ayuthaya, 242
Kasem Prunratanamala, 128-9
Kassapa, 529
Kat Met, 513
Kathin festival, 361, 362, 401
Kavee Chukijiasem, 235
Kedah Sultan, 51
Kee Fa, 43

Keiza Obachi, 328
Kelaniya, 381
Kern Dabbaransi, 108, 124, 158, 184-5, 196
Ketagama, 517
Ketumala, 442-3, 457
Khamphaeng Phet, 11
Khamtay Siphandone, 244
Khanchit Assavasamvarn, 180
Khaṇḍasīmā, 383
Khānti, 88
Khao Banemrung, 354
Khao HO, 355
Khao Prabat Yai, 367
Khelang Nakhon, 7, 9
Khelāṅganagara, 382, 489
Khelāṅgapura, 494
Khemangala Mahathera, 380
Khettagama, 517
Khienti, 22
Khien-Yimsiri, 480
Khin Maung Thein, 137
Khmer Angkor Vat, 425
Khmer Prang, 424
Khmer Thai, 408
Khmer, 344, 350, 355, 360, 372, 375, 408-9, 411, 421-7, 430, 432-3, 439-40, 444, 455-65, 479, 530, 539, 544
Khoi, 435-6, 474, 476, 548
Khon, 437, 482
Khuang Aphaiweng, 93
Khun Ram Khamheng, 363
Khun Sen Tong, 504
Khun Tan Range, 7, 9
Khun Vilangka, 7
Khun Werawongsa, 29
Khunyibg (Lady) Pankura, 126
Kiatnakin Finance and Securities Co. Ltd., 235
Kichi Miyazawa, 326
Kiettisak Chaenonart, 548
Kilana, 371, 520
Ki-lok, 436
Kim Dae Sung, 328
King And I, 118, 327
Kinnara, 437
Kirti Śrī Rājasiṁha, 387-9, 542
Kittisirimeghavanna, 495
Klaus Kinkel, 193
Kobsak Chutikul, 125, 280, 324
Kodah, 52, 76
Koe Fa, 29
Kohkum, 244
Korat, 42, 47-8, 50, 70, 354
Korea, 94, 159, 188, 439
Kosa Pan, 38
Kosit Panpiemras, 196-7
Kotmai Phrasough, 394
Krairit Uchukanendchai, 114
Krirkkiat Pipathseritham, 284
Krishna Kant, 329
Krom Somdet Phra Paramanujit, 526
Krung Ratanakesin, 490
Krung Thai Bank Plc., 130, 132, 320, 323
Krungthai Thanakit Plc., 129, 132, 259-60, 313
Ku, 442

Kuala Lumpur, 138, 142, 192, 240, 242, 244, 248, 327
Kubera, 420
Kublai Khan, 11, 17, 531
Ku-Bua, 412
Kuenā, 371, 520, 522
Kunjaraj, 439
Kusinarai, 500
Kuthep Saikrajang, 211, 282
Kuwait, 307

Labapuri, 378
Lai Rad Nam, 5, 455
Lajonquiere, 14
Lak, 484
La-Khung, 508
Lakhung, 512
Lakkhana, 517
Lakshman Kadirgamar, 335
Lamjiek, 436
Lampang, 7, 9, 47, 382, 492, 494, 508, 524
Lamphang, 439
Lamphun, 4, 8-9, 11, 413, 439, 487, 503
Lamp'un, 505, 508
Lampun, 4
Lampoon, 4, 344, 382, 487, 494-5
Lampang, 7, 9, 47
Lan Na, 8
Lanchang, 444
Land of Yellow Robes, 538
Land of Yellow Renes, 339
Lanka, 541
Lanka Theravāda form of Buddhism, 366, 380-1, 390, 397, 405
Lanka, 516-17, 528, 541
Laṅkādīpacatutthavarasangha-niddesa, 490
Laṅkādīparājavaṁsaniddesa, 499
Lankapakara Press, 402
Lankarama, 379, 528-9
Lankasasanapavatti, 495
Lankavong, 366-9, 374, 380-2
Lankavong Nokaya, 445
Lankavong sect, 540-1, 543
Lankavong Theravada sect, 445, 346
Lanna Thai, 485, 497, 500-1
Lanna, 447, 496
Lannat'ai, 513
Lan-na-thai, 439-40, 444, 455
Lan-natnai kingdom, 357
Lao, 2-3, 55, 59, 61, 90, 502-3, 506
Laos, 1-3, 33, 53, 89, 90, 92, 94, 116, 118, 127, 142, 184, 240, 303, 307, 323-4, 328-9, 435, 478-9, 523, 533
Laotine chronicles, 524
Laotian, 340
Laq Code, 403
Lava, 496, 499, 538
Lavavamsakatha, 495
Lavavamsarajaniddesa, 499
Lavo, 3-4, 7-8, 24, 344, 346, 348, 351, 353, 377, 412, 421, 458
Law Code, 403
Lawa, 504

Lawrence Palwar Briggs, 25
Lawrence Summers, 176, 240
League of Nations, 79, 89
Liberal Democratic Party, 277
Liddyya, 519
Ligor, 22, 51, 361, 363, 365, 374, 409, 540
Lila, 450
Lithai, 371
Lo T'ai, 23
Lo Thai, 23
Lo Thai or Lothai, 365, 369-71
Lodaiya, 369, 501
Loe Thai, 23
Lohapasada, 499
Lohaprasad, 470
Loi Rot Nam, 428
Lokeśvara, 354
Lomsak, 32
London, 36, 74, 95, 296
Lopburi, 10-11, 25, 42, 70, 312, 344, 346-8, 350-5, 357, 359, 374, 395, 412, 421-7, 433, 435, 445, 453-4, 456, 460, 463-5, 488, 496, 538-9, 544
Lopburi O'ra Itarai, 4
Louis Napoleon of France, 63
Louis XIV of France, 386
Louis XIV, 36-8, 41, 463
Lovok, 32, 386
Lu Thai, 23-4, 446-7, 450
Lua, 7
Luang Boribal Buribhand, 377
Luang Prabang, 22, 32-3, 47, 75, 431, 444
Luang Pradist Munudharn, 81
Luang Praset, 525
Luang Rachapirom, 491
Luang Thammapinion, 491
Luang Udom Chinda, 491
Lum, 22
Lut'ai, 23-4
Luthai, 370-4, 501

Ma Wang, 29, 52
Madras, 39
Mae Hla, 321
Mae Hong Son, 309, 321
Mae Khan, 6, 9
Mae Kwung, 9
Mae Ohing, 494-6
Mae Phing, 11, 393
Mae Ping, 6, 9
Mae Sariang district, 279
Mae Set, 309, 321
Mae-Hong-Song province, 279, 309, 321
Mae-La Luang, 279
Maha Chakrap'at, 29, 30, 385
Maha Chakrapat, 380
Maha Chakri Srindhorn of Thailand, 116
Maha Cham Dongamvarna, 375
Maha Dhammaraj, 385-7
Maha Dharmaraja, 380
Maha Mongkut, 51
Maha Sakarat, 31
Maha T'ammaraja, 30, 44, 387
Maha Tewi, 29
Maha Uparat, 28, 33

Maha Vajiralongkorn, 329
Maha Vajiravudh, 76, 498
Mahabodhārāma, 383
Mahabodhi Temple, 441
Mahabodhi tree, 383
Mahabrahma, 515-16, 520, 522-3
Mahacera, 500
Mahadevi, 519
Mahadhammaraja, 500
Mahadhammarajabbata Monastery, 522
Mahadhammarakkhita, 343
Mahadhat, 487
Mahādhātu Cetiya, 384
Mahādhātu Monastery, 352
Mahādhātu, 377, 499, 540
Mahākālarājādhirāja, 500
Mahakukamanasara, 501
Mahākūṭasatriya, 401
Mahamahinda, 500
Mahamakutarajavidyalaya, 402
Mahanagarattha, 343
Mahanam, 355
Mahanama, 487
Mahanikaya sect, 402, 404
Mahantayasa, 489
Mahaparinibbana, 347, 397, 405, 495, 543
Maharakkhita, 343
Maharastra, 344
Maharattha, 343-4
Mahasamana, 403
Mahasami Sangharaja, 372-3, 380, 385
Mahasurasimhanada, 395
Mahathera Samagam, 406
Mahathera Sri Sraddharajaculamuni Sriratanalankadipa mahasami, 373
Mahathera, 363-5, 370, 373
Mahathir Mohamad, 159, 244-5, 247, 282, 325
Mahaupada, 500
Mahauttamapanna, 381
Mahavajrunhisa, 402
Mahāvaṁsa, 340, 343
Mahavihāra, 441
Mahāvikkamabāhu, 381
Mahawongse, 487
Mahāyāna, 339, 347-50, 352-5, 360, 365, 411-12, 419-20, 422, 424-5, 439, 440, 538-40
Mahayuddhakar, 526
Mahim, 380
Mahin, 30
Mahindra, 377
Mahinda, 499, 529
Mahinyangana Thupa, 499
Mai Yang, 504
Maitreya Bodhisattva, 420, 422, 424, 467
Malacca, 28, 52, 374
Malay Archipelago, 418
Malay Peninsula, 340, 342-3, 348-9, 361, 363, 365, 374, 418, 540
Malay, 1-3, 19, 25, 28, 41-2, 45, 50, 61, 54, 57, 59, 61, 70, 74-6, 88-90, 94, 533
Malaysia, 142, 145, 151, 158-60, 166, 188, 192, 230, 235, 240, 245-7, 250, 255, 260, 262, 265,

277, 282, 284, 308, 317-18, 325-9, 334-6
Manchuria, 89
Mango Grove monastery, 370, 372-3
Mangalartha Temple, 15
Maṅgalasīlavaṁsa, 383
Mangrai, 6, 18, 24
Mangroi, 3
Manila Plan, 225
Manila, 94, 137, 226, 228, 318
Manop Thongyen, 233
Mantrisavinnanaka Mahathera, 379
Māra Vijaya Mudrā, 443-4, 450, 458, 461
Māra, 420, 450, 457
Māravijaya, 420
Marble Temple, 470
Marc Lovine, 311
Maricavatti Cetiya, 499
Marshal Desfarges, 38-41
Martaban, 32, 44, 200
Masatsugu Nagato, 257
Masatsube Ngate, 280
Mathura, 410
Maurice of Nassau, 33
Maurya, 340-1, 343, 346, 499, 529, 538
May, 503-4
McDonnell Dougles, 289
Me Ping, 504
Me Set, 22
Me'an Rat, 373
Medhamkaranna, 9, 383
Meditation *mudrā*, 435, 450
Mekhlong, 46
Mekhong, 22
Mekong Valley, 486
Mekong, 1, 3, 18, 22, 65, 88, 438, 439
Menam valley, 2-6, 11, 18, 25, 36, 45, 48
Menam, 342-4, 347-8, 350-2, 355, 357-8, 360, 374, 408, 420, 439, 455-6, 458, 494-5, 538-9
Meng, 6, 7
Meng Rai, 6
Mengrai, 8, 407, 439, 441, 484, 486, 499, 503
Meping, 22
Mergui, 28, 38-40, 45, 48
Mettā, 358
Mexico, 146, 168, 230, 247, 317, 319, 327
Mi, 397
Michel Camdessus, 169, 171-2, 177, 216-18, 220, 230, 235, 286, 303, 316, 325, 327
Migasangara, 488
Migasangha, 488
Migkhasangara Nakhon, 7
Mike Jondrzejezyk, 225
Milakkaraja, 488
Milinda, 523
Minh-Mong, 53
Misiem Yipintsai, 481
Missions Etrangeres, 40, 43
Mitsu Sate, 257, 308
Mlou-pray, 50

Mo Kha, 504
Mo'an Pan Yan, 17
Mo'an Rat, 17, 373
Moci, 321
Mohamad Al Fayed, 274
Mohamad Bolkiah, 142
Mon, 4, 5, 8, 10, 18-23, 31, 44, 52, 342-4, 346, 348, 351, 355-61, 407-8, 411, 413, 417, 421-2, 427, 445, 456, 458, 539, 544
Monastery of Aruna, 402
Monastery of Bang Va Jai, 392
Monastery of Bot, 393
Monastery of Great Relic 395-8, 402-4
Monastery of Indrama, 393
Monastery of Mahabuddharupa, 522
Monastery of Nirvana, 391, 393
Monastery of of Pho, 393
Monastery of Phra Kao, 394
Monastery of Rae Khang, 392
Monastery of Rajapurana, 396
Monastery of Sa: Ket, 397
Monastery of Samorai, 399
Monastery of Sri Sarvajna, 393
Mondop, 427, 430-1, 462, 467
Mongol, 408
Mongkol, 110
Mongkolbaurey, 49
Mongkut, 59-62, 64-7, 69, 118, 345, 367, 396, 398-402, 404, 413, 469-70, 490, 532-3
Mongol, 531
Mongols, 23
Mon-Indian, 408-9
Mon-Khmer, 408, 410, 439
Montree Pongpanich, 196
Moody's, 185-6, 250, 256, 261
Moslems, 474
Moulmoin, 31-2, 66
Muan Laken, 385
Muang Ban Yang, 17
Muang Fa Due Sung Yang, 412
Muang Keo, 494
Muang Lawa, 504
Muang Ma, 505
Muang Nakon, 512
Muang Ngoen Yang Chiangsaen, 486, 548
Muang Rat, 11, 17
Muang Sau, 454
Muang Thathong, 342
Mueng Chava, 22
Mueng Chot, 22
Mueng Man, 22
Mueng P'le, 22
Mueng P'lua, 22
Mukhasan, 460
Mulasasana, 500-2, 548
Mun Dong, 512
Mun Nangsu Vimala Kitit, 512
Musica, 46
Muslim Institute for Consumer Protection, 325
Muslim Law Society, 325
Mutual Security Act, 94
Myanmar, 1, 4-5, 25, 28-2, 34-6, 42, 44-8, 51-2, 57, 59, 68, 72-3, 88, 90, 94, 110-13, 118, 120-1,

127, 137, 142, 154, 159, 184, 198-200, 240-1, 244, 257-8, 277, 279-80, 287, 307-9, 321-3, 340-4, 356, 361, 370, 374, 381, 385-7, 389-91, 395, 399, 486, 494, 496, 526-7, 532-3, 539-42

N.A. Jayawickrema, 494, 496
Na Htun, 285
Nabbisipura, 6, 371, 381-6, 487-8, 494, 496, 499, 501, 520-2
Naga, 420, 423-6, 441-2, 452, 469, 514, 516, 518
Nagara Jum inscription, 14
Nagara Pathama, 343
Nagara Prathama, 344
Nagarainda, 500
Nagarama Patha, 4, 344, 538
Nagaravasigana, 384-5
Nagarjun, 372
Nagarjun inscription, 372
Nagasena, 523
Nagata Prathama, 4
Nai Khan Kwaya, 7
Nai Khuang Aphaiwong, 92
Nai Pote Sarasin, 96-7
Nak Dharma, 396
Nakon Sri Tammarat, 349-50, 353, 361, 365
Nakon Pathom, 340-1, 343-7, 357-60, 412-14, 416, 433, 470
Nakon Raychasima, 422, 426
Nakon Sawan, 346
Nakon Si Thammarat, 365-8, 382, 385, 409, 418-19, 440, 466-7, 514
Nakon Śrī Dharmarāja, 363, 365-6, 487, 514, 540
Nakon, 508, 515
Nakorn Pathom, 341, 344
Nakorn Patom, 4
Nakorn Rajasima, 352
Nakhon Lamp'ang, 29
Nakhon Nayek, 42
Nakhon Pathom, 155
Nakhon Savan, 22
Nakhon Sithammarat, 514
Nakhon Sritammarat, 28, 42, 46, 47
Nakhon Sri Thammarat, 515
Nalanda Copper Plate of Devapala, 440
Nam Thai Party, 109
Nam Ya, 437
Nan, 22, 485
Nanaanisamasacetiyathanapancantaradhananiddesa, 500
Nānagambhira mahāthera, 380
Nanchao, 2, 11, 17, 360, 531
Nanda Bayin, 31-2
Nanda Sayin, 386
Nang Cham T'evi, 505
Nang Hai, 482-83
Napoleon, 65
Narai, 35-40, 42, 380, 463-5, 478
Narakiri, 510
Narasuen, 380, 386
Naraya, 500
Narayana, 478
Narongchai Akrasanee, 178, 196

Naresuan, 32
Nari, 380
Naris, 470
Narissa, 500
Narodam, 53
Narongchai Akrasorani, 105, 123, 127, 128
Nation newspaper, 100, 110, 117, 154, 165-6, 178, 217, 233, 241, 259, 275, 285, 301, 303
National Finance and Securities, 129
National Museum, 476
Nationalist Socialist Party, 96
Nava Finance and Securities, 129, 305, 312
Navadhammasanghaniddesa, 500
Nekkhamma, 388
Nelson Mandela, 140
Nepal, 277
New Aspiration Council, 543
New Aspiration Party, 98-100, 102-4, 106-9, 180, 185, 197-8, 210-11, 219, 284, 292-3, 301-2, 535
New Delhi, 125
New Straits Times, 244
New Sunflower Group, 197-8
New Wat, 398
New York, 81, 287, 290
New Zealand, 184, 230, 317, 327
Ngam Muang, 18, 486
Nguenpodduang, 465
Nguyen Anh, 48
Nguyen Nan Cam, 142
Nguyen, 43, 49
Nibbana, 499, 516-17
Nicco Park, 335
Ninth Buddhist Council, 391-2, 394, 543
Nipa, 496
Nirantaraya, 545
Nirvāṇa, 449
Nisit Wattanachariya, 117
Nivas Hemavachiravarakorn, 113
Nomura Research Institute, 159
Nong Khai, 147
Nong Sa Rai, 32
Nong Tao, 122
Non-Proliferation Treaty, 319
Nonthaburi, 544
Norodom Sihanouk, 141, 329
North Korea, 184
Norway, 64
Nukul Prachuabmoh, 284
Nyanakamip'on, 510

O.W. Walters, 25
Ohn Gyaw, 241
Olarn Chaiprawat, 251
Ong Kham-Mang, 53
Order of St. Michael, 39
Osaka, 228
Oudh, 458
Oudong, 53
Overseas Economic Co-operation Fund, 277

P. Chidambaram, 125

P. Dupont, 434
P. Patithuguenin, 14
P.M. Bose, 492
Pacific islands, 428
Padharangsi, 492
Padumavana, 401
Padumuttara Mahathera, 379
Pagan, 356-60, 407, 440-2, 523
Pahang, 75
Paiteen Maungsomboon, 480, 547
Pakaee sect, 381-2
Pakistan, 318
Paknan, 70
Pakorn Saedan of Bangkok's Ramkamhaeng University, 173
Pakua P'o, 22
Pala, 10, 416, 439-42, 453, 467, 519
Palace of the Golden Horses Hotel, 242
Palembang, 348
Pala-Sena, 410, 419-20, 453
Pali Buddhism, 365
Pallankadipaka, 522
Pallava Script, 346
Pallava, 410
Pallu, 36-7
Pan Klan Dav, 17
Pan Puongsachart, 300
Pandyas of Madurai, 410
Pang Mapha district, 309
Pankura Yongchaiyudh, 127, 150, 153-5
Panna, 388
Pany Vijinthanasarn, 482
P'ao Sriyanon, 92, 94, 96
Papua New Guinea, 230, 317, 327
Parakramabahu the Great, 527, 529
Paramacakrabarti, 377-8
Paramanuxit Xinoret, 526-7
Paramaraja I, 374
Paramaraja, 25, 528-9
Paramarājādhipati-Sri-maha-Cakrabarti, 378
Paramarajadhiraja, 374, 378-9, 500, 528
Paramatilokanatha, 500
Paramatthapitaka, 393
Paramis, 387
Paramitas, 387
Paris, 64, 74, 81, 375, 456
Parliament, 479
Patalung, 348, 350, 382
Patani, 28, 33-5, 38, 349
Pathama Chetiya, 341, 345
Pathamasambodhi, 526-27
Pathom Chedi, 341, 413
Patjana Suansri of the Thai Volunteer Service Foundation, 122
Pattaya, 119, 123
Paul Volker, 303
Pavaranivesa monastery, 398-99, 401-4
Pavararajadhiraja, 379
Pavaresvariyalankarana, 401
Pavaret, 401-2
P'ayao, 18

Pechabun, 91
Pegu, 5, 22, 30-2, 52, 61, 340, 361, 385, 399, 456
Peking, 94
Penang, 50-2, 68, 88
P'engsawadan, 42
Pennsylvania University, 346
People's Bank of China, 145
People's Liberation Army, 93, 115
People's Party, 81
Perak, 51-2
Perlis, 76
P'etchaburi, 22, 33, 45, 70
Petracha, 466
Petroleum Authority of Thailand, 200
Periphong Lamsam, 27
Pha Manng, 111
Pha Mo'an, 17
Pha Muang, 12-13, 16-17, 373
Phaga Prachakitch Korachakr, 524
Phaijit Sriverakarn, 180
Phaisit Phipatanakul, 212-13
Phak Hai Temple of Ayuthia, 120
Phan Van Khai, 244
Phatra Thanakit, 129
Phaulkon, 37-41
Phaya or P'ya Bahal, 84-7
Phaya Tak sin, 45, 390
Phaya Tak, 391
Phaya, 486, 492-3
Phetburi, 374, 544
Philip Bowring, 262
Philip McClelland, 102
Philippines, 135, 141-2, 145, 151, 166, 170, 175, 184, 284, 304, 308, 317, 326, 329, 336-7
Philips of Penang, 51
Phitnu Pathanopas, 240
Phnom Penh, 47, 53, 141
Pho Khun Bang Klang Thao, 11-12
Pho Khun Pha Muang, 11-12
Phongsavadan Krung Kao, 549
Phonnarat, 497
Phonsavadan Krun Kao chabab Praset Aksaraniti, 525-6
Phonsavadan Krun Kao, 549
Phonsavadan Yonok, 492, 524, 549
Phonsavadan, nu'a, 524, 549
Phra Baht Samdoch Phra Paramender Maha Mongkut Phra Bhem Klao Chao Yu Hua, 62, 400
Phra Brahma Rajapanna, 522
Phra Buddha Yotfa Chulalok, 524
Phra Chao Kuena, 371
Phra Chedi, 413, 428-30
Phra Chom Klao, 62, 400
Phra Devamodi Dit, 402
Phra Dhatu, 14
Phra Dhammatrailokacarya Hong, 403
Phra Khampaeng Khayong, 451
Phra Maha, 396
Phra Mahadhatu (Maha Tat), 349
Phra Mahathat, 419, 456
Phra Mahathen (Mahathera), 363

Phra Nang Klao, 397, 526-7
Phra Nangklao, 118
Phra Narai, 386, 478
Phra Naret, 386
Phra Nirantaraya, 472
Phra or Ora Sam Yet, 423
Phra or Pra Prang, 430, 447-8, 456, 460, 469-70
Phra or Pra Puttha Sihing, 450, 467
Phra Panya Vihan, 470
Phra Pariyati Dharmadhata, 525
Phra Pathom Chedi, 345, 414, 470
Phra Pathom, 4, 344, 346, 538
Phra Phuttha Sihing, 514
Phra Pim, 350
Phra Rajaphongsavadan Krung Kao Chabab Hluang Prasot, 525
Phra Ram, 483
Phra Ruang, 14-5, 514
Phra Sihing, 513
Phra Tripitaka Chabab Thai, 405
Phra Vichien Prescha Phraya Potachanapinon, 491
Phra Vichien Pricha or Preecha, 525
Phra Vimaladhamma, 404
Phrabad Somdet Phra Buddha Yod Fa Chulalok, 490-1
Phrah Thammarat, 14
Phraya Maha Dharmaraja, 14
Phraya Pariyattidharmadhata, 513
Phujao, 492
Phuk, 489, 491
Phum-Kha-Bin, 446
Phya Prajakich Korachakr, 524
Phya Tak Sin, 542
Pichai Nirand, 547
Pichai Niranf, 481-2
Pichit, 22
Pimai, 352, 354, 422, 426, 478
Piman Mulapramuk, 480
P'imp'akan, 506
Pisanulok, 380
Pisnulok, 22
Pitak Intrawityanunt, 125-6
Pitok, 47
Pitsanulok, 26, 28, 30, 46-7, 450, 462
Piyasvasti Amranand, 137
Pli, 429
Plong Chanai, 429, 447
Pojrapuri, 374
Polonnaruva, 448, 451
Pondicherry, 39, 41
P'ong Tuk, 346-7
Pong T'uk, 409, 433
Pope, 63
Pora Tachard, 38, 41
Portugal, 66, 532
Portuguese, 474
Pra Bodhisattva Haroi Prachat, 461
Pra Borom That Chaiya, 419
Pra Chedi, 413
P'ra Indra, 504
P'ra Keo Se Tang Kamani, 502-3
P'ra Maha Mun, 503, 506-7

P'ra Maha P'ot'a Lang Ka, 507
P'ra Muang Sam P'ya, 505
P'ra Muang, Yot, 505
Pra Nag Prok, 424
P'ra Nang Klao, 51, 60-1
Pra Naret, 31
Pra Niran Tarai, 472
Pra Patom, 409
P'ra Petraja, 40-2
P'ra P'ut't arup Se Tang Kamani, 504-5
P'ra P'utta yet Fa Chulalok, 48, 390
Pra Puttha Chibasat, 450
Pra Sambuddhaberni, 472
Pra Samputthapanni, 472
Pra Sat, 430
P'ra Sihing, 502, 505, 513-14, 516, 523, 549
P'ra Sila, 459, 502-3, 505, 507, 549
Pra Song Khrueng, 456, 466
P'ra Wutinyan, 507
Pracha Prommek, 323
P'rachae Sua, 42
Prachakorn Party, 101, 198, 213, 291
Prachothipok, 79
Prachuab Chaiyasarn, 141-2, 145, 193
Prachup Khairi Khan, 482
Pradoch Phayakvichien, 143-4
Pradit Charoenthaitawee, 205
Pradit Pataronpasit, 271
Prah Kham, 460
Prai, 69
Prajadhipok, 79, 80, 86, 403
P'rajai, 29
Prajñāpāramitā, 424-5
Prajum Silacarik, 375
Prang, 376-7, 379, 423, 427, 434, 433, 456, 461, 469-71
Prapan Bomyakiet, 170
Prapass Charueetthiara, 326
Prasad Hin, 422
Prasat, 427, 469
Prasat T'ong, 34-5, 386, 459-60, 463-4
Prateung Emjaroen, 481-2
Pravaj Wasee, 122
Prayeon Ulshata, 481
Preah Khan, 479
Preecha Thaothong, 482
Pre-Angkor Vat period, 354
Prem Tinsulananda, 149, 152, 206-7, 323
Premsak Jermsawatdi, 357
Pridi Banemyong, 81-7, 91-2
Prime Finance and Securities, 130
Prince Damrong, 15
Prince Khun, 20
Prince T'ien, 29
Princess Galayani Vadhana Kromluang Narathiwat Rajanakarin, 325
Priya Tantisuk, 481, 547
Prohm, 439, 455
Prohn-Top, 50
P'rok, 22
Prome, 4, 344
Prussia, 64

Pubbārāma, 384, 389
Pukam, 356-7, 360
Puket, 41
Puppet, 482-3
Puppet Theatre, 548
Puppharamevasigana, 384-5
Purachatra, 81
Put't'aga, 512
P'ya Anurata, 511
P'ya Anutat'a, 508
P'ya Bodin, 53
P'ya Dok Chai, 507
P'ya Kosa Tibodi, 37
P'ya Mangrai, 505
P'ya Manopakern, 82-4
P'ya Sam Lan, 507
P'ya Sank'aburi, 47
P'ya Suriya, 48
P'ya Suriyawong, 505
P'ya T'aksin, 45-8, 391
P'ya Tilok, 512
Pyo of Ava of Myanmar, 36
Pyu, 344

Queen Elizabeth II centre, 296
Queen Fabiola of Belgium, 326
Queen Sirikit, 317

R.C. Majumdar, 13, 15
R.L. Morant, 73
Rabi, 74
Rachakena, 509
Rachakrut, 507-10
Rachatani, 99
Radhanasin Bank (RAB), 331
Radra, 517
Rai Et, 482
Raiprasok, 461
Rajabhat Institute, 99
Rajabhiramya, 491
Rajaburi, 74, 374
Rajadhirajapavaro, 376, 379
Rajaguru, 355, 385, 498
Rajapratistha, 401
Rajapuri, 346
Rajib Kaul, 335
Ram Khamheng, 3, 20, 514
Ram Khamheng or Khamhaeng, 446-7, 450-2, 478
Ram Raja, 26
Rama I, 390, 391, 393, 395, 468-9, 471, 477-9, 498, 523, 543, 546
Rama II, 395-7, 570-1, 477-8, 483, 546
Rama III, 387-400, 470-2, 477-8, 483, 490, 544, 546
Rama IV, 345, 367, 398, 400, 413, 469, 472, 477-8, 483, 532, 545-6
Rama V, 402-3, 405, 414, 470-3, 477-9, 483, 498, 532, 546-7
Rama VI, 374, 403, 469-70, 473, 478, 483, 498, 547
Rama VII, 403-4, 470, 478
Rama VIII, 404-5, 478
Rama IX, 405, 470, 478, 543
Rama Khamheng, 3, 14-8, 20, 22-3, 173, 204, 206, 361-2, 364-9, 373-4, 531, 540, 543
Rama the Brave, 514

Rama Tibodi I, 374, 395
Rama T'ibodi, 25, 28-9, 46, 48
Rama Tibodi, 455, 458-60, 462-3, 478
Rama, 3, 48-56, 59-62, 67-81, 84-6, 345, 458, 478, 517-19
Ramadhipati Suvannadola, 500
Ramadhipati, 25, 46-7, 377, 378, 380, 500, 519
Ramakien, 49, 437, 462, 473, 476, 478, 545-6
Ramanna country, 540-1
Ramanna sect, 384
Ramannadesa, 342, 370-1
Ramannanagara, 5, 9, 347-8
Ramaraja, 378, 380, 500
Ramasisuddhavasa Monastery, 403
Ramassura, 500, 528
Ramasuen, 374, 380, 460, 478
Ramavasi Mahathera, 380
Rāmāyaṇa, 49, 437
Ramesuen, 25-6
Ramesvara, 378
Ramon Magsaysay Award, 158
Ramong, 115
Rangoon, 69, 112, 121, 257-58, 280
Ra-not, 419
Ranaridh, 140-2
Ratana Bimbawamsa, 522-23, 549
Ratana Bimbawongs, 487, 522, 549
Ratana Mahavihara, 492
Ratana Pannanama, 487
Ratanacetiya, 355
Ratanakesin, 468
Ratanapanna, 488-89, 492-3, 496-7, 501
Ratburi, 22, 46-7, 348, 374, 390, 412, 414, 416, 456
Ratchaburi, 111, 113, 199-200
Ratnakesin, 465
Ratsada, 29
Rattavanamahavihara, 382
Ratthadhirajakumara Jayarajasi, 500
Rayong, 45
Reginald Le May, 455
Renato Ruggiero, 335
Rev. Phra Khrn Prasrrnaawikhat, 232
Revatta, 510
Revolutionary Party, 97
Rice Festival, 140
Riksa, 401
Robert Morant, 67
Robert Rountree, 159
Robert Rubin, 174, 176, 183, 286
Robert, de Ocampo, 170
Roberts, 53
Robin Cook, 158
Roca, 517-19
Rocaraja, 515
Rock Edict XIII, 340
Rolin Jacquenins, 72
Rorngchai Merakanand, 113, 115, 129, 136, 306
Royal International Finance and Securities, 130

Royal Saka Era, 517
Royal Thai Navy, 115-16
Ruan, 46
Ruang, 46
Rusi, 484
Russel Kopp, 273
Russia, 288, 319, 327
Ryutare Hashimote, 244

S.G. Macfarland, 66
S.K. Roy, 126
Sa dung Mara, 443
Sabbadhisiddhi, 8, 355
Sabbasiddhi, 355
Sacca, 388
Sachanalai, 496, 512
Sachart Chaowiait, 165, 166
Saddavaisesana, 393
Saddhammasamgaha, 379, 527-9
Saeng Manavidura, 488-9, 492, 497, 500, 502
Sai Yok National Park, 198, 199
Saigon, 70, 84
Sailendra dynasty, 348, 350
Sailendra, 440, 538
Saivism, 424
Sajjanalaya, 12, 17, 371, 494, 496, 519, 523
Sakdi Na, 27
Sakon-Nakorn, 352
Sakti, 398
Sakyas, 442
Sal Cau, 351
Sala Gong, 470
Sala Kan Parian, 427
Sala, 427, 431
Salt Lane in Calcutta, 126
Salween, 1, 279, 309, 321
Salwin, 8, 10
Sam Fang Ken, 38
Sam Rainsy, 262
Sam Roi Yot, 65
Samadhi Rab, 443, 449-50
Samadhi, 435
Samak Sundaravej, 198, 213, 291
Samannasarajaniddesa, 499
Samarang, 68
Samgha Mantri, 406
Samghakamma, 369
Samgharaja Medhamkara, 372
Samsak Soisup, 120
Samuel George White, 39
San Cau, 351
San Kampaeng, 444
San Thong, 444
Sanam Kajornprasart, 216, 219, 238
Sanam Luang Park, 328
Sanam Ngophainan, 158
Sanan Kachomprasart, 323
Sanchi, 345
Sanci, 429
Sandalwood image, 499
Sangalok, 452
Sangchai Ekkapatanapanit, 161, 165
Sangitikalakatha, 495
Sangitivamsa, 393, 497-8, 548
Sangitiyavamsa, 497

Sangrama, 431
Sankalok, 452
Sanoh Thientong, 109, 119, 163, 193, 195, 301
Santisuk Sanguanruang, 156
Sanwa Bank, 260
Saraluang, 22
Saranamkara, 387
Saraburi, 42
Saranburi, 456
Sarasakka, 500
Sarawak, 54
Sarit Thamarat, 82, 96, 97
Sarnath, 415, 417, 418
Sasanavamsa, 340, 345, 527
Sastras, 372
Satchanalai, 370
Sation Tantanasarit, 239
Savatthi, 416
Sawaeng Songmangmae, 480, 547
Sawankalok, 17, 23, 70, 352, 367, 370, 381-2, 452, 508, 572, 539
Sawi district, 232
Sayahm Sami, 69
Seamice Securities, 270
Sekha, 22
Semphab Amaetayakul, 128
Sempop Chareenkul, 255
Sen Muang-Ma, 516, 523
Sen Muong Ma, 381
Senabodi, 57, 72
Senauraksa, 395
Senchai Montriwat, 128
Sett'at'irat, 30
Seven Pagodas, 357
Seven Spired Temple, 441
Shahbandar, 43
Shammayutti, 399
Shan, 3, 343, 357, 494
Shin Arahan, 356
Shinantra Group, 233
Shwe Dagon Pagoda, 69
Si Satchanalai, 17, 23, 446-7, 449, 452
Si Thammarat, 22
Si, the Sangharaja, 393
Siam City Bank, 196, 258, 322
Siam Cement Plc., 233, 246-47
Siam Commercial Bank, 260
Siam Directory, 69
Siam Htaw Saming, The, 44
Siam Times, 63
Siam Weekly Register, 69
Siam, 1, 3, 13, 18-23, 42-3, 64, 68-9, 89, 341, 398, 408, 455, 487, 502, 515, 523-4, 532
Sidviratna, 500
Siemreap, 46, 49, 65, 75, 80
Sihala Buddhism, 495-6
Sihala Buddhism-sangha, 495, 499
Sihala image, 496, 516-22
Sihala Samgha, 370-72, 382, 384-85
Sihalasasana Jotanakatha, 495
Sihala, 516, 518, 527
Sihanouk, 138
Sihinganidana, 513-14, 549
Sikkha, 499
Sila, 388

Silawangso, 510-12
Silom Road, 191
Silpa Bhirasi, 473
Silpakorn University, 476
Silpakorn, 480
Silver Flower, 444
Silver Pond Wat, 447
Simon de La Loubero, 38
Simon Flint 274
Singapore, 50, 55, 64, 68, 70, 127, 142, 159, 175, 182, 184, 192, 209, 230, 240, 244, 439, 535
Singhanawati, 486
Singhanawatieuman, 548
Singora, 35, 38, 374
Singu, 47
Sinhalese, 410
Sinhalese Buddha, 514
Sir Harry Ord, 65
Sir John Bowring, 63-4
Siri Garnjaranendee, 303
Siridhamma, 383, 517-18
Siridhammanagara, 365-66, 540
Sirikhetta, 4, 344
Sisophon, 49
Sithammarat, 363
Sithop Thangsuban, 261
Sittang Valley, 30
Sitthidot Saenghiran, 480, 547
Siva, 409, 420, 423, 425, 451, 469, 478
Sivaism, 365
Siyam sect, 389, 542
Siyamagama sect, 389, 542
Siyamapasampadavat, 389
Siyamavamsa, 389
Siyamopali sect, 389
Social Action Party, 101
Solanger, 51
Solomb Crosby Securities, 256, 311
Solomb Smith Burney, 266
Solomon Brothers, 129
Somanassa, 401
Sombat Thamrongtanyawong, 325
Somchai Khunpluem, 323
Somdet Krem Phaja Pavaret, 401
Somdet Phra Rajagana, 398
Somdet Phra Samgharaja, 397
Somdet Phra Vanaratana, 402, 403
Somdet Phra Wammaratma, 497, 526
Somkid Jatusipitak, 190, 196
Somnath Chatterjee, 126
Somphob Manarangsan, 200
Sompong Amernvivat, 137
Somsak Kaiseek, 164
Somsak Soisup, 120
Sona Thora, 340, 343
Song K'we, 22
Songkha, 419
Songt'am, 33-4
Soni Promoj, 83, 91-2
Sonthaya, 323
SooGen Grosby Securities, 256, 311
Sop Moci district, 321
Sor Sivalak, 199

Soraida Salwala, 199, 200
South Korea, 184, 227, 232, 235, 230-240, 246, 250-2, 256, 261, 263, 277, 284, 296, 304, 308, 317, 326-8, 336
South-East Asia Treaty Organisation (SEATO), 94, 96-7
South-East Asian Nuclear Weapon Free Zone Treaty, 324
South-East: Its Historical Development, 341
Soviet Union, 278
Sri Deva, 352, 409
Sri Dhana DBS Securites, 234
Sri Dharmanagara, 365
Sri Dharmaraja, 22, 540
Sri Indraditya, 4, 17, 351, 361
Sri Indrapati, 13
Sri Indrapatindraditya, 12
Sri Indtaditya, 450
Sri Int'arat'itya , 17
Sri Lanka, 1, 62, 125, 277, 304, 335, 340, 343, 347, 356, 364, 368, 370, 372-3, 379, 381-3, 385, 387, 389, 396-7, 400, 402, 407, 409, 417, 433, 436, 445-8, 450-1, 456, 464, 470, 487-8, 494-6, 499, 514, 527, 529, 540-2, 548
Sri Ratanamahadhatu, 372
Sri Sachanalai, 17, 351, 382
Sri Sakyamuni Buddha, 478
Sri Suriyendra, 59
Sri Surya Phra Maha Dharmarajadhiraja, 14
Sri Suryavamsa Rama Mahadharmarajadhiraja, 23
Sri Sut'ammaraja, 35
Sri Top, 352, 354
Sri Vijaya, 10-11, 348-50, 352-4, 411, 418-20, 414, 424, 427, 435-6, 445-7, 453, 456, 464, 538-40
Sri Vijaya Rajasimha, 387
Srilankan Tamil Tigers, 116
Srindravarman, 12, 14, 16-17
Srisakra Vallibhetana, 6
Srisudhammaraja, 380
Sriyan Pietersz, 256
St. Petersburg, 74
Stanley Fischer, 163
State Law and Order Restoration Council (SLORC) of Myanmar, 120-21
Stone Buddha, 506, 508, 510-13, 549
Stone temple, 422
Stone Wheel of the Law, 341
Stubg Trong, 50
Sua T'ai, 23
Suan Dok, 447
Subarnapuri, 374, 377-79
Suchit Bunbongkarn, 148, 219, 148
Sudhammanagara, 5, 9, 340
Sudhammaraja, 500
Sudhammavati, 358
Sugandha, 520-2
Suhala sect, 493
Suharto, 121, 225, 244, 276, 283

Sui, 69
Sukh, 395
Sukhodaya, 3, 4, 11-25, 28-30, 47, 86, 351-2, 360-74, 379, 381-2, 390, 405, 407-9, 417, 419, 421-2, 427, 432, 442, 452, 456, 458, 464, 466, 468, 471, 478, 494, 496, 501, 514, 517-20, 531-2, 539-41, 543-4, 546
Sukhot'ai, 11
Sukhothai, 3, 11, 18, 21, 408, 432, 445, 478, 487, 494, 499, 515
Sukhumbhand Paribatra, 266
Sukkadanta, 488
Sukum Naunsakul, 204, 206
Sultan of Brunei, 150, 317
Sultan of Kedah, 50
Sultan of Perak, 52
Sumangala Mahathera, 380
Sumana kuta, 367, 370, 372
Sumana, 370-1, 409, 496, 499, 517
Sumanadeva-Mahathera, 380
Sumatra, 32, 342, 348-9, 411, 418, 439
Sunandalaya, 73
Sunaparanta, 342
Supachai Punitchapakdi, 216, 218, 219, 233, 239, 248, 254, 278, 335
Supanburi, 341-2, 412, 416, 419, 454-5
Sup'annaphum, 22, 455
Supat Thampet, 325
Suphan, 374
Supoto Isarankura, na Ayudhya, 333
Suppachai Pisitvanich, 164, 304
Suradit Sonakong, 482
Surahma, 488
Surakirat Sathirathai, 105
Suraphel Thipvilai, 130
Suraporn Dunaitangtrakul, 187
Surasinghananda, 525
Surathami, 342, 349
Surathani, 419-20
Surin Pitsuwan, 152, 222, 241, 265, 276
Surya Mahathera, 380
Suryavamsa I, 350-3
Suryavarman II, 4
Suttantapitaka, 393
Suvannabhumi, 519
Suvannacanda, 500
Suvannamali *cetiya*, 499
Suvannapasada, 500
Suvannaramsi, 527
Suvarnabhumi, 340-3, 455
Suwannakomkhan, 486
Suwat Liptapallop, 104, 184, 187, 196
Suwit Hinkiti, 196
Svankalok, 3
Svargalok, 351, 382
Swami Sadananda, 18-19, 408
Sweden, 64
Switzerland, 86
Syam Kut, 4
Syam, 3
Syama, 3
Syriam, 41
Szechwan, 2, 531

Ta Tong Nielloware, 467
Tabinshwehti, 385
Tabinshwohti, 30
T'ai Sra, 42-3, 386
Tai Yuan, 485, 500
Taipei, 305
Taiwan, 182, 230, 217, 277, 295, 304-5, 317, 327
Takkpura, 521-2
Taksin, 468, 476
Ta-Kua-Pa, 419
Talaing, 19
Tamalinga, 418
Tamalingamu, 365
Tambalinga, 365
Tambarattha, 365
T'ammaraja, 23-4, 31
Tamnan Muang Suvannakham, 485, 548
Tamnan Munsasana, 6
Tamnan P'ra P'ut't'arup Se Tang Kamani, 549
Tamnan, 485-86, 502-3, 506-7
Tamra Thopharup, 476
T'anaburi, 45
Tanhankara Mahathera, 379
T'annaburi, 46
Tantric, 439-40
Tanya Sirivedhim, 256, 257
T'ao Sri Suda Chan, 29
Taoism, 339
Tapodarama, 383
Tara Nakayama, 277
Tarrin Nimmanahaeminda, 216-17, 219, 232, 235, 250-1, 259, 265, 267, 273-4, 276-8, 282, 284, 286, 300, 303, 309-10, 313, 316, 323, 326
Tasachat, 462, 476, 545
Tavatimsa heaven, 451
Tavoy, 25, 31-2, 44, 46, 48, 374
Tayson, 48, 49
Tenasserim, 25, 28, 32, 44-5, 48, 51, 54, 88, 111, 374
Thai Citizens' Party, 210
Thai Conduk General in Calcutta, 333
Thai Farmer's Bank, 258-59, 295, 326
Thai Financial Trust, 130
Thai Fuji Finance and Securities, 130
Thai Military Bank, 258
Thai Oil, 233
Thai Olefins Co (TOC), 188
Thai Petro-Chemical Industry (TPI), 188
Thai Polyethylene (TPE), 188
Thai, 408
Thaimex Finance Securities, 224
Thaksin Shinawatra, 310
Thalang, 395
Thambalinga, 365
Thamers Research Centre, 99
Than Shwe, 244
Thana One Finance and Securities, 130
Thanaporn Promyamyai, 102
Thanathip Vidhyasirinun, 148
Thanawat Patchimkul, 234

Thanon Kittikachern, 97, 326
Thanong Bhidaya, 129, 134, 155-6, 170, 175, 183, 190-1, 194
That Dnu Bank, 239
Thathong, 342
Thaton, 5, 340, 342-3, 356-60
Thawan Duchanee, 481-2, 548
Thawatchai Yongkittikul, 319
Thed Pha Pa dundraising campaign, 231-2
Thon Buri, 470
Theravada Buddhism, 538-42
Theravada, 21, 339, 341, 344, 346-8, 352-3, 357, 360-1, 364-6, 368-70, 373-4, 381-2, 384, 398, 403-5, 412, 445, 456, 488
Thihathura, 47
Third Buddhist Council, 340, 538
Thonburi, 532
Thot Krathin Ceremony, 325
Three Baskets, 366
Three Pagodas Pass, 35
Thuparama, 447
Tibet, 230, 531
Tika, 490
Tilaka, 383
Tilakabaddhasima, 490
Tilakapanattu, 383
Tilakaraja, 382, 393
Tilok, 494, 500, 513, 524
Tilokarat, 486, 512
Tipanna, 519-22
Tipitaka Chabab Tongyei, 394
Tipitaka, 366, 391-2, 394, 402-4
Tissaraja, 21, 381-2
Tju Mahathera, 356
Tokyo, 74, 145, 179, 183, 251, 255, 455
To-lo-po-ti, 344
Ton De Beer, 295
Tong Dham, 459
T'ong Lan, 25
Tonga, 277
Tonle Ropou, 50
Tony Blair, 296
Tooth Relic, 388, 495, 499
Total Access Communication Plc., 233
Toungee dynasty, 385
Toungee, 32
TPI Group, 233
Trai Sra, 459, 463
Trailok, 26-28, 380, 382, 459, 461, 541
Traiphun, 476
Traiphun-P'a Ruang, 372
Traibhumikatha, 372
Trang, 100, 349-50
Trengganu, 52, 75-6
Tripatch Isuzu and Tuntwz Plc., 233
Tripitaka, 490
Twatchai Yongkittikul, 235-6

Udakajjotthata, 518
Udon Tantiprasengchai, 254
Udon Thani Water Project, 147
Udon, 98-9
Udong, 43, 49
Udumbara Mahasami, 370-2

Udumbara Swami, 409
Udumbarapuppha, 500
Ujung Salang, 41
Ulfa, 116
Uma, 451
UNDP, 285
Unionist Party, 96
United Finance, 130
United Nations, 94, 125, 184
United States of America, 53-4, 79, 90-1, 94-5, 97, 113, 147, 151, 159, 172, 175-6, 197, 201-2, 215-16, 227, 229-30, 232, 240, 242, 249, 254-5, 262, 274, 278, 280-2, 285-92, 294, 297, 303, 305, 307, 310, 316-17, 319, 327, 332, 334, 337
Upali Mahathera, 388-9
Upalivamsa Nikaya, 389
Uparat, 27, 42-3, 387
Upari-arama-monastery, 383
Upasampada ordination, 370, 379, 381-2, 384, 388
Upasampada Ordination, 541-2
Upasika Kaew, 317
Upatasanti, 527
Upekkha, 388
Uposatha Hall, 355
Uposatha, 389
Upper Godavari, 344
Uprat, 57
US Federal Reserve Bank, 303
USA, 346
Usnisa, 473
Ussu, 504
U-Thong, 341-2, 374, 454, 544
U-Tong, 412, 414, 419, 427, 454-60, 471
Utradit, 544
Uttar Pradesh, 458
Uttara Thera, 340, 343
Ut'ump'on, 44

Vacana Vimala, 491
Vaiṣṇava, 409, 458
Vaiṣṇavism, 424
Vajiravudh, 403
Vajrananavararasa, 402-3
Vajrapakara, 519-22
Vajrasena, 346
Vajrayana, 439
Vajravudh School, 78
Vajrayana, 79
Valagam-aba, 529
Vamsa Kavya, 494
Vanaratana Sukh, 393
Vanaratnavong, 381-82
Vanatavong, 542
Vanavāsī, 369
Vancouver People's Summit, 230
Vancouver, 219, 224, 229-30, 298
Varanana muni, 388
Varapol Sirivat, 178
Varathep Ratanakoon, 162
Vasabha Mahathera, 379
Vasudeva, 5, 342, 488
Vasukri, 526
Vasuthep, 6, 7
Vat Mahadhatu, 373
Vat Rajapuranah, 379

Vat Srirathnamahadhatu, 375
Vat Xetuphon, 527
Vattaraja, 522
Vattiteja, 519-22
Vaychai Matwa, 293
Ve Van Kiet, 116
Vedas, 372
Versailles, 37-8, 40
Vichieb Fangadtaisak, 234
Vickers Ballas, 128, 130, 180, 237
Victory Monument, 480
Vieng Chan, 22
Vieng Chang, 30
Vieng Kham, 22
Vieng Mane, 9
Vieng the Karn, 9
Vieng Thoh, 9
Vientiane, 444
Vietnam, 43, 47, 49, 53-4, 61, 84, 92, 94, 116, 142, 184, 240, 244, 257-8, 304, 327-8, 336-7, 342, 419, 533
Vihan Phra Mongkon Bopit, 459
Vijaya mudrā, 463
Vimala Dhamma, 393
Vimaladhamma, 498
Vinaya, 529
Vinayadhara, 406
Vinayapiṭaka, 372, 393
Vinhlong, 53
Vipasanadhura, 369
Virabhongso Ramangkura, 153, 205
Viriya, 386, 388
Viṣṇu, 409, 423, 425, 451, 458, 467, 469, 489
Visuddhacariya Mahathera, 388-9
Visuddhi Pusyakula, 375
Viśvakarmā, 425
Vitarka mudrā, 415, 422, 435, 451
Vittaya Thienthong, 162
Viwntiane, 45, 53

W.A.R. Wood, 29
W.G. Johnson, 73
Wachirawut, 76
Walden Belle, 229-30
Wall Street, 290, 334
Wallop Tangananaurak, 162
Walter F. Vella, 58
Wang River, 9
Wan-Muhammad Noor Matha, 108, 210, 212-13
Washington, 74, 83, 91, 225, 240, 246, 267, 285-6, 290, 303, 313-14, 326
Wat Mun San, 507-8, 512-13
Wat Arannika, 363
Wat Arun, 470
Wat Ban Hlui, 356
Wat Benchamabopit, 470-1
Wat Bon, 383
Wat Bovornivet, 470
Wat Cedi Cet Yod, 383
Wat Cgedi Sung Phra Bhat Yai, 449
Wat Chai Watena Ram, 464
Wat Chalerm Phra Kiet, 470
Wat Chamatewi, 453-4

Wat Chanasongkram, 449
Wat Chang Lom, 367, 447, 449
Wat Chang Rob, 449
Wat Chang, 449
Wat Chatawan, 325
Wat Chedi Si Hong, 449
Wat Chetupon, 449, 546
Wat Chiengmai, 502-3, 507
Wat Chot Yot, 441, 446-7
Wat Chulamani, 380
Wat Don inscription, 355
Wat Ho T'am, 503
Wat Kathom, 407
Wat Khotawanaram, 504
Wat Krabuang Khlaub, 466
Wat Kukut, 355, 413, 453
Wat Mahadhatu, 395
Wat Mahathat, 478
Wat Mongkon, 449
Wat Na Phramama, 460
Wat Om Rob, 447
Wat Pa Daeng Luang, 383
Wat Pa Tan, 504
Wat Padeng Mang, 512
Wat Pavaranivesa, 62, 398
Wat Phara Dhat Lamphun, 8
Wat Phra Chedi Si Samphat, 407
Wat Phra Kaew, 407, 469-70, 472, 545
Wat Phra Maha-Tat, 423, 446, 460
Wat Phra Ram, 460
Wat Phra Si Samphet, 459-60
Wat Phra Singh, 407, 444
Wat Phra Sri Sampot, 462-3
Wat Phra That, 453-4
Wat Pra or Phra Boromothat, 450
Wat P'ra Sihing, 502, 514, 516
Wat Pra Sri Ratana Mahathat Chalieng, 447, 450
Wat Pra Sri Ratana Mahathat, 450, 456, 463
Wat Pra Yuon, 442
Wat Raja Oros, 470
Wat Rajapradit, 471
Wat Ram P'oneng, 503
Wat Rathburama, 460-1
Wat Sadet, 451
Wat Samorai, 61, 399
Wat Sen Khaot-te, 355
Wat Si or Sri Chum, 452
Wat Si Pichit Kiti Kalayamin, 449
Wat Siri Kot, 507
Wat Sri Chum, 448
Wat Sri Chun, 365
Wat Srisathobg Temple, 155
Wat Suan Dok, 512
Wat Suthat, 478
Wat Swam Utayam Noi, 447
Wat Thiptidaram, 470
Wat Thong Nophakum, 470
Wat Traikum, 449
Wat Trakuan, 450
Wat Trapang Nagaem, 447
Wat Traping Tong Lang, 451
Wat Wang Phra That, 447
Wat Yai Chaimonkol, 462
Wattachak, 170, 310
Webel, 126
West Bengal, 125

Wheel motifs, 341
Wheel of the Law, 346, 414, 416, 433-4, 451
White House, 289
Wieng Kalong Kilu, 444
Wieng Lhet Lin, 505
Wieng Pa Pao, 444
Wild Tiger Scout Corps, 77-8
Windsor Castle, 39
Wiratham, 89
Wisaka, 503
World Bank, 146, 155, 158, 175, 218, 252-3, 255, 273, 294, 302-4, 316
World Buddhist Association, 405
World Economic Outlook, 167
World Trade Organisation, 226, 335
WWW Chuan Th Org, 318

Xieng Mai, 6, 371, 381, 409, 487, 492
Xieng May, 6
Xieng Rai, 382, 494
Xieng Saen, 374, 382, 494
Xumphon, 395

Yadnam-Khang, 429
Yakkha, 409, 463
Yakṣas, 437
Yakṣiṇīs, 437
Yamada, 34
Yapapattana, 381
Yatra, 450
Yodaya, 528
Yona, 343-4, 495
Yonok, 439, 495, 524
Yonaka, 343, 494, 495, 524
Yonana, 490
Yonrattha, 494-5
Yor Mum, 456
Yot, 430
Young Muslim Association of Thailand, 325
Yugi Morimote, 277
Yunnan, 11, 387, 531